CANADIAN ENTREPRENEURSHIP & SMALL BUSINESS MANAGEMENT

NINTH EDITION

D. Wesley Balderson
UNIVERSITY OF LETHBRIDGE

Peter Mombourquette
MOUNT SAINT VINCENT UNIVERSITY

McGraw-Hill
Ryerson

McGraw-Hill Ryerson

CANADIAN ENTREPRENEURSHIP AND SMALL BUSINESS MANAGEMENT
Ninth Edition

Statistics Canada information is used with the permission of Statistics Canada. Users are forbidden to copy the data and redisseminate them, in an original or modified form, for commercial purposes, without permission from Statistics Canada. Information on the availability of the wide range of data from Statistics Canada can be obtained from Statistics Canada's Regional Offices, its World Wide Web site at www.statcan.gc.ca, and its toll-free access number 1-800-263-1136.

The Internet addresses listed in the text were accurate at the time of publication. The inclusion of a Web site does not indicate an endorsement by the authors or McGraw-Hill Ryerson, and McGraw-Hill Ryerson does not guarantee the accuracy of the information presented at these sites.

ISBN-13: 978-0-07-133886-8
ISBN-10: 0-07-133886-1

2 3 4 5 6 7 8 9 WEB 9 8 7 6 5 4

Printed and bound in Canada.

Care has been taken to trace ownership of copyright material contained in this text; however, the publisher will welcome any information that enables them to rectify any reference or credit for subsequent editions.

Director of Product Management: Rhondda McNabb
Group Product Manager: Kim Brewster
Marketing Manager: Cathie Lefebvre
Product Developer: Tracey Haggert
Senior Product Team Associate: Christine Lomas
Supervising Editor: Jessica Barnoski
Photo/Permissions Researcher: Indu Arora
Copy Editor: Erin Moore
Proofreader: Rohini Herbert
Plant Production Coordinator: Tammy Mavroudi
Manufacturing Production Coordinator: Lena Keating
Cover Design: Greg Devitt
Cover Image: Compassionate Eye Foundation/Robert Kent/Getty Images (RF)
Interior Design: Liz Harasymczuk
Page Layout: Aptara®, Inc.
Printer: Webcom

Library and Archives Canada Cataloguing in Publication

Balderson, D. Wesley (David Wesley), 1948-, author
    Canadian entrepreneurship and small business management / D.
Wesley Balderson, Peter Mombourquette.—Ninth edition.
Includes bibliographical references and index.
ISBN 978-0-07-133886-8

    1. Small business—Canada—Management—Textbooks. 2. New business
enterprises—Canada—Textbooks. 3. Entrepreneurship—Canada—Textbooks.
I. Mombourquette, Peter, author II. Title.
HD62.7.B34 2014   658.02'20971   C2013-906033-2

BRIEF CONTENTS

CHAPTER 1
The Role of Entrepreneurship and Small
Business in Canada   2

CHAPTER 2
The Small Business Decision   31

CHAPTER 3
Evaluation of a Business Opportunity   53

CHAPTER 4
Organizing a Business—The Business Plan   88

CHAPTER 5
Buying a Business and Franchising   150

CHAPTER 6
Financing the Small Business   196

CHAPTER 7
Marketing Management   242

CHAPTER 8
Managing the Marketing Mix   271

CHAPTER 9
Financial Management   301

CHAPTER 10
Operations Management   331

CHAPTER 11
Human Resources Management   351

CHAPTER 12
Managing Taxes and Getting
Management Assistance   382

CHAPTER 13
Managing Growth   412

CHAPTER 14
Managing the Transfer of the Business   430

CONTENTS

PREFACE WITH WALKTHROUGH ix

PART ONE The Decision To Start A Business 1

CHAPTER 1 The Role of Entrepreneurship and Small Business in Canada 2

Learning Objectives 2

Small Business Profile 3

Introduction to Entrepreneurship and Why Students Will Want to Study the Subject 4

Nature and Development of Entrepreneurship in Canada 4

Increases in the Number of Business Establishments 8

Increases in the Number of Employees of Small Businesses 10

Increases in Government Interest and Programs 10

Increases in the Number of Small Business-Related Courses at Colleges and Universities 11

Increases in Entrepreneurial Activities Known as Intrapreneurship in Large Businesses 11

Increases in the Political Power of Small Business 12

Improvement in the Image of Small Business 12

What Is Small Business? 13

Comparison and Evaluation 13

Government Programs 13

Lending Programs 13

Current State of Small Business in Canada 14

Young Entrepreneurs 15

Senior Entrepreneurs 17

Female Entrepreneurs 17

Immigrant Entrepreneurs 19

Entrepreneurial Activity by Industry 20

Entrepreneurial Activity by Region 20

Contributions of Small Business 21

Labour Intensity 21

Innovations and Inventions 21

Productivity and Profitability 22

Flexibility 23

Canadian Ownership 23

Small Business Health as a Link to Economic Growth 24

Social Contributions 24

Small Business and the Future 24

Change 25

Technology 25

Intranet and Mobile Technology 25

Consumer Demographics and Buying Patterns 26

Competitive Aspects of Markets 26

The Economy 27

The Political Climate 27

The Social Climate 28

Time to Take Action 29

Learning Objectives Summary 29

Discussion Questions 30

Application Questions and Hands-On Activities 30

CHAPTER 2 The Small Business Decision 31

Learning Objectives 31

Small Business Profile 32

The Small Business Decision: Personal Evaluation 33

Advantages of Small Business Ownership 33

Disadvantages of Small Business Ownership 36

Demographic Characteristics of Entrepreneurs 39

Personality Characteristics Required by Successful Entrepreneurs 39

The Small Business Decision: Organizational Evaluation 44

Small Business Successes 44

Small Business Failures 46

Entrepreneurship and Small Business Management 48

Entrepreneurial Skills 48

Managerial Skills 48

Entrepreneurial Success in Large Businesses 49

Time to Take Action 50

Learning Objectives Summary 51

Discussion Questions 51

Application Questions and Hands-On Activities 51

Appendix 2A: Entrepreneur Suitability Checklists 52

CHAPTER 3 Evaluation of a Business Opportunity 53

Learning Objectives 53

Small Business Profile 54

Entrepreneurial Process 55

Ideas 55

Sources of New Ideas 55

Assessment of Business Opportunities 58

Qualitative Assessment 58

Opportunity Assessment 59

Evaluating How to Break Into the Market 60

Developing a Strategic Competitive Advantage   61
  The Right Industry   61
  The Right Business   62
  The Right Aspect of the Business   62
Collecting Information   64
  Sources of Information   64
  Secondary Data   64
  Primary Data   66
Quantitative Assessment of Business Opportunities   70
  Preparing the Feasibility Analysis   70
  Step 1: Calculate Market Potential   71
  Step 2: Calculate Market Share   72
  Step 3: Calculate Net Income and Cash Flow   75
Time to Take Action   79
Learning Objectives Summary   79
Discussion Questions   80
Application Questions and Hands-On Activities   80
Comprehensive Case—Dan Kim: Part 1   81
Cases for Part 1   83
Petite Shop (A)   83
Petite Shop (B)   83
Big D's Painting Company   84
Katie's Custom Engraving Logos   85
Appendix 3A: Small Business Reference Books and Sources of Information   Online

PART TWO Preparing for Small Business Ownership   87

CHAPTER 4 Organizing a Business— The Business Plan   88

Learning Objectives   88
Small Business Profile   89
Getting Started: Establishing the Business   90
  Advantages of Organizing a Small Business from Scratch   90
  Disadvantages of Organizing a Small Business from Scratch   92
The Small Business Plan   92
  Writing the Plan   93
Components of the Plan   94
  Prepare a Table of Contents   96
  Prepare a Synopsis of the Plan in an Executive Summary and Background Statement   97
  Describe the Management Team   97
  Establish Business Objectives   97
  Plan the Marketing Approach   98
  Describe the Selection of the Location   101
  Determine the Physical Facilities   104
  Plan the Financing   106

Plan the Personnel   107
Investigate the Legal Requirements   107
Assess the Risk   116
Using and Implementing the Business Plan   117
  Measuring Plan Progress   117
  Updating the Plan   118
Time to Take Action   118
Learning Objectives Summary   119
Discussion Questions   119
Application Questions and Hands-On Activities   119
Appendix 4A: Checklist for a Small Business Plan   121
Appendix 4B: Sample Business Plans   124
  Business Plan 1—Retail Stocking Store, The Sock Hop   124
  Business Plan 2—Quality Cuts   139

CHAPTER 5 Buying a Business and Franchising   150

Learning Objectives   150
Small Business Profile   151
Purchasing an Existing Business   152
  Advantages of Purchasing   152
  Disadvantages of Purchasing   153
Sources of Businesses for Sale   156
Evaluating a Business for Sale   157
  Industry Analysis   157
  The Previous Owner   157
  Financial Condition of the Business   158
  Condition of the Assets   159
  Quality of Personnel   160
  External Relationships—Suppliers and Customers   160
  Condition of the Records   161
Determining the Price or Value of a Business   161
  Market Value   161
  Asset Value   161
  Earnings Value   162
  Combination Methods   163
The Purchase Transaction   165
  Negotiating the Deal   166
History and Background of Franchising   166
What Is Franchising?   169
Advantages of Franchising   170
Potential Disadvantages of Franchising   173
Finding a Franchise   177
Evaluation of a Franchise Opportunity   178
The Entrepreneur as Franchisor   183
  What Businesses Can Be Franchised?   183
  How Does One Become a Franchisor?   184

Franchising in the Future 186

Time to Take Action 186

Learning Objectives Summary 187

Discussion Questions 188

Application Questions and Hands-On Activities 188

Comprehensive Case—Dan Kim: Part 2 189

Appendix 5A: Checklist of Considerations in Purchasing a Business 190

Appendix 5B: A Checklist for the Potential Franchisee: Questions to Answer Affirmatively before Going into Franchising 192

CHAPTER 6 Financing the Small Business 196

Learning Objectives 196

Small Business Profile 197

Small Business Financing 198
The Importance of Capital and Planning 198

Determining the Amount of Funds Needed 199
Start-up Costs 199
Ongoing Operating Costs 201
The Owner's Net Worth 201

Determining Types of Financing 202
Business Stages and Financing 202
Equity Financing 205
Bootstrap Financing 222
Debt Financing 223

Determining the Term of Financing 228

Preparing a Proposal to Obtain Financing 229
Lender Relations 231

Time to Take Action 232

Learning Objectives Summary 232

Discussion Questions 233

Application Questions and Hands-On Activities 233

Comprehensive Case—Dan Kim: Part 3 235

Cases for Part 2 236

Clark's Sporting Goods 236

Jensen Roofing 236

Conrad's Photographer's Supplies 237

Kelly's Grill 238

Second Cup 239

Appendix 6A: Provincial Equity Capital Programs Online

Appendix 6B: Federal Government Assistance Programs for Small Business Online

PART THREE Managing the Small Business 241

CHAPTER 7 Marketing Management 242

Learning Objectives 242

Small Business Profile 243

The Role of Marketing Management in the Small Business 244

The Marketing Plan 245
Characteristics of a Marketing Plan 251
The Marketing Mix 255

Steps in Preparing the Marketing Plan 256
Defining the Business Situation 256
Market Segmentation and Target Marketing: Beyond the Basics 257
Customer Profile 260
Considering Strengths and Weaknesses 262
Customer Relationship Marketing 262
The Database Information System 263
Database Marketing for the Small Business 263
CRM Databases and Retention 265
Establishing Goals and Objectives 266
Defining Marketing Strategy and Action Programs 267
Budgeting the Marketing Strategy 267
Monitoring Progress of Marketing Actions 267

Contingency Planning 268
Why Some Plans Fail 268

Time to Take Action 268

Learning Objectives Summary 269

Discussion Questions 269

Application Questions and Hands-On Activities 270

CHAPTER 8 Managing the Marketing Mix 271

Learning Objectives 271

Small Business Profile 272

The Role of the Marketing Mix in Small Business 273

Developing the Product or Service 273

Developing the Distribution System 276
Channel Options 277
Channel Length 277
Channel Intensity 277
Multi-Level Marketing 277

Setting the Price for the Good or Service 278
Cost-Based Pricing 279
Demand-Based Pricing 280
Competition-Based Pricing 280
Value-Based Pricing 281

Promotion   281
  Steps in a Promotional Campaign   281
  Types of Promotion   283
Time to Take Action   299
Learning Objectives Summary   299
Discussion Questions   300
Application Questions and Hands-On Activities   300

CHAPTER 9 Financial Management   301

Learning Objectives   301
Small Business Profile   302
The Need for Financial Records   303
The Accounting Cycle   303
  Recording Transactions   303
  Classifying Transaction Totals   305
  Summarizing Data   305
Accounting Systems for the Small Business   308
  Manual Systems   308
  Outsourcing Financial Activities   309
  Small Business Computer Systems   310
Management of Financial Information for Planning   311
  Short-Term Financial Planning   311
  Long-Term Financial Planning   312
Evaluation of Financial Performance   316
  Management of Current Financial Position   316
  Evaluation of Financial Statements   317
Credit and the Small Business   321
  Advantages of Credit Use   321
  Disadvantages of Credit Use   321
  Management of a Credit Program   321
  Use of Bank Debit and Credit Cards   323
Time to Take Action   324
Learning Objectives Summary   324
Discussion Questions   325
Applications Questions and Hand-On Activities   325
Appendix 9A: Use of Financial Ratios for a Small Business
  (Automotive Dealer)   327
Comprehensive Case—Dan Kim: Part 4   329

CHAPTER 10 Operations Management   331

Learning Objectives   331
Small Business Profile   332
Management of Internal Operations   333
The Production Process   333
  Total Quality Management   334
Physical Facilities   335

Layout   336
  Layouts for Manufacturing Firms   337
  Layouts for Retail Firms   339
  Layouts for Service Firms   342
Purchasing and Controlling Inventories   343
  Sources of Supply   343
  Evaluating Suppliers   343
  Determining Order Quantities   344
  Inventory Control   346
  The Small Business-Supplier Relationship   348
  Supply Chain Management   348
Time to Take Action   348
Learning Objectives Summary   348
Discussion Questions   349
Application Questions and Hands-On Activities   349
Comprehensive Case—Dan Kim: Part 5   350

CHAPTER 11 Human Resources Management   351

Learning Objectives   351
Small Business Profile   352
Human Resources Management and the Small Business   353
Planning for Human Resources   354
The Hiring Process   357
  Sources of Employees   357
  The Screening Process   359
  Notification of the Hiring Decision   362
Personnel Management   363
  The Introduction Period   363
  The Probationary Period   363
  Training   363
  The Owner-Manager as Leader and Personnel Manager   364
  Organization Culture   366
  Motivation, Engagement, and Loyalty   367
  Paying Employees   369
  Fringe Benefits   370
  Controlling and Evaluating Employee Performance   372
Handling Grievances   373
  Terminating the Employee   373
  Unionization and the Small Business   374
Government Requirements and Assistance   374
  Federal Government   374
  Provincial and Territorial Governments   375
  Municipal Governments   376
Record Keeping for Employers   376
  Contract Employees   378
Time to Take Action   379

Learning Objectives Summary   379

Discussion Questions   380

Application Questions and Hands-On Activities   380

Comprehensive Case—Dan Kim: Part 6   381

CHAPTER 12 Managing Taxes and Getting Management Assistance   382

Learning Objectives   382

Small Business Profile   383

Advisers and Small Business   384

Use of Advisers   384

Taxation and Small Business   387

General Tax Management Principles   389

Continual Tax Planning   389

Tax Deferral   390

Income Splitting   390

Marginal Tax Rates   390

Deductibles   391

Government Tax-Related Programs   393

The Incorporation Question   395

The Remuneration Question   395

Transferring the Business: Capital Gains   396

Goods and Services Tax (GST) and Provincial Sales Taxes (PST)   396

Time to Take Action   396

Learning Objectives Summary   397

Discussion Questions   398

Application Questions and Hands-On Activities   398

Cases for Part 3   399

Derocher's Market   399

Home Mart Hardware Store   400

Martha's Designs   401

Sadie's Country n' Western   402

Dale's Sport Pursuit   403

Susie's Fashions   403

Taylor Construction Company   405

The Barrel Bracket   405

Threadz   406

Garner Men's Wear   407

Boomerang Bouncers Entertainment   408

PART FOUR Looking to the Future   411

CHAPTER 13 Managing Growth   412

Learning Objectives   412

Small Business Profile   413

Small Business and Growth   414

The Business Cycle   414

Problems Created by Growth   417

Evaluating the Growth Question   421

Planning for Growth   422

The Expansion Plan   423

Understanding the Requirements of Growth   423

Time to Take Action   427

Learning Objectives Summary   427

Discussion Questions   427

Application Questions and Hands-On Activities   428

Comprehensive Case—Dan Kim: Part 7   429

CHAPTER 14 Managing the Transfer of the Business   430

Learning Objectives   430

Small Business Profile   431

Long-Range Planning   432

Alternative Outcomes for the Business   433

Succession Planning   433

Transferring Ownership to Family Members   435

Selling the Business to an Employee   444

Selling the Business to Outsiders   444

Closing Down or Going Bankrupt   446

Time to Take Action   447

Learning Objectives Summary   447

Discussion Questions   447

Application Questions and Hands-On Activities   448

Cases for Part 4   449

Bailey's Office Supply   449

Baker Hardware Ltd.   450

Brian Luborsky—Premier Salons International Inc.   452

ITI Educational Corporation   453

Company's Coming Cookbooks   453

Directory of Supplementary Cases   CA-1

Clovis Jewellers   CA-2

Thomson Greenhouse   CA-9

Robinson Test Prep Co.   CA-13

Blake Lock and Security Systems   CA-14

The Beach Carrier   CA-16

Gourmet Express   CA-18

The Winslow Clock Company   CA-26

Window Tech Inc.   CA-34

The Framemakers   Online

Top Human Technology Limited   Online

ENDNOTES   EN-1

INDEX   IN-1

PREFACE

Canadian Entrepreneurship & Small Business Management, ninth edition, is the result of many years of teaching entrepreneurship business classes at the college and university levels; of starting and managing several successful small businesses, working closely with numerous owners of small businesses in a consulting role; and, of course, of experience with all the previous successful editions. This edition has gone through a significant revision with a focus on currency, generating and maintaining student interest in the subject matter, and improving academic rigour. All changes were made while staying true to the book's vision of being easy to follow and absorb.

To accomplish these sometimes diverse aims, the text draws upon theory from the fields of entrepreneurship, small business management, and the major functional areas of business, including management, marketing, accounting, and finance. The text supports theory with over 100 real-life business examples, featured in box-inserts, and opening profiles. These inserts have been carefully selected to include both a mix of young inspiring entrepreneurs with experienced high-profile business owners. In addition, 40 of the box-inserts have become small-to mid-sized cases featuring thought-provoking discussion questions to generate student interest in the subject matter. The chapters now feature over 200 additional in-text examples about current business owners, trends in small business, and emerging topics in entrepreneurship.

The book is also supported by numerous end-of-chapter cases that illustrate the small business management concepts discussed in the text. These concepts are stated at the beginning of each case in the Instructor's Manual to aid in teaching. Each case proceeds in a logical order from start-up of the business, through management of the existing business, and finally to planning for the future.

WHAT'S NEW IN THIS EDITION

The ninth edition introduces several improvements to the previous editions based on professor and student feedback. Specifically, the ninth edition includes the following:

Chapter 1: The Role of Entrepreneurship and Small Business in Canada

- Enhanced discussion on the benefits of studying small business and entrepreneurship.
- Enhanced discussion on social entrepreneurs, immigrant entrepreneurs, and female entrepreneurs.
- New in-chapter cases on:
  - Crowd-funding and the Pebble Watch, a smartwatch invented by Canadian Eric Migicovsky
  - Young Canadian social entrepreneurs
  - HootSuite.com
  - Mompreneurs

Chapter 2: The Small Business Decision

- Enhanced discussion on the advantages and disadvantages of entrepreneurship.
- Enhanced discussion on small business failure.
- Enhanced discussion on entrepreneurial characteristics.
- New in-chapter cases on:
  - Well.ca, a growing Canadian online retailer
  - Canadian Jordan Satok, who raised $2 million in investment for his company AppHero when he was 18

Chapter 3: Evaluation of a Business Opportunity

- New and enhanced information on idea generation.
- Enhanced information on opportunity assessment.
- Inclusion of social media and Internet tools to conduct market research.
- Enhanced market research section.
- New in-chapter cases on:
  - Spotting new consumer trends
  - Gord Dickie and his web company goalline.ca
  - The Internet's impact on market research

Chapter 4: Organizing a Business—The Business Plan

- New information on the importance of business planning.
- Information which links the chapter on business planning to supporting material in other chapters.
- Expanded information on risk assessment.
- New information on the need to update and revise business plans.
- New in-chapter cases on:
  - Noteable.ca and its planning strategy
  - Shockbox, a concussion sensor for hockey and football helmets
  - Quicksnap and the progression of the company from a sole proprietorship to a partnership to a private corporation
  - The use of shotgun clauses in partnerships and whether they should be included in partnership agreements

Chapter 5: Buying a Business and Franchising

- Combined buying a business and franchising into one chapter.
- New and expanded information on evaluating a business that is for sale.
- Enhanced discussion on the advantages and disadvantages of buying a business.
- New and expanded information on evaluating franchise opportunities.
- New table on evaluating franchise opportunities.
- New in-chapter cases on:
  - NovaScotian Crystal and if the new purchaser can save the troubled company
  - Booster Juice as a franchise opportunity

- Tim Hortons and a group of unhappy franchise owners who are suing the company
- Trends in franchising
- Unhappyfranchise.com and A&W restaurants

Chapter 6: Financing the Small Business

- New information about the size of business, stage of growth, and impact on type of financing.
- New information on equity financing, including information on crowd-funding, and expanded information on other sources of equity.
- New information on Canadian angel investors, pitching to angel investors, and angel organizations.
- Enhanced information on debt as a source of financing.
- New in-chapter cases on:
  - Underuse of equity financing by Canadian entrepreneurs
  - *Dragons' Den* investors as angel investors
  - The willingness of chartered banks to lend money to entrepreneurs

Chapter 7: Marketing Management

- Significant enhancements to the sections on market segmentation, target markets, and customer profiles.
- New information, including an in-chapter case on social media monitoring.
- New information on customer relationship management.
- New in-depth tables illustrating the full list of steps in establishing a successful marketing plan for a retail or service company.
- New information on why some marketing plans fail.

Chapter 8: Managing the Marketing Mix

- New enhanced coverage of all aspects of the marketing mix, including product, place, price, and promotion.
- Large amount of information on promotions for small business. Chapter 8 opens with an emphasis on traditional marketing and extends to include Internet and digital marketing.
- New information on the use of the Internet including enhanced coverage of Internet marketing, digital marketing, and marketing using social media.
- New information on using mobile devices to market a business.
- New information on guerrilla marketing and public relations.
- Enhanced information on steps in the promotional campaign.
- New in-chapter cases on:
  - Groupon and Team Buy and if they are effective marketing tools for SMEs
  - The *Dragons' Den* Effect—the case deals with the positive impact appearing on the show has on a company's sales and brand
  - Pinterest versus Flickr versus Instagram—which is a more effective tool for promoting your business?
  - Stealth marketing and the difference from street or guerrilla marketing

Chapter 9: Financial Management

- New information on cash flow management.
- New information on the various forms of payment firms accept and the implications of acceptance.
- New in-chapter cases on:
  - Legendary story of Ted Rogers and cash flow management
  - Reward credit cards and their impact on SMEs
  - Inbox Marketer's case about the company's cash flow problems and turnaround

Chapter 10: Operations Management

- New information on supply chain.
- New in-text examples.

Chapter 11: Human Resources Management

- Enhanced information on human resources planning.
- Enhanced information on the employee selection process, including information on interviewing and recruitment and a review of the important steps in staffing.
- New information on the use of social media and human resources management.
- New information on leadership and its importance in building a great company.
- Enhanced information on organizational change.
- New in-chapter cases on:
  - Use of LinkedIn and employee recruitment
  - Social media and reference checking
  - Purdy's Chocolates and building employee loyalty
  - Bringing your pets to work as a motivational strategy

Chapter 12: Managing Taxes and Getting Management Assistance

- New information on Canadian taxes.
- New information on boards of directors and advisers.
- New information on mentors.
- New in-chapter case on:
  - Victoria Sopik and Jennifer Nashmi and their Kids and Company

Chapter 13: Managing Growth

- New information on the importance of growth in small and medium businesses.
- Enhanced information on problems created by growth.
- Enhanced information on growth strategies.
- New in-chapter cases on:
  - BeyondtheRack.com, a Canadian flash retailer that is enjoying significant growth
  - Business concerns that arise because of growth

- Secure Key Technologies, a Canadian company that is working to grow by creating security in and around online transactions
- Enviro Paving, a company seeking growth by franchising—the company repaves driveways with recycled rubber
- Bnotions.com, a growing Canadian app and game developer

Chapter 14: Managing the Transfer of the Business

- New information and statistics on family business in Canada.
- New information on creating a successful succession plan.
- New information on successfully selling a business.
- New in-chapter case on disputes in succession.

This text remains appropriate for any entrepreneurship or small business management class at the college or university undergraduate or graduate level. It can also be adapted easily to continuing education classes for those who are thinking about or are currently involved in running their own businesses. In many cases, the text would also be a useful resource book for practitioners outside the classroom setting.

CHAPTER STRUCTURE OF *CANADIAN ENTREPRENEURSHIP & SMALL BUSINESS MANAGEMENT*

Canadian Entrepreneurship & Small Business Management is divided into four parts. Each part covers an essential aspect of starting or managing a small business.

Part 1 provides background information essential to the decision to undertake small business ownership. Chapter 1 reviews the characteristics of small business and its contribution to Canadian society. Chapter 2 covers areas required for a personal evaluation of one's suitability for small business ownership. Chapter 3 presents a systematic procedure for determining whether a small business opportunity is feasible. It includes numerous sources of information essential in carrying out a feasibility analysis.

The three chapters in Part 2 discuss important aspects of starting or obtaining a business. Chapters 4, 5, and 6 review the three methods of establishing a small business. Chapter 4 discusses organizing the small business from scratch, including a special emphasis on the preparation of the business plan. Chapter 5 covers buying a business and franchising as types of small business ownership. Chapter 6 discusses financing concerns in starting the business and includes a listing of sources of financing for entrepreneurs.

Part 3 includes six chapters that discuss the fundamental management practices used in operating the already established business. Chapters 7, 8, 9, 10, 11, and 12 cover in detail the small business applications in marketing, finance, internal operations, and personnel management. Chapter 12 focuses on tax considerations for the small business owner-manager.

Part 4 discusses the future and long-term aspects of small business. Chapter 13 deals with the principles underlying effective growth management. Chapter 14 discusses methods of terminating or transferring the ownership of the enterprise, with a special emphasis on family businesses.

FEATURES OF THIS BOOK

The Incidents contain current examples of small business and entrepreneurship successes and challenges and discuss relevant issues related to the chapter topic. Many Incidents have been expanded to include Discussion Questions.

INCIDENT 1-1

YOUNG CANADIAN SOCIAL ENTREPRENEURS

More and more young Canadians are turning toward social entrepreneurship as a way to make a difference in society and earn a living. For example, Greg Overholt, founder of Toronto-based Students Offering Support, or SOS (www.studentsoffer-ingsupport.ca), recruits volunteers to set up on-campus tutoring sessions for groups of students rather than traditional one-to-one tutoring. This results in a reduction in tutoring costs as students pay on average $10 to $20 for help compared with $50 to $75 charged by for-profit tutors for a similar session. Overholt's company retains a small portion of the fee and uses the rest of the money to build education projects in developing nations, by volunteers on two-week outreach trips. To date, the company has taught more than 25,000 students and raised more than $1 million for projects in Latin America. Twenty-six-year-old Al Roback, owner of Grass Frames (http://grassframes.ca), a socially responsible bike manufacturing company, is another example of a social entrepreneur. Roback's company shuns traditional bike materials, which he believes are not environmentally friendly and makes bike frames entirely out of bamboo tubing and hemp fibre. The firm, which has grown quickly, hopes to continue to expand by selling its environmentally friendly bikes worldwide.

Discussion Questions

1. How would you define social entrepreneurship? Do you think there is a difference between social entrepreneurs and regular entrepreneurs? Why, or why not?
2. Can an entrepreneur consider themselves social entrepreneurs if they retain all the profits from their business?
3. Either in groups or individually, list some ideas for a social enterprise. If time permits, discuss the marketing mix for the social enterprises, including the product or service you will sell, how you will promote the business, the price you will charge, and where the business will

STUDENTS OFFERING SUPPORT IS A SOCIAL ENTERPRISE THAT RAISES MONEY FOR EDUCATION PROJECTS IN DEVELOPING COUNTRIES.

The Small Business Profiles demonstrate real-life examples and real-person profiles, the epitome of applied learning.

SMALL BUSINESS PROFILE

DANI REISS *Canada Goose*

Rick Madonik/GetStock.com

Imagine a company whose products never go on sale, even though competitive products sell for far less. In fact, the business intentionally undersupplies the marketplace to ensure there is always a demand. A firm which does not spend a great deal of money on advertising and relies on word of mouth from customers to sell products. A CEO who insists on producing all of its products in Canada, even though production costs are much higher than many competitors who have outsourced manufacturing to China and other countries. Do you think these strategies or decisions would lead to success? Dani Reiss, current CEO Canada Goose, thought so, and the Canada." As a result, Dani convinced his father to change the name of the business to Canada Goose. Within the year, Dani's father asked him to take over as CEO of the business.[2]

Once he assumed control of the company, Dani faced a major decision—should he follow his competitors and outsource production, or should he continue to manufacture jackets in Canada? Dani says he struggled with the decision as many experts advised him to manufacture in China where he could save substantially on costs. He opted to follow his instinct and continue to produce the coats in Canada. "We took that opportunity to stay in Canada, and by doing that we became successful. The strategy of sticking around [helped] the perception that we are the champions for "Made in Canada," and people appreciate that. You can't be a luxury brand without the history and the heritage."[3]

Dani then opted to change the way the company was marketing its products by focusing on telling a story about the company and its coats. The stories were based on feedback from customers and featured the tagline: "Ask anyone who knows," which is a reference to any customer telling you how great the product is. "We tell the stories of the people who actually use our products. . . . People who live and work in the coldest places on earth, like Antarctica and Northern Canada, our original market."[4]

The company's savvy marketing, combined with some luck, resulted in the company's coats being used in the hit

LEARNING OBJECTIVES SUMMARY

LO1 The entrepreneurial revolution is evidenced by the growing numbers of business establishments, employees in small businesses, government small business programs, college and university small business classes, and entrepreneurial activities of large companies.

LO2 Although defining a small business is difficult, having a definition is important when comparing and evaluating small business, as well as when taking advantage of various lending and assistance programs. Some common criteria for defining small business are gross sales, number of employees, profitability, and type of management structure.

LO3 Small business accounts for 98 percent of all businesses, 30 percent of gross domestic product, and 48 percent of the labour force in Canada.

LO4 Small business can provide jobs, innovations, high productivity, flexibility, a higher proportion of Canadian ownership, and more contributions to society.

LO5 The climate for starting a small business should continue to be strong despite some competitive disadvantages.

Each chapter contains a Summary that clearly reinforces important concepts covered in the chapter.

DISCUSSION QUESTIONS

1. Why do you think entrepreneurial activity has increased? Do you think these trends will continue? Why, or why not?
2. What excites or interests you about being an entrepreneur? What are your major concerns?
3. Under what conditions would the various definitions of small business be more appropriate (e.g., the level of profit may be used by the Canada Revenue Agency to determine the small business tax rate)?
4. What is meant by the statement, "Small business is the backbone of the Canadian economic system"? Give evidence to support this statement.
5. The computer-consulting business is becoming more and more fragmented. In data processing, for example, there are hardware versus software consultants, batch versus time-sharing service bureaus, and mainframe versus microcomputer specialists. What effect does this type of industry fragmentation have on the small business community?

The Discussion Questions and Application Questions and Hands On Activities allow students to use applied and lateral thinking and to come up with unique solutions to typical small business issues.

APPLICATION QUESTIONS AND HANDS-ON ACTIVITIES

1. Form groups of two to three, and start a small business or mini-venture that will run for a period of four to six hours. The only rules are:
   a. The business has to be legal
   b. No lotteries
   c. Maximum investment of $1
   d. Businesses must cease operations at day's end.
   After completing the project, write a reflection stating what you did, whether you made a profit, and what you learned. You may also present this information to the class.
2. Ask three small business owners about their projections for the future of small business. What problems and opportunities do they foresee?
3. Using Internet resources, find out how different Canadian organizations define social enterprise. After preparing a summary report on your findings, draft your own definition of the term.
4. Write a short essay discussing your views on the future of small business given current trends in society *and* in your geographic area.

CLOVIS JEWELLERS

D. Wesley Balderson, *University of Lethbridge*

Clovis Jewellers is a small jewellery store located in Brandon, Manitoba.* You have been called on by the owner to prepare an analysis of the business. The owners have supplied you with a detailed description of their operation and strategy. Critically evaluate each area described in the case.

Structure
Legal Structure.

Clovis Jewellers is an incorporated company under the name of Clovis Jewellers (1988) Limited. It is a privately held corporation. The only shareholders are Mr. and Mrs. Neudorf, each of whom owns 50 percent of the outstanding shares. As a corporation, Clovis Jewellers is authorized to issue an unlimited number of Class A, B, and C common shares. The only outstanding shares are 100 Class A shares. In the case of Clovis Jewellers, the shareholders are the owners, directors, and managers.

Financial Structure.

The capital structure of Clovis Jewellers is financed by a com-

and is filled by Mr. Neudorf. The duties of this position include accounting and financial management, management of day-to-day store operations, and gemologist/diamond expert. Mr. Neudorf works together with both the assistant manager and the sales staff.

The second level in the organization is the assistant manager and is filled by Mrs. Neudorf. She works as the assistant manager approximately 50 percent of the time and as a salesperson the remaining 50 percent. The duties of the assistant manager include purchasing merchandise and controlling inventory. The inventory control function is done on a very informal basis, usually by a simple visual check.

The third level in the organization includes the sales staff and the repair service administrator. The job of overseeing the repair service is held by one of the full-time salespersons and requires approximately 20 percent of her time. The number of salespersons varies with the time of year, ranging from six to seven at Christmastime to two or three during the summer months.

The fourth level in the organization is the goldsmith and repairperson. This position is filled by Mr. Neudorf and requires a great deal of his time. Mr. Neudorf works together with the repair service administrator when acting

The end-of-part Cases, as well as the supplementary end-of-text Cases, provide numerous opportunities for students to apply the theory covered in the text.

The Comprehensive Case runs throughout the text and is updated for the ninth edition. Following a typical small business person's progress and challenges, this case allows students to build upon the concepts as their course progresses.

COMPREHENSIVE CASE | **DAN KIM: PART 3**

Dan is quite proud of his business plan and realizes that he has learned a lot in preparing it. He also realizes, however, that for the business to get off the ground, he needs financing. Suzie will only let Dan use $20,000 of their savings for the venture, but Dan is of the opinion that this will at least help them get started. Once the business is up and running, additional funds will be generated through sales of the Ladder Rail.

Dan decides that he would rather establish the manufacturing facility from scratch than purchase the plant that is for sale. This way he can arrange the facility in a way that suits him, and he will not have to spend money to retrofit. In addition, Dan lives on an acreage and he already owns enough property on which to construct the building. He estimates that constructing a small building of 2000 square feet will cost about $100,000. Although he can use some of the metal-cutting and -bending equipment that he already has, another $30,000 is required to obtain the equipment required to move to commercial production of the Ladder Rail. Dan also thinks that he will need a truck to haul inventory to the plant and to deliver the finished product to purchasers. The esti-

FIGURE 3-B	Ladder Rail Income Statement
Revenue: 5000 units at $40	$200,000
Cost of goods sold: 5000 units at $10	50,000
Wages (Sid: $50,000; 2 workers at $30,000 each)	110,000
Utilities and phone	15,000
Net income	$ 15,000

When Dan takes this statement to the banker, he is still told that more work needs to be done. Dan goes home to Suzie feeling pretty discouraged and is not sure what to do next.

Suzie and Dan decide to spend some time researching other potential sources of money online. Both are surprised to learn about the number of angel investors and angel groups in their region. Suzie thinks pursuing angel support for their business would be ideal as the couple will not be burdened with interest costs, which are associated with traditional bank financing. Furthermore, if the business fails, they

INSTRUCTOR AND STUDENT SUPPORT FOR STUDENTS

McGraw-Hill Connect™ is a web-based assignment and assessment platform that gives students the means to better connect with their coursework, with their instructors, and with the important concepts that they will need to know for success now and in the future.

With Connect, instructors can deliver assignments, quizzes, and tests online. Instructors can edit existing questions and author entirely new problems. Track individual student performance—by question, by assignment, or in relation to the class overall—with detailed grade reports. Instructors can integrate grade reports easily with Learning Management Systems (LMS).

By choosing Connect, instructors are providing their students with a powerful tool for improving academic performance and truly mastering course material. Connect allows students to practise important skills at their own pace and on their own schedule. Importantly, students' assessment results and instructors' feedback are all saved online—so students can continually review their progress and plot their course to success.

Connect also provides 24/7 online access to an eBook—an online edition of the text—to aid them in successfully completing their work, wherever and whenever they choose.

KEY FEATURES

Simple Assignment Management

With Connect, creating assignments is easier than ever, so you can spend more time teaching and less time managing.

- Create and deliver assignments easily with selectable end-of-chapter questions and test-bank material to assign online.
- Streamline lesson planning, student progress reporting, and assignment grading to make classroom management more efficient than ever.
- Go paperless with the eBook and online submission and grading of student assignments.

Smart Grading

When it comes to studying, time is precious. Connect helps students learn more efficiently by providing feedback and practice material when they need it, where they need it.

- Automatically score assignments, giving students immediate feedback on their work and side-by-side comparisons with correct answers.
- Access and review each response; manually change grades, or leave comments for students to review.
- Reinforce classroom concepts with practice tests and instant quizzes.

Instructor Library

The Connect Instructor Library is your course creation hub. It provides all the critical resources you will need to build your course, just how you want to teach it.

- Assign eBook readings and draw from a rich collection of textbook-specific assignments.
- Access instructor resources, including ready-made PowerPoint® presentations and media to use in your lectures.
- View assignments and resources created for past sections.
- Post your own resources for students to use.

eBook

Connect reinvents the textbook learning experience for the modern student. Every Connect subject area is seamlessly integrated with Connect eBooks, which are designed to keep students focused on the concepts key to their success.

- Provide students with a Connect eBook, allowing for anytime, anywhere access to the textbook.
- Merge media, animation, and assessments with the text's narrative to engage students and improve learning and retention.
- Pinpoint and connect key concepts in a snap using the powerful eBook search engine.
- Manage notes, highlights, and bookmarks in one place for simple, comprehensive review.

FOR INSTRUCTORS

Canadian Small Business & Entrepreneurship, ninth edition, offers a complete, integrated supplements package to address all your needs.

- **Instructor's Manual:** The Instructor's Manual, prepared by the text author, Peter Mombourquette, accurately represents the text's content and supports instructors' needs. Each chapter includes the learning objectives, glossary of key terms, a chapter synopsis, complete lecture outline, and solutions to the end-of-chapter discussion questions.
- **EZ Test Computerized Test Bank:** This flexible and easy to use electronic testing program allows instructors to create tests from book specific items. Created by Morden Shapiro, University of Ontario Institute of Technology, the Test Bank has undergone a rigorous auditing and revision process for the ninth edition. It contains a broad selection of multiple choice, true/false, and essay questions, and instructors may add their own questions as well. Each question identifies the relevant page reference and difficulty level. Multiple versions of the test can be created and printed.
- **Powerpoint® Presentations:** Prepared by Nicole Roarke, St. Clair College, these robust presentations offer high-quality visuals from the text and highlight key business concepts from each chapter to bring them to life.

- **Videos:** Accompanying the text, and accessible within Connect or on an instructor DVD with closed captioning, a series of videos from the CBC and other sources demonstrate real life situations and how the concepts work in the world of business. All segments are tied in by concept to the chapters in the text.

SUPERIOR LEARNING SOLUTIONS AND SUPPORT

The McGraw-Hill Ryerson team is ready to help you assess and integrate any of our products, technology, and services into your course for optimal teaching and learning performance. Whether it's helping your students improve their grades, or putting your entire course online, the McGraw-Hill Ryerson team is here to help you do it. Contact your Learning Solutions Consultant today to learn how to maximize all of McGraw-Hill Ryerson's resources!

For more information on the latest technology and Learning Solutions offered by McGraw-Hill Ryerson and its partners, please visit us online: www.mcgrawhill.ca/he/solutions.

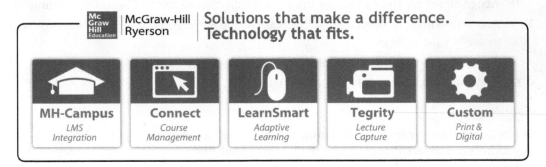

ACKNOWLEDGEMENTS

Many people contributed to *Canadian Entrepreneurship & Small Business Management*, ninth edition. I am as always particularly grateful to my beautiful wife who serves as an editor, idea generator, and friend. I am, of course, indebted to the wonderful people at McGraw-Hill Ryerson, including especially Kim Brewster, Tracey Haggart, Jessica Barnoski, Erin Moore, and Rohini Herbert. Reviewers of the ninth edition and reviewers and users of the previous eight editions also provided valuable suggestions. Reviewers include the following:

Robert Anderson, *University of Regina*

Dan Doiron, *University of New Brunswick, Saint John*

Larry Drew, *Conestoga College*

Jon Kerr, *York University*

Angie Lyrette, *Algonquin College*

Michael Madore, *University of Lethbridge*

Mario Pascucci, *George Brown College*

I thank Wes Balderson and Professor Jim Clark, University of Lethbridge, who authored some of the cases.

I also thank the many authors and entrepreneurs who granted us permission to use diagrams, tables, profiles, and article excerpts to illustrate the text concepts.

Dr. Peter Mombourquette

PART
I

THE DECISION TO START A BUSINESS

The decision to start one's own business is a difficult one. It often involves leaving secure employment to face an uncertain financial future. Such a decision can have far-reaching effects on the physical, emotional, and financial aspects of one's life. To provide a better understanding of the implications and preparation for this decision, Part 1 discusses three topics.

Chapter 1 reviews the role of small business in Canadian society. It examines current trends and the probable future environment for small business.

Chapter 2 describes the characteristics of successful and unsuccessful small businesses, and the personal characteristics that make up the majority of successful entrepreneurs. The chapter also reviews the potential advantages and disadvantages of operating one's own business. Understanding this information can help one make an informed small business career decision.

Once an individual understands the relative merits of starting a small business and feels suited to such a career, he or she can do several things in pursuit of the best business opportunity. Generally, a person needs to gather a considerable amount of information to evaluate business opportunities. Chapter 3 presents ideas that can improve information collection and analysis skills for this purpose.

THE ROLE OF ENTREPRENEURSHIP AND SMALL BUSINESS IN CANADA

LEARNING OBJECTIVES

By the end of this chapter, you should be able to:

LO1 Discuss the level of interest and activity in the small business sector.

LO2 Evaluate common methods of defining small business and explain why a definition is important.

LO3 Describe the current extent of entrepreneurship and small business in Canada.

LO4 Discuss the benefits a healthy small business sector can offer society.

LO5 Explain the probable future environment for entrepreneurship and the small business community.

SMALL BUSINESS PROFILE

DANI REISS *Canada Goose*

Rick Madonik/GetStock.com

Imagine a company whose products never go on sale, even though competitive products sell for far less. In fact, the business intentionally undersupplies the marketplace to ensure there is always a demand. A firm which does not spend a great deal of money on advertising and relies on word of mouth from customers to sell products. A CEO who insists on producing all of its products in Canada, even though production costs are much higher than many competitors who have outsourced manufacturing to China and other countries. Do you think these strategies or decisions would lead to success? Dani Reiss, current CEO Canada Goose, thought so, and the results have been outstanding. Since Reiss has taken over as CEO of the family-run business, sales have soared 3500 percent and have recently surpassed $150 million. Just last year Canada Goose sold 400,000 coats in 44 countries.[1]

Canada Goose can trace its origins to Dani's grandfather, Sam Tick, an immigrant who started an apparel business in 1957. David Reiss, Sam's son-in-law, eventually took over the business and developed a niche product, "Snow Goose" parkas, which were down-filled coats for public sector workers such as police and park rangers. Dani, a Bachelor of Arts student, had little desire to work in the family business but agreed to work for the company for a short period of time to make some money so he could travel. During this brief stint with the company, Dani learned more about the firm and the connection many customers had with the "Made in Canada" label. Dani noted that many customers associated the product with their ideal image of the Canadian wilderness. "I realized people had an emotional connection to 'Made in Canada.' The experience of owning one of these jackets was like trying on a piece of

Canada." As a result, Dani convinced his father to change the name of the business to Canada Goose. Within the year, Dani's father asked him to take over as CEO of the business.[2]

Once he assumed control of the company, Dani faced a major decision—should he follow his competitors and outsource production, or should he continue to manufacture jackets in Canada? Dani says he struggled with the decision as many experts advised him to manufacture in China where he could save substantially on costs. He opted to follow his instinct and continue to produce the coats in Canada. "We took that opportunity to stay in Canada, and by doing that we became successful. The strategy of sticking around [helped] the perception that we are the champions for "Made in Canada," and people appreciate that. You can't be a luxury brand without the history and the heritage."[3]

Dani then opted to change the way the company was marketing its products by focusing on telling a story about the company and its coats. The stories were based on feedback from customers and featured the tagline: "Ask anyone who knows," which is a reference to any customer telling you how great the product is. "We tell the stories of the people who actually use our products. . . . People who live and work in the coldest places on earth, like Antarctica and Northern Canada, our original market."[4]

The company's savvy marketing, combined with some luck, resulted in the company's coats being used in the hit movie, *The Day After Tomorrow*. In addition, a number of celebrities were photographed wearing the coats, including Kate Upton on the cover of *Sports Illustrated* Swimsuit edition, as well as Matt Damon and Sacha Baron Cohen. As sales grew, Dani's next decision was on how to maintain momentum. Business experts wondered if the company would revisit the question of producing products in other countries or diversify by licensing out the brand. Rather than diversify or license out, the younger Reiss is opting to stay the course as a niche brand manufactured in Canada. Dani says, "I believe a lot of brands have lost an element of their soul by outsourcing to Asia. If you look at some of the world's greatest brands, like Louis Vuitton—it is all made at 27 factories in France…we are not a mass brand. The strongest brands in the world are true to what they say."[5] Canada Goose is staying focused on selling winter jackets and creating complementary products such as spring and fall jackets, branded toques, and gloves. The strategy is working, and Dani notes he is happy with the results of the new products.

CANADA GOOSE
www.canada-goose.com

INTRODUCTION TO ENTREPRENEURSHIP AND WHY STUDENTS WILL WANT TO STUDY THE SUBJECT

This chapter provides an overview of the importance of and trends toward small business. The terms "entrepreneurship" and "small business ownership" will be used interchangeably throughout the chapter. Entrepreneurs typically start small businesses, but sometimes they establish larger enterprises. At the same time, many small business owners may not be considered very entrepreneurial. The differences between entrepreneurs and small business owners or managers will be discussed in detail in Chapter 2. In addition, the distinction between the entrepreneur and the small business is often difficult to make because the owner-manager and the business are frequently very much intertwined. This relationship between entrepreneur and business will also be discussed in the next chapter.

What you may be asking yourself is, "Why should I study entrepreneurship?" Perhaps you are interested in owning a business or are curious about why some businesses succeed and others fail. What you should know is entrepreneurship is an exciting field and there are many benefits to studying about small business such as:

- Students who study entrepreneurship are more likely to start a business.
- Students who enrol in entrepreneurship courses earn more money.
- Students who enrol in entrepreneurship courses learn about important topics such as business planning, managing growth, and family business.
- Students who study entrepreneurship develop critical thinking and problem solving skills.
- Due to trends in the workforce, such as outsourcing and subcontracting, many would-be employees end up working for themselves. People who study entrepreneurship are more likely to succeed in today's workforce.
- Ninety-nine percent of businesses in Canada are considered small or medium enterprises (SMEs), so even if you never become an entrepreneur, you are likely to work in a small firm. Studying entrepreneurship will provide you with the knowledge and skills to be successful in small companies.
- Research indicates that students enjoy learning about entrepreneurship.

To better understand entrepreneurship and small business, it is important to consider the nature and development of the subject, particularly as it pertains to Canada.

NATURE AND DEVELOPMENT OF ENTREPRENEURSHIP IN CANADA   LO1

Since the mid-1970s, there has been a reawakening of interest in entrepreneurship and business ownership in Canada, the United States, and abroad. After the Second World War, the philosophy in many circles was that bigger was better in both business and government. As a result, for several years, government increased in size, and the climate for big business improved.

The critics of "bigness," however, have gathered support because big government and big business have failed to provide the expected panacea for society's economic problems. The result has been that more people and more governments are looking to small business to provide a catalyst for their stagnant economies and to enable faster economic growth. As John Naisbitt stated in *Global Paradox*, "The entrepreneur is the most important player in the building of the global economy, so much so that big companies are decentralizing and reconstituting themselves as networks of entrepreneurs. Huge companies must break up to become confederations of small, autonomous, entrepreneurial companies if they are to survive."[6]

In a recent survey conducted by Ernst and Young, 8 out of 10 influential North Americans indicated that they believe entrepreneurialism will define twenty-first-century business.[7] Many other countries share in this growth and increased awareness.[8] This growth trend for entrepreneurial interest and behaviour is also evident in Canada. The Global Entrepreneurship Monitor places Canada third in entrepreneurship progress out of 53 countries studied but second only to the United States among the G8 countries.[9] Canada has one of the highest levels of entrepreneurial activity in innovation-driven economies, according to recent Global Entrepreneurship Monitor guidelines.[10] Currently, over 15 percent of the Canadian workforce is self-employed with no paid employees.[11] While this percentage may seem small, it does not include those who are planning to start small businesses, or those who are employed by small businesses. By any measure, however, the trend toward improved entrepreneurial attitude, self-employment growth, and small business formation is all positive in Canada. Starting a business is now seen as a preferred occupational alternative for a majority of Canadians (Figure 1-1) and self-employed people make up over 15 percent of the labour force (Figure 1-2).

This growth in entrepreneurial attitudes, along with the significant growth in self-employment and small business formations, illustrates that entrepreneurship is firmly established in Canada. Except for a brief slowing of this growth from 1999 to 2002 and from 2008 to 2010, the growth of small businesses has consistently surpassed that of larger organizations and the economy as a whole.[12] As a result, the importance of the small business sector of Canadian society is now more widely acknowledged than ever.

What has fuelled this growth? Throughout this text, we will use many examples of entrepreneurs to illustrate why an increasing number of people are establishing their own businesses. The dream of starting small and developing a successful business, such as that of Eric Migicovsky,

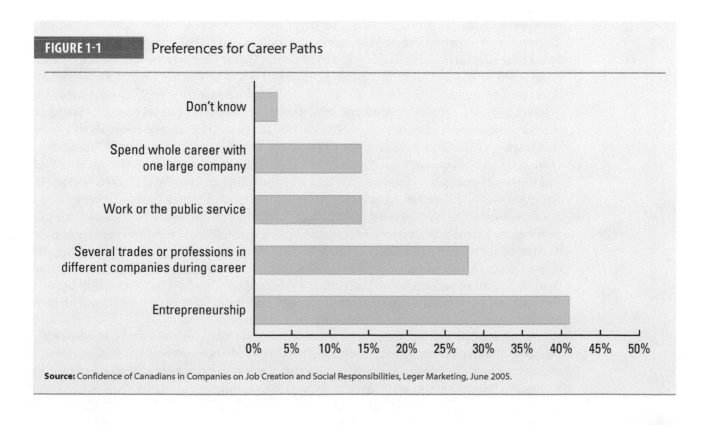

FIGURE 1-1   Preferences for Career Paths

Source: Confidence of Canadians in Companies on Job Creation and Social Responsibilities, Leger Marketing, June 2005.

FIGURE 1-2   Self-Employed as a Percent of the Labour Force

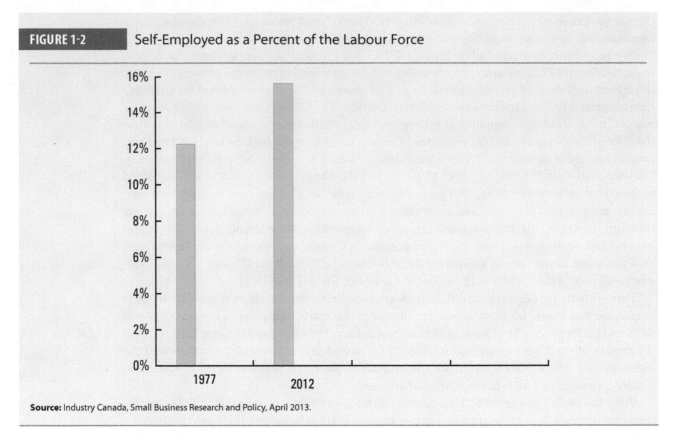

Source: Industry Canada, Small Business Research and Policy, April 2013.

who invented the Pebble Watch, a smartwatch that links to iPhone, Android, and BlackBerry devices (see below), is shared by many. However, many individuals have become successful entrepreneurs due to the downsizing of larger organizations. A recent survey found that 22 percent of small businesses are started for this reason.[13] For example, Ted Nugent, a Vancouver computer games developer, started Genius Factor Games (www.geniusfactorgames. com) when he was laid off from a gaming company. He was able to use his experience and his interest in being his own boss to launch his first product—Gravity Well. Ted describes the product as a cross between pinball and mini-golf.[14] Genius Factor Games has since launched several games for smartphones and mobile devices and in 2011 developed Heart Hero, a game that teaches people how to administer CPR, for the Canadian Heart and Stroke Foundation. During the past recession, from 2008 to 2010, many companies downsized, and many college and university graduates who were unable to secure employment started their own businesses. For example, David McDonald of Halifax started his own landscaping business after he could not find work when he graduated from Mount Saint Vincent University (www.msvu.ca/business) with a Bachelor of Business Administration degree. McDonald used his business skills to determine there are people who are interested in environmentally friendly landscaping and offered lawncare using organic products and push mowers. A recent labour force survey found that 12 percent of self-employed individuals were "pushed" into business ownership because there was no work available.[15] Others chose to leave secure employment and strike out on their own because of a natural interest or a desire for a challenge.

While some people are drawn to starting a business from scratch to make money or are pushed into entrepreneurship when they cannot find a job, others are attracted to entrepreneurship as a means to make a living and help solve some of society's problems. This trend of earning money and helping society has given rise to the term "social entrepreneurship." A social entrepreneur is a person who applies the skills of entrepreneurship such as risk taking, problem solving, and business planning to create a social change. Social entrepreneurs not only strive to make money, but they also work toward making the world a sustainable community. For example, Jim Reid of Green Solutions Inc. (www.gsnai.com), a North American reuse and recycling company in Bridgewater, Nova Scotia, noticed that many large firms were not only throwing used office furniture such as chairs and desks into landfills, but they were also disposing of workable electronic devices such as smartphones and laptops in a similar fashion. Reid saw this as an opportunity to help society and make money. His company diverts used office furniture and electronic devices from landfills and distributes them to charities that are in need of such products. Rather than charge the charities for the supplies, Reid gets paid by the large firms who are looking for an environmentally friendly way to get rid of furniture and equipment they no longer want. When Reid first started the company, many business experts told him that corporations would not pay for such a service, but Reid has proven them wrong by signing up some of Canada's largest companies, including RBC and TD Bank. Reid says, "Green Solutions recognizes the need for a simple, turnkey, cost-effective way to eliminate and re-purpose no-longer-needed facility assets . . . and we are seeing a large increase in organizations across the board wanting to be part of what we do."[16] Canadian philanthropist, and eBay's first employee and eventual CEO, Jeff Skoll, believes so much in the idea of social enterprise and social entrepreneurship that he created the Skoll Foundation (www.skollfoundation.org) to invest in social entrepreneurs. The Foundation is the world's largest organization dedicated to social entrepreneurship and makes annual grants of $40 million to social entrepreneurs and social organizations throughout the world. Skoll thinks that many of society's problems are complex and need to be addressed with innovative solutions.[17] Who better to develop these solutions than entrepreneurs? Entrepreneurs are known for their hard work, problem solving skills, and innovativeness, which is needed in today's society. Social entrepreneurs are usually ambitious people who value helping society over making a profit and are driven to produce results.

EBAY'S FIRST CEO, CANADIAN JEFF SKOLL, HAS SET UP THE SKOLL FOUNDATION TO PROMOTE SOCIAL ENTERPRISE.
Dick Loek/GetStock.com

INCIDENT 1-1

YOUNG CANADIAN SOCIAL ENTREPRENEURS

More and more young Canadians are turning toward social entrepreneurship as a way to make a difference in society and earn a living. For example, Greg Overholt, founder of Toronto-based Students Offering Support, or SOS (www.studentsoffer-ingsupport.ca), recruits volunteers to set up on-campus tutoring sessions for groups of students rather than traditional one-to-one tutoring. This results in a reduction in tutoring costs as students pay on average $10 to $20 for help compared with $50 to $75 charged by for-profit tutors for a similar session. Overholt's company retains a small portion of the fee and uses the rest of the money to build education projects in developing nations, by volunteers on two-week outreach trips. To date, the company has taught more than 25,000 students and raised more than $1 million for projects in Latin America. Twenty-six-year-old Al Roback, owner of Grass Frames (http://grassframes.ca), a socially responsible bike manufacturing company, is another example of a social entrepreneur. Roback's company shuns traditional bike materials, which he believes are not environmentally friendly and makes bike frames entirely out of bamboo tubing and hemp fibre. The firm, which has grown quickly, hopes to continue to expand by selling its environmentally friendly bikes worldwide.

STUDENTS OFFERING SUPPORT IS A SOCIAL ENTERPRISE THAT RAISES MONEY FOR EDUCATION PROJECTS IN DEVELOPING COUNTRIES.
Photo courtesy of Students Offering Support

Discussion Questions

1. How would you define social entrepreneurship? Do you think there is a difference between social entrepreneurs and regular entrepreneurs? Why, or why not?
2. Can an entrepreneur consider themselves social entrepreneurs if they retain all the profits from their business?
3. Either in groups or individually, list some ideas for a social enterprise. If time permits, discuss the marketing mix for the social enterprises, including the product or service you will sell, how you will promote the business, the price you will charge, and where the business will be located.

Sources: www.profitguide.com/startup/success-stories/profile-greg-overholt-2012-fuel-award-winner-45299; www.studentsofferingsupport.ca; and http://grassframes.ca.

Recently, governments have been promoting social enterprise at the national and provincial levels, and several provinces such as Nova Scotia have developed strategies to assist social entrepreneurs. Prominent Canadian social enterprise organizations include the Social Enterprise Council of Canada (www.secouncil.ca/en) and the Canadian Social Enterprise Foundation (www.csef.ca).

The above information and examples provide evidence of the growth of small business and how entrepreneurs such as Eric Migicovsky and Jim Reid can overcome hurdles to be successful—a detailed discussion regarding the evidence of small business growth follows.

INCREASES IN THE NUMBER OF BUSINESS ESTABLISHMENTS

Considerable research has been done to determine the number of new businesses established each year. This has proved a difficult, if not impossible, task because of the many different types of businesses as well as the varied methods of estimating business start-ups. Some indicators of business start-ups that researchers have used include tax returns, new employer registrations, phone hookups, new incorporations, and business registrations.[18]

CROWD-FUNDING HELPS A CANADIAN BUILD A SMARTWATCH

Eric Migicovsky, a Canadian and University of Waterloo graduate, was driven by a dream to build a smartwatch that would link to iPhones and Android smartphones. Migicovsky, who managed to build a simpler version of the product for BlackBerry devices, wanted to develop a more complex product called "the Pebble," a smartwatch that would display text, alert users about incoming emails, and control music on their phone (http://getpebble.com). A big challenge for Migicovsky was raising the funds needed to develop the product, as traditional lenders such as banks were leery about investing in the idea and in the young entrepreneur. When Migicovsky failed to raise the funds needed to start the business from conventional sources, he turned to the Internet and a new fundraising solution called "crowd-sourcing." Crowd-sourcing or crowd-funding is a relatively new funding concept where people donate or invest money in start-up companies for a future reward. The reward in this case, was an actual Pebble watch that Migicovsky had yet to build. People who donated $115 would receive the new watch that was supposed to retail at $150 once the product was finished.[19]

THE PEBBLE WATCH, WHICH WAS JUST RELEASED THIS YEAR, IS HOPING TO PROVIDE CONSUMERS WITH A SMARTWATCH TO GO ALONG WITH THEIR SMARTPHONES. THE COMPANY RECENTLY RAISED $10 MILLION ON CROWD-FUNDING SITE KICKSTARTER.
© Mlenny/iStockPhoto

Using the crowd-funding website, Kickstarter (www.kickstarter.com), Migicovsky hoped to raise $100,000 in a month or enough money to produce 1000 watches. What happened next was almost impossible to predict; as Migicovsky's idea was shared among Kickstarter followers, contributions started to roll in, and he surpassed his original goal in less than two hours. A month later, at the end of the fundraising period, Migicovsky managed to raise over $10 million. Migicovsky says that the process of using crowd-funding was simple compared with other methods of raising funds. "Previously the method of bringing a hardware product to market was to create a demo, show it off . . . If they said 'yes,' you worked for another two years to make the product and then spent a lot of money on marketing and worried about having a distribution channel in place. Whereas we just skipped all of that and went directly to the consumer. It's a straight-forward process: you put a video together and figure out what rewards to give to attract backers. You submit it, you post it, and the next thing you know people are pledging money. They're voting with their wallets that this is what they want to see."[20]

Now with $10 million in start-up capital, Migicovsky went from trying to create a small profit to building a large company—something he always wanted to achieve. Rather than build the watch in North America, Migicovsky outsourced production to China and started working with application developers to build additional apps for the watch. The result was a delay in production, which bothered some of the company's donors who regularly communicate on Kickstarter. Migicovsky opted to use his blog to update contributors about the company's progress and recently announced they would be shipping 15,000 watches a week. He has also announced that app developers are lining up to offer useful tools for the watch, and so far the Pebble comes with a preinstalled function that can measure exercise output while cycling, GPS, and a golf range finder. Additional apps, according to Migicovsky, are in development and will be available in the near future.[21]

The case of Migicovsky and the Pebble smartwatch highlights the most successful crowd-funding story to date. The use of crowds of people donating or investing small amounts of money into a company appears to be ideal for entrepreneurs. Yet readers should recognize the term is relatively new, and while some entrepreneurs see the money coming in as a donation or a pre-order, as in the case of the Pebble watch, other entrepreneurs are asking people to invest money into their company for a share of future profits. Given the blurring of lines, the Canadian government is studying crowd-funding and considering regulations aimed at protecting both the entrepreneur and the investor.

Discussion Questions

1. Do you think the Pebble watch will be a successful product? Why, or why not?

2. Why do you think some traditional lenders did not want to lend money to Migicovsky?

3. Why do you think Migicovsky's use of crowd-funding was so successful?

4. What do you think are some of the advantages and disadvantages of crowd-funding?

5. Do you consider crowd-funders to be donors or investors? Why?

6. Visit the Kickstarter website, and report back to the class some of the best ideas that are being pitched. What are the terms associated with the ideas? Would you personally donate or invest money using crowd-funding?

7. Should the government create rules and regulations for crowd-funding? Why, or why not? What are some advantages and disadvantages of creating rules?

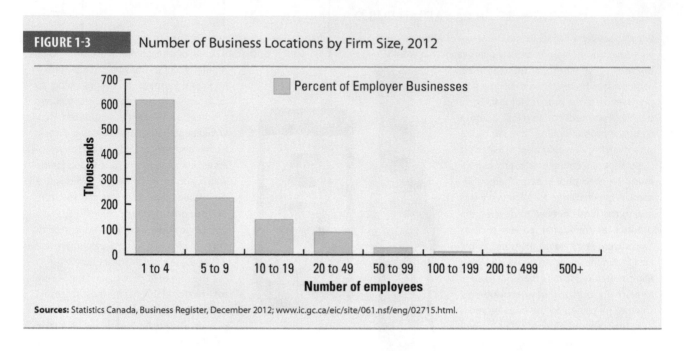

FIGURE 1-3   Number of Business Locations by Firm Size, 2012

■ Percent of Employer Businesses

Thousands

Number of employees: 1 to 4, 5 to 9, 10 to 19, 20 to 49, 50 to 99, 100 to 199, 200 to 499, 500+

Sources: Statistics Canada, Business Register, December 2012; www.ic.gc.ca/eic/site/061.nsf/eng/02715.html.

Figure 1-3 illustrates the number of small businesses in Canada in 2012. Small businesses with few employees constitute the vast majority of all businesses with employees, but small businesses with no employees make up an even larger number. In addition, the number of businesses with fewer than 50 employees has increased substantially over the past decade. Similar trends for the United States show even more increases in small business formations than in Canada.[22] During the recent recession, even though job losses were significant among small businesses, the overall net change in the self-employed increased by close to 2 percent per year, while employees totals dropped over 2 percent per year.[23] Statistics Canada has estimated that 98.1 percent of all existing businesses have fewer than 100 employees, 75 percent have fewer than 10 employees, and 55 percent have from one to four employees.[24] By 2012, 48 percent of the total workforce, or 5 million Canadians were employed by small business.[25] A recent CIBC report indicated that the self-employment growth rate has been double that of the growth in the number of firms with paid employees.[26] Further, recent Statistics Canada data indicate the growth rate of the self-employed to be 57 percent, from 1987 to 2011.[27]

INCREASES IN THE NUMBER OF EMPLOYEES OF SMALL BUSINESSES

The number of Canadians employed by small and medium sized businesses has grown substantially in recent years[28] and has been estimated at slightly over 5 million.[29] In addition, there is a marked shift in new job creation from a reliance on big firms and projects to small firms and entrepreneurs. Statistics Canada indicates that more than 42 percent of total job growth from 2000 to 2011 was due to small businesses.[30]

INCREASES IN GOVERNMENT INTEREST AND PROGRAMS

Politicians recognize the importance of small business to a healthy economy and are beginning to offer various financial and non-financial programs to assist the small business owner.[31] Recently the Canadian government announced that it had achieved a 20 percent reduction in government paperwork burden for small business.[32] The Entrepreneurship and Small Business Office in the Department of Industry Canada coordinates and administers programs designed to aid small business at the federal level. Likewise, all the provinces and territories have departments that perform the same function for small businesses within their jurisdictions. Appendix 3A (on Connect) lists some of these agencies. In addition, Canada Revenue Agency provides a number of tax breaks to entrepreneurs and investors who lend money to small and growing firms.

INCREASES IN THE NUMBER OF SMALL BUSINESS-RELATED COURSES AT COLLEGES AND UNIVERSITIES

The level of interest in small business-related courses at Canadian colleges and universities has risen dramatically in the past few years. The trend of increasing the number of entrepreneurship courses in business schools appears to be continuing.[33] Traditionally, such courses were housed in management and commerce faculties and attracted only students of those faculties. However, as a result of the growing general interest in small business, many non-business majors now take these courses. In addition, entrepreneurship courses have become increasingly common in Arts and Science programs throughout the country. This growth has been attributed to a number of factors, including a strong likelihood that these students, particularly those studying fine arts and engineering, may one day become entrepreneurs. As such, many schools have added entrepreneurship courses as a matter of practicality. Demand has also been fuelled by Arts and Science students who see studying entrepreneurship as a way to linking career development to their chosen field of study. Entrepreneurship courses are also becoming common at high schools throughout Canada, and some entrepreneurial topics are being discussed in K–9 classrooms.

INCREASES IN ENTREPRENEURIAL ACTIVITIES KNOWN AS INTRAPRENEURSHIP IN LARGE BUSINESSES

Intrapreneurship can be defined as entrepreneurship within an existing organization. Intrapreneurs are employees, who use entrepreneurial skills to solve problems or create additional revenue streams for a company. Ali Asaria was acting as an intrapreneur when he created the mobile game *Brick Breaker* for BlackBerry (http://ca.blackberry.com/). Many large, successful companies have developed or altered their organizations to promote creativity, entrepreneurship, and individual initiative.[34] These businesses have realized considerable productivity gains by encouraging this type of intrapreneurship. For example, 3M Canada (www.3m.com/ca) encourages employees to act intrapreneurially and will give them time away from their traditional jobs if it believes the employee's ideas could lead to costs savings or additional revenue. In their extensive study of successful large companies, which resulted in the best-selling book *In Search of Excellence,* Thomas Peters and Robert Waterman found that one common characteristic of these organizations was their formal encouragement of entrepreneurship within and among departments. These companies were quick to recognize increases in productivity and innovativeness by rewarding employees who engaged in such entrepreneurial behaviour.[35] Canadian companies such as Bombardier and CGI Group are examples of companies that have incorporated these practices into their organizations. Other large companies have struggled with the implementation of intrapreneurship because of their size and bureaucratic structure. This difficulty also exists within spin-off entrepreneurial divisions of the main company.[36] This will be discussed further in Chapter 2.

INCREASES IN THE POLITICAL POWER OF SMALL BUSINESS

The small business community is a significant economic force in Canadian society. Several organizations are currently attempting to advance the small business cause through lobbying efforts and educational programs. The largest and most visible organization is the Canadian Federation of Independent Business (CFIB), which boasts a membership of more than 109,000. Current concerns of CFIB members include high tax rates, sales tax harmonization initiatives, government regulations, and employment insurance premiums.[37] Lobbying has resulted in many government programs and some legislation beneficial to small business. Many industry associations made up primarily of small businesses are also very active in lobbying activities and have influenced the directions of government initiatives.

IMPROVEMENT IN THE IMAGE OF SMALL BUSINESS

Small business owners and entrepreneurs are viewed very positively today. The benefits of entrepreneurship are being proclaimed by universities and colleges, governments, and corporations. Entrepreneurship careers are considered to be honourable and, in some cases, prestigious pursuits. An increasing number of Canadians recognize the economic benefits of a healthy small business sector (Figure 1-4). As people continue to recognize the benefits that small businesses provide to society, the occupation of entrepreneur will carry more prestige. Evidence of the prestige associated with entrepreneurship can be found in a recent survey carried out by *Business Week*, which found that small business leaders were more trusted by the general public than leaders of religious institutions, big business, the news media, labour unions, and governments.[38]

A significant influencer on the public's positive attitude toward entrepreneurship has been the increased coverage of entrepreneurship in the media. The media have played a powerful role by engaging in discussions about impact of entrepreneurship on society, highlighting entrepreneurial

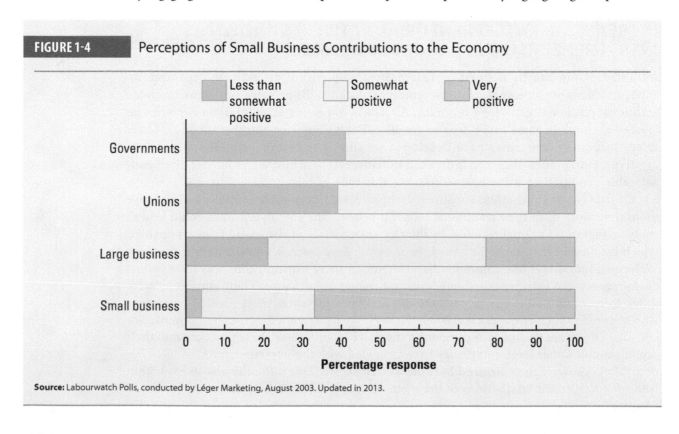

FIGURE 1-4 Perceptions of Small Business Contributions to the Economy

Source: Labourwatch Polls, conducted by Léger Marketing, August 2003. Updated in 2013.

success stories, and offering entrepreneurs and potential entrepreneurs advice and stories on emerging trends. *The Globe and Mail, National Post, Canadian Business Week,* and *Profit Magazine* all regularly publish content both in print and online highlighting entrepreneurial success stories and offer advice to current and aspiring entrepreneurs.

Television networks are increasingly offering shows that celebrate the achievements of entrepreneurs and promote business ownership. For example, CBC's hit series, *Dragons' Den* (www.cbc.ca/dragonsden), has would-be entrepreneurs presenting their business ideas to a panel of wealthy investors, better known as the Dragons. Entrepreneurs who appear on the show are hoping to get the Dragons to invest money and time into their business for a share of future profits. Presenters on the show also benefit from airtime on CBC, and estimates are businesses that appear on the show see sales increase by 30 percent after an episode airs.[39] While the show has its share of critics, as some do not care for the personalities of the Dragons, most people agree that *Dragons' Den* has positively promoted entrepreneurship as a career coast-to-coast. Other Canadian television shows such as *Venture, Marketplace,* and *The O'Leary and Lang Exchange* also promote business ownership.

WHAT IS SMALL BUSINESS? LO2

What size of business qualifies as a small business? This question is not easy to answer because most organizations and agencies concerned with small businesses use different definitions. It is essential, however, to understand some of the common characteristics of these definitions to better appreciate what constitutes a small business. These characteristics are outlined in the following paragraphs.

COMPARISON AND EVALUATION

To compare the performance of a small business with that of other small businesses, it is necessary to understand the sizes and characteristics used by data collection and dissemination agencies such as Statistics Canada and Dun and Bradstreet. Ensuring that firms are relatively the same size allows a more meaningful monitoring of sales levels, performance, and productivity in relation to other similar firms in the industry. Currently, Statistics Canada publishes operating data for incorporated and unincorporated businesses with average net sales of $1 million or less.

GOVERNMENT PROGRAMS

Knowing how various government departments define a small business enables an entrepreneur to take advantage of the tax incentives and other government assistance programs designed for small business. Examples of differences in definitions among government agencies are given below.

LENDING PROGRAMS

A small business owner needs to know the size of business that lenders require in their lending programs to take advantage of favourable small business provisions. Programs are available to small businesses from the Business Development Bank of Canada (BDC), provincial or territorial government lending agencies, and chartered banks. Therefore, it is important to understand the criteria commonly used to distinguish a small business from a large one. At least four criteria exist.

1. Number of Employees.

Industry Canada specifies a small business as one that employs fewer than 100 people in a manufacturing industry and fewer than 50 employees in a non-manufacturing industry. The Ministry of State for Small Business also uses the guideline of 50 employees, while the BDC (www.bdc.ca) considers a business that employs fewer than 75 people to be eligible for its Counselling Assistance for Small Businesses program. Other organizations such as the Canadian Bankers' Association (www.cba.ca) classifies a company as small if it qualifies for a loan authorization of less than $250,000. Microbusinesses are classified as businesses that employ fewer than five employees, while businesses employing fewer than 500 are classed as SMEs (small and medium-sized businesses).[40]

2. Total Revenue.

Although the limits vary by industry, total revenue is a common basis for defining small business. The Ministry of State for Small Business uses $2 million in revenue as a benchmark. The Small Business Loans Act in Canada applies to firms with revenues of less than $5 million. The Small Business Administration in the United States uses the following revenue guidelines:

Retailing: $3.5 million to $13.5 million

Services: $3.5 million to $14.5 million

Construction: $7 million to $17 million

3. Profits.

Canada Revenue Agency uses operating profits as a guideline to define which businesses qualify for the small business deduction. This special deduction allows a reduced tax rate (the small business deduction is discussed in detail later in the text). This limit is presently set at a net operating profit of $300,000.

4. Type of Management-Ownership Structure.

Another criterion used to define small business is the degree to which the owner is also the day-to-day manager of the business. With some exceptions, the majority of small business owners are also the managers.[41] Because the guidelines differ among industries and agencies, the Committee for Economic Development in the United States uses a slightly different and less specific approach in defining small business. Its definition states that if any two of the following characteristics exist, the business may be classified as small business:

1. Independent management (i.e., the owner is the manager)
2. Owner-supplied capital
3. Local area of operations
4. Relatively small size within its industry

It is no easy task to define the size limits of small business. The definition used will depend on the purpose and the agency or program concerned.

CURRENT STATE OF SMALL BUSINESS IN CANADA   LO3

Although the size and extent of small business in Canada depends on the definition used, a review of the data compiled by Statistics Canada and Industry Canada illustrates that small business comprises a significant part of the Canadian economy. This is shown in Figure 1-5 and

FIGURE 1-5 Significance of Small Business to the Canadian Economy in Gross Domestic Product

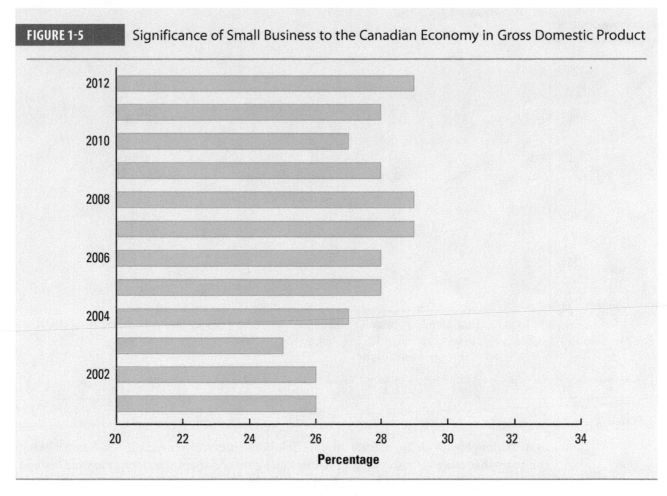

Figure 1-6. The pertinent facts derived from these figures show the strong position held by the small business community (percentages are approximate):

- 99.8 percent of business in Canada can be classified as small or medium enterprises, that is, they have less than 500 employees.
- 98.1 percent of all businesses operating in Canada employ fewer than 100 employees, while 75 percent of all businesses have fewer than 10 employees.[42]
- 48 percent of the labour force is employed in small business, or slightly over 5 million people.[43]
- 30 percent of gross domestic product (GDP) is provided by small business.[44]
- 32 percent of all business profits are made in small businesses.[45]
- 29 percent of gross sales in Canada are made by small businesses.[46]
- 86 percent of exports were from small businesses, accounting for $77 billion in sales.[47]
- 52 percent of net job creation is from small business.[48]
- 100,000 new small businesses are started annually.[49]

YOUNG ENTREPRENEURS

In addition to the large general increases in the number of small businesses in recent years, more small businesses are being started by young people. For example, Bryan McCrea and

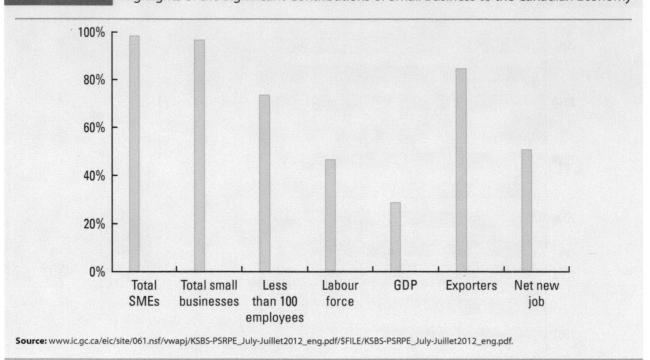

Source: www.ic.gc.ca/eic/site/061.nsf/vwapj/KSBS-PSRPE_July-Juillet2012_eng.pdf/$FILE/KSBS-PSRPE_July-Juillet2012_eng.pdf.

Evan Willoughby, both 26, operate 3twenty Solutions (http://3twenty.ca/), a Saskatoon-based company that takes steel shipping containers and converts them into temporary offices and housing for the booming resource industry.[50] The modular units come with heat and plumbing and replace tents or flimsy wood structures. The pair cannot keep up with the demand for their product and have expanded their manufacturing space 10 times since the company's inception. Similarly, 30-year-old Rebecca Cotter of Toronto is experiencing success in her business Water-on-Wheels, or WOW (http://wateronwheels.blogspot.ca). Cotter started the mobile water station business after becoming disgusted with the amount of plastic bottles in garbage cans at special events. Her company allows people to fill-up reusable water containers for free, and she charges event partners for her service. Event planners like the turnkey solution WOW provides with its own cooling system, tents, and staff—all of which results in less clean-up costs for picking up discarded water bottles when an event ends.[51]

In 2007, close to 10 percent of the self-employed were under the age of 30 as shown in Figure 1-7. As youth unemployment remains high, starting one's own business is an attractive career option for many younger Canadians. Further, a recent survey of Canada's fastest-growing small businesses indicated that the average age of the owners was about 40.[52] Organizations such as Enactus (www.enactus.ca) have been formed in Canada to provide networking and information for these young entrepreneurs. In addition, government and private organizations have recognized the importance of young entrepreneurs in lending programs offered by the Business Development Bank of

YOUNG ENTREPRENEURS BRYAN MCCREA AND EVAN WILLOUGHBY HAVE FOUND AN INNOVATIVE USE FOR STEEL SHIPPING CONTAINERS. THEIR BUSINESS TAKES CONTAINERS AND TURNS THEM INTO TEMPORARY HOUSING FOR REMOTE USE IN THE RESOURCE INDUSTRY.
Photo courtesy of 3twenty Solutions Inc.

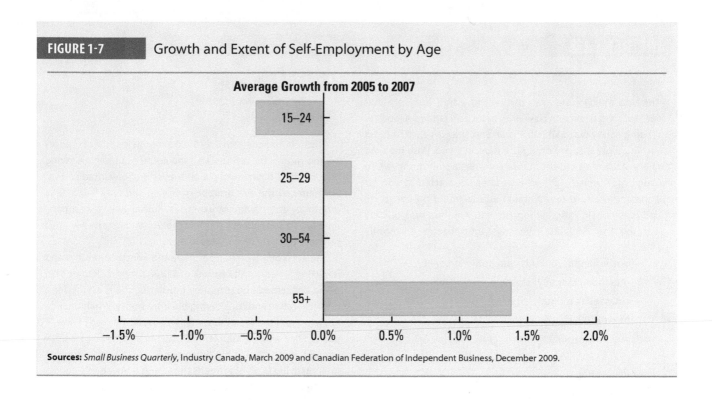

FIGURE 1-7 Growth and Extent of Self-Employment by Age

Average Growth from 2005 to 2007

Sources: *Small Business Quarterly*, Industry Canada, March 2009 and Canadian Federation of Independent Business, December 2009.

Canada (BDC) as well as the Canadian Youth Business Foundation (www.cybf.ca). Annual awards are also made to top Canadian youth entrepreneurs by the BDC.

SENIOR ENTREPRENEURS

Recently, more senior citizens have become entrepreneurs in Canada. Older entrepreneurs are currently the fastest growing segment in the small business sector, and long-term demographic trends indicate that they will become an even more significant part of the economy in the future. In addition, a large number of non-retired Canadians are strongly considering working in some capacity after they retire.[53] For example, Corin and Brian Mullins founded HapiFoods Group Inc. (http://holycrap.ca/), a B.C.-based firm that is best known for its breakfast cereal Holy Crap. The retired couple came up with their idea for a healthy breakfast cereal after Brian was diagnosed with diabetes. The cereal was originally sold at farmers' markets, netting the couple approximately $60,000. A trip to CBC's *Dragons' Den* quickly accelerated growth for the business, and the day after their segment aired they had $1.5 million in sales and reached over $5 million within a year.[54] Unlike the Mullins, a unique characteristic of many older entrepreneurs is that they do not want their businesses to grow. They are content to have a business that will provide some income but also allow them to maintain a balanced lifestyle.

FEMALE ENTREPRENEURS

Self-employment among women has increased rapidly in recent years. From 1976 to 2012, the number of self-employed women tripled from 311,600 to 910,000.[55] While the likelihood of being self-employed has grown considerably for both men and women over the past 20 years, the rate of growth has been stronger for women. In addition, more and more women have a desire to start a business. Statistics Canada has found that 46 percent of small and medium

WHY RECENT STUDENTS AND GRADUATES SHOULD START A BUSINESS

Amanda MacDonald was thrilled. She had just received her teaching licence in New Brunswick and landed a job. Her starting salary was $50,000 a year, and she was excited to be earning a great salary doing the job she loved. With her new salary, Amanda thought that her worries about money were over. Unfortunately, a short time later, she started to wonder if she could afford to maintain her apartment on her salary and was considering selling her car. Amanda was quickly learning that $50,000 a year was not that much money after all.

Here is Amanda's monthly cash flow statement:

Amanda's monthly take-home pay $2,300

Less Amanda's monthly expenses:

Rent $600

Car and insurance $400

Gas $150

Food $400

Phone/cable/Internet $200

Student loans $150

Entertainment $100

Clothing $100

This left Amanda with only $200 a month for other expenses and no money for savings, and she could not imagine saving enough for a downpayment on a condo she wanted to buy. Furthermore, she was disappointed that she only had $100 a month for entertainment expenses. Rather than take a part-time job to supplement her income, Amanda started a small business teaching 4-year-olds to read.

Amanda only works on Saturday and Sunday mornings and is making an extra $300 a week or $1200 a month. Rather than being concerned about money problems, she is saving for a dream vacation and considering buying a house. What Amanda has learned is the secret that many Canadians already know. If you can find a way to supplement your income, even by a small amount, it can make a big difference in your lifestyle. You can go from living in an apartment to owning a house or a condo, driving a new car versus driving an old car, and saving money versus living paycheque to paycheque.

sized businesses in the country have some degree of female ownership, with 16 percent majority-owned by females. A great number of women are also aspiring entrepreneurs, as a recent survey found that 71 percent of women would like to start a business. In another study, many women in corporate settings intend to start their own businesses. A recent study of Canadian female managers found that 27 percent intend to leave their employer to start their own businesses. Reasons cited are dissatisfaction and frustrations with their current employment.[56] Increasingly, female entrepreneurs are well educated (24 percent have a university education), and many are over age 55.[57] Many of the examples and profiles in this text describe the significant contributions of Canadian female entrepreneurs. See Figure 1-8 for summary facts on women entrepreneurs.

This growth in female entrepreneurship is not limited to North America; a recent Global Economic Entrepreneurship study recently found that over 40 percent of entrepreneurs starting new businesses were female.[58] Organizations such as Women Entrepreneurs of Canada (WEC) and Women Presidents Organization (WPO) have increased the political power and networking opportunities for female entrepreneurs.

The majority of self-employed women in 2013 worked in the service sector, while four in 10 businesses operated by men were in the goods sector, but this was the case for only two in 10 self-employed women. This difference mostly reflects the greater concentration of men in the construction industry, since similar proportions of self-employed men (16 percent) and women (14 percent) worked in agriculture.[59] The backgrounds of men and women entrepreneurs tend to be similar, but women have a tendency to start their businesses later in life. Women are also more likely to work at their businesses on a part-time basis compared with

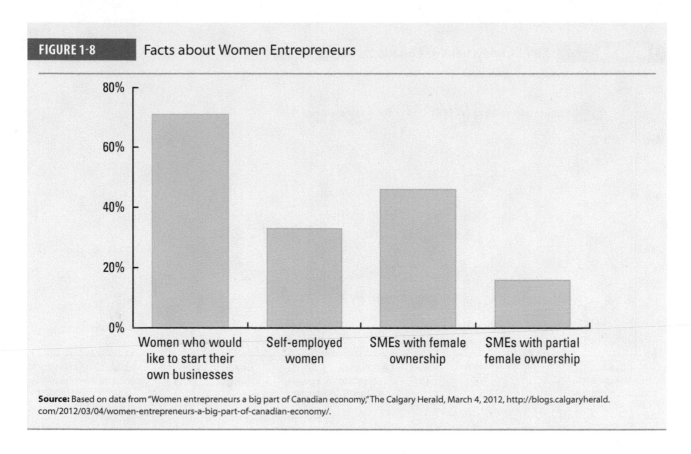

FIGURE 1-8   Facts about Women Entrepreneurs

Source: Based on data from "Women entrepreneurs a big part of Canadian economy," The Calgary Herald, March 4, 2012, http://blogs.calgaryherald.com/2012/03/04/women-entrepreneurs-a-big-part-of-canadian-economy/.

men and as a result work fewer hours. Statistics Canada reports that roughly 40 percent of women run their businesses part-time compared with less than 15 percent for men. While some women are running part-time businesses, many are working full time managing growing companies. *Profit Magazine's* annual ranking of top female entrepreneurs found that the top 100 women entrepreneurs in Canada had combined revenues of $1.4 billion and an annual three-year growth rate of 140 percent.[60]

IMMIGRANT ENTREPRENEURS

A large number of Canadian entrepreneurs are immigrants to Canada or have parents who were immigrants. Close to one in five of the self-employed in Canada are immigrants, almost double the rate observed in the 1980s. For example, Frank Stronach, one of Canada's most successful entrepreneurs, came to Canada in his early 20s. He started a small Toronto machine shop, where he logged such long hours that he often slept on a cot rather than go home. Stronach grew this small machine shop into Magna International, a global supplier of automobile parts, and accumulated a net worth of $1.2 billion.[61] Other examples include Arlene Dickinson and Robert Herjavec, both of whom have become famous on CBC's *Dragons' Den* as investors and successful entrepreneurs. Dickinson has made her fortune in the communications industry, while Herjavec's success came mostly in Information Technology (IT). Both share a similar story, as they came to Canada as children with little more than the clothes on their backs. Dickinson, who emigrated from South Africa, recalls that her parents arrived in Canada with $50 to support a family of five, while Herjavec's family emigrated from Croatia arriving in Canada with $20. Many immigrants become

FIGURE 1-9 Self-Employment in Canada by Sector

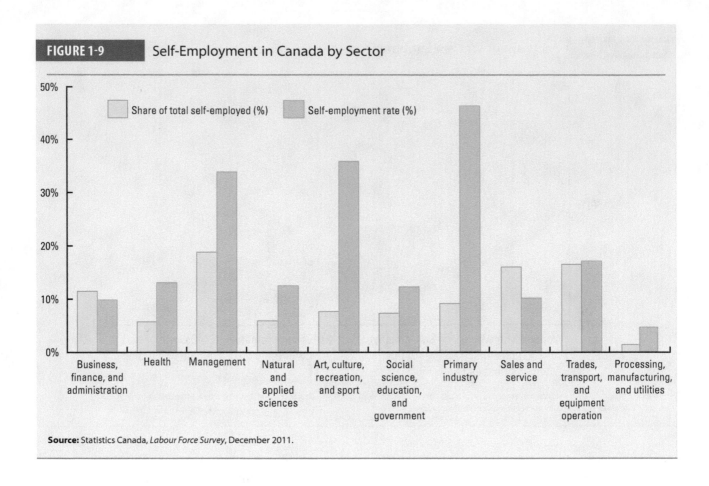

Source: Statistics Canada, *Labour Force Survey*, December 2011.

entrepreneurs because they often lack English-speaking skills or networks to find traditional employment. In addition, many immigrant communities in large Canadian cities offer support for would-be entrepreneurs, including advice, start-up funds, and access to established networks.

ENTREPRENEURIAL ACTIVITY BY INDUSTRY

As in other countries, Canadian small business activity is more dominant in sectors that are not capital intensive, such as the service industry. As noted in Figure 1-9, self-employment is more prevalent in the trades, sales, and management sectors.

ENTREPRENEURIAL ACTIVITY BY REGION

Although small businesses exist in all areas of Canada, some regions seem to be more fertile areas for growth. Figure 1-10 shows that the economies of all provinces are dominated by small business. Manitoba has a slightly smaller percentage of businesses with fewer than five employees, while Newfoundland and Labrador has a slightly higher share. These small businesses make up more than 70 percent of the total share, while businesses with fewer than 50 employees represent more than 90 percent of the total businesses in each province. The regional distribution of growth in self-employment over the past decade shows that Alberta and Ontario have seen the most rapid growth. This trend is predicted to continue.[62]

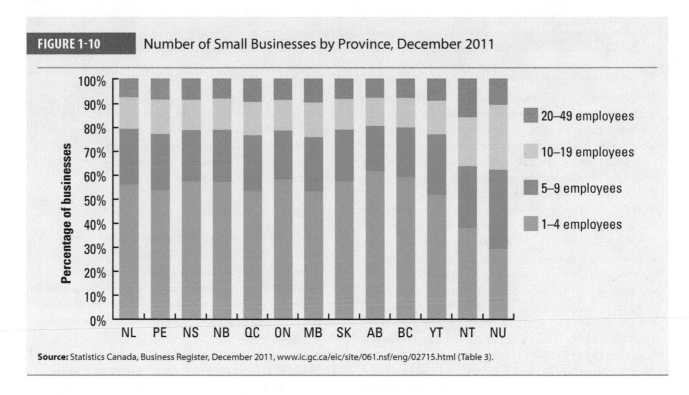

FIGURE 1-10 Number of Small Businesses by Province, December 2011

Legend:
- 20–49 employees
- 10–19 employees
- 5–9 employees
- 1–4 employees

y-axis: Percentage of businesses

x-axis: NL, PE, NS, NB, QC, ON, MB, SK, AB, BC, YT, NT, NU

Source: Statistics Canada, Business Register, December 2011, www.ic.gc.ca/eic/site/061.nsf/eng/02715.html (Table 3).

CONTRIBUTIONS OF SMALL BUSINESS   LO4

The size of the small business sector is not the only reason why it is important to Canada. The following sections discuss other significant benefits of small business to Canadian society.

LABOUR INTENSITY

Small businesses are generally more labour intensive than large companies. This means they typically employ more people to produce a certain level of output than a larger business does. In addition, small firms accounted for a significant portion of the new jobs created in Canada over the last decade. From 2001 to 2011, small business in Canada created over 550,000 jobs, close to 48 percent of the jobs created in the country.[63] Most of these new jobs were created in the trade and services sectors. In this era of concern about employment levels, it is not surprising that current government policy includes incentives to promote the establishment of small businesses.

INNOVATIONS AND INVENTIONS

Individuals in small businesses have been responsible for a majority of the inventions and innovations that society benefits from today. Small firms produce approximately 55 percent of innovations.[64] Among important twentieth-century innovations by Canadian small firms are the smartphone, insulin, the snowmobile, the pacemaker, the washing machine, the IMAX movie system, and the television. Potential innovations being developed by Canadian entrepreneurs include a portable Zamboni for backyard rinks, an underwater communications system, a one-handed ice cube tray, and a space craft docking system. Even innovations within larger companies are often made by individuals, who are rewarded for their entrepreneurial creativity. Studies show that small businesses have six "innovation enablers" that make them more likely than large corporations to innovate.[65] These are personal passion, customer connection,

INNOVATION IN NEW BUSINESS—A SOCIAL MEDIA SUCCESS STORY

Ryan Holmes, CEO of Vancouver-based HootSuite (http://hootsuite.com), a social media dashboard, is hoping his innovative company will grow into an Internet giant. Holmes' social media dashboard allows companies to manage multiple social media campaigns from one central website. Essentially, HootSuite allows companies to send messages to a variety of social media sites, including Twitter, Facebook, LinkedIn, Google+, Foursquare, MySpace, WordPress, and Mixi, from one central location. HootSuite can also be used with YouTube, Instagram, MailChimp, Reddit, Storify, Tumblr, and Vimeo. The business offers some of its services for free but charges a premuim if a company wants to post information to more than five sites. In addition, HootSuite bills clients for its social media analytical tools, which provide companies with insight as to what consumers are saying about both their social media campaigns and the company in general. Businesses like the ability to send messages to multiple sites using HootSuite, which saves them time and money. To date, both large and small businesses are using HootSuite, and the company boasts that both the Prime Minister's Office and the U.S. President's Office, as well as over 80 of the Fortune 100 companies, are using its services. Holmes, who founded the company in 2008, has seen a rapid appreciation of the firm's value as HootSuite was estimated to be worth $6 million in 2010 and, in 2013, estimates have the company worth between $200 and $500 million.[66]

Discussion Questions

1. What are some of the advantages and disadvantages of using a product like HootSuite for your company?

2. Given that many consumers are becoming increasingly concerned about privacy rights, do you think HootSuite or companies that use its social media tracking tools could be subject to public backlash against monitoring social media use and activities?

3. If time permits, visit HootSuite's website, and try out the free tools. Report back to the class if the tools worked as you expected. Prepare a summary of the features HootSuite can offer businesses.

flexibility, experimentation, resource limitations, and information sharing. Recent studies show that small- and medium-sized businesses do, in fact, invest more money in research and development as a proportion of their revenue compared with large firms.[67]

PRODUCTIVITY AND PROFITABILITY

During the twentieth century, the conventional wisdom was that the larger the organization, the greater is the opportunity to be more productive and profitable. As a result, both business and government have tended to increase in size. However, the validity of this thinking has been seriously questioned in recent years and shown to be empirically weak.

Large businesses are also recognizing the gains in productivity associated with smallness. Of the eight attributes of success listed by Peters and Waterman in their study of successful corporations,[68] no fewer than six are commonly found in small businesses.[69] These six attributes are:

1. Bias for Action.

These organizations have found that a preference for doing something—anything, rather than sending an idea through endless cycles of analyses and committee reports—encourages new ideas and creativity. This principle seems typical of most successful businesses.

2. Staying Close to the Customer.

Small businesses learn about customer preferences and cater to them. They are generally closer to and have more contact with the customer. Larger organizations spend considerable amounts of money to maintain this closeness.

3. Autonomy and Entrepreneurship.

Breaking the corporation into small companies and encouraging each unit to think independently and competitively has become a strategy of many large businesses.

4. Productivity through People.

Creating the awareness in all employees that their best efforts are essential and that they will share in the rewards of the company's success is a major goal of successful companies. In small businesses, owner and employees typically share in the rewards of success and the disappointments of failure.

5. Hands on–Value Driven.

Many organizations insist that executives keep in touch with the firm's essential business and promote a strong corporate culture. A popular method of management, known as management by walking around (MBWA), testifies to the realization that management needs to be familiar with the firm's employees and the operation of the business. The successful owner-manager follows this principle faithfully.

6. Simple Form–Lean Staff.

Few administrative layers, with few people at the upper levels, is characteristic of many successful businesses. In many small businesses, employees have direct access to the owner-manager. This arrangement increases the flexibility of the organization as well as employee morale.

FLEXIBILITY

Small businesses are generally able to respond more quickly than large businesses to changes in the economy, government policies, and competition. For example, Kelsey Ramsden, owner-operator of B.C.-based Belvedere Place Development (www.bpdltd.ca) and one of *Profit Magazine's* Top 2012 Women Entrepreneurs, reinvented her business when the economy went into recession between 2008 and 2010. At that time, almost all of Ramsden's clients came from government sources, and the number of competitors doubled almost overnight. Competitors were desperate for work and they were driving down the price of government contracts. Rather than compete, Ramsden expanded the company into private sector work, which resulted in a three-year growth rate of 804 percent.[70] In addition, many markets can only be served by small businesses because the areas are too small or too localized for large companies to serve profitably. This situation alone presents countless opportunities for entrepreneurs. For example, Ingonish in Cape Breton sits on the world famous Cabot Trail (www.cabottrail.com), a vacation destination which draws thousands of visitors each year with its majestic coastal drive, national parks, and golf courses. Yet the tourism operators are not large businesses or national chains, as the region, even with strong tourist numbers, is too small to support big firms.

CANADIAN OWNERSHIP

The percentage of Canadian ownership, a major concern of economic nationalists in Canada, tends to be much higher in small business than in large business.[71] Of businesses operating in Canada with less than $2 million in sales, less than 1 percent is foreign owned.

SMALL BUSINESS HEALTH AS A LINK TO ECONOMIC GROWTH

Considerable evidence exists that economies that provide the most encouragement for entrepreneurship and small business have experienced the highest growth rates since the 1950s.[72] Recognition of this fact by many centrally planned economies has resulted in more encouragement of entrepreneurship, with the associated potential of rewards for those engaged in this type of productive activity.[73] This recognition may also have contributed to the dramatic changes that have occurred in these countries in recent years. One key finding of the *Second Annual Global Entrepreneurship Monitor*, which examines new and growing business in 21 countries, was that a country has a better chance of achieving economic well-being if it supports entrepreneurial activities.[74]

SOCIAL CONTRIBUTIONS

Small business owners often have a long-term interest in the communities in which their businesses operate. As a result, they contribute to those communities in non-business ways to a greater extent than an employee of a large corporation might do. In a recent survey conducted by *Profit Magazine,* 76 percent of entrepreneurs think they have a moral obligation to give back to their communities through philanthropic endeavours. When asked about the amount their business contributed to social causes in the last year, entrepreneurs reported they donated an average of 9.3 percent of revenues, including cash donations, in-kind donations, and employee time.[75] Some entrepreneurs such as Kalen Emsley, David Luba, and Derrick Emsley are using their philanthropic donations as part of their overall marketing strategy. The three young business partners are co-owners of Ten Tree Apparel, an environmentally friendly clothing brand that plants 10 trees for every item it sells. The company's website, www.tentree.com, maintains an active count of the trees the company has planted to date and highlights the business's ongoing success. The business was recently featured on CBC's *Dragons' Den,* where the entrepreneurs won accolades for being one of the top 10 presentations in the history of the show.[76]

SMALL BUSINESS AND THE FUTURE   LO5

An important question for present and future entrepreneurs, as well as for policymakers, is, What effects will future changes in our society have on the small business community? As mentioned at the beginning of this chapter, the 1970s and 1980s were a period of entrepreneurial

KALEN EMSLEY, DAVID LUBA, AND DERRICK EMSLEY ARE USING DONATIONS AS PART OF THEIR MARKETING STRATEGY. THEIR COMPANY DONATES 10 TREES FOR EVERY PRODUCT YOU PURCHASE. CONSUMERS LOVE THE CONCEPT, AND THE TRIO'S BUSINESS IS GROWING MORE QUICKLY THAN THEY COULD HAVE IMAGINED.
Photo courtesy of Ten Tree

revolution. Moreover, the late 1990s determined that change to have been a permanent adjustment to the Canadian business environment.[77] Several developing trends have potentially positive implications for entrepreneurs. At the same time, many of these trends will be advantageous only if entrepreneurs' actions are the result of insight, research, and careful planning.

Some of the more significant factors that will affect the future of small business are discussed briefly in the following sections.

CHANGE

The world is now undergoing a period of rapid change, and this trend is expected to continue. Businesses carry out their various activities very differently today from how they will 10 years from now. This means that being flexible will likely continue to be a competitive strength for the entrepreneur.

As the following sections discuss, changes are occurring in technology, the Internet and mobile technology, consumer demographics and buying patterns, the competitive aspects of markets, and the economy.

TECHNOLOGY

Technology has revolutionized the activities of both small and large businesses. Computers allow the entrepreneur to manage large amounts of information as effectively as a larger business. Such advances have signalled significant small business opportunities. Financial management and accounting, marketing research and planning, promotion, and consulting are areas in which small businesses, many of them home-based, have succeeded. As computer technology becomes more affordable, more small businesses will take advantage of computer applications in these areas.

New technology has also allowed small businesses to obtain subcontracts for many services from larger businesses and government organizations that are unable to or choose not to carry out these activities themselves. Despite these potential opportunities, however, small businesses must be prepared to embrace new technology or face the possibility of obsolescence and lack of competitiveness.

Increased performance in the areas of customer service, marketing, and manufacturing, and improved communications are all benefits an entrepreneur can achieve through the use of technology.

INTERNET AND MOBILE TECHNOLOGY

The Internet and mobile technologies such as cloud computing, smartphones, and tablets have forever changed how businesses operate and has levelled the playing field between large and small firms. Small businesses can now reach global markets once out of reach, create professional marketing and social networking campaigns, and communicate with stakeholders at a fraction of what it used to cost. A recent article in the *National Post* sums this up when the author notes, "The Web has lowered the bar for people with skills and ideas. People don't need a development team or a big budget; they just need a good idea and a laptop."[78] For example, Mike McDerment of Toronto founded FreshBooks (www.freshbooks.com), an online accounting company aimed at servicing small businesses, when he was 23 years old. FreshBooks, while located in Toronto, has 5 million customers spread throughout the globe, all of whom pay approximately $19.95 a month for its accounting services. The Internet has also provided entrepreneurs with opportunities that did not exist in the past. For example, Vincent Cheung started ShapeCollage Inc. (www.shapecollage.

com), an online application that allows users to download photos and arrange them into a collage in a variety of shapes. Cheung's software has been downloaded over a million times, and he has recently won the Ontario Entrepreneur of the Year award.

CONSUMER DEMOGRAPHICS AND BUYING PATTERNS

The level of retail expenditures is a key to the growth of the small business sector; a 1 percent increase in the growth of consumer spending results in a 0.7 percent increase in small business activity.[79] Of particular interest to most businesses are the baby-boomers born between 1946 and 1964, and their children, known as the "echo generation" or "millennial generation," who were born between 1980 and 2000. These groups are of interest to entrepreneurs due to their sizes and spending habits. Baby-boomers are the largest and most significant demographic group, comprising close to two-thirds of the Canadian population. This group has entered its highest income-earning period, resulting in large expenditures for certain types of goods and services. As the baby-boomers age entrepreneurs can create or tailor businesses to appeal to their changing needs. Baby-boomers are known to be materialistic and interested in health care, fitness, and travel. The millennial generation is also another attractive market for business owners. This generation is well educated and interested in the environment, social causes, and technology. This group is just starting to get married, buy homes, and have families. Millennials are interested in career coaching, investing, travel, and the betterment of their children. Since this group is having fewer children than their parents, and having them later in life, they are willing to spend more money and time on their development. For example, Shaindy Alexander, owner of Toronto-based Ringley Natural Teething (http://ringley.ca), produces a premium line of teethers made from organic cotton and maple. Alexander, who now sells her teethers in 13 countries, says, "Millennials will invest in quality and in products that are healthier for their children."[80]

COMPETITIVE ASPECTS OF MARKETS

Two major occurrences in recent years have affected the already intensely competitive environment that most small businesses face. The first is the worldwide movement to global markets, augmented by recent developments in Europe. The second is big business's response to the growth of the small business sector.

Global Markets.

The world is currently experiencing a major shift to the globalization of markets. The erosion in domestic and international market boundaries means that smaller businesses should have increased opportunities to source, produce, and deliver to international markets. As a result, many small businesses will eventually include an international aspect in their operations. The signing of the North American Free Trade Agreement (NAFTA) was a major occurrence for Canadian businesses, as it gave them access to more than 380 million consumers in the United States and Mexico.[81] The agreement eliminates tariffs, offers Canadian companies much greater and surer access to government markets in Mexico and the United States,[82] and disallows prohibitions of most services.[83] Other events which have led to trade liberalization include the defeat of communism in the Eastern European bloc countries, which led to a number of new opportunities for entrepreneurs. Consumers in these countries have an insatiable demand for Western products and services. As remaining barriers and purchasing power problems are overcome, these areas will offer huge untapped markets.

Another development that has affected Canadian entrepreneurs is the European Union (EU). The EU is the largest single common market with a $17 trillion economy and 500 million consumers. The EU allows for free trade between member nations and uses protective tariffs to keep out goods from non-member countries. While Canada is not a member of the EU, it is currently negotiating a free trade agreement called the Comprehensive Economic and Trade Agreement (CETA). If signed, Canadian business owners would have access to a large market that would likely be interested in many Canadian products and services.

The market with perhaps the most potential for Canadian entrepreneurs in the future is in Southeast Asia in countries such as Singapore, Thailand, Taiwan, South Korea, India, and, most notably, China. China's population alone of more than 1 billion represents a massive market. These areas are also increasingly receptive to Western goods and services.

Large Business Response.

Small businesses have always had difficulty competing with large businesses, particularly for such things as capital, raw materials, and labour. This situation is not expected to change appreciably in some industries. Financing problems continue to plague small businesses. Despite new programs, influence over suppliers by large businesses is strong, and wage rates paid by larger organizations and government are often too high for the smaller business to meet.

In addition to the difficulty of matching wage rates, labour shortages continue. This will increase the competition for competent employees even more. Small businesses will need to find ways to retain top employees through nonfinancial methods. One survey of small business owners indicated that close to half see labour shortages as a major concern for small business.[84]

One positive and often overlooked aspect is that many large businesses and government agencies are increasingly downsizing and subcontracting (outsourcing) the purchase of products and services to small business. It is estimated that close to one-half of small businesses become established through outsourcing with another business.[85] There is also evidence that many small businesses are joining together through such means as industry associations in an attempt to be more competitive. Such a collaborative relationship, however, often runs against the grain of the entrepreneur's independent nature.

Large businesses in some industries have recently adopted strategies employed by smaller businesses to recoup lost market share. The adoption of entrepreneurial programs in product development (intrapreneurship), the increased attention to customer service, and the addition of some small business operating policies have enhanced the growth and success of smaller enterprises.

THE ECONOMY

The performance of many small businesses is directly related to the Canadian economy. Recently, the Canadian economy is experiencing a period of slow growth as it recovers from the 2008–2010 recession. During slow periods and downtimes small companies increase their focus on innovation to a greater degree than large business.[86] However, certain economic occurrences affect many small businesses negatively by adding to increased costs and decreased customer traffic for some of Canada's key industries and industrial areas.

THE POLITICAL CLIMATE

Over the last decade, the political climate for small business ownership seemed to be improving. This was evidenced by attempts to reduce the burdens of paperwork (mentioned previously)

ECONOMIC DOWNTURN PRESENTS OPPORTUNITIES

While many businesses suffer significantly when a recession or downturn in the economy occurs, Warren Industries Ltd. (www.warren-ind.com) is an exception. Warren is an automobile parts manufacturer located in Concord, Ontario, that is predicting a three-fold increase in sales contracts over the next three years and a doubling of its staff over the next four. The secret, according to David Freedman, is that a couple of years before the recession, they began developing a strategy to make the company more resilient and adaptable to change. They became more aggressive in obtaining business rather than sitting back, cutting costs, and waiting until the tough times past. The company bolstered its engineering staff so that it could develop more of its own products and move up the value chain rather than rely on outsourcing as it had done in the past. It became more aggressive in negotiating with hungry suppliers. The result has transformed Warren into a Tier 1 supplier that develops innovative and highly engineered products that it can now sell directly to customers.

Source: Adapted from Jean-Rene Halde, Business Development Bank of Canada, Special Supplement to *The Lethbridge Herald*, October 19, 2009, p. 2.

and provide tax incentives to small businesses. According to the Global Entrepreneurship Monitor, entrepreneurship is fostered as governments reduce state involvement in economic activities and instead promote entrepreneurship at the cultural level.[87] The World Bank states that out of 181 countries, Canada has a second place ranking in ease of starting a new business.[88]

The federal government has attempted to encourage entrepreneurship with incentives for immigrant entrepreneurs to enter the country. Special visas are provided for immigrants who invest in small business. These entrepreneurs have injected considerable capital into the Canadian economy.

Although there is considerable interest in government circles in reducing government involvement in business and encouraging entrepreneurial activity,[89] most small business proponents are still waiting for significant action to take place.[90] A recent CFIB report states that small businesses are especially hard hit by regulation, as it takes time and money away from other more productive activities. This also puts them at a competitive disadvantage with respect to larger businesses that can afford individuals or whole departments devoted to regulatory compliance.[91] Small businesses state repeatedly that some of the major concerns about the business environment are high taxes, regulations, and paper work burdens imposed by government, and ineffective government programs.[92] A recent study by CFIB estimates that Canadian businesses spend $31 billion per year to comply with regulations imposed by government.[93] Continued collective lobbying efforts through organizations such as the Federation of Independent Business are required to achieve a political environment more conducive to the establishment and successful operation of small businesses.

THE SOCIAL CLIMATE

Society tends to look favourably on small business and entrepreneurial activities as a legitimate way to make a living. A recent Angus Reid survey indicated that entrepreneurs have the highest level of respect from Canadians, edging out doctors, police officers, and teachers.[94] More and more college and university graduates are beginning their careers by starting their own businesses, joining the ranks of the many people who left the once secure confines of large business to strike out on their own. Although this trend is expected to continue, adequate preparation and planning will increasingly be required to achieve success following this route. In addition, a structural shift has occurred in Canada to a strong culture of individualism and self-betterment that has resulted in a more accepted and positive attitude toward the small business sector.[95]

The onus is now on entrepreneurs as prospective owner-managers to sharpen their skills in this competitive and rapidly changing society. An owner-manager in today's world cannot survive on guesswork. Numerous programs, courses, and types of assistance are available to allow the owner-manager to acquire this training. The remaining chapters in this book cover the critical areas a prospective owner-manager should be familiar with in starting and operating a successful small business.

LEARNING OBJECTIVES SUMMARY

LO1 The entrepreneurial revolution is evidenced by the growing numbers of business establishments, employees in small businesses, government small business programs, college and university small business classes, and entrepreneurial activities of large companies.

LO2 Although defining a small business is difficult, having a definition is important when comparing and evaluating small business, as well as when taking advantage of various lending and assistance programs. Some common criteria for defining small business are gross sales, number of employees, profitability, and type of management structure.

LO3 Small business accounts for 98 percent of all businesses, 30 percent of gross domestic product, and 48 percent of the labour force in Canada.

LO4 Small business can provide jobs, innovations, high productivity, flexibility, a higher proportion of Canadian ownership, and more contributions to society.

LO5 The climate for starting a small business should continue to be strong despite some competitive disadvantages.

1. Why do you think entrepreneurial activity has increased? Do you think these trends will continue? Why, or why not?

2. What excites or interests you about being an entrepreneur? What are your major concerns?

3. Under what conditions would the various definitions of small business be more appropriate (e.g., the level of profit may be used by the Canada Revenue Agency to determine the small business tax rate)?

4. What is meant by the statement, "Small business is the backbone of the Canadian economic system"? Give evidence to support this statement.

5. The computer-consulting business is becoming more and more fragmented. In data processing, for example, there are hardware versus software consultants, batch versus time-sharing service bureaus, and mainframe versus microcomputer specialists. What effect does this type of industry fragmentation have on the small business community?

APPLICATION QUESTIONS AND HANDS-ON ACTIVITIES

1. Form groups of two to three, and start a small business or mini-venture that will run for a period of four to six hours. The only rules are:
   a. The business has to be legal
   b. No lotteries
   c. Maximum investment of $1
   d. Businesses must cease operations at day's end.
   After completing the project, write a reflection stating what you did, whether you made a profit, and what you learned. You may also present this information to the class.

2. Ask three small business owners about their projections for the future of small business. What problems and opportunities do they foresee?

3. Using Internet resources, find out how different Canadian organizations define social enterprise. After preparing a summary report on your findings, draft your own definition of the term.

4. Write a short essay discussing your views on the future of small business given current trends in society *and* in your geographic area.

For more information on the resources available from McGraw-Hill Ryerson, go to www.mcgrawhill.ca/he/solutions.

THE SMALL BUSINESS DECISION

By the end of this chapter, you should be able to:

LO1 Discuss the advantages and disadvantages of business ownership as a starting point in making the small business decision.

LO2 List the personal and organizational attributes of a successful small business owner.

LO3 Explain the reasons some businesses succeed and others fail.

LO4 Identify the differences between an entrepreneur and a manager.

LO5 Discuss entrepreneurial development in large businesses.

SMALL BUSINESS PROFILE

CHRIS YE *Uken Games*

Chris Ye, 25-year-old owner of Toronto-based Uken Games (www.uken.com), was recently announced as winner of Profit *Magazine's* Young Entrepreneur of the Year award. Chris's company, which he co-founded with his partner Mark Lampert, specializes in developing cross-platform mobile games. Cross-platform games allow users to play the same games on multiple devices. Games can be started on an iPhone, continued on a BlackBerry or Android device, and completed on Facebook. Chris says, "Our users love to play our games in a seamless fashion," whether they're using their phones on a train or loading up Facebook on their home computer, they have the ability to access the same player account."[1]

Chris and Mark's business partnership started when the pair met at a Facebook development camp. They quickly struck a relationship and developed a gifting app

Photo courtesy of Uken Games

where users could go trick-or-treating at their friends' virtual doors for fun gifts. Within two weeks, the app went viral and reached over a million users and companies paid for in-game advertisements. While the popularity of the game quickly waned, it provided Chris and Mark with their first successful venture and some insight into the future of mobile and social gaming. Chris says, "We had some success. We had a million active users, we made money, and that got us excited."[2]

Uken's first game, *Superheroes Alliance,* was released on Facebook a short time later. While the game did not get as many subscribers as the trick-or-treating app, it was far more engaging, and Chris used it to create a "game engine" from which the company would go on to rapidly launch 6 more

titles. "We basically built a game engine that supported cross-platform play. After we launched on iOS (Apple), we were able to launch quickly on Android and on BlackBerry and on iPad. So, our users were able to use one device, then switch to another device seamlessly, and it would just work. That really gave us a leg up."[3]

Besides competition, which is constantly emerging in the industry, Uken's other challenge is attracting top talent. While the company has grown to over 55 employees now, the ability to continue growing a world class team is top of mind. Uken employs a rigorous hiring process to ensure smart decisions are made on the front end of employee selection. Uken then offers employees a competitive salary, meaningful responsibilities, and a fun culture that respects shared ideas, meritocracy, and both personal and professional growth. So far this strategy appears to be working, as very few employees have left the company.[4]

To date, Uken Games has launched 9 titles including hits Bingo Pop, Crime Inc., and Forces of War. The company has over 1 million monthly active users around the globe and has achieved revenue in the millions. What may be more impressive is they have been profitable for the past three years and have not had to raise any extra money. At the current time, Chris plans to re-invest profits back into the company to fuel the continued growth. Uken's next generation of games are already being developed. Chris believes the next few years will see accelerated growth in mobile games, and he thinks his company is uniquely positioned to capitalize.[5]

UKEN GAMES
www.uken.com

THE SMALL BUSINESS DECISION: PERSONAL EVALUATION

An important but often difficult part of making the small business decision is to separate this decision into two parts—personal considerations and those related to the business or the opportunity. Each will be discussed in this chapter. In contemplating whether to start their own businesses, individuals are well advised to consider the potential consequences of such a move, both for themselves and for their families and friends. Failure to do this can lead to disillusionment, frustration, and an unsuccessful attempt to capitalize on a viable business opportunity. Frequently, the entrepreneur finds that the reasons for continuing in a small business are different from the reasons for start-up (Figure 2-1). Therefore, a good way to begin this evaluation is to learn the potential advantages and disadvantages of starting and operating one's own business. In addition, understanding the personality characteristics and abilities required of an entrepreneur, as well as an honest self-appraisal of one's own suitability, is essential in making an intelligent small business decision.

ADVANTAGES OF SMALL BUSINESS OWNERSHIP

Running one's own business offers some unique advantages over being an employee. Numerous small business owners cite the following potential advantages.

Independence.

Often, independence is the primary reason for going into business for oneself. This includes the freedom to make one's own decisions without having to ask a superior. One study of successful entrepreneurs indicated that the majority started their businesses to "control their own lives" or to

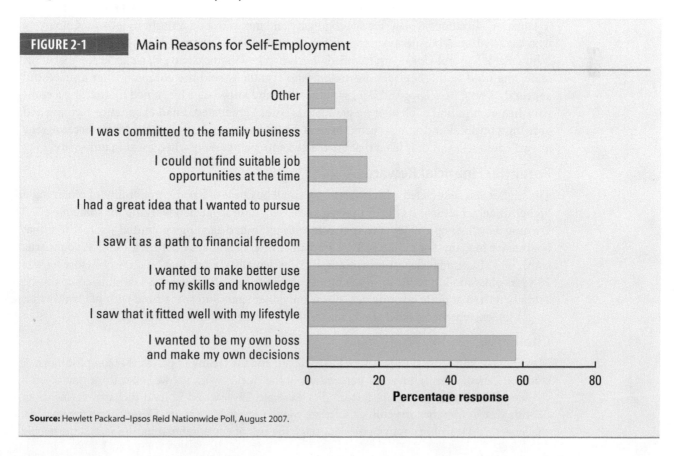

FIGURE 2-1 Main Reasons for Self-Employment

Source: Hewlett Packard–Ipsos Reid Nationwide Poll, August 2007.

"be their own boss."[6] Kenzie MacDonald left his job as vice-president at Colliers International, a global commercial real estate firm, to branch off and start his own company in Halifax. MacDonald stated the main reason for leaving his job was a strong desire to be his own boss: "I wanted to be in charge, to do things the way I wanted to do them . . . when you work as an employee for years, you're always answering to someone . . . its nice to be able to make all the decisions, to be in control."[7] Young Toronto entrepreneur Bill Hennessey, owner of RoyalPak (www.royalpak.com), a cleaning-products manufacturer, and Oxford Beach (http://oxfordbeach.com), an events planning company, echoes MacDonald's comments about independence. "As an entrepreneur, you control your own destiny. I work the hours I want to work, and I take vacations when I want to take vacations."[8] In a recent TD Bank survey, 95 percent of entrepreneurs cited being their own boss and independence as the main reasons they like being an entrepreneur. Additionally, Statistics Canada has cited the desire for independence as the main motivator for starting a business. Entrepreneurs should realize, however, that even though they own their businesses, they must still answer to customers, suppliers, key employees, and creditors. Incident 2-1 illustrates this point. Increased independence allows many entrepreneurs to better balance work and family commitments. A recent study by CIBC World Markets found this to be important to 79 percent of entrepreneurs.[9]

More Personal Contact with People.

Running a small business usually means making contact with a large number of people, including customers, suppliers, and employees. Those who enjoy and are skilled at working with people find such interactions the most rewarding aspect of their businesses.

Skill Development.

Abilities in many functional areas of management are necessary to run a small business and can be developed during the process. Often, possessing such skills makes an individual more sought after in larger organizations. Today, many progressive and innovative organizations look for employees who have had small business experience. For example, David Reynolds of Halifax, while attending Mount Saint Vincent University, founded Quicksnap (www.quicksnap.ca), a plastic clip that eliminates the need to tie shoelaces. Reynolds, who eventually sold the company after a successful appearance on CBC's *Dragons' Den,* says the skills and knowledge he gained by running a company helped him find a job after he graduated. "After I graduated, I had experience running and growing a business and a track record in sales. Several companies wanted to hire me because they knew I could sell, and they liked that I had acted entrepreneurially when I was in university."

Potential Financial Rewards.

The higher risk associated with operating a small business offers the possibility of obtaining a higher financial return. As the old saying goes, "you cannot get rich working for someone else." Owning a business provides entrepreneurs with unlimited earnings potential—something that is attractive to many. For example, Ryan Smolkin, owner of Smoke's Poutinerie (smokespoutinerie. com), one of Canada's fastest growing franchises actually started two businesses before he was 25 years old. Smolkin made so much money from the sale of Amoeba, a branding company, he actually retired at quite a young age. It was only after spending some time with his family that he got the entrepreneurial itch again to start his growing restaurant franchise.

Challenge.

Many people start small businesses for the challenge and the feeling of personal accomplishment. A study of Canadian entrepreneurs' perceptions of the "ideal" work showed that work that offers a challenge is the most important factor.[10] For example, 29-year-old Ronald Richardson, owner of Benbria Corp. (www.benbria.com), a software company based in Kanata, Ontario, says the rewards, challenges, and learning opportunities outweigh the risk of entreprenurship.[11] In fact, some people leave larger companies because their positions lack the opportunities and challenges a small business can offer. Kenzie MacDonald, as discussed above, left a vice-president's job to pursue his entrepreneurial dream. Other examples include Doug Lacombe, founder of Calgary-based Communicatto Inc. (www.communicatto.com), a digital marketing firm, who states he enjoys the challenge of trying to run his own business given the high failure rate among start-ups. It is a challenge he enjoys on a daily basis.[12] A recent Angus Reid poll of entrepreneurs indicated that the most common reason for starting a business was "the appeal of doing something interesting and challenging."[13]

Enjoyment.

Most successful entrepreneurs enjoy what they do. In fact, entrepreneurs tend to get their best ideas from their hobbies.[14] While researching this text and reading countless interviews with entrepreneurs, both successful and unsuccessful entrepreneurs told us they loved being their own boss. Recent research indicates that 90 percent of entrepreneurs would start their business again, and in a national survey conducted by TD Bank, two-thirds of business owners described themselves as very happy. For example, 27-year-old Reid Campbell, owner of Toronto-based VMG Cinematic (www.vmgcinematic.com), a world leader in creating viral marketing strategies using social media such as YouTube, says he loves being an entrepreneur. Campbell notes that it is both challenging and rewarding and that the enjoyment he gets from running his own business beats late nights at the office.[15] The Entrepreneurial Research Consortium found that one of the top motivators for starting a business was, in fact, having a passion for the field.[16] This factor explains, in part, why financial rewards are not necessarily the prime motivation for establishing a business.

INCIDENT 2-1

MOMPRENEURS

As discussed in Chapter 1, some women are attracted to entrepreneurship as a way to achieve work–life balance. For example, many mothers have started their own businesses so they could be personally in charge of their own work schedule, which allows them to spend more time with their families. In fact, mother entrepreneurs have become so common that they have become known in the mainstream media as "mompreneurs." *Mompreneur* is defined as a female business owner who is actively balancing the role of mom and the role of entrepreneur.[17] Sometimes when people hear the term "mompreneur," they imagine a mother operating a very small business, but this is not always the case, and many mompreneurs are managing growing businesses. For example, Maria Locker is the founder and CEO of Mompreneur Showcase Group Inc. (www.themompreneur.com), a company that operates *MOMpreneur Magazine*, which is dedicated to assisting other mompreneurs in running successful companies in Canada.[18] Other examples include Sarah Davis, owner of FashionPhile.com, an online site that sells used high-end purses and bags. Davis's company, which guarantees its products are authentic, had sales in excess of $4.5 million last year.[19]

MOMPRENEURS SUCH AS SARAH DAVIS HAVE STARTED BUSINESSES TO ACHIEVE WORK–LIFE BALANCE.
AP photo/Lenny Ignelzi/CP Photo

Discussion Questions

1. Given the challenges associated with starting and running a business, do you think being a mompreneur allows for more work–life balance compared with traditional work or part-time employment?

2. What do you think are some of the advantages and disadvantages of being a mompreneur?

3. What do you think are some business ideas that would allow work and life balance?

DISADVANTAGES OF SMALL BUSINESS OWNERSHIP

Although there are many advantages to owning and operating a small business, there are several often overlooked disadvantages. A discussion of some of these and other disadvantages is found below.

Risk.

The failure rate of small businesses is very high. One of the key reasons for Canadians' hesitancy to start a small business is the risk of failure.[20] In Canada, about 85 percent of small to medium businesses survive the first year, 70 percent make it through year two, and 50 percent last more than five years. There are many potential reasons for these failures, but the major causes appear to be inexperience and unbalanced management.

Stress.

Studies show that small business owners have high stress levels, a high incidence of heart disease, and a high rate of divorce owing to the increased pressures of managing their businesses.[21] Sources of stress for entrepreneurs are illustrated in Figure 2-2. As evident below, many sources of stress are due to the individual nature of entrepreneurship, where the business owner ultimately makes final decisions and is responsible for the success or failure of the company. For example, Josh Horowitz, owner of Sell My Stuff Canada (www.sellmystuffcanada.com), a Toronto-based company that specializes in content or estate sales, says that while he loves being his own boss, he does feel the pressure of being responsible. "There's no one higher up," he says. "You're the last line of defence when a tough question comes up. It's a quick learning curve."[22] Colin McDonald, co-founder of Clearwater (www.clearwater.ca), a Halifax firm he grew from a small business to a publicly traded company, echoes Horowitz's comments, "Being your own boss is stressful. When we were a small company, I would look around the room and think that I had to make sure there was enough money to pay everyone at the end of the week. I still think that from time to time."[23]

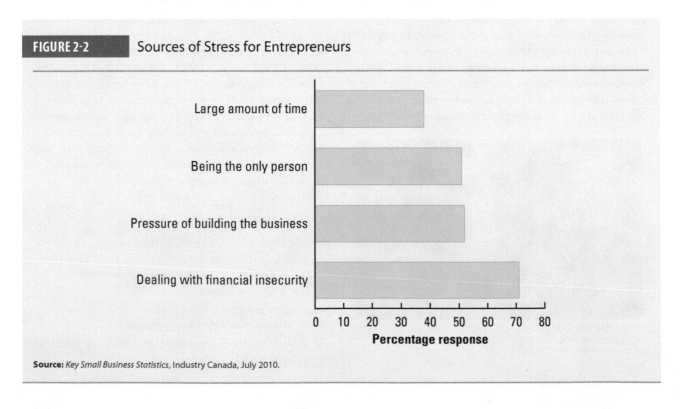

FIGURE 2-2   Sources of Stress for Entrepreneurs

Source: *Key Small Business Statistics*, Industry Canada, July 2010.

In owning a business, it is difficult, if not impossible, to confine concerns about the business to the workplace. Typically, these pressures will affect one's personal life and family situation as well.

Need for Many Abilities.

Acquiring the required skills such as accounting, finance, marketing, and personnel management, is a difficult task that many owner-managers never master. This is particularly true for the countless businesses that start out very small. In these situations, entrepreneurs generally cannot afford to hire people with specialized expertise. Failure to acquire these skills, either personally or through recruitment, can seriously hinder the growth of the business.[24]

Limited Financial Rewards.

Although the possibility of high earnings exists, relatively few small business owners become extremely wealthy. The financial rewards are often very meagre, especially during the first few years. A recent Royal Bank of Canada survey found that while 42 percent of new entrepreneurs expected their income to be higher after starting their business, only 34 percent of them achieved this.[25] Even businesses that grow rapidly are not necessarily as profitable as one might think. The Canadian Federation of Independent Business reports that although a small number of small business owners do very well financially, the majority earn less than the average paid employee.[26] Statistics Canada also found that median income of self-employed individuals was

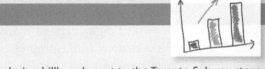

INCIDENT 2-2

TAKING THE PLUNGE

On the surface, it seemed that Ali Asaria was content in his lucrative job as a software engineer at Research In Motion, where he was best known for designing the game *Brick Breaker* for BlackBerry, which was the most successful mobile game of its time. However, Asaria wanted to be an entrepreneur, so he subsequently quit his job to start his own company Well.ca, an online health, beauty, and baby store. Ali says he left RIM out of frustration that his work benefitted the company, but not necessarily himself. "I got to the point where I just couldn't work for someone else. I think it's great for some people, but it wasn't right for me," he says.[27]

Asaria, who initially raised $10,000 in capital to start Well.ca, later sold his car and Toronto home to raise additional funds for the business. While Asaria had some experience building online stores for other companies, he knew little about the health and beauty industry. Luckily for Asaria, who had to move in with his father after the sale of his house, had identified an area in Canada which was being significantly underserved with little competition. Consumers had a strong demand to order personal care items such as adult diapers, condoms, and other products online and have them delivered the next day. By 2009 revenues reached $2 million and the company had roughly 30,000 customers. Asaria, ever the innovator, continued to push sales using a variety of non-conventional marketing campaigns

such as placing billboards next to the Toronto Subway stops promoting products some people would normally not want to buy in public. Well.ca urged people to purchase products now, in public, on their mobile phones.[28]

Well.ca has continued to grow and the company recently announced it attracted $5 million from investors who like the site's long-term business prospects. Asaria has recently opted to step down as CEO to pursue another start-up, as he enjoys the entrepreneurial process.[29]

Discussion Questions

1. Asaria notes one of the disadvantages of being an employee is your work sometimes benefits the company, but the financial rewards may not flow back to you the employee. Based on this statement, what would you say was Asaria's primary motive for starting a business?

2. What are some of the reasons that Asaria's business succeeded?

3. Given how easy potential competitors can enter the marketplace and the increasing competition from American online retailers would you have invested money in Well.ca? Why or why not?

Sources: Adapted from Charles Mandel, "Some Things Come For Free," *The Globe and Mail*, February 24, 2009, pp. 1–3 and Becky Reuber, "Keeping Corporate Culture Unified Across Several Locations," *The Globe and Mail*, June 1, 2012.

only 91.4 percent of the median income of paid employees[30] and that employees of small businesses earned only 85 percent of the income of employees in large businesses.[31]

People Conflicts.

Because owning a small business tends to require more contact with people, the potential arises for more conflicts with employees, suppliers, and customers. This factor could turn what is often thought of as an advantage into both a disadvantage and a frustration.

Time Demands.

At least initially, almost all small businesses require long hours of work. Owner-managers of small businesses often have a much longer workday than if they were working for someone else. On average, the self-employed worked 39.5 hours per week in 2011 compared with 35.3 hours for employees. Even more striking is the large difference in those who usually worked over 50 hours per week in 2011—30.3 percent of self-employed persons worked over 50 hours compared with less than 4.1 percent of employees.[32] Further, small businesses with paid help tended to work five to 10 hours longer per week than those self-employed with no employees.[33] For example, Adrienne D'Amico, co-founder of We Bake in Heels (www.webakeinheels.com/), an Ontario-based high-end cake shop says while she loves being an entrepreneur, the hours are a lot longer and more stressful compared with traditional employment. "…I didn't think it would be this much work. The hours have been crazy [7 a.m. to 9 p.m.], and you have to make the hard decisions you're used to other people making." In a recent national survey of owners of with small- and medium-sized businesses, *Profit Magazine* found that entrepreneurs worked on average 54 hours a week.[34] The Entrepreneurial Research Consortium found that the main reason entrepreneurs voluntarily stopped operating their own business was that they were working too hard at the business.[35] Figure 2-3 illustrates that long hours are part of owning a small business, particularly in the early years of its existence. Another study of 650 small

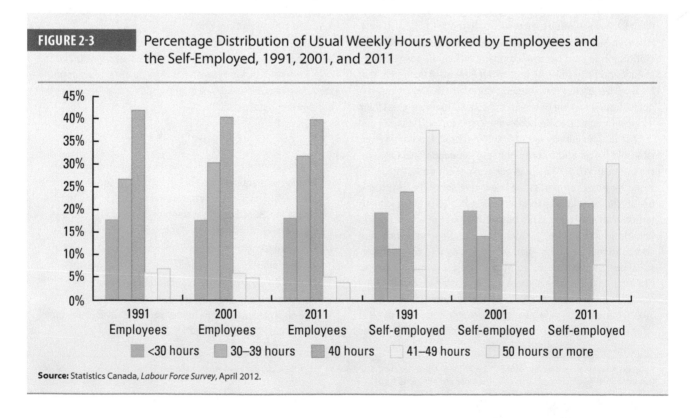

FIGURE 2-3 Percentage Distribution of Usual Weekly Hours Worked by Employees and the Self-Employed, 1991, 2001, and 2011

Legend: ■ <30 hours ■ 30–39 hours ■ 40 hours ☐ 41–49 hours ☐ 50 hours or more

Source: Statistics Canada, *Labour Force Survey*, April 2012.

businesses in the service and retail sector found that the most frequently mentioned advice to potential entrepreneurs was to "be prepared to work hard and put in long hours."[36]

DEMOGRAPHIC CHARACTERISTICS OF ENTREPRENEURS

LO2

Although entrepreneurs come from all demographic backgrounds, there are some conditions that seem to be correlated with entrepreneurial activity. Entrepreneurs are more likely to come from families in which parents set high standards for their children's performance, encouraged habits of self-reliance, and avoided being strict disciplinarians.[37] A recent significant trend is that the greatest growth of small business start-ups comes from those who have post-secondary education.[38] Statistics Canada reports that the education level of entrepreneurs has improved significantly in recent years.[39] The percentage of self-employed workers who have university degrees increased by 33 percent from 2000 to 2008.[40] Several recent reports have found that entrepreneurs are more likely to have a degree, with 53 percent of business owners having studied at university.[41] In addition, entrepreneurs tend to be children of parents who owned their own businesses. Some of the relevant demographic characteristics of entrepreneurs are shown in Figure 2-4.

PERSONALITY CHARACTERISTICS REQUIRED BY SUCCESSFUL ENTREPRENEURS

What are the personality traits of the successful owner-manager? In his book *Peak Performers*, Charles A. Garfield estimates that 70 percent of the 1500 peak performers he studied were

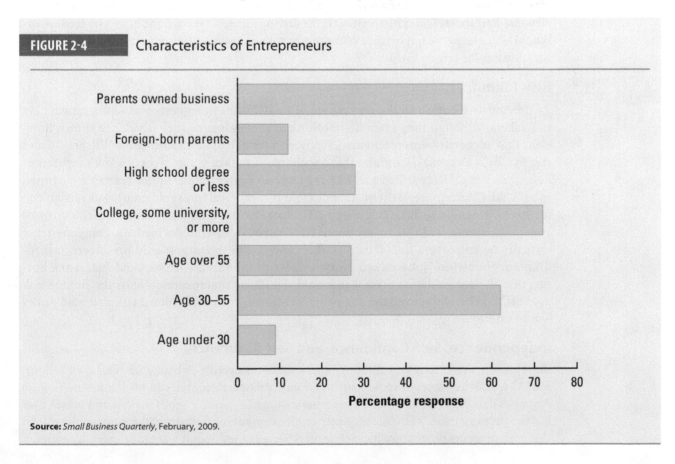

FIGURE 2-4 Characteristics of Entrepreneurs

Source: *Small Business Quarterly*, February, 2009.

entrepreneurs. These individuals exhibited some common characteristics that confirmed the results of previous studies.

In discussing the following characteristics, note that Canadian entrepreneurs have many different traits and come from diverse backgrounds. Very few entrepreneurs, if any, possess all the traits discussed, but many possess at least a few of them. However, even possessing such characteristics does not guarantee success in small business.

Individuals contemplating small business ownership would do well to evaluate their own suitability to operate a small business by noting the following personality characteristics. Keep in mind, however, that being an entrepreneur is less about being a type of individual and more about possessing an attitude of "pursuit of opportunity."

Achievement Orientation.

Those who place a high value on achievement, competition, aggressiveness, and hard work may be ideal owner-managers. Such people tend to be disciplined goal setters and have a bias for action. For example, Andrew Doyle, co-founder of 2nd Act Innovations (www.2ndactinnovations. com), a data storage company that enables firms to search through all their data for useful information, wants to build a billion-dollar company in Atlantic Canada. Since having opened an office in Silicon Valley, Doyle has demonstrated that he has the drive and ambition shared by many entrepreneurs. Doyle, who was previously president of the marketing company Extreme Group, talks about his love of starting a new company, "I loved playing offense. I loved building a business, making something big, new, exciting. The thrill was staying one step ahead of the competition."[42] Business owners also tend to possess above-average focus and drive, as well as the initiative to make things happen. Because they are hard workers, they generally strive to maintain good health to sustain this high level of energy. As Terence Corcoran, writer for the *National Post* states, "The entrepreneur is the driving force, the mover, the hero who sees opportunity, who grasps the importance of the product, knows when to assume risks, and, in the end, accumulates the largest fortunes."[43]

Risk Taking.

As previously mentioned, the very nature of small business suggests that entrepreneurs are risk takers, although they often do not think of themselves as such. Evidence shows, however, that successful entrepreneurs usually do take calculated risks. Brett Wilson, former star of CBC's *Dragons' Den* states that a willingness to take smart risks is a key to entrepreneurial success.[44] Recent Ernst and Young Ontario Entrepreneur of the Year award winner, John A. McCluskey, president of Alamos Gold Inc. (www.alamosgold.com), was recognized for his willingness to take calculated risks to grow his business. Colleen McMorrow of Ernst and Young had this to say about McCluskey, who transformed his company from virtually no employees to 500 paid workers and one of the largest gold producers in three different countries: "John risked everything when founding Alamos Gold Inc. at the bottom of a 20-year gold bear market and amid significant macroeconomic issues. But the risk paid off."[45] When he started the company, McMorrow took a calculated risk that gold prices would improve.

Independence, Self-Confidence, and Self-Assurance.

Entrepreneurs tend to resent authority and want to take credit or blame for their own actions. Karl Vesper, a well-known spokesperson for entrepreneurship, states in his book *New Venture Strategies* that "the entrepreneur ... has a basic human appetite ... for freedom and power over his/her circumstances."[46] In fact, an American Express survey found that the number one reason that entrepreneurs do not take more time off is because they do not want to relinquish control.[47]

LISA PATEL SAYS WATCHING HER PARENTS RUN AND MANAGE NUMEROUS
COMPANIES INSPIRED HER TO BE AN ENTREPRENEUR.
Photo courtesy of Lisa Patel, Property Princess

Other characteristics of successful small business ownership strongly correlated with independence are self-confidence and self-assurance. Often these traits are acquired through parents who were also small business owners. A recent study found that 50 percent of Canadian entrepreneurs' parents owned businesses. For example, Lisa Patel, owner of the Property Princess team (http://propertyprincess.ca), an Ontario-based real estate company, credits watching her parents start and sell 18 businesses as her inspiration to become an entrepreneur. "Growing up I knew I'd own my own business," she says. "My parents raised four children, and each of us worked in the family businesses. They taught us that ambitious people can have what they want in life."[48]

Innovativeness.

Successful entrepreneurs tend to be creative and willing to try new ideas. They are not afraid to evaluate an idea in a non-traditional way and to ask questions such as "why not?" They also tend to experiment and test their ideas. Such entrepreneurs are sensitive to new trends in society arising from how consumers experience products and to potential opportunities that result from these trends. For example, Wilson Wood, founder of Ottawa's Vrtucar (www.vrtucar.com), noticed that car sharing was becoming a trend across North America. Wood, who admits to not actually liking cars, was more than happy to build a profitable company around the growing trend. Interestingly, the major reason given by Canadian entrepreneurs for starting their own businesses was that they had found an attractive market niche and wanted to pursue it.[49]

INCIDENT 2-3

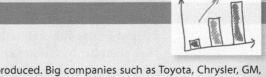

SIGPOD INNOVATION

It has been said that what electrocardiography does for the heart is what SigPod does for car engines. In 2006, Ottawa-based Sciemetric (www.sciemetric.com) introduced SigPod, an analysis software system that locates defects in products at the manufacturing and assembly stages. This highly innovative technology allows car makers to identify and graph defects in engines, brakes, transmissions, and drive shafts as the parts are being produced. Big companies such as Toyota, Chrysler, GM, and Ford are all among Sciemetric's clientele. The average cost of a SigPod is only $10,000, a pretty good price considering Nissan spent $14.4 million to recall 131,000 cars for a defective steering system. Sciemetric is now ready to expand into the world of medical devices and has adapted the SigPod software for use in the manufacture of cardiac implants.

Source: Adapted from Olivia Stren, "Auto Be Perfect," *Report on Small Business*, Summer 2007, p. 3.

For example, Derrick Fung, owner of Richmond Hill-based Tunezy (www.tunezy.com), was well aware that many new musicians were using the Internet to gain fans and yet failing to capitalize or make money from the attention. Fung's company allows independent musicians to earn money by providing fans with online concerts. Fung sells advertising and customer information from these events and shares the revenue with the musicians.[50]

Strong Verbal and Numerical Skills.

Successful small business owners are able to communicate their thoughts well. One study of 264 Canadian entrepreneurial companies found that communication skills were judged to be the most important contributor to the success of entrepreneurs.[51] Their numerical skills help them solve many of the problems that arise in operating a small business. Whether or not they have achieved a high level of formal education, successful entrepreneurs have usually acquired the necessary skills and knowledge from various sources. Increasingly, however, the educational background of Canadian entrepreneurs is rising. The CIBC Economic Analysis division recently found that the majority of the owners of small business start-ups had at least some post-secondary education.[52] Statistics Canada has also found that the growth in the number of self-employed persons with graduate degrees was higher than for other educational levels.[53]

Selling Skills.

Most successful entrepreneurs have above-average marketing and selling skills. Selling skills are not only helpful in promoting the business to customers but are also essential for obtaining debt or equity capital, securing suppliers, and maintaining employee loyalty. Saeed El-Darahali, founder of Halifax-based Simplycast (www.simplycast.com), a specialized digital marketing company, says sales and marketing skills are essential to growing a business. They are also very valuable in establishing networking contacts or sources of assistance for the operations. Lisa Patel, previously discussed, says, "Business today is all about connections. Networking is a long-term process and the key is to establish relationships. If you don't connect, it doesn't work,"[54] Successful entrepreneurs tend to handle rejection well, realizing that when they hear a "no," they cannot take it personally.

Problem-Solving Abilities.

Entrepreneurs identify problems quickly and respond with effective solutions. Typically, they rank above average at sorting through irrelevant details and getting to the heart of a problem.

Strategic Planning.

Successful small business owners tend to excel at setting business objectives and developing different ways of achieving them. They adapt to change easily and know their industries and products thoroughly. For example, Janet MacMillan, owner of Halifax-based MTL Communications (www.mtlcommunications.com), a communications and public relations firm, states that planning has been key to her company's long-term success. Companies, especially businesses in ever-changing fields such as communications, have to anticipate changes in the marketplace and be ready to respond accordingly."[55]

Perseverance.

Because of the difficulties in starting and operating a small business, successful entrepreneurs tend to have perseverance. They do not quit amid adversity. For example, Jim Trevling, owner of Boston Pizza (www.bostonpizza.com), could not find the money to purchase his first store. Rather than give up, Trevling convinced his friends to lend him half the money to buy the business and then he convinced the original owner to lend him the other half. Trevling went on to build Boston Pizza into the most successful Italian franchise in Canada. On a smaller scale, Eryn Green and Tamar Wagman, founders of Sweetpea Baby Food, had difficulty raising funds from traditional sources. The pair eventually wrote a business plan that they pitched to their family and friends on the opportunity to invest in their business. The partners eventually raised $150,000, which was enough to kickstart their successful company. One study found that successful entrepreneurs "average 3.8 failures before the final success."[56] Business owners tend to view these failures as part of their entrepreneurial education and point out that many millionaires failed several times before becoming successful. Successful business owners also tend to have greater self-discipline, as they often forgo paying themselves or taking vacations in the early months of the life of the business.

To assess the suitability of their personalities for starting a small business, entrepreneurs should evaluate their own capabilities in the areas just described. Completing a checklist from a number of checklists that are available allows for a quantitative evaluation of these characteristics. A simple example of one such checklist appears in Figure 2-5. A longer, more comprehensive checklist can be found in Appendix 2A.

FIGURE 2-5   Personality Characteristic Checklist

1. If the statement is only rarely or slightly descriptive of your behaviour, score 1.
2. If the statement is applicable under some circumstances, but only partially true, score 2.
3. If the statement describes you perfectly, score 3.

		Score
1.	I relish competing with others.	_____
2.	I compete intensely to win regardless of the rewards.	_____
3.	I compete with some caution but will often bluff.	_____
4.	I do not hesitate to take a calculated risk for future gain.	_____
5.	I do a job so effectively that I get a feeling of accomplishment.	_____
6.	I want to be tops in whatever I elect to do.	_____
7.	I am not bound by tradition.	_____
8.	I am inclined to forge ahead and discuss later.	_____
9.	Reward or praise means less to me than a job well done.	_____
10.	I usually go my own way regardless of others' opinions.	_____
11.	I find it difficult to admit error or defeat.	_____
12.	I am a self-starter—I need little urging from others.	_____
13.	I am not easily discouraged.	_____
14.	I work out my own answers to problems.	_____
15.	I am inquisitive.	_____
16.	I am not patient with interference from others.	_____
17.	I have an aversion to taking orders from others.	_____
18.	I can take criticism without feeling hurt.	_____
19.	I insist on seeing a job through to the finish.	_____
20.	I expect associates to work as hard as I do.	_____
21.	I read to improve my knowledge in all business activities.	_____

A score of 63 is perfect; 52 to 62 is good; 42 to 51 is fair; and under 42 is poor. Obviously scoring high here is not a guarantee of becoming a successful small business owner, since many other personal qualities must also be rated. But it should encourage you to pursue the matter further.

INCIDENT 2-4

PERSEVERANCE PAYS OFF

Deland Jessop and Adam Cooper, while they were taking their MBA at the University of Western Ontario, hatched the idea of Police Prep (www.policeprep.com), an Internet training course for prospective police officers. Jessop had been a police officer and knew how difficult it was to become an officer because there were no Canadian application and testing materials on the market. Cooper had experience providing preparation for exams such as the GMAT and the LSAT, so they decided to start the business. Sales were slow in the beginning. During 2002, the partners travelled across Ontario and met with every college that would see them. Few were interested. "It was very discouraging and frightening to be consistently rejected," Mr. Jessop says. However, they did not quit, and Conestoga College in Kitchener finally agreed to buy their product after three meetings with the school and an information session with its police program students. After one more meeting and an agreement to slightly modify their program, Police Prep had its first college client. This deal was the springboard for new business, allowing the partners to quit their day jobs to devote time to Police Prep. Programs have now been developed for other provinces and preparation courses for other occupations are in the works.

Source: Adapted from Rasha Mourtada, "Tracking A Lucrative New Niche," *The Globe and Mail*, March 10, 2009, p. 1–4.

THE SMALL BUSINESS DECISION: ORGANIZATIONAL EVALUATION   LO3

It is important not only to evaluate one's personal capabilities to operate a small business successfully but also to investigate what makes some businesses succeed and others fail. The following discussion reviews what some businesses do right and what others do wrong. The potential small business owner should incorporate the things successful businesses do right and avoid the mistakes other businesses have made.

SMALL BUSINESS SUCCESSES

Despite the high risk associated with starting a small business, many small businesses operate successfully. Numerous examples of these successes appear throughout this book. These examples illustrate many of the characteristics of successful businesses and their owners. The characteristics discussed next are compiled from reviews of successful small businesses.

Alertness to Change.

Small businesses that are flexible and plan ahead are able to adapt to changing environmental conditions more quickly and, in many cases, more effectively than larger businesses. The success of many small computer software companies is a good example of companies that can embrace change. Specific examples include Ben Baldwin and Jamie Schneiderman, owners of ClearFit (www.clearfit.com), a Toronto-based software company that makes applicant screening software. After engaging in discussion with clients, the pair realized that an industry trend of ramping up sophistication in systems was pushing many small clients away. As a result, the partners re-thought their strategy and better aligned their software with their clients' needs.[57] The computer industry changes very rapidly, and the new needs that emerge offer many opportunities for small business. Albert Iannantuono, owner of Tri-Media (www.tri-media.com), has managed to remain successful through the re-invention of his company by jumping into new technologies. Iannantuono says, "I call (re-invention) an evolution. What we are today is not what you're going to be tommorow."[58]

Ability to Attract and Hold Competent Employees.

Small businesses tend to be labour intensive. Thus, the value of employees cannot be overstated. Small businesses face increasing competition from large firms and even government in attracting and holding good employees. A recent survey of Canadian entrepreneurs found that attracting good employees is a challenge for 43 percent of small- and medium-sized businesses in Canada. Entrepreneurs who have mastered employee recruitment and retention are generally more successful. Many of the owner-managers profiled in this text have retained their good employees by using creative personnel management techniques. For example, Schleese (www.schleese.com), an Ontario manufacturer of custom saddles, uses flextime as a way to attract and retain employees. Employees at the company can work longer hours and bank them to use against Fridays or to attend family events or other appointments. Since implementing the strategy, the company reports they have experienced very little turnover.[59]

Staying Close to the Consumer.

Business owners who have a good knowledge of consumers' wants and needs and are able to incorporate them within the operations of their companies tend to be more successful. This skill involves constant monitoring of and responding to the market. The success of Molly Maid, a maid service franchise, can be attributed to the owners' knowledge of consumers' wants and needs. Molly Maid spends $80,000 a year on consumer research and is looking to expand into other areas.

Thoroughness with Operating Details.

Successful businesses have a very detailed and highly controlled operating plan, whether in the plant or out in the market. Goals, reports, evaluations, and adjustments are made constantly. College Pro Painters' success can be attributed to the very thorough operating plan the founder, Greig Clark, set up while testing the business concept. Many successful entrepreneurs subscribe to the "management by walking around" (MBWA) technique, with which they remain on top of operations details. Also, most successful small business owners have a strong technical background relating to their business.

Ability to Obtain Needed Capital.

A potential constraint on the operation and growth of any business is a lack of funds. Businesses destined to succeed, however, often have little difficulty obtaining start-up and operating capital. Their owners are aware of the sources of available financing and are able to make an acceptable presentation of their requirements to both equity and debt sources as the situation requires. As illustrated in Chapter 1, young Canadian entrepreneurs such as Eric Migicovsky who raised over $10 million using crowd-funding to build his smartwatch and as seen in the example of Jordan Satok below, money is available for entrepreneurs who have good ideas.

Effective Handling of Government Laws, Rules, and Regulations.

Owners of successful small businesses keep abreast of legislation and programs that may affect their operations. They realize that ignorance of certain regulations can cost their organizations not only in a direct financial sense but, perhaps more importantly, also in terms of a tarnished reputation or a missed opportunity.

YOUNG ENTREPRENEUR APPEARS TO POSSESS ALL THE KEYS TO SUCCESS

Eighteen-year-old Jordan Satok appears to have mastered most, if not all, of the keys to entrepreneurial success discussed above. Satok's company, AppHero (http://apphero.com/), has built an interactive iPhone and iPad app bearing the company's name. AppHero assists people in identifying which apps are best for them based on their online habits. The app also works with Facebook, as AppHero tracks usage, likes, dislikes, and so forth and identifies the apps that users most likely will use. The software also allows users to view the apps their friends use and to share the apps they use with their friends. Satok, who also owns the company App of the Day (www.appoftheday.com), has managed to raise $1.8 million in start-up money for his firm.[60] Satok believes his product is better than traditional ways of finding apps, which include online searches, as these rely on the consumer's knowledge to enter key words. Satok offers, "… people don't know what they don't know."[61] Satok's further states that his app will recommend many apps that users may like but are not aware of.

EIGHTEEN-YEAR-OLD JORDAN SATOK HAS ALREADY MANAGED TO RAISE CLOSE TO $2 MILLION FOR HIS COMPANY APPHERO. APPHERO HELPS PEOPLE FIND APPS THAT THEY WILL BE USEFUL TO THEM.
Vince Talotta/GetStock.com

Discussion Questions

1. Review the keys to entrepreneurial success above. Does Satok possess most of these characteristics?

2. Do you think AppHero is a strong product? Will the company succeed? Why, or why not?

3. Were you surprised that an 18-year-old was able to raise $1.8 million for a business? What do you think are some of the challenges with trying to raise money while still in high school?

4. Mobile business offers entrepreneurs incredible opportunities. List and, if time permits, develop an explanation of some mobile-based businesses you may want to start. For example, for a similar project, an Acadia University student actually developed a beer appreciation app that he is now selling.

SMALL BUSINESS FAILURES

Despite the considerable appeal of operating one's own business, it can also be disappointing if adequate preparations are not made. This section discusses some of the causes of small business failure. It is hoped that prospective entrepreneurs will avoid making the same mistakes as they start their own businesses. Readers should also recognize that businesses start and cease to exist all the time. It is a natural occurrence in the business community for businesses to exit the marketplace and new businesses to appear. As previously mentioned in Chapter 1, the Canadian economy sees an increase of approximately 100,000 businesses a year, which traditionally outnumbers the number of small businesses that exit the marketplace.

Often, when we hear about business failure, we think bankruptcy, but very few business closings actually end in bankruptcy. The reality is that, on average, 11,000 business declare bankruptcy in Canada each year. More businesses simply cease to exist, some are bought out by competitors, and others just close. For example, The Book Room, Canada's self-proclaimed oldest book store located in Halifax, had been in operation for 169 years prior to closing. The store that survived two world wars, the Great Depression, and a massive fire could not compete with online retailers, and its owner decided to close rather than suffer any more financial losses. Often customers and area residents are surprised when a business closes, as they fail to see it as part of a normal business life cycle. For example, it would have been doubtful that Canadians in the 1970s and 1980s would have predicted the end of Eaton's or Zellers.

Why do so many new businesses fail? While there is a variety of problems that cause businesses to fail, including external shock, a downturn in the economy, or an entrepreneur's lack of management experience, there is another problem that causes the demise of many companies— the failure of the entrepreneur to identify and deal with problems quickly. Often business owners ignore or not see problems until they are too late. Thus it is important that entrepreneurs become aware of problems so that they can make develop solutions effectively.

Factors That Cause Business to Fail

While various studies indicate there are numerous reasons a business can fail, most of them can be classified as external shocks or management problems.

EXTERNAL SHOCKS: Statistics Canada estimates that roughly 68 percent of businesses fail due to some type of external shock. These commonly include a downturn in the economy, changes in the economy such as interest and/or currency rates, new competition, loss of customers, loss of suppliers, new competition or substitute product, and/or change in laws or regulations.

MANAGEMENT PROBLEMS: Management problems usually revolve around issues such as starting a business without raising enough funds, inability to raise additional capital, failure to control costs, problems attracting or retaining employees, growing too quickly, and/or poorly planned expansion. Additionally, some entrepreneurs will also suffer from burnout associated with working too many hours.

If an entrepreneur is paying attention to their business plan and carefully monitoring the firm's financial progress, they may notice a number of warning signs indicating their business may be in trouble. Such signs include a failure to achieve objectives in the firm's business plan, a decrease in sales, an inability to pay some bills, or so forth. When this happens, an entrepreneur should take immediate action to solve the problem. Entrepreneurs should spend some time identifying the major problem at hand and engaging in some corrective actions. Often business owners who are struggling to survive will have to re-draft business plans, cut costs, raise additional funds sometimes by selling excess products at a discount, and engage in discussions with lenders. If business owners take the necessary steps they may prevent the closure of their business.

A study of failing Canadian small businesses sheds further light on the specific types of management weaknesses that exist (Figure 2-6).

FIGURE 2-6	Common Failure Factors for a Small Business

1. Poor or non-existent management information systems (inventory and accounts receivable control)
2. Poor controls on management expenses
3. Overreliance on a few key customers
4. Lack of financial skill (cash flow and profitability management)
5. Company is overleveraged (high debt), and debt is not being reduced
6. Poor cash flow management
7. Company management does not ask for help

Source: Julia Geller, "Failure Factors—Seven Signs Your Business Is Sinking," *Profit*, December/January 2003, pp. 31–33.

ENTREPRENEURSHIP AND SMALL BUSINESS MANAGEMENT

Up to this point in the text, the terms *entrepreneurship* and *small business management* have been used interchangeably. However, considerable confusion exists among these two terms, the types of skills they describe, and the type of training required to develop such skills. This section distinguishes between these terms. Understanding this distinction can be valuable in establishing and maintaining a business. Although they differ, both entrepreneurial and managerial skills may be necessary at different stages of the business's life cycle. This is the primary reason that both types of skills and traits were discussed together earlier in this chapter.

ENTREPRENEURIAL SKILLS

Entrepreneurial skills are required to start or expand a business. The specific traits that describe entrepreneurship are creativity, flexibility, innovativeness, risk taking, and independence. Entrepreneurs who have a high tolerance for ambiguity and change tend to think and plan with a long-term perspective. Entrepreneurs are generally idea oriented.

Those who start their own businesses are known as *founders* of the business, and there are two types. The first, sometimes called the *artisan* entrepreneur, has expertise in the technical or operations side of the business. He or she may have invented the product and tends to be passionate about it and confident of its success. The second is the *promoter*, who identifies a product or service he or she feels has potential and teams up with the founder to assist with initial financing or marketing expertise. Many small businesses are established following this pattern.

MANAGERIAL SKILLS

The skills of a manager are useful in maintaining and solidifying the existing product or service or business. The effective manager knows how to develop strategy, set organizational goals, and develop methods for achieving those goals. Managers require skill and knowledge in several functional areas of a business, including finance, marketing, personnel, network development, research, teamwork development, and operations. Such skills are most valuable after the business has been established.

As can be seen, although the entrepreneur's and the manager's skills differ, they are, nevertheless, essential for the long-run success of the business. Entrepreneurial skills help get the business started, while managerial skills help ensure that the business continues to operate successfully. Entrepreneurial skills may be essential once again to promote the growth of the business. Figure 2-7 summarizes the distinction between entrepreneurial and managerial skills and the situations to which they apply.

A major problem associated with small business is that individuals who have strengths in both areas are rare. Because most small businesses are started and operated by the same person, skills or characteristics that the person might lack must be found in others who are hired or otherwise acquired. Failure to do so may doom the venture. A study by the Harvard Business School found that only one-tenth of 1 percent of the ideas patented and listed in the *Patent Gazette* had actually made money or could be considered successful.[62] This suggests that many of the businesses established to develop these ideas may have lacked the necessary managerial skills. Part 2 of this text discusses essential considerations in starting a business (the

FIGURE 2-7 Small Business Skills

TYPE	CHARACTERISTICS	APPROPRIATE SITUATIONS
Entrepreneurial	Creativity and innovativeness	Generating ideas or solutions to problems
	Independence	Starting new business
	Risk taking	Expanding or adding new products
	Being idea oriented	
Managerial	Ability to develop strategy and goal setting	Reaching performance objectives
	Preferring to know outcomes of actions or activities	Maintaining control of operations
	Being a team player	
	Ability to work through others	
	Having skills in finance, marketing, personnel, operations	

entrepreneurial side). These chapters refer to the individual as the entrepreneur. Part 3 covers the managerial skills required for the established enterprise (the management side). It refers to the individual as the owner-manager or the small business manager.

ENTREPRENEURIAL SUCCESS IN LARGE BUSINESSES   LO5

Many individuals may possess the characteristics and desire to be an entrepreneur but find themselves part of an already established company or organization. In addition, many larger organizations realize that to remain competitive, they need to adopt many of the entrepreneurial traits discussed in Chapter 1 and what was referred to as "intrapreneurial" activity.

Because attempts by large organizations to incorporate intrapreneurialism are not always successful, the following suggestions have been made to increase the chances of success.[63] These were first developed by management consultant Gifford Pinchot and have been referred to as the "Ten Commandments for Intrapreneur Success."[64] Many large companies have followed these "commandments" to successfully develop and manage products and organizations. Figure 2-8 compares traditional managers to entrepreneurs and intrapreneurs.

Ten Commandments for Intrapreneur Success

1. Do any job needed to make your project work, regardless of your job description.
2. Share credit wisely.
3. Remember, it is easier to ask for forgiveness than to ask for permission.
4. Come to work each day willing to be fired.
5. Ask for advice before asking for resources.
6. Follow your intuition about people; build a team of the best.
7. Build a quiet coalition for your idea; early publicity triggers the corporate immune system.
8. Never bet on a race unless you are running in it.
9. Be true to your goals, but be realistic about ways to achieve them.
10. Honour your sponsor.

	FIGURE 2-8	Comparison of Traditional Managers to Entrepreneurs and Intrapreneurs	

	TRADITIONAL MANAGERS	**ENTREPRENEURS**	**INTRAPRENEURS**
Primary motives	Promotion and other traditional corporate rewards such as office, staff, and power	Independence, opportunity to create, and money	Independence and ability to advance, gain corporate rewards
Time orientation	Short term—meeting quotas and budgets, weekly, monthly, quarterly, and the annual planning horizon	Survival and achieving 5- to 10-year growth of business	Between entrepreneurial and traditional managers, depending on urgency to meet self-imposed and corporate timetable
Activity	Delegate and supervise more than direct involvement	Direct involvement	Direct involvement more than delegation
Risk	Careful	Moderate risk takers	Moderate risk takers
Status	Concerned about status symbols	Not concerned about status symbols	Not concerned about traditional status symbols—desire independence
Failure and mistakes	Try to avoid mistakes and surprises	Deal with mistakes and failures	Attempt to hide risky projects from view until ready
Decisions	Usually agree with those in upper management positions	Follow dream with decisions	Able to get others to agree to help achieve dream
Who serves	Others	Self and customers	Self, customers, and sponsors
Family history	Family members worked for large organizations	Entrepreneurial small-business, professional, or farm background	Entrepreneurial small-business, professional, or farm background
Relationship with others	Hierarchy as basic relationship	Transactions and deal making as basic relationship	Transactions within hierarchy

Source: An extensively modified version of a table in G. Pinchot, *Intrapreneuring* (New York: Harper & Row, 1985), pp. 54–56.

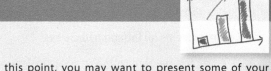

TIME TO TAKE ACTION

In this chapter, you have learned about some of the advantages and disadvantages of entrepreneurship, the keys to entrepreneurial success, how to avoid business failure, and the difference between entrepreneurship and small business.

After reading this chapter, you should start to consider some of the ideas you have for a business. Write down these ideas, and begin conducting research on any potential changes or innovations in and around your product or service. Can you identify any types of niches that you may want to explore?

At this point, you may want to present some of your ideas to entrepreneurs or former business owners. Ask them what they think about your idea. What did they say was good about your idea? What suggestions did they make for improvement? Remember networking is a key to business success, and by engaging in this exercise, you are building these networks.

You may want to begin attending some entrepreneurship events such as guest lectures or discussions in your community. Talk to like-minded entrepreneurs at these events, and see what they see as potential good ideas for businesses.

LEARNING OBJECTIVES SUMMARY

LO1 There are many advantages and disadvantages to owning a small business. Some of the most common advantages are frequent contacts with people, independence, skill development in many areas, potential financial rewards, challenge, and enjoyment. The possible disadvantages include high risk, higher stress levels, the need for many abilities, conflicts with people, limited financial rewards, and time demands.

LO2 Certain personality characteristics are associated with a successful owner-manager. These include an achievement orientation, risk taking, independence, self-confidence and self-assurance, innovativeness, strong verbal and numerical skills, problem-solving abilities, strategic planning ability, and perseverance.

LO3 The major causes of business failure are generally related to management problems and external shocks. Businesses that identify problems and try to resolve them are more likely to survive.

LO4 Entrepreneurs are creative, independent, and idea oriented, whereas managers possess strengths in problem solving, working with others, and developing strategies.

LO5 Large businesses must develop intrapreneurship activity to retain employees who would otherwise leave to start their own businesses.

DISCUSSION QUESTIONS

1. What are the advantages and disadvantages of small business ownership?
2. Which characteristic of successful small business owners do you think is the most important? Why?
3. How do managerial skills differ from entrepreneurial skills? When would an entrepreneur's skills be more useful than a manager's? Why?
4. Select a successful small business, and discuss the reasons for its success, drawing on the success characteristics outlined in the text.
5. What are the most common reasons for small business failure?

APPLICATION QUESTIONS AND HANDS-ON ACTIVITIES

1. Investigate a local business that has recently failed. Using Internet sources and other research methods, identify why the business ceased to exist.
2. Complete the checklist in Figure 2-5. Do you possess the personality characteristics necessary for successful small business ownership?
3. Interview a local small business owner about what he or she feels are the advantages and disadvantages of small business ownership.
4. Interview a local entrepreneur, and attempt to identify his or her entrepreneurial characteristics and leadership style.
5. Select a successful small business, and discuss the reasons for its success, drawing on the success characteristics outlined in the text.

APPENDIX 2A

ENTREPRENEUR SUITABILITY CHECKLISTS

– Business Development Bank of Canada—Entrepreneurial Self Assessment—www.bdc.ca
– Da Vinci Method—www.davincimethod.com
– Canada One—Assessing Your Business Readiness—www.canadaone.com/tools/assessments/self_assessment.html
– Small Business Canada—http://sbinfocanada.about.com/library/startbusinessquiz.htm
– American Express Entrepreneur—www133.americanexpress.com/usbn/tools/articles/entrepreneur.asp

CHAPTER 3

EVALUATION OF A BUSINESS OPPORTUNITY

LEARNING OBJECTIVES

By the end of this chapter, you should be able to:

LO1 List the four stages of the entrepreneurial process.

LO2 Identify the various sources of ideas for new ventures.

LO3 Summarize the non-quantitative aspects of evaluating business opportunities.

LO4 Describe the methods by which an entrepreneur can enter a market with a product or service.

LO5 Recognize the ways that an entrepreneur can develop a strategic competitive advantage.

LO6 Discuss the types of information available to assist in the quantitative analysis of selecting a small business and illustrate how that information can be used.

LO7 Identify a systematic way to quantitatively assess an industry and evaluate the financial feasibility of a specific small business opportunity.

SMALL BUSINESS PROFILE

LINDA HIPP *Lija Style Inc. (www.lijastyle.com)*

Linda Hipp was a business development manager for Orca Bay Sports and Entertainment, which owned NBA and NHL teams, when she arrived at the idea of providing more stylish apparel for female golfers. Being an avid golfer herself, Linda recognized what she thought was a market niche that had not yet been filled.

As a result, Hipp extensively researched the statistical trends provided by the U.S. National Golf Foundation and discovered that in the late 1990s, younger women were starting to play the game in large numbers. Because of this demographic shift, there was a need and demand for more fashion-forward, stylish yet functional apparel for younger women.

Linda quit her job at Orca Bay in 1997 and started her own company, Hyp Golf. She ventured out onto the trade show circuit marketing a small line of women's golf apparel that was influenced by European trends and West Coast style. Sales were slow for the first couple of years while the brand gained momentum. However, within three years, performance improved and the company experienced rapid growth of 50 percent per year, which has continued since then.

This rapid growth allowed her to expand both Spring and Fall collections by increasing the number of styles and

Photo courtesy of Linda Hipp

selection. She also began to hire key employees to help with production, finance, and marketing. Linda still manages the product development and marketing departments, while her partner focuses on the sales.

In 2004, Linda's company went through a brand and name change due to its notable successes outside of the golf industry. HYP Golf became LIJA (pronounced *Lee-zha*) a spin on the word *leisure*. These changes again resulted from further research and a clear focus of the market in the development of a competitive strategy. Growth has been outstanding over the last five years. Lija has been voted in the top 100 fastest growing companies in Canada in each of those years, and Hipp was recognized as one of Canada's top women entrepreneurs in 2008 as well as Executive of the Year in 2008 by *Score Magazine*.

Lija's products are now worn by many professional golfers and product lines have been added in the leisure, tennis, and active wear categories. Markets have been expanded to include the U.K., South Africa, the United Arab Emerites, as well as Canada and the U.S. The company has recently introduced an online showroom to facilitate information and sales.

LIJA STYLE INC.
www.lijastyle.com

Sources: Used with permission of Linda Hipp, as well as the Lija website, 2013.

ENTREPRENEURIAL PROCESS   LO1

The process of starting a new venture can be referred to as the *entrepreneurial process*. The process involves four specific stages that include (1) identification and evaluation of an opportunity, (2) development of a business plan, (3) determination of the resources required, and (4) management of the business. While the stages proceed sequentially, no one stage is dealt with in isolation or completed before work on the next stage begins. For example, some elements of evaluating an opportunity complement elements of business planning. The text will deal with ideas and opportunity evaluation in this chapter and proceed with business planning and the other elements in the entrepreneurial process in subsequent chapters.

IDEAS

All businesses start with one thing—an idea. Without ideas there would be no businesses or entrepreneurship. This chapter wants to encourage students and entrepreneurs to see all the ideas that surround them. Since many traditional employers ask employees to think creatively and develop new concepts, this chapter should be helpful to those who have no intentions of starting a business in the near term. Studying about idea generation should be enjoyable. You are looking for ideas, both big and small. Most entrepreneurs and innovators agree that looking for innovative ideas is a fun learning experience. Students should try to develop as many ideas as possible when using the techniques below. Do not worry if they appear to be impossible to create, sound silly, or are insignificant as many great ideas originally sounded this way—think about bottled water, mini vans, and the Internet. Do you think 50 years ago that any of these ideas would have sounded practical?

SOURCES OF NEW IDEAS   LO2

Some of the more frequently used sources of ideas include: past or current occupations, hobbies, personal experiences, observing consumers, existing products and services, and engaging in deliberate searches for ideas. Distribution channels and federal government sources are discussed later in the chapter.

Occupations.

Work experience, whether current or prior, is the most common source of new business ideas. It is estimated that over 80 percent of new businesses are based on an entrepreneur's current or previous job. Since entrepreneurs have the greatest chance of being successful if they start a business in which they have some past experience, it makes sense to seize opportunities from your work experience. For example, recent Ernst & Young's Entrepreneur of the Year Dr. Alan Ulsifer started Fyidoctors (www.fyidoctors.com) after graduating from optometry school and starting his own practice. Ulsifer saw an opportunity for independent eye doctors to combine knowledge, buying power, and patient care under one brand that has grown to include 200 optometrists from coast to coast.[1]

Hobbies.

Getting an idea from a hobby ties back to the notion of starting a company in an area in which you have previous knowledge. Furthermore, one can assume that you enjoy your hobby, so perhaps working in that industry will

ALAN ULSIFER CAME UP WITH THE IDEA FOR FYIDOCTORS AFTER WORKING AS AN OPTOMETRIST AND SEEING FIRST-HAND THE OPPORTUNITY TO FORM A NATIONAL ORGANIZATION.
Photo courtesy of Dr. Alan Ulsifer

provide similar enjoyment. Sometimes starting a business based on a hobby can be as simple as a comic book collector starting a comic book website or an avid hiker starting a backpacking business.

Drawing from Experience.

One of the best ways to develop a new idea is to reflect on past experiences and think about consumer habits and demands. Sandra Wilson did this when she created Robeez Inc. (www.myrobeez.ca), from her home in British Columbia. She had recently quit her job to be a stay-at-home mom and noticed that her son kept slipping in traditional children's shoes. Sandra proceeded to make him a pair of soft-sole leather shoes that enabled him to grip the floors better. Her son loved the shoes so much that she decided to make 20 pairs and bring them to a trade show. The response—15 retailers wanted to sell her product. Sandra recently sold her company, one that she started from her kitchen table, one that was based on a simple experience with her toddler, for $30.5 million.

Observations.

Entrepreneurs should continually pay close attention to potential customers. This attention can take the form of informally observing consumers to identify gaps in the marketplace, monitoring potential ideas and needs, or formally arranging for consumers to have an opportunity to express their opinions. One of the best methods of finding business ideas is to simply observe your current environment. Often, some of the best ideas can come from your day-to-day activities. For example, Jay Gould, founder of NY Fries (www.newyorkfries.com), a Canadian fast-food company that can be found in almost every mall coast to coast, says that when he was growing up, he observed that everyone loved French fries, especially from trucks that focused on their production. Thus the concept of a specialized French fry store made perfect sense to him. So when he discovered a restaurant selling what he would describe as the perfect fry in NY City, he returned to Canada and built a company around the idea. Gould says entrepreneurs should not be detracted when others criticize their ideas. "The one thing all my ideas had in common is that everyone I told about them thought they were dumb. That includes my bankers, my lawyers and accountants."[2] Matthew von Teichman, owner of Toronto-based company Life Choices Natural Foods (www.lifechoicesfoods.com), also used observation to identify a business opportunity. Teichman, observed the trend in society toward organic foods. By doing so, he noticed a gap in the marketplace—very few companies were producing child-friendly organic food. Teichman proceeded to address this gap by developing organic pizza, chicken nuggets, hot dogs, and cookies. The company now sells products throughout Canada and the United States.[3]

Existing Products and Services.

Potential entrepreneurs should monitor and evaluate existing products and services on the market. Frequently, this analysis uncovers ways to improve on these offerings that may result in a new product or service that has more market appeal. For example, Vancouver native Andrew Scott founded Digital Payment Technologies Corp. (www.digitalpaytech.com), a company that developed a replacement for traditional grey parking meters. Scott spent $1 million in research and development to build his new improved parking meters, which enable remote monitoring by parking enforcement officials, six locking points to deter theft, full-colour graphic screens, surveillance cameras, and a wide variety of payment options, including text, coins, bank cards, and credit cards. Consumers can register their cellphone numbers with a parking meter, and it will call to notify them that more money is required. The company currently has meters set up in 250 municipalities in North America, many of whom are motivated by the fact that the new

INCIDENT 3-1

CONSUMER TRENDS

Entrepreneurs should pay attention to consumer trends. Duplicating an existing trend or designing a product to meet a trend in consumers' lifestyles can be extremely profitable. Some methods of looking for trends include paying attention to what is happening in the mainstream media. For example, CBC's *Dragons' Den* frequently discusses new products and trends that entrepreneurs could build a company around. The show's website, www.cbc.ca/dragonsden provides visitors with a great deal of information on the businesses that have been on the show including old episodes. Other opportunities to view the latest trends include various print and online media sources such as:

Wired magazine (www.wired.com): Focuses on news about innovative concepts.

Small biztrends (http://smallbiztrends.com): Discusses the latest trends impacting small and medium businesses including business ideas.

Josh Pear (http://joshspear.com/): A site that highlights truly original products.

www.trendwatching.com: Site uses trend watchers around the globe to find new emerging trends.

www.springwise.com: The site has 15,000 trend watchers posting the latest business ideas for both products and services.

Other entrepreneurs are relying on social media sites such as Pinterest (www.pinterest.com), Digg (www.digg.com), Instagram (www.instagram.com), and Facebook to identify new and emerging trends.

Discussion Questions

1. Do you think entrepreneurs can identify business opportunities by visiting media sites such as the ones mentioned above?

2. Many businesses have become quite successful by taking an idea from someone else and making it their own. If you observe a great business opportunity on *Dragons' Den*, do you think it is ethical to simply duplicate the idea under a new business name? Why, or why not? What if a student talks about an idea she has in class? Would it be ethical for you to start a business based on your peer's idea?

3. Visit some of the trend sites mentioned above individually or in small groups. Report back to the class what ideas you found which have the most business potential. What ideas were you surprised by? Did you think any ideas were really bad?

4. What do you think are some of the advantages and disadvantages of using social media sites to discover trends? What social media sites would you recommend to trend watchers?

meters are not only appreciated by consumers for their convenience but also that they collect more cash due.[4]

Deliberate Searches.

Entrepreneurs deliberately searching for an idea may discuss ideas with friends and family, search through specific publications, and attend presentations and/or conferences. Entrepreneurs may also engage in formal idea generation methods such as focus groups or brainstorming.

Focus Groups.

A moderator leads a group of people through an open, in-depth discussion rather than simply asking questions to solicit participant response. For example, one company interested in the women's slipper market received its new product concept for a "warm and comfortable slipper that fits like an old shoe" from a focus group of 12 women from various socioeconomic backgrounds in the Boston area. In addition to generating new ideas, the focus group is an excellent method for initially screening ideas and concepts. The Internet has also made the practice of holding focus groups much less costly and more convenient. Business owners and potential entrepreneurs can now bring people from diverse backgrounds together online saving time and money and getting input from an increased number of participants.

Brainstorming.

Brainstorming, allows people to be stimulated to greater creativity by meeting with others and participating in organized group experiences where the goal is to produce new business ideas or solve problems. Both aspiring entrepreneurs and existing businesses use brainstorming to develop ideas. For example, Crelogix Credit Group Inc. (www.crelogix.com), a B.C.-based firm, which provides lending to consumers in a number of niche markets, uses online brainstorming to generate ideas. The firm makes use of Chatter, an online social media tool, where employees post ideas and information for new products. Crelogix's CEO, Karl Sigerist, credits Chatter with the development of loans for families to hire elementary school tutors for their children.

ASSESSMENT OF BUSINESS OPPORTUNITIES

An idea is just that—an idea. It may be something that can be turned into a profitable business, or it could just be something interesting. An opportunity is much more; it is an idea that if managed correctly can result in a successful new business. Prior to writing a full business plan, entrepreneurs will normally engage in an opportunity assessment process to determine if their idea actually has merit. Opportunity assessment normally consists of a qualitative assessment, and a detailed analysis, including quantitative measures. After completing a full assessment of an idea, entrepreneurs will then decide whether to proceed with writing a business plan.

QUALITATIVE ASSESSMENT   LO3

A qualitative assessment looks at non-quantitative factors to determine if the idea for a business aligns with an individual's goals and expectations. The major factors considered in a qualitative assessment are as follows:

Goals.

Individuals should examine their personal goals regarding income earned from the business. The question to address is: How well will the type of business I choose allow me to achieve not only my financial goals but also my occupational status goals?

Content of Work.

Individuals should assess their suitability for the business's working conditions. What type of work will the business involve? Will the business require hard physical work or considerable contact with people?

Lifestyle.

What type of lifestyle will the business allow? Will the hours be long or concentrated in the evenings or on weekends? Will the business allow family members to be involved? Remember that most small businesses take much more time to operate than the owner anticipates before start-up.

Capabilities.

In addition to the personal characteristics needed to run a small business that were discussed in Chapter 2, at least two other capabilities are required.

The first requirement is good health. As mentioned earlier, managing a small business usually involves long hours and is often physically and mentally stressful. Good physical health and stamina, as well as the ability to withstand high levels of stress, are all essential.

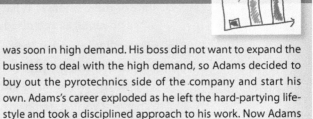

WHAT A BLAST

Doug Adams, president of Pyrotek Special Effects Inc., can be said to have one of the coolest jobs in the world. He designs and sets off the explosions, fireballs, and laser blasts that have become a large part of pop concerts. He has handled the special effects for the Grammy Awards for the past seven years and has worked for the music industry's biggest names such as Metallica, Beyonce, Prince, Kiss, and Kid Rock, among others.

Adams started out in Quebec as a 17-year-old in a rock band. MCA signed him to a record deal that did not work out, so Adams ended up working for a sound and lighting company in Ottawa. His boss was doing pyro, and Adams found he enjoyed the work and was good at it. Because of his musical background, Adams was able to detonate in time to music and was soon in high demand. His boss did not want to expand the business to deal with the high demand, so Adams decided to buy out the pyrotechnics side of the company and start his own. Adams's career exploded as he left the hard-partying lifestyle and took a disciplined approach to his work. Now Adams can pick and choose which big name artists he will work for. His incredible talent and his ability to outwork his competitors have helped him reach the top of the entertainment industry.

Over the past few years, Pyroteck has been busy providing special effects for many big name concerts around the world, including the last Britney Spears Circus World Tour. In 2009, Doug decided to step back from the business somewhat, as he resigned his post as CEO.

Sources: Adapted from Jeff Sanford, "What a Blast," *Canadian Business*, April 11–24, 2005, pp. 57–60, and Pyrotek website, 2013.

The second requirement is expertise in the fundamentals of management, including administration, marketing, and finance. Although numerous courses can provide valuable training, many successful small business managers have acquired expertise in these areas through self-education. For example, Ryan Smolkin, owner of Smoke's Poutinerie, a Canadian poutine franchise, says one of the reasons his company has been so successful is he understands marketing and branding. While he did not know much about actually running a restaurant, he had strong business skills that have enabled him to build his company across Canada.

Experience.

Potential entrepreneurs may want to consider starting businesses in areas where they have experience either through work or as volunteers. Lack of experience and unbalanced experience are two major causes of business failure. One of the best preparations prospective small business operators can make is to acquire knowledge of the type of business or industry they plan to enter. For example, Jill Strong of Halifax-based Wild Flower clothing (http://wildflowerclothing.com) worked part-time in retail prior to starting her own store. Strong credits this experience with helping her successfully own and operate an independent clothing store for over 13 years.

OPPORTUNITY ASSESSMENT

After completing a qualitative assessment or at the same time, an entrepreneur should complete a full opportunity assessment. A full assessment should have the entrepreneur prepare answers to the following questions. Remember, while this may seem like a lot of work, research indicates entrepreneurs who conduct full evaluations of business ideas are more likely to be successful.

Entrepreneurs will normally want to be able to discuss the following:

1. What product or service will the business provide? How will the business offer value to customers?
2. How will you enter the market? What will your competitive advantage be?

3. Who will the customers be? Why will they buy from you?

4. Assess the industry and environments your business will be operating in: What is the state of the economy? What are the economic trends? Who will your competitors be? What advantages and disadvantages do they have? What are the key success factors?

5. How will you market your product or service? What will your marketing mix look like?

6. Where will you get your major supplies? What will your costs be? Will suppliers sell to a new firm? What terms are offered?

7. What will your start-up costs be? Where will you get the money? Project your income over the next three years?

After answering the questions above, entrepreneurs should have a good sense if the idea they are assessing is just that an idea—or something much more valuable, an opportunity. Small business owners know that market entry, competitive advantage, and accessing information are particularly important to starting a successful venture, and these will be discussed in more detail below. This will be followed by information that will help you calculate important financial statements.

EVALUATING HOW TO BREAK INTO THE MARKET　　　LO4

There are three ways an entrepreneur can enter a market. The first is to offer a totally new product to the market. This involves "inventing" a product that meets a need that is not being fulfilled. Thousands of successful products have resulted from someone's dissatisfaction with the a lack of an existing product. For example, Canadian, Ron Foxcroft invented the first pealess whistle, the Fox 40, after becoming dissatisfied with a malfunctioning pea-whistle. "I always had a problem with whistles. They have a cork pea in them, and when you blow a pea-whistle really hard, nothing comes out. When they're frozen or wet or get some dirt inside, they lose their efficiency." Not only did Foxcroft manage to invent a new whistle, but he also successfully built the idea into a company. Fox 40 (www.fox40world.com) produces whistles for almost every major sporting league and the Olympics.[5]

Sometimes entrepreneurs can enter the market selling fad or novelty types of products. The needs these types of products satisfy are often emotional or subjective rather than rational. For example, Holey Sole shoes was a Canadian company that reached millions in revenue selling Styrofoam shoes similar to Crocs when the product was the latest trend. Holey Sole has since changed its name to Holeys (www.holeys.com) and now sells specialized Styrofoam boots and other products. While revenue levels are much lower than when the Styrofoam shoes were trendy, the company is still in business.

A second approach is to offer an existing product to a different market or industry. Phillip Kives, founder of K-tel International, was the master of this type of approach. His company initially achieved success by acquiring products sold abroad and marketing them in North America. Tim Kimber, founder of PlaSmart Toys (http://plasmarttoys.com), is another example of someone using this business strategy. Kimber discovered plastic cars that could be propelled using hand motions were popular in several global markets. He brought the car to North America, renamed it Plasma Car, and built a successful company around the product. Another form of this approach is to offer an existing product or service in the same geographic market but to a different age or income group or to use the product for a different purpose.

The third way to enter the market is to offer a product or service similar to those already existing in the same market. In this case, the prospective small business owner attempts to obtain some competitive advantage over the existing products or businesses in the industry to maintain viability. For example, Michael Kay founded Toronto-based Alexa Translations, a company that offers translation services and stands out by focusing on quality. Alexa Translations (www.alexatranslations.com), which operates in a growing and fragmented market, only uses translators who have degrees in translation or are certified, and they must have experience with the subject matter they are working with. Kay says the company's fees are higher than average, but they stand out from the crowd by focusing on quality service.[6] Other times the market is large and or growing enough to accommodate an additional business, or the level of satisfaction with existing businesses or products in the industry is low. For example, one of the authors of this text, Peter Mombourquette, noticed that there was a growing market for specialized cross-training for young athletes. As a result, he formed a company, Halifax Explosion (www.halifax-explosion.com), which offers younger athletes high level hockey, soccer, and martial arts training. Other examples of this type of entry into the market include establishing a retail store that stocks brand-name, conventional merchandise and manufacturing a product so that it can be sold at a lower price.

THE PLASMA CAR WAS SOLD IN SEVERAL COUNTRIES THROUGHOUT THE WORLD UNDER VARIOUS NAMES. IT WAS NOT UNTIL TIM KIMBER ACQUIRED THE NORTH AMERICAN RIGHTS TO DISTRIBUTE THE PRODUCT DID SALES SOAR.
Hixson/Dreamstime.com/GetStock.com

DEVELOPING A STRATEGIC COMPETITIVE ADVANTAGE LO5

An important part of being successful with a start-up business is selecting an industry, a business, or a part of a business that will provide a competitive advantage. A competitive advantage exists when a firm has a product or service that is viewed as better than its competitors'. More will be discussed about the specifics of developing the competitive advantage in the next chapter, as part of preparing the business plan. However, an entrepreneur can save valuable time and energy by identifying the most appropriate area to develop that advantage by selecting (1) the right industry, (2) the right business, and (3) the right aspect of the business to focus on. A brief discussion of each follows.

THE RIGHT INDUSTRY

Some industries tend to be conducive to small business success and may provide a competitive advantage over larger businesses:

- *Businesses or industries in which the owner's personal attention to daily operations is essential to success.* In a service business, for example, the expertise of the owner-manager is a major factor in generating revenue.

- *Businesses in which owner contact with employees is important to the motivation of staff and the quality of work done.* Specialized or custom-made manufacturing processes or service businesses and other businesses in which employees have direct contact with customers fit into this category. As evident in the example above, Alexa Translations is building a competitive advantage by offering superior service to clients.

- *Markets in which demand is small or local, making large businesses generally reluctant to pursue them.* For example, many shuttle services have sprung up in rural parts of the country in recent years. These services offer transportation to and from rural communities to larger urban centres.

- *Industries that require flexibility.* These include industries with high growth rates, erratic demand, or perishable products. For example, there has been high growth in businesses that appeal to parents of young children who are seeking to maximize their personal development. Many specialized tutoring companies, dance and music instruction, and sports training businesses have started small and been quite successful.

- *Businesses that are more labour intensive and less capital intensive.* Because of the above points, a business that relies heavily on people rather than machines to provide its product or service may be easier to manage if it is small. For example, many specialized businesses have remained quite small. Simply Sweet (www.simply-sweet.ca) is a Montreal bakery that has managed to be quite successful baking specialized wedding and occasion cakes. The amount of labour and expertise involved has served as barriers to larger businesses.

- *Industries that receive considerable encouragement from the government in the form of financial, tax, and counselling assistance.* Much of this assistance is directed at smaller businesses in the manufacturing, processing, exporting, and tourism industries. Such industries represent potential opportunities for small businesses.

While these specific industries above tend to offer competitive advantages to small business, readers should realize they are not essential to small business success. Many entrepreneurs have started small and medium businesses using technology to leverage the playing field between themselves and competitors. Technology such as the Internet has allowed many firms to compete on an International scale while maintaining some of the advantages of staying small. For example, Jad Saliba has built a successful software company Magnet Forensics Inc. (www.magnetforensics.com), based in Waterloo, Ontario, into a fast growing firm. Saliba, a former police officer, used to spend hours reading though computer files and social networks of suspects to look for evidence and thought there had to be a better way to search for clues. He eventually built an Internet Evidence Finder (IEF), working part time at home—the product is now being used by the RCMP, FBI, CIA, and U.S. Homeland security.

THE RIGHT BUSINESS

To identify a business that may provide a greater chance of success for a small business, the entrepreneur should be aware of those areas that are predicted to grow rapidly in the future. The following are some of the top Canadian business ideas for the future as reported by *Profit Magazine*:

1. Health care
2. Services for small business
3. Mobile business
4. Services that appeal to parents with children
5. Green products and services

THE RIGHT ASPECT OF THE BUSINESS

Once the industry and type of business are selected, the entrepreneur should decide which aspect(s) of the business to focus on to ensure the company performs better than the

INCIDENT 3-3

WEB SUCCESS

When Gord Dickie was growing up he dreamed about being a professional hockey player. While this dream did not come true, he did manage to combine his love of sports and his IT skills to build North America's leading sports-administration company— Goalline (www.goalline.ca). Goalline, which is located in Halifax, provides amateur sports teams with website administration, registration, and statistics. Dickie, who played university varsity hockey, noticed after graduation that there was an opportunity to administer websites for amateur sports teams throughout North America. Goalline's original premise was they would provide teams and organizations with a consistent and professional site, allow for online registration, and track player statistics. At the time, many amateur sports teams were struggling with creating a web presence, and Dickie offered them a turnkey package that solved their needs. Dickie felt Goalline would be able to offer top quality service in a growing market. Goalline originally targeted minor hockey teams throughout North America and quickly became the web-hosting site of choice for hockey teams and organizations. Recently, the company has been aggressively expanding into other sports, including soccer and baseball, ramping up its online advertising sales and working in partnership with Pac Rim Hospitality to develop an online team travel booking service called the Team Travel Centre (TTC). So far, Goalline's strategies appear to be working, as Dickie is managing sites for 1200 sports organizations, 60,000 teams, and year over year revenue has been doubling.[7] Online advertising efforts have also been paying off, as online ads now account for roughly one-third of Goalline's revenue. Dickie says, "We have 20 million page views a month, and while it took us sometime to demonstrate we had a base of web users, the strategy is working." Goalline's latest offering, booking team travel through their site, is still in its infancy stage, but Dickie believes it has tremendous growth potential. The TTC will allow teams to book hotels, cars, and make other arrangements through one point of contact. For example, rather than have a team call several hotels to compare rates, TTC will be able to check rates at several hotels electronically and allow team managers to make entire travel arrangements from one central site.[8]

Discussion Questions

1. Review the information in this chapter on market entry and competitive advantage. How did Dickie choose to enter the market, and how has he achieved a competitive advantage?

2. Goalline's original business was web hosting for sports teams, specifically hockey teams. The company has recently expanded into several other businesses. Do you think this is a good strategy for the company? Why, or why not?

3. Why do you think Goalline has been aggressively looking for other revenue streams?

4. What do you see are the primary advantages of TTC to consumers?

5. TTC has yet to catch on with sports teams that are used to making travel arrangements through traditional methods. Do you think TTC will ultimately be successful? Why do you think some sports teams have been slow to use the service?

competition. Natural advantages for the small business typically are flexibility, innovation, customer service, and product quality. Aspects such as price, selection, and location may also provide a competitive advantage, although they are typically more difficult for small businesses to achieve. The entrepreneur should be aware of the aspect of the business that is the most important to the consumer and attempt to develop superiority in that aspect of the business relative to competitors. A related question is to determine the scale of operations (size and scope) that the entrepreneur will attempt to establish. The results of the analysis in this chapter will allow the entrepreneur to formalize the strategy into the initial development of the business model, which is a critical part of the business plan. The business model is the framework for creating the economic, social, and/or other form of value. This includes a broad range of core aspects of the business, including purpose, offerings, strategies, infrastructure, organizational structure, trading practices, and operational processes and policies. The business model is the method of doing business by which an organization can sustain itself by specifying where it is positioned in the value chain. Considerable research should be carried out to finalize the business model and then develop the comprehensive business plan (see Chapter 4).

COLLECTING INFORMATION

The key to making a wise decision regarding which industry to enter and the type of business to start as discussed above is the gathering and analysis of information. The more relevant the information, the less uncertainty about the results of this decision. One study showed that the overwhelming majority of small business owners do no formal marketing research, although many do informal, unsystematic information gathering.[9] Recent studies indicate that research carried out by small firms is only 1.35 percent of value added, much lower than large businesses.[10] Failure to do adequate or appropriate market research is frequently cited as one the most common reason for small business failure.[11]

Some reasons entrepreneurs commonly cite for not researching and investigating a business are that it is too time consuming, too expensive, too complicated, and irrelevant. Although each of these claims has some substance, there are some simple, inexpensive, but effective methods of collecting and analyzing data available to the entrepreneur. Cassandra Rush, owner of Sassy Cassy's Boots Inc. (www.sassycassys.com), a B.C.-based company that specializes in selling boots for women with different calf sizes, credits market research with helping her company succeed. She notes research helped her make better decisions and helped her to be prepared when it came time to sign contracts.[12]

SOURCES OF INFORMATION

The first thing entrepreneurs should be aware of is the many sources of information available to assist them in their investigations. Two general types of information can help prospective small business owners select the right small business—secondary data and primary data. Secondary data consist of data previously published by another organization. Primary data are collected by the entrepreneur. The following sections discuss both types of information in detail.

SECONDARY DATA

Secondary data take the form of reports, studies, and statistics that another organization or individual has already compiled. There is no shortage of secondary data available to the entrepreneur, and collecting is usually inexpensive. A major problem, however, is finding information relevant to a particular situation. The secondary data available may be too general or may not apply to the type of business being established. Also, some reports are out of date and thus will need to be adjusted to make them useful. Such data can be updated by projecting past trends.

Secondary information is inexpensive, which makes it very attractive to the prospective small business owner. Much of the secondary information available in Canada is provided by the federal and provincial governments. However, much valuable secondary information is available from private and semi-private sources. Appendix 3A (found on Connect) presents a listing of those sources most relevant for small businesses. Figure 3-1 gives an example of using secondary data to begin the feasibility analysis for a business. This example uses Statistics Canada reports to estimate the market potential for a bookstore in Toronto.

In addition to obtaining published secondary information, entrepreneurs can consult several agencies for counselling in both starting up a business and ongoing operations. The most inexpensive and often most valuable source is the counselling provided to entrepreneurs by federal and provincial governments. The Business Development Bank of Canada can provide start-up counselling as well as analysis of an existing business. For example, Jim Ochitwa and Mark Bishop, owners of Calgary-based Maryn International Ltd. (www.maryngroup.com), a leading developer and manufacturer of industrial lubricant additives and finished fluids for all

Assessing Market Feasibility of Opening a Bookstore in Toronto Using Secondary Data

Problem	To estimate the size of the market for a bookstore in Toronto		
Step 1:	Determine the population in Toronto		
	Population of Metropolitan Area of Toronto	=	5,500,000
	(Source: Metro Toronto Information)		
Step 2:	Determine the number of families in Toronto		
	5,500,000 divided by 3 (average size of families in Ontario)	=	1,833,000
	(Source: Statistics Canada Census information)		
Step 3:	Estimate total bookstore sales for Toronto		
	1,833,000 × $300 (average household expenditures on books and magazines)	=	$549,000,000
	(Source: Average Household Expenditures, Market Research Handbook)		

This shows that a total of $549,000,000 could be expected to be spent in the Toronto area in bookstores.

Sources: *Market Research Handbook,* 2009, Statistics Canada; Metro Toronto Information, 2009; and *Average Household Expenditures,* 2009.

types of equipment, went to the BDC with questions about strategic planning and growth. After meeting with advisers and consultants, they left with clear marketing strategies and plans around improving cash flow, distribution, and succession. "The consultant helped us see where we were performing well and not so well. It's very useful to have an external person pushing you further," says Ochitwa.[13]

Most provincial and territorial governments also employ small business consultants to assist the small business (see Appendix 3B on Connect for information on some of these agencies in each province and territory). Many of these agencies provide start-up and business plan preparation assistance similar to that offered by the federal government.

Another potentially valuable source of assistance comes from universities and colleges. Many universities have student consulting programs designed to help small business owners. Using the expertise of graduating or graduate students, these programs can assist in preparing feasibility analyses or evaluating a business problem for a minimal fee, usually the cost of materials used. Some businesses such as Laval-based Ergoresearch Ltd. (www.ergoresearch.com), a manufacturer of orthotics and orthopedic products that help manage pain, are partnering with faculty and students to develop new business ideas. Sylvain Boucher, president and CEO, says partnering with universities makes sense, as they can provide firms with new business ideas or further develop ideas that are in progress. Boucher also notes that various government programs such as the National Research Council (www.nrc-cnrc.gc.ca/eng) and the Natural Sciences and Engineering Research Council of Canada (www.nserc-crsng.gc.ca/index_eng.asp) often cover much of the cost. "Partnering on research is a great way for an entrepreneurial company to innovate, because you can really leverage your money," says Boucher. "For every dollar you invest in a project, government programs may invest two or three times that."[14]

Other helpful counselling sources are lawyers, accountants, or bankers. Some of these sources may be more expensive than government services, however. Numerous consulting firms also specialize in small business operations. Industry Canada has found that small businesses that use professional advisers experience sales of 76 percent more than those that do not.[15]

An informal source of valuable information for the entrepreneur that is gaining popularity includes social networking sites such as LinkedIn, Facebook, and blog websites. Networking with other entrepreneurs on these sites can be an excellent source of ideas and information. Similarly, many cities hold entrepreneur forums and speaker series such as entrepreneur "igniter" meetings.

In addition to the types of assistance just described, another concept appears to promise considerable help in establishing new enterprises: the incubation centre. The incubation centre consists of an organization—usually a municipal or provincial agency—that provides essential services for new small businesses, either free or at minimal cost. Office space, secretarial services, computer capabilities, and financial and business counselling are examples of these services. For example, Innovate Calgary (www.innovatecalgary.com) is a business incubation centre dedicated to helping researchers, entrepreneurs, and businesses within the advanced technology sector. The centre offers entrepreneurs access to more than 50 years of combined experience supporting the technology community and was recently recognized as Canada's top incubation centre.[16] A Statistics Canada study found support for using incubation centres, concluding that 80 percent of businesses nurtured by incubators were still operating after five years.[17]

There are currently more than 500 incubators operating in North America.[18] These include more than 1000 incubator tenants, and estimates indicate that new incubators are opening at a rate of one per week.[19] In Canada, more than 40 business incubation centres operate across the country,[20] although this recent growth may be difficult to maintain because of cutbacks in funding from government sources. For a complete listing, see the Canadian Association of Business Incubators website at www.cabi.ca. Business incubators allow the small business community to work, individually or collectively, through the chamber of commerce and with municipal (city or town) governments, provincial or territorial governments, universities, and colleges. Statistics show that businesses receiving assistance from incubator centres have a 30 percent greater chance of success after five years over those who do not use them.[21]

PRIMARY DATA

Primary data are information collected through one's own research. Although usually more costly to obtain than secondary data, these can be more relevant to one's business and more current. Primary research is essential if secondary sources do not provide the information required for the feasibility analysis. It may also be beneficial to supplement the information obtained from secondary sources. Despite these advantages, small business owners have traditionally hesitated to do much primary research because of their lack of knowledge about how to do it and its relatively high cost. The Internet and social networking sites have gone a long way in reducing the costs associated with collecting information, but some entrepreneurs still cite cost as a deterrent.

Some research methods, however, are not complicated and can be of great value to the entrepreneur in evaluating the feasibility of a potential business opportunity. Three general methods that can be used to collect information through primary research are observation, surveys, and test marketing.

1. Observation.

Observation involves monitoring the who, what, where, when, and how relating to market conditions. For the small business, this method might involve observing auto and pedestrian traffic levels or customer reactions to a product, service, or promotion. It may also entail simply observing sales or expenditure levels. The Internet has allowed entrepreneurs to engage in online observation of consumers for a fraction of the cost. Businesses that once monitored customer reaction to a product or service can visit review sites such as Yelp or TripAdvisor to learn what customers are saying about their products. They can also monitor Facebook, Twitter, Instagram, and so forth to review customer feedback on various aspects of their marketing mix, including products and promotions. The observation method, especially traditional observation, may be fairly expensive, as it requires that time be spent monitoring events as they occur. Another limitation of observation research is that it only allows the small business owner to make inferences about the reasons people respond in certain ways. There is no two-way interaction with the subject of the research that might shed light on such motivations.

2. Surveys.

To obtain more detailed information from potential consumers and to better understand their motivations for purchasing a product or service, a small business owner can carry out a survey. The entrepreneur should clearly define the objectives of the research before questionnaire construction and ensure that each question addresses one of the objectives. Usually, it is not possible to survey each potential customer or the total market; therefore, only a part of the market is surveyed. It is essential, however, that the responses obtained be representative of the total market. Figure 3-2 illustrates a simple but accurate method for determining a representative sample for a research project for a small business. Such a survey might give the entrepreneur a general indication of the extent of demand for a new business. Of course, more detailed research should be carried out before a decision to start the business is made. Many businesses have failed because the owners acted on their own feelings or the opinions of a few acquaintances. In some cases, these responses do not represent the opinions of the total market.

Occasionally, through design or necessity (e.g., limited funds), a non-representative group of people is surveyed as part of the primary research project. This could involve surveying only experts or knowledgeable people in an industry rather than an equal cross-section of consumers. This method is also often used in surveying shopping mall customers. The most obvious drawback is that the findings may not be representative of the total market.

Three types of surveys are used to collect market information: mail surveys, telephone surveys, and personal interviews.

| FIGURE 3-2 | Calculating a Representative Survey Sample for a Small Business |

Step 1: Use the following chart to determine the number of surveys that should be completed to achieve a 95 percent confidence level at 0.05 degree of precision.

POPULATION SIZE	SAMPLE SIZE
50	44
100	80
500	222
1,000	286
5,000	375
10,000	385
100,000 and over	400

Step 2: Choose the respondents. If a phone survey is being conducted, there are two ways to choose the respondents. The first is to use the phone book and choose every nth individual. The second is to use a random number generator to come up with the phone numbers. Both of these methods have advantages and disadvantages, but both allow the surveyor to obtain a representative sample.

Mail and Internet Surveys.

These surveys are most appropriate when:

- Only a small amount of information is required.
- Questions can be answered with "yes–no" or "check the box" answers, or brief responses.
- A picture of the product may be required.

One problem with mail and Internet surveys is their poor response rate—typically well under 50 percent—and the lack of control over who fills out the questionnaire. Also, the preparer needs to make sure that the survey is not too long or too complicated.

Telephone Surveys.

Telephone surveying has become the most popular survey method in recent years, most likely because of its low cost and quick response time. However, it is even more restricted than a mail survey in the amount and detail of information the entrepreneur can obtain. The telephone interviewer should follow a survey guide to ensure consistency. As with the example of the mail survey, this phone survey might give the entrepreneur an indication of the acceptance of the concept. Further research and analysis is required before a decision can be made.

Personal Interviews.

The most expensive type of survey is the personal interview. Although this method generally costs more and requires greater expertise, it is the best approach for obtaining more detailed information and opinion-oriented responses. Since the number of people surveyed typically is smaller than in mail or phone surveys, this method is more suitable for interviewing knowledgeable people in an industry as opposed to surveying a cross-section of potential consumers. This type of research is known as *customer-focused interview,* or CFI. Personal interviews may involve surveying one individual at a time or, as many companies do, surveying several people together in what is called a *focus group*. The personal interview may be used for purposes such as testing a new product concept or advertisement or evaluating a company's image.

Entrepreneurs are often unsure about what types of questions to use in a survey. Some areas in which information should be obtained are the following:

- Respondents' reactions to the product or service
- The price respondents are willing to pay for the product or service
- Respondents' willingness to purchase the product or service (answers to such questions are often overly positive and should be adjusted downward by as much as 20 percent)
- Frequency of purchase
- Level of satisfaction with current product or service
- Demographic characteristics of respondents

3. Test Marketing.

Test marketing involves an attempt to simulate an actual market situation. For an inventor, it may mean letting a number of people try a new product and then finding out their reactions. For a business, it may mean marketing a product on a limited basis and observing sales levels or surveying to find out the level of satisfaction with the product or service. This method is fairly costly in that the product must be developed and marketed, albeit on a limited basis. The main advantage of experimental research, or test marketing, is that it measures what people actually do, not just what they say they will do, concerning the product. Small businesses have successfully used this method when taking prototype products to tradeshows, exhibitions, or potential customers to assess potential acceptance. The Internet, in particular crowd-funding sites have enabled many small business owners the opportunity to test market products with wide audiences for a fraction of the traditional cost. As discussed in Chapter 1, crowd-funding sites enable entrepreneurs to illustrate what a potential product may look like without having a finalized product ready for market. Consumers are often asked to comment on the product, and

INCIDENT 3-4

THE INTERNET'S IMPACT ON COLLECTING INFORMATION

Developer Robert Fung wanted to know what type of retail establishments local residents wanted in his new 8000 square feet of space he had recently built in New Westminster, B.C. Rather than turning to traditional market research, Fung opted to use Facebook, Twitter, and blogs to ask residents what types of establishments they wanted in their community. The response, according to Fung, was quick and informative providing insight into what type of retail community residents wanted.[22]

While Fung's use of social networks is interesting, it is certainly not groundbreaking, as more entrepreneurs are turning toward the Internet to get consumer opinions on various topics instead of relying on traditional market research. For example, Mike Bric, owner and operator of Toronto-based Sacred Rides Mountain Bike Adventures (www.sacredrides.com), was designing a new poster campaign and was not sure which picture he should use. Rather than using traditional means of collecting data such as presenting various pictures to focus groups and listening to their opinions, Bric decided to post some pictures on Facebook and informed his followers he was going to crowd-source his new poster. This meant that followers would select the new poster picture for his company by selecting "like" or "dislike" on Facebook and/or commenting on the images.[23]

Other examples of firms using the Internet to collect information are plentiful. For example, rather than paying market research firms to conduct surveys, many businesses are using online survey tools such as SurveyMonkey (www.surveymonkey.com) to create and conduct online surveys with consumers. Small firms are using crowd-funding sites, as discussed above, as a means to test market products and other businesses are using online focus groups, and/or observing customer reviews and comments on sites such as Yelp and Facebook all with the goals of collecting meaningful information at a low cost.

Some market research experts point out there are problems with entrepreneurs relying on the Internet and their own judgment in collecting data. Luke Zukowski, co-owner of Reveal Research Inc. (www.revealresearch.com), a firm which specializes in small business research, says many entrepreneurs lack the knowledge to use online tools to collect information. Furthermore, Zukowski points out that not all consumers are online, so relying solely on online sites could lead to businesses making the wrong conclusion. Other experts disagree with Zukowski, stating online data are easier and cheaper to access than traditional data and almost all Canadians are, in fact, online.[25]

Discussion Questions

1. What do you think are some of the advantages and disadvantages of entrepreneurs using online information to assess an opportunity?

2. Do you think Robert Fung and Mike Bric obtained enough information online to make the correct business decision for their companies? Why, or why not?

3. A lot of business owners are spending countless hours reading and, in many cases, responding to online reviews about their companies. Do you think reading and responding to online reviews is a good business strategy? Why, or why not?

4. If you were going to start a travel company catering to university students, how would you use the Internet to evaluate the opportunity? How could you use social media and online information to improve your marketing mix?

MIKE BRIC OFTEN USES SOCIAL MEDIA TO GET INPUT FROM CONSUMERS ON POTENTIAL PROMOTIONAL CAMPAIGNS.
Photo courtesy of Mike Bric, Sacred Rides

in many cases, companies can pre-sell finished products prior to manufacturing them. This pre-purchase provides entrepreneurs with a real sense of the market potential for their business. Perhaps the most famous use of crowd-funding is the Pebble watch example in Chapter 1, where the entrepreneur pre-sold over $10 million worth of smartwatches in a short period of time on the crowd-funding site Kickstarter. Another example is Ben Grynol's use of the crowd-funding site Indiegogo (www.indiegogo.com) to determine if his concept of a new cane called Top & Derby would sell. The cane quickly racked up over $14,000 in pre-orders and illustrated to Grynol that a market did exist.[24] Grynol's company, Winnipeg's Top & Derby (www.topandderby.com), then had several months to produce the canes prior to shipping them to customers. Test marketing is especially appropriate where little capital investment is required, such as with a small service business or online marketing to other businesses and consumers.

The proper collection of secondary and primary data can be invaluable to entrepreneurs as they assess business opportunities. It can provide a base of data that, if analyzed correctly, may allow for the capitalization of a successful opportunity or the avoidance of a disaster. The types of market research just described require an investment in time and money, but many successful entrepreneurs are convinced research is a worthwhile investment.

Although owner-managers often use these information collection methods before starting their businesses, they can and should use them on an ongoing basis after the businesses have been established to stay abreast of changes in market conditions. Many successfully established businesses become complacent and, as a result, eventually fail because they lose touch with consumers or market conditions. To avoid this, small businesses should set aside the effort and money required to regularly collect and use relevant market information. Chapter 7 discusses this subject further.

QUANTITATIVE ASSESSMENT OF BUSINESS OPPORTUNITIES   LO7
PREPARING THE FEASIBILITY ANALYSIS

Once the entrepreneur has collected the relevant information about the market, the next step is to use this information as quantitatively as possible to assess the financial feasibility of the proposed venture. The purpose of this assessment is to determine whether the business will earn the income the entrepreneur desires. The financial feasibility analysis as described in this section is most appropriate for starting a new business from scratch, but much of it could be applied to the purchase of an existing business or the operation of a franchise. The first step in doing a feasibility analysis for a small business is to prepare a sales or revenue forecast. This is a very important estimate, as it will become the foundation for the projected income and cash flow statements, which will ultimately indicate the feasibility of the venture.

There are two methods of forecasting sales. Both secondary and primary information may be required to follow either method. The first is the build-up method. To use this method of forecasting, the entrepreneur identifies each target market and estimates potential daily sales to each. This estimate may be obtained by observing similar businesses, or from industry experts, suppliers, or government sources. The daily sales estimate is then projected to compose an annual amount.

The second method of sales forecasting is referred to as the *breakdown method*. When choosing this method, the entrepreneur may not be as familiar with the specific target market and so begins with the total population and "breaks down" this large market by eliminating demographic or buyer markets that would be less likely to purchase. Figure 3-1 showed an example of a breakdown method of sales forecasting using secondary information only.

The procedure and example that follow are more similar to the breakdown method of sales forecasting than to the build-up method. Keep in mind that the following and accompanying example are simplified to allow the entrepreneur to follow more easily. Difficulty in obtaining relevant data and rapidly changing market conditions can increase the uncertainty of the result.

Three steps are required to estimate the financial feasibility of a proposed business venture. The first step is to determine potential revenue (demand) for the total market. The second is to estimate the share of total market revenue that the new business might obtain. The third is to subtract the associated expenses from the revenue estimate to arrive at a projected estimated net income for the prospective business. A more detailed explanation of the steps in calculating a feasibility analysis is presented next. A detailed example of such an analysis is given in Figure 3-4 later in the chapter. In carrying out the feasibility analysis, remember to be conservative with all estimates.

STEP 1: CALCULATE MARKET POTENTIAL

The purpose of this step is to arrive at a dollar or unit sales estimate for the total market. It may involve three substeps:

1. *Determine the market area and its population.* Delineate the geographic area or target market the business will serve. This can be done by obtaining a map and marking off the size of the market. Then estimate the population (numbers) within that market that might conceivably purchase the type of product or service to be offered. This process yields an estimate of the size of the target market.

2. *Obtain revenue (sales) statistics for this market area for the product type or service.* Usually, federal, provincial or territorial, or municipal governments have this information for many standard types of products or businesses. For example, Statistics Canada publishes retail expenditure and manufacturing data for many products and services. If total revenue or sales figures are not available for the proposed type of business or product, but per capita or per family expenditures are obtainable, simply multiply this figure by the population estimate obtained in substep 1 (population of market × per capita expenditures).

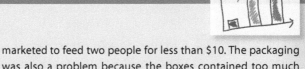

INCIDENT 3-5

CRAZY PLATES

When Crazy Plates frozen meals flopped, their inventors started over, but this time they used a recipe. Crazy Plates had high expectations, with the meals being an extension of two of the most successful Canadian cookbooks ever—*Crazy Plates* and *Looneyspoons*, written by Janet and Greta Podleski. The team behind the meals also included David Chilton, author of *The Wealthy Barber*.

Chilton and his team had made the all-too-familiar error of creating a product for themselves rather than for the researched market. "Almost all of them (problems) came about because we didn't research our market," says Chilton. The meal kit could feed a family of about four or five for about $14. However, research could have told them that 85 percent of frozen food is marketed to feed two people for less than $10. The packaging was also a problem because the boxes contained too much visual clutter and had no wax coating, making the box look cheap and fragile.

The team decided to start again and, using market research, reformulated the meals and redesigned the packaging. Chilton also created a 24-page business plan that outlined what exactly went wrong. After only a year, the sales of Crazy Plates were up 400 percent over those of the old product. "The real lesson is you can't replace solid research with pure instinct," says Chilton. Crazy Plates continues to be a successful company by marketing numerous products worldwide.

Sources: Adapted from Lee Oliver, "Appetite for Resurrection," *Profit*, November 2003, pp. 19–20, and Crazy Plates website, 2013.

If the product or service is new and no secondary data are available, use secondary data about a similar product. If there is no similar product, primary research—in the form of a survey, for example—may be used to assess consumer acceptance of the concept. If the results of such a survey indicate that a certain percentage of the market shows a purchase interest, multiply that percentage by the size of the market to obtain the market potential estimate.

Many entrepreneurs have started Internet businesses. Obtaining an estimate of market potential for this type of business may be difficult because many markets are untested and hard to define. There are some methods, however, that can be helpful in determining the size of the market for an Internet business. Data are emerging which indicate Internet usage for various types of products and services. This information can be used to help attain market revenue estimates as described above, although the geography for the market size may be more difficult to estimate. Figure 3-3 provides an example.

3. *Adjust the market potential total as necessary.* If a small business owner is able to obtain actual revenue statistics for the market, usually the only adjustment needed is to update the data. As mentioned previously, secondary data are typically a year or two out of date. A simple way to update sales and expenditure data is to increase the amount of sales by the annual rate of inflation for the years involved. This might also include a forecast of trends that will affect demand in the future. Such trends could be included in the estimate.

If national averages of per capita expenditures are used, make adjustments for local shopping patterns. A common adjustment in this regard is to adjust for those living in the market area who purchase outside the market, and vice versa. For example, if it is estimated that 20 percent of the market buys the product or service outside the market area, reduce the market potential by 20 percent.

Projections should include one-year and five-year estimates to reflect trends that may exist in the industry. Projections should also include trends with respect to growth of the competition that might affect future market share.

STEP 2: CALCULATE MARKET SHARE

The purpose of this step is to estimate the percentage of the total market potential the proposed business will obtain. Because the method of calculating market share differs significantly,

---

| FIGURE 3-3 | Calculating a Representative Survey Sample for a Small Business |

Background: An entrepreneur wants to estimate the market potential for a website that provides information and booking services for the 60 ski areas in the province of British Columbia.

Step 1: Using the Internet, the B.C. Skiers Profile 2003–04, and Ski Market Study 2007 were located. These studies indicated that 4.5 million skiers visited ski areas in B.C. annually.

Step 2: Using the Internet, the Travel Activities and Motivation Study (Government of Ontario) indicates that 78 percent of U.S. and Canadian skiers and snowboarders used the Internet for research, and 36 percent of those used the Internet to book their latest trip.

Step 3: Using the information collected in steps one and two above, make the following estimate:

$$4,500,000 \times 78\% \times 36\% = 1.26 \text{ million}$$

The market potential estimate is 1.26 million customers. Of course, adjustments should be made to this estimate to update the data, using skiing trends as well as adjustments to reconcile natural and B.C. skiing differences. However, the estimate provides a good starting point for the analysis.

depending on the type of business, market share calculations for retail, manufacturing, and service firms are illustrated separately.

It is important to remember that the market share calculations as described below are preliminary estimates only. They serve as a simple starting point from which significant adjustments must be made. Some of the required adjustments may be difficult to arrive at due to lack of current information and their possible subjective nature. Collecting the information to make these adjustments typically requires primary information with qualified sources such as industry experts and personal experience. The amount of the required adjustment may also be difficult to establish. However, arriving at a quantitative and objective initial market share percentage and recognizing that appropriate adjustments are necessary will lend confidence to the entrepreneur and credibility to the outside observer.

Retail Firm.

1. *Estimate the total amount of selling space in the market devoted to the merchandise the new business will sell (usually in square feet or square metres).* This involves taking an inventory of space of competing stores (specialty and department stores) devoted to this product. This estimate may be obtained informally by observation or by asking the owners. In some areas, secondary information about retail selling space may be available through the municipal or city government or department.

2. *Estimate the size of the proposed store (in square feet or square metres).* It is likely that the entrepreneur will have a good idea of the size of the proposed store. The actual size, of course, may depend on the availability of outlets.

3. *Calculate the market share based on selling space.* Integrate the information collected in steps 1 and 2 in the following formula:

$$\frac{\text{Proposed store selling space}}{\substack{\text{Total market selling space} \\ \text{(including proposed store)}}} = \text{Percentage market share}$$

4. *Make adjustments to reflect any competitor strengths and weaknesses regarding the proposed store.* Typical adjustments might include the following:

   a. Decrease percentage share if the competition has a better location, is larger in size, or has considerable customer loyalty. Also, decrease the percentage because the proposed store is new and will take time to build customer loyalty.

   b. Increase percentage share if the proposed store will offer unique products, services, location, advertising, or other advantages over the competition.

   The amount of the adjustments may be arbitrary and somewhat subjective, but typically they are fractions of a percentage of the market share.

5. *Multiply the revised market share percentage by the market potential estimate obtained in step 1.* The result is a dollar revenue estimate for the proposed business for the first year of operations. By applying market trends to this figure, a one- to five-year estimate can be obtained, if required.

Manufacturing Firm.

1. *Estimate the total productive capacity in the market for the product to be manufactured.* Typically, this will be calculated in units, but it may be in dollars. This will involve estimating the production size of competitors (both domestic and foreign).

   If the product is a new innovation and no competition exists, market share obviously is the same as the market potential calculated previously.

2. *Estimate the productive capacity of the proposed manufacturing plant.*

3. *Calculate the market share based on productive capacity.* Integrate the information obtained in steps 1 and 2 into the following formula:

$$\frac{\text{Production capacity of proposed business}}{\substack{\text{Total production capacity} \\ \text{(including proposed business)}}} = \text{Percentage of market share}$$

4. *Make adjustments to reflect competitive strengths and weaknesses that the proposed plant may possess.* The market share percentage estimated in step 3 will likely need to be adjusted. Determine the strengths and weaknesses of competitors, and compare them with the proposed business. Primary research is often required to obtain this type of information.

    Generally, a higher market share can be obtained in industries in which competitors are smaller in size, the product can be differentiated from competitors' products, and primary research shows a particular level of dissatisfaction with existing products.

    Market share will tend to be smaller if the industry is made up of a few large and powerful competitors who hold key contracts, or where consumer satisfaction with the existing product is determined to be high.

    Even though the existing market may look formidable, some sectors of the economy look favourably on purchases from small businesses. The federal government, for example, is a very large potential purchaser that should not be overlooked. These types of markets are discussed in Chapter 7. For a manufacturing firm, success at obtaining key contracts may provide the certainty required to calculate the market share and bypass some of these calculations.

5. *Multiply the estimated market share percentage by the market potential estimate obtained in step 1.* This figure projects estimated dollar sales for the first year of operations. As in the retail example, industry trends can assist in estimating this figure for more than one year.

Service Firm.

1. *Estimate the total capacity of the service available in the market area.* The base used to calculate capacity will vary, depending on the type of service being offered. For example, restaurant capacity may be measured by number of seats, tables, or square footage; motel capacity by number of rooms; and beauty salon capacity by number of employees or number of workstations. It is important to determine which base most accurately reflects the service capacity. Obtain this estimate by observing existing businesses or talking to owners.

2. *Estimate the service capacity of the proposed business.* This involves projecting the size of the proposed business in terms of service capacity.

3. *Calculate market share based on the capacity base.* Integrate the information obtained in steps 1 and 2 into the following formula:

$$\frac{\text{Proposed business service capacity}}{\substack{\text{Total production capacity} \\ \text{(including proposed business} \\ \text{service capacity)}}} = \text{Percentage of market share}$$

4. *Make adjustments similar to those made for a retail store.* The adjustments in the service industry tend to be more significant than in retailing. The opportunity to differentiate

from competitors in the service industry is much greater than in retailing, which tends to deal with more standardized products. Therefore, the percentage adjustments may be larger for service industry market share calculations.

5. *Multiply the estimated market share percentage by the market potential estimate obtained in step 1.* This figure projects estimated dollar sales for the first year of operations. As in the retail example, industry trends can assist in estimating this figure for more than one year.

STEP 3: CALCULATE NET INCOME AND CASH FLOW

1. *Using the market share revenue figure obtained in step 2 as the starting point, calculate the expenses expected to be incurred for the business.* Obtain most of these figures by checking with suppliers and other similar businesses. However, some secondary sources such as those provided by Statistics Canada provide typical operating statements for many types of small businesses. Often these statements express expenses as a percentage of revenue and thus can be easily adapted to the proposed business. Some of the more important required expenses are as follows:

   • Cost of goods sold and gross profit percentages—these can be obtained from secondary data but should be confirmed with suppliers.

   • Cash operating expenses such as rent, wages, utilities, repairs, advertising, and insurance—these expenses can also be obtained from secondary sources but should be verified by checking with vendors of these services, as they may differ for the market area of the proposed business.

   • Interest and depreciation—a list of the costs of capital items (i.e., building and equipment) and total start-up costs needs to be made so that yearly depreciation and interest expenses can be calculated. Chapter 6 presents information on determining start-up costs and the subsequent interest calculation.

   Remember that only the portion of these assets estimated to be used during that period should be included as the depreciation expenses. Using these start-up costs as a basis, determine an estimate of the amount of debt and annual interest costs using current rates.

2. *Subtract expenses from revenue to determine the projected net income from the proposed business in the first year and subsequent years, if required.* Once a projected income figure is calculated, the prospective entrepreneur is in a position to evaluate and compare this result with other types of available investments. Compare return (income) as a percentage of investment (funds put into the venture) with other types of businesses or safe uses of money such as the return obtained by placing the funds with a bank. The rate of return of the business should be higher than bank interest, however, to compensate for the risk factor that accompanies a new business.

   It is conceivable—and not uncommon—that the projected income for the new business will be negative, at least in the first few years of operation. Usually, the entrepreneur is taking a long-term view of the business, and thus long-term projections may be required to evaluate financial feasibility. In addition to a net income projection, many feasibility analyses include a projected cash flow statement. This document is of particular interest to potential lenders and investors. The cash flow simply describes the cash in minus the cash out on a chronological basis. Usually cash flow statements are shown monthly (see Chapter 6).

   A quantitative financial feasibility analysis for a retail pharmacy is presented in Figure 3-4. This example illustrates the steps described in the preceding sections.

FIGURE 3-4 Feasibility Analysis for a Pharmacy in Lethbridge (approximately 300 square metres)

Step 1: Calculate Market Potential

1. *Market area.* The market area is the population of Lethbridge plus outlying regions. This region includes towns within a 100 km radius of Lethbridge. The population of this total market area is about 200,000. (Source: City of Lethbridge estimate.)

2. *Sales for market area.* The per capita sales for pharmacies in the market area can be determined through two sources. First, the actual sales figures may be published and available from the municipality concerned. Second, if that information is not available, find the per capita sales by taking Canadian or provincial sales of pharmacies divided by the respective population. This information is available from Statistics Canada.

$$\frac{\text{Pharmacy sales for Alberta (2009)}}{\text{Population Alberta (2009)}} = \text{Per capita pharmacy sales}$$

$$\frac{\$31,400,000}{3,650,000} = \$860$$

Once per capita sales have been determined, this number can be applied to the market area population.

$$\begin{aligned}
\text{Lethbridge} &= \text{Population} \times \text{Per capita sales} \\
&= 85,000 \times \$860 \\
&= \$73,100,000
\end{aligned}$$

$$\begin{aligned}
\text{Outlying area} &= \text{Population} \times \text{Per capita sales} \\
&= (200,000 - 85,000) \times \$860 \\
&\quad (\text{Total market} - \text{Lethbridge}) \\
&= 115,000 \times \$860 \\
&= \$98,900,000
\end{aligned}$$

Since only 30 percent of people in the outlying area made their purchases in Lethbridge (primary research), multiply this figure by 0.3:

$$\$98,900,000 \times 0.3 = \$29,670,000$$

$$\begin{aligned}
\text{Total market potential} &= \$73,100,000 + \$29,670,000 \\
&= \$102,770,000 \text{ (rounded to \$100,000,000)}
\end{aligned}$$

3. *Adjustments.* Typical adjustments might include updating secondary information regarding population and purchases by applying past trends.

Step 2: Calculate Market Share

1. *Estimate selling space in market.* There are a total of 45 pharmacies and pharmacy departments in Lethbridge, with a total estimated size of 17,000 square metres. (Primary research collected by observation.)

2. *Size of proposed store.* The size of the proposed pharmacy is 300 square metres.

3. Calculation of market share. Percentage share of the market:

$$\frac{\text{Proposed store selling space}}{\substack{\text{Total market selling space} \\ \text{(including proposed store)}}} = \frac{300\text{m}^2}{17,000\text{ m}^2 + 300\text{ m}^2} = 1.7\%$$

4. *Adjustments.* The percentage of market share would probably have to be decreased slightly, because the proposed pharmacy is new and would not have built up clientele and the reputation of an existing store.

Based on the above factors, market share has been adjusted to 1.5 percent.

5. *Multiply market share percentage by the market potential.*

Market share $\times$ Market potential = Estimated market share
1.5% $\times$ $100,000,000 = $1,500,000

Therefore, market share is approximately $1,500,000.

Step 3: Calculation of Net Income and Cash Flow

NEW PHARMACY
Projected Income Statement
For the Period Ended December 2009

		PERCENT OF SALES	SOURCE OF INFORMATION
Sales	$1,500,000	100.0	From calculation in step 2
Less: Cost of goods sold	1,080,000	72.0	Dun and Bradstreet Key Business Ratios (2007)
Gross margin	420,000	28.0	
Expenses:			
Manager's salary	80,000		Primary information (talked to owners)
Employee wages (Schedule 1)	200,000		Schedule 1, primary information
Fringe benefits	15,000	0.75	Stats Canada operating results for pharmacies (2007)
Rent	50,000		Primary information (talked to owners)
Utilities and telephone	20,000		Primary information (talked to owners)
Accounting, legal, taxes and licence	6,500		Primary information (checked with agencies)
Insurance	6,500		Primary information (checked with agencies)
Repairs and maintenance	6,500	0.65	Stats Canada (operating results etc.)
Advertising	6,500	0.65	Stats Canada (operating results etc.)
Depreciation (Schedule 2)	24,000		Schedule 2
Interest, exchange, and bank charges	7,500		Schedule 3
Office and store Supplies	5,000	0.5	Stats Canada (operating results etc.)
Contingency	5,000	0.5	Stats Canada (operating results etc.)
Total expenses	432,500		
Net income (loss) before tax	(12,500)		

Schedule 1 (obtained through primary research)

Employee wages	
1 Full-time pharmacist	80,000
1 Part-time pharmacist	40,000
1 Full-time cashier @ $20,000	20,000
2 Part-time cashiers @ $10,000	20,000
1 Bookkeeper	20,000
2 Marker/receiver/delivery persons	20,000
Total	$200,000

Schedule 2 Depreciation Schedule

Equipment cost = $150,000 Capital cost allowance (CCA) = 20% (obtained from Master Tax Guide)

YEAR	UNDEPRECIATED AMOUNT	$\times$	CCA	=	DEPRECIATION
2009	$150,000	$\times$	0.20	=	$30,000
2010	120,000	$\times$	0.20	=	24,000
2011	96,000	$\times$	0.20	=	19,200
2012	76,800	$\times$	0.20	=	15,360
2013	61,440	$\times$	0.20	=	12,288

The above process is continued until the entire item is depreciated.

Schedule 3

Interest schedule

Amount borrowed = $100,000

Interest rate = 5%

Interest 2009 = 100,000 $\times$ 5%	=	$5,000
Estimated bank and service charges	=	$ 500
Debit machine lease	=	$2,000
Total		$7,500

Another potentially important part of the feasibility analysis, particularly for the manufacturing firm, is to estimate the level of production and sales required to break even financially. A detailed discussion of break-even analysis is included in Chapter 9. Once the feasibility analysis is completed, the prospective entrepreneur should have enough information to decide whether to pursue a particular business opportunity. The areas covered up to this point can be used to make this decision. Figure 3-5 presents a checklist for personal and opportunity evaluation.

FIGURE 3-5 Self-Assessment for a Small Business Opportunity

Personality:	Do I possess most of the personality characteristics of successful entrepreneurs introduced in Chapter 2?
Nature:	Does this business opportunity meet my occupational and lifestyle goals and interests?
Abilities:	Do I have the expertise in the fundamentals (financial, marketing, personnel, production) needed to manage this business opportunity? If I do not, am I able and willing to acquire or hire such expertise?
Experience:	Do I have experience with the business or industry? If not, am I able and willing to obtain it or find someone who can help me get started?
Financial base:	Do I currently have, or can I obtain, the necessary funds to finance the venture?
Feasibility:	Does the financial feasibility of the business opportunity meet my expectations and financial goals?

TIME TO TAKE ACTION

In this chapter, you learned about idea generation and opportunity assessment.

If you have not done so already, prepare a list of ideas that you may want to develop further into a business plan.

Start to narrow down the list of ideas by reviewing your qualitative goals. Then start to review each idea by answering some of the question identified in this chapter around opportunity assessment.

After narrowing down your list to one or two ideas, complete a full opportunity assessment of the idea. If you can, access both primary and secondary research.

LEARNING OBJECTIVES SUMMARY

LO1 The process of starting a new venture can be referred to as the entrepreneurial process. The process involves four specific stages which include (1) identification and evaluation of an opportunity, (2) development of a business plan, (3) determination of the resources required, and (4) management of the business.

LO2 All businesses start with an idea. Some of the more frequently used sources of ideas include: past or current occupations, hobbies, personal experiences, observing consumers, existing products and services, engaging in deliberate searches for ideas, distribution channels, and federal government sources.

LO3 Before deciding which small business opportunity to pursue, entrepreneurs must consider some non-quantitative factors such as their goals, the content of the work, the lifestyle the business offers, and their capabilities and experience.

LO4 There are three ways to enter a market with a new product or service. The first method is to offer a totally new product. The second is to offer an existing product to a different market or industry. The third is to offer a product or service similar to those that already exist in the same market.

LO5 An entrepreneur can develop a competitive advantage by choosing the right industry to enter, the right kind of business to pursue, and the right aspect of the business to focus on.

LO6 Two general types of information are available to help a potential small business owner to select a business opportunity. The first and most inexpensive method is to collect secondary data about a potential market. Many government documents and other sources can provide valuable secondary data. When little current secondary data are available, prospective small business owners can collect primary data to help determine the feasibility of their businesses. Primary data are information collected through one's own research. Although usually more costly than secondary data, these can be more relevant and current to the analysis. Three general methods of doing primary research include observation, surveys, and experiments. Surveying is usually the most effective method for a small business.

LO7 There are three steps in estimating the financial feasibility of a proposed business venture. The first step is to determine potential revenues for the total market. The second step is to estimate the proposed business share of that total market. The third step is to subtract the associated expenses from the revenue estimate to determine an estimated net income for the prospective business.

DISCUSSION QUESTIONS

1. Briefly explain the ways of entering a market. List examples that fit these methods other than those mentioned in the text.

2. J&J Inc. is thinking of developing a new coin laundry. The firm first needs to do some market research to determine the demand for the product. What kind of information should it collect?

3. Why is it important to make adjustments in market potential and market share figures?

4. For a small business of your choice, show how you would evaluate non-quantitative factors such as goals, experience, lifestyle, and content of work.

5. Discuss the difficulties of preparing a feasibility analysis for an e-commerce business.

APPLICATION QUESTIONS AND HANDS-ON ACTIVITIES

1. Form groups and brainstorm ideas that you could turn into a business. Select two or three ideas from the group and develop the marketing mix for the idea along with some justification why the business will be successful (competitive advantage). Present the ideas to the class.

2. Design a simple mail-in questionnaire to assess demand for a carpet-cleaning business in your city.

3. From Statistics Canada Small Business Profiles, find the Return on Sales, Gross Profit, and Current Ratios for a jewellery store, a clothing manufacturer, and a grocery store.

4. Contact an entrepreneur of your choice, and ask what the person feels is his or her competitive advantage.

Dan Kim has worked for a carpentry company building homes in Hamilton, Ontario, for the past five years. Although he has moved up in the organization to be a project manager, he is becoming increasingly frustrated with the negative aspects of working for a small company with little room for advancement. Dan has offered advice to the business owner that he should consider expanding, perhaps consider moving into commercial construction and that Dan himself could handle more duties under his proposed expansion plans. Dan has even offered he would be willing to become a partner in the business or eventually buy the company from the owner. The owner, who is nearing retirement age, prefers to maintain business as it is. He recognizes Dan as ambitious, dependable, and hardworking, but he has little desire to grow his company at this stage in his life.

Dan, while making a good wage, is certain that he could make more money if he worked on his own. Having grown up with parents who owned their own restaurant, he also fondly remembers the freedom that his father had in taking time off to attend Dan's hockey games and to take family trips. His father's restaurant had been successful and had grown to the point where he added four additional locations and eventually sold them all for a significant profit. Dan is not certain he wants to work for someone else for the rest of his life, nor is he even certain he wants to be a carpenter. Dan has recently started to think about ideas to start his own business and has been searching the Internet late into the evening for information on the latest trends in the construction and housing industries. Dan is certain that his experience and hands-on ability will help him identify an opportunity he could turn into a company, and he has started making notes on his iPhone about various business ideas he has during the course of the day.

After spending six months thinking about various ideas for a business, Dan believes he has found one that would work. After watching extension ladders wobble, lean, and sometimes move, Dan thought there had to be a better way to increase their stability without having someone stand and hold a ladder all day long. Dan spent the next few months building various prototypes that would solve this problem, and he finally developed a set of rails that could be easily attached to extension ladders to make them more stable and increase their safety. The rails are made of lightweight aluminum, bent so that they attach to a ladder through the holes of the ladder rungs. Dan was thrilled with his invention, which he intends to call the Ladder Rail. Dan is sure that the product will especially appeal to those in the construction industry as well as to homeowners. Dan is confident that he

can produce enough ladder rails in his garage out of lightweight aluminum (the same material that ladders are made from) with metal cutters and benders to launch a viable business.

Dan brought the Ladder Rail to work and showed it to his boss. His boss thought it was an interesting invention but stated he did not think people would buy them. This reaction concerned Dan, and while he was excited about the product's potential, he decided to post some information about the concept on several crowd-sourcing sites and on his Facebook page asking for input. While most respondents agreed the idea was a good one, many entrepreneurs stated that Dan would never be able to produce enough of the ladders himself to meet demand. Others suggested that rather than trying to make the extension, he should bring his concept to some of the larger ladder manufacturers and see if they would buy the idea from them. At this point, Dan was satisfied he had done enough research to determine the idea was a good one, and he believed people would buy them. While he appreciated all the advice he received online, he wanted to be the one to build the ladders, and he was not interested in selling the idea. After all, if he sold the idea, he would just be back working at the same company again, albeit with a little more money in his pocket.

Dan is more determined than ever to start his own business. He feels that his invention has great potential. He discusses the possibility of becoming an entrepreneur with his wife Suzie. Suzie is somewhat apprehensive about the idea, as she and Dan both have good jobs and have accumulated some savings. Furthermore, Suzie is concerned that Dan has not done enough work to assess if the idea is good enough for Dan to quit his job and start a business. Suzie states that Dan's only real market research came online from friends and family and other entrepreneurs and they would, of course, be encouraging. She would prefer if Dan engaged in more traditional market research or tried to pre-sell some of his ladders on a crowd-sourcing site. Dan is confident that he has collected enough information to determine there is a market for the product; and given that he is unsure how he will ultimately sell the Ladder Rail, he does not want to take any pre-orders at this time on crowd-funding sites. While Suzie says she has reservations, she agrees that Dan should at least do some additional research on the feasibility of the product. Dan has learned by reading blog posts from successful entrepreneurs that he needs to collect some information to find out whether the Ladder Rail can provide a large enough income so he can quit his job and make a living at it.

Dan feels that the primary market for the Ladder Rail is construction and home renovation companies. He also wonders whether homeowners will buy the Ladder Rail. This market would likely purchase ladders at their local hardware stores such as Canadian Tire, Home Depot, or Home Hardware. Dan believes that while the Ladder Rail would have global appeal, he should likely focus his business on Canada in the near term. Dan is also starting to realize that he will likely have to build a facility to manufacture in large quantities. Dan thinks that he should start small by attempting to market the product initially in the Hamilton area.

Dan goes to the local library and obtains some data regarding construction, population, households, and expenditures for Canada and for Hamilton. The information that he collected is found in Figure 1-A below.

Dan is not quite sure what to do with this information or what additional information he needs. He is aware that the company he worked for had 20 ladders and employed 100 people, so he estimates that one ladder is purchased per five employees in a construction or roofing company. Dan estimates that one out of 10 households would buy an aluminum ladder for such things as roof repairs, TV antennae adjustments, and putting up Christmas lights. He thinks that at least 20 percent of these ladder owners will be interested in the Ladder Rail. It costs Dan about $10 to make the standard Ladder Rails, and he estimates that he could sell them for about $40. A breakdown of his costs is shown in Figure 1-B. He feels that he could surely get 1 percent of the market. If so, he would be a rich man.

Questions

1. If Dan came to you asking for advice about whether to pursue this idea, what advice would you provide?

2. What aspects of Dan's background and personality traits are suited to owning his own business? What aspects might hinder his success?

3. Briefly discuss aspects of the product and business that may contribute to or hinder the success of the business.

4. What positive things has Dan done in investigating the new business?

5. What additional information should Dan obtain before completing his feasibility analysis?

6. With the information provided, prepare a feasibility analysis for the homeowner market.

7. What other information would make this calculation more accurate?

FIGURE 1-A	Dan's Market Research		
	CANADA	**ONTARIO**	**HAMILTON**
Population	31,413,990	11,410,046	662,401
Households	11,552,010	4,302,710	260,968
Household expenditures (Hardware tools per annum)	$1,655	$1,928	$1,848

FIGURE 1-B	Manufacturing Expenses for the Ladder Rail
Metal	$7 per unit
Labour	$2 per unit
Overhead	$1 per unit

Petite Shop (A)   Big D's Painting Company
Petite Shop (B)   Katie's Custom Engraving Logos

Petite Shop (A)

D. Wesley Balderson, *University of Lethbridge*

Alice Wood is concerned. She has worked in a women's clothing store for several years and is now considering opening a store of her own. Her investigations have yielded considerable secondary information, but she is not sure how to go about estimating the potential for another women's clothing store in Prince George, British Columbia. Prince George is a city of 86,100 surrounded by a large trading area. It currently has 17 clothing stores and five department stores that retail women's clothing. During the past few years, Alice has been saving her money and learning all she could so that her Petite Shop ladies' wear store would be a success.

In anticipation of starting her own store, Alice enrolled in a small business management course at a local college. The instructor stressed the importance of market research and mentioned several sources of secondary information that could assist in determining market potential for a new business. Alice obtained the reports she felt were relevant to her prospective business from the Provincial Department of Small Business, Statistics Canada, and the city hall in Prince George. This information is presented in Figures 1 and 2.

Now that Alice has this information, however, she is not sure how to proceed. She does not want to retail all kinds of ladies' clothing, but plans to cater to the "petite" woman who wears dress sizes 3 to 9. Alice herself is petite (5 feet, or

---

FIGURE 1   Selected Data for the City of Prince George

Population	86,100
Number of families	29,200
Per capita income	$15,000
Retail sales	$737,700,000
Per family expenditure on women's clothing	$1,000

Source: *Financial Post Canadian Markets and Urban Family Expenditure Report;* and *Market Research Handbook, 2009,* Statistics Canada.

FIGURE 2   Estimated Retail Space for Selected Retail Establishments (in square feet) City of Prince George

Food stores	1,200,000
Apparel stores:	
Men's clothing stores	145,000
Women's clothing stores	180,000
Hardware stores	600,000
Department stores	1,650,000

Source: City of Prince George; and *Market Research Handbook*, 2009, Statistics Canada.

1.55 metres), and she feels she understands the difficulties women of her size have in shopping for clothing. From her retailing experience, she estimates that about 60 percent of all clothing sales are in women's clothing and 20 percent of all women fit in the size 3 to 9 category. She arrived at her decision to select a store directed at the petite woman after she visited all of the 17 clothing stores in Prince George and the clothing departments of the city's five department stores. She estimates that only about 10 percent of clothing stores' stock is sized 3 to 9, and the five department stores devote only about 6500 square feet of selling space to this size range. She believes a small shop of about 1000 square feet could provide a much better selection to this market than those outlets presently provide.

Questions

1. Using the information provided, prepare an estimate of the market potential for the target market at which Alice Wood is aiming.
2. What portion of this market potential could Alice expect for Petite Shop's market share?
3. What non-quantitative considerations should be brought into this analysis?

Petite Shop (B)

D. Wesley Balderson, *University of Lethbridge*

Now that Alice Wood has a better idea of market potential and market share for her proposed retail store, she wants to be satisfied that the Petite Shop will provide an adequate return on her savings of $25,000. She begins investigating the typical costs she would incur in operating the store. Alice thinks she can operate her new store with one other full-time person and some part-time help at an estimated monthly cost of $2000. In looking at potential rental costs, she came across a retail outlet for lease on a busy street in the central business district of Prince George that seems ideal for the Petite Shop. She learns that the site leases for $20 per square foot, with no royalty payments except $550 per year to cover municipal taxes. The estimated utility expenses the owner provided were $300 per month, and the insurance for the retail shoe store that had previously been located there was $1500 per year.

Although Alice is excited about the potential of this site, she estimates she will need to spend approximately $12,000 for leasehold improvements, of which $8,000 will be depreciable items (20 percent). When obtaining the secondary information from the Prince George city hall, she learned that the business licences will be $100. Alice estimates all miscellaneous expenses such as stationery, bad debt expense, credit expense, and telephone to be about $5000 per year. These figures are based on her experience in the store she currently works in.

Alice knows she will have to borrow some money to purchase inventories. She visited her local bank and found out that the interest rate for a business loan was 10 percent. She also learned that until she had a more concrete proposal, her banker was not interested in considering her for a loan. He mentioned that in addition to leasehold

improvements, she would need one-fourth of the year's cash expenses as operating funds. Although a bit surprised at the bank's reaction, Alice is determined to prepare such a proposal. She knows the new store will need to be promoted, but does not know how much she should spend on advertising. The banker suggested the average for ladies' clothing stores was about 2 percent of sales and gave her a copy of a recent Dun and Bradstreet financial ratio sheet to assist her (Figure 1).

Alice now finds herself in the same dilemma she was in when determining market potential and market share. She has a lot of information but is not sure how to proceed.

Questions

1. Using the information presented in "Petite Shop (A)" and this case, prepare an estimated income statement and return on investment calculation for the Petite Shop's first year of operation.

2. What areas has Alice overlooked in her investigation?

3. Given your analysis, what would you recommend to Alice?

Big D's Painting Company

D. Wesley Balderson, *University of Lethbridge*

Dave Valdon lives in Maple Ridge, British Columbia, and is contemplating starting his own painting business. Having worked for a national painting franchise during his summers while attending college, Dave feels that he has the experience and skills necessary to be successful with this venture. Because he knows the area, he would like to establish the business in Maple Ridge and the surrounding communities of Pitt Meadows, Port Coquitlam, and Coquitlam. He will concentrate on providing professional and high-quality residential painting services. He intends to base the business out of his home and to set up a home office, as his work will be done at the site of the homeowner. In addition, Dave has been told that part of his home expenses (utilities, rent, insurance, etc.) can be deductible business expenses if he does this.

Although Dave is pretty sure that a viable opportunity exists, he knows that he should prepare an estimate of income for the first year of operations. From his industry experience, he estimates that an average painting job for a residential project is about $1700. His main concern is whether he will be able to obtain enough of these projects to make this a financially viable business. To that end, he has collected some information from outside sources as well as

FIGURE 1	Key Business Ratios, Canada— Corporations

LINE OF BUSINESS CLOTHING, WOMEN'S

(Number of concerns reporting)	(2,323)
Cost of goods sold	58.4%
Gross margin	41.6
Current assets to current debt	1.4
Profits on sales	2.7
Profits on tangible net worth	15.6
Sales to tangible net worth	5.9
Sales to inventory	5.7
Fixed assets to tangible net worth	63.6
Current debt to tangible net worth	127.6
Total debt to tangible net worth	177.3

from his experience working in the industry. This information is found below.

HOMES IN THE MARKET AREA

Maple Ridge	19,865
Pitt Meadows	3,496
Port Coquitlam	27,134
Coquitlam	15,828

Dave feels that one-third of all homeowners initiate painting projects each year in his area. He is not sure how to verify this percentage, however.

Dave estimates there are 100 painting companies in his intended market area. He feels that all will be his competition. He has also made the following estimates concerning his operating expenses for his first year.

Wages (himself and 1 other employee)	$60,000
Utilities/phone	1,500
Licence/accounting/insurance	3,000
Vehicle expense	3,000
Advertising	4,000
Equipment/supplies	5,000
Rent	2,500
Contingency	1,000
Total	$80,000

Questions

1. Using the information provided, prepare an estimate of total market revenue and Dave's share of market revenue for the first year of operations.
2. What adjustments should Dave make to the above information to be more accurate with total market revenue?
3. What adjustments or additions should be made to the information to be more accurate with the market share and projected income statement for the first year of operations?

Katie's Custom Engraving Logos

James D. Clark, *University of Lethbridge*

Katie Clark needs to make a decision to either start her new small business venture or return to university to pursue a graduate education. She really likes the idea for her new business. It plays into her skills and education in her just completed undergraduate degree in "New Media." Katie really needs to firm up her numbers to make sure that this venture has a great chance of being feasible and

earning her a nice living. Her decision needs to be made within the week.

Katie is 23 years old and has a degree in new media. She is very skilled in creating, designing, and producing digital media. While going to school, Katie worked part time and in the summer for her uncle who owns a trophy and awards store called Bullet's Awards Inc. in Red Deer, Alberta. Katie was responsible for the engraving and personalization of the various products. This family business has been in operation for over 40 years and has done very well. The business has evolved from very personal and hand-engraved products to one that is totally computerized.

Katie became very skilled at this business by using the computer hardware and software that drove this business. As she gained experience at the store, she noticed that the one way to differentiate Bullet's products from their competitors' was to customize the products to the customer as much as possible.

Using her skills, Katie was able to create custom logos for Bullet's customers that could then be engraved on metal, wood, and so on. Katie found that when she created these logos or just reproduced a customer's own logo in very specialized computer formats, those customers were almost certain to return for repeat business year after year because of the unique customization. Bullet's also earned higher margins on those customized and personalized products.

Creating these logos is not an easy task. It requires specialized software and hardware, coupled with technical skills, to create vector images that work on the various brands of engraving equipment. The logos are also in various file formats that are not widely distributed or used outside of the engraving industry.

Stock images of the engraving hardware are available when purchasing machines or engraving software from the manufacturers. These images are very generic, and every engraver has them, therefore no competitive edge is gained from these images.

This gave Katie the idea to start her own business producing custom image files for engraving businesses. Katie feels she could obtain between $40 (for simple logos) and $80 (for more complex images). After some investigation, Katie determines that she needs to invest about $27,000 in hardware and software to produce these images commercially. All the production and sales would be done digitally. The business would use the Internet to receive orders and to deliver the finished product to the customer. Seeing that this is really an e-commerce business, Katie determines that her market would not be local only but really anywhere in North America. The prospects of this business really excite

Katie. She also determines some of the other costs to starting this business.

Rent in Bullet's	$300/month
Internet and phone	$100/month
Accounting software	$400
Insurance	$300/year
Supplies	$100/month
Internet marketing	$200/month
Desks, chairs, etc.	$500
Web page development	$300
Katie's wage	$3000/month

Katie also gathers intelligence on who would be her competition in this business. To her surprise, she finds very little, if any, competition for this service. Most of the competition comes in the form of people engraving custom images for themselves. Katie's target market is other engraving shops that would use her logos to then engrave products customized to their local market. The industry comprises many producers of trophies but no dominant industry players; this tends to be a very localized and independent business.

As Katie ponders her decision to open this business, she feels she needs more information to make a correct decision. She really has very little money to start this business. She knows she would have to borrow from family, friends and, with any luck, she would also obtain funds from the bank. As she talks over this idea with her uncle, he looks at the few numbers she has and tells her that she would have a break-even point of 876 images per year. He tells her that if she could sell 1000 images/year, she would make a profit $6200 on top of paying herself $36,000 per year.

Katie knows from a production point of view she could produce 1200 to 1400 images per year. She does not know what her sales would actually be. She needs to find out how big the market is for custom images and what market share she would need to break even.

Katie has a few numbers that might give her an indication of sales. She knows that she created about 25 custom images a year for her current employer, Bullet's Trophy & Awards. Katie also knows that in the Red Deer market of 90,000 people, there are five other trophy and award outlets. Katie wonders how she might determine the market potential of her venture and then realistically estimate her market share of that potential.

Questions

1. What sources of information should Katie use?
2. How should Katie gather the needed data?
3. What is the market potential for this product?
4. What share of the market does Katie need to break even?

For more information on the resources available from McGraw-Hill Ryerson, go to www.mcgrawhill.ca/he/solutions.

PART II

PREPARING FOR SMALL BUSINESS OWNERSHIP

Once the entrepreneur has assessed an opportunity, the next important consideration is selecting from among three methods of assuming ownership of the business: organizing the business from scratch, buying an existing business, or signing a franchise contract. Chapters 4 and 5 provide information to help evaluate each of these methods. The last, but equally important, start-up consideration is obtaining financing. Chapter 6 discusses the critical factors the entrepreneur should consider in obtaining the financing needed to establish and operate the venture.

CHAPTER 4

ORGANIZING A BUSINESS— THE BUSINESS PLAN

LEARNING OBJECTIVES

By the end of this chapter, you should be able to:

LO1 Describe the advantages and disadvantages of organizing a business from scratch compared with purchasing a business or becoming a franchisee.

LO2 Discuss the importance of formulating and following a business organizational plan.

LO3 List the essential components of a small business plan.

SMALL BUSINESS PROFILE

JONATHAN BLANSHAY *Revision Military*

Jonathan Blanshay has always been interested in business. He graduated from the University of Western Ontario with a Bachelor's degree in Economics and obtained his Chartered Financial Analyst designation. In 2001, after 10 successful years in the financial services industry, Blanshay left this sector to start his own business in Montreal. "I had spent more than 10 years in the finance industry and had gotten a little bored of it and wanted a new challenge. I had always felt that I would eventually start my own business that actually made something useful, and so looking around and checking into different opportunities, this one came up. So I grabbed it."

Although he admits he knew little about eyewear, he teamed up with a friend who had 30 years' experience in eyewear manufacturing. With Blanshay's financial and business experience, they launched a successful venture.

By 2002, Revision Eyewear, now Revision Military (www.revisionmilitary.com), was manufacturing products for consumer niches such as glasses for motorcycling, paintball, racquetball, and the military. It was this latter market niche that has achieved phenomenal growth and success for the company. Blanshay describes the military business as a happy accident, as he had originally not thought of the market when he started the company. "I can certainly say when it all started ten years ago, we weren't even thinking of the military at that time. That was something that came up after a year in." Blanshay credits his experience with evaluating business plans in his previous occupation as a key to Revision's success. He ensured that a focused business plan was developed; this helped the company identify and target growing niche markets. As a result, the company has a clear vision, mission, and values statement on their website that reflects the overall company plan.

Revision develops high-quality protective glasses for military and tactical clients worldwide. Serving this unique customer group, the company also makes substantial efforts to supply

Photo courtesy of Revision Military Ltd.

products to specification such as changing style or colour to suit customer preferences.

To have better access to the large domestic U.S. market, in 2004, Revision established its first U.S. branch of operations with a new facility in Williston, Vermont. In 2007, their growth necessitated a move to a larger facility in Essex Junction, Vermont, and in 2008, the company began its own manufacturing. Blanshay admits the move was not an easy one, and it involved a great deal of careful planning and hundreds of hours of work with lawyers, consultants, and accountants. Although the company's operational headquarters are located in the U.S., Revision maintains offices in Montreal, The Netherlands, the U.K., and Germany.

Current military customers include the U.S. military (for combat troops in Iraq and Afghanistan) as well as defence departments in Canada, the U.K., Belgium, South East Asia, and numerous others.

Marketing for Revision's products consists of developing relationships with foreign sales agents, attending numerous trade shows, and maintaining an excellent website, in addition to using traditional advertising and strong community support. Future directions for the company include adapting to the changing needs of military customers. This includes developing integrated head protection systems that incorporate the helmet, protective eyewear, visors, and jaw and neck protection.

Revision has recently earned a place in Canada's 100 fastest growing companies for three consecutive years, and the company is continuing to grow through product development and expansion. Revision recently announced it has developed a new helmet system that is the most advanced in the world, and in 2012, it purchased MSA, North America's combat helmet division located in Newport, Vermont, and immediately landed a $21-million contract from the U.S. military. Blanshay says, "I think we will continue to add new products and new technologies. We're definitely still growing, and I don't see any signs that that will stop anytime soon."

REVISION MILITARY
www.revisionmilitary.com

Sources: Andy Holloway, "Perfect Vision," *Profit Magazine,* June 2008, pp. 78–79; the Revision Eyewear website, 2010; Eleanor Beaton, "The Overseas Office: How to Make the Launch Successful," *Profit Magazine,* May 2012; Patrick Leahy, United States Senator, "Leahy And Shumlin Applaud Revision's Turnaround of Newport Helmet Manufacturing Facility and Planned Doubling of Workforce," Press Release, October 16, 2012; Laura Burgess, "Jonathan Blanshay, CEO of Revision, Talks Growth, International Markets and Digital Capabilities of Eyepro with Laura Burgess Marketing," The LBM Blogger, April 27, 2011; and Revision Military, "Revision Introduces New Batlskin Head Protection System," Press Release, November 12, 2011.

GETTING STARTED: ESTABLISHING THE BUSINESS LO1

Once the entrepreneur has assessed the feasibility of a business opportunity and found it to be favourable, the next step is to select the method of establishing the business. There are essentially three methods from which to choose. The first is to organize a business from scratch, the second is to purchase an existing business, and the third is to become a franchisee. This chapter discusses the essential steps in organizing a business from scratch and details the steps in creating a business plan. Chapter 5 deals with purchasing an existing business and franchising. Although the topics covered in Chapter 5 are treated separately, a business plan resulting from the strategy development business model and feasibility analysis as discussed in the previous chapter should be employed regardless of which method is chosen.

Students should also recognize that business planning is an essential business skill. Whether you start your own company or work as an employee, being able to write a business plan will assist your career aspirations. For entrepreneurs, writing a business plan is essential to raise money and to assist them in the day-to-day management of their company. For students who are pursuing a job upon graduation, the ability to write a business plan will help them in their careers.

Organizing a business from scratch gives an entrepreneur greater independence in the establishment and operation of the business, but it also poses more risk (Figure 4-1). For example, if you are starting a homecare business for seniors in your area, you will have to create your own marketing and staffing plans, find customers, and create your own operations systems. If you buy a pre-existing business, or a franchise such as Nurse Next Door (www.nursenextdoor.com), then some of these things are already established.

The option to organize from scratch is often chosen by entrepreneurs who want the satisfaction of creating a business and adding their personal touch to all its aspects. It may also be the preferred route when few suitable businesses are for sale or there is little chance of obtaining a franchise for the market area. Another motive for starting from scratch include limited financial resources—entrepreneurs can sometimes start a business for a lot less money when compared to other forms of entering a market. A recent survey of small business owners by Statistics Canada indicates that about two-thirds of them started their business from scratch.[1] In making this decision, the entrepreneur should be aware of the advantages of organizing the business from scratch as well as the potential drawbacks.

ADVANTAGES OF ORGANIZING A SMALL BUSINESS FROM SCRATCH

Organizing a business from scratch offers several advantages. First, this option allows the small business owner to define the nature of the business, the competitive environment in which the business will operate, the appropriate market, and the size and extent of operations.

Second, the owner can obtain the exact types of physical facilities—building, equipment, and location—preferred. Buildings and equipment can be precisely tailored to meet requirements.

FIGURE 4-1	Independence versus Risk		
	ORGANIZING	**BUYING**	**FRANCHISING**
Level of independence	Higher	Medium to high	Lower
Level of risk	Higher	Medium	Lower
Chance of survival	20%	70%	90%

The owner can also choose the most appropriate location for the market, a very important competitive tool in retailing.

Third, the owner can obtain fresh inventory tailored to the target market. Thus, the risk of products becoming obsolete or difficult to turn over is minimized.

Fourth, the owner can personally select and train employees for the business rather than having to rely on the existing personnel of an established business.

Fifth, the owner can develop his or her own information systems such as the methods used for bookkeeping and for evaluating the operation. The owner also can take advantage of the latest technology in equipment and materials.

Finally, starting a business from scratch can be cheaper. The owner can choose to operate out of his home, start with little cash, and grow the business when he chooses to. For example, Brian Scudamore, founder of 1-800-Got-Junk? (www.1800gotjunk.com), started his business with a truck and a plan to professionalize garbage pick-up. Scudamore, who eventually grew the company into the largest home garbage removal service in North America, had very little in the way of start-up costs. If he was going to buy an existing business, he would likely have to pay for their assets, customer lists, and income. Buying a franchise likely would have been even more money. Interestingly enough, buying Scudamore's 1-800-Got-Junk? franchise costs owners approximately $100,000 to $150,000 to start.[2]

BRIAN SCUDAMORE STARTED A JUNK REMOVAL BUSINESS AS AN UNEMPLOYED STUDENT AND ONE TRUCK. HE HAS GROWN THE COMPANY TO BE THE LARGEST CANADIAN AND U.S. HOME JUNK REMOVAL SERVICE.
The Canadian Press/Jeremy Hainsworth

DISADVANTAGES OF ORGANIZING A SMALL BUSINESS FROM SCRATCH

Starting one's own business also carries substantial risks. First, the owner lacks historical information on which to base future plans. This can be a drawback if the owner has uncertainties regarding market demand, supplies, and operations. It is also generally more difficult to obtain financing if projections are based on estimates rather than on the extension of trends from existing operations.

Second, the advantage of personally assembling physical facilities can become a liability because of the time required. In some industrial situations in which prompt establishment is critical, purchasing a business or signing a franchise contract may be more advisable.

Third, a new business always has start-up problems or bugs that have to be worked out.

Fourth, establishing outside relationships with financial institutions, suppliers, and other key professionals is often time consuming. For example, new small businesses typically are not granted trade credit initially, whereas an existing business or franchise has far less difficulty. The savings in interest costs can be substantial.

Finally, the owner faces the risk that there will be insufficient demand for the product or service. Even if a feasibility analysis is to be carried out before business start-up, some uncertainty regarding the extent of the market may remain.

THE SMALL BUSINESS PLAN   LO2

Regardless of whether an entrepreneur starts the business from scratch, buys an existing business, or signs a franchise contract, a business plan is essential. Research data point to the crucial need for entrepreneurs to formulate business plans, not just for raising capital but also for organization and classification of long- and short-term goals. A business plan is a vital tool for entrepreneurs—a blueprint to be referred to again and again to keep business growth on course.[3]

For example, Kent Groves, founder of Maritime Trading Co., notes that for a business plan to work, people must use them not only to get initial financing but also to assist them in running their business. He says that his company constantly checks his business plan to see if their projections are on track and adjusts accordingly. Gary Kaye, partner in Ernst & Young's Assurance and Advisory Business Services in Ontario, says that street smarts and gut feel are not enough to run a company. He says that in order to be successful entrepreneurs must plan where they are going and how they will get there. He compares business planning to a roadmap for entrepreneurial success.[4] The use of business plans by Canadian entrepreneurs is increasing. A recent study of 100 successful Canadian small business owners found that 53 percent used full-scale plans— 91 percent had a timeframe, and 98 percent were written down. Only 4 percent of Canadian entrepreneurs did not prepare a business plan.[5] Business plans have both internal and external purposes. For example, when Jonoke Software (www.jonoke.com), an Edmonton-based medical billing company, went through a business planning process with the Business Development Centre, the company developed a new plan which included internal measures to improve productivity and a means to deal with increased competition from the external environment.[6]

Internally, the business plan provides a blueprint for the business that can help maintain a focus essential to success. The plan can help the entrepreneur in a business start-up as well as serve as a reference document to assist in the management of the ongoing business. A business plan can also help the entrepreneur by providing a vehicle to evaluate the performance of the operation over time. Business plans should contain both short-term and long-term or growth components for the business. A business plan may also serve an external purpose in that lenders and investors generally require one before lending or investing capital in the venture. There are several other reasons why a business plan should be developed. A business plan provides a sense of direction for the business, a test of the idea's viability, assistance in achieving financing, and a clear-cut implementation plan. Successful entrepreneurs also know that business plans need updating if they are going to assist you in running a business. As few things go as perfectly as planned, as entrepreneurs revise their goals and markets, a business plan will need updating. Julian Brass, founder and CEO of Notable.ca, an online company that informs people about notable events and people in and around Toronto, sums up this sentiment: "Every entrepreneur needs to start with a business plan, and like when you're seeking advice and mentorship, it's an ongoing process. You can say, 'This is a golden plan and we're going to be rich in a year,' but often times when you hit the market, things are very different than what you perceived before starting out. It's then that you have to return to the drawing board and tweak some things and go from there."[7]

His comments are echoed by Jeremy Koenig, co-owner of I Promise Performance (www.ipromiseperformance.com), a Halifax-based healthy lifestyle consultant, who states, "...you can have a plan, but things are going to change. You can't stick to your plan if the market is telling you something different.[8] Writing a plan gives you a starting point, once the business is running, you make changes as the market changes."[9]

The format and emphasis of the business plan vary depending on the user. A plan prepared for a lender should emphasize the entrepreneur's security or collateral position and the cash flow statement. It should show how the loan will be serviced in addition to the other areas. A plan prepared for a potential investor generally requires more detail to compensate for greater risk and a thorough description of the manager's or management team's capabilities, with emphasis on the projected rate of return. A venture capitalist will be interested in knowing the above items as well as in knowing how to liquidate ownership interest in a few years. (More is said about venture-capital firms in Chapter 6.)

WRITING THE PLAN

The business plan should be prepared by the entrepreneur, although it often makes sense for him to consult with others in its preparation. Sean Wise, entrepreneurship professor, author, and consultant who specializes in helping entrepreneurs find financing, states, "Entrepreneurs should write their own plans. By writing their plans they will gain from the process, they will ask themselves many of the same questions investors would ask them...entrepreneurs must go through the writing and investigation process to understand their business."[10] Some aspiring business owners will hire a consultant to write the business plan for them, but this is not advisable. As stated above by Wise, by drafting the business plan, an entrepreneur really gains a firsthand understanding of the opportunity and will have to answer important questions. Additionally, as entrepreneurs draft their business plan, they have the ability to make changes to their business model. For example, Tracy MacKinnon dreamed of opening a high-end wedding store in a small town in Nova Scotia. After starting out to write her business plan, she realized the market was not large enough for a premium dress store and further discovered there was a gap in decorating for weddings and other events. Rather than create a new wedding boutique, MacKinnon now runs a profitable decorating and party rental company. She says that if she had not written a business plan that forced her to investigate her idea, she likely would have opened the bridal store and failed.

Writing a business plan can take a significant investment of time. Many aspiring business owners and students look at the different sections and wonder where to start and when, or if, they can possibly finish. Perhaps one of the best ways to deal with this issue is to develop a plan for writing your business plan. The plan should include timelines and break the larger sections of the business plan into smaller, more manageable tasks.

Remember that a business plan starts with a number of headings and what you are doing is filling in the headings and analyzing information. Entrepreneurs will find this process will go a lot easier if they work on one small piece at a time and maintain separate files for each section. The best advice is to start with the marketing plan, as this is the most important section, and go from there. See an excerpt from a sample below:

TOPIC	INFORMATION NEEDED/ACTION REQUIRED	DUE DATE
2. Executive Summary	Make sure it is written for investors; highlight key concepts and sustainable advantage.	December 1, 2013
3. Industry Analysis	Review completed analysis with a peers in a similar industry.	September 1, 2013
3a. Future outlooks and trends	Assess the economy and culture in the area; check for any pending legal restrictions; interview potential customers; read trade journals; interview suppliers; make sure to collect Statistics Canada information, and talk to local regional development agent.	July 1, 2013
3b. Analysis of competitors	Determine who the competitors are, determine their marketing mix, interview their customers and suppliers, and assign strengths and weaknesses.	July 1, 2013

COMPONENTS OF THE PLAN   LO3

Although each user of the plan may require a different format or emphasis, the components of a compressive plan are as follows:

1. Introductory Page
2. Executive Summary
3. Industry Analysis
    A. Future outlooks and trends
    B. Analysis of competitors
    C. Market segmentation
    D. Industry and market forecasts
4. Description of Venture
    A. Products and services
    B. Size of the business
    C. Background of the entrepreneur
5. Production Plan
    A. Manufacturing process
    B. Physical plant
    C. Machinery and equipment
    D. Name of suppliers
6. Operational Plan
    A. Description of operations
    B. Flow of goods and services
    C. Technology utilization

YOUNG. PROFESSIONAL. CONNECTED.

As Julian Brass was getting ready to start NotableTV, an online site focusing on trendy events and people in Toronto, he spoke the following words, "Every entrepreneur needs to start with a business plan, and like when you're seeking advice and mentorship, it's an ongoing process. You can say, 'This is a golden plan and we're going to be rich in a year,' but often times when you hit the market things are very different than what you perceived before starting out. It's then that you have to return to the drawing board and tweak some things and go from there."[11]

NotableTV did launch, and true to its original vision, much of the focus was on video content, and the only market covered was Toronto. The site attracted much fanfare in the Toronto area as it quickly became popular among its target group of young, aspiring professionals. While the site, according to Brass, was making money, he became aware that a company of this nature, focusing solely on one city, even Canada's largest, had limited growth potential and other large Canadian markets were becoming ripe for expansion. True to his words above, Brass revisited his business plan, and relaunched NotableTV as a national company with a new name Notable.ca and expanded markets to Canada's largest cities, including Montreal, Calgary, and Vancouver. Notable's website now attracts 1.5 million visitors a month and features news and information about notable entrepreneurs, celebrities, events, and restaurants. In addition, and staying somewhat true to its original premise, the site provides links to a vast amount of video content covering everything from trendy events to inspirational lectures. Brass has also incorporated social media into the site with links to Facebook, Twitter, Instagram, and YouTube. Brass's strategy of national expansion appears to be paying off, as the national launch coincided with the announcement that Lexus and Gray Goose had signed on to advertise on the site. The company's site, which features the tagline "YOUNG. PROFESSIONAL. CONNECTED." is appealing to businesses looking to tap into Notable's target market of successful 25–45-year-olds who are interested in what is "notable."

Discussion Questions

1. Do you think Brass should have started with a national site, or was he correct in originally only focusing on the Toronto market? Why?

2. Why would advertisers want to promote their products on Notable's site? What are the advantages and disadvantages?

3. While Noteable.ca does have a national page, it clearly has separate pages and a focus on the Toronto, Montreal, Calgary, and Vancouver markets. Would this negatively impact visitors from other regions of the country? Why, or why not?

4. Given the small size of many of Canada's cities, should Notable focus on becoming a national site, or should it continue to focus on large urban areas?

5. Instead of branching out to other Canadian cities, would it be a better strategy to expand to larger American urban markets? Why, or why not?

6. Visit the Noteable.ca site, and note the company's strengths and weaknesses. What recommendation would you make to the company's owner Julian Brass?

7. Marketing Plan
   A. Target markets and customer profile
   B. Marketing mix (product, price, promotion, place)
   C. Forecasts

8. Organizational Plan
   A. Form of ownership
   B. Identification of partners
   C. Description of management team
   D. Personnel plans, including organizational chart, staffing plans, and so forth

9. Assessment of Risk
   A. Weakness of the business
   B. New technologies
   C. Contingency plans

10. Financial Plans
    A. Pro forma income and cash flow statements
    B. Pro forma balance sheet
    C. Break-even analysis
    D. Sources and application of funds

11. Appendix (contains back-up material)
    A. Letters from customers and/or suppliers
    B. Market research data
    C. Additional information

Often an entrepreneur will not need this level of comprehension and will opt for a more condensed plan. The general components of a condensed plan are below. The rest of the chapter will present a summary of the highlights of this condensed plan, but readers should be aware that many topics will be further developed throughout the book. For example, while this chapter briefly discusses target markets and customer profiles, Chapter 7 deals with this in much more depth and detail.

- Prepare a table of contents.
- Prepare a synopsis of the plan in an executive summary and background statement. This should include a mission statement indicating in general what type of business it is and what it is going to do.
- Describe the management team.
- Establish business objectives.
- Plan the marketing approach.
- Describe the selection of the location.
- Determine the physical facilities.
- Plan the financing.
- Plan the personnel.
- Investigate the legal requirements.
- Assess the risk.

As noted above, this chapter gives a brief overview of these components. Chapters 7 through 11 discuss the operating aspects of these areas in detail and should be consulted before preparing a business plan. Appendix 4A at the end of this chapter presents a checklist for a small business plan, and Appendix 4B shows two actual business plans following this format. In addition to the business plan outline provided in the appendix, several other business plan templates are available online. Examples are the Canadian Business Service Centres' "Interactive Planner," The Entrepreneurship Centre Business Plan, and the Business Development Bank of Canada's "Business Plan." The websites for this information are found on Connect in Appendix 3A. Note that a business plan may also be critical when purchasing a business, obtaining a franchise, acquiring financing, and performing other essential activities of the business. The format of the business, however, may vary, depending on whom the plan is intended for.

PREPARE A TABLE OF CONTENTS

This is mainly for the benefit of outside users of the business plan. It not only provides an overview of what is included in the plan, but it also provides quick access to various parts of the plan.

PREPARE A SYNOPSIS OF THE PLAN IN AN EXECUTIVE SUMMARY AND BACKGROUND STATEMENT

The executive summary, written at the conclusion of the preparation of the business plan, provides a short summary of the highlights of the plan for the reader. Depending on the length of the business plan, the executive summary can be anywhere from one to four pages in length and should stimulate the interest of the reader, especially if the entrepreneur is using the business plan to raise money. The executive summary should sell the business to investors and sell the entrepreneur. This is a very important section of the business plan and should not be taken lightly by the entrepreneur, as some investors use the summary to determine if the entire business plan is worth reading. For example, Colin MacDonald, co-founder of Clearwater, a national seafood company, is often presented with business plans from aspiring entrepreneurs looking to raise funds. Mac-Donald states he sees hundreds of business plans a month and often does not get past the executive summary. Generally, the executive summary should address a number of issues or questions that anyone picking up the written plan for the first time would want to know. For example:

- What is the business?
- How will it make money?
- How is this business unique?
- Why will you be successful?
- What advantages does the business have?
- Who are your customers, and why is this segment attractive?
- Who are the individuals starting the business, and why should investors believe in them?
- How much money will you make?
- What are your long-term exit strategies?

DESCRIBE THE MANAGEMENT TEAM

This section should describe the background of the entrepreneur and the management team. For the smaller business, it may simply include a resumé. The qualifications relating to the experience and education of the owner-manager are important aspects. For example, Kevin O'Leary, one of Canada's most famous investors who stars in CBC's *Dragons' Den* and ABC's *Shark Tank,* says he wants to invest in business owners who have relevant experience in the industry in which they hope to start a business.

ESTABLISH BUSINESS OBJECTIVES

Have clearly thought-out and formally written objectives for the business. The objectives identify goals to be met to achieve the mission and vision of the enterprise. The mission of the business indicates in a general, long-term way what the business is and what it intends to do. A mission statement should guide the firm through long-term decision making. Chris Bart, a management guru, notes that 24 years of studying business has led him to conclude that successful companies must be able to articulate their mission statement and their mission should reflect what the firm stands for. While a vision statement is the ultimate goal for a company, a mission statement is about how a company plans on reaching their vision. Bart states that successful mission statements should focus on customers and staff, provide guidance and inspiration to stakeholders, and assist in the allocation of resources.[12]

After creating mission and vision statements, an entrepreneur will focus on creating goals or objectives. To be effective, an objective must be specific. Specific and quantitative objectives allow meaningful evaluation of the business's performance. Objectives can be set in the following areas for the initial year and for a few years following start-up:

- *Business size.* This includes the size of the physical facilities, financial commitments, and number of employees.
- *Production levels.* The plan should include the number of products, product lines, and unit production anticipated.
- *Performance levels.* Sales, market share, and profit level should all be estimated and may form part of the plan.

PLAN THE MARKETING APPROACH

The next step in the business plan is to develop a marketing plan. Considerable information regarding the calculation of market potential and market share, both essential parts of the marketing plan, is provided in Chapter 3. The research and analysis carried out in the previous chapter resulted from an evaluation of the industry. In addition, the business plan should include the growth trends of the industry, the degree of confidence in predicting such trends, the strength and potential entry of new competitors, and a clear statement of the unique position the business is expecting to have within the industry as based on the business model. More is discussed about the industry analysis in Chapter 7. The following additional key aspects of a marketing plan should be investigated before starting the business.

Have a Clear Concept of the Target Market.

It is important that the prospective small business owner have a clear idea of who the target customer is and have a well-developed customer profile. This profile should include such demographic information as age, income, occupation, and social class, as well as certain personality and lifestyle characteristics.

After determining the target market, the owner can perform the steps discussed in Chapter 3: determining market area, market area population, market potential, and market share. Sometimes this information can be obtained using secondary data alone, but often primary research will be required. Chapter 7 illustrates a more detailed target market profile.

Understand the Target Market's Needs, Wants, and Purchasing Habits.

Understanding the target market's needs, wants, and purchasing habits is essential in formulating a marketing strategy. Answers to the following questions may prove valuable:

- Where do, or where will, the target customers purchase the product or service?
- When do, or when will, they purchase it?
- What product or service attributes influence the purchase decision?
- In what quantities will purchases be made?
- Most important, why do customers, or why will they, purchase the product or service?

Once again, the answers to some of these questions may be obtained using secondary data, but primary research may be required.

Be Aware of Any Uncontrollable Factors That Might Affect the Marketing of the Product or Service.

Several factors external to the business can affect the marketing plan and should be investigated, including those discussed below.

OWNERS OF SHOCKBOX HELMET SENSOR APPEARS TO HAVE THE PERFECT PLAN

Impakt Protective was founded in 2010 when co-owner Scott Clark's son was injured in a hockey game. Scott asked his son if he was OK, and his son responded in the affirmative and went back out to play. It was not until later that night he started to show signs of a concussion. The very next day, Scott and his friend Danny Crossman started working on a helmet sensor that would measure the impact of a collision on a player's head to help in determining if further medical attention is warranted.[13]

A short time later, the pair developed Shockbox (www.theshockbox.com), a sensor that attaches to helmets and can measure impact and display the results on a smartphone. If a player gets hit in the head, Shockbox will tell the parents, coach, or trainer whether the impact occurred on the front, back, or side and will display the g-force associated with the hit. If the g-force exceeds 50g, Shockbox will display a yellow warning, and if the force exceeds 90g, then the sensor displays an orange signal noting the player should receive further medical attention. While co-founder Crossman says there is no precise science to determine the g-force that causes a concussion, they used 50g based on research in Junior Hockey. Crossman says, "There is no magic threshold on concussions. Just a certain amount of research and information. A normal hit in the junior or college level shows 96% of impacts are below 50g. You have to draw a line in the sand somewhere in order to get a quantitative measure."[14]

Not everyone is convinced the product will be a success, as some potential users are concerned that the device only measures direct contact to the head. Others wonder if the price-point is not too high especially in expensive sports like hockey. But Crossman and Clark remain excited about the long-term potential for the company, as they appear to have excellent answers for anyone assessing their business opportunity. The business is unique, as it is the only helmet sensor for sale focusing on youth sports. A clear market exists among athletes, parents, sports associations, and insurance companies, who are all interested in preventing head injuries, in particular untreated concussions. Furthermore, the market is large and reachable, and there appears to be a great deal of demand for the product.[15]

The future prospects for the company appear to be strong. The partners have recently developed a Shockbox for football helmets, expanding the potential market to all youth football players. Additionally, a NHL team and several junior and university teams are testing the product, and some minor sports associations are ordering Shockbox sensors for entire teams. Crossman and Clarke are also in negotiations with a major helmet manufacturer to have the product installed directly into helmets. The pair recently appeared on CBC's *Dragons' Den* and managed to secure a $350,000 investment from Dragon Jim Treliving for 10 percent of their business, which values their company at roughly $3.5 million.

Discussion Questions

1. Do you think this product will ultimately be successful? Why, or why not?

2. Review the major aspects of the marketing plan cited in the chapter, and answer the following questions: Who will be the target market for the product? How should they promote Shockbox?

3. Given the price tag of $150 for one sensor, do you think parents or sports teams will be willing to pay this much for a product that does not prevent concussions?

4. In groups or as individuals, draft an executive summary for Shockbox that could be used in a business plan. Present this to the class.

SHOCKBOX APPEARS TO HAVE THE PERFECT BUSINESS PLAN. THE SENSOR, WHICH HELPS PEOPLE DETECT POSSIBLE CONCUSSIONS, HAS A STRONG COMPETITIVE ADVANTAGE AND IS IN DEMAND BY ATHLETES AND PARENTS WHO ARE WORRIED ABOUT HEAD INJURIES.
Photo courtesy of Impakt Protective Inc.

Existing or Pending Legislation Relevant to the Business.

New laws relating to marketing practices such as advertising, pricing, and manufacturing can have a significant impact on the business and cannot be ignored. This information may be obtained from an office of the federal government or the equivalent provincial agency.

State of the Economy in the Market.

The prospective small business owner should investigate whether the state of the economy is in a recovery or recessionary period. This trend also can influence the effectiveness of the marketing plan. Statistics Canada and private reports can provide this information.

Extent and Strategies of the Competition.

The entrepreneur should attempt to evaluate the competition and look for competitive strengths in the prospective business. A recent study found that 33 percent of Canadian entrepreneurs omit this important aspect from their business plans.[16]

Cultural Norms of the Market.

The entrepreneur should ensure that the new business conforms to the social and cultural norms of the market. This is especially important for exporters and for companies moving into new markets. An important aspect in today's business world relates to ethics and social responsibility. This should be an essential part of the business plan and subsequent policies. The business should have a code of ethics covering all operational functions of the business, ensuring honest and ethical behaviour. This code of ethics should be clearly communicated to employees, documented, monitored, enforced, and regularly reviewed. Studies have shown that organizations that display a clear commitment to ethical conduct consistently outperform companies that do not.[17]

Another cultural trend that small businesses should consider addressing relates to environmental issues. As concern for the environment increases, there is mounting evidence that environmental efficiency of organizations leads to reduced waste and operating costs. Although a key concern for small businesses adopting environmental policies has been large capital expenditures, a recent study found that small business could become involved in such things as recycling of materials and energy conservation without incurring significant costs.[18]

New Technology That Might Affect the Business.

Regularly review and monitor new technology, as it can represent either opportunities for the business or detrimental competitor strategies. Trade magazines and competitor strategies are good sources of information concerning new technology.

Plan the Marketing Program.

After collecting the above information, the entrepreneur can formulate a marketing program. The essential aspects of the marketing program are as follows:

- *The product or service.* This includes such information as how the product or service is developed, sources of material, and level of quality, variety, and packaging.
- *The distribution system.* This includes determining the path the product or service will take to reach the consumer or ultimate user and may involve selection of wholesalers and retailers.
- *Promotion.* This involves decisions regarding promotion budgets, advertising versus personal selling, and developing appropriate communications.
- *Pricing.* The development of pricing policies, including the calculation of specific price levels, should be planned. These elements of the marketing program are discussed in more detail in Chapter 7.

DESCRIBE THE SELECTION OF THE LOCATION

The next component of a business plan is selecting the location for the business. In setting up a new business, the prospective owner needs to determine the trading area or city in which to locate. Then the owner selects the specific site within the trading area. New Internet services such as Google Maps may be helpful in identifying and selecting suitable locations.

The Trading Area.

Several criteria are commonly used to select the trading area. Choosing the general trading area is often more critical for manufacturers than for retailers or service firms, whereas the selection of a specific site within the trade area is generally more important for retailers. The following information is valuable in selecting the trading area.

Economic Base.

Information on population, employment levels, income levels, retail sales, and house values within the trading area may be needed. These elements help small manufacturers determine the availability of employees and expected pay scales. For retail and service firms, they indicate the potential for future sales. One should also examine the trends relating to these key indicators. Most of this information may be obtained from secondary data such as the government sources listed in Appendix 3B on Connect.

Attitude of Trading Area toward New Businesses.

Many communities are eager to attract new industry and offer various kinds of incentives for new businesses. Although this benefit is usually more important for manufacturers, any small business owner should contact the local city administration or chamber of commerce regarding incentives. Often these agencies are aware of specific types of businesses their communities need.

Competition.

Competitive firms in a trading area should be noted. A retail or service firm with a fixed geographic market should evaluate various trading areas on the basis of saturation levels for the type of outlet it will establish. There are many methods of calculating the saturation index. A method commonly used in the retailing industry is to divide retail sales of all competitors by the selling space of the trading area:

$$\text{Saturation} = \frac{\text{Competing retail sales}}{\text{Competing retail space}}$$

The saturation index can be compared with other trading areas or industry norms. The higher the index, the more attractive is the opportunity. The statistics needed to compute a saturation index can be obtained from city and provincial or territorial licence and tax records, Statistics Canada reference books, or personal visits.

Costs.

Obviously a key consideration in selecting a trading area is the cost of land and buildings. Another is the cost of required services and expenses once the business is operating. These include such items as utilities, business taxes, and insurance.

The trading area decision can be quantified to allow evaluation among several alternatives.

The Site.

After selecting the trading area, the prospective owner should investigate the following items in selecting the specific site.

Accessibility.

For the manufacturer, this means accessibility of transportation services for incoming supplies and materials, as well as ease of shipping the finished product. It might also include the site's accessibility to necessary services, employees of the business, and protection services such as the fire department.

For the retailer, proximity to major arteries and transit lines and availability of parking is important to ensure maximum customer traffic. Assessing traffic patterns, both pedestrian and vehicular, may be critical to success, especially for retailers of certain types of merchandise (Chapter 7 further discusses the location considerations for retail goods). Often the chamber of commerce can provide information on traffic flows.

Site Costs.

The costs of sites within a community usually vary considerably. Generally, the higher-traffic areas are more expensive to buy or lease. One should also investigate other possible costs such as utilities, taxes, and licences.

Restrictions.

When evaluating a site, any restrictive ordinances such as zoning by-laws should be investigated. Such restrictions may hinder current operations as well as future expansion.

Site History.

The prospective owner should find out whether the site has had several tenants or owners over the years. If this is the case, investigate the reasons for the turnover before proceeding to purchase or lease the site.

Proximity to Other Businesses.

Will the surrounding businesses have a positive or negative influence on the business? Levels of competitiveness and complementarity are two significant factors. Figure 4-2 gives examples of the positive and negative effects of these factors for both non-competitive and competitive businesses.

Physical Characteristics.

Size, frontal footage, external facade, contour, and shape are all important considerations in site selection. The business should blend in with surrounding businesses, but it should also be distinctive.

The Buy-or-Lease Decision.

In selecting the specific site, a major consideration is whether to own or lease the premises. Because ownership is generally more expensive, most small businesses find that to reduce the

FIGURE 4-2	Influence of Neighbouring Businesses	
	POSITIVE INFLUENCE FROM NEIGHBOURING BUSINESSES	**NEGATIVE INFLUENCE FROM NEIGHBOURING BUSINESSES**
	Complementary—for example, a pharmacy by a doctor's office	Uncomplementary—businesses such as a mortuary, tavern, and factory
	Competitive—could be positive for shopping goods such as clothing, automobiles, and motels	Competitive—for non-shopping goods such as convenience stores

already high risk at the initial stages, leasing is the more attractive option. The small business owner should investigate several factors before signing a lease contract.

Cost of the Lease.

The owner-manager should investigate the cost of the lease, how the rent is calculated, when the payments are due, and what taxes and utilities apply. Most leases are calculated on a per-square-footage basis. In retailing, a percentage of gross sales is often added to the cost of the lease in the form of royalties.

Length of the Lease.

Questions concerning the length of the lease include these: For how long is the contract? Is there a provision for renewal at the end of that time? What notice is required for renewal, termination, or rent increase?

Restrictions.

Potential restrictions on the use of the property should be investigated. Can the site be sub-leased to someone else? Does anyone have the right to use a part of the property? Are there certain services or products that cannot be sold or manufactured at the site?

Repairs and Leasehold Improvements.

Who is responsible for any repairs and improvements required? When the lease expires, who will own such improvements?

Insurance Coverage.

What insurance does the lessor have on the property? What about liability insurance coverage? What insurance coverage will be required by the lessee?

Running the Business from One's Home.

The final important consideration in site selection is the possibility of operating the business out of one's home. A recent study found that home businesses were operated in 2.8 million Canadian households, a 33 percent increase from 1995 and that 44.6 percent of Canadians who work at home are self-employed.[19] In addition, a recent estimate pegs the percentage of self-employed Canadians who operate out of the home at 33 percent.[20] And estimates are that soon two out of every three households will be running either a part-time or full-time business.[21] Some of the best home-based businesses are business services and consulting, computer-related services, marketing and public relations, alternative medicine, independent sales, and online sales. A primary reason for the increase in home-based businesses is the use of computer technology. Such equipment allows the entrepreneur access to information and communication capabilities on par with larger businesses.[22]

Some situations are particularly suitable for a home-based business. First, if the business is started on a part-time basis, as many are, the costs associated with establishing a home office are minimal. Second, the lower costs associated with starting a business in one's home reduce the financial risks of a venture that may already carry a high degree of risk. Thus, a home office can serve as a temporary office until the business is more firmly established. Third, a home office is suitable for many businesses for which location is of minimal importance. Many service and some small manufacturing businesses fit in this category. Fourth, locating the business in the home offers several tax-related advantages. Chapter 12 gives more details on such advantages.

INCIDENT 4-3

ENTREPRENEUR RUNS BUSINESS FROM HOME

Karen Start was becoming frustrated trying to get her baby's squirmy arms into a jacket, and she began to wonder if there was a better way to deal with the problem. As a result, she came up with the idea of creating a line of ponchos for kids that would easily slip over the head and snap under the arms and neck. Although Ms. Stark, from Vancouver, had little experience in design or sewing, she developed a prototype of the product and sampled them with some friends. Reaction was very positive, so she invested her savings into the business, enlisted the services of some people to sew the products and started selling them at trade shows. Success was immediate, so Karen quit her job to devote herself full-time to the business. She works out of an office in her home as do those contracted to make the ponchos. Po Po's Ponchos (www.poposponchos.com/) are now sold in colourful designs, are named after ice cream flavours, and are made of high-quality micro fleece. One of the keys for her successful start-up has been keeping costs down by working out of her home, having no employees, and advertising through web coupons, mommy blogs, and local baby magazines.

Source: Adapted from Roma Luciw, "Po Po's Ponchos Owner Starts Slowly, Treads Carefully," *The Globe and Mail*, May 29, 2009, pp. 1–2.

DETERMINE THE PHYSICAL FACILITIES

In preparing the feasibility analysis outlined in Chapter 3, the entrepreneur should already have prepared a detailed estimate of the total capital needed to acquire the building, equipment, furniture, fixtures, and possibly initial inventory. The size of investment in buildings and equipment is typically larger for a manufacturing firm, while the investment in inventory tends to be larger for the retail firm.

Before constructing buildings and purchasing equipment, investigate the relevant building codes and construction standards and obtain required permits.

In addition to these capital requirements and standards, a plan should be made of the operation's flow within the business. This includes such factors as purchasing, inventory control, the production process, the interior layout, and distribution of the finished product. Chapter 10 discusses all these items in detail.

Insurance.

Small businesses face several risks. Figure 4-3 illustrates four ways that an entrepreneur can deal with risk. The entrepreneur should analyze the extent of such risks and determine whether they threaten the existence of the company. Generally, entrepreneurs transfer risk by buying insurance when the loss would be serious. Insurance coverage for such risks should be purchased before the start-up of the business.

FIGURE 4-3	Ways to Manage Risk

METHOD	TYPE OF RISK
Self-insurance	Cover losses out of cash flow (asset values small)
Prevention	Burglar alarms, inspections, education, hiring practices
Avoidance of risk	Leasing, incorporation
Transfer of risk	Purchasing insurance (asset values large)

Types of Insurance.

Common insurable risks for a small business include the following:

Loss or damage of property. This type of coverage protects the business in the case of fire, theft, and similar occurrences.

Business interruption. If one of the above problems occurs, this type of insurance protects the earning power lost due to the occurrence for a short period of time.

Liability and disability. This coverage includes bodily injury to employees or customers, and could include liability coverage for company officials such as members of the board of directors of the company.

Life insurance. This insurance is usually bought in the form of a group insurance plan or occasionally key employee life insurance. Partners of a business may also want to purchase life insurance for the other partner(s).

Insurance Decisions.

The entrepreneur faces three insurance-related decisions:

1. What kind of insurance to purchase
2. How much coverage to take out
3. From whom to purchase the insurance

In making these decisions, the following rules of thumb commonly used in the insurance industry are helpful. The first and most important rule is: Do not risk more than you can afford to lose. In other words, if the prospective loss will put the business into bankruptcy or serious financial difficulty, take out insurance. Usually the probability of these losses occurring is low, and the associated insurance premiums are also low. The maximum sustainable loss will, of course, vary across firms and times in a particular business.

A second rule of insurance management is: Do not risk a lot for a little. In implementing this second rule, the premium should be related to the potential loss and treated as savings or costs. For this reason, it is usually advisable to purchase the largest deductible the business can afford. This can result in substantial premium savings.

The third rule is that insurance should be taken out only when absolutely necessary. Insurance always costs more than the expected value of a loss because the premium must also include the insurer's administration and selling costs, plus profit. This insurance is economically feasible only when the probability of loss is low and the severity of a potential loss is high. Therefore, in the opposite situation, the best approach may be to take preventative measures and build these losses into the cost or expense structure of the business.

The fourth rule is to buy adequate coverage. The reason is that all property insurance contracts contain a co-insurance clause. The co-insurance clause states that if the amount of insurance purchased on the property is less than some stated percentage (usually 80 percent), the insured will share all partial losses up to the face value of the policy. The purpose of co-insurance is to encourage the small business owner to buy adequate insurance coverage for the business.

The last insurance purchasing rule involves adequately investigating both the insurance company and the agent. Choosing an insurance company with financial stability, satisfactory claims service, and competitive premiums is important, and the selection of the agent may be even more critical. The agent should have a thorough knowledge of insurance, be located where he or she can provide prompt service on claims and enquiries, and possess a genuine interest in clients' needs. Question the agent regarding the claim settlement procedures, cancellation procedures, and premium rates. Many insurance companies now have special policies tailored to small businesses.

Care should be taken to ensure that coverage is current. As replacement costs rise, the level of coverage should increase. Most insurance companies now automatically adjust policies for inflation.

PLAN THE FINANCING

Four major financial aspects of the new business should be planned in advance of opening.

Establish Capital Requirements and Make Feasibility Projections.

As indicated previously, these calculations are made when preparing a feasibility analysis. The results of these calculations form an integral part of the projected income statement for at least the first year of operations and in some cases five years into the future. Although making financial projections involves considerable uncertainty, using average industry financial benchmarks and ratios can increase the reliability of these estimates. These benchmarks and ratios are available through Statistics Canada, Industry Canada, Dun and Bradstreet, and some provincial or territorial government economic development departments. The website addresses for these are found in Appendix 3A on Connect, and further explanation of the use of these numbers is made in Chapter 9 dealing with financial management. In conjunction with the income statement projection, enough information would have likely been obtained to prepare a projected balance sheet and cash flow statement. Although these statements are described fully in Chapter 9, Figure 6-2 in Chapter 6 shows the format of a cash flow that would be required in a business plan. It may be advisable for the entrepreneur to enlist the services of an accountant in completing these financial statements. Proper preparation of this financial data is key to obtaining funding from investors and lenders.

Determine Sources of Funding.

The projections discussed above provide an estimate of the funds required to get started and to operate the business. After calculating the required funds, the owner will need to determine a balance between his or her own funds (equity) and borrowed funds (debt). Because raising funds is such a critical area for the small business, Chapter 6 is devoted entirely to the types of funds required, sources of funding for the small business, and methods of evaluating those sources. Sufficient start-up funding is of critical importance to a new small business.

Plan the Accounting and Bookkeeping Systems.

An essential part of any business is record keeping. Bookkeeping is the recording and classifying of the internal and external transactions of the business. This may be an area that requires professional advice. Chapter 9 reviews the types of financial records kept and the different types of bookkeeping systems used by small businesses.

Determine Financial Evaluation Measures.

One area crucial to the success of the small business is the financial evaluation of operations. To perform this evaluation, the owner should determine the key indicators of the financial health of the business. These indicators include profit margins, return on investment, and inventory turnover. The owner should also set up a system of regular monitoring and reporting of these areas. This system may also require professional assistance to establish and is discussed in detail in Chapter 9.

PLAN THE PERSONNEL

Chapter 11 discusses the operating details of personnel administration for a small business. The following are the major considerations in organizing for the management of personnel.

Administrative Structure.

This involves setting up the responsibility and reporting procedure for all employees of the business. If there are only two owners, the administrative structure takes the form of a clear division of responsibilities. A business with several employees might require an organizational chart.

Employee Recruitment and Training.

Determine the plan for hiring, training, and managing those who will work in the business.

Personnel Policies.

Explicitly state and formally prepare operating policies affecting employees before the business begins operations.

INVESTIGATE THE LEGAL REQUIREMENTS

A small business can be significantly affected by the legal environment in which it operates. Considerable legislation in Canada applies to the ongoing management of the business. Typical areas covered are advertising and promotion, credit, sales contracts, pricing, distribution channels, personnel, record keeping, and financial relationships. Legislation pertaining to each of these aspects of managing the ongoing business is covered in later chapters.

This section discusses the legal requirements relating to the establishment of the business that should be included in the business plan. Some of the most important aspects are selecting the legal structure, investigating which licences are required, and filing for patent protection if necessary. The legal information provided here and in later chapters is intended not to replace the advice and direction of a lawyer but merely to provide a background against which the entrepreneur can work with such professionals more knowledgeably. Care should be taken in the selection of a lawyer. References from business acquaintances or a lawyer referral service could ensure that you enlist the services of a lawyer who has small business experience and expertise.

Legal Structure.

The owner must decide under which legal structure the business will operate. Five types of legal structures can be used. Figure 4-7 (found later in this chapter) compares the most common legal structures for small and medium businesses.

1. Sole Proprietorship.

In a sole proprietorship, the business is owned by a single individual. The proprietor has perfect freedom of operation; when business decisions are made or when actions are taken, it is not necessary to get anyone else's consent. Similarly, all profits are the property of the owner and need not be shared with anyone else. There are, however, certain disadvantages to the one-owner organization. Limited personal assets, for example, do not encourage lenders and cannot always provide the capital needed to meet the needs of the business. But perhaps the biggest disadvantage is the proprietor's personal liability for business debts; in case of business failure, the owner's home, automobile, stocks, cash, and other personal assets may be seized by creditors to satisfy the debts of the business. Registration with the provincial or territorial government is

FIGURE 4-4   Advantages and Disadvantages of a Sole Proprietorship

ADVANTAGES	DISADVANTAGES
1. Simple and inexpensive to start	1. Unlimited liability
2. Offers individual control over operations, profits, and so on	2. Often more difficult to obtain financing
3. Fewer forms and reports to fill out	3. The personal tax rate may be higher than the corporate rate
4. Some tax advantages	4. The life of the business terminates on owner's death

normally required and can help protect the name of the business. Figure 4-4 lists the advantages and disadvantages of a sole proprietorship.

2. Partnership.

In most ways, partnerships are similar to sole proprietorships except that partnerships include two or more partners. Partnerships typically provide increased resources and complementary abilities. For example, Mississauga-based PolicePrep (www.policeprep.com), a provider of online training to help people with pre-employment exams for policing, firefighting, and public service, was founded by three partners—Adam Cooper, who had previous experience in the standardized testing industry; Kalpesh Rathod, who brought e-commerce and technology experience to the business; and Deland Jessop, who previously worked as a police officer. As evident in the example, the three partners brought complementary skills to the business. Cooper notes, "We went into business together because our skill sets were so complementary."[23] Partnerships can also allow people to share the heavy workload that is involved in running a company. Shane Graham, Karl Moussa, and brothers Aaron and David Hardy founded Golf Without Limits (www.golfwithoutlimits.com), a Waterloo, Ontario–based company that operates an interactive indoor golf centre. The partnerships works as they share a similar vision of franchising their concept, and they divide the workload with Graham running the centre, Moussa looking after client services, Dave managing the physical facilities, and Aaron overseeing marketing and finance. One major drawback of partnerships is the increased possibility of conflict. A recent study found that less than 20 percent of partnerships last past the five-year mark. It is therefore essential to have a conflict resolution strategy worked into a partnership agreement and perhaps a buyout clause where one partner can purchase the business from the other. Figure 4-5

FIGURE 4-5   Advantages and Disadvantages of a Partnership

ADVANTAGES	DISADVANTAGES
1. Simple and inexpensive to start	1. Unlimited liability
2. Pooling of financial and skill resources	2. Death of a partner terminates the partnership unless a provision to the contrary is specified in the partnership agreement
3. Tax advantages (i.e., income splitting)	3. Greater possibility for disagreements (buy-sell agreements should be drawn up in the event that a partner wants to leave the business)

QUICKSNAP: THE EVER CHANGING OWNERSHIP STRUCTURE

When David Reynolds of Halifax, Nova Scotia, started university he had no idea what he wanted to do with his life. Reynolds says, "I went to university with no real plan or ambition to do anything. I went to university because it's what all my friends were doing." A short time after enrolling at Mount Saint Vincent University, Reynolds attended a lecture on entrepreneurship, and as part of a class assignment, he had to create and run a small business for a day. Reynolds immediately fell in love with the concept of entrepreneurship and being his own boss. He notes, "I loved the thoughts of being my own boss. I was always inventing little things, but it never really occurred to me that I could create a company from one of my ideas. That class lecture and the small assignment showed me I could."

Reynolds now knew he wanted to be an entrepreneur but did not have a business idea. A short time later, while waiting impatiently for his friend to tie his shoes, Reynolds had a light bulb moment. Reynolds states, "People hate tying their shoes. What if they didn't have to do this? What if there was a way to clip the laces together?" A short time later Quicksnap (www.Quicksnap.ca), a shoe-fastening device, was born. When the company first started, it was structured as a sole proprietorship; as Reynolds quips, "It was just me and my idea." Reynolds says the advantage of being a sole proprietor allowed him to work when he wanted to work, and since he was a full-time student, this was important to him. Reynolds soon realized that starting a company, especially a manufacturing business, was a lot of work, and he brought in his friend and his brother as partners. The partners brought in some additional capital and, more importantly, some extra help in getting the business off the ground. Together they shared the work and combined their strengths. Reynolds says that forming a partnership was cheaper and easier than forming a corporation. "We drafted a partnership agreement, we all signed it, and we became partners." Together the three managed to bring the product to market, albeit in a small way, in local sporting goods stores.

Reynolds felt that the business needed some additional marketing dollars and soon started pursuing outside investors. He pitched his business idea to a variety of banks and traditional lenders and managed to sell his concept to a fellow student, Riad Byne, who was attending Mount Saint Vincent University after completing military duty in Afghanistan. Reynolds notes, "At this time, I knew that we needed a formal structure, and the business went through the process of incorporating. We needed the advantages of a private corporation, we needed to be able to issue shares to investors, ensure that everyone involved in the ownership group had limited liability and so forth."

The business partners eventually brought their idea to the mainstream media pitching the product on CBC's *Dragons' Den*, where they successfully brokered a deal for $125,000 investment in return for 50 percent ownership in the company. While Reynolds is no longer the CEO, something he attributes to giving up too much ownership control too early to outside investors, he does say he has done well on his investment in the business and is pleased to report that Quicksnap landed several large deals after *Dragons' Den*, including Walmart and Sport Chek.

Discussion Questions

1. Based on the information in the case, what are some of the advantages and disadvantages of the three major forms of business (sole proprietorship, partnership, and corporation)?

2. What do you think are some of the potential markets for Quicksnap? How would you promote the product?

3. Were you surprised to learn the entrepreneurs agreed to give up 50 percent ownership of their business for $125,000? Why, or why not?

4. Would you have sold off shares in your business like Reynolds, who was trying to grow his business quickly, or would you prefer the slow growth method where you maintain 100 percent ownership of your company? Why?

summarizes the advantages and disadvantages of partnerships. There are two kinds of partnerships a small business might use:

1. *Limited partnership.* In a limited partnership, one or more partners obtain limited liability in exchange for not taking an active part in the day-to-day management of the business or acting on behalf of the company. These partners, often called *silent partners*, usually provide only the financial investment as their part of the ownership interest. Small businesses are increasingly using this form of ownership because silent partners constitute an important source of equity funding. In addition, limited partnerships

POSITIVE PARTNERSHIP

In the realm of small business, partnerships often go awry. However Jason Cunningham and Derek Brock have found that their partnership in establishing Jugo Juice (www.jugojuice.com), a successful Calgary-based juice-bar chain, has made life easier for both of them. Cunningham and Brock had both been managers for the Starbucks franchise when they decided to leave the company to start Jugo Juice as a franchise in 1999. Brock indicates that each of their personalities and skill sets complement one another. "Jason is the more serious one and I'm more friendly." They also say that having a partner to take over when you're not having any luck can be a distinct advantage. When the dynamics behind one personality fail, the other can step in. They have found that the partnership can more effectively manage staff and create and maintain business relationships. They have also found that the partnership provides increased flexibility to get away from the business knowing there is someone to take over. "It definitely helps to get some feedback instead of making a solo decision," says Mr. Cunningham. These partners seem to work well together and share the same values and vision for the company. This relationship has led to a successful business with over 100 franchises in operation today.

Source: Derek Sankey, "Good Partnership Juices Up Profits," *Financial Post*, August 25, 2009, pp. 1–2.

offer some tax advantages for the silent partner while retaining the positive aspects of sole proprietorship for the entrepreneur.

2. *General partnership.* When the partners share in the management or control of the business, it is referred to in legal terms as a *general partnership.* The most obvious advantage to this form of organization over the proprietorship form is that added capital is made available by combining the assets of the partners, and money is usually easier to borrow because the partners share debts. Similarly, the personal abilities of the partners are complemented, and they may succeed together when neither could alone. However, each partner by law is equally responsible for all the debts of the partnership, regardless of the amount of capital contributed and regardless of any agreement among them to the contrary. Also, any one partner can bind the entire partnership in a business arrangement, even if it is contrary to the wishes or judgment of the majority. The general partnership has other disadvantages as well, such as the termination of the business by the death or withdrawal of any one of the partners and the inability of a partner to sell or assign his or her interest in the partnership without the consent of all the other partners. However, both of these conditions or eventualities can be circumvented by appropriate provisions in a written partnership agreement, which should be prepared with the consultation of a lawyer. Although not legally required to form a general partnership, such an agreement is nonetheless advisable, even among relatives and close friends. At a minimum, it should specify the following:

1. Duration of the partnership
2. Administrative responsibilities and authority of each partner
3. Withdrawals and salaries of the partners
4. Provision for the arbitration of policy disputes among the partners
5. Provisions for the withdrawal of partners or the admission of additional partners
6. Amount of capital invested by each partner
7. Division of profit or loss. (Regardless of the amount of capital invested, general partners must share profit or loss equally unless there is an agreement among the partners to the contrary.)

SHOULD PARTNERS HAVE A SHOTGUN?

"Should partners have a shotgun?" Perhaps the question makes you think of the Old West or organized crime movies, but the term "shotgun" has a very different meaning in partnership agreements.

Essentially, the term is used to describe a clause where one business partner can make a cash offer for the other partner's share of the business. The person being offered the money for their share of the business is usually left with only two choices: (1) Accept the offer and take the money; or (2) match the partner's offer and assume the partner's share of the business. People's opinions of shotgun clauses in partnerships differ. Some argue that they are useful tools, which allow for a quick end to a partnership that is no longer working. Furthermore, the cash offer is usually at a premium as the person making the offer risks getting removed from the business if he or she makes a low offer. Others argue that shotgun clauses are often used too quickly when other dispute resolutions could be used to save partnerships, that shotguns favour the partner with the

most resources, and that executing a shotgun clause normally ends any personal relationships among partners. For example, when partners Michel Boucher and Chuck Buchanan had a falling out over future plans for their London, Ontario–based company Flightexec (www.flightexec.com), Boucher exercised the partner's shotgun clause. The 10-year partnership that saw the pair take Flightexec out of receivership to a company with over $20 million in sales quickly ended. Buchanan admits that the use of the shotgun clause left him unsettled.

Discussion Questions

1. If you were to ever join a partnership, would you want to have a shotgun clause?

2. What are some of the advantages and disadvantages of a shotgun clause?

3. What alternatives would you suggest to using a shotgun clause?

8. Distribution of assets in the event of dissolution. (As in the case of profits or losses, this distribution must be on an equal basis unless otherwise agreed on in writing.)

9. Settlements in the event of death or disability of a partner. This might include a buy-sell agreement funded with business life insurance in amounts equal to the interest of each partner; thus the surviving partner(s) would be assured of full title to the business, and the deceased partner's estate would be assured of receiving the full value of his or her share of the business. In the absence of such an agreement, the business might well be forced into liquidation to satisfy the demands of the deceased partner's estate.

In a general partnership, unlimited liability applies to all partners.

3. Corporation.

The corporation, or limited company, is becoming an increasingly popular form of structuring a small business. Industry Canada reports that more than 40 percent of all self-employed businesses with paid help and 24 percent of small business without paid help in Canada were incorporated in 2008.[24] Moreover, Statistics Canada reports that incorporated companies grew at an annual rate of 3.9 percent compared with 1 percent for unincorporated businesses.[25] The corporation is a legal entity that is separate and distinct from the shareholders of the business. The chief advantages of the corporation are (1) continuity in existence, (2) easy transferability of ownership interest, and (3) limited liability of shareholders. The corporation is long-lived, being able to continue in existence up to the time limit granted in its charter, which may even be granted in perpetuity. In contrast, other forms of organization may cease abruptly with the death of the proprietor or a partner. Ownership in a corporation is easily transferred merely by the sale or exchange of stock; permission of other shareholders is not required. Care should be taken in drafting a shareholder agreement to facilitate the smooth transition of the ownership of the company in the event that a key owner leaves the business. Legal liability of owners or shareholders for suits for personal injury or other activities connected with operating the business is limited to the amount of funds invested in the business. The corporate form of business organization is also more attractive for raising equity capital because capital can be more readily obtained from many more sources and because of the legal limited liability of corporate shareholders. A corporation has certain disadvantages, however. Its activities are limited to those specifically granted in its charter. Similarly, its geographic area of operations is limited to the province or territory granting its charter until permission is secured from each of the other provinces or territories in which it desires to operate; this means that additional filing fees must be paid and additional legal requirements observed. The corporation must make numerous reports for taxation and other purposes in each jurisdiction in which it does business; not only has federal and provincial or territorial regulation of corporations been increasing for some time, but the paperwork required also increases greatly as the corporation grows in size.

The day-to-day operations of a corporation are handled by a manager who is appointed by and reports to a board of directors. The board of directors is elected by the shareholders. Often in very small businesses, the manager, director, and major shareholder are the same person. Many small businesses have found it valuable to enlist the services of lawyers, accountants, and other non-competing businesspeople to serve on their boards of directors.

The vast majority of incorporated small businesses are private companies. For a business to qualify as a private company, the following conditions must exist:

- The right to transfer shares is restricted, usually requiring the approval of the board of directors.
- The number of shareholders is limited to 50. The company cannot sell new shares publicly.

Figure 4-6 summarizes the advantages and disadvantages of a corporation.

FIGURE 4-6	Advantages and Disadvantages of a Corporation

ADVANTAGES	DISADVANTAGES
1. The continuity of the business exists even if the owner dies.	1. The cost to incorporate generally ranges from $800 to $1,200.
2. The owners have limited liability.	2. There is a greater reporting requirement by government.
3. The business may have a manager with professional training or expertise.	3. Flexibility may be reduced because of the binding provisions of the corporate charter.
4. It is easier to raise funds, as lenders and equity investors usually look more favourable on incorporated companies.	4. Losses cannot be deducted from other personal income of the owner.
5. The corporate tax rate on small businesses (see Appendix 12B on Connect) can be lower than one's personal rate.	5. Lenders often require a personal guarantee, negating the advantage of limited liability.
6. Incorporation can assist in establishing commercial credibility.	
7. Liability insurance may be less expensive.	

Steps in Incorporation.

Most entrepreneurs regard incorporation as a very complex process that requires a lawyer's assistance. Although it is advisable for a small business to enlist the services of a lawyer to assist in incorporating the business, some entrepreneurs with relatively uncomplicated businesses have incorporated their businesses successfully on their own. Recently, incorporation software has been developed to assist entrepreneurs with self-incorporation. Incorporating a business involves four steps:

1. *Selection of a name for the business.* This name must be submitted to and approved by the provincial or territorial government department that handles incorporations (see Appendix 4C on Connect). The selection can be facilitated by doing a computer search to ensure that no similar names are currently being used.

2. *Development of the share structure, directors, restrictions on share transfers, and so on.* The owner must determine the number of shares to authorize, the number of shares to issue, the number of directors, the timing of meetings, and approvals required for shares to be bought or sold.

3. *A description of company operations.* This section describes what the business can and cannot do.

4. *Acquisition of the necessary supplies.* This includes such items as the corporate stamp, the minute book, and the necessary journals and ledgers.

Figure 4-7 offers a comparison of the most common legal structures of small and medium businesses.

4. Cooperative.

The cooperative is used infrequently by small businesses although with the growing trend in social entrepreneurship, which was discussed in previous chapters, this may start to change. One example of a small and growing cooperative is Just Us! Coffee Roasters Co-op (www.justuscoffee.com), located in Nova Scotia. The company was started by several friends who wanted to make a difference in how coffee was sold and purchased and help farmers in developing countries. The owners say, "We called ourselves Just Us! because we were just a small group of friends who had very little in the way of business experience or resources, but really believed we could do our bit for social 'justice.'" The co-op's roasted coffee recently won the

JUST US! COFFEE ROASTERS CO-OP HAS ENJOYED SIGNIFICANT GROWTH WHILE OPERATING AS A COOPERATIVE IN NOVA SCOTIA. VISIT THEIR WEBSITE TO READ ABOUT THEIR BEGINNING AND RECENT SUCCESS.
Photo and logo courtesy of Just Us! Coffee Roasters

FIGURE 4-7

FIGURE 4-7   Factors of Three Forms of Business Formation

FACTORS	PROPRIETORSHIP	PARTNERSHIP	CORPORATION
Ownership	Individual.	No limitation on number of partners. There must be at least one general partner.	No limitation on number of shareholders.
Liability of owners	Individual liable for business liabilities.	In general partnership, individuals all liable for business liabilities. In limited partnership, partners are liable for amount of capital contribution.	Amount of capital contribution is limit of shareholder liability. In closely held corporations, owners may have to become personally liable for some debts.
Costs of starting business	None other than filing fees for trade name.	Partnership agreement, legal costs, and minor filing fees for trade name. Limited partnership requires more comprehensive agreement, hence higher cost.	Created only by statute. Articles of incorporation, filing fees, taxes, and fees for provinces in which corporation registers to do business.
Continuity of business	Death dissolves the business.	Death or withdrawal of one partner terminates partnership unless partnership agreement stipulates otherwise. In limited partnership, death or withdrawal of one of limited partners has no effect on continuity.	Greatest form of continuity. Death or withdrawal of owner(s) will not affect legal existence of business.
Transferability of interest	Complete freedom to sell or transfer any part of business.	General partner can transfer his/her interest only with consent of all other general partners. The terms for transferring interest in limited partnerships are outlined in the partnership agreement.	Public corporations allow for flexible transfer on open exchanges. Closely held corporations usually stipulate rules that govern the transfer of shares.
Capital requirements	Capital raised only by loan or increased contribution by proprietor.	Loans or new contributions by partners require a change in partnership agreement.	Public corporations may raise capital by selling stock or bonds or borrowing debt. Closely held corporations may sell shares or acquire debt, but the shareholders often have to personally guarantee debt.
Management control	Proprietor makes all decisions and can act immediately.	All partners have equal control and majority rules. In limited partnership, only the general partners have management control of the business.	Majority shareholders have most control from legal point of view. Day-to-day control in hands of management who may or may not be major shareholders.
Distribution of profits and losses	Proprietor responsible and receives all profits and losses.	Depends on partnership agreement and investment by partners.	Shareholders can share in profits by receipt of dividends. Will often depend on shareholders' agreement.
Attractiveness for raising capital	Depends on capability of proprietor and success of business.	Depends on capability of partners and success of business.	With limited liability for owners, more attractive as an investment opportunity.

award for the best Fair Trade product in Canada, and the co-op has enjoyed significant growth while staying true to its mission, "People and the Planet before Profits."[26] In most respects, the strengths and weaknesses of a cooperative are similar to those of a corporation (see Figure 4-6). The distinguishing feature is that in a cooperative (which needs a minimum of six members) each member has only one vote, whereas in a corporation each voting share has a vote.

5. Joint Ventures.

A joint venture is an agreement between one or more sole proprietors, partnerships, or corporations to participate in a business venture. Although similar to a partnership in many ways, this form of business allows for individual ownership of assets in the venture. Items such as capital cost allowance can be used by either party, depending on the need. Other advantages and disadvantages are similar to those in a partnership (see Figure 4-5).

Licences and Taxes.

Before starting a business, the prospective owner should investigate the required licences and the taxes that may be payable to the government. Licences and taxes can be levied by federal, provincial or territorial, and municipal governments, and these requirements differ among various industries. The following are the most common licences and taxes that apply to the small business. For a more detailed listing, see Appendix 4D on Connect.

Federal Government.

1. *Income tax.* The income tax is a tax on both companies and individuals earning income from a business operating in Canada. The rates vary by province or territory and by industry (see Chapter 12). Although the income tax payments are made to the federal government, part of this amount is transferred to the province or territory in which the business earns income. Some provinces and territories now collect their own business income tax.

2. *Goods and services tax.* The goods and services tax (GST) is a value-added tax levied on many sellers of goods and services by the federal government. The tax, which currently is 5 percent of the sale price, is collected from the purchaser by the seller and remitted to the government quarterly. Although the GST has met with considerable resistance from business and consumers, it has been an effective method for increasing government revenues. Certain exemptions from the GST, relating to the size of the business and type of merchandise sold, are available. Small business owners should consult Canada Revenue Agency (CRA) for the information about how the GST applies to their business and for information about obtaining a GST remittance number.

3. *Excise tax.* The excise tax is an extra tax imposed on certain goods sold in Canada. Payment is made by the manufacturer and is a hidden component in the cost of purchasing those goods.

Provincial or Territorial Government.

1. *Income tax.* A percentage of federal income tax payable is assessed by the provinces and territories. Some (Ontario, Quebec, and Alberta) collect this tax. In other provinces and territories, the federal government collects the tax and remits a portion to the province or territory.

2. *Licences.* Many types of businesses require a provincial or territorial licence to operate. Some of these businesses may also require bonding.

3. *Sales tax.* Most provinces and territories levy retail sales taxes on tangible property sold or imported. This tax is collected by the retailer from the purchaser at the time of the sale and remitted to the government in much the same manner as the goods and services tax. Many businesses have found the administration of the sales tax more difficult since the introduction of the GST.

Municipal Government.

1. *Licences.* Municipalities (cities) are authorized to license all businesses operating within their boundaries.
2. *Property taxes.* Municipalities are also authorized to levy property taxes on the real estate on which a business operates.
3. *Business taxes.* Other taxes levied on businesses by a municipality might be for water use or other services.

Intellectual Property Protection.

As many entrepreneurs create new products or processes, a critical measure for ensuring their success is to secure legal protection. This protection could be required for a patent, trademark, industrial design, or copyright. Copyrights are for literary, artistic, musical, and dramatic works. Industrial designs include shapes, patterns, or ornamentation of an industrially produced object. Trademarks are words, symbols, or slogans that represent origins of goods and services. A patent, the most commonly obtained protection for a small business, is a right granted by the government to an inventor to exclude others from making, using, or selling his or her invention in Canada for 17 years.

It is important for the inventor to record the date of the invention and file for the patent as soon as possible. Registration of a patent may be made through a Consumer and Corporate Affairs office or the Commissioner of Patents, Ottawa-Hull, Canada, K1A OE1. Other helpful information about intellectual property protection may be obtained through the Strategies website listed on Connect. In Canada, if the patent has been used publicly or sold within the previous two years, it may not be granted. A patent agent or lawyer can provide valuable assistance in the patenting process and may be essential if infringement on the patent occurs later. Careful screening to ensure that the invention is new, useful, and a result of inventive ingenuity is used in the patent approval.

Two steps are required to register a patent:

1. Conduct a search at the patent office to ensure that the idea is not already registered.
2. File an application, the formal request for the patent, which includes a description of the idea.

A patent application may take from one to three years to receive an approval. Nearly 29,000 patent applications are received each year in Canada, and approximately 24,000 are approved. A listing of patents is available for public perusal at most public libraries. Similar procedures for obtaining patents are followed in registering trademarks, industrial designs, and copyrights. Applications for these items are also obtained through Consumer and Corporate Affairs or the Commissioner of Patents.

ASSESS THE RISK

Every new venture will be faced with some potential hazards, given the particular industry and competitive environment. It is important that the entrepreneur make an *assessment of risk* in the following manner. First, the entrepreneur should indicate the potential risks to the new venture. Next should be a discussion of what might happen if these risks become reality. Finally, the entrepreneur should discuss the strategy that will be employed to either prevent, minimize, or respond to the risks should they occur. Major risks for a new venture could result from a competitor's reaction; weaknesses in the marketing, production, or management team; changes in government policies; and new advances in technology that might render the new product obsolete.

One way to identify risk in an industry or marketplace is to use Michael Porter's forces model. The model assesses risk and the nature of competition in a number of important categories. These categories include the following:

- *Rivalry among competitors:* This deals with the strength and intensity of rivalry between competitors. Are competitors pursuing a price penetration strategy or a profit maximization strategy? How do the competitors react to new competition? For example, one entrepreneur decided to start manufacturing Styrofoam plates and cups for the Quebec and Atlantic Canada markets. He thought that since there were only two competitors in the industry who also manufactured a number of other products, they would not deal aggressively with a new entrant who could only take a small portion of their market share. Unfortunately, he did not pay enough attention to past history; previously another entrepreneur tried a similar strategy only to see the competitors drop their prices dramatically to force the new entrant out of business. Shortly after introducing his products to the market, both competitors started selling their plates and cups below cost and forced him out of business.

- *Threat of new entrants:* How easy is it to enter the marketplace? What financial and knowledge barriers exist? If your business starts to thrive, how quickly can someone else jump in and compete in the same niche?

- *Supplier power:* How dependent would you be on suppliers? How far are suppliers from your operation? What would you do if you were to lose important suppliers or if a supplier started competing against you?

- *Buyer power:* How dependent are you on your buyers? For example, if you start a book publishing company, you will be very dependent on Indigo. How many buyers are there? What position are they in to negotiate discounts? How far away from your buyers are you?

- *Threat of substitutions:* Are there readily available substitute products in the marketplace? What is the pricing strategy for the substitutes? Is there a chance of consumers demanding a substitute product?

USING AND IMPLEMENTING THE BUSINESS PLAN

The business plan is designed to guide the entrepreneur through the first year of operations. It is important that the implementation of the strategy contain control points to ascertain progress and to initiate contingency plans if necessary. Some of the controls necessary in manufacturing, marketing, financing, and the organization are discussed in subsequent chapters. Most important to the entrepreneur is that the business plan not end up in a drawer somewhere once the financing has been attained and the business launched.

MEASURING PLAN PROGRESS

During the introductory phases of the start-up, the entrepreneur should determine the points at which decisions should be made as to whether the goals or objectives are on schedule. Typically, the business plan projections will be made on a 12-month schedule. However, many successful entrepreneurs know they cannot wait 12 months to see whether the plan has been successfully achieved. Instead, on a frequent basis (i.e., the beginning of each month), the entrepreneur should check the profit and loss statement, cash flow projections, and information on inventory, production, quality, sales, collection of accounts receivable, and disbursements for the previous month. This feedback should be simple but should provide the business owner with current information in time to correct any major deviations from the goals and objectives outlined. Roger Pierce, co-founder of Toronto-based BizLaunch, a company that trains entrepreneurs in business start-ups notes, 'Measures, especially ones that relate to your customers are crucial. The more detailed information that you have about your business, particularly your customers may determine if you succeed or fail."[27] Knowledge is, as they say, power. A brief description of each of these control elements is given below:

- *Inventory control.* By controlling inventory, the firm can ensure maximum service to the customer. The faster the firm gets back its investment in raw materials and finished goods, the faster that capital can be reinvested to meet additional customer needs.

- *Production control.* Compare the cost figures estimated in the business plan with day-to-day operation costs. This will help to control machine time, worker hours, process time, delay time, and downtime cost.

- *Quality control.* This will depend on the type of production system but is designed to make sure that the product performs satisfactorily.

- *Sales control.* Information on units, dollars, specific products sold, price of sales, meeting of delivery dates, and credit terms is useful to get a good perspective of the sales of the new venture. In addition, an effective collection system for accounts receivable should be set up to avoid aging of accounts and bad debts.

- *Disbursements.* The new venture should also control the amount of money paid out. All bills should be reviewed to determine how much is being disbursed and for what purpose.

UPDATING THE PLAN

The most effective business plan is outdated on the day it is finished. The very next day brings changes in the market, economy, and customer base. Successful entrepreneurs know that they

TIME TO TAKE ACTION

If you have completed a thorough opportunity assessment, then you have narrowed down your idea and have thought about who your customers may be. Start to examine these potential customers—speak to them, and if possible, visit where they shop. Some entrepreneurs find it useful to interview potential customers. (This is recommended in Chapter 7 on marketing.)

Get to know your people in the industry that you are considering entering, including your competition, suppliers, distributors, and so forth. Start to speak to as many people as possible. Examine any opportunities for partnerships or alliances.

Review your competitive advantage. Does it still make sense in light of any new facts? Discuss your competitive advantage with your mentors. Expand your mentors to include potential suppliers of money.

Start to write your business plan! If you have completed your opportunity analysis section, then you should have already conducted some research on your industry, customers, and competitive analysis. If you have not completed it, then this may serve as a good starting point.

cannot update their plans every day, but they should continuously monitor their plans, making small adjustments and notes as needed. At the very minimum, plans should receive significant updates twice a year, with many entrepreneurs doing so on a quarterly basis. Of particular importance is the need to update the marketing plan as the year unfolds. Many key goals and strategies are encompassed in this section of the business plan, and they need to be reviewed and controlled throughout the year.

LEARNING OBJECTIVES SUMMARY

LO1 Organizing one's own business has several advantages and disadvantages. The advantages of having a hand in determining the type of business, equipment, employees, inventory, and market are balanced against the disadvantages of uncertainty concerning demand, unforeseen problems, and the time required to establish the business.

LO2 A business plan provides a sense of direction for the business, determines the viability, assists in obtaining financing, and helps the owner to evaluate progress.

LO3 The basic steps in preparing a business plan are preparing a table of contents and providing a synopsis of the plan in an executive summary and background statement (best done when the plan is complete), setting the overall mission of the business, establishing business objectives, planning the marketing approach, selecting the location, determining the physical facilities, planning the financing, planning the personnel, investigating the legal requirements, and assessing the risk.

DISCUSSION QUESTIONS

1. Given the difficulties in accurately predicting the future, is a business plan useful?
2. What makes an excellent business plan?
3. Would the entrepreneur be better off spending more time selling his or her product rather than investing so much time in writing a business plan?
4. If a business plan is to be used to raise capital, then why would the entrepreneur want to advertise the firm's major risks by detailing them in the business plan?
5. What is the purpose of the business plan if the audience is (a) the entrepreneur, (b) an investor, and

(c) a key supplier? How might the plan be adapted for these different audiences? Or do you believe that it is better to simply have one business plan that serves all audiences?
6. What do you think are some of the advantages of buying a business or a franchise compared with starting a business from scratch?
7. You are thinking of opening up a small business consulting company. What uncontrollable factors might affect your decision? Explain.

APPLICATION QUESTIONS AND HANDS-ON ACTIVITIES

1. Using Internet resources find a business that is for sale. Compare the costs of buying the business to starting the business from scratch. What do you think is a better choice? Why?

2. The saturation index is useful to a prospective small business owner in selecting a trading area.
   a. Using the information in the following table, which trading area would you recommend to the prospective owner?

LOCATION	1	2	3
Number of customers for the store	100,000	50,000	25,000
Average purchase per customer	$5	$7	$9
Total square footage of the drugstore (including the proposed store)	20,000	15,000	10,000

b. If you excluded the proposed store (3000 square feet), which area would you select?

c. Which index of saturation is more accurate—the calculation with the proposed store square footage or the calculation without it? Why?

3. Which variables are important in site location for a pharmacy?

4. Interview a small business owner about the details of his or her start-up plan. Find out what aspects were omitted from the plan that should have been included.

5. Choose a specific type of small business, and obtain advice from an insurance agent on the types of insurance needed and the precise costs. Write a short report on your findings.

6. Visit the Canadian Intellectual Property Office (CIPO) website, and find out the requirements for registering a patent.

7. Contact local chartered bankers and entrepreneurs about coming to class to listen to the various business ideas that students have. Students should prepare two ideas each and pitch the concept in less than one minute to the visitors. Each visitor should then be given 3 to 5 minutes to provide feedback. If the class is large, this can be done in small groups on an informal basis. Assign one entrepreneur and one commercial banker to a group of five to eight students, and have them complete the activity within the group.

8. Have student(s) write and present a written business plan.

9. Have student(s) write and prepare a small written business plan for a charitable event that they can run for a period of five to 15 days. Have the students run the event and assess the following:
   - Did planning help?
   - Did you follow the business plan? Why, or why not?
   - Was the event a success?
   - Did you meet the goals described in the business plan?

CHECKLIST FOR A SMALL BUSINESS PLAN

INTRODUCTION

1. Have a table of contents, executive summary, and description of the management team been prepared?

BUSINESS OBJECTIVES

1. Have specific business objectives been set? At the end of one or five years, what will the size of the business be in gross sales? in production level? in number of employees? in market share? in profit?

MARKET APPROACH

1. Who is the target market in terms of occupation? income level? education? lifestyle?
2. What is the target market's purchasing behaviour for this product or similar products? Where are purchases made? When are purchases made? What quantities are purchased?
3. Why does the target market purchase this product or similar products? Which characteristics are preferred? What other factors influence the purchase?
4. What external constraints will affect the business? existing or pending legislation? state of the economy? competition? social or cultural trends? new technology?
5. Which product characteristics will be developed? quality level? amount of depth? type of packaging? patent protection? extent of warranty protection? level of service?
6. How will the product get to the consumer? What channel of distribution will be used? length of the channel? intensity of channel distributors? legal arrangement within the channel? type of physical transportation?

7. How will the product be promoted? What are the promotional objectives? Which media will be used? How much will be spent on production? Who is the target of the promotion? What is the promotional theme? What is the timetable for the promotion?

8. What price levels will be set for the product? Which pricing policies will be instituted? What factors will influence pricing? How important is price to the target market?

LOCATION

1. Has the location been selected?

2. In what trading area or community will the business be established? What is its economic base? its attitude toward new businesses? its saturation level in terms of competing businesses? its costs?

3. What specific site will be selected? Is it accessible to suppliers, employees, and the target market? What is the site cost? What restrictions on site use exist? What is the history of the site? What are the neighbouring businesses? What are the physical characteristics of the site?

PHYSICAL FACILITIES

1. Have the physical facilities been determined?

2. What building, equipment, and start-up supplies will be needed? What are the costs? What are the depreciation rates of the fixed assets? Which building codes or standards are relevant? Which permits are required? What insurance is required?

3. How will the physical facilities be organized? Is the production process efficient and safe? Has the interior layout been carefully planned? Is the exterior facade attractive?

4. How will inventories be managed? What initial inventory is required? How will inventory levels be monitored? How will inventory be valued? What method will be used to order inventory?

FINANCIAL

1. Has a financial plan for the business been made?

2. What are the financial requirements of the business? What are the start-up costs? ongoing operating costs? What are projected sales, expenses, income, and cash flow?

3. Which sources of funding will be used? how much equity? how much debt? Which sources will be used? private? commercial? government?

4. What bookkeeping system will be instituted?

5. How will the financial information be used? Which accounts will be evaluated? how often? by whom?

PERSONNEL

1. Has a personnel plan been developed?

2. What is the administrative structure? Is there an organizational chart? a responsibility and reporting procedure? Have job descriptions and specifications been developed?

3. Have personnel policies been developed? What are the hours of work? pay levels? employee benefits? conditions and standards of employment? grievance procedures?

4. How will the business recruit employees? Where will employees be found? How will they be screened? What guidelines will be used in selection? How will employees be trained?

LEGAL REQUIREMENTS

1. Have legal requirements been investigated?

2. Has the legal structure for the business been determined?

3. Have the relevant licences and taxes been researched?

4. Has patent protection been obtained, if necessary?

APPENDIX 4B

SAMPLE BUSINESS PLANS

BUSINESS PLAN 1—RETAIL STOCKING STORE, THE SOCK HOP

TABLE OF CONTENTS

Executive Summary and Background
Description of the Management Team
Business Objectives
Market Approach
Location
Physical Facilities
Financial
Personnel
Legal Requirements

EXECUTIVE SUMMARY AND BACKGROUND

The Sock Hop is a store totally devoted to socks. The product is in the medium price range, and emphasis is on variety and quality. The Sock Hop will be located in the new Park Place Mall, Lethbridge, Alberta, which is close to the downtown core. The mall, which opened in August 1988, has a variety of products and services. It contains beauty salons, shoe repair shops, movie theatres, one anchor store (Sears), jewellery stores, men's apparel, ladies apparel, children's stores, toy stores, a food fair, as well as many other specialty stores.

The majority of the customers of The Sock Hop will be between the ages of 15 and 64, both male and female. The 2009 city census estimates that there are 48,436 people between the ages of 15 and 64.[1]

---

[1] City of Lethbridge Census, estimate 2009.

The feasibility analysis shows that The Sock Hop could be a viable business within five years as it becomes well known and builds a clientele.

DESCRIPTION OF THE MANAGEMENT TEAM

The owner-manager of The Sock Hop is Sharon Stockwell. She holds a management degree from the University of Lethbridge and has eight years of full- and part-time experience working in the retail clothing industry. She has prepared this business plan to assist in the start-up of this venture.

BUSINESS OBJECTIVES

The Sock Hop's business plan consists of a number of objectives. The first objective relates to opportunity costs for the owner-manager. The owner would like to obtain returns that would exceed that of a salary obtained through alternative employment and the cost of capital on her equity investment in the business. Therefore,

> Salary at The Sock Hop ($24,000) + Additional profits > Salary if working for someone else + Cost of capital on equity

It should be noted that the cost of capital on equity investment is included because had the person placed her life savings in a savings account, it would have been earning a stated interest amount. Thus, for the owner-manager to remain in the business, the total tangible benefits derived from the business must be greater than they would have been without the business. This objective should be met in approximately five years.

The second objective is based on performance. Market share should increase from the present adjusted 22 percent to 33 percent within five years (medium-term goal). It is hoped that as the business grows, it will have a loyal following of customers along with a good business reputation to overcome some of the weaknesses.

As a result, the sales and profits should also increase. The sales per square foot should increase from the present estimate of $278/sq. ft. As a way to increase overall profit, a minor objective is to increase the efficiency in selling the merchandise.

A third objective is a five-year long-term goal for future expansion. By the year 2015, the owner hopes to be able to work out a system to franchise The Sock Hop in Western Canada. By then, the bugs should be worked out of the system and a franchising plan can be established. This is dependent on the Lethbridge prototype store being successful.

A fourth (short-term) objective involves the method of financing the business. The owner-manager of The Sock Hop will not be the sole contributor of equity capital to the business. However, she wants to retain as much independence and control as possible while spreading the risk. Thus, even when equity capital is obtained, the owner-manager will retain in excess of 51 percent of the control, and there will be an option for the owner-manager to buy out other equity investors.

MARKET APPROACH

Description of the Target Market.

The geographic market area for The Sock Hop is Lethbridge. However, this must be further defined into a demographic target market, since a consumer-oriented marketing strategy is to be adopted by The Sock Hop.

For The Sock Hop, the target will be anybody between the ages of 15 and 64 who lives in Lethbridge. Income level, occupation, social class, and education are basically irrelevant for this necessary product.

The fact that this target market will be interested in quality socks at a moderate price is important. Furthermore, The Sock Hop is targeted at those who are looking for variety and fashion in socks. In addition, a good part of inventory will be devoted to high-quality socks, catering to the business community.

Uncontrollable Factors.

There are four uncontrollable factors that the small business owner must understand. The owner must gather information about these uncontrollable, predict or monitor trends, and adjust the internal operations to them.

Economy.

At this point, the economy in Lethbridge is positive. The type of merchandise that The Sock Hop is selling, however, tends to be recession proof. Because socks are not a high-cost item, the market should remain steady. The economic environment will be continually monitored, however, with respect to its effect on this business.

Competition.

There are several stores in Lethbridge that sell socks. A lot of these stores have built up their reputation and convenient location as strengths. Reputation is one of The Sock Hop's weaknesses. However, its main strength is greater variety, particularly in fashion socks.

The Sock Hop plans to monitor the competition closely through primary observation and by reviewing industry reports on a regular basis. Competitor reactions to its entrance into the market will also be noted.

Legal Restrictions.

The specific legal restrictions are discussed in the legal section of this paper. Keeping abreast of new and existing laws that affect retailers and the sock industry is important. Talking to intermediaries in the industry and reading association magazines and newspapers are effective ways to monitor legal effects.

Social/Cultural Trends.

Since The Sock Hop has decided to adopt a consumer-oriented marketing strategy, it is imperative that new trends be monitored. Because the product is very fad-oriented at times, trends are going to be vital, especially to the portion of the target market that is young and attracted by the fashion stock. To keep up with these trends, industry and fashion magazines, social statistics, and government reports will be of particular help. Furthermore, observing the competition and the general surroundings will help to keep The Sock Hop management up to date on lifestyle trends, demographic changes, and purchase patterns.

Marketing Strategy.

Product.

The product strategy for The Sock Hop involves offering a product that can be differentiated from the competition and that will ensure a reasonable profit, anticipating the market's changes in preference and continuing product innovations.

The product will be differentiated by being more fashion-oriented. There will be more variety, greater selection, and better services offered at The Sock Hop than are found with competitors. The customer will be able to choose socks from both the fashion stock and the basic stock. There will be a full money-back guarantee to complete this total package offered to the customer—a package that will sway the consumer's choice toward The Sock Hop.

Distribution.

It is an advantage that The Sock Hop is located close to other stores that carry socks, since it facilitates comparison. The Sock Hop is small and new and thus will have some disadvantages compared with department stores and chains. For this reason, it would be best for The Sock Hop to take part in a buying group. There are a lot of sock stores in Calgary and Edmonton, and many are operated as small businesses. The Sock Hop intends to investigate joining a buying group. In this way, it can obtain volume discounts, pass the savings on to customers, and thus remain competitive. Purchasing with a buying group will help keep a lower inventory, as slow-moving items can be purchased in minimum quantities.

In addition, The Sock Hop will use a more direct channel for purchasing, in accordance with the belief that the fewer the number of intermediaries, the higher the profit margin available to the retailer. It will use a manufacturer/supplier in Canada, if one with a good reputation for quality and dependability exists. The Sock Hop will avoid foreign suppliers, if possible, since it is The Sock Hop's policy to buy Canadian.

Pricing.

Price is not the means of differentiating The Sock Hop from the competition. The Sock Hop is competing on the basis of selection, quality, service, and specialization.

Sales will be held at various times of the year to improve overall profit, to promote certain items, to counter competition, to dispose of excess inventory of inactive stock, and to improve cash flow. However, in the long term, pricing based on the full cost will be used. The economic situation, competition, market demand, and price sensitivity of the customers also have to be taken into account when establishing a markup percentage.

Promotion.

The objective here is to inform, persuade, and/or remind the target market. Five percent of sales has been devoted to advertising for the first year. This is in spite of the fact that the Dun and Bradstreet average for small businesses for advertising is 1.5 percent. Extra advertising support is needed in the first year of business because sales will not be large compared with those of other clothing stores, and the public needs to be informed about The Sock Hop and its total offering. In the next four years, advertising will be reduced to 3 percent of sales, but it will still be above the Dun and Bradstreet average.

A variety of advertising methods will be used. The normal outlets such as newspapers, radio, television, and the Yellow Pages will be used. A door-to-door flyer campaign will be considered, as Lethbridge is relatively small. For television and radio, The Sock Hop hopes to be involved in any promotional efforts in conjunction with the Park Place Mall.

At the start of the business, various contests can be held to get ideas on new designs for socks, which will help renew the product life cycle. In addition, sponsoring sock hops at the local high schools will improve public relations. This will be especially advantageous, since the younger, fashion-conscious portion of the target market are high school youth. Moreover, a lot of these youngsters are innovators and thus have the power to influence a major portion of the target market.

Finally, price promotions can be used in busy months such as January, when clearances are usually held, during August and September, when it is back-to-school time, and during November.

LOCATION

Trading Area.

Economic Base.

The City of Lethbridge's economy is strongly based on agriculture. The agricultural economy is supported by the food processing, packaging, distilling, and brewing industries. The city has good road and rail connections to various markets as well as to producers, and these have been important in maintaining Lethbridge's economic position. In addition, Lethbridge is in a prominent position in its region, and growth is expected in the area.

Competition.

In terms of general retail and service competition in the trading area, there are 36 major retail/service clusters in Lethbridge, and they have been evaluated at a total of 3,479,000 square feet of retail and service space in addition to the square footage covered by Park Place.[2] The 3,479,000 square feet are allocated in the trading areas as follows:

2,650,000 sq. ft.	in the city of Lethbridge
829,000 sq. ft.	in the surrounding area, which composes the trading area
3,479,000 sq. ft.	

Attitudes of the Trading Area toward Having a New Business.

The new mall has increased the trading area and has shown a positive attitude toward development of the area. Lethbridge is moving ahead, and as a result, most of the community is anxious for new businesses.

Specific Site.

Accessibility.

Park Place Mall is centrally located in the city of Lethbridge, north of the central business district (CBD). There are major roads on all sides with good connections to the city. Careful consideration to traffic flows was given by the city before construction of the mall took place. Lethbridge is also well served by the major highway system serving Southern Alberta. Therefore, vehicular traffic is facilitated both in and around Lethbridge. The transit system facilitates customers who do not own vehicles. There is a major transit station downtown within walking distance of the mall. A proposal to move the station north of Galt Gardens has also been considered, which would bring this station to the street facing this mall. In addition, bus routes include the mall.

Thus, all customers will have good access to the site, which is fairly visible from the major thoroughfares (Stafford Drive, Crowsnest Trail, First Avenue).

---

[2] Lethbridge Community Profile. City of Lethbridge, Economic Development Department, estimates 2009.

Site Costs.

The specific site costs (information obtained from Park Place Mall administration and the city of Lethbridge) include the following:

Rent	$20–$30/sq. ft. per year ($30 × 400 sq. ft. = $12,000 per year)
Utilities	$5–$10/sq. ft. per year ($10 × 400 sq. ft. = $4,000 per year)
Business taxes	4.2% of fair rental value [4.2% × (400 × 30)] = $504
City business licence	$53 per year
Business Revitalization Zone fees	$3.78 per month–$45.36 per year (0.75% of business tax)
Insurance	$87.39 per year

The total site and operational costs add to $16,689.75.

Total rent of The Sock Hop will be $12,000 per year. In addition, the mall offices generally set a break-even point for the store, and once this point is reached by the store, a royalty of 5 percent to 8 percent of sales in excess of the break-even point is charged in addition to the normal rent.

The typical term of this lease is between five years and 10 years. Since this aspect of the lease is negotiable, an attempt should be made to have the term reduced. In addition, advance rent of two months is required by the mall administration. In terms of recharges, the total cost of utilities, electricity, and upkeep of the common area is $4000 ($10.00 × 400 sq. ft.).

Insurance for The Sock Hop covers the business contents such as merchandise, fixtures, furniture, and equipment. The insurance also applies to the actual business loss sustained by the owner and the expenses incurred to resume normal business operations. Thus, the insurance provides coverage when the damage caused by an insured peril results in the interruption of business. The money and securities are also covered against loss by robbery, safe burglary, and theft from a night depository in a bank or from the custodian. The insurance further covers liability for bodily injury and property damage claims arising out of the maintenance and use of premises.

Total insurance per year is equal to:

$$\$3.70 \times (\$23,618.77/\$1,000) = \$87.39$$

It should be noted that the mall administration insures the common area. (The various taxes and licences will be covered in the final section of this business plan.)

Proximity to Other Businesses.

Park Place Mall has many products and services. This is advantageous in that it will generate customer traffic essential to the success of the business. Socks are defined as a shopping good, which means that consumers will usually shop around and compare before making the final purchase decision. Therefore, by locating close to competing businesses (see Figure 1), consumers will be able to compare and choose the superior product. The Sock Hop offers good quality socks at a reasonable price, which, when compared with other stores, will draw a loyal following.

Furthermore, other stores will be selling complementary articles of clothing (shoes, pants), which will generate customer traffic for The Sock Hop by creating a need for socks. Other than the businesses in Park Place Mall, there are no other stores offering socks in the immediate vicinity of the site.

PHYSICAL FACILITIES

Start-up Costs.

The start-up costs for a retail store are made up of two things—capital assets and inventory. The following is a detailed breakdown of the physical items required to furnish the store. (This list was obtained from Roll-It Catalogue, National Signs, and Consumers Distributing.)

ITEM	NO.	EACH	TOTAL VALUE
Furniture and Fixtures			
Multimerchandiser (48″ × 54″)	6	$ 507.00	$ 3042.00
End frame pegboard (48″ × 66″)	4	146.65	587.00
Miscellaneous hardware (pegs)	1	1000.00	1000.00
Used bargain bunk	1	200.00	200.00
Counter	1	500.00	500.00
Sign	1	500.00	500.00
Filing cabinet (4 drawer, legal 24″ deep)	1	190.00	190.00
Desk (30″ × 60″, steel)	1	250.00	250.00
Swivel chair	1	50.00	50.00
Equipment (obtained from Cypress Business Equipment, AGT Business Office, Office Depot, General Fasteners)			
Software (Bedford)	1	$ 300.00	$ 300.00
Computer and printer (IBM clone)	1	2000.00	2000.00
Cash register	1	1200.00	1200.00
Telephone installation	1	40.00	40.00
Adding machine	1	75.00	75.00
Pricing gun	1	80.00	80.00
Vacuum cleaner	1	280.00	$ 280.00
Total			$10,294.00

Initially The Sock Hop will invest about 15 percent of projected sales in inventory. This is standard.

Inventory = Sales × 15%

$13,324.70 = $88,831.33 × 15%

Layout.

In the case of The Sock Hop, the layout is designed to display the merchandise effectively. Although browsing is somewhat encouraged by the multimerchandisers, there is not enough selling space to encourage a lot of creativity in layout (see Figure 2).

FINANCIAL

Feasibility Analysis

Target Market and Trade Area.

Geographically, the trade area for Lethbridge is delineated. The competitive influence of retail and service facilities in the city of Calgary limit the extension of the trade area to 70 kilometres to the north. To the east, competitive retail facilities in the city of Medicine Hat limit the trade area to 95 kilometres. In the south, the trade area extends some 80 kilometres to the Canada–United States border. The trade area to the west extends 130 kilometres from Lethbridge. Here, it is primarily limited by the distance and driving times and is bounded by the Alberta–British Columbia border. The study by Larry Smith and Associates Ltd. indicates that Park Place Mall expects to derive the majority of its sales volume (80 percent to 95 percent) from this area. The remaining 5 percent to 20 percent of market support normally reflects customer shopping derived from visitors, tourists, or people working in Lethbridge but not residing in the delineated trade area.

Market Potential

- Total 2008 Lethbridge retail apparel and accessories estimated sales were $32,260,000 (City of Lethbridge Economic Development). At an inflation rate of 4 percent per year (Alberta Retail and Service Trade Statistics), the retail sales for 2009 will be:

$$\$32,260,000 \times (1.04)^5 = \$40,000,000$$

- The 2009 population of Lethbridge is 85,000 (city statistics).
- The 2009 population for the trade area excluding Lethbridge is 115,000 (city statistics).
- The amount of the regional population that shops for socks in Lethbridge was estimated by clothing retailers to be 33 percent.
- It is estimated by clothing retailers and the personal experience of the owner-manager that between 3 percent and 5 percent of the expenditures on clothing are for socks. However, 3 percent may be on the high side for a low-price item such as socks, so a more conservative figure would be 2 percent. Based on these figures, the 2009 Lethbridge per capita socks sales figure can be calculated as follows:

$$\frac{\$40,000,000 \times 2\%}{[85,000 + (11,500 \times 33\%)]} = \$6.50$$

The market area for The Sock Hop can be safely defined as Lethbridge. Thus, in the remaining calculations, Lethbridge population figures will be used. Total market potential calculations:

- 2009 per capita socks sales in Lethbridge is $6.50 (as calculated above).
- 2009 population for Lethbridge is 85,000 (see above).

Therefore, the 2009 unadjusted total market potential figure for The Sock Hop can be calculated as follows:

$$\$6.50 \text{ per person} \times 85,000 = \$552,500$$

An adjustment must be made to this figure to take outshopping into account. Outshopping is the result of a consumer in a particular market area going to another area to make purchases. Based on interviews with store managers, the outshopping figure was said to be 20 percent. This is quite conservative, since the presence of Park Place Mall has two implications. Thus, the adjusted 2009 total market potential for Lethbridge will be:

$$\$552,500 \times 0.80 = \$442,000$$

This figure is the most accurate market potential figure. It takes into account inflation, outshopping buying habits (figure determined by primary research), and 2009 population figures.

Market Share.

No statistics were available on the amount of retail space devoted to socks. Therefore, estimates were obtained through primary research (see Appendix 2). The proposed store will have an area of 400 square feet, with 300 square feet devoted to selling space. Based on these figures, the unadjusted market share of The Sock Hop should be the following:

$$\frac{320 \text{ sq. ft.}}{872 \text{ sq. ft.} + 320 \text{ sq. ft.}} = 26.8\%$$

This figure represents the unadjusted market share available to The Sock Hop. To adjust the figure, the strengths and weaknesses of the various aspects of the business must be considered.

The major weakness of The Sock Hop is that it is a new store. It does not have a loyal customer following, has no reputation, and has plenty of established competition. In addition, this specialty store will more than likely have higher prices than some of the discount department stores selling socks.

The major strength of The Sock Hop is its location. It is going to be located in a new major shopping mall, Park Place Mall. The customer traffic in the mall is above average. The store will be in an attractive setting with good exposure. Furthermore, there is a vast amount of parking space available for the satisfaction of the consumers. The Sock Hop provides a variety of socks in one location that is convenient and pleasant for consumers. Another area of strength is the growing trading area. The outlook is very positive for the Lethbridge economy, and this can only aid The Sock Hop.

Based on this analysis, the adjusted market share can be said to be a very conservative 20 percent. This is based on present conditions. In the future, the owner-manager hopes that this percentage will increase as the business becomes more established.

Projected Income.

The projected income statements for the next five business years are in Figure 3. The figures have been derived through primary and secondary research. The revenue figure was calculated by multiplying the adjusted market potential and the adjusted market share figures together:

$$\$442,000 \times 20\% = \$88,400.00$$

Financing.

This section pertains to the financing plan for The Sock Hop. Business start-up costs are needed to determine the financing needed. These costs are made up of the following:

CASE program	$ 400.00
Inventory	13,324.77
Incorporation fees	1,000.00
Physical facilities	10,294.00
Rent (last 2 months of lease + 1 month rent)	3,000.00
Total	$28,018.77

Most lenders require the borrower to prepare a financing proposal. This will provide answers to questions the lender will have about the owner and about the proposed business. In order for the lenders to know how a loan will be repaid, they need to look at income and cash flow projections for evidence of earnings that will support the loan. These are shown in Figures 3 and 4.

Sources of Financing.

The Business Development Bank of Canada (BDC) offers term loans to allow small business owners to acquire fixed assets such as land, building, machinery, and equipment. The loans are offered at floating rates or at fixed rates. BDC may also provide assistance through its CASE program. CASE is a counselling service offered exclusively to small- and medium-sized businesses. This program employs experienced counsellors who advise the small business owner on any aspect of business.

The interest rate for the loan is approximately 8 percent with a minimum repayment period of four years.

The term of the amount borrowed must match the actual lifetime of what is being financed. Thus, the inventory portion will be financed by an operating loan with a term of two years. This will be financing from a chartered bank. It should be noted that although $13,325 is being borrowed for this purpose, a lesser amount will be needed. This is because The Sock Hop will endeavour to finance a good portion of inventory from suppliers who, because of competition in the industry, are willing to market their products through new outlets. The remaining $7500 will be borrowed from BDC on a term of five years. The equity investment will thus be $7500.

Accounting System.

Rather than employ a bookkeeper, the manager of the business will record on a computer all transactions that occur every day. The Bedford accounting software will be used, which is priced at less than $300 (quote from computer dealer). The computer and a suitable printer priced at $2000 will also be used.

The Bedford accounting software is a fully integrated package for the small business. It is easy to use and very user friendly. It consists of the General Ledger, Payroll, Receivables, Payables, and Inventory modules that are all posted, as applicable, through single entries. It is very versatile and easily adaptable to small business needs. It produces full audit trails and a number of other management information reports. The vendors have a good track record of maintenance and support. Computing magazines such as *PC Magazine* and *InfoWorld* have given good reviews to this software.

The services of a public accountant (CA or CGA) will be used for annual reviews, for tax advice, and on special occasions when necessary. The business will follow Generally Accepted Accounting Principles in maintaining the financial records.

Credit Policy.

The Sock Hop does not intend to allow any credit to customers, since it is not a practice in the industry. It does not intend to start a trend in this area, as the volume per customer would not justify it. However, it will accept all major credit cards (VISA, MasterCard, American Express, etc.). With this facility to customers, there would be no need to extend direct credit, which, in any case, would entail taking some risk on the part of The Sock Hop.

Financial Evaluation.

Monthly financial statements will be prepared and reviewed by the owner-manager in an effort to monitor and evaluate progress. Several financial ratios will be calculated and compared with similar businesses as well as with previous performance.

PERSONNEL

Administrative Structure.

Since The Sock Hop is not a big store, initially the number of staff employed will be limited. Store hours for The Sock Hop will be as follows:

- Monday–Wednesday, 9:30 a.m.–5:30 p.m.

    Thursday and Friday, 9:30 a.m.–9:00 p.m.

    Saturday, 9:30 a.m.–5:30 p.m.

Thus, the basic salary and wage expenses will be

Store manager	$24,000.00
1 full-time clerk ($8.00 × 35 h/week)	13,440.00
1 part-time clerk ($7.00 × 10 h/week)	3,360.00
Total salary and wage	$40,800.00

With this staffing plan in mind, the organizational chart will be as follows:

```
                    Owner-manager
        ┌───────────────┴───────────────┐
Full-time clerk                    Part-time clerk
```

Employee Recruitment and Training.

Job Descriptions.

A typical job description is as follows:

Duties: Greets and helps customers, keeps shelves organized and stocked, rings up sales and bags items, opens and closes store when manager is away, cleans counters and vacuums

Responsible to: Store owner/manager

Requirements: Must have previous sales experience, be available to work nights and weekends, be able to use a cash register, be able to learn store procedures

Personal: Must be friendly, appropriately dressed and groomed, punctual, and reliable

Recruitment.

The channels of recruitment used by The Sock Hop will include write-ins (applicants), walk-ins, want-advertising, and educational institutions. Job application forms will be used to collect information about recruits. These application forms will attempt to gather information pertaining to personal data, employment status, education, skills, work history, memberships, awards, hobbies, and references.

Evaluation.

The first three months of employment are a period of observation for the employee as well as the owner-manager. The employee will receive professional sales training and will be taught the basics of The Sock Hop store procedures.

Beginning at the end of week three of employment, the owner-manager will initiate a coaching discussion. The employee's job performance will be evaluated, and discussions will be held to help the employee understand the job. In addition, any questions the employee has will be answered.

Training.

Training will be carried out by the owner-manager and will consist of three general areas. First, the employee will be provided with information about the business and its philosophy and goals. Second, the employee will receive training about the merchandise, including such things as the material they are made of, washing instructions, and so on. The third area of training involves the teaching of specific selling skills—such things as approaching the customer, presenting the merchandise, closing the sale, and suggestion selling.

Policies.

The following policies will be followed by The Sock Hop employees:

- An employee is assigned an identification number consisting of four digits to be used for all cash register operations.
- Work schedules will be posted at least one week in advance.
- Scheduling conflicts are to be reported to the manager as soon as possible.
- The wages for regular full-time clerks will consist of an hourly rate of $8 plus a 2 percent commission on sales.
- The wages for part-time clerks will be an hourly rate of $7 plus a 2 percent commission on sales.
- An employee who has completed six full months of continuous service by June 30 will be entitled to one week's vacation during the summer vacation period.
- Any employee who has completed one full year of continuous service with the company by June 30 will be entitled to two weeks or 4 percent of earnings as vacation pay (whichever is greater).
- Employees who have completed less than six months service with the company by June 30 must be paid 4 percent of their gross earnings from the date of hire until the last pay period in June.
- All full-time employees must receive vacation pay in the last pay period before leaving for their vacations.
- The employee will be expected to have a professional appearance. This includes proper grooming, clean and pressed clothing (no jeans), name tags, clean and proper footwear, and above all else, a smiling, pleasant attitude.
- The Sock Hop emphasizes customer satisfaction. Therefore, the employee should ask all customers to retain their sales receipts. The Sock Hop will provide a full cash refund or merchandise exchanges on all returns with receipts.
- All staff will be entitled to a 20 percent discount on purchases from The Sock Hop.
- All purchases by staff members must be handled by the owner-manager. At no time is the staff member to "key in" their own purchases. These purchases are to be conducted during breaks or at the end of shifts.
- The phone is to be answered promptly, giving the store name and the employee's name. It is important that the employee be cheerful, helpful, and courteous.

- Personal calls are to be kept to an absolute minimum!
- The employee should practice the following prevention activities: (1) approach and greet all customers promptly and never leave the sales floor without coverage, and (2) be aware of customers carrying merchandise from one location to another.

LEGAL REQUIREMENTS

The Sock Hop will be an incorporated business. This decision was made after looking at the relative pros and cons of incorporation. The main reason for incorporating is the limited liability of shareholders. Thus, the owner is protected should the business fail. By incorporating, the owner is not risking her life savings; she is only liable for the amount invested in the business.

Regulations.

Since The Sock Hop is a retail store, the regulations that apply to it are those common to any regular small business in Lethbridge. The municipal government requires that the small business owner hold a business licence ($53 per year). In addition, the city requires building and electrical inspections after renovations have been made. Municipal taxes include a business tax of about $504 per year and a Business Revitalization Zone (BRZ) fee of $45.36 per year, since the mall is within the BRZ. In addition, the small business is required to pay various taxes. The federal and provincial government require the filing of yearly income tax returns. The federal GST will need to be collected on sales and remitted to the federal government. Provincial sales tax is not charged in Alberta.

FIGURE 1	Selling Space in the Market	
STORE	**NUMBER OF STORES**	**TOTAL SQUARE FEET**
Zellers	1	323
Safeway	3	22
Walmart	1	161
Smart Set	2	11
Reitmans	2	11
Winners	1	54
Sears	1	75
Shoppers Drug Mart	1	32
Tip Top	3	32
Jack Fraser	2	22
The Bay	1	32
Mariposa	3	11
Error factor	00	237
Total		1,023

FIGURE 2   Selling Space

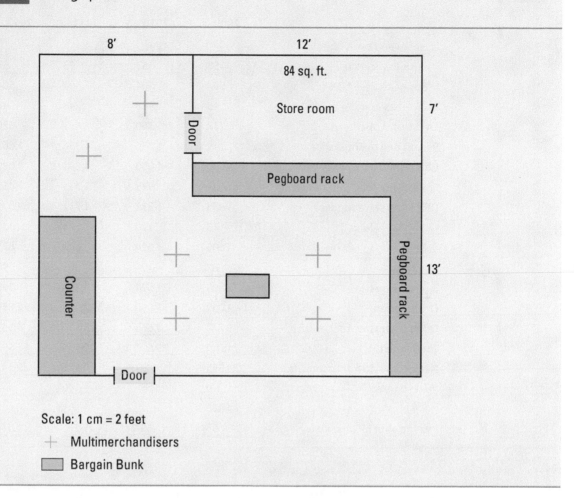

Scale: 1 cm = 2 feet
+ Multimerchandisers
▨ Bargain Bunk

FIGURE 3   Projected Income Statement for Five Years (in dollars)

	2009	2010	2011	2012	2013
Sales	$ 88,400	$133,248	$173,222	$207,866	$228,654
Cost of goods sold	43,984	66,624	86,611	103,933	114,327
Gross margin	44,416	66,624	86,611	103,933	114,327
Less expenses					
Rent	12,000	12,000	12,000	12,000	12,000
Staff wages	16,800	17,268	17,911	18,579	19,274
Owner's salary	24,000	24,000	24,000	24,000	24,000
Employee benefits	3,960	4,007	4,071	4,138	4,207
Advertising	4,442	3,997	5,197	6,236	6,860

FIGURE 3

FIGURE 3   (continued)

	2009	2010	2011	2012	2013
Licences and taxes					
Business licence	53	53	53	53	53
Business tax—4.2% of rent	504	504	504	504	504
BRZ fees	45	48	48	48	48
Credit-card discounts	213	360	433	520	572
Repairs and maintenance	711	1,066	1,386	1,663	1,829
Utilities and occupancy costs	4,000	4,000	4,000	4,000	4,000
Professional fees	622	933	1,213	1,455	1,601
Office and store supplies	888	1,332	1,732	2,079	2,287
Telephone—Rent	115	120	124	129	135
Estimated toll charges	600	624	649	675	702
Insurance	87	91	95	98	102
Interest expense	2,593	1,594	1,396	398	199
Depreciation	2,059	2,059	2,059	2,059	2,059
Other expenses	1,777	2,665	3,464	4,157	4,573
Total expenses	74,269	75,521	79,135	81,591	83,805
Net income (before income taxes)	(29,853)	(8,897)	7,476	22,342	30,522
Income taxes	0		0		1,500
	4,468				6,104
Income after income taxes	$(28,653)	$ (7,697)	$ 5,776	$ 16,674	$ 23,218

FIGURE 4   Projected Cash Flow for Five Years (in dollars)

	2009	2010	2011	2012	2013	TOTALS
Cash in						
Net income	$(29,853)	$(8,897)	$7,476	$22,342	$30,522	$18,138
Add noncash items:						
Depreciation	2,059	2,059	2,059	2,059	2,059	10,294
Cash flows from operations	(27,794)	(6,838)	9,535	24,401	32,581	28,432
Equity contribution	35,000	15,000				50,000
Loan receipts —Operating	13,325					13,325
—BDC	7,500					7,500
Total cash inflows	28,031	8,162	9,535	24,401	32,581	99,257
Cash out						
Loan repayments—Operating	0	6,662	6,663	0	0	13,325
—BDC	0	1,500	1,500	1,500	1,500	6,000

	2009	2010	2011	2012	2013	TOTALS
Return of equity	0	0	0	20,000	30,000	50,000
Start-up costs						
Legal	1,000					1,000
CASE counselling	400					400
Furniture and fixtures	10,294					10,294
Inventory	13,325					13,325
Two months' advance rent	2,000					2,000
Total cash outflows	27,019	8,162	8,163	21,500	31,500	96,344
Net cash flows	$ 1,012	$ (0)	$1,372	$ 2,901	$ 1,081	$ 2,913

BUSINESS PLAN 2—QUALITY CUTS

TABLE OF CONTENTS

Executive Summary and Background

Description of Management Team

Business Objectives

Market Approach

Location

Physical Facilities

Financial

Personnel

Legal

EXECUTIVE SUMMARY AND BACKGROUND

Quality Cuts is a new beauty salon located in the city of Lethbridge, Alberta. It operates from the College Value Mall in south Lethbridge, employs five full-time hairdressers, and is managed by Sue Holland. Quality Cuts provides haircuts, styles, perms, and colour, as well as hair products supplied by well-known manufacturers. It also provides cosmetic and manicuring services. Quality Cuts attempts to target the middle- to older-aged women in the Lethbridge area, which is currently the most rapidly growing part of the market. Quality Cuts uses a computer database to build knowledge of customers and improve customer service. The feasibility analysis and business plan projections show that Quality Cuts will be a viable entry to the beauty salon market.

DESCRIPTION OF MANAGEMENT TEAM

Quality cuts is owned and operated by Sue Holland. She has her hairdressing certification from the Alberta School of Hair and Beauty Design and has worked as a hairdresser for 10 years in the Lethbridge area. Before leaving her current employment to plan the establishment of Quality Cuts, Sue was supervising four other hairdressers. Sue is assisted in the financial and computer management aspects of the business by her husband, who is a chartered accountant. Preliminary consultations indicate that a high percentage of Sue's current clients will continue with her in the new business.

BUSINESS OBJECTIVES

The objectives for Quality Cuts are as follows: The first objective is to have a positive cash flow for the first year of operations. Cash flows consist of receipts and payments attributed to operating, investing, and financing activities. As can be seen from the cash flow statement, it is estimated that there will be a positive net cash inflow for each of the four sectors of the first year of operations.

A second objective deals with the prices charged to the customers of the business. The prices will be competitive with other salons. Each hairdresser will have some input into prices charged for his or her clients to ensure that pricing is competitive.

A third objective is to achieve a market share of at least 3 percent by the end of the first year of operation, moving up to 5 percent within five years.

MARKET APPROACH

Description of Target Market.

The target market geographically consists of the city of Lethbridge and some of the surrounding trade area. Lethbridge is an agricultural service centre with a high market draw for many smaller communities within a 48-kilometre radius.

The demographic characteristics include middle- to older-aged women in the middle- to higher-income classes. Approximately 80 percent of Sue Holland's current clients fall into this range. The location of Quality Cuts is ideal for this market because the College Value Mall is adjacent to some very large seniors' apartment buildings and upscale housing projects. It is located on the south end of Lethbridge where new housing developments are being built. The purchase characteristics for this market include concern over quality and service in a clean and friendly atmosphere.

Uncontrollable Factors.

There are two uncontrollable factors that would most affect Quality Cuts. The competition is the first. There are currently 35 other beauty salons or shops in the city employing 150 hairdressers/stylists. Because this is a personal service industry, customer patronage is determined to a large extent by the quality of the service provider and the level of confidence the client has in the hairdresser. Quality Cuts has determined that it will attain a competitive edge through careful hiring and training of its employees. Proximity of competitors may be a secondary factor to customer patronage, and Quality Cuts is the only beauty salon in the College Mall, which should be an advantage.

The second relevant uncontrollable is the social/cultural factor. Concern over one's looks is a major trend in North America. This suggests a continued and growing use of beauty salons. In addition, the Lethbridge market is an aging one. Both of these should be a positive influence on Quality Cuts' performance.

Product.

The product that makes up a beauty salon comprises three distinct parts: hair service, manicures and cosmetic work, and hair products. The hair service side is by far the most important, as it includes such things as haircuts, styles, perms, and colours. This will make up 80 percent to 90 percent of the entire revenue of the beauty salon. Selling hair products and providing cosmetic and manicure services, although less important, are still vital as they may serve as a draw for passing consumers. The products include such things as gels, shampoos, conditioners, moisturants, hair-repair treatments, protectors, sculpting lotions, and hairsprays. These type of products are available to the consumer in pharmacies but the quality of the professional products that are only found at beauty shops makes them attractive, even if the price is slightly higher. The brands that will be stocked include Paul Mitchell, Matrix, Lanza, Zotos, and Mahdeen. Because hair grooming is a service, Quality Cuts emphasizes superior customer service with its clients. Frequent follow-up communications with consumers is maintained through computer tracking and database programs.

Pricing.

Prices are set close to competitors' prices during the first year to ensure the transfer of existing clients with their hairdresser. Price will eventually rise to 5 percent to 10 percent above the competitors' as the clientele of the business stabilizes. This, in turn, is in harmony with the image Quality Cuts wants to project. Markup on the products is 50 percent of retail selling price.

Promotion.

Advertising takes place at approximately the average for hair salons in Alberta. This amount is 1.9 percent of sales, or approximately $2836 for the first year of operations.

In addition to this amount in the first year, there extra "opening" advertising will be conducted for the first month. This is to get the name of the business out to the public and to let the hairdressers' old clients know where their hairdressers have moved. The cost of this opening advertising is an additional $500, making the total advertising budget for the first year $3336.

This advertising will take a couple of forms. First, the Yellow Pages is a must, as it is an easy way for the public to see where certain salons are located. There are currently seven pages full of advertising just for beauty salons, with the average large advertisement occupying approximately 26 square centimetres.

The TV guide within the Friday edition of the *Lethbridge Herald* is also a favourite place for beauty salon advertising.

Business cards and extensive use of single-sheet advertising will also be used. These printed sheets of paper will be slid under the doors of apartments in neighbouring buildings, containing information and possible coupons to attract new customers. As mentioned previously, a sophisticated tracking system is set up on computer to monitor customers' purchases and improve customer service efforts.

Distribution.

There are four main suppliers that Quality Cuts deals with, three from Calgary and one from Lethbridge. They are the following:

Emerald Beauty Supplies (Lethbridge)

Monarch Messenger Beauty Supplies (Calgary)

Consolidated Beauty Supplies (Calgary)

Obsco Beauty Supplies (Calgary)

All these distributors can supply within two days. Quality Cuts will attempt to take advantage of quantity and cash discounts where possible.

LOCATION

Trading Area.

Lethbridge has a fairly stable population into which many older people from the surrounding areas retire. The socioeconomic level of the community is above average. Both of these factors will have a positive effect on Quality Cuts's performance.

Specific Site.

Quality Cuts is located in the College Mall in the southeast corner of the city. Quality Cuts is located where North West Trust was located, as moved to a different location within the mall.

Accessibility.

This location has access from within the mall and private access from outside. It also allows for a neon sign on the outside of the mall to help attract customers. Traffic flow should be quite high, as Walmart is not too far away.

Site Costs

ITEM	COST ($)	
Rent	18.50	per square foot (includes property tax)
Utilities	3,000	per year (plus $150 deposit)
Telephone	540	per year
Insurance	605	per year
Business taxes	420	per year
Licences/permits	113	per year

Proximity to Other Businesses.

There are no other beauty shops within the mall, but there are many businesses that draw traffic and would be complementary to Quality Cuts.

Physical Characteristics of the Site.

The store size is 1200 square feet. It has the front opening into the mall and a side door open to the outside.

PHYSICAL FACILITIES

Equipment, fixtures, and supplies are an integral part of the business, and a list of these items is included below. The costs have been obtained from prospective suppliers.

ITEM	COST ($)
9 hydraulic chairs	4500
9 styling stations	2997
10 hair dryers	2490
10 dryer chairs	1480
4 shampoo chairs	592
4 sinks	1476
9 mirrors	1350
washing machine	650
dryer	450

2 neon signs	3000
4 lounge chairs	400
computer system	2000
air exchanger	5000
reception desk	300
layout additions	3000
shelving	500
miscellaneous supplies	6000
(includes start-up product)	

Layout.

The layout of the shop is shown in Figure 1. The layout diagram shows that the shop consists of three areas. The first is the reception area, which houses the reception desk, the shelves of products, the coat rack, and the waiting chairs. The second contains the hair salon itself, with the nine stations, four sinks, 10 dryer stations, and coffee area. The third section is at the back of the location and includes a bathroom, washer/dryer area, and an 18 foot by 18 foot office/lunchroom/storage area.

The salon is set up in a way to accomplish three goals: to use the space, to be convenient for the patron, and to be pleasing to the eye. The image projected is one of cleanliness and class, as appropriate for the target market.

FINANCIAL

Feasibility.

Market Potential.

The estimate of average family expenditure on hair grooming for Alberta in 2005 was $375 (source: Statistics Canada Catalogue 62-555). It is also estimated that 45.5 percent of this amount is for women's hair grooming (source: Statistics Canada Catalogue 63-555). Using a percentage of 50 percent should be conservative as Quality Cuts's revenue will also include sales of hair care products and cosmetic/manicuring services as well as some haircuts to male customers. The population for the target market includes approximately 20,000 households (source: City of Lethbridge). Market potential estimate is as follows:

Households $\times$ household expenditures $\times$ percent of expenditures for target market
$= 22,000 \times 375 \times 0.50 = \$4,125,000$

Market Share.

The number of beauty salons and hairdressers/stylists in the market area were obtained through calls to all the shops, a total of 35 shops and 150 hairdressers/stylists. An estimate of Quality Cuts proposed market share is shown below:

$$= \frac{6 \text{ hairdressers/stylists (Sue } + 5 \text{ employees)}}{6 + 150}$$

$$= \frac{6}{156} = 3.8\%$$

This share should be decreased to 3.6 percent because the business is new and will take some time to build sales. The start-up delay should not be significant, however, because all five hairdresser/stylists are currently working in the market area and will bring the majority of their clients to the new business.

$$\text{Projected share in revenue} = \text{market share} \times \text{market potential}$$
$$= 3.6\% \times \$4,125,000 = \$148,500$$

Projected Income.

Below are the projected income statements for the first five years of operation. Revenue figures from above are used as the basis behind this information. Amounts and sources of expenses are as follows:

Cost of Goods Sold	10% (Statistics Canada Small Business and Special Surveys Division, confirmed by primary research)
Wages and Salaries	53.5% of sales (Alberta Business Profile, *Barber & Beauty Shops*, July 2006)
Depreciation	See schedule for calculation
Repairs and Maintenance	0.8% of sales (Alberta Business Profile, *Barber & Beauty Shops*)
Utilities	$3000 per year, 5% increase yearly (Primary information from College Mall management)
Phone	$540 per year, 5% increase yearly (Primary information from phone company)
Rent	$10 per sq. foot flat rate for first 2 years, $11 for years 3 and 4, $12 for year 5. $8.50 per sq. foot variable rate, 5% increase yearly (Primary information from College Mall management)
Interest Expense	See table for calculation
Legal Fees	0.7% of sales (Alberta Business Profile, *Barber & Beauty Shops*)
Advertising	1.9% of sales (Alberta Business Profile, *Barber & Beauty Shops*)
Insurance	See legal section for details
Licences/Permits	See legal section for details
Business Taxes	$0.35 per sq. foot (City of Lethbridge Taxation Department)
Other Expenses	1% of sales (Statistics Canada Small Business and Special Surveys Division)

The projected income for Quality Cuts is as follows:

	YEAR 1	YEAR 2	YEAR 3	YEAR 4	YEAR 5
Sales	$148,500	$156,702	$164,537	$172,764	$181,402
Cost of Goods Sold	14,850	15,670	16,454	17,276	18,140
Gross Margin	$133,650	$141,032	$148,083	$155,488	$163,262
Expenses:					
Wages and Salaries	$ 79,448	$ 83,836	$ 88,027	$ 92,429	$ 97,050
Depreciation	1,749	1,749	1,749	1,749	1,749
Repairs and Maintenance	1,188	1,254	1,316	1,382	1,451
Utilities	3,000	3,150	3,308	3,473	3,647
Phone	540	567	595	625	656
Rent	22,200	22,710	24,444	25,008	26,796

Interest Expense	1,894	1,056	829	578	303
Legal Fees	1,040	1,097	1,152	1,209	1,270
Advertising	2,822	2,977	3,126	3,283	3,447
Insurance	605	635	667	700	735
Licences/Permits	113	113	113	113	113
Business Taxes	420	420	420	420	420
Other Expenses	1,485	1,567	1,645	1,728	1,814
Total Expenses	$116,504	$121,131	$127,391	$132,697	$139,451
Net Income	$ 17,146	$ 19,901	$ 20,692	$ 22,791	$ 23,811

DEPRECIATION SCHEDULE

ASSETS	CAPITAL COST	LIFE (YEARS)	YEARS 1–5	6–10	11–15	16–20
Equipment:						
Hydraulic chairs (9)	$4500	20	$1125	$1125	$1125	$1125
Workstations (9)	2997	20	749	749	749	749
Hair dryers (10)	2490	20	623	623	623	623
Dryer chairs (10)	1480	20	370	370	370	370
Shampoo chairs (4)	592	20	148	148	148	148
Sinks (4)	1476	20	369	369	369	369
Washing machine	650	10	325	325		
Dryer	450	10	225	225		
Computer system	2000	5	2000			
Air exchanger	5000	20	1250	1250	1250	1250
Fixtures and furniture:						
Shelves	500	20	125	125	125	125
Neon signs (2)	3000	20	750	750	750	750
Lounge chairs (4)	400	10	200	200		
Mirrors (9)	1350	20	338	338	338	338
Reception desk	300	10	150	150		
Total			$8747	$6747	$5847	$5847

Financing.

Start-up costs are as follows:

ITEM	COST	SOURCE
Initial equipment and fixtures	$30,185	See Physical Facilities section
Miscellaneous supplies and product (includes opening inventory)	6,000	See Physical Facilities section
Rent (one month)	1,850	See Location section
Utility deposit	150	See Location section
Business licences and permits	113	See Legal section
Legal fees	754	See Legal section
Advertising and promotion (first month)	500	See Promotion section
Insurance (first quarter)	151	See Legal section
Total start-up costs	$39,703	

A cash flow statement has also been calculated to determine the cash situation that might arise during the first year of operations. This is shown below:

QUARTER ENDING	MAR 31	JUNE 30	SEPT 30	DEC 31
CASH INFLOWS:				
Sales	$29,848	$37,310	$37,310	$44,772
Bank Loan	37,000	0	0	0
Equity Investment	5,000	0	0	0
Mall Payback	25,000	0	0	0
TOTAL CASH INFLOW	$96,848	$37,310	$37,310	$44,772
CASH OUTFLOWS:				
Equipment and Supplies	$36,185	$ 0	$ 0	$ 0
Inventory	2,985	3,731	3,731	4,477
Wages and Salaries	15,969	19,961	19,961	23,953
Advertising	1,334	834	834	834
Licences/Permits	113	0	0	0
Business Taxes	0	0	0	420
Insurance Expense	151	151	151	151
Interest Expense	925	323	323	323
Legal Fees	209	261	261	313
Rent	5,550	5,550	5,550	5,550
Repairs and Maintenance	239	298	298	358
Utilities	900	750	750	750
Telephone	135	135	135	135
Loan Repayment	24,075	788	788	788
Other Expenses	$ 298	$ 373	$ 373	$ 448
TOTAL CASH OUTFLOW	$89,068	$33,155	$33,155	$38,500
NET CASH INFLOW	$ 7,780	$ 4,155	$ 4,155	$ 6,272

Financing.

Sue requires approximately $40,000 to finance Quality Cuts. She intends to invest $10,000 of her own money and borrow $30,000 from the Royal Bank. Current interest rates are 8 percent and the term of the loan is five years. The loan repayment schedule is shown below:

YEAR	PAYMENT	PRINCIPAL	INTEREST	BALANCE
1	$28,333	$25,933	$2,400	$4,067
2	1,340	1,014	326	3,053
3	1,260	1,015	245	2,038
4	1,180	1,016	164	1,022
5	1,104	1,022	82	0

Bookkeeping/Accounting System.

The computer system that is purchased will take care of all aspects of a beauty salon, including the financial aspects. The ACCPAC software program for small businesses will be used to monitor and evaluate performance. Monthly financial statements will be prepared and reviewed by Sue and her husband.

The credit policy for the shop is quite simple: cash, cheque, or charge. No credit is granted, except for clients in very good standing and then only with Sue's approval. Cheques are accepted with identification for unknown customers. Also, major credit cards such as Visa, MasterCard, and bank debit cards are accepted.

PERSONNEL

Quality Cuts will begin operations with five hairdressers and Sue Holland as owner-manager. The organizational chart for the staff is shown below:

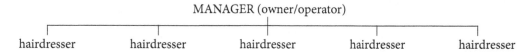

The salon hours follow those of the mall: 9:30 a.m.–5:30 p.m. Monday to Wednesday and Saturday; 9:30 a.m.–9:00 p.m. Thursday and Friday. It is not open on Sundays and will not extend its hours during the Christmas season.

Hairdressers work on commission, so the estimate of wages paid out over a year makes up a percentage of total sales. As stated earlier in this plan, secondary data suggest that this percentage averages 53.5 percent of total sales in Alberta, which is used to calculate the wages and salaries paid out over the first year of $79,844.

Hairdressers work 16 to 24 hours per week. This is in accordance with industry averages as most hairdressers/stylists prefer to work part time. A work schedule is drawn up at least one week in advance and accommodates client preference for certain hairdressers/stylists.

Employee Recruitment and Training.

Skill training is limited in this field of work as hairdressers have to attend a qualified beauty school and earn their certificate. However, Quality Cuts devotes extra effort to stressing to each employee the importance of customer service and projecting the right image. Explanation of company procedures and the commission payment plan is also be a part of the training.

Recruitment also stresses that the workers project the image that the beauty salon itself projects. Sue has already made contact with three hairdressers/stylists who fit the Quality Cuts image and have agreed to work for her. Interviews will be held to select the remaining employees. This should lead to the hiring of those who work well with the customers and other hairdressers.

Policies.

The following policies will be in effect at Quality Cuts:

1. Employees must appear neat and clean.
2. No smoking is allowed in the customer area of the shop.
3. The approved uniform top must be worn at all times.
4. No food or drink is allowed in the customer area.
5. Employees will receive a 20 percent discount on all hair care products.
6. The customer is always right.

Evaluation.

Employees' performance will be evaluated monthly on the basis of revenues generated, referrals, sales of hair care products, customer complaints, and progress toward employee objectives. As mentioned previously, employees' pay will be based partly on commissions of appointments as well as other sales.

LEGAL

Legal Structure.

Quality Cuts will operate as a sole proprietorship. This will allow Sue to maintain flexibility and control of operations in the first few years.

Licensing.

The licences necessary to operate this business are as follows:

Development application	$ 31.00
Occupancy permit	20.00
Business licence	62.00
Total licensing costs	$113.00

Insurance.

Insurance is a legal necessity for this business. The breakdown of insurance is as follows:

Commercial general insurance (covering stock and building)	$190.00
Money and security insurance	75.00
Employee dishonesty bond	150.00
Malpractice insurance	190.00
Total insurance (for the first year)	$605.00

FIGURE 1 Shop Layout

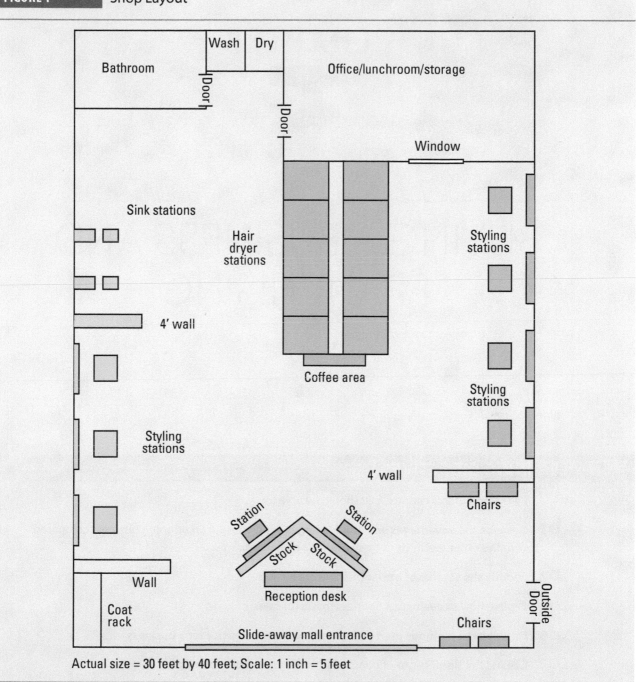

Bathroom

Wash | Dry

Office/lunchroom/storage

Door

Door

Window

Sink stations

Hair dryer stations

Styling stations

4' wall

Styling stations

Styling stations

4' wall

Chairs

Station   Station

Stock   Stock

Coffee area

Wall

Coat rack

Reception desk

Slide-away mall entrance

Outside Door

Chairs

Actual size = 30 feet by 40 feet; Scale: 1 inch = 5 feet

For more information on the resources available from McGraw-Hill Ryerson, go to www.mcgrawhill.ca/he/solutions.

CHAPTER
5

BUYING A BUSINESS AND FRANCHISING

LEARNING OBJECTIVES

By the end of this chapter, you should be able to:

LO1 Describe the advantages and disadvantages of purchasing an ongoing business compared with the other methods of small business ownership.

LO2 Identify the sources of businesses that are for sale.

LO3 Explain how to evaluate a business that is for sale.

LO4 Describe the methods used in determining the price to pay for a business.

LO5 Discuss the significance of franchising in the Canadian economy.

LO6 Explain the various types of franchises available for small business.

LO7 List the relative strengths and weaknesses of franchising as a method of starting a small business.

LO8 Explain how to evaluate a franchise opportunity.

LO9 Discuss how to organize a franchising system.

SMALL BUSINESS PROFILE

ANNE CAMPBELL *NovaScotian Crystal*

Well, as the saying goes, second time's the charm, but you can likely forgive Anne Campbell if she changes the words slightly to "second time is crystal." Campbell recently purchased NovaScotian Crystal (NS Crystal, www.novascotiancrystal.com), Canada's only mouth-blown crystal, from receivership. Campbell, who was originally involved with starting the company in Halifax, saw an opportunity to buy the company's assets and rescue the business from closing. "I've always had a passion for the business, and when I heard about what was happening, I wondered if there might be a place for me here."

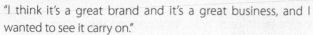
Republished with permission from The Halifax Herald Ltd.

"I think it's a great brand and it's a great business, and I wanted to see it carry on."

NS Crystal has a long history in the province and in Canada. The company was founded over 20 years ago as craftsmen from Ireland established the business with the goal of maintaining the traditional mouth-blown process while creating a premium Canadian branded crystal. While enjoying periods of success, the company has recently fallen on hard times in 2008 and again in 2013. During the financial crisis of 2008, previous owner Rod McCulloch placed the firm into receivership to protect it from its creditors while he negotiated a repayment plan. McCulloch who has invested and lost over $1 million in the business settled his firm's debts when creditors agreed to accept shares in the company instead of payment. Given that the other alternative was likely closing the business down, creditors no doubt saw this as a way to give the business time to recover with the hopes of eventually receiving some payment. Now in 2013, the business is back into receivership owing creditors slightly less than $2 million. McCulloch cites the lack of efficient manufacturing along with the burden of managing a large debt as two factors contributing to the company's financial problems.

Why would Campbell buy a company that was failing? Common reasons cited by entrepreneurs for purchasing a struggling business is they believe the company's financial situation can improve or they can add needed capital to push the business forward. Campbell believes she can do both. As past owner Rod McCulloch states, the firm was in desperate need of a second furnace to increase efficiency

and production during busy times. Unfortunately for McCulloch, while they did add the furnace, the learning curve for the new equipment was steeper than he thought, and the business did not get to benefit from its purchase. According to McCulloch, "What we didn't have then was a second blowing operation; we believe we're on the verge of getting it there. We just didn't quite make it. So I think the learning has been done and that someone coming in should be able to pick up from that point forward." McCulloch further states the company has a great brand and a loyal following but he has been unable to produce crystal at low prices—something which the new furnace could change.

Campbell also hopes to add some capital to the business and will benefit from not having to take over the unsecured debt of the company. While the terms of the sale are private, Campbell has stated she will not be assuming the debt as part of her purchase. As stated above, a major challenge for McCulloch was managing his high debt load, especially during slow sales months of January through April. Even though sales were slow, the company had to meet its debt obligations and continue to pay all of its fixed costs, including wages, as it had to manufacture 12 months a year, even though most revenue only came in for six. McCulloch says, "From January through June, because we are a production facility, the money keeps going out the door. We don't cut back in our expenses the way a normal retail store would, for example. So we've got the production side, and yet there's no money coming in. So we really need a lot of cash to fund the operation through the first six months of the year so that we can then collect all that money back in the last six months of the year. And we just got to the point where we didn't have enough and I didn't have any more to put in." While Campbell will likely have to continue with this boom-and-bust cycles of sales, she will be doing so without dealing with the company's debt.

Campbell is quite optimistic the company can be turned around and is hoping to grow the business moving forward. She notes that the firm has a great brand and a strong web presence, and she hopes to increase both online and corporate sales. Campbell says the new furnace will enable NS Crystal to produce larger and more expensive items and this will help grow revenue in the future.

NOVASCOTIAN CRYSTAL
www.novascotiancrystal.com

Sources: Melanie Patten, "Buyer Steps Forward for NovaScotian Crystal," *Metro News*, March 14, 2013; Roger Taylor, "New Owner May Revive Beloved NovaScotian Crystal," *Chronicle Herald,* February 21, 2013; and Chris Lambie, "NovaScotian Crystal to Go Into Receivership," *Chronicle Herald*, February 15, 2013.

PURCHASING AN EXISTING BUSINESS   LO1

An alternative to organizing a business from the ground up is to purchase an existing business. Many entrepreneurs prefer this method of becoming small business owners. Thirty-eight of Canada's fastest-growing companies have acquired other firms in recent years. Of these, 22 firms can attribute more than 20 percent of their growth to mergers and buyouts.[1]

ADVANTAGES OF PURCHASING

The following are some reasons that buying a business may be an attractive alternative.

1. Reduction of Risk.

The most significant advantage is that the acquired firm has an established image and track record. If the firm has been profitable, the entrepreneur would need only to continue its current strategy to be successful with the existing customer base. When compared with starting a business from scratch, buying a business is often preferred because the entrepreneur will have actual knowledge that a market exists and what amount of revenue can be expected.

2. Reduction in Start-up Time.

Since an ongoing business already has employees, a location, and products, it will take much less time to acquire the business than start a venture from scratch. For example, if a furniture store feels the cost of transport is too high and it would be a good complementary business to own, it would take much less time to purchase an ongoing shipping company than start one from scratch.

3. Financing.

Finding financing dollars to buy an existing successful business is easier than finding money to start a company from scratch. Since the entrepreneur is buying an existing company then potential financers of the deal will know if the business is profitable and will be able to calculate a rate of return on their investment. It may be challenging, however, to find financing to purchase a struggling business.

4. Location.

New customers are already familiar with the location.

5. Established Marketing Structure.

An acquired firm has its existing channel and sales structure. Known suppliers, wholesalers, retailers, and manufacturers' reps are important assets to an entrepreneur. Additionally, the business may have already established credit terms with suppliers, something that is often difficult for new businesses to initiate. With this structure already in place, the entrepreneur can concentrate on improving or expanding the acquired business.

6. Cost.

The actual cost of acquiring a business can be lower than other methods of expansion or starting from scratch.

7. Existing Employees.

The employees of an existing business can be an important asset to the acquisition process. They know how to run the business and can help ensure that the business will continue in its successful mode. They already have established relationships with customers, suppliers, and channel members and can reassure these groups when a new owner takes over the business.

8. More Opportunity to Be Creative.

Since the entrepreneur does not have to be concerned with finding suppliers, channel members, hiring new employees, or creating customer awareness, more time can be spent assessing opportunities to expand or strengthen the existing business and tap into potential synergies between the businesses.

9. Reduce the Number of Competitors.

By buying an ongoing business, the entrepreneur can reduce the number of competitors operating in a market. For example, if there are five industrial cleaning companies in your area and an entrepreneur starts a new business from scratch, he will have five competitors and perhaps a sixth of the market share. But if he buys one of the existing businesses, he will have only four competitors and perhaps a fifth of the market share. For example, Darren Throop owner of eOne (www.entertainmentone.com), a Toronto-based distributor of independent movies and TV shows, became the largest player in Canada when the company acquired its major competitor Alliance Films. Throop states, "By buying Alliance, we took out our main competitor in our two primary markets."[2]

DISADVANTAGES OF PURCHASING

A prospective purchaser should also be aware of the potential disadvantages of purchasing a business. Many of these problems concern the condition of the assets and other aspects of the business.

1. Marginal Success Record.

Most ventures that are for sale have an erratic, marginally successful, or even unprofitable track record. It is important to review the records and meet with important constituents to assess that record in terms of the business's future potential. For example, if the store layout is poor, this factor can be rectified; but if the location is poor, the entrepreneur might do better using some other expansion method. Merging two businesses also comes with a host of complicated issues such as: Will the cultures of the firms work together? Will the new business drain capital and time for the on-going business? Don Lenz, a Toronto-based consultant points out that 50 percent of business buyouts result in failure.[3]

2. Physical Facilities.

The building and equipment may be old, obsolete, or below current standards. In addition, they may not be completely paid for or may have charges or liens against them. If the prospective buyer is unfamiliar with how to evaluate the condition of such facilities, he or she should enlist the services of a professional appraiser.

TAKEOVER HELPS COMPANY MEET ITS TARGET

Mel Mogil's Toronto-based company California Innovations (www.californiainnovations.com) was a successful manufacturer of coolers, freezer bags, diaper bags, and lunch bags, with sales in more than 25 countries. However, they were prevented from being the market leader because of stiff competition from the Chicago company Arctic Zone, which had the giant Target Store account in the U.S. tied up. Repeated attempts to break into this market had failed. However, in 2004, Mogil learned that Arctic Zone might be up for sale, and even though he had never participated in a takeover, he immediately pursued the opportunity. The acquisition took place along with the large contract with Target, and it has propelled California Creations into the market leadership position. Sales increased 22 percent in the first year, and increased enthusiasm was evident with employees as they saw the company growing and progressing. Being the market leader has also led to more credibility with off-shore manufacturers and new customers.[4]

CALIFORNIA INNOVATIONS HAS USED AN ACQUISITION OF THEIR MAIN RIVAL TO GROW MARKET SHARE.
AP Photo/Larry Crowe/The Canadian Press

Discussion Questions

1. What are some of the questions Mogul should have asked prior to buying the business?
2. Given the complexity of integrating one business into another would you have recommended Mogul pursue this strategy? Why, or why not?

3. Personnel.

The business's employees may be incompetent or unmotivated. They may also resist the new ownership and reduce their productivity or even quit once the transfer of ownership is completed. The potential buyer is well advised to visit with current employees to ascertain their attitudes toward change.

4. Inventory.

The inventory may be obsolete or hard to sell. This factor may be especially critical in a retail store or a high-technology firm. The age of inventory can often be determined through internal records or by price-tag coding.

5. Accounts Receivable.

The outstanding accounts may be uncollectible or at least costly and time consuming to collect. An evaluation of the length of time these accounts have been outstanding can be helpful in evaluating this potential problem.

6. Financial Condition.

The financial health of the business may be deteriorating or less positive than it appears in the financial statements. Always conduct an in-depth evaluation of the firm's financial condition before purchase.

7. Market and Key Customers.

The market for the business's product or service may be deteriorating, or a strong new competitor may be about to enter the market. In addition, factors such as the economic state, interest rates, or government policy could adversely affect the market. In addition, some firms are reliant on one or two key customers for the majority of their revenue. The prospective purchaser will want to ensure status of these customers prior to buying the business.

8. Overvalued.

It is possible that the actual purchase price is inflated due to the established image, customer base, channel members, or suppliers. If the entrepreneur has to pay too much for a business, it is possible that the return on investment will be unacceptable. It is important to look at the investment required in purchasing a business and at the potential profit and establish a reasonable payback to justify the investment.

9. Paying Too Much for Goodwill.

Many businesses that are for sale include some element of goodwill in the sale price. Goodwill is essentially the favourable reputation the business has established under the tenure of the previous owner. Often the seller overestimates the goodwill associated with his business. A good

---

INCIDENT 5-2

ROCKY MOUNTAIN SOAP COMPANY INC.

Karina Birch and Cameron Baty purchased Rocky Mountain Soap Company (www.rockymountainsoap.com) in January 2000. This company, located in Canmore, Alberta, just beside the beautiful Rocky Mountains, had been in existence since 1995 and had established a small niche in the natural handmade soap products market, with gross sales of $90,000 annually.

Although the business was successful before the purchase, Birch and Baty realized that there was potential to substantially expand the business after they attended a tradeshow in the United States. They saw a growing market that was virtually untapped by Canadian manufacturers and that had not been recognized by the previous owners of the company.

The pair bought the business and set plans in motion to expand all phases of the business. Taking the business to the next level required updating their processes, buying specialized equipment, and learning to become more efficient with the staff they had. A key to the successful purchase and growth strategy involved carrying out extensive research with similar companies in the United States. By doing this, they were able to find out what these companies were

KARINA BIRCH (PICTURED HERE) AND CAMERON BATY PURCHASED ROCKY MOUNTAIN SOAP COMPANY AND EXPANDED THE BUSINESS BY TAKING ADVANTAGE OF OPPORTUNITIES THEY SAW IN THE MARKETPLACE.
Photo courtesy of Rocky Mountain Soap Company & Craig Douce

doing in the areas of manufacturing, marketing, and distribution.

Cameron and Karina's efforts have led to growth and success for the company, which is now the largest manufacturer of handmade soaps in Canada. Revenues are over $7 million annually. The product line has expanded to 27 scents that are marketed through eight company-owned stores in Western Canada, as well as the Internet. Rocky Mountain Soap Co. products have been featured in many magazines such as *Chatelaine, Western Living,* and *Fashion.* The owners also take an interest in the community and a close relationship with their customer base by sponsoring community events and maintaining an extensive customer database.[5]

Discussion Questions

1. Why was the acquisition of Rocky Mountain Soap Company Inc. such a success?

2. What are the advantages of buying a successful company compared with buying a company that may be struggling?

3. Use Internet resources to find out the current state of Rocky Mountain Soap Company. What are the company's major strengths, weaknesses, opportunities, and threats?

rule of thumb suggested by some financial advisers is that no more than 20 percent of the selling price should be allocated for goodwill. Other small business experts go a step further and claim that you should not spend any money on goodwill when buying a business. For example, Jeanne Lawrence bought what she thought was a successful clothing store in Winnipeg. But when she took over the store, she was inundated with complaints from current and past customers. Within two years, she lost most of her clientele due to the actions of the previous owner.

Many of the above potential problems associated with buying a business can be uncovered through a detailed investigation of the operations of the business before purchase. Some of the key evaluation areas are discussed later in this chapter.

SOURCES OF BUSINESSES FOR SALE   LO2

Where can the entrepreneur who has decided to purchase a business find out which businesses are for sale? The following are common sources.

Internet.

Numerous ads for businesses for sale can be found on the Internet, including such sites as Kijiji, online newspaper classified ads, and a host of other websites. The Multiple Listing Network (MLS) (www.mls.ca) maintains a list of commercial properties and businesses for sale on its sister site ICX (www.icx.ca). Entrepreneurs looking to purchase a business can likely find many opportunities by using search engines such as Google (www.google.ca) or Bing (www.bing.com).

Government Departments.

The small business or industry department in most provinces and territories is usually aware of businesses for sale. They may also know of communities that want to attract a particular type of business.

Trade Journals.

Trade journals frequently carry listings of businesses that are for sale in that industry. This may be a more effective source than more general classified ads.

Real Estate Brokers.

Many entrepreneurs purchase their businesses with the assistance of a broker whose job is to get buyers and sellers together and help negotiate the sale. If the prospective purchaser knows a certain broker fairly well, he or she might request that this individual be on the lookout for the type of business desired. Brokers are aware of most businesses that are, or soon will be, for sale that and some brokers even specialize in businesses. Toronto-based consultant Ken Smith says that brokers can be particularly helpful when entering a new market in which an entrepreneur may lack business contacts. While there is a cost of using a broker, generally the seller will pay their commission out of the purchase price.[6]

Other Professionals.

Other professionals such as lawyers, accountants, business appraisers, and bankers often know of businesses for sale. Some prospective purchasers have found excellent opportunities by sending these professionals letters requesting information about businesses for sale. In addition, organizations such as chambers of commerce may offer match-up services. One example is COIN (Canadian Opportunities Investment Network).

Word of Mouth.

In their association with businesspeople, entrepreneurs often learn about business opportunities through word of mouth. For example, Jim Iredale was a frequent customer of Ware House Hobbies, a Winnipeg-based hobby store. During one visit, he was chatting with the owner who was looking to sell the business. During the course of the conversation, the owner offered to sell the store to Iredale. A short time later, Iredale purchased the business due to his personal interest in the hobby business. Toby Chu, president and CEO of Vancouver-based CIBT Education Group (http://cibt.net), a private college, takes a direct approach to purchasing businesses. Chu uses the Internet to find prospective companies he may want to purchase and investigates their reputation, brand, and financial performance. If he is happy with what he learns, he contacts the company to see if he can buy the business.[7]

EVALUATING A BUSINESS FOR SALE   LO3

A wise purchase decision may require considerable investigation. The prospective buyer should look into several key areas of a business before making a decision to purchase.

INDUSTRY ANALYSIS

The entrepreneur should be well informed about the industry in which the business operates. Ideally, this information should come from an extensive background or experience in that industry. Some specific areas to investigate are discussed below.

Sales and Profit Trends of the Industry.

- The degree of competition, the number of competitors entering or leaving the industry, and the nature of competitors' strategies
- The state of the economy in the market area and the extent to which changes in the economy affect the industry
- Legal restrictions currently affecting the operations of the business as well as relevant pending legislation or political pressure
- Social concerns that may adversely affect the industry in the future

One or more of these areas could be significant in determining the future success of the proposed purchase. As a result, each should be thoroughly investigated unless the buyer has considerable experience in the industry.

THE PREVIOUS OWNER

The entrepreneur should ask the following questions about the previous owner of the business:

- Why is the previous owner selling the business? The often advertised reason, "because of poor health," may refer to financial rather than physical health.
- Is the previous owner a well-known and respected member of the community? Has this reputation contributed significantly to the success of the business? Will this success continue once that individual is no longer associated with the business?
- Will the previous owner be available—temporarily, at least—to provide assistance and advice to the new owner? This help can be invaluable, especially to a purchaser who

lacks experience in the industry or market. For example, Doug Robbins, president of Hamilton-based Robbinex Inc. (www.robbinex.com), a business brokerage and consulting company, says in an ideal situation, the owner will remain involved as a full-time employee for a short period of time following the sale of the firm. He will then gradually reduce his involvement over time. Robbins actually recommends that a management contract be signed where the seller has to provide strategic advice for a period up to five years.[8]

- Is the previous owner willing to finance the purchase by spreading it over a number of years? This may be helpful to the purchaser and advantageous tax-wise to the seller.

- What will the previous owner do after he or she sells the business? To guard against the previous owner starting a similar business in the same market area, the prospective purchaser might insist that a non-competitive clause be included in the sales agreement.

FINANCIAL CONDITION OF THE BUSINESS

The financial condition of a prospective business is perhaps the most important area to evaluate. Care should be taken in evaluating the financial statements and assessing their validity.

Validity of Financial Statements.

Since accountants can use a variety of methods in increasing or decreasing the net income of a business, an entrepreneur should attempt to validate as much of the reported information as possible. Entrepreneurs should ask for audited financial statements. In many cases, most small and medium businesses will not have audited statements and would usually be unwilling to undertake the costs associated with producing them. Instead, entrepreneurs can ask to see income tax receipts, sales receipts, and any other financial records that are available. If the seller of the business is not willing to provide any of this information, the entrepreneur should complete a very thorough evaluation of the business prior to buying it. One entrepreneur recounts that he considered buying a takeout restaurant when he was informed that the business, located in a busy waterfront location, was quite profitable. When he asked to see the financial records for the company, he was handed a one-page income statement for the previous year. The seller became upset when the interested entrepreneur asked to see further financial statements and proof that the business was, indeed, profitable. The entrepreneur refused to buy the business and a short time later watched the seller close the business. Small business consultant Don Letz says prospective buyers should pay attention to the condition of the financial records and how long it takes sellers to respond to questions. Letz states if a seller appears to be scrambling to find key information it may be a sign that the firm is poorly managed.[9]

Financial Performance of the Business.

To judge the financial performance of the business, the entrepreneur will want to see income statements, balance sheets, and cash flow statements. If possible, the entrepreneur would like to see or calculate on his own complete liquidity, productivity, and profitability debt ratios. These ratios should be compared with industry benchmarks, when available, to determine if the business is in good financial shape. The entrepreneur should look for other clues to determine the financial health of the business. He should consider trends in profits, costs, revenue, and so forth. Ideally, the business has been experiencing growth in revenue and profits. After seeing these documents, entrepreneurs will very quickly be able to determine their potential return on investment and often decide whether they should investigate the business further.

Naturally, one would hope the business is strong financially and profitable in its operations. In some situations, however, a business may be a good purchase even if it is unprofitable or has a negative reputation at the time of evaluation. Such situations might include the following:

- The current owner is incompetent or lacks knowledge about the industry, and the purchaser has the competence and knowledge to turn the business around.

- The industry is, or will shortly be, in a growth position that might improve the firm's profitability or resale value.

- The major contributor to the firm's unprofitability is lack of capital leading to high interest costs, and the purchaser has the needed capital to inject into the business.

CONDITION OF THE ASSETS

Several business assets may require thorough inspection and, for non-liquid assets, possibly an appraisal by an independent appraiser. The fee for this service is generally reasonable and may be well worth it. Assets to value in this manner are discussed below.

Liquid Assets (Cash and Investments).

An important question to a prospective purchaser concerns how easily the liquid assets can be converted to cash. There may be special terms or conditions with respect to these assets, such as the period on a term deposit.

INCIDENT 5-3

WILL NOVASCOTIAN CRYSTAL BE SAVED?

As discussed in the opening Small Business Profile, Anne Campbell has recently acquired NovaScotian Crystal (NS Crystal), Canada's only mouth-blown crystal company. Campbell is hoping that a new furnace and an injection in capital will turn the business around. While the terms and conditions of the sale are private, Campbell has bought the company out of receivership. Receivership is a form of credit protection for businesses enabling them to keep operating while they negotiate a settlement with their creditors. In this case, NS Crystal owed roughly $1.7 million to investors, lenders, and suppliers. As part of the sale, Campbell has indicated she has not assumed any of this liability and will now be able to operate the company without having to meet these debt obligations. Interestingly, this is the second time NS Crystal has gone into receivership in the past five years. The last time, most creditors were not paid and took shares in the company in lieu of money. These creditors, much like their current creditors, would be lucky to get any of their money back as a result of Campbell's purchase. Campbell is now optimistic that the business will succeed and she will be able to grow the fine crystal company, which employs 46 people and whose retail store serves as a tourist attraction on the Halifax waterfront.

Discussion Questions

1. Re-read the opening Small Business Profile; based on this information and the material above, do you think Campbell will be able to turn the business around? Why, or why not?

2. Based on the information in the chapter, would you have purchased the business? Why, or why not? What are some of the negative and positive characteristics of the business from a purchaser's standpoint?

3. Do you think it is ethical for Campbell to take over the operations of the business in a deal that likely saw unsecured creditors and investors left with next to nothing, in terms of payment? Why, or why not?

4. Given NS Crystal is both a local employer and a tourist attraction, should the government have stepped in and provided the business with some financial assistance? Note that some government agencies are listed as creditors of the firm but the amounts would not be classified as significant. Why, or why not?

5. What are the key success factors for the company moving forward?

Accounts Receivable.

Have accounts receivable been aged? How many may be uncollectible? (Accounts receivable aging is discussed in detail in Chapter 9.) Enlisting the services of a professional accountant to assist in this regard may be well worth the cost.

Inventory.

Is any inventory old, obsolete, or damaged? A detailed evaluation of inventory should be done by someone with knowledge and experience in this area.

Building and Equipment.

Are the buildings and equipment old or obsolete? Are they comparable to competitors' facilities? Are there any liens against them?

Systems and Processes.

Examine the accounting and reporting systems in the business. Are they efficient, accurate, and timely? Are they compatible with your own system? What will be the cost of changing the system, if necessary?

Real Estate.

What are the land taxes and service costs? If the premises are leased, is the lease transferable? What are the terms and conditions of the lease? Has the location experienced a high turnover of businesses in the past?

Goodwill.

What value does the owner place on goodwill? Goodwill is the intangible value of such things as reputation, past experience, expertise, and prominence in the industry or community. Is this value realistic and reasonable? Generally, goodwill costs should not exceed 20 percent of the cost of the assets, even for well-established businesses. Further assistance to evaluate the value of the assets and even the value of the entire business may be obtained by enlisting the services of a qualified chartered business evaluator.

QUALITY OF PERSONNEL

The prospective purchaser should evaluate the efficiency of the business's personnel. How do they compare with employees in other similar businesses? An important factor is personnel reaction to the new owner after the purchase. It may be wise for the buyer to meet with key personnel to better evaluate their reaction to the sale of the business. What is the staff turnover? Peter Bryne, CEO of Edmonton-based Andersons Liquor (www.ruminvestor.com/andersons-liquor), says he looks at the staff of all the firms he is buying. Not only is Bryne looking for talent which he can use to stay on and help manage the business but he is also looking for managerial gaps. He says many small business owners have limited experience in larger operations and he often needs to recruits external people to help in managing the acquired companies. The strategy appears to be working, as Bryne has acquired 38 businesses, and sales have grown by $40 million over the past eight years.[10]

EXTERNAL RELATIONSHIPS—SUPPLIERS AND CUSTOMERS

The investigation should include a review of those organizations or agencies currently essential to the operations of the business. Will these relationships continue, and if so, under what terms or conditions? Some organizations to contact include suppliers, financial institutions, and key customers. For example, Dave Miller, CEO of Toronto-based Sentry Metrics (www.sentrymetrics. com), has been involved in numerous acquisitions. Miller states he requests a customer list of any firm he is considering acquiring and then meets with some of the customers. Miller used these meetings as part of his assessment of the firm, as he notes that a company that has strong customer relations is an indication of good management and employees.[11]

CONDITION OF THE RECORDS

Other records to review are credit files, personnel files, sales reports, contracts, and customer lists. These items can be very valuable to the operations of the business and should be included with the business when it is purchased.

Appendix 5A at the conclusion of this chapter presents a comprehensive checklist of considerations in purchasing a business.

DETERMINING THE PRICE OR VALUE OF A BUSINESS   LO4

If the preceding evaluation of the business shows positive results and the prospective purchaser decides to buy the business, he or she must make a decision concerning the price to pay for it. Is the asking price reasonable? Should a lower counter-offer be made? Several methods can be used to arrive at a price for a business.

There are four approaches to valuing a business. The first is by market value. The second relies heavily on asset value. The third uses the earnings potential of the business as a basis for determining value. The fourth uses a combination of asset value and earnings potential. Each method can help the entrepreneur make a general estimate of the purchase price. It should be kept in mind, however, that the buyer, the seller, or the business may possess unique characteristics that cannot be incorporated into a formula. Such situations will require adjustments to a formula-determined price. More detailed coverage of the financial terms used in price determination is found in Chapter 9.

MARKET VALUE

In a free market, the right price is the one on which the purchaser and seller agree or, in other words, where demand and supply meet. When applied to a business purchase, this price is called the *market value*. To use the market value method effectively, the prospective purchaser must collect data on the market values of many similar businesses. In many markets, the number of sales transactions of similar businesses is fairly small; thus, little data may be available. In such cases, other methods of valuation will be more useful.

ASSET VALUE

There are two approaches to valuing a business using value of assets as a base: book value and replacement value.

Book Value.

The book value method lists the business at the net balance sheet value of its assets minus the value of its liabilities (Chapter 9 provides the fundamentals of balance sheet assets and liabilities). This method generally understates the value of the business by a significant amount. For this reason, the book value price may form a lower limit to determining the price of the business.

Replacement Value.

The replacement value method lists the replacement cost of the assets at their value. Because the assets of an existing business typically are not new, the replacement value method tends to overstate the value of the business. When coupled with the liability side of the balance sheet, the replacement cost method may result in an upper limit for the price to pay for the business.

EARNINGS VALUE

The prospective purchaser is interested not only in asset value but also in how the business will perform in the future. Therefore, earnings potential is another factor to be taken into account in setting the price of a business. Pretax earnings or income should be used, as tax rates vary by province or territory and by industry.

It is also important to use average earnings in calculating earnings potential rather than just the most recent year's net income figure. When using average earnings, extraordinary items that have affected income should be deleted to make the estimate a "true" average. This is called *normalizing earnings*. Many analysts will use the previous five years' average of earnings. If earnings appear to be unstable from year to year, a weighted-average calculation might be used. The determination of average earnings using the weighted-average approach is shown in Figure 5-1. This method gives a greater weight to the most recent year's earnings in arriving at average earnings.

Two specific methods of estimating the purchase value of the business use earnings as a base.

Capitalization of Earnings Method.

This method is commonly used to arrive at a quick estimate of the price of a business. The capitalized value is found by dividing average earnings of the business by a specified rate of return expressed as a decimal. This specified rate of return figure can be obtained by using bank interest (a risk factor of a few percentage points should be added) or another required rate of return percentage for the investment. It can also be obtained by using average return on tangible net worth statistics from such sources as Dun and Bradstreet and Statistics Canada. Generally,

| FIGURE 5-1 | Calculating Weighted-Average Earnings for a Business |

	AVERAGE EARNINGS	WEIGHTED AVERAGE EARNINGS (EARNINGS × WEIGHTS FACTOR)				
Last year	$5,000	5,000	×	5	=	25,000
Two years ago	4,000	4,000	×	4	=	16,000
Three years ago	7,000	7,000	×	3	=	21,000
Four years ago	10,000	10,000	×	2	=	20,000
Five years ago	$14,000	14,000	×	1	=	14,000
	$40,000			15		96,000
	Average Earnings		Weighted Average Earnings			
	40,000/5 = 8000		96,000/15 = 6,400			

FIGURE 5-2

Capitalization of Earnings Formula

$$\frac{\text{Average earnings}}{\substack{\text{Predetermined interest rate or} \\ \text{rate of return required for investment}}} = \text{Capitalized value}$$

capitalization rates are 12 percent to 20 percent for well-established businesses and 25 percent to 50 percent for a new unproven business.[12] Figure 5-2 illustrates the capitalization of earnings formula.

Figure 5-3 illustrates a calculation of capitalized earnings value using industry averages. This method measures the firm's ability to earn profits in relation to the capital invested. For example, for a book and stationery store, it will take $45,450 paid for the business to earn $10,000 after taxes if the store were run at the median level. Figure 5-3 also illustrates Dun and Bradstreet averages for various industries.

Times Earnings Method.

This method arbitrarily multiplies average earnings by a number, usually between 1 and 10, based on past sales and industry experience, to arrive at the price for the business. This is often called the *price-earnings ratio*. Small businesses are usually sold at between four and five times earnings, according to the U.S. Small Business Administration, although recently some Internet companies have sold at much higher multiples. This number can vary significantly for very small businesses. Therefore, the advice of an experienced business broker or accountant valuator should be sought.

COMBINATION METHODS

Because both the asset value and the earnings value are important components of the true value of the business, some methods attempt to combine both values to estimate an appropriate price. Two combination methods can be used to arrive at such a price. The first is an analytical approach, and the second is a method based on historical transactions or experience in the industry. Each will be discussed briefly.

Analytical Method.

This method combines three factors to arrive at the value for the business: adjusted net worth, past earnings, and future earnings.

To obtain adjusted net worth, take the market value of tangible assets, subtract liabilities, and then add goodwill. If the business's assets are worth $220,000 with liabilities of $60,000 and goodwill of $40,000, then the adjusted net worth is $220,000 − $60,000 + $40,000 = $200,000.

To arrive at a value for past earnings, these earnings (net income) are "capitalized" by multiplying earnings by a number usually between 5 and 10. If the firm is judged to be very solid, the factor used should be closer to 10, and if considerable risk exists, a factor of 5 would be more appropriate. If average past earnings are $40,000 and a capitalization rate of 8 is used, the earnings value is $320,000.

A future earnings value is established by discounting future earnings of the business. This is done by applying a discount factor to current earnings. Such factors reflect the fact that future earnings flows are worth more today than they will be in the future. If the business earns

FIGURE 5-3 Capitalized Earnings Value

LINE OF BUSINESS	NET PROFITS TO TANGIBLE NET WORTH AS A PERCENTAGE*	CAPITALIZED EARNINGS VALUE†
Retail		
Book and stationery stores	22.0	$45,450
Clothing, men's	12.9	77,520
Clothing, women's	12.8	78,125
Drugstores	20.7	48,310
Food stores	10.8	92,595
Gasoline service stations	23.1	43,290
Hardware	14.5	68,965
Jewellery store	8.3	120,480
Manufacturers		
Appliances, small	18.4	54,350
Bakery products	17.8	56,180
Machine shops	19.7	50,760
Meat products	11.8	84,745
Sash, door, and millwork plants	29.0	34,480
Soft drinks	34.9	28,655
Sporting goods and toys	11.0	90,910
Construction		
Building contractors	23.3	42,920
Services		
Hotels	15.5	64,515
Agriculture, forestry, and fishing		
Agriculture	12.2	81,965

Sources: Adapted from Paul Harmon, *Small Business Management—A Practical Approach* (New York: D. Van Nostrand), p. 76. Figures updated from Dun and Bradstreet, *Key Business Ratios.*

*Tangible net worth is net worth less intangibles, that is, copyrights, goodwill, trademarks, and patents. This figure can be found in Dun and Bradstreet, *Key Business Ratios.*

†Represents the investment or tangible net worth required to earn $10,000 in profits after taxes, assuming the firm is operating at median level, calculated in the following manner:

$$\frac{\$10,000}{\text{Net profit to tangible net worth as percentage}} = \text{Capitalized earning value}$$

$40,000 today and a discount factor of 10 percent is applied, the future earnings flow make the business worth $400,000 today.

To combine the above factors into one value reasonable for the business requires experience, judgment, and insight. For example, if the business has considerable assets, more emphasis should be given to the net worth method, whereas if the business is a service business, the earnings methods will be given more prominence in the combination. In the above examples, if a 50 percent emphasis is used for assets and 25 percent for each of the earnings factors is used, the combined value for this business would be:

$$(\$200,000 \times 0.50) + (\$320,000 \times 0.25) + (\$400,000 \times 0.25) = \$280,000$$

Historical Method.

This method uses historical experience in determining relevant indicators of the components of the value of a business. Figure 5-4 illustrates such an example.

As mentioned previously, determining the price of a business by using a formula may provide a good estimate of a business's worth, but the unique characteristics of each situation may alter the price offered and paid for the business.

THE PURCHASE TRANSACTION

The entrepreneur should enlist the services of professionals such as lawyers and accountants to assist in the purchase decision. Once a purchase price and other terms and conditions have been agreed on, the buyer should enlist the services of a lawyer to draw up the purchase agreement and close the transaction. This helps ensure that clear title to the business is transferred and post-purchase difficulties are minimized. The purchase agreement should cover the following areas:

- The purchase price, including principal and interest amounts
- Payment date(s)—when and to whom payments are to be made
- A detailed list of all assets to be included in the purchase. It may be advisable to purchase the assets of the business rather than the business itself. By doing this, the purchaser may avoid potential negative intangibles associated with the business.

FIGURE 5-4	Combination Methods for Pricing a Business

TYPE OF BUSINESS	PRICE OFFERING RANGE
Accounting Firms	100–125% of annual revenues
Auto Dealers	2–3 years' net income + tangible assets
Book Stores	15% of annual sales + inventory
Coffee Shops	40–45% of annual sales + inventory
Courier Services	70% of annual sales
Daycare Centres	2–3 times annual cash flow
Dental Practices	60–70% of annual revenues
Employment and Personal Agencies	50–100% of annual revenues
Florists	34% of annual sales + inventory
Food/Gourmet Shops	20% of annual sales + inventory
Furniture and Appliance Stores	15–25% of annual sales + inventory
Gas Stations	15–25% of annual sales + equip/inventory
Gift and Card Shops	32–40% of annual sales + inventory
Grocery Stores	11–18% of annual sales + inventory
Insurance Agencies	100–125% of annual commissions
Janitorial and Landscape Contractors	40–50% of annual sales
Law Practices	40–100% of annual sales
Property Management Companies	50–100% of annual revenues
Restaurants (non-franchised)	30–45% of annual sales
Sporting Goods Stores	30% of annual sales + inventory
Travel Agencies	40–60% of annual commissions

Source: Excerpted from 2003 *Business Reference Guide* (Wilmington, NC: Business Brokerage Press).

- Conditions of the purchase—what non-financial requirements, if any, are part of the purchase (many purchase contracts are signed subject to the purchaser obtaining suitable financing)

- Provisions for non-compliance with conditions, including penalties for breaches of the contract

- Collateral or security pledged in the transaction (if the seller is financing the sale)

NEGOTIATING THE DEAL

In purchasing a business, the first formal step is to make the offer to purchase. The offer may be made directly by the buyer or through a realtor or a lawyer. In either case, the offer to purchase should be made only after consulting a lawyer and an accountant. As part of the negotiating strategy, the potential buyer should have calculated (preferably financially) the maximum amount he or she can offer for the business using one or more of the methods previously cited. This value is generally somewhat higher than the original purchase offer. As negotiations continue, the purchase price or other aspects of the agreement may have to be altered.

Rather than settling on a firm price, buyers are increasingly turning to performance-based guarantees whereby they not only agree to pay a certain price if sales or profits reach certain levels but also set a floor price that applies if targets are not met.[13]

Once the purchase price has been agreed on, the transaction is usually closed, and legal transfer of title to the business takes place. Typically, this is carried out by both the buyer's and the seller's lawyers. The purchaser should exercise caution if the seller's lawyer is to close the deal. The buyer's lawyer should be permitted to review the details of the transaction in this case.

The buyer is normally required to make a deposit of 5 percent to 10 percent of the purchase price as a show of good faith. This amount should be minimized at least until the seller has met the conditions of the agreement.[14]

HISTORY AND BACKGROUND OF FRANCHISING   LO5

Franchising is becoming an increasingly popular method of establishing and operating a small business. Many entrepreneurs find the opportunity to operate their own business with slightly less risk an attractive option. Others enter franchising out of necessity, having lost jobs with larger organizations. Franchising now occurs in most industries and is experiencing rapid growth in the service sector.

Franchising has not only been successful for the entrepreneur. Many large organizations also recognize that this method of doing business benefits their operations.

From the franchisor's point of view, franchising provides a source of capital and a stable and motivated workforce, usually leading to higher performance. Mac Voisin, co-founder of the successful M&M Meat Shops Ltd. (www.mmmeatshops.com), says that franchising allows the franchisor to expand quickly as the franchisee provides the capital for growth and serves as a motivated manager with a vested interest in the business.[15] For the franchisee, it offers a turnkey operation with valuable assistance from the franchisor. For example, William Borque, owner of a New Brunswick-based Little Caesar's (www.littlecaesars.ca) franchise, says it is doubtful he would have gone into business for himself without the assistance of the franchisor who helped him get his business up and running quickly and provides ongoing assistance.[16]

Although the concept has been around for decades, franchising has experienced its most rapid growth in North America only since the 1950s. It began with the automobile manufacturers, oil companies, soft drink bottlers, and breweries, and has since spread to many different industries throughout the world. Through franchising, many organizations with a proven concept or product were able to expand much more rapidly to meet demand. This growth was so rapid that toward the end of the 1960s, several problems developed in the industry that resulted in the formation of franchisee associations and the passage of legislation to protect the rights of both franchisees and franchisors. Currently, several provinces are looking at requiring greater financial disclosure by franchisors to better protect potential franchisees.[17] Five Canadian provinces, including Manitoba, Ontario, Alberta, New Brunswick, and Prince Edward Island, have passed such legislation.[18]

Franchising has become an important factor in the Canadian economy. According to research provided by the Canadian Franchise Association (www.cfa.ca), franchise businesses account for 40 percent of retail sales and there are roughly 80,000 franchise units in the country. These franchises employ close to one million people, account for one out of every five consumer dollars spent, and contributes 10 percent to Canada's GDP.[19] Estimates are that the impact of franchising on retail sales will continue to grow and may reach as high as 60 percent of sales in the future.[20] Studies by Price Waterhouse and Peat Marwick Thorne show that franchising is growing faster than the general economy.[21] In addition, more than 100 Canadian companies are now franchising internationally, with the United States being the prime location,[22] whereas 500

INCIDENT 5-4

THE JOY OF GIVING

When Zora Brouwer and Patrick Lamoureux started their company, Original Basket Boutique, in 1989, they had no experience and a shaky business plan. Brouwer, who had studied floral arranging, bought the Edmonton franchise with selling rights for the rest of Alberta. A few phone calls established a need for its services, especially in the corporate sector, as companies liked the idea of a client or employee reward program that acknowledged milestones—such as birthdays, marriages, or big corporate deals—with a gift basket. Brouwer worked on product research, design, website administration, and finances, while Lamoureux was in charge of sales, marketing, and developing a customer base. In 2004, Basket Boutique's success allowed them to begin selling franchises across Canada. Today, the Original Basket Boutique has 40 franchises all over the world, and revenues have increased 30 to 40 percent every year. The couple would like to someday see a franchise in every U.S. state, Canadian province, and country in the world.

The entrepreneurs cite that a franchise provides many things that assist the franchisee, such as training, purchasing advantages through a cooperative, and help with field operations. These and other sources of assistance from the franchising company lead to a success rate much higher than a small business operating without the connection of the parent franchise.[23]

FIGURE 5-5

Franchise Sales in Canada (in billions)

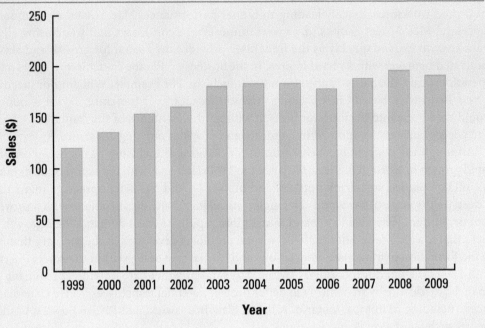

Source: Canadian Franchise Association.

of the largest U.S. franchisors have introduced their franchised systems into Canada.[24] Canada has the second largest franchising industry next to the U.S.[25] See Figure 5-5.

Figure 5-6 illustrates the industries in which franchising has had the most significant impact. The percentages denote industry sales as a percentage of total franchise sales. Traditional franchising includes motor vehicle, oil, and soft drink companies, which sell their products through franchises.

FIGURE 5-6

Franchising by Industry

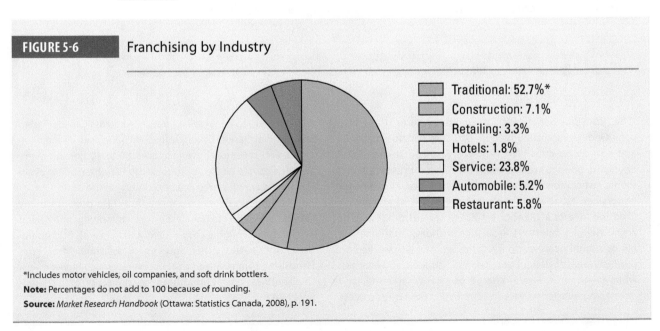

*Includes motor vehicles, oil companies, and soft drink bottlers.

Note: Percentages do not add to 100 because of rounding.

Source: *Market Research Handbook* (Ottawa: Statistics Canada, 2008), p. 191.

Franchises exist in almost all industries today. A major reason for the large recent increase in the number of franchises is expansion into the service sector, which is the fastest-growing sector in the Canadian economy.

WHAT IS FRANCHISING? LO6

Franchising is a system for selectively distributing goods or services through outlets owned by the franchisee. A common definition for a franchise arrangement is a patent or trademark licence entitling the holder to market particular products or services under a brand or trademark according to prearranged terms or conditions. In addition to products and services, the franchise may consist of or may include a "system" or method of providing the product or service. Today, many applications of this definition translate into a broad range of franchising relationships. The brand identification is an important aspect of this form of distribution. It consists of standardization throughout the system. The various outlets in the system are similar as to class of trade, merchandise carried, or services rendered, and other factors that have a bearing on joint merchandising and management through common policies. Also, all the outlets in a franchise system are identified as members of the system. They operate under a common name or insignia, and the establishments often have a distinctive appearance common to all members of the system. This standardization is ensured and controlled by the terms of the franchise contract.

A franchise system is therefore a "voluntary" chain, that is, a chain of individually owned businesses. Franchising, in fact, has been the salvation of many independent wholesale and retail merchants in the face of increasing competition from corporate chains and discount operations. By joining a jobber-sponsored voluntary chain, for example, an independent retailer can get all the benefits that are available to a corporate chain store: central buying and assistance in merchandising, promotion, and management.

The franchising or licensing technique is more often used today, however, when a company comes up with an idea for a product or service and finds that it does not have adequate resources to market its own idea. By licensing prospective entrepreneurs to perform the marketing function for it, the franchising company is able to achieve rapid expansion at relatively low cost, with a substantial part of the investment being contributed by the franchise holder. The various types of franchises are grouped into three categories.

Manufacturer-Directed Franchise.

In this type of franchise, the manufacturer (producer) of a product grants a dealer the right to sell the product. This right, which tends to be geographically exclusive, often requires no initial fee. (See Figure 5-7 for further details of this type of franchising.) Manufacturer-directed franchising is common in such industries as automobile sales, gasoline distributorships, and farm implement dealerships. This type of franchising is successful only when the manufacturer has an established name, a solid reputation, and considerable consumer loyalty.

Wholesaler–Retailer-Directed Franchise.

In this arrangement, one member of the distribution channel such as the wholesaler or retailer initiates the organization of the franchise. The primary purpose of such an organization generally is to centralize many managerial and operational functions and take advantage of volume buying for a group of sellers. As with the manufacturer-owned franchise, there is usually no initial fee, but an equity investment in the franchise may be required. Figure 5-7 illustrates some of the other operating details for this type of franchise and the industries in which it is prevalent.

FIGURE 5-7

Types of Franchises

TITLE	METHOD OF FRANCHISING	DETAILS OF AGREEMENT		EXAMPLES	
		FRANCHISOR PROVIDES	FRANCHISEE PROVIDES	INDUSTRY	COMPANY
Manufacturer	Franchisee has right to sell product	Product sales support Exclusive territory	Selling function Facilities	Automobile Oil companies	Ford GMC ESSO Petro Canada
Wholesaler-retailer	Franchisee owns equity in supplier company and purchases product from the franchise	Product and other technical assistance and service	Selling function Buys equity Board of directors	Retail grocery Hardware	Associated Grocers Home Hardware
Franchising company	Franchisee buys the right to sell service or product	Method of operations Training Location, building, etc. Financing Proven name Advertising	Fee Royalties Compliance with conditions of contract	Fast food Auto rental	McDonald's Tim Hortons Avis Budget Hertz

Franchising Company.

This type of franchise usually involves a company (the master licensor) that sells a product or service in exchange for an initial predetermined fee and an ongoing royalty. The franchisee gains the right to sell under the franchisor's name and receives the franchisor's assistance and managerial expertise. Franchising companies are commonly found in the retail and service industries. In recent years, many companies using this method of franchising to expand their operations have experienced rapid growth. See Figure 5-7 for further details of the franchising company arrangement.

ADVANTAGES OF FRANCHISING   LO7

Compared with the other two methods of starting a small business (buying and organizing), franchising offers many specific advantages.

Proven Market for the Product or Service.

Except for newly established franchises, a known market and instant brand recognition for the franchisor's product or service exists. Information about the performance of existing franchises is normally supplied or can be obtained by the franchisee. Such a track record makes it much easier to make projections for future operations. For example, successful franchises such as Tim Hortons, Boston Pizza, and Subway can usually provide reliable estimates for franchise sales based on market size and other conditions. For entrepreneurs this is very valuable knowledge, as it will help them in making a decision to invest in the business.

The instant pulling power of the product also greatly helps the small business owner shorten the duration of the initial stage of the business, when the market is being developed and resulting revenues are low. A study by the University of Toronto showed that franchised businesses had higher sales per outlet than independents in almost all types of businesses.[26] Another study of franchisors found that during the last recession, franchised outlets were less affected than non-franchised outlets.[27]

Services the Franchisor May Provide.

A franchising company typically provides many valuable services to a franchisee. A description of franchisor services follows.

Selection of Location.

Assistance in selecting the location can be very important, especially if location is critical to the success of the business, such as in retailing and often in the service industry. Often a franchisor has considerable site selection expertise that can be used in establishing the business. Additionally, landlords are more likely to provide entrepreneurs with prime locations if the franchisor guarantees the lease to the landlord.

Purchase or Construction of Site, Buildings, and Equipment.

The franchisor's experience and financial resources in this area may mean considerable savings of time and money. In addition to providing expertise, the franchisor may even purchase or construct the facilities for the franchisee. For example, Tim Hortons (www.timhortons.com) takes full responsibility for the construction and development of its stores, and its franchise agreement actually prohibits franchisees from developing or constructing locations.[28]

Provision of Financing.

Some franchisors will provide financing for franchisees, and their association with the franchisees often helps the franchisee obtain financing. For example, the Royal Bank (www.rbc.ca), through its Franchise Assistance Program, allows favourable interest rates on franchisee loans because of a franchisee's association with a well-known franchisor.

Standardized Methods of Operating.

Standardized operating procedures and manuals are often part of the services the franchisor provides in the areas of cost accounting, control systems, and customer service standards. Such methods can result in considerable savings for the small business. For example, Boston Pizza (www.bostonpizza.com) franchise owners are trained in a system that produces the lowest food costs in the industry. As a result Boston Pizza franchisees enjoy food costs of 25 percent, this compares quite favourably with the industry average of 38 percent.[29]

Advertising.

Most franchisors will provide national advertising that may benefit the franchisee. Such a level of promotion may be difficult and costly for the franchisee to develop unassisted. For example, Tim Hortons spends millions every year supporting its brand by advertising its products and restaurants.

Purchasing Advantages.

Because the franchising company purchases large volumes of inventories for its franchisees, it can pass the resulting cost savings on to franchisees on purchases made from the franchisor.

Training.

Most franchisors provide training to new franchisees. This may take the form of an instruction manual, site visits, and/or training at a franchisor's facility. Previous to opening any Boston Pizza franchise, head office sends nine trainers to assist the staff and the franchisee.[30] Cora (www.chezcora.com), a Quebec-based breakfast and lunch franchise that has been expanding throughout Canada, operates three corporate stores that they use as training facilities. The company's founder, Cora Tsouflidou, says they use these facilities to provide

INCIDENT 5-5

BOOSTER JUICE—A CANADIAN FRANCHISE SUCCESS STORY

Dale Wishewan grew up wanting to be a baseball player. After completing his degree in mechanical engineering at Portland State University, which he attended on a baseball scholarship, he founded Booster Juice with a partner, John Amack. Dale felt that there was a market for a healthy alternative to traditional fast food. Booster Juice provides a menu of juices and smoothies consisting of such nutritional ingredients as natural fruits as well as wheat grass and Acai berry. Booster Juice's mission statement is: "To provide customers with an incredible, healthy alternative to fast food that's great tasting, convenient, and nutritious, making it perfectly suited for today's active lifestyle." The first Booster Juice outlet was opened in Sherwood Park, Alberta, in 1999. Since then, the concept has grown with the help of a well-developed franchise system.

Growth was rapid with 15 outlets added in the first year and 35 in the next. In 2002, however, Wishewan decided to reduce expansion to ensure that the business was on firm footing. "We consciously slowed down after our second year, wanting to be sure our concept grew into something solid,"

BOOSTER JUICE HAS USED FRANCHISING TO BECOME THE LARGEST JUICE AND SMOOTHIE COMPANY IN CANADA.
© Shane Shaw/iStockPhoto

he reported. Wishewan and his management team spent about a year ironing out various kinks in the business plan. He secured better deals with food distributors and improved quality control by hiring permanent staff to visit each franchise on a regular basis. Wishewan understands that successful franchising is all about systems, and Booster Juice provides good training and support for franchisees. This includes hands-on training as well as assistance in the marketing, legal, logistics, and real estate aspects of the franchise. To decrease competition, Booster Juice bought out two smaller smoothie chains. Today, Booster Juice is the top juice and smoothie franchise in Canada, with 211 outlets operating across Canada (over twice as many as its nearest competitor) and nearly 300 stores overall.

Booster Juice has also expanded internationally, with several outlets in the U.S. as well as successful franchises in Saudi Arabia and planned entrances into the United Kingdom and China. Expanding internationally has been a challenge, however. Wishewan indicates that it is a big hurdle to find suitable overseas partners. "It is challenging to qualify an individual franchisee in Canada, but it is 10 times as important to choose the right master franchisor in another country." Booster Juice is now Canada's premium juice and smoothie franchise and plans call for the addition of 40 to 50 new locations each year.[31]

Discussion Questions

1. What do you think are some of the strengths and weaknesses of the Booster Juice franchise?

2. Do you think Booster Juice grew too fast in the early years? What are the disadvantages to rapid growth from a franchisor–franchisee perspective?

3. The company originally started out serving fresh fruit, but has since moved to frozen produce to control costs. Do you think this is a good idea? Why, or why not?

potential franchisees with insight into how busy a restaurant can be and everything that it takes to make it successful.[32] Other examples include McDonald's (www.mcdonalds.ca) franchisees, who receive training at Hamburger University in Illinois and can even receive a bachelor's degree in Hamburgerology! Because of the extra training provided, franchising (as opposed to buying or organizing) is often more suited to someone who lacks experience in the industry. Recently, knowledge-based businesses such as consulting or research have experienced rapid growth in franchising. The capital investment to get established in these businesses is typically low and flexibility is high.

Ongoing Support.

In addition to initial training many franchises provide ongoing services and support to franchisees. This support can include follow-up training, assistance in managing the business, and, in some cases, help in the day-to-day operations. For example, both Vancouver-based franchise 1-800-Got-Junk? (www.1800gotjunk.com), a junk removal business, and Nurse Next Door (www.nursenextdoor.com), a home care company, offer call centre support for franchisees. The support enables owners to focus on generating sales and not answering the phone. Nurse Next Door's call centre, which is open 24 hours a day and staffed by professional agents, saves franchisees an estimated 240 hours of work a month.[33] Both the above-mentioned Boston Pizza and Cora provide ongoing training and support. For example, Cora has corporate managers visit on a weekly basis, and if a store shows signs of financial trouble, corporate consultants are brought in to help manage costs and, if the need arises, to invest in additional local advertising.[34]

Because of the foregoing advantages, a franchisee's chance of success in the business is higher than with the other two methods of starting a small business. The franchising industry advertises a failure rate of only 4 to 8 percent, which is much lower than the rate for non-franchised businesses.[35] Some claim, however, that this low failure rate is greatly exaggerated by franchising companies. In the United States and Canada, an increasing number of franchisees are complaining—sometimes in court—about the problems incurred when signing a franchise contract.

POTENTIAL DISADVANTAGES OF FRANCHISING

Because of the apparent advantages just discussed, many individuals have signed franchise contracts. However, some have suffered disillusionment and failure a short while later. The level of franchise litigation is growing. Often franchisees misinterpret the franchise agreement concerning such things as use of advertising funds, restrictions, and services provided by the franchisor. In other cases, the franchisor has acted inappropriately, leading to a dispute. It is critical that the prospective franchisee be aware of the difficulties that can arise when entering the world of franchising. There are several areas of potential conflict discussed in this section. Often, as in the case with a recent class action lawsuit by franchisee owners of Edible Arrangement (www.ediblearrangements.com), a North American company that sells fruit bouquets, there are more than one complaint. In this specific case, franchise owners are claiming Edible Arrangements has made several decisions such as forcing them to stay open for longer hours, implementing new software systems, and raising supply prices. All of these things have increased the costs of operating the stores. The franchisees further state that the corporation has started an online competitor, www.dippedfruit.com, which competes with the bricks and mortar stores.[36] The franchisee should have a clear understanding of how disputes will be resolved in the event that they occur. The following are some of the more common dangers.

Lack of Independence.

In signing a franchise contract, the franchisee can expect to receive a certain amount of assistance from the franchisor. The franchisor will monitor the business, however, to ensure that the conditions of the contract are being met. This condition restricts the franchisee's freedom and independence.

Cost of the Franchise.

Most franchises have a price that often consists of an initial fee and ongoing royalties based on operations. To enter most franchise organizations, individuals have to accumulate a certain amount of capital either to pay the fee or to provide the facilities and the associated set-up costs.

Unfulfilled Promises.

Most franchising companies indicate they will provide such services as training and advertising. In some cases, however, this assistance does not materialize or is inadequate.

Restrictions of the Contract.

The franchise agreement may contain some restrictions that inhibit the franchisee's freedom. Such restrictions are discussed below.

Product or Service Offered.

The franchisee may not be allowed to offer for sale any products not procured by the franchisor.

Line Forcing.

The franchisee may be required to offer the franchisor's complete line of products for sale, even if some are not profitable in the franchisee's market area.

Termination.

The franchisee may not be able to terminate the franchise contract without incurring a penalty. The franchisee may also be prohibited from selling the business or passing it on to family members.

Remodelling Clauses.

Many franchise agreements force the franchise owner to update their facilities often at a significant cost to the franchisee. Boston Pizza forces franchisees to update their stores every seven years at a cost of approximately $800,000.[37]

Saturation of the Market.

In some industries, franchising companies have allowed oversaturation to occur in a particular geographic market. For example, David Joseph, an outspoken former owner of a Kumon franchise, a North American franchise that assists children in math and reading, has posted his concerns about Kumon on www.UnhappyFranchisee.com. Joseph, who eventually sold his franchise, cited oversaturation as an ongoing concern stating that Kumon had embraced a major expansion plan and he suddenly found new stores in close proximity to his franchise.[38] Saturation in established markets is a growing problem in North America. Careful examination of the franchise contract should be made to ensure that this does not occur. This puts financial pressure on those franchisees operating within that market. In some cases, oversaturation has occurred when franchisees failed to understand their rights to protect their territory in their franchise agreement. Sometimes, franchisees get what is known as "right of first refusal." What this means is that if someone else wants to build a franchise near the original franchisee, the owner of the first franchise can purchase the proposed location instead. If they decline the location for any reason, including lack of financing or their franchise is not succeeding, anyone else can open a second franchise. An upset former Robin's Donuts franchise owner describes how he got out of the franchise business at a loss when the chain opened up seven stores in his area in a short timeframe. When asked if he could have prevented this in any way he says, "No, the only thing I could have done was bought them all myself." John Sotos, a franchise lawyer in Toronto, thinks that companies such as Subway (www.subway.com) have expanded so much that they are putting franchisees at risk. If a franchisor has a large initial fee and no royalties, its major concern may be the selling of franchises rather than their ongoing success. Such franchises seem particularly vulnerable to oversaturation.[39]

Lack of Security.

A franchisor may elect not to renew a franchise contract once it has expired, or may terminate the contract before its expiry if the franchisee has violated the terms or conditions. Many franchising companies operate company-owned outlets as well as franchised outlets. The number of company-owned outlets is only about 18 percent of total franchise outlets, but recent figures show slight increases in this percentage.[40] Some argue that franchising companies take over the outlets after the franchisees have successfully established them. This practice has led to some lawsuits between franchisors and franchisees. For example, Timothy's Coffees of the World Inc. was recently successfully sued by a franchisee in Ontario for failure to renew the franchise agreement. Other examples include a group of Pizza Pizza franchisees who successfully sued Pizza Pizza for interference in store operations and wrongful termination of franchise agreements without cause. In one of the more infamous franchisor–franchisee disputes, Subway corporate employees went into a franchisee's store overnight, changed the locks on the door, and hired a security guard to keep the franchise owner out of the store because he had failed to make a $4600 royalty payment.[41]

Cost of Merchandise.

The cost of merchandise purchased from the franchisor may exceed the price the franchisee can obtain elsewhere. However, the contract may require the franchisee to purchase solely from the franchisor. For example, two well-known Canadian franchisors, Pet Valu Canada Inc. (www.petvalu.com) and Quiznos (www.quiznos.ca), have been involved in legal disputes with franchisees who claim they are either overpaying for supplies or are not getting access to expected volume rebates.[42]

Effectiveness of Promotion.

Most franchisors provide promotion and advertising for their franchisees. In some situations, however, the promotion is not effective for the franchisee's market and may be time consuming and

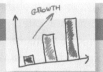

TIM HORTONS' FRANCHISEES ATTEMPT TO SUE FRANCHISOR FOR $2 BILLION

A group of Tim Hortons' franchisees have failed in their attempt to sue the franchisor for $2 billion in a class action lawsuit. The franchisees were upset that Tim Hortons had forced them to stop baking fresh doughnuts in their stores and instead required them to use shipped frozen products, which they warmed-up or finished baking. Tim Hortons' co-founder, Ron Joyce, said he did not like the taste of the new doughnuts and it flew in the face of the company's motto, "Always Fresh."

What likely upset the franchisees even more than deviating from the "Always Fresh" model is the cost of the frozen doughnuts is more than double the cost of baking doughnuts in stores—something that was at the heart of the lawsuit. The franchisees claimed that forcing them to sell frozen doughnuts

was eating into their profits. Franchisees further claimed Tim Hortons was setting the price of some lunch items so low that they were losing money on the sale of goods. The low prices were seen as particularly problematic as franchisees still had to pay Tim Hortons a royalty on sales, creating a larger loss. For example, some franchisees were saying they were selling items such as soups and some sandwiches below cost and then they had to turn around and pay Tim Hortons a royalty on the sale, creating a deeper loss. In responding to the lawsuit, Tim Hortons stated that their franchise agreement allowed them to stipulate the costs of supplies and determine the selling price of its products.

The Ontario court found in favour of Tim Hortons, the franchisor, stating franchisees have a right to earn a reasonable return, and their coffee sales, which have significant markup, allow them to do so. The court further noted franchisees do not get to make money on all items they sell and they should be willing to sell some items below cost in return for the right to sell Tim Hortons' branded coffee.

A GROUP OF TIM HORTONS' FRANCHISEES UNSUCCESSFULLY TRIED TO SUE THE COMPANY AFTER TIM HORTONS FORCED THEM TO SELL FROZEN DOUGHNUTS. FRANCHISEES WERE UPSET THAT THE DOUGHNUTS WERE DOUBLE THE COST OF THE ONES PRODUCED FRESH IN STORES.
Burke/Triolo Productions/Getty Images

Discussion Questions

1. Were you surprised that the judge agreed with the franchisor in this particular case?

2. Do you think it's fair that Tim Hortons, the franchisor, is setting the price of menu items below cost and then taking a royalty on the sale of these items, furthering the franchisees' loss?

3. While many Tim Hortons' franchisees are no doubt quite successful, the ones that are struggling would have been negatively impacted by the change in donut prices. What if anything could Tim Hortons do to help these franchisees?

4. Based on what you have read in this case, would the information deter you from buying a Tim Hortons' franchise? Why, or why not?

costly for the franchisee to participate in. Often a franchisee does not want to participate in these programs but is required by the contract to do so. For example, a Wendy's franchisee expressed frustration with the franchisor's marketing fee. This is a fee that he had to pay every month as his contribution to Wendy's national and provincial marketing programs. At the time, his store was operating in a French-language community and Wendy's was not advertising in French.

Exaggeration of Financial Success.

Most franchising companies provide promotional literature for prospective franchisees. This information generally contains financial statements for the typical franchisee. In some cases, these estimates have been overly optimistic, and the actual results for the franchisee are disappointing. For example, a Mr. Sub (www.mrsub.ca) franchisee successfully sued the franchisor after the courts found, in part, the franchisor provided financial statements that were misleading. The judge ordered the franchisor to return the owner's initial investment along with additional damages.[43]

FINDING A FRANCHISE

Entrepreneurs searching for a franchise opportunity may use the same opportunity search techniques discussed in previous chapters. They can evaluate franchises that they come into contact with during their daily activities, conduct a search, and seek advice from business contacts, colleagues, and friends. As part of a search entrepreneurs may use the Internet to search for ideas, buy magazines that discuss franchising, and/or attend franchise shows. Some helpful directories include *The Franchise Annual Directory* and *The Canadian Franchise Dealership Guide*. Figure 5-8 lists the hot trends in franchising.

The entrepreneur will usually short list some franchises that she is interested in and contact the company for a promotional kit. Most companies will provide the entrepreneur with basic information and ask the entrepreneur to fill out an application form (often found on the company's website) that must be approved prior to receiving additional documents. The application form usually asks for the entrepreneur's work, financials, and education histories. If the company feels the entrepreneur is a good candidate for a franchise, then they will send her a full information kit.

After the entrepreneur receives the information, she should evaluate the documents and ask the franchisor for any clarification that is required. It should be noted that just because an entrepreneur decides to buy a franchise it does not mean that the franchisor will sell her one. The franchisor may engage in a lengthy evaluation of the entrepreneur and decide that she is not a suitable franchisee in their business. For example, Second Cup and Robin's Donuts, both successful Canadian franchises, have potential franchisees take personality tests to determine if candidates are a good fit in their franchise system. Figure 5-9 lists the Top 10 new franchises for 2013.

FIGURE 5-8	Hot Trends in Franchising

1. Commercial and Residential Services—Such as junk removal, cleaning, and restoration work has seen the number of franchises grow by 47 percent year over year.
2. Advertising/Marketing/Promotional Services—Typically provides marketing and other services to business. Growth has been 45 percent over the past year.
3. Children's Products and Services—An emphasis on families and the development of children has resulted in 37 percent growth.
4. Business Consultants/Services/Training—As small business grow, they need more services. The result is year over year growth of 29 percent.
5. Seniors/Home Care Services—Aging demographic and a desire to stay at home is fuelling demand for these franchises, which has climbed by 29 percent.

Source: Adapted from Jim McElgunn, "Franchising: Canada's Hottest Industry," April 12, 2011, www.profitguide.com/opportunity/franchising-canada%E2%80%99s-hottest-industry-30138.

FIGURE 5-9

Top 10 New Franchises for 2013 According to *Entrepreneur Magazine* and the Investment Required

1.	Kona Ice	$103.7K–$119.1K
2.	Menchie's	$300K–$320K
3.	Orange Leaf Frozen Yogurt	$274.5K–$408.5K
4.	ShelfGenie Franchise Systems LLC	$70.1K–$125.25K
5.	Bricks 4 Kidz	$33.8K–$51.05K
6.	Smashburger Franchising LLC	$560.5K–$909.5K
7.	GameTruck Licensing LLC	$119.5K–$310.5K
8.	Paul Davis Emergency Services	$41.78K–$147.82K
9.	Signal 88 Security	$84.81K–$104.61K
10.	Mac Tools	$87.74K–$206.23K

Source: Top 10 New Franchises for 2013, *Entrepreneur Magazine*, www.entrepreneur.com/franchises/topnew/index.html#.

EVALUATION OF A FRANCHISE OPPORTUNITY   LO8

In view of the potential disadvantages discussed earlier, it is critical to make a thorough investigation of the prospective franchise before signing the contract. Several key areas should be examined in evaluating a franchise. Thorough investigation of the franchisor, the product or service, the franchise contract, and the market should be carried out.

Franchising involves many risks to an entrepreneur. Although we often read and/or hear about the success of Tim Hortons or Canadian Tire, for every one of these successes, there are many failures. Franchising, like any other venture, is not for the passive person. It requires effort and long hours, as any business does, since duties such as hiring, scheduling, buying, accounting, and so on are still the franchisee's responsibility.

Not every franchise is right for every entrepreneur. He or she must evaluate the franchise alternatives to decide which one is most appropriate. A number of factors should be assessed before making the final decision.

1. Unproven versus Proven Franchise.

There are some trade-offs in investing in a proven or unproven franchise business. Whereas an unproven franchise will be a less expensive investment, the lower investment is offset by more risk. In an unproven franchise, the franchisor is likely to make mistakes as the business grows. These mistakes could inevitably lead to failure. Constant reorganization of a new franchise can result in confusion and mismanagement. Yet a new and unproven franchise can offer more excitement and challenge and can lead to significant opportunities for large profits should the business grow rapidly. A proven franchise offers lower risk but requires more financial investment. For example, Nurse Next Door, a relatively new Vancouver-based franchise operating in the home health care market, is pursuing a high growth strategy and striving to expand across Canada and into the United States. Currently, almost all of the locations have been open less than five years, the exception being two model stores in Vancouver and Kamloops. While this franchise may represent a great opportunity for an entrepreneur to own a growing franchise with relatively low start-up costs, she must also realize that Nurse Next Door will not be able to provide substantial information (e.g., long-term sales figures, profit statements) on other franchisees, as many have been open for only a short time.

2. Financial Stability of Franchise.

The purchase of a franchise should entail an assessment of the financial stability of the franchisor. A potential franchisee should develop answers to the following questions:

- How many franchises are in the organization?
- How successful is each of the members of the franchise organization?
- Are most of the profits of the franchise a function of fees from the sale of franchises or from royalties based on profits of franchisees?
- Does the franchisor have management expertise in production, finance, and marketing?

Some of the above information can be obtained from profit-and-loss statements of the franchise organization. Face-to-face contact with the franchisor can also indicate the success of the organization. It is also worthwhile to contact some of the franchisees directly to determine their success and to identify any problems that have occurred. If financial information of the franchisor is unavailable, the entrepreneur may purchase a financial rating from a source such as Dun and Bradstreet. Generally, the following are good external sources of information:

- Franchise association
- Other franchisees
- Government (especially provinces with franchise legislation)
- Accountants and lawyers
- Libraries
- Franchise directories and journals
- Business exhibitions

3. Potential Market for the New Franchise.

It is important for the entrepreneur to evaluate the market that the franchise will attract. A starting point is evaluating the traffic flow and demographics of the residents from a map of the area. Traffic flow information may be observed by visiting the area. Direction of traffic flow, ease of entry to the business, and the amount of traffic (pedestrian and automobile) can be estimated by observation. The demographics of the area can be determined from census data, which can be obtained from local libraries or the town hall. It can also be advantageous to locate competitors on the map to determine their potential effect on the franchise business. Marketing research in the market area is helpful. Attitudes about and interest in the new business can be assessed in the market research. In some instances, the franchisor will conduct a market study as a selling point to the franchisee.

4. Profit Potential for a New Franchise.

As in any start-up business, it is important to develop pro forma income and cash flow statements. The franchisor should provide projections in order to calculate the needed information. The entrepreneur will also want to consider the start-up money required, the terms for any royalty payments, and sources and costs of supplies.

5. Territorial Protection.

Does the franchise offer any territorial protection? As previously discussed some franchisors will only offer "right of first refusal" protection, which means that a franchisee owner is given the chance to open up another franchise in their territory. If the original franchisee does not want to or cannot for any reason, then the franchisor can open another business or sell the rights to another franchisee. Entrepreneurs should try to find franchises that grant them excusive regions—but they should also realize that the number of franchisors that do this is shrinking.

6. Training and Operations Assistance.

Most, if not all, franchises offer some type of training and operations procedures. Entrepreneurs should be looking for comprehensive, documented training that occurs both prior to and after opening the business. Good training programs are easy to follow and have accompanying metrics. In addition, the franchise should provide ongoing operations assistance and managerial controls. Entrepreneurs should seek out franchises that offer superior operating profits to their benchmarks. This will indicate that the company's operating systems are providing the franchisee with value.

7. Contract Length and Renewal and Termination Terms.

The duration of franchise agreements can vary significantly. Some franchise agreements offer terms of less than five years, while others offer 20-year-plus terms. Entrepreneurs should look for franchises that offer terms of at least 10 years, with a 20-year term being more acceptable. Additionally, entrepreneurs must also be concerned over the renewal process for a franchise. Sometimes the renewal is automatic, but in some cases, it is up to the franchisor's discretion. One Second Cup franchisee in Toronto was shocked to learn that Second Cup was not renewing his franchise, resulting in a significant financial loss. Furthermore the entrepreneur will want to consider any additional fees that must be paid upon the renewal of the agreement. The entrepreneur will also want to clarify if the contract comes with a termination clause and what these terms entail.

8. What Current Owners Are Saying About Their Franchise.

When investigating a franchise, it is important to talk to other franchise owners to find out if they are happy with their decisions. Sometimes the franchisor will supply some contact information, but it is highly recommended that potential franchisees seek out their own contacts, as it is unlikely that a franchisor would provide contacts who are unhappy with the system. Some questions to consider asking a current or former franchisee include the following:

- Why did you choose this franchise?
- Are you happy with the choice?
- Did you have any problems with the franchisor? If so, how were they resolved?
- Are there any hidden costs or fees?
- Are you satisfied with the training and marketing assistance provided by the franchisor? Why, or why not?
- Would you invest in this franchise again?

In general, most of the above information should be provided in the disclosure statement or the prospectus. If the franchisor refuses to answer these questions, a potential franchisee should take a lot more time evaluating the franchisor.

Figure 5-10 presents a risk assessment table that can be used to determine if a franchise opportunity is worth further investigation.

FIGURE 5-10

Franchise Risk Assessment

Criteria	Low Risk/Avg. Market Return –20%	Acceptable Risk/ Incremental 30% Return	High Risk/Marginal 40–50% Return	Extreme Risk/Large Return 60–100%
Outlet pro forma disclosed or discerned	National	Regional	Province	Local
Market share	Yes, 90%+ apparently profitable Number one and dominant	Yes, 80% + apparently profitable Number one or two, with a strong competitor	Yes, 70% + apparently profitable Lower than number two	No, less than 70% profitable Lower than number three, with a dominant player
National marketing program	Historically successful creative process, national media buys in place	Creative plus regional media buys	Creative plus local media buys	Local media buys only
National purchasing program	More than 3% + gross margin advantage in national purchasing contract	1–3% gross margin advantage versus independent operators	Regional gross margin advantage only	No discernible gross margin advantage
Margin characteristics	50% + gross margin and 18% net outlet margin	40–50% gross margin and 12–17% net outlet margin	30–40% gross margin less 12% net outlet margin	Declining gross margin detected, erratic net outlet margin
Business format	Sophisticated training, documented operations manual(s), identifiable feedback mechanism with franchisees	Initial training and dynamically documented operations manual, some field support	Training and operations but weak field support	Questionable training and field support and static operations
Term of licence agreement	20 years with automatic renewal	15 years with renewal	Less than 15 years or no renewal	Less than 10 years
Site development	Quantifiable criteria clearly documented and tied to specific markets	Market prioritized with general site development criteria	General market development criteria outlined	Business format are not tied to identifiable market segment(s)
Capital required per unit	$15,000–$25,000 working capital	Working capital plus $50,000–100,000 machinery and equipment	Working capital plus machinery and equipment plus $.5–1 million real estate	Erratic, highly variable, or ill-defined
Franchise fee and royalties	Present discounted value* of the fees are less than the demonstrated economic advantages (reduced costs or increased revenue) of the franchise versus stand-alone	Present discounted value of the fees are less than the demonstrated economic advantages (reduced costs or increased revenue) of the franchise versus stand-alone	Present discounted value of the fees are only projected to be less than the expected economic advantages (reduced costs or increased revenue) of the franchise versus stand-alone	Present discounted value of the fees are not discernibly less than the expected value of the franchise

*If franchising is a risk-reduction strategy, then the discount of future revenue should be less. Concurrently, the economics of scale in marketing should increase the amount of revenue a franchise can generate versus a "stand-alone" operation.

Source: New Venture Creation, 7th Edition, © 2007, by Jeffry A. Timmons and Stephen Spinelli (McGraw-Hill). Reprinted with permission.

Front-end procedure fees, royalty payments, expenses, and other information should be compared with those of franchises in the same field, as well as in different business areas. If a franchise looks good as an investment, the entrepreneur may request a full franchise package from the franchisor, which usually contains a draft franchise agreement or contract. The contract or franchise agreement is the final step in establishing a franchise arrangement. Here, a lawyer experienced in franchising should be used. The franchise agreement contains all the specific requirements and obligations of the franchisee. Things such as the exclusivity of territory coverage will protect against the franchisor's granting another franchise within a certain radius of the business. The renewable terms will indicate the length of the contract and the requirements. Financial requirements will stipulate the initial price for the franchise, the schedule of payments, and the royalties to be paid. Termination of franchise requirements should indicate what will happen if the franchisee becomes disabled or dies

INCIDENT 5-7

UNHAPPYFRANCHISEE.COM

The name of the site says it all. UnhappyFranchisee.com is a website where unhappy franchise owners can vent their frustrations about their franchisor. In addition to allowing visitors to post both anonymous and signed complaints, the website maintains an active list of legal cases concerning franchisor–franchisee disputes and publishes research about franchising. The site also allows franchisors to dispute some of the posted information or to defend their franchising track record and/or practices. For example, UnhappyFranchise.com recently published a report noting the following information about A&W franchises:

A&W RESTAURANTS FRANCHISES 2008–2011

Franchises open January 2009	910
Franchises added 2009–2011	31
Franchises terminated/closed 2009–2011	167
Franchises terminated/closed (%)	18%

Source: A&W Franchise Disclosure Documents (FDDs).

UNHAPPYFRANCHISSEE.COM IS ATTRACTING MORE ATTENTION AS A SOURCE OF INFORMATION FOR POTENTIAL FRANCHISEES. SOME CEOS, LIKE A&W'S KEVIN BAZNER, MONITOR THE SITE'S INFORMATION ABOUT THEIR COMPANY.
© AWSeebaran/iStockPhoto

The information, which it took from A&W's disclosure documents, indicates a high termination/failure rate, something that would likely deter future franchisees. Kevin Bazner, president and CEO of A&W Restaurants, actually responded to this report on the website and cited several reasons to explain the store's poor performance, including co-branded stores (shared with another restaurant) and corporate restructuring issues.[44]

Discussion Questions

1. Given that not all posts are signed, how much credibility would you give to the reviews on the site? Would you consider them at all? Why, or why not?

2. Given that the information published about A&W was part the company's internal records, would this impact your decision to purchase an A&W franchise? Why, or why not?

3. Given the fact that Bazner responded to the website, does he add credibility to the report and the website itself? Does Bazner's response offer enough to put potential franchisees at ease with their decision to purchase an A&W franchise?

4. Use the Internet to visit the site, look at Bazner's complete response. Does his response explain the high failure rate of A&W stores? Why, or why not?

FIGURE 5-11	Top 10 Franchises According to *Entrepreneur Magazine* for 2013 and the Investment Required

1. Hampton Hotels	$3.7M–$13.52M
2. Subway	$85.2K–$260.35K
3. Jiffy Lube Int'l. Inc.	$196.5K–$304K
4. 7-Eleven Inc.	$30.8K–$0.5M
5. Supercuts	$103.55K–$196.5K
6. Anytime Fitness	$56.3K–$353.9K
7. Servpro	$133.05K–$181.45K
8. Denny's Inc.	$1.18M–$2.4M
9. McDonald's	$1.03M–$2.18M
10. Pizza Hut Inc.	$295K–$2.15M

Source: "Entrepreneur 2013 Franchise 500," *Entrepreneur Magazine,* www.entrepreneur.com/franchise500/index.html.

and what provisions are made for the family. Terminating a franchise generally results in more lawsuits than any other issue in franchising. These terms should also allow the franchisee to obtain fair market value should the franchise be sold. Even though the agreement may be standard, the franchisee should try to negotiate important items to reduce the investment risk.

Because the signing of a franchise contract is a major step for the entrepreneur, the investigation should be thorough. Appendix 5B at the end of this chapter provides a comprehensive checklist for the prospective franchisee to use in this evaluation.

Figure 5-11 lists the Top 10 franchises for 2013.

THE ENTREPRENEUR AS FRANCHISOR   LO9

An increasingly popular method of entrepreneurship in franchising is not being a franchisee but, rather, selling franchises and becoming a franchisor. For example, John DeHart and Ken Sim, founders of Nurse Next Door, started the company with the goal of establishing a large franchisor company. After establishing three stores on Canada's West Coast, the pair immediately went into hyper-expansion mode and quickly added 50 franchises in a short period of time. Before a prospective franchisor attempts to sell franchises, several requirements must be met. Is the type of business franchisable? What information is required? How much capital is needed? All these questions should be addressed in the process of becoming a franchisor.

WHAT BUSINESSES CAN BE FRANCHISED?

Franchises abound in many industries today. This phenomenon is reflected in the following statement by the U.S. Commerce Department: "Any business that can be taught to someone is being franchised."[45] The franchise business must have a sound concept. The franchise should be distinct, be practical, and fill a need. It must also be easy to teach and clearly communicated to others. It must be capable of being replicated and transferred to other geographic areas. Suzy Okun, a co-founder of the franchise Treats (www.treats.com), which specializes in desserts, elaborates on this idea: "We sell a concept. We take what the palate already knows, and we make it electric! We take what the customer has already seen and do it differently."[46] Consumer research may be required to solidify the concept. Estimates based on sound research will be much more attractive to the prospective franchisee.

HOW DOES ONE BECOME A FRANCHISOR?

Once prospective franchisors are satisfied that the business is franchisable, they must take several steps to develop the franchise. Some of the most important steps are discussed below.

1. Establish a Prototype.

The franchisor should set up and operate a prototype business long enough to iron out the bugs and get a clear picture of market demand. This business can also serve as a reference point for prospective franchisees to use in their evaluations. To be useful, the prototype should be earning a consistent profit.

2. Selling Franchises.

Entrepreneurs often get established in business by operating a single franchise. However, selling franchises after successfully managing their own has been the preferred route to follow for some. Such is the case with master franchisor Nicole Matta, who has obtained the rights to sell a U.S.-based line of high-tech, low-touch spa centres in Ontario for Planet Beach Contempo Spas (www.planetbeach.com). Planet Beach's services are fully automated. There are no massage therapists, but the company still provides body wraps, facials, full-body and deep-tissue massages, and UV therapy using high-tech equipment to deliver the treatments in private rooms. Growth for Planet Beach's Spas has been dramatic, and Matta is confident that this growth will be evident in Ontario. She is planning to award eight to 10 franchises in the next year and to have about 40 locations in the next four to five years. With the company's help, Matta is able to provide marketing, financial, and operational assistance to prospective franchisees, which increases their chance of success.[47]

3. Prepare the Necessary Information.

Information prospective franchisees will require includes promotional literature regarding the franchise and detailed financial data not only for the company but also for a typical franchise. A prospective franchisee requires information on capital needed, potential income, cash flow projections, and future trends in the industry to make an informed decision. It is recommended that someone with accounting expertise be retained to assist in preparing this information.

4. Investigate the Legal Requirements.

The franchisor should investigate the legal requirements in setting up a franchising company. Some of these requirements include the following:

- Registration and disclosure with government agencies; as mentioned earlier, some provinces require detailed information before franchising can begin
- The required business licences and incorporations
- Other laws regulating the operations of franchises

In addition, the franchise contract should be drawn up by someone with legal expertise to ensure that the rights of both parties are protected. The legal operations of the franchise and the responsibilities of both franchisor and franchisee are formalized in the franchise contract. The franchisor needs to decide which services and what assistance to provide, what restrictions to impose, and what to require from the franchisee in return.

5. Develop a Planned and Standardized Program of Operations.

Standardization of procedures is an essential part of a successful franchise and enables the franchisor to monitor operations more easily. The following quote about Molly Maid (www.mollymaid.com), a maid service franchise, illustrates the effective use of professionals in the development of the franchise system:

> MacKenzie made full use of experts in setting up his company. He used two well-known accounting firms, one to develop an internal accounting system, and the second to construct a package for franchisees. A legal expert on franchising developed the franchise agreement, and a firm specializing in trademarks and patents set up the rules for use of the logo.[48]

The operations manual is generally developed using the experience of the prototype business. As mentioned above, the methods or "system" used are typically the "service" that is franchised. The franchisor must ensure that the operations manual is understandable and easy to integrate into franchisee operations. The following quote about College Pro Painters (www.collegepro.com) shows the time and care taken in preparing the operations manual:

> After graduation in 1974, he took a year off to travel around the world, and started to put together a manual for the operation of College Pro Painters. Drawing on the knowledge he had acquired at school, he developed a chronology for starting a business and systematically attached every topic from "Business Plan" to "Close Down" in what would become his corporate bible.[49]

6. Establish a Support System.

After establishing standard operations, entrepreneurs will have to create a support system to assist franchisees in training and managing their company. Most successful franchisors have initial and ongoing training in place for franchisees and provide assistance in managing the ongoing operation of the business, including, but not limited to, staffing, marketing, and financial planning. As noted above, Boston Pizza one of Canada's most successful franchises, provides training for new franchisees in a corporate store and then sends a nine-person team to help train the staff prior to opening. Additionally, the franchisees can expect to be visited a minimum of four times a year for an assessment of operational performance and food quality. Boston Pizza also sends in secret shoppers throughout the year to help improve restaurant performance and maintains an advisory council to provide advice to store owners.[50] Nurse Next Door, as discussed above, established a call centre and staffed it with trained operators to assist franchisees in managing their business. Boston Pizza and Nurse Next Door are not alone in this support, and other successful franchisors such as Tim Hortons, Subway, and Harvey's actively provide franchisees with a considerable amount of assistance in running their business.

7. Obtain Adequate Financing.

To franchise successfully, the franchisor will need capital to set up the prototype business, do the necessary market research, prepare the promotional literature and financial estimates, and develop the system of operations. A rapid expansion program may even require outside equity financing from a venture-capital company or other financial institution.

8. Find Franchisees.

After establishing standard operations, obtaining capital, and creating a support system, franchisors must find franchisees. A common method to do this is to advertise in trade publications, on the Internet, or to rely on word of mouth. Franchisors should recognize that the selection of franchisees is very important to the long-term success of their firm. George Melville, co-owner of Boston Pizza, says, "You want somebody who is entrepreneurial and yet can work within a system. A lot of times you need some business acumen and some money, but you also need a personality."[51] Successful franchisors will spend significant resources finding and then selecting franchisees. Cora restaurant will spend two months evaluating franchise candidates and only one in 15 actually make the cut. Douglas Fisher, a Toronto restaurant consultant, says, "Franchisees are your partners and you need to pick them wisely. A heartbeat and money does not make a good franchisee."[52]

FRANCHISING IN THE FUTURE

Franchising is expected to continue its rapid growth as new types of businesses incorporate franchising principles into their operations. Several trends are expected to surface in the future. The retail food industry, the largest sector of Canadian franchising, is expected to continue its growth, but in more specialized areas such as ethnic foods. This growth will provide numerous opportunities for entrepreneurs, but it also means greater competition for existing small businesses in certain industries. As mentioned previously, more and more service businesses are expected to become franchises. A high percentage of Canada's fastest-growing franchises are in the service industry.

Some franchises are experimenting with "piggybacking," in which two or more franchises operate in one outlet. This concept has been tried with gas stations/convenience stores and restaurants/video stores. The practice of converting existing chain outlets to franchises, or "branchising," is expected to continue as chains search for new sources of interest-free capital. Additional growth areas in franchising are "mini-franchises," which are small satellite versions of larger franchisees (e.g., a McDonald's in a Walmart) and mobile franchises that move from location to location on a seasonal basis.

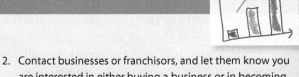

TIME TO TAKE ACTION

If you are interested in becoming an entrepreneur as a franchisee, learning more about franchising, or growing a business through acquisition, then this is the time to act. You may want to consider using some or all of the steps outlined below:

1. Start to study the industry in which you are interested in owning a business. Narrow the search down to a few franchises or specific businesses. Conduct some research specific to the company, including identifying and assessing their marketing mix, value chain, and competition. Then look at the target market, and identify who the customers are, talk to them to determine if they are satisfied, if they will continue to visit the location, and so forth.

2. Contact businesses or franchisors, and let them know you are interested in either buying a business or in becoming a franchisee. If you are looking to buy a business, then you should start to investigate the financials of the company and the personnel using the methods discussed in this chapter. If it is a franchise, then you will ask to see additional information and to speak to franchisees.

3. Speak to people who have engaged in similar business decisions in the past. If you are buying a business, talk to people who have bought businesses about the pros and cons, how to structure a deal, and where to get financing. If you are interested in franchising, then speak to people who have owned and operated a franchise.

LEARNING OBJECTIVES SUMMARY

LO1 The potential advantages of buying a small business include the reduction of risk, time, set-up expense, and competition; capitalization of business strength; possible assistance from the previous owner; and easier planning. Potential disadvantages include problems with physical facilities, personnel, inventory, and accounts receivable; deterioration of the business's financial condition or market; and difficulty in negotiating a purchase price.

LO2 The common sources for locating a business for sale include classified ads, government departments, real estate brokers, word of mouth, and professionals such as lawyers, accountants, and bankers.

LO3 The key areas an entrepreneur should investigate in carrying out an industry analysis are sales and profit trends, degree of competition, state of the economy in the market area, legal restrictions, and social concerns that may adversely affect the industry in the future. To evaluate the internal aspects, the following should be addressed: previous owner's reputation, why the owner is selling the business, validity of the financial statements, condition of the assets, personnel, external relationships of the business, and existing records.

LO4 There are three general approaches to valuing a business. The first method uses the asset value to determine the price. The second method uses the earnings of the business. The third method uses a combination of assets and earnings.

LO5 Franchising has enjoyed phenomenal growth in recent years. One reason franchising is popular is the increased incentives for franchisees. Franchising continues to allow many organizations with a proven concept or product to expand much more rapidly to meet demand.

LO6 The three types of franchises are (a) the manufacturer-directed franchise, in which the manufacturer of a product grants a dealer the right to sell the product; (b) the wholesaler–retailer-directed franchise, in which one member of the distribution channel, such as the wholesaler or retailer, initiates the organization of the franchise; and (c) the franchise company, in which a company sells a product, service, or system in exchange for an initial predetermined fee and an ongoing royalty.

LO7 Franchising offers the following advantages over the other two methods of starting a small business: a proven market and services such as selection of location, purchase or construction of the site, financing, standardized methods of operating, advertising, volume purchasing, and training. The potential disadvantages of franchising are lack of independence, cost of the franchise, unfulfilled promises, restrictions of the contract, saturation of the market, lack of security, cost of merchandise, and possible exaggeration of financial success.

LO8 Several key areas should be examined in evaluating a franchise. Information can be obtained from several sources, including the franchising company, the Association of Canadian Franchisors, professionals such as lawyers and accountants, other franchisees, and government agencies.

LO9 Becoming a successful franchisor entails five steps. The first step is to develop a franchise prototype to iron out any difficulties. The second is to prepare the necessary information for the prospective franchisee. The third is to investigate the legal requirements in setting up a franchise company. The fourth is to plan and standardize the program of operation to facilitate the monitoring of operations. The last step is to ensure that adequate financing is available to keep up with possible rapid expansion.

DISCUSSION QUESTIONS

1. Why are there so many different techniques for determining the worth of a firm? In any given situation, is there one "right answer" for a company's value? What effects do your answers to these questions have on the entrepreneur making an acquisition?

2. Being a franchisor seems to be a mechanism for growth, but what are the growth prospects for entrepreneurs that are franchisees? Isn't the entrepreneur limited in his or her ability to pursue all the different types of growth strategies?

3. Is being a franchisee simply substituting one type of employment for another type of employment?

4. What do you think is the best method of becoming an entrepreneur? Starting a business from scratch? Buying an existing business? Buying a franchise? Why?

5. Discuss in detail the steps you would follow in developing a house-cleaning franchise system.

6. What possible benefits does a franchise realize in franchising its businesses instead of expanding through company-owned outlets? What method of expansion would you prefer? Why?

APPLICATION QUESTIONS AND HANDS-ON ACTIVITIES

1. Find a local business that is for sale, and investigate and evaluate the company. Determine whether the business is overvalued, fairly valued, or undervalued. If you had the capital, would you buy this business? Have other groups evaluate each business, and compare the results.

2. John Van Goegh wants to own his own business. His area of expertise is the sporting goods market. He has checked into opening his own store versus purchasing an existing store in the downtown area. The existing store is a seven-year-old proprietorship with sagging sales. There are four main sporting goods shops in the city (60,000 people). The existing business is in a prime location, and the market and product line are well established. The financial condition, however, includes a large number of accounts receivable. With this information, John turns to you as a consultant. What advice would you give John regarding whether to purchase the existing business or start his own? What additional factors should he consider? Justify your answer.

3. You are investigating the purchase of a fertilizer manufacturing plant. The results of your analysis of the firm are extremely positive, except for an unidentifiable annual payment of $100,000. On further investigation, you learn that the $100,000 is being paid in fines for dumping toxic waste. The previous owner has determined that it costs less to pay the fines than it would to properly dispose of the waste by deep-well injection. In light of recent government actions, how would this situation affect your decision to purchase? Explain.

4. Sally's Bar and Grill is available for purchase. Sally's earnings for the past five years were as follows:

    Last year, $50,000   Four years ago, $40,000
    Two years ago, $60,000   Five years ago, $25,000
    Three years ago, $30,000

    Determine the value of the business, using the following methods (use current bank interest rates) and both general and weighted averaging methods:
    a. Capitalized earnings formula
    b. Times earnings method

5. Do an industry analysis for the existing grocery stores in your area. Complete your analysis using all the areas mentioned in the text. Refer to the checklist in Appendix 5A.

6. Have students visit the website, www.Entrepreneur.com, and complete a search for the top franchises for the year, fastest-growing franchises, and low-cost franchises. The students can proceed to engage in a number of activities, including the following:
    - Select one franchise from each category, and complete a profile of the company that can be submitted or presented to class.
    - Select on franchise and complete a full investigation, and conclude whether the franchise would be a good investment for the geographic region.
    - Compare the support, training, costs, and so forth associated with a low-cost franchise with one of the top or high-growth companies. Have the students determine if the added costs are justified.

7. Visit a local franchise in your city, and ask the manager what he or she thinks are the advantages and disadvantages of franchising.

Although the numbers Dan put together indicated that the Ladder Rail business might face several challenges, he decides to devote all his spare time to the venture. This is primarily because of the positive response that he has received from his co-workers, the local Home Hardware dealer, as well as numerous comments on the Internet, all agreeing that the product has potential. Dan is particularly excited about some of the positive comments on crowd-sourcing sites, as they had come from all over the world, and he is convinced the product could have global appeal. Dan was so enamored by the response that he decided to put up a few units for sale using Kijiji and some Internet sites used by inventors. He quickly had to pull the ads down, as he sold 10 units within a few short days, essentially running out of product. Feedback from customers has been positive, and this is encouraging Dan.

One of the decisions that Dan is concerned about is whether to build a manufacturing plant or purchase an existing facility. He is aware of a small plant close to his home that is for sale. It has much of the metal-bending equipment that he needs, and he could retrofit the plant to suit his purposes for $10,000. However, when he learns that the owner of the plant is asking $200,000 and that its net worth is only $180,000, Dan feels that it is just too much money and is leaning toward building his own plant. Dan's wife, Suzie, has been pressuring Dan to consider manufacturing the product in China to reduce costs, but Dan is insistent that the product be made in Canada.

Regardless of how he establishes the manufacturing facility, one thing that Dan learned in his small business management class was that he should prepare a business plan. He therefore sets to work preparing the plan. The outline of Dan Kim's business plan for the Ladder Rail is found below.

Introduction

My objective in starting this business is to become independent and develop a business that will provide an adequate living for my family and me. I anticipate that within three years, the product will experience high awareness and demand throughout Southern Ontario and Canada. At that time, I will look to expand globally. I have considerable expertise in construction and roofing, which has allowed me to be knowledgeable about the safety and convenience concerns associated with the use of ladders.

Marketing

The product is a light metal handrail that will attach to most aluminum extension ladders commonly used in the construction industry and by many homeowners. It can be made inexpensively (estimated at $10 per unit) and has great profit potential (selling price estimated at $40 per unit). I anticipate that anyone who owns a ladder would see the Ladder Rail's benefit and would be interested in purchasing it. I intend to promote the product on the Internet during the early days of the company, making use of social media sites, sites that allow for free advertisements such as Kijiji, and perhaps make use of some traditional promotion such as newspapers and perhaps television advertising. I am also hopeful that I will be able to generate some publicity for the product, as there is currently no other product like it on the market.

Physical Facilities

Although I now can manufacture the Ladder Rail in my garage, as sales increase, I will need to build or purchase a small factory to meet the demand. I estimate that an adequate production facility, including the required equipment, will cost approximately $170,000. I already own the land that the plant would be built on.

Financial

I currently have $20,000 of my own money to invest in the business and will borrow the rest from the local bank. I am certain that the business will be able to generate the required income to make the interest payments on the loan plus provide a good living for my family.

Legal

I plan to operate the business as a sole proprietorship for the first few years until incorporation looks positive. I will need a business licence to operate the manufacturing plant.

Personnel

The business will employ three people initially, including me. I will be in charge of the production process, assisted by two others. I will also handle the marketing and financial aspects of the Ladder Rail with the help of my wife, Suzie.

Questions

1. What aspects about this situation would suggest that Dan should buy the plant instead of building it from scratch?

2. If Dan decided to purchase the building and estimated that income from the plant would be $20,000, is the asking price reasonable, assuming he wanted to make a 10 percent return on the investment? (Use the capitalization of earnings formula.)

3. Evaluate the business plan that Dan has prepared. Suggest improvements.

CHECKLIST OF CONSIDERATIONS IN PURCHASING A BUSINESS

THE INDUSTRY

1. What are the sales and profit trends in the industry?
2. What is the degree of competition? What competitive changes have taken place?
3. What is the nature of competitor strategies?
4. What is the state of the economy in the market? How is the business's performance affected by changes in the economy?
5. What existing or pending legal restrictions affect the operations of the business?
6. What social or cultural concerns affect the industry?
7. Are there any potential competitive or trading area changes that might affect the business?

THE PREVIOUS OWNER

1. Why is the previous owner selling the business?
2. Has the reputation of the previous owner contributed to the success of the business?
3. Will the previous owner help you by providing assistance and advice after the sale?
4. Is the previous owner willing to finance all or part of the purchase?
5. Will the previous owner start a competitive business after the sale?

FINANCIAL CONDITION OF THE BUSINESS

1. Is the financial information provided accurate and indicative of the business's performance?
2. What is the history of profits going back at least five years?

3. Has the business gained or lost market share in the past five years?

4. How do the various financial ratios for the business compare with industry averages?

5. Does the business have a strong identity with customers or clients? Can this identity be maintained?

6. What prospects does the business have for increasing market share and profitability in the future?

7. If the business is currently unsuccessful, what are the chances of improving it with an infusion of capital or managerial expertise?

8. What value does the business place on goodwill?

CONDITION OF ASSETS

1. Are any special terms or conditions associated with the liquid assets?

2. Are the accounts receivable collectible?

3. Is the inventory old or obsolete?

4. Are the building and equipment up to date and paid for?

5. Are taxes and service costs paid on land?

6. Is the location good? Is it increasing or decreasing in value?

7. Is the lease good? What are the terms and conditions of the lease?

8. Have you verified the value of assets with a qualified chartered business evaluator?

9. Are the systems and processes efficient, timely, and compatible with your own?

QUALITY OF PERSONNEL

1. Do the employees of the business compare favourably with the industry in productivity and expertise?

2. Will the employees stay on with the business after the sale?

3. Has the business been progressive in meeting competitive demands regarding wage rates and employee benefits?

CONDITION OF EXTERNAL RELATIONSHIPS

1. Can favourable relations with suppliers be maintained?

2. Are financial sources appropriate and adequate? Can they be maintained?

3. Does the business have a strong support staff such as a lawyer, an accountant, and a consultant? Can these people be retained, if needed?

CONDITION OF RECORDS

1. Can the purchaser obtain key records such as credit files, personnel files, customer lists, sales reports, and contracts?

A CHECKLIST FOR THE POTENTIAL FRANCHISEE: QUESTIONS TO ANSWER AFFIRMATIVELY BEFORE GOING INTO FRANCHISING

THE FRANCHISOR

1. Has the franchisor been in business long enough (five years or more) to have established a good reputation?

2. Have you checked better business bureaus, chambers of commerce, government agencies, Association of Canadian Franchisors, industry associations, or bankers to find out about the franchisor's business reputation and credit rating?

3. Did the above investigations reveal that the franchisor has a good reputation and credit rating?

4. Does the franchising firm appear to be financed adequately so that it can carry out its stated plan of financial assistance and expansion?

5. Have you found out how many franchisees are now operating?

6. Have you found out the "mortality" or failure rate among franchisees?

7. Is the failure rate low?

8. Have you checked with some franchisees and found that the franchisor has a reputation for honesty and fair dealings among current franchisees?

9. Has the franchisor shown you certified figures indicating exact net profits of one or more going operations that you have checked yourself?

10. Has the franchisor given you a specimen contract to study with the advice of your legal counsel?

11. Will the franchisor assist you with:

    a. A management training program?

    b. An employee training program?

    c. A public relations program?

    d. Obtaining capital?

    e. Good credit terms?

    f. Merchandising ideas?

    g. Designing store layout and displays?

    h. Inventory control methods?

    i. Analyzing financial statements?

12. Does the franchisor provide continuing assistance for franchisees through supervisors who visit regularly?

13. Does the franchising firm have experienced and highly trained management?

14. Will the franchisor help you find a good location for your business?

15. Has the franchising company investigated you carefully enough to assure itself that you can successfully operate one of its franchises at a profit both to it and to you?

16. Have you determined exactly what the franchisor can do for you that you cannot do for yourself?

THE PRODUCT OR SERVICE

17. Has the product or service been on the market long enough to gain broad consumer acceptance?

18. Is it priced competitively?

19. Is it the type of item or service the same consumer customarily buys more than once?

20. Is it an all-year seller in contrast to a seasonal one?

21. Is it a staple item in contrast to a fad?

22. Does it sell well elsewhere?

23. Would you buy it on its own merits?

24. Will it be in greater demand five years from now?

25. If it is a product rather than a service:

    a. Is it packaged attractively?

    b. Does it stand up well to use?

    c. Is it easy and safe to use?

    d. Is it patented?

    e. Does it comply with all applicable laws?

    f. Is it manufactured under certain quality standards?

g. Do these standards compare favourably with similar products on the market?

h. If the product must be purchased exclusively from the franchisor or a designated supplier, are the prices for you, as the franchisee, competitive?

THE FRANCHISE CONTRACT

26. Does the franchisee fee seem reasonable?

27. Do continuing royalties or percent of sales payment appear reasonable?

28. Is the total cash investment required and the items for financing the balance satisfactory?

29. Does the cash investment include payment for fixtures and equipment?

30. If you will be required to participate in company-sponsored promotion and publicity by contributing to an advertising fund, will you have the right to veto any increase in contributions to the fund?

31. If the parent company's product or service is protected by patent or liability insurance, is the same protection extended to you?

32. Are you free to buy the amount of merchandise you believe you need rather than required to purchase a certain amount?

33. Can you, as the franchisee, return merchandise for credit?

34. Can you engage in other business activities?

35. If there is an annual sales quota, can you retain your franchise if it is not met?

36. Does the contract give you an exclusive territory for the length of the franchise?

37. Is your territory protected?

38. Is the franchise agreement renewable?

39. Can you terminate your agreement if you are not happy for some reason?

40. Is the franchisor prohibited from selling the franchise out from under you?

41. Can you sell the business to whomever you please?

42. If you sell your franchise, will you be compensated for the goodwill you have built into the business?

43. Does the contract obligate the franchisor to give you continuing assistance after you are operating the business?

44. Are you permitted a choice in determining whether you will sell any new product or service introduced by the franchisor after you have opened your business?

45. Is there anything with respect to the franchise or its operations that would make you ineligible for special financial assistance or other benefits accorded to small business concerns by federal, provincial or territorial, or local governments?

46. Did your lawyer approve the franchise contract after studying it paragraph by paragraph?

47. Is the contract free and clear of requirements that would call on you to take any steps that your lawyer thinks are unwise or illegal in your province, county, or city?

48. Does the contract cover all aspects of your agreement with the franchisor?

49. Does it really benefit both you and the franchisor?

YOUR MARKET

50. Are the territorial boundaries of your market completely, accurately, and understandably defined?

51. Have you made any study to determine whether the product or service you propose to sell has a market in your territory at the prices you will have to charge?

52. Does the territory provide adequate sales potential?

53. Will the population in your territory increase over the next five years?

54. Will the average per capita income in your territory remain the same or increase over the next five years?

55. Is the existing competition in your territory for the product or service not too well entrenched?

56. Are you prepared to give up some independence of action to secure the advantages offered by the franchise?

57. Are you capable of accepting supervision, even though you will presumably be your own boss?

58. Are you prepared to accept rules and regulations that you may not agree with?

59. Can you afford the period of training involved?

60. Are you ready to spend much or all of the remainder of your business life with this franchisor, offering this product or service to the public?

For more information on the resources available from McGraw-Hill Ryerson, go to www.mcgrawhill.ca/he/solutions.

CHAPTER 6

FINANCING THE SMALL BUSINESS

LEARNING OBJECTIVES

By the end of this chapter, you should be able to:

LO1 Discuss financing problems experienced by small businesses.

LO2 Identify the types of start-up capital the entrepreneur may require.

LO3 Explain the stages of venture funding.

LO4 Illustrate a method for determining the amount of capital required.

LO5 Identify the sources of equity and debt funds available to start and operate a small business.

LO6 Explain the considerations in obtaining equity or debt financing.

LO7 Discuss what elements to include when preparing a proposal to obtain financing for the small business.

SMALL BUSINESS PROFILE

RAZOR SULEMAN *Achievers*

Razor Suleman, 35, is the founder and CEO of Achievers (www.achievers.com), an employee recognition company that was originally called I Love Rewards Inc. Suleman began his first business at 15, importing and selling hockey cards between Canada and the United States. The profit he generated from his first of many ventures paid his tuition to Wilfrid Laurier University, where he studied Business and Economics.

Out of Suleman's Bricker Residence dorm room, he started his own campus-branded apparel company, Razor's Edge. After graduating from university, Suleman expanded his business to include supplying corporate-branded items for large businesses. Suleman soon discovered that nobody works harder for a coffee mug, and his clients needed more to give their employees an incentive for doing a job well. Branded apparel was not influencing behaviour or motivating employees to do a better job. Challenged by this obvious demand in the industry, Suleman created I Love Rewards in 2002.

I Love Rewards grew to become the leading web-based employee rewards and recognition solution provider. It works with top employers in North America to drive the behaviours and results most important to their organization and build a motivated and aligned workforce.

By mid-2005, I Love Rewards had 18 employees and $5 million in sales. This rapid growth created several internal management problems that led Suleman to reorganize and clearly set out his vision for the company. Much of the reorganization took the form of creative employee management practices, allowing Suleman to obtain financing to break into the U.S. market, which was integral to the company's growth vision. For the financial backing the company needed, he decided that venture capital was the best route to follow.

In 2008, I Love Rewards received $4 million during its Series A financing round led by JLA Ventures with

Photo by Peter Power/The Globe and Mail/
The Canadian Press

participation by Lawrence Capital. Success came rapidly after that, with sales nearly tripling in two years. In the summer of 2009, I Love Rewards accepted its Series B funding led by Grand Banks Capital, with participation from the Ontario Venture Capital Fund, Lawrence Capital, and JLA Ventures. Although this financing has allowed I Love Rewards to achieve an increase in sales, it did cost Suleman his majority interest in the company he had founded. However, Razor states, "You either have to give up control to get big, or you stay small."

In 2011, I Love Rewards opted to change its name to Achievers as Suleman felt the new name better described the company's goal of increasing employee engagement and driving performance. Suleman says, "The new name highlights the values and philosophy that we use to help our customers to build great corporate cultures every day." Achievers shows no signs of slowing down, as the firm recently reported continued rapid growth including a 105 percent increase in year over year revenue, 162 percent increase in employees, and an additional capital injection of $14 million from investors. According to Suleman, not only is the company growing but it is retaining customers, as 84 percent of firms who work with Achievers return. "Our platform is sticky. Eighty-four percent of our entire user base comes back every quarter. Our churn is less than one percent."[1]

Suleman's one piece of advice to Canadian entrepreneurs is to think bigger. In a recent interview he refers to the famous line in the *Social Network* movie where Mark Zuckerberg's character realizes that while a million dollar company is cool. . . . what is really cool is a billion dollar company. Suleman says Canadian entrepreneurs should think bigger and try to create businesses that make lasting change to how things are done.[2]

ACHIEVERS
www.achievers.com

SMALL BUSINESS FINANCING   LO1

The inability to obtain adequate funding has often been cited as a major small business frustration, if not a primary cause of some small business failures. The entrepreneur may require financing not only to start the business but also to provide capital to fund ongoing operations.

One dilemma the entrepreneur often faces is that as the business grows, funds are needed for expansion. As the previous chapter illustrated, franchising is one solution to this financing problem.

Although many small businesses experience difficulties due to their inability to obtain needed funds, statistics show that financing woes are often a symptom of other management problems.[3] Lack of managerial competence and experience can often result in the following specific financial problems:

- Underestimating financial requirements. This typically leads to undercapitalization (shortage of cash) and is a major cause of failure.

- Lack of knowledge of sources of equity and debt capital, leading to either an inability to obtain funds or the failure to obtain them at the lowest cost.

- Lack of skills in preparing and presenting a proposal for financing to a lender or investor.

- Failure to plan in advance for future needs, resulting in last-minute financial crises.

- Poor financial control of operations, leading to failure in payment of loan obligations.

This chapter discusses each of these important areas to help the entrepreneur obtain financing for establishing his or her business. Most of the information in this chapter is also applicable to the purchase of a business or for signing a franchise contract. Readers should recognize that while obtaining financing is not always easy, perseverance and hard work will usually pay off in the form of an investment. For example, when Christopher Frey, Kisha Feruson, and Matt Robinson began searching for the $300,000 they needed to fund their Toronto-based Canadian adventure travel magazine, Outpost (www.outpost-magazine.com), they had to be determined. In less than three months, the three owners telephoned over 200 potential investors. While the trio was initially unsuccessful in raising all the money needed, they did manage to come up with $50,000 in bridge financing. Two years later, after many failed attempts, the company managed to raise a $1 million equity injection from BHVR Communications, a Montreal media and entertainment company.

THE IMPORTANCE OF CAPITAL AND PLANNING   LO2

Entrepreneurs have probably heard the saying "cash is king," but until you are actively starting or managing an enterprise, a potential entrepreneur may not fully understand the statement. For a start-up venture, cash is what is needed to gain access to supplies and to purchase inventory and assets, while growing businesses need cash to pay employees, restock inventory, and conduct day-to-day operations. While profits are important, cash is the heart of the business; without it, a business will fail to exist. For example, Display Partners (www.displaypartners.com), an Ontario company that specializes in moving tradeshow booths, generated $573,000 in sales in their first year but they could not finance the growth because they were receivable rich and cash poor. The business eventually had to find a U.S. company that would purchase their receivables to provide needed cash. Entrepreneurs should be aware of the following issues when trying to raise capital:

- How much do you need? Entrepreneurs should determine the amount of funds needed. Investors will want to see a documented plan noting exactly what the money will be used for. If entrepreneurs are purchasing assets, investors will want to make sure they are providing exact costs and not rough estimates.

- When will the funds be used? Investors will want to know exactly when the money will be spent.

- How long will the money last? Entrepreneurs and investors have a vested interest in determining how long the requested money will last. For example, when Mitomicsinc (www.mitomicsinc.com), an Ontario biotechnology company, was searching for $3.3 million, they informed investors that the financing was to get their product from the science stage to proof-of-concept, and then more financing would be required at that point.

- Where can the money be raised and what type of financing (debt versus equity) will be used? When first looking at the financial landscape, there appears to be many sources of financing, but as discussed below, the stage of the company will usually dictate the choice of funding available.

- Do you need funds immediately? If the company does not need money right away, they will be in a stronger bargaining position with both debt and equity investors. As such, entrepreneurs should pay attention to their burn rate, or how much money they are spending a month, and anticipate when they will be out of cash. By monitoring these factors, entrepreneurs will know the urgency associated with obtaining financing.

- Will I get anything else besides money? Often investors will contribute their knowledge and experience along with their money to a business venture. Equity investors in particular will often insist on overseeing if not contributing to the management of a company. For an entrepreneur, especially an entrepreneur with limited contacts or experience, these contributions are particularly useful.

DETERMINING THE AMOUNT OF FUNDS NEEDED

As indicated above, the first step in securing capital (funds) for the business is to determine the amount of money needed. Any lender or investor will want to see evidence of a systematic and thoroughly prepared statement of fund requirements. In this regard, it is helpful to divide required funding into two categories: start-up costs and ongoing operating requirements. The entrepreneur's own funds available for the venture can then be subtracted from the projected required amounts to obtain the capital needed from outside sources, as shown in the following formula:

$$\text{Capital requirements} = \text{Start-up costs} + \text{Operating requirements} \\ - \text{Owner assets available for investment}$$

START-UP COSTS   LO3

Capital is required to finance land, buildings, equipment, and other items needed to start up the business. Figure 6-1 illustrates an example of a start-up schedule for a small retail

FIGURE 6-1 Start-up Cost Schedule

ITEM	COST	SOURCE
Land and buildings	No cost—leased	If purchased, a similar business or quotes from suppliers
Equipment	$ 34,000	Other similar businesses or quotes from suppliers
Initial inventory	70,000	Other similar businesses or quotes from suppliers
		Use the formula Inventory = Projected sales/Inventory turnover (300,000/4.3)
Wages (first two months)	6,000	Other similar businesses or current wage rates
Utilities and telephone		
First deposit	100	Quotes from provider
First two months	680	Quotes from provider
Rent (deposit)	500	Quotes from lessor
First two months	3,000	Quotes from lessor
Advertising agency/media	960	Quotes from advertising agency or media
Insurance (prepaid)	975	Quotes from insurer
Licences and permits	200	Quotes from municipal agency
Other prepaids	285	Other similar businesses
Contingency	3,300	
Total start-up requirements	**$120,000**	

THE FIRST STEP IN FINANCING IS DETERMINING THE START-UP FUNDS NEEDED. A GOOD RULE OF THUMB IS TO ADD UP ALL THE CAPITAL COSTS AND ALLOW FOR SIX MONTHS, WORKING CAPITAL.
© Ariel Skelley/Blend Images LLC

store. Note the source provided for each number in the schedule. The owner should obtain and verify quotes from sellers of these assets with owners of existing similar businesses. Add a contingency factor for potential price increases during the planning and start-up phase.

Start-up capital is also required to finance some of the operating costs during this period. Usually a delay in sales revenues occurs for a start-up business, but many operating expenses are incurred before the business begins operating. The entrepreneur needs to estimate these types of expenses and include them in the capital requirements. The length of time until operations provide sufficient cash flow to finance expenses will vary, but it may be two to six months. Some of these types of expenses are:

- Initial inventory
- First few months' payroll, including owner's salary
- First few months' utilities
- First few months' rent
- Initial advertising
- Prepaid items such as utility deposits, rent deposits, and insurance
- Licences and permits
- Other operating costs to be paid before revenues are generated

Start-up costs may be difficult to project. Note the sources of information used to prepare this statement. Also note that operations of the business in the first two months should provide some cash to offset the initial start-up requirements, although this has not been included in this example.

ONGOING OPERATING COSTS

The entrepreneur should prepare a cash flow statement to calculate financial operating requirements after the start-up period. A cash flow statement, explained in more detail in Chapter 9, is simply a record of all projected cash inflows and outflows. An example of such a statement for the same business for which the start-up schedule appears is found in Figure 6-2. In this monthly cash flow for a hypothetical business, it has been calculated that up to $34,000 may be needed to finance operations. This occurs in the first month.

If debt financing were used, the entrepreneur would most likely attempt to arrange a $35,000 line of credit (operating loan) with a lender to cover this amount when required. Such a method of financing would allow the business to withdraw and deposit funds on an ongoing basis as long as the total amount withdrawn at any point in time did not exceed $35,000.

THE OWNER'S NET WORTH

After estimating start-up and operating capital requirements, the owner should prepare a personal net worth and capability statement. Preparing this statement will not only help determine the amount of the owner's funds to invest in the business but will also probably be required by a lending institution if the owner needs to borrow the necessary capital. The essentials of the personal net worth statement are the same as those for a business's balance sheet. An example of a net worth statement appears in Figure 6-3.

FIGURE 6-2	Sample Cash Flow Statement					
	BEFORE START-UP	**FEB.**	**MARCH**	**APRIL**	**MAY**	**JUNE**
Opening balance	$ 0	$(69,000)	$(65,285)	$(48,595)	$(31,905)	$(55,173)
Bank loan	$ 35,000	0	0	0	0	0
Sales: Cash	0	12,000	12,000	12,000	13,750	13,750
Credit	0	0	12,000	12,000	12,000	13,750
Total receipts	$ 35,000	$(57,000)	$(41,285)	$(24,595)	$ (6,155)	$(27,673)
Disbursements						
Furniture and fixtures	$ 34,000	$ 0	$ 0	$ 0	$ 0	$ 0
Rent		1,500	1,500	1,500	1,500	1,500
Utilities		200	200	200	200	200
Promotion (2% of sales)		480	480	480	550	550
Telephone		140	140	140	140	140
Wages and salaries		3,000	3,000	3,000	3,000	3,000
Inventory	70,000	0	0	0	41,820	0
Maintenance and repairs		240	240	240	270	270
Professional fees		330	330v	330	330	330
Insurance		975	0	0	0	0
Interest and bank charges		1,420	1,420	1,420	1,208	1,208
Loan repayment						
Total disbursements	$104,000	$ 8,285	$ 7,310	$ 7,310	$ 49,018	$ 7,198
Cash (+/−)	$ (69,000)	$(65,285)	$(48,595)	$(31,905)	$(55,173)	$(34,871)

Note: 50% of monthly sales are cash and 50% are credit. The credit sales are collected in the next month.

DETERMINING TYPES OF FINANCING

Two general sources of funds can be used to finance a small business. The first is equity or ownership financing. The second is funds obtained from borrowing, usually referred to as debt financing (including trade credit). Many small businesses use both forms of financing to get established, although, as discussed below, the stage the business is in (start-up compared with high growth) will often impact the type and source of financing used.

BUSINESS STAGES AND FINANCING   LO4

The type of financing entrepreneurs can access is usually dictated by the stage the business is in and the type of opportunities the company is pursuing. In Canada, start-up businesses are traditionally self-funded, with 73 percent of new ventures relying on personal savings, while ongoing business are often using personal investment and retained earnings (64 percent and 54 percent). In addition, entrepreneurs who are just starting a business are more likely to be turned down for bank financing (40 percent rejection rate compared with 13 percent overall) and usually have to sign a personal guarantee for debt.[4]

FIGURE 6-2 — Sample Cash Flow Statement (concluded)

	JULY	AUG.	SEPT.	OCT.	NOV.	DEC.	JAN.
	$(34,871)	$(14,569)	$(36,839)	$(17,289)	$ 2,261	$(20,311)	$ 1,467
	0	0	0	0	0	0	0
	13,750	13,750	13,750	13,750	13,750	14,250	14,250
	13,750	13,750	13,750	13,750	13,750	14,250	14,250
	$ (7,371)	$ 12,931	$ (9,339)	$ 10,211	$ 29,761	$ 8,189	$ 29,967
	$ 0	$ 0	$ 0	$ 0	$ 0	$ 0	$ 0
	1,500	1,500	1,500	1,500	1,500	1,500	1,500
	200	200v	200	200	200	200	200
	550	550v	550	550	570	570	570
	140	140	140	140	140	140	140
	3,000	3,000	3,000	3,000	3,000	3,000	3,000
	0	41,820	0	0	43,350	0	0
	270	270	270	270	270	270	290
	330	330	330	330	330	330	330
	0	0	0	0	0	0	0
	1,208	1,960	1,960	1,960	712	712	712
	0	0	0	0	0	0	35,000
	$ 7,198	$ 49,770	$ 7,950	$ 7,950	$ 50,072	$ 6,722	$ 41,742
	$(14,569)	$(36,839)	$(17,289)	$ 2,261	$(20,311)	$ 1,467	$(11,775)

As illustrated in Figure 6-4, start-up companies are much more likely to rely on personal savings and personal lines of credit when compared with SMEs with a history.

Figure 6-5 illustrates the types of financing used to maintain company activities in 2007.

Figure 6-6 offers a more detailed analysis of the types of financial instruments used by SMEs in 2007.

In addition to the stage a business is in, the type of opportunity that the company is pursuing is very likely to dictate the type of financing sought (Figure 6-7). Entrepreneurs who are starting or managing a relatively small business that is pursuing a slow growth strategy will often be limited to debt as their main source of capital, although they may use equity when dealing with small business angels, friends, and relatives. These smaller start-ups also pass through fewer stages as they travel from idea inception to an ongoing business (examples of these businesses include service companies, retail operations, and food and beverage businesses).

Entrepreneurs who are pursuing a high growth venture are much more likely to use equity and debt in financing their business. These businesses are usually in technology, health care, or knowledge-based industries, and they pass through numerous stages of financing and operations compared with low growth SMEs.

FIGURE 6-3

Suggested Format for a Personal Net Worth Statement

Personal Net Worth Statement for _____

As of _____, 20_____

ASSETS		LIABILITIES	
Cash on hand and in banks	$ _____	Accounts payable	$ _____
Savings account in banks	_____	Notes payable to banks	_____
Canada savings bonds	_____		
Accounts and notes receivable	_____	Notes payable to others	_____
Life insurance—cash surrender value only	_____		
Other stocks and bonds	_____	Instalment account (auto)	
		Monthly payments $ _____	_____
Real estate	_____	Instalment accounts (other)	
		Monthly payments $ _____	_____
Automobile—present value	_____	Loans on life insurance	_____
Other personal property	_____	Mortgages on real estate	_____
Other assets	_____	Unpaid taxes	_____
		Other liabilities	_____
		Total liabilities	_____
		Net worth	_____
Total	$ _____	Total	$ _____

The three types of funding as the high growth business develops are indicated in Figure 6-8. The funding problems, as well as the cost of the funds, differ for each type. *Early-stage financing* is usually the most difficult and costly to obtain. Two types of financing are available during this stage: seed capital and start-up capital. Seed capital, the most difficult financing to obtain through outside funds, is usually a relatively small amount of funds needed to prove concepts and finance feasibility studies. Since venture capitalists usually have a minimum funding level of above $500,000, they are rarely involved in this type of funding, except in the case of high-technology ventures of entrepreneurs who have a successful track record and need a significant amount of capital. The second type of funding is start-up financing. As the name implies, start-up financing is involved in developing and selling some initial products to determine if commercial sales are feasible. These funds are also difficult to obtain. Angel investors are active in these two types of financing.

Expansion or development financing (the second basic financing type) is easier to obtain than early-stage financing. Venture capitalists play an active role in providing funds here. As the firm develops in each stage, the funds for expansion are less costly. Generally, funds in the second stage are used as working capital to support initial growth. In the third stage, the company is at break-even or a positive profit level and uses the funds for major sales expansion. Funds in the fourth stage are usually used as bridge financing in the interim period as the company prepares to go public.

Acquisitions and leveraged buyout financing (the third type) is more specific in nature. It is issued for such activities as traditional acquisitions, leveraged buyouts (management buying out the present owners), and going private (a publicly held firm buying out existing stockholders, thereby becoming a private company).

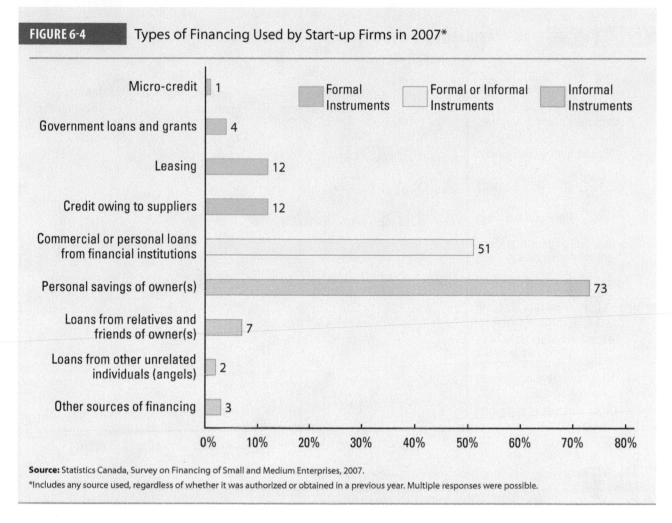

FIGURE 6-4 Types of Financing Used by Start-up Firms in 2007*

Micro-credit: 1
Government loans and grants: 4
Leasing: 12
Credit owing to suppliers: 12
Commercial or personal loans from financial institutions: 51
Personal savings of owner(s): 73
Loans from relatives and friends of owner(s): 7
Loans from other unrelated individuals (angels): 2
Other sources of financing: 3

Formal Instruments · Formal or Informal Instruments · Informal Instruments

0% 10% 20% 30% 40% 50% 60% 70% 80%

Source: Statistics Canada, Survey on Financing of Small and Medium Enterprises, 2007.

*Includes any source used, regardless of whether it was authorized or obtained in a previous year. Multiple responses were possible.

There are three *risk-capital markets* that can be involved in financing a firm's growth: the *informal risk-capital market or angel investors*, the *venture-capital market*, and the *public-equity market*. Although all three risk-capital markets can be a source of funds for stage-one financing, the public-equity market is available only for high-potential ventures, particularly when high technology is involved. Recently, some clean technology and biotechnology companies raised their first-stage financing through the public-equity market, since investors were excited about the potential prospects and returns in this high-interest area. This also occurred in the areas of oceanography and fuel alternatives when there was a high level of interest. Although venture capital also provides some first-stage funding, the venture usually requires the minimum capital level of $500,000. A venture-capital company establishes this minimum level of investment due to the high cost in evaluating and monitoring a deal. By far, the best source of funds for first-stage financing is the informal risk-capital market.

EQUITY FINANCING   LO5

Equity financing involves giving up ownership of the business in return for capital. The sources of equity financing are private investors, including using personal funds, friends and family, informal investors better known as angel investors, corporate investors commonly called venture capitalists, and government.

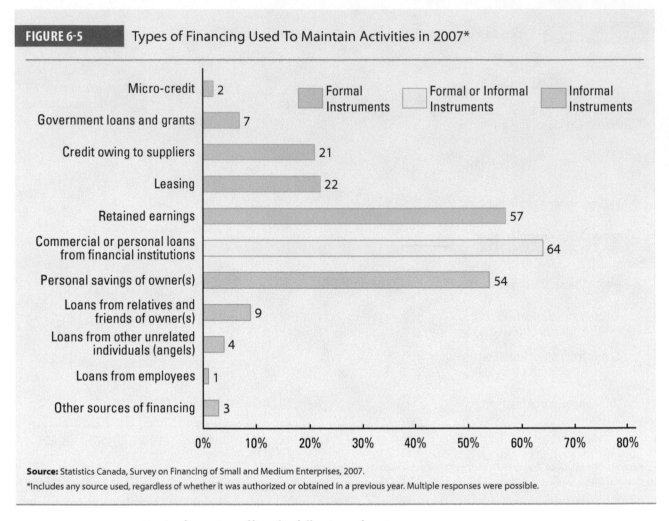

FIGURE 6-5   Types of Financing Used To Maintain Activities in 2007*

Micro-credit — 2
Government loans and grants — 7
Credit owing to suppliers — 21
Leasing — 22
Retained earnings — 57
Commercial or personal loans from financial institutions — 64
Personal savings of owner(s) — 54
Loans from relatives and friends of owner(s) — 9
Loans from other unrelated individuals (angels) — 4
Loans from employees — 1
Other sources of financing — 3

Legend: Formal Instruments, Formal or Informal Instruments, Informal Instruments

Source: Statistics Canada, Survey on Financing of Small and Medium Enterprises, 2007.

*Includes any source used, regardless of whether it was authorized or obtained in a previous year. Multiple responses were possible.

Equity financing offers the following advantages:

1. There is no obligation to pay dividends or interest. This flexibility allows the firm to invest earnings back into the business in its early years, when these funds are usually needed most.

2. Often the original owner benefits from the expertise the investor brings to the business in addition to the financial assistance.

3. Equity capital expands the borrowing power of the business. Most lenders require a certain percentage of equity investment by the owners before they will provide debt financing. Thus, the more equity a business has, the greater is its ability to obtain debt financing.

4. Equity financing spreads the risk of failure of the business to others.

Disadvantages of equity financing include the following:

1. Equity financing dilutes the ownership interest of the original owner and leads to decreased independence. Because of this drawback, many owner-managers are hesitant to follow this route in obtaining capital.

2. With others sharing the ownership interest, the possibility of disagreement and lack of coordination in the operations of the business increases.

3. A legal cost may be associated with issuance of the ownership interest.

FIGURE 6-6 **More Detailed Analysis of Types of Financial Instruments Used by SMEs**

START-UP SMEs	PERCENTAGE USED	SMEs	PERCENTAGE
Personal savings	66%	Commercial loans and lines of credit	49%
Personal credit cards	32%	Trade credit from suppliers	39%
Commercial loans and lines of credit	29%	Personal savings of owners	35%
Personal loans of owners	23%	Personal credit cards of owners	33%
Trade credit from suppliers	18%	Business retained earnings	31%
Leasing	12%	Commercial credit cards	26%
Loans from friends and relatives	12%	Personal lines of credit	21%
Commercial credit cards	8%	Leasing	16%
Government loans and grants	5%	Personal loans of owners	14%
Other sources	5%	Loans from friends and relatives	10%
Loans from employees	3%	Other sources including factoring, loans from employees	8%
Loans and investment from other individuals	1%	Government loans and grants	7%
		Loans and investment from other individuals	4%

Personal Funds and Retained Earnings.

Few, if any, new ventures are started without the personal funds of the entrepreneur. As indicated at the beginning of this chapter, 73 percent of start-ups use personal savings, and three out of the four most common financing strategies involve personal guarantees. Entrepreneurs

FIGURE 6-7 **Financing Small, Slow Growth Businesses**

Early Stage
- Seed capital — Relatively small amount to conduct market research and develop the business plan. Most likely sources are personal savings, personal lines of credit and/or credit cards, money from friends and relatives either in the form of equity or debt, and government programs.
- Start-up — Funding to get the business running. The business is operating but it is unlikely that it is profitable. Financing is usually needed for working capital, inventory, and marketing. Most likely sources are personal savings, personal lines of credit and/or credit cards, loans from a chartered bank that are personally guaranteed, trade credit, money from friends and relatives either in the form of equity or debt, government programs, and retained earnings.

Expansion/Maintaining Operations
- First stage — Funding to maintain operations as the business is striving to become profitable. Financing is used primarily for working capital, marketing, and other day-to-day activities. Most likely sources are personal savings, retained earnings, trade credit, personal or business lines of credit, and loans from chartered banks.
- Second stage — The business is profitable and may be starting a slow to medium-paced expansion. Financing is used for working capital and to fund expansion ideas. Most likely sources of financing are retained earnings, commercial lines of credit, and trade credit.

FIGURE 6-8   Stages of Business Development Funding

Early-Stage Financing: Most likely sources of funding are personal investment by the entrepreneur, friends and family, angel investors, and some venture-capital funding.

- Seed capital   Relatively small amounts to prove concepts and finance feasibility studies.
- Start-up   Product development and initial marketing, but with no commercial sales yet; funding to actually get company operations started.

Expansion or Development Financing: Most likely sources of funding are personal investment, venture capital, and government programs.

- Second stage   Working capital for initial growth phase, but no clear profitability or cash flow yet.
- Third stage   Major expansion for company with rapid sales growth, at break-even or positive profit levels but still private company.
- Fourth stage offering   Bridge financing as the company prepares to go public.

Acquisitions and Leveraged Buyout Financing: Most likely sources of funding are venture capital and bank financing.

- Traditional acquisitions   Assuming ownership and control of another company.
- Leveraged buyouts (LBOs)   Management of a company acquiring company control by buying out the present owners.
- Going private   Some of the owners/managers of a company buying all the outstanding stock, making it a private company.

should realize that personal funds are not just used in small businesses—96 percent of the fastest growing businesses in Canada as identified by *Profit Magazine* partly financed their business with a cash infusion from the owner. Not only are these the least expensive funds in terms of cost and control, but they are absolutely essential in attracting outside funding, particularly from banks, private investors, and venture capitalists. The typical sources of personal funds include savings, life insurance, or mortgage on a house or car. Pam Streeter, owner and operator of a small Halifax daycare and private school company, noted that she had to rely almost exclusively on personal savings when starting her daycare and private school. In addition, growing firms are using retained earnings to keep the business growing. For example, Vincent Fiore, owner of Partner in Credit (www.partnersincredit.com), a Markham-based debt collection company says, "We've self-generated all our financing. It's all sexy to go out and want to get bigger, but I'm kind of old school. We use what we have to grow. Yes, it's a slower climb, but I don't have to worry about making payments to anyone at the end of the month." Fiore, much like 54 percent of Canadian entrepreneurs, are re-investing profits back into their business.

Some entrepreneurs take this a step further and use personal credit cards to finance their start-up or to build their company. Kevin Fitzgerald, founder and president of Aurora Micro-systems (www.auroramicro.com) in Sudbury, Ontario, originally applied to several banks for financing. After he was rejected by all of them, he used his credit cards to provide much-needed capital. He estimated in year one that he charged approximately $1 million to various credit cards.[5] As personal funds are often the easiest and cheapest type of financing available, entrepreneurs should monitor their own investment in the business. Some entrepreneurs end up relying more on personal funds than they originally planned and put their financial future at risk. Entrepreneurs have to be careful to balance the risks associated with pursuing their dream of owning a business and their financial future. Gerry Schwartz, one of Canada's most successful entrepreneurs and current chairman and CEO of Onex Corporation (www.onex.com), argues the opposite point though noting that entrepreneurs should be willing to put their finances at risk as it is often the only way they can follow their dreams. "Invest in yourself—don't be afraid to take virtually all of your assets, everything you can scrape together, and put it into your business."[6] For example, the co-founders of SweatPea, an Ontario firm that produces and sells frozen organic baby food, both lament that they have put much more money into the business than originally planned. But the pair is hoping that their financial contributions will lead to a bigger payoff in the future. Thus they are willing to risk their money in hopes of fulfilling their dreams.

Outside providers of capital feel that the entrepreneur may not be sufficiently committed to the venture if he or she does not have money invested. Entrepreneur Michael Cerny states, "Be prepared to put your money where your mouth is.… The reality is that any reputable grade-A financial institution is going to expect you to put some kind of your own money up front to show your commitment and belief in your venture."[7] As one venture capitalist succinctly said, "I want the entrepreneurs so financially committed that when the going gets tough, they will work through the problems and not throw the keys to the company on my desk." A complete lack or very small commitment of personal funds invested in a project may hinder an entrepreneur's ability to gain financing.

Family and Friends.

After the entrepreneur, family and friends are a common source of capital for a new venture. They are most likely to invest due to their relationship with the entrepreneur. This helps overcome one portion of uncertainty felt by impersonal investors—knowledge of the entrepreneur.

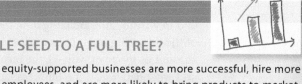

INCIDENT 6-1

DO CANADIAN ENTREPRENEURS PREFER AN APPLE SEED TO A FULL TREE?

Would you rather own 100 percent of an apple seed or a percentage of an apple tree? In other words, would you rather own a large share of a small business or a smaller share of a large business? To many the answer is pretty straightforward: It is almost always better to own a percentage of a larger business compared with full ownership in a much smaller one.

But for many Canadian entrepreneurs, the answer appears to be the former rather than the latter. Canadian entrepreneurs have traditionally shunned equity sources of financing, as they do not want to exchange ownership for capital. Studies consistently indicate that small firms often refuse to share ownership in exchange for capital, and the majority of SMEs are dependent on debt for long-term financing. Many entrepreneurs view equity investors as individuals and companies that are looking for a quick return and care little about the actual business in which they are investing. As noted above, successful entrepreneur Vincent Fiore, owner of Partner in Credit, has shunned debt and equity in growing his firm and instead relied on retained earnings. Other companies such as Original Joe's restaurant opted to issue debt and franchise their company to fund growth rather than sell equity in their firm.

Yet entrepreneurs may be missing out as numerous studies in both Canada and the United States have revealed that equity-supported businesses are more successful, hire more employees, and are more likely to bring products to market. Razor Suleman, who is featured in the opening Small Business Profile, recognized that equity financing was an important step in growing his business. Suleman notes that he had a choice: He could stay small and fund his business through retained earnings, debt, and some small injections of equity financing, or he could take on large equity partners and grow his business into a much larger firm. Suleman eventually gave up majority ownership in his firm for the capital and assistance that helped him grow his business into the leading employee recognition company in North America.

Discussion Questions

1. If entrepreneurs knew all the facts, do you think they would be so quick to dismiss equity as a source of capital?

2. If you owned a growing business would you make use of equity financing from investors? Why, or why not?

3. Would you sell majority control of your business like Suleman did to access the capital to grow? Why, or why not?

Young entrepreneurs often have to rely on family and friends as their main source of capital as they usually do not have any significant personal savings. For example, when Amanda Harburn started her Calgary-based dance school, Prestige Dance Academy Inc. (www.prestigedance.com), she was only 21 years old and had difficulty raising money. Harburn says that while lending agencies such as banks say they like young entrepreneurs, this is mostly lip-service and they do not want to lend young people money. Rather than giving up on her dream of running a dance studio, Harburn brought her proposal to her parents, and they readily invested in their daughter.[8]

Although it is relatively easy to obtain money from family and friends, like all sources of capital, there are positive and negative aspects. Although the amount of money provided may be small, if it is in the form of equity financing, the family members or friends then have an ownership position in the venture and all rights and privileges of that position. This may make them feel they have a direct input into the operations of the venture, which may have a negative effect on employees, facilities, or sales and profits. Although this possibility must be guarded against as much as possible, frequently family and friends are not problem investors and, in fact, are more patient than other investors in desiring a return on their investment.

To avoid problems in the future, the entrepreneur must present the positive and negative aspects and the nature of the risks of the investment opportunity to try to minimize the negative impact on the relationships with family and friends should problems occur. One thing that helps to minimize possible difficulties is to keep the business arrangements strictly business. Any loans or investments from family or friends should be treated in the same businesslike manner as if the financing were from an impersonal investor. Any loan should specify the rate of interest and the proposed repayment schedule of interest and principal. The timing of any future dividends must be disowned in terms of an equity investment. If the family or friend is treated the same as any investor, potential future conflicts can be avoided. It is also beneficial to the entrepreneur to settle everything up front and in writing. It is amazing how short memories become when money is involved. All the details of the financing must be agreed upon before the money is put into the venture. Such things as the amount of money involved, the terms of the money, the rights and responsibilities of the investor, and what happens if the business fails must all be agreed upon and written down. A formal agreement with all these items helps avoid future problems. For example, when Eryn Green and Tamar Wagman, founders of Sweetpea Baby Food (www.sweetpeababyfood.com), an Ontario firm that produces and sells frozen organic baby food, went looking for investment dollars from their friends and family they prepared and formally presented a full business plan outlining the opportunity. The pair wanted people to invest in their business because they believed in the concept and not just because of their relationship. By treating friends and family like formal investors, Green and Wagman managed to raise $150,000 for 10 percent equity in their company.[9] In September 2013, Green and Wagman sold Sweetpea to One Earth Farms Corp., a fully integrated, farm-to-fork Canadian food company offering natural and organic products under the "Beretta," "Last Rep," and "Protein Puck" labels.

Finally, the entrepreneur should carefully consider the impact of the investment on the family member or friend before it is accepted. Particular concern should be paid to any hardships that might result should the business fail. Each family member or friend should be investing in the venture because they think it is a good investment, not because they feel obligated.

CO-FOUNDERS ERYN GREEN AND TAMAR WAGMAN SUCCESSFULLY RAISED MONEY FROM THEIR FRIENDS AND FAMILY FOR THEIR FROZEN ORGANIC BABY FOOD COMPANY, SWEETPEA BABY FOOD, BY PREPARING A FORMAL BUSINESS PLAN AND TREATING FRIENDS AND FAMILY LIKE FORMAL INVESTORS. IN 2013, SWEETPEA BECAME PART OF THE ONE EARTH FAMILY OF BRANDS.
Photo courtesy of Eryn Green and Tamar Wagman

Some entrepreneurs receive funding, consultation, and from time to time manual labour from their friends and family. When Craig Flinn was opening his award-winning restaurant, Chives (www.chives.ca) in Halifax, his friends and family pitched in with more than just money. They helped him physically get his location ready, and many were his first customers. His grandmother pitched in as well with a recipe for the restaurant's now famous biscuits.

Crowd-Funding.

As discussed in previous chapters, a new and emerging trend in equity investment for business is crowd-funding. Crowd-funding occurs when an entrepreneur solicits small donations from the public to fund the start-up or growth of their company or social enterprise. Originally crowd-funding was used by social entrepreneurs and artists who solicited support from investors who donated funds over the Internet. Generally, investors or donors received little in the way of a return for their investment outside of a thank you and the knowledge that they had contributed to society's greater good. As crowd-funding websites such as Kickstarter (www.kickstarter.com) and Indiegogo (www.indiegogo.com) grew in popularity some entrepreneurs such as Canadian Eric Migicovsky made use of the site to pre-sell products or services in return for up-front money. As discussed in Chapter 1, Migicovsky raised the largest amount of money on Kickstarter to date, over $10 million to produce a smartwatch. While being perhaps the most successful entrepreneur to use crowd-funding, Migicovsky is far from alone, as contributions on Kickstarter topped $320 million in 2012 and the total value of contributions on crowd-funding sites is expected to surpass $3.5 billion in 2013.[10] Many Canadian entrepreneurs have successfully used crowd-funding to raise start-up money and to test market their products. For example, Alex Kennberg and Joshua Moore, two University of Waterloo students, recently raised in excess of $51,000 pre-selling their sleek Cobra wallet design on Kickstarter. Entrepreneurs are now starting to use crowd-funding to sell shares in their fledging businesses or to borrow money a practice sometimes referred to as *peer-to-peer lending*.[11]

A major constraint for entrepreneurs who want to sell equity using crowd-funding is technically, it is not yet legal in North America. Currently, entrepreneurs who want to sell shares to the public in Canada have to create a prospectus, which is a document that explains the opportunity to the investor. Given that these are expensive and timely to create, many smaller companies and start-ups do not draft these documents. These entrepreneurs, rather than sell shares to the public, often target friends and family and accredited investors (angels and venture capitalists), who are exempt from the prospectus requirements when selling equity to raise funds. The U.S. government appears to be ready to finalize legislation called the Jumpstart Our Business Start-ups (or JOBS) Act, which would allow companies to source up to $1 million from investors via crowd-funding, with the U.S. Securities and Exchange Commission (SEC) regulating the operation. In Canada, legislation appears to be much slower in arriving. A major barrier in Canada is the lack of a national regulator such as the SEC in the U.S. In Canada, each province establishes its own security regulations, and for crowd-funding to be legal coast to coast, each province would have to agree to a set of rules governing the process. This type of agreement appears to be difficult to establish as not all provincial exchange commission's appear to be willing to consider the matter.

Even with the legal ambiguity, there is little question U.S. and Canadian entrepreneurs are engaging in the practice of selling shares to the general public using crowd-funding. Some entrepreneurs are using social networking sites to avoid the rules as mentioned above—in Canada, you can legally sell shares in a company to close friends. Given that social networking sites has allowed people to form relationships with hundreds if not thousands of people, these friends could also be investors in a business. Other entrepreneurs are using international crowd-funding sites to sell shares in their company, or relying on peer lending. In response to the growing demand of Canadian entrepreneurs who want to legally sell equity in their business and investors who want to invest in start-up companies using crowd-funding, David Geertz, a B.C. entrepreneur, developed the site SoKap (www.sokap.com). SoKap is a legal site where investors can purchase geographic locations in Canada, referred to as "towns" on the SoKap website. The entrepreneur will receive the money from the purchase of the towns by investors, and in return, the investor will receive a percentage of sales or profit that occurs in the designated geographic area. For example, an entrepreneur could solicit funds for a T-shirt company. An investor could invest in the company and in return receive the rights to a percentage of sales in the Ontario marketplace. The entrepreneur would receive the investment and the investor would get a legal financial stake in the company.

The major advantages of crowd-funding include the capital it can provide entrepreneurs, an increase in public profile, a way to test market a product, and an opportunity to get valuable feedback and advice from the public. The major disadvantages of crowd-funding include the lack of laws in Canada allowing entrepreneurs to sell equity in their firm, the potential damage to an entrepreneur's reputation if he fails to meet his goal or build his product, and possible negative comments or publicity based on unmet products or poorly produced products. For example, the three entrepreneurs discussed above, Eric Migicovsky (Pebble Watch), Alex Kennberg, and Joshua Moore (Cobra wallet), were all late in producing their products leading to some negative publicity for their companies on crowd-funding and social networking sites. While the entrepreneurs maintained open communication with their donors or investors explaining the delay, inevitably not everyone was happy, and some voiced their opinions online.

Informal Risk-Capital Market (Angels).

The informal risk-capital market is the most misunderstood type of risk capital. It consists of a virtually invisible group of wealthy investors, often called *business angels,* who are looking for equity-type investment opportunities in a wide variety of entrepreneurial ventures. Typically investing anywhere from $10,000 to $500,000, these angels provide the funds needed in all stages of financing, but particularly in start-up (first-stage) financing. In Canada, angel investors became prominent with the emergence of CBC's hit show *Dragons' Den.* The show features five well-known business angels called "Dragons," who, as a group, listen to pitches from entrepreneurs who are hoping to get them to invest both their money and expertise into their business. While the show does have its share of detractors, it is one of the most popular shows on the network and regularly attracts over a million viewers to each episode. Similarly, angel investors are known in the U.S. due to the popularity of *Shark Tank,* a show on ABC which is quite similar to *Dragons' Den.* In fact, two of the original Dragons, Kevin O'Leary and Robert Herjavec, also appear on *Shark Tank.* When Mark Chaplin, founder and president and CEO of Disc-Go-Tech (www.discgotech.com), a manufacturer of DVD, CD, and video game repair kits based in Surrey, British Columbia, started his business, he found money by first draining his bank account and then asking family and friends for help. After exhausting his personal finances and raising as much money as he could from friends and family, Chaplin attempted to find capital from banks or venture capitalists with no success. He notes, "Neither myself nor my partners had any credit or assets, so the banks wouldn't look at us, and venture capitalists weren't interested unless we were looking at $1 million to $5 million." Chaplin then started looking for angel financing to get the funds needed to start his company. He eventually succeeded and raised $300,000 for 20 percent of his company from a pair of angel investors.[12] In addition to start-up financing, angels can bring a wealth of experience and knowledge to a venture. The majority of angels are entrepreneurs themselves and can offer advice on such important issues as strategic planning, management, and marketing. For example, angel investor Robert Herjavec says, "The best deals for me are the ones where I can leverage my investment with my network, experience and facilities. That way I can increase their and my chances of making money."[13] In addition, since most angels are over the age of 50, they have usually accumulated a wide variety of contacts that the entrepreneur can use.[14] Firms funded from the informal risk-capital market frequently raise second- and third-round financing from professional venture-capital firms or the public-equity market.

To date, there has been very little research done on the total amount of capital available to entrepreneurs through angel financing, but some research has indicated that the dollar amount may exceed the total venture-capital pool in the country. This notion has been supported by research in the United States that has indicated the amount of money available through angel financing surpasses the total amount available through venture capitalists.

The characteristics of these informal investors, or angels, are indicated in Figure 6-9. They tend to be well educated; many have graduate degrees. Although they will finance firms anywhere in Canada (and a few in other parts of the world), most of the firms that receive funding are within one day's travel. Business angels will make one to two deals each year, with individual firm investments ranging from $10,000 to $500,000 and the average being $125,000. If the opportunity is right, angels might invest from $500,000 to $1 million. Angel investors are quite selective and fund only between 1 and 3 percent of the proposals that they screen. Angels traditionally prefer equity to debt financing, but sometimes they will offer a combination of the two, or just debt financing. Unlike venture capitalists, angel investors usually do not want to assume control of a venture and will usually structure their investment as a limited partnership or hold shares in a private corporation. Angels may or may not play an active role in the management of the firm, although they will often sit on a board of advisors or directors. In some cases, angels will join with other angels, usually from a common circle of friends, to finance larger deals.

Is there a preference in the type of ventures in which they invest? While angels invest in every type of investment opportunity, from small retail stores to large oil exploration operations, some prefer manufacturing of industrial and consumer products, energy, service, and the retail/wholesale trade. In general, angels such as venture capitalists prefer ideas that are difficult to duplicate, offer some form of intellectual property protection, and are in a leading-edge sector such as IT or clean energy. Additionally, angels prefer to invest in entrepreneurs with a proven track record. Angels want to see a history of success in running a business. The returns expected decrease as the number of years the firm has been in business increases, from a median five-year capital gain of 10 times for start-ups to three times for established firms over five years old. These investing angels are more patient in their investment horizons and do not have a problem waiting for a period of seven to 10 years before cashing out. This is in contrast to the more predominant five-year time horizon in the formal venture-capital industry. Investment opportunities are rejected when there is an inadequate risk/return ratio, a subpar management team, a lack of interest in the business area, or insufficient commitment to the venture from the principals.

Finding and Soliciting Angels.

It is estimated that there are approximately 200,000 Canadian angels who are willing to invest thousands of dollars in entrepreneurial start-ups. This number is also set to grow as more and more senior executives retire and look to invest their savings. Jason Aparaga, president and CEO of Spara Capital Partners Inc. (www.sparacapital.com), an Oakville-based company, says the number of retired people taking buyouts as well as the encouragement of other angels is fuelling the growth of angel investors across Canada. Still even with the strong growth, most entrepreneurs claim the only thing more difficult than finding an angel is successfully

FIGURE 6-9   Characteristics of Canadian Angel Investors

Demographic Patterns and Relationships

- 99 percent are male.
- Most are at least 50 years old.
- Most are or were entrepreneurs.
- Most are well educated, with many having graduate degrees.
- Most have a net worth of at least $1 million and earn approximately $150,000 a year.
- Most are likely to invest in firms about which they have some background knowledge.
- Angels have the potential to bring much more than capital to a firm; they usually have a strong background in management and a variety of useful business contacts.
- Most will finance firms just about anywhere, particularly in Canada, though generally within one day's travel.
- Many belong to angel clubs.

Nature of Investment

- Most angel investments will either become limited partnerships or receive shares in a closely held corporation.
- Angels may or may not want to be actively involved in the management of the firm.
- Angels will usually sit on a firm's board of advisers or directors.

Investment Range

- Range of investment: $10,000–$2,000,000.
- Average investment: $125,000.
- One to two deals each year.

Venture Preference

- Mostly finance start-ups.
- Most interested in financing manufacturing, technology, and knowledge-based companies.

Approval Rate

- Most angels will reject anywhere from 97 to 99 percent of proposals they review.
- Of the 1 to 3 percent that are eventually approved, most have to go through an extensive due diligence process to ensure that they are reliable and the information presented in the business plan is accurate.

Risk/Reward Expectations

- Median five-year capital gains of 10 times for start-ups.
- Median five-year capital gains of six times for firms under one year old.
- Median five-year capital gains of five times for firms one–five years old.
- Median five-year capital gains of three times for established firms over five years old.

Reasons for Rejecting Proposals

- Risk/return ratio not adequate.
- Inadequate management team.
- Not interested in proposed business area.
- Unable to agree on price.
- Principals not sufficiently committed.
- Unfamiliar with area of business.

negotiating a deal with one.[15] Thus entrepreneurs should consider the following when seeking out and negotiating with an angel investor:

- *Prepare in advance.* Make sure that you have a complete business plan prior to attempting to contact angels and that you have fully investigated the idea. While angel investors will invest in start-ups, they do not usually just hand over money based on a poorly researched idea. Prior to investing, most angels will insist on a due diligence process that is quite thorough, and entrepreneurs should assist them, whenever possible, by providing a complete business plan in advance. Yasmine Kustec of the National Angel Capital Organization (www.angelinvestor.ca) recommends that entrepreneurs plan for capital well in advance and start to network with potential angel investors prior to needing money. Kustec notes that this will help establish a relationship with potential investors, build trust, and increase the likelihood of success when asking for money.[16]

- *Ask for referrals.* Angel investors, like most successful entrepreneurs, enjoy their privacy and it is often difficult to access their contact information. The best way to find an angel investor is through networking with existing contacts such as bankers, accountants, lawyers, and financial planners. Since most angels rely on trusted friends and business partners to steer potential investments their way, they often let their associates know that they are looking to invest in start-up companies. In addition, many angels belong to angel clubs or groups, and by accessing the information for one angel, you may gain access to an entire group.

- *Screen potential angel investors.* Try to get as much background information as possible before contacting a potential angel investor. Since most angels limit investments to areas with which they are familiar, your chances of successfully receiving financing improves if you approach an angel who has either working or investment experience in the industry. If a potential angel lacks this knowledge, the entrepreneur may have a harder time accessing financing.

- *Prepare for the first contact.* When making initial contact with an angel, it is best to use the referral's name (after getting permission). Prior to making a contact, the entrepreneur should prepare a short list of points that they want to cover over the course of the conversation. The main goal of the conversation is to arrange a meeting where the entrepreneur can pitch his or her idea.

- *Pitch the idea.* Prior to your meeting with an angel investor, he will most likely ask to see a brief business plan or an outline of the business model. The key to this is being as precise as possible while clearly outlining the potential of the business. When it comes time to pitch the idea face to face, entrepreneurs must focus on key points that emphasize their ability to succeed. Entrepreneurs should be able to explain in a very short time period using layman's words the size of the market and the problem that they are solving. Sean Wise, a financing expert, provides this example of an ideal pitch for the pill Viagra: "People want to have sex longer than their bodies will allow. Our aspirin-sized, government approved tablet is extremely effective at letting them do so." Kevin O'Leary says he put a great deal of emphasis on the entrepreneur's pitch. "If you can't stand up in front of people and communicate what the deal is and how it works in four minutes, you're not going to be successful. All the rest—finance, marketing, system integration—is secondary, because you can always hire a systems person or an accountant. But someone has to be able to set the course and communicate the vision."

Jim Treliving, who is an avid angel investor outside of the television show *Dragons' Den* notes that entrepreneurs should not hesitate to bring third party validation for their product. Treliving says, "I don't know anything about software but if Bill Gates said (your software) was good, who would I be to argue?" Audry Lacrocque and Louis Brun, founders of Neuralitic Systems Inc. (www.neuralitic.com), a Montreal-based IT company whose products and apps assist marketing managers in identifying customer needs, have recently raised $20 million in money from investors and note that they used testimonials from early adopters to help investors see the potential of their idea. Current Neuralitic CEO Luc Filiatreault, founder of four well-financed IT firms states, "The more strong testimonials you have, the better your chances of convincing investors of the validity of your idea."[17]

Entrepreneurs should come fully prepared to answer a variety of complex questions. Entrepreneurs also have to display a willingness to accept advice during the pitch. As discussed above most angels will want to contribute not only money but knowledge to the business. Bob Chaworth-Musters, founder of the Vancouver Angel Forum (www.angelforum.org), states, ". . . a CEO's demonstrated ability to accept advice can make or break an application."[18]

- *Prepare for a response.* Angels will usually respond to an idea pitch rather quickly. If the answer is no, entrepreneurs should ask why and react accordingly. Some common reasons for rejection and suggested responses are the following:

  1. *Incomplete proposal or lack of funds at this time*: The entrepreneur may ask if she could pitch the concept again after completing the proposal or at a time when the angel thinks he may have more money to invest.

  2. *Weak management team*; insufficient return on investment: The entrepreneur could offer to repitch the idea after addressing these issues.

  3. *Not interested in that particular industry*: The entrepreneur could ask the angel if he could provide a reference to any potential investors who are familiar with that industry.

  4. *Not a good idea*: The entrepreneur should ask the angel for input—be polite and thank him for his time.

If the answer is yes, the entrepreneur should assist the angel investor in completing his due diligence of the business and the entrepreneur himself. The entrepreneur should have the following ready:

- A list of 10 to 15 personal and business references including contact information.

- Any letters from customers, suppliers, and creditors, including patent information, financial records, and so on.

- Any other information that will allow the process to move forward.

- Draw up an agreement. After the investigation of the concept is complete, the angel investor and the entrepreneur will draw up a legal agreement. Entrepreneurs should realize in advance that while angel investors are willing to be flexible with their terms and invest in start-ups, they will still demand a much higher rate of return than a traditional lender. One angel investor who was participating in a research project on Canadian angel investors clearly stated, "A guy phoned the other day and asked me to consider a project. I said, 'I'll look at the venture, but I'll tell you right now, I'll want between 20 and 25 percent on my money.' The guy said, 'We can go to the bank and get better than that.' I said, 'What did you call me for?'" These comments are reinforced by Kevin O'Leary, who states he is looking for returns of 10–20 and perhaps 100 times his original investment. He says angels need these kinds of returns as only 20 percent of firms they invest in will actually become successful companies. Research conducted

ANGEL INVESTOR GROUPS: HEAVENLY BODIES

Pray really hard, and an angel might come down from on high and invest in your business. But if you don't believe in miracles—or can't wait for your prayers to be answered—then do what I recommend to my clients, and get thee in front of one of Canada's 20 angel investor groups.

Historically, angel investors were as hard to find as a heavenly spirit at a Heavy Metal concert. That's because, as private investors in early-stage companies, typically with long entrepreneurial or executive careers under their belts, angels did not advertise; entrepreneurs usually found them only through extensive networking and professional referrals. In recent years, however, angels have banded together to pool their knowledge of various sectors, share best practices in such investor-critical areas as due diligence, board representation, and shareholder agreements, and to spread their risk by making smaller placements in more companies.

How do angel groups work? Consider a typical alliance such as the Toronto-based Maple Leaf Angels (www.mapleleafangels.com), of which I'm a member. It's a group of 40 or so investors who meet to receive presentations from companies looking for money. Hopeful entrepreneurs fill out an application to make their pitch and submit their business plans online; those proposals are ushered through a committee that selects the three or four companies that will present their investment opportunity at the group's monthly breakfast meeting. If you have a good management team, a clearly defined product or service that has some sort of defensible competitive advantage, and huge revenue potential, you could make the cut.

On the big day, each entrepreneur makes a 15-minute pitch, followed by a Q&A session. The angels discuss the opportunity in private and decide whether it's worth graduating to a due-diligence committee that further explores the opportunity on behalf of the group. Typically, only a handful of the members will like a particular opportunity, but they are free to move forward as a smaller syndicate or individually.

The committee reviews the firm's financials and projections, talks to employees and customers, and generally kicks the tires to satisfy the interested investors that they want to move to the next phase: negotiating a term sheet. Analogous to a letter of intent, a term sheet outlines the principal points of the agreement between a company and its potential investors. If a final agreement is reached, the financed company pays 2 percent of the amount raised to the Maple Leaf Angels, thus funding the group's operations in part.

Although deals that come out of angel groups typically involve multiple investors, the amounts invested rarely top $1 million. That's because the angels form a syndicate to spread their risk rather than make bigger investments. However, another trend has evolved: namely, the syndication of the investment to other angel groups across the country. Companies have been known to get funded by members of the Okanagan Angel Network in Kelowna, B.C., and then present in Toronto and get further funding. Once one of the angel groups in one part of the country has voted with their wallets, another angel group is more likely to invest as well. They typically invest on the same terms as previous groups and become signatories of a unanimous shareholders' agreement that governs the relationship between the angels and the company.

While it seems like a high-potential business would be crazy not to approach an angel group, there is a price to pay. With strength in numbers, angel syndicates are better able to dictate financial and other terms of a deal. They also share the cost of legal counsel and other consultants they might involve in the process, allowing them to dig deeper into your business.

If you can find angels who'll invest independently, you can avoid the shift in bargaining power. That could not only get you a better valuation, but it may also allow you to avoid a unanimous shareholders' agreement and, therefore, a lot of potential interference in the day-to-day operation of your business. The challenge with a divide-and-conquer approach is that unless you have a pretty good Rolodex of investors like I do, finding individual angels is like finding a needle in a haystack.

Whichever route you choose, remember what the typical angel investor seeks in an opportunity:

1. A strong management team with a good track record
2. A product that relieves a major "pain" in the market
3. Clear use of proceeds (what you'll spend the money on)
4. Huge market opportunity (a.k.a. "hockey stick" projections)
5. A unique technology or other sustainable competitive advantage or barrier to entry
6. Fit with the expertise of the investor
7. An exit strategy

Sources: Jeff Dennis, *Profit Magazine*, December/January 2008 and Canadian Business Online, December 5, 2007.

INCIDENT 6-3

FIVE WAYS TO GET YOUR PITCH ON *DRAGONS' DEN*[20]

OK, you have the perfect business idea, you are excited, all you need is money and you are good to go. Wait a minute, there is a TV show, *Dragons' Den,* if you get on that you will surely not only get the money you need but millions of Canadians will know about your product. So. . . . how do you get on the show? Every year there are thousands of would-be entrepreneurs who audition to be on the air and get in front of the Dragons. So how do you stand out? What can you do to ensure you make the cut and appear on TV? *Profit Magazine* author Deborah Aarts offers the following advice:

1. Go easy on gimmicks such as models and children. Focus on the business idea.
2. Do your homework. Make sure you know who your competitors are and how you are different.
3. Have a good story. Be certain you and your idea are interesting to the audience.
4. Prove that you really need help. The show's executives state they are looking for companies that really need the money not just entrepreneurs looking for publicity.
5. Keep your cool. Make sure you can answer questions and pitch under pressure.

by the National Angel Capital Organization (NACO) also echoes these claims. The organization found that while angels can earn a healthy return on their investment most of the return can usually be attributed to one or two successful companies that exceed expectations. NACO found that roughly 50 percent of angel investments fail to yield any return.

Angel Organizations.

A new trend that has emerged in angel investing over the last decade is the formation of angel clubs or associations. Angels use these clubs to network with other angels, share investment opportunities, and pool money to invest in start-up ventures. The above mentioned Canadian National Angel Captial Organization, or NACO, is probably the best-known angel organization, although its mandate focuses more on networking opportunities and creating national guidelines to assist angels rather than investing in opportunities. Yasmine Kustec of the NACO says that entrepreneurs who are looking for angels should contact NACO; NACO serves as a matchmaking service between companies in need of angels and angels in need of companies.[20]

Angel clubs usually meet monthly to network and review one or two venture pitches from aspiring entrepreneurs. In a recent survey with angel groups, research found they contributed at least $35.3 million in 2010 to 88 businesses, and this amount increased to $82.4 million in 2011. The research conducted by the NACO also found that the size of the average investment has increased to $614,000 and many angel groups are contributing follow-up or additional capital to existing entrepreneurs. Angel groups favour technology with their investments as 43 percent of their funds were directed to IT firms, 18 percent in life sciences, and 16 percent in clean technology.[21] One example of an angel group is Ottawa's Purple Angel (www.purpleangel.com). The group is made up of former Bell executives who offer entrepreneurs two types of venture financing. They will invest approximately $150,000 in start-up companies that are having problems attracting venture capital, or they will invest upwards of $1 million in companies that are successfully raising capital from other sources. Along with capital, the Purple Angel club will contribute ideas and contacts and assist in managing the venture. The founder of the group, Irving Ebert, describes the club as active angel investors who bring decades of experience to portfolio companies. To date, the Purple Angel club has provided funding to such notable companies as KidsFuture (www.kidsfutures.ca) and BTI Photonic Systems Inc. (www.btiphotonics.com).

Generally, an idea pitch to an angel organization will follow this pattern:

1. Entrepreneurs hoping to pitch their idea to an angel group have to be sponsored by at least one member to get their idea on the agenda. The sponsoring member usually meets with the entrepreneur prior to the meeting and completes an initial screening process. Getting to the pitch stage is not easy. Angel investor and member of NACO Parm Gil states that most angel groups receive 100 business plans a year and on average only formally review one to five of them. Gil says there is value in entrepreneurs just trying to get your business reviewed as they will receive valuable feedback that should help them manage their business.[22] Some clubs now ask the entrepreneur to pay a fee to present to the organization. The organizations that charge entrepreneurs will usually assist entrepreneurs in putting together their presentation and sometimes their business plan.

2. Prior to the meeting, the entrepreneur will provide investors with a summary of the company and key financial information.

3. Entrepreneurs will get 30 to 60 minutes to pitch their idea.

4. Angels will spend at least another 60 minutes asking further questions.

5. If the group makes investing decisions together, then they will vote whether to invest in the idea. Voting members usually vote either for or against the idea, or for the idea upon hearing further information. Some angel groups do not invest as a group and after the entrepreneur's presentation individual angels will decide on their own whether to pursue the idea.

6. If the majority vote "yes" or "yes, but . . . ," two to three angels will be assigned to the project to complete further due diligence and ensure that it meets the requirements of the group.

Refer to Figures 6-10 and 6-11 for more information on Canadian angel investment groups.

Corporate Investors.

Many companies are interested in investing in a small business in the hope that the value of their investment will increase over time. Often they then sell their ownership interest back to

FIGURE 6-10	Some Canadian Angel Investment Groups

National Angel Capital Organization https://nacocanada.com/	Maple Leaf Angels, Toronto, ON www.mapleleafangels.com
BC Angel Forum, Vancouver, BC www.angelforum.org	Mindfirst Angels, Toronto, ON www.mindfirst.com
First Angel Network, Halifax, NS www.firstangelnetwork.ca	
Golden Horseshoe Venture Group Burlington, ON www.ghvf.org	

FIGURE 6-11   Information on Canadian Angel Groups

- The vast majority operate on the basis of individuals doing their own due diligence, sometimes with group support, and making their own investment decision. However, in most angel groups, two or more angels will invest together in the same company.
- The groups collectively had just under 1500 investors. Three large groups accounted for 58 percent of the total. The majority of groups had fewer than 50 investors.
- The groups had a portfolio of over 250 investments. The three largest groups accounted for 55 percent of this total.
- In 2010, the groups collectively received around 1850 business plans from companies seeking finance. Four groups accounted for 48 percent of the total. Only 14 percent of these business plans passed the initial screening and were considered in detail.
- The group made over 80 investments, with most groups making between one and five investments. This is equivalent to 4.5 percent of the overall number of business plans received but 32 percent of the business plans that had been seriously considered. Only around one-quarter of the group members invested in these businesses. The proportion was significantly higher in the smaller groups.
- The vast majority (90 percent) of investments were new as opposed to follow ups.
- The majority of investments (61 percent) were in Ontario, with a smaller concentration in British Columbia (17 percent). The remainder of provinces had just a handful of investments. The amounts invested by business angels are much greater in Ontario than in the rest of Canada.
- The amounts invested by angels in a single deal ranged from less than Can$50,000 to over Can$5 million, but clustered in the $100,000 to $999,000 range. Over half of the investments had just one angel investor, while at the other extreme, 30 percent had more than five angels.

Source: National Angel Capital Organization, *Investment Activity by Canadian Angel Groups: 2011 Report* https://nacocanada.com/wp-content/uploads/2012/12/NACO-2011-Report-Investment-Activity-By-Canadian-Angel-Groups.pdf.

the original owners when the owners are in a better position to finance the business independently.

Companies whose major activity is investing in smaller and medium-sized businesses are called *venture-capital companies*. These companies use highly sophisticated evaluation techniques and accept only a small percentage of applications.[23] A venture-capital company typically looks for a business within a growth industry, with sound management and the potential for a return on investment of between 20 percent and 40 percent.

In 2012, the members of the Association of Canadian Venture Capital Companies (www.cvca.ca) invested some $1.5 billion in almost 395 businesses in Canada. Of the investments, information technology (IT) sector led the way with $719 million invested, investments in the biotechnology, life sciences, and medtech sectors totalled $368 million, and clean technology sector had $144 million. Regionally, Ontario accounts for the majority of venture-capital (VC) activity in Canada with $603 million of invested capital representing 41 percent of all disbursements.[24] Refer to Figure 6-12 for guidelines on dealing with venture capitalists.

Government.

Government has traditionally hesitated to provide equity funding to small businesses. However, programs have been developed in recent years that permit government funding and incentives for venture-capital firms or allow for direct equity investment by government in the business. Some of these programs and agencies are described next.

FIGURE 6-12   Guidelines for Dealing with Venture Capitalists

- Carefully evaluate the venture capitalist to approach for funding the particular type of deal. Screen and target the approach. Venture capitalists do not like deals that have been excessively "shopped."
- Once a discussion is started with a venture capitalist, do not discuss the deal with other venture capitalists. Working several deals in parallel can create problems unless the venture capitalists are working together. Time and resource limitations may require a cautious simultaneous approach to several funding sources.
- It is better to approach a venture capitalist through an intermediary who is respected and has a pre-existing relationship with the venture capitalist. Limit and carefully define the role and compensation of the intermediary.
- The entrepreneur or manager, not an intermediary, should lead the discussions with the venture capitalist. Do not bring a lawyer, accountant, or other advisers to the first meeting. Since there are no negotiations during this first meeting, it is a chance for the venture capitalist to get to know the entrepreneur without interference from others.
- Be very careful about what is projected or promised. The entrepreneur will probably be held accountable for these projections in the pricing, deal structure, or compensation.
- Disclose any significant problems or negative situations in this initial meeting. Trust is a fundamental part of the long-term relationship with the venture capitalist; subsequent discovery by the venture capitalist of an undisclosed problem will cause a loss of confidence and probably prevent a deal.
- Reach a flexible, reasonable understanding with the venture capitalist regarding the timing of a response to the proposal and the accomplishment of the various steps in the financing transaction. Patience is needed, as the process is complex and time consuming. Too much pressure for a rapid decision can cause problems with the venture capitalist.
- Do not sell the project on the basis that other venture capitalists have committed themselves. Most venture capitalists are independent and take pride in their own decision making.
- Be careful about glib statements such as "There is no competition for this product" or "There is nothing like this technology available today." These statements can reveal a failure to do one's homework or can indicate that a perfect product has been designed for a non-existent market.
- Do not indicate an inordinate concern for salary, benefits, or other forms of current compensation. Dollars are precious in a new venture. The venture capitalist wants the entrepreneur committed to an equity appreciation similar to that of the venture capitalist.
- Eliminate to the extent possible any use of new dollars to take care of past problems such as payment of past debts or deferred salaries of management. New dollars of the venture capitalist are for growth, to move the business forward.

Business Development Bank of Canada (BDC).

The BDC (www.bdc.ca) participates with other investors as a principal in the provision of investment capital in businesses it views as promising. Generally, the purpose of such financing is to provide an adequate equity base for the firm to receive funding from additional sources. The BDC is an important source of equity capital, and as of 2012 the corporation has invested $15.8 billion in Canadian firms.[25] Chris Murumets, owner of LOGiQ3 (www.logiq3.com), a Toronto-based insurance company that has been consistently identified as one of the fastest growing firms in Canada, says the BDC provides more than money to entrepreneurs. "We raised some money with the BDC. I like the BDC because it feels like they are on your side. That sounds fluffy but, as a business owner, it's nice to have these people guiding you through the process and helping you along the way." His comments are echoed by entrepreneurs, Lee Van Iderstine of New Gen Technologies (www.newgen.ca) and David Ciccarelli of Voices.com (www.voices.com). Both owners of growing Canadian IT/Internet firms agree that the BDC is

NEURALITIC OFFERS ENTREPRENEURS A ROADMAP TO VC SUCCESS

Montreal based-Neuralitic, an IT company which helps mobile operators understand customer behavior to ensure long-term success, offers business owners and inspiring entrepreneurs a model to follow when looking for VC investment. The company, which was co-founded by Audry Lacrocque and Louis Brun, managed to raise $20 million in just three years between 2008 and 2011 when VC money was not easy to come by. They did it by building an innovative product, Seven Flow, and then targeting VC investors who had a history of investing in the industry. When meeting with VCs, rather than focus on the product, the co-founders focused on how profitable the app could become and secured $12 million in investments from five investors. While sales were growing, the entrepreneurs soon needed additional capital and went back to the original investors along with other contacts. This time the pair faced some tough questions about why the original $12 million was not enough. The Neuralitic founders countered this by offering testimonials from early adopters and again focused their pitch on the potential financial success of the product and not the technology behind the app. The strategy worked as investors could see the long-term capital appreciation that could be made investing in the company. In 2013, the company was bought out by a larger American firm Guavus, who just prior to the purchase raised $30 million to fuel its own growth. While the terms of the deal have remained confidential reports indicate that the investors and founders of Neuralitic were happy with the sale of the firm.

Discussion Questions

1. Why do you think Neuralitic was successful in raising capital?

2. Do you think the sale of Neuralitic, a Canadian company, to a U.S. firm is a positive development? Why, or why not?

3. If you were the owner of Neuralitic would you have preferred to keep the company for yourself, or would you have jumped at the opportunity to sell your shares at a profit to a larger company? Why?

more open to financing and supporting entrepreneurs compared with traditional banks. Iderstine, whose BC-based company provides IT solutions to small and medium businesses says, "We've used the BDC to fund product launches and sales efforts. A normal bank doesn't try to make it work, in our experience."

BOOTSTRAP FINANCING

One alternative to acquiring outside capital that should be considered is bootstrap financing. This approach is particularly important at start-up and in the early years of the venture when capital from debt financing (i.e., in terms of higher interest rates) or from equity financing (i.e., in terms of loss of ownership) is more expensive.

Bootstrap financing involves using any possible method for conserving cash. While some entrepreneurs can take advantage of any supplier discounts available, entrepreneurs with restricted cash flow need to take as long as possible to pay without incurring interest or late payment fees or being cut off from any future items from the supplier. The entrepreneur should always ask about discounts for volume, frequent customer discounts, promotional discounts for featuring the vendor's product, and even "obsolescence money," allowing upgrade to an enhanced product at no additional cost.

Savings can also be obtained by asking for bulk packaging instead of paying more for individually wrapped items as well as using co-op advertising with a channel member so that the cost of the advertisement is shared. Some entrepreneurs have also encountered significant savings by locating their business in a smaller city and/or by buying used equipment. RECYC PHP INC. (www.recycphp.ca) of Drummondville, used both strategies to

ENTREPRENEURS OFTEN PREFER TO BANK WITH THE BDC AS IT IS OFTEN MORE OPEN TO LENDING MONEY TO SMALLER BUSINESSES.
The Canadian Press Images/Francis Vachon

save money. The business, which recycles disposable diapers, considered locations in both Montreal or Drummondville but after considering the costs, the management team decided to locate in the smaller city saving the company a lot of money. The owners then purchased used production equipment at an estimated savings of $750,000 compared with purchasing new equipment.[26]

Consignment financing can also be used to help conserve cash. Some vendors allow entrepreneurs to place a standing order for the entire amount of goods to be used over a period of time but take shipment and make payment only as needed, therefore securing the lower price of a larger order without having to carry the cost of the inventory. These are just some examples. The only possible limitation in bootstrap financing is the imagination of the entrepreneur. Another type of bootstrapping is for the entrepreneur to get paid as quickly as possible from outstanding accounts and getting overdue accounts to pay up.

DEBT FINANCING   LO6

Few small businesses are able to get established and continue operations without some sort of debt financing. About 30 percent of the money loaned to business in Canada is held by small businesses.[27] A national survey found that 85 percent of small and medium businesses used a bank for financial support, 75 percent have lines of credit, and 50 percent have loans.[28] According to a survey carried out by Statistics Canada, the average debt outstanding for firms with fewer than five employees is $187,000, and for firms with 5–20 employees, it is $489,000.[29] Because of the high possibility that debt financing will be required, it is essential that entrepreneurs be aware of the advantages and dangers of using it. It is also important that they understand the sources of debt capital and the characteristics and requirements of various financial lenders.

Advantages and Disadvantages of Debt Financing.

Some of the positive benefits of using debt are as follows:

1. It is possible to obtain a higher return on investment by using leverage debt. If borrowed funds earn a higher return than the associated interest cost, it is possible to increase the overall return on investment for the business through debt financing. The $10,000 investment could be any productive asset or change in the business.
2. Interest costs in a business are tax-deductible expenses (assuming a profit is being made), whereas dividends paid as a result of equity ownership are not tax deductible.
3. Debt financing may allow greater flexibility in that there is no loss of ownership control.
4. Many small businesses have found it is often easier to obtain debt capital than equity capital. A recent study by Statistics Canada found that 86 percent of small business loan applications were approved.[30]

Some of the potential negative aspects of debt financing are as follows:

1. Interest must be paid on borrowed money. Interest costs can be high, and high interest expenses are a common problem in many failing businesses. Interest rates have been high in the past in Canada, and this caused serious hardship for many small businesses. The inability to pay interest costs resulted in the foreclosure or bankruptcy of many businesses. Although interest rates are currently low, the small business owner must monitor rate changes closely.
2. Debt financing creates additional paperwork requirements for the entrepreneur, and the lender may monitor the business.
3. When using debt financing, the total risk of the venture lies squarely on the owner's shoulders. There are no other partners or shareholders to assume some of this risk.

Sources of Debt Financing.

Several sources of debt financing are available to small businesses, including private lenders, corporate lenders, private lending institutions, and government agencies.

Private Lenders.

One increasingly common source of debt capital for small business is the borrowing of funds from the owners of the business. These funds are called shareholders' loans, and they offer some unique advantages. It is estimated that approximately one-third of small business owners make a start-up loan to their own businesses.[31] Although the interest paid is a tax-deductible expense for the business, the repayment terms are often flexible. In addition, lenders often view shareholders' loans as equity as long as the funds are left in the company. Some believe this method combines the advantages of equity and debt financing.

Another source of private debt is borrowing from other individuals such as friends or relatives. As with shareholders' loans, it may be possible to structure flexible repayment terms.

Corporate Lenders.

In some circumstances, other companies may lend funds to a small business. Often these are larger firms that have established some connection or working relationship with the small business. One example of such funding would be the granting of trade credit by a company to a small business that purchases merchandise from that company. Most small businesses use this source of financing wherever possible. Trade credit for inventory is normally financed for 30,

60, or 90 days, with discounts for prompt payment. Equipment is usually financed for up to five years, with a 20 percent to 30 percent downpayment required.

Another type of lender associated with accounts receivable is a factor. Factor companies purchase accounts receivable from a business at a discount. The business obtains needed cash, and the factor collects the accounts receivable. An increasing number of businesses in Canada are enlisting factoring companies to obtain short-term financing.

The sale and leaseback is another form of financing involving other businesses. In this arrangement, the business sells an asset to another company, which, in turn, leases it back to the seller. The advantage of the sale and leaseback is that the seller not only has the use of the funds of the sale but also benefits from the tax deductibility of the lease payments.

Regular Private Lending Institutions.

This category includes companies whose major purpose is the lending of funds. The most common of these firms are the following:

- *Chartered banks.* A major source of small business financing is Canada's chartered banks. Banks have currently extended over $88 billion in credit to 1.6 small and medium companies. At present, six major Canadian chartered banks and a multitude of foreign-controlled banks operating in Canada account for the majority of all small business lending.[32] While this is a sizeable amount of money, banks normally have stringent requirements for approving financing for new or small businesses. *Profit Magazine* recently noted that banks require a business plan, a good to excellent credit rating, a personal guarantee, loan security, and a reasonable request.

- *Trust companies.* Trust companies are geared primarily for mortgages on long-term capital assets such as land, buildings, and equipment.

- *Credit unions.* Credit unions are usually locally owned. They tend to be concerned primarily with personal loans and working with smaller companies. Since credit unions have a tendency to be more local in their approach, they tend to offer better financial service to small companies. In fact the Canadian Federation of Independent Businesses recently concluded a study on access to capital in Canada and found that credit unions outperform all of the big five banks in financial service to small firms.[33] Matt Mould, founder of Sport Systems Canada (www.sportsystemscanada.com), an Ottawa-based manufacturer of sports pads and floors, supports these findings. Mould says, "The credit unions listened to us in the beginning, when the chartered banks didn't . . . credit unions were instrumental in getting us started."

- *Finance companies.* These are high-risk lenders that charge a higher rate of interest than other agencies. As with credit unions, the majority of their loans are personal loans.

An additional source of small business financing that seems to be increasing is the entrepreneur's use of their credit cards to provide temporary assistance. The Canadian Bankers Association states that 59 percent of small businesses help finance their start-up in this way,[34] and a growing number of start-up entrepreneurs report credit cards as their most important source of financing.[35]

Government Lenders.

As discussed above government agencies at both the federal and the provincial or territorial levels invest in Canadian small business. The BDC is the major source of federal money for aspiring and growing entrepreneurs and in addition to money the agency provides counselling assistance to small businesses. Two other significant programs are the Canadian Small Business Finance Program and the Canadian Youth Business Foundation.

DO CHARTERED BANKS LEND MONEY TO ENTREPRENEURS?

This is a rather simple question but the answer appears to be complex.

According to the Canadian Bankers Association, banks are major lenders to entrepreneurs, and as of 2012, banks had approved credit in excess of $88 billion to 1.6 million small and medium businesses. The Association points out that approval ratings are quite high at 88 percent and the average loan is in excess of $300,000. The banks through their national association state they are important partners in small business financing in Canada.[36]

So, based on these statement above, one may assume that banks are strong supporters of Canadian entrepreneurs.

The Canadian Federation of Independent Businesses (CFIB) begs to differ. The non-profit agency recently completed a report titled, "Battle of the Banks" in 2013, where they surveyed roughly 12,800 small business owners and concluded access to financing was problematic for small businesses and particularly problematic for smaller firms. For example, on a scale of 1 to 7, microbusiness, firms with less than five employees, ranked their access to bank financing as almost non-existent. For example, microbusiness owners actually gave CIBC a score of zero in assessing the banks willingness to lend money and TD Bank's score was 0.09 out of 7. CFIB's report did conclude that access to capital appears to increase with firm size, and age of the firm, but ultimately concluded that banks need to do more to assist small Canadian firms. CFIB CEO Dan Kelly says, "Access to affordable financing and banking services is essential for hard-working entrepreneurs, and it's clear that all of the banks should do more to serve small business clients."[37]

Evidence both statistical and anecdotal appears to support Kelly's assertion that banks are not overly supportive of smaller businesses and start-ups. As discussed earlier in the chapter, banks only supply approximately 33 percent of funds to start-up companies and of this most, if not all, of the money is guaranteed by personal assets of the business and/or the entrepreneur. Additionally, the provincial and federal governments have all invested in various funding programs to assist start-up enterprises that cannot access traditional capital through banking institutions. As stated by serial entrepreneur Chris Neville, banks really are not interested in lending money to start-ups or small companies. Furthermore, while the Banker's Association states that banks provide funding to 1.6 million firms, research by Statistics Canada has concluded that there are roughly 2.5–3 million companies operating in Canada of which 99 percent are small. Given this information, one can conclude there are approximately one million business who are not accessing financing through banks.[38]

Anecdotal evidence that banks do not lend money to aspiring entrepreneurs or small business is much stronger and perhaps best summed up by Michael Duck, CEO of SureShot Dispensing (www.sureshotdispensing.com), a growing Halifax company that manufactures restaurant equipment. Duck says, " . . . some people have this idea in their heads, they go into a bank with a business plan and good credit, the plan has strong projections and he will sell himself and his idea to the banker. Based on his business idea and credit, the bank will lend the entrepreneur the money. This is not how it works. Banks don't lend money based on business plans. They lend money based on assets, what the owner can pledge against the loan. If they cannot pledge anything then they do not get any money. It's that simple." HSBC commercial banker Richard Dawson agrees with Duck saying, banks will lend money against assets, including receivables and inventory, but they have to have something pledged against the loan. Dawson notes banks do not make money by offering loans based on unproven projections.

Discussion Questions

1. Do you think banks should be willing to lend money based on a strong business plan and credit scores alone? Why, or why not?

2. Since many angel investors make a healthy return on investing in start-ups, are banks missing out on an opportunity for profits by not investing in new or small companies? Why do you think banks are not doing this?

3. Since Canadian banks tend to be highly profitable and appear to benefit from some federal laws that limit competition, should they as a group be more willing to invest in small business given its importance to the Canadian economy. Do you think rather than invest in small business themselves that government should stipulate a percentage of bank loans be made to new businesses? Why, or why not?

Canadian Small Business Finance Program (CSBF).

CSBF (www.ic.gc.ca/eic/site/csbfp-pfpec.nsf/eng/Home) is a loans program that aims to increase the availability of capital for existing small and medium businesses that are looking to improve and/or expand their small business (start-ups can qualify for the program). The program allows business owners to apply for a maximum loan of $500,000 at any of the participating lenders, including banks, credit unions, and caisses populaires, with the federal government acting as a guarantor for 85 percent of the lender's losses. The financial institutions make all lending decisions and are responsible for providing the funds and registering the loans. Both start-ups and existing businesses are eligible to apply for funding as long as they meet the program's requirements. Many entrepreneurs have successfully used this program to gain access to much needed funds and are happy with the interest terms of no more than 3 percent above prime for floating rates or 3 percent above residential mortgages for fixed rates. For example, Jim MacAulay used the CSBF program to open the True North Diner, a Halifax-based 1950s style diner. MacAulay says that traditional banks would never have lent him money without the CSBF program. MacAulay eventually sold his profitable business to an expanding restaurant chain. Cozy Corner Saunas used a CSBF loan to gain access to much needed start-up capital. The Dartmouth Nova Scotia-based business had a difficult time securing initial funds and relied on the CSBF program to get the business up and running. The firm's owner, Catherine Whittaker, says if it weren't for the loan from the program, she would not have been able to start her company. "Our business plan had just been approved, but the bank was uncomfortable lending us the entire amount requested," she says. "One of the bank officers offered to look into the Canadian Small Business Financing program for us. A few weeks later, we were accepted into the program and the deal went through!" "We had a perfect vision of what we wanted to do with our business and were determined to go forward. But as first-time business owners, we had very little capital or history to back us up," Ms. Whittaker explains. "The Canadian Small Business Financing program was really the deciding factor as to whether we were going to be able to move forward."[39]

Canadian Youth Business Foundation (CYBF).

The CYBF (www.cybf.ca) is a national non-profit organization funded by the federal government, which provides access to start-up and growth funds to young entrepreneurs who are 39 or younger. The foundation will provide new businesses with access up to $50,000 in funds and growing businesses up to $30,000 in expansion money. CYBF is particularly attractive as a financing option to young entrepreneurs as they consider the applicant's character and the merits of their business plan not collateral. In addition to capital, the CYBF ensures that all successful applicants work with a business mentor to assist them in running their business. To date, the CYBF has invested in more than 5600 young entrepreneurs, whose businesses have created more than 23,000 new jobs, $163.3 million in tax revenue, and hundreds of millions of dollars in sales and export revenue.[40]

Provincial Programs.

Provincial governments have provided tax and rebate incentives for the formation of small business investment companies, which function similarly to venture-capital companies.

The potential advantages of approaching a government agency are the following:

1. The agency may finance higher-risk or lower-equity ventures, which characterize many small businesses.

2. Government lenders may be more willing to rewrite loan terms and conditions if the business gets into trouble. They also tend to be less quick to foreclose on a failing business.

3. Government agencies may provide a lower interest rate than the chartered banks. Many provincial and territorial government lenders fall into this category. BDC rates, which are adjusted periodically, are usually similar to chartered bank rates.

4. Government lenders may provide some equity capital in the form of temporary owner-ship or grants, depending on the type of business and its location. (See Government Grants Canada website.)

5. Government lenders may provide management counselling along with funding to assist the business.

Although the above advantages may make borrowing from government agencies attractive, there are some potential disadvantages that the small business owner should be aware of:

1. A government agency usually requires more information to review a loan application than other lending institutions do.

2. The time required for approval of a loan tends to be longer than with private lending institutions.

3. Most government agencies exert more monitoring and control over the businesses they lend to and often require regular reports on operations.

In addition to the government agencies established to provide both debt and equity financing, several specific federal government programs also provide financial help for small businesses.

Most provinces and territories also have various programs designed to provide financial assistance to the small business community.

DETERMINING THE TERM OF FINANCING

The small business owner should carefully evaluate the characteristics of the above sources of financing to ensure their suitability to the needs of the business.

The length of term and type of financing required may assist in making the decision among lenders, as Figure 6-13 shows. This figure also illustrates the typical assets covered by the various

| FIGURE 6-13 | Matching Financing to Assets |

TYPE OF LOAN	SOURCES	USE	SECURITY	LOAN CHARACTERISTICS
Short-term (demand) loans (3–6 months)	Banks, private sources, factoring houses, confirming houses	Receivables, line of credit, inventory (working capital items)	Assignment of receivables and inventory, personal guarantees, assignment of life insurance	Can be withdrawn on short notice; no fixed payment terms; interest, principal rates fluctuate
Medium-term (3–10 year) loans	Banks, term lenders, financial houses, leasing companies, foreign banks, private sources, and government programs	Equipment, furnishings, vehicles, leaseholds, and new business investments	Chattel mortgages, conditional sales contracts, or assignment of equipment insurance	Specific repayment terms; interest either fixed or floating with prime rate
Long-term (15–25 year) mortgages, bonds, debentures	Trust companies, foreign banks, private sources	Property, land and buildings, new business investments	Collateral mortgages, assignment of property insurance	Fixed repayment terms; fixed interest rates

terms of financing. The length of the term allowed by a lender is normally equivalent to the useful life of the asset, except in the case of land, which is often carried on a 20-year term.

An often costly mistake that some owner-managers make is to use funds obtained for long-term purposes to get them through short-term crises. Inevitably, this practice creates a more serious financial crisis a short while later. If capital requirements were underestimated, the owner should approach the lender again with this information and attempt to have the lender adjust the funds provided.

PREPARING A PROPOSAL TO OBTAIN FINANCING   LO7

In attempting to obtain financing, a small business owner should be aware of those areas about which the lender requires information. In addition to completing the loan application, the owner should include the financial projections. A detailed and well-prepared loan proposal goes a long way toward ensuring the approval of a loan application.

1. The Applicant's Management Ability.

The lender will want to be sure the applicant has the skills, education, experience, and ability to make the business succeed. To evaluate the applicant's managerial ability, the lender will specifically want to know the following:

How Much the Applicant Knows about the Business.

The lender will probably ask questions about the business or industry to ascertain the applicant's level of knowledge. The lender will also be interested in any previous experience the applicant has had that relates to the proposed business.

How Much Care Was Taken in Preparing the Proposal.

The lender will want to see a detailed plan of what the loan is for, as well as a listing of the other sources of financing for the project. The steps of a business plan outlined in Chapter 4 should provide the basis for the financing proposal. Several statements will be required, and it is important that the applicant document the source of the information in those statements. The first statement is the lending proposal, which typically follows the format shown in Figure 6-14.

In addition to the lending proposal, the lender will probably want to see a proposed income and cash flow statement for at least the first year of operations, and probably longer. A balance sheet may also be required. These statements should be carefully prepared following the formats discussed in Chapters 3 and 9. As mentioned above, each item on the statement should be well researched and well documented. The lender will want to know what provision has been made for the owner's salary and for potential contingencies. Often an entrepreneur is advised to enlist an accountant if he or she is weak in financial statement preparation.

FIGURE 6-14   Loan Proposal Format

PROGRAM		FINANCING	
Land	$20,000	Bank loan	$60,000
Building	$50,000	Own funds	$20,000
Equipment	$10,000	Total	$80,000

2. The Proposal.

Obviously, the lender will assess the idea or proposal itself. Using the income statement and cash flow projections, the lender will assess the chances of repayment of the loan. The lender will evaluate not only the specific business but also industrial trends, including the extent of competition and the experiences of similar businesses. The lender may also check with experts in the industry. Many chartered banks now have industry specialists on staff to assist in this type of evaluation.

Some specific types of evaluation used in the lending industry are:

- *Level of working capital*—the dollar difference between current assets and current liabilities. Working capital should be sufficient to meet current obligations as they become due and to finance delays in revenue caused by such items as accounts receivable.
- *Current ratio*—current assets compared with current liabilities. A healthy current ratio is 2:1.
- *Quick ratio*—current assets less inventories compared with liabilities. A healthy quick ratio is 1:1.
- *Debt-to-equity ratio*—percentage of owner's equity compared with debt. A minimum debt-to-equity ratio is 4:1 (25 percent equity). For smaller businesses, most lenders prefer to see 50 percent equity.

The lender will also want to see projections for the basic financial statements such as the balance sheet and income statement. The fundamentals of these statements are also covered in Chapter 9.

Collateral.

Because of the security position on the loan, the lender will want to know whether another lender is also providing funding for the project and, if so, what collateral it has taken as security for the loan. The lender will want to ensure that the funds loaned will be secured by some form of saleable collateral. On capital assets, a lender generally allows no more than 80 to 90 percent of the value of the assets as security. The reason is that if the lender needs to realize on

INCIDENT 6-6

FINDING CAPITAL

Michael Dinn and Heidi Noble, co-owners in the restaurant industry for years, shared a dream of building a winery in the Okanagan Valley in British Columbia. Through their industry experience, they had built up some close connections with winemakers that they assumed would help them to get started. The only problem was that they did not have the finances to get started. At first, they went to their families and got enough for a downpayment on a five-acre farm. However, it was not long before they were using their credit cards and had resumed their day jobs in Vancouver. On weekends, they began processing their first sample vintage on a limited basis with the help of a winemaker. Everyone agreed that the product was excellent. However, they needed substantial financing to construct the winery. They had difficulty obtaining the needed funding due to weaknesses in their proposal that included their lack of understanding of the business and the market, failure to show a positive cash flow, being short on equity, and not having a sound business plan. Eventually, after finding a bank that was familiar with the industry, Michael and Heidi received the required funding and have now realized their dream of building a successful wine business.

Source: Adapted from Alexandra Lopez-Pacheco, "Good Palate and Tenacity," *Financial Post*, September 21, 2009, pp. 1–2.

(repossess) the security, obsolescence, selling, and administration costs will reduce its value. The level of collateral may also vary by industry type, reflecting risk and type of asset.

At this point the entrepreneur may realize that he or she does not possess the required equity to secure adequate financing. In such cases, an investigation of the possibility of leasing instead of buying could be made. An increasing number of businesses are leasing assets to free up capital for other purposes. A recent study carried out by Trimark Seg Fund found that more than one-half (53.5 percent) of small business entrepreneurs have given personal guarantees to secure loans. Forty percent have used their homes, while 20 percent have used their savings.[41]

3. The Applicant's Background and Creditworthiness.

In addition to the project itself and the applicant's managerial ability, the lender will require some additional information in judging the applicant's creditworthiness.

Personal Information.

In filling out a loan application, an applicant is usually required to file information typically included in a personal resumé—items such as age, marital status, education, and work experience. (Be careful to check the legal implications of certain questions.)

Present Debt and Past Lending History.

The lender will want a list of the current state of any loans outstanding and may require information about the applicant's past loan history as well. Most lenders are members of credit bureaus that can provide a complete credit history of the applicant. Lenders will generally use this source to verify the information provided by the applicant.

Amount of Equity the Applicant Has Invested.

All lenders want to know the amount of the applicant's personal funds going into the project. Usually, cash equity is required, but occasionally, capital assets or even "sweat equity" may be acceptable. The amount of equity funds required will vary depending on the risk associated with the project, but as mentioned above, few lenders will provide financing if the applicant has less than 20 percent to 25 percent equity to invest in the business.

Will the Applicant Bank with the Lender?

Many lenders will request that the applicant's business accounts be transferred or opened with the lending bank. They may also require that a compensating balance be held in the account as collateral. If the loan request is turned down, it is important that the entrepreneur find out the reasons for the refusal and make adjustments to the proposal. Alternatively, several lenders should be visited to secure the necessary funding.

LENDER RELATIONS

Once financing has been obtained, it is important that the business provide up-to-date information to the lender regarding current operations and future plans. Regular financial statements and lease contracts can help establish trust between the banker and the owner-manager. Many businesses have found that maintaining a close working relationship with lenders helps ensure adequate levels of financing in the long run. A recent survey by the Canadian Bankers Association found that 78 percent of small businesses had positive relationships with their financial institutions.[42]

TIME TO TAKE ACTION

If you are interested in finding money for starting a business or to grow an existing business, it is time to take action. You should focus on doing the following from this chapter:

1. Determine your own net worth. Establish your cash position as it will impact how much money you need to raise.

2. If you have not done so already, determine how much money you need. Then decide on your optimal capital mix.

3. Start to discuss financial plans with potential sources of capital as early as possible, including bankers, potential family and friend investors, and so forth.

4. Prepare your fundraising pitch, and start looking for capital; and remember—you will be successful if you work hard enough!

What do entrepreneurs do if they have investigated both equity and debt sources and are unable to obtain the needed capital? Probably the first thing to do is find out the reasons for refusal and possibly rework the proposal to bring it more in line with the lender's requirements.

Changes may be necessary to make the proposed business more attractive to lenders or investors. One option that is increasingly being used to reduce the amount of funds required for capital purchases is to consider leasing or renting the asset. Leasing the asset generally does not require a downpayment. The ability to obtain the lease is usually based more on the earning power of the asset and the business than on the background of the owner. Later, when the company is in a more stable condition, the owner may succeed in obtaining funds to make a purchase if he or she desires.

LEARNING OBJECTIVES SUMMARY

LO1 Lack of managerial competence and experience can often result in such financing problems as underestimation of financial requirements, lack of knowledge of sources of capital, lack of skills in preparing and presenting a proposal for financing to a lender, failure to plan in advance for future needs, and poor financial control in payment of loan obligations.

LO2 Start-up capital includes initial inventory, deposits, and first month's payments for payroll, utilities, rent, advertising, insurance, licences, and permits. Accounts receivable and any other operating costs that need to be paid before revenues are generated should also be planned for.

LO3 The type of financing entrepreneurs can access is usually dictated by the stage the business is in and the type of opportunities the company is pursuing. In Canada, start-up businesses are traditionally self-funded, while ongoing businesses often use personal investment and retained earnings. The type of opportunity that the entrepreneur is pursuing is also likely to dictate the type of financing sought. Entrepreneurs who are starting or managing a relatively small business that is pursuing a slow growth strategy will often be limited to debt, while entrepreneurs who are pursuing a high-growth venture are much more likely to use equity and debt in financing their business.

LO4 An essential step in determining the amount of capital needed is to calculate the owner's net worth. This helps determine the amount of funds the owner(s) has to invest in the company and will probably be required by a lending institution.

LO5 Three general sources of equity financing are private investors, corporate investors, and government programs. Sources of debt financing include owners of the business, corporate lenders, regular lending institutions, and government agencies.

LO6 The advantages of equity capital over debt financing include interest obligation, expertise of the investor(s), expanded borrowing power, and spreading of risk. The disadvantages of using equity financing include dilution of ownership, increased potential of disagreements, and the cost incurred in the issuance of the ownership interest. The potential advantages of debt financing over equity capital are a possible higher return on investment, deductibility of interest, flexibility, and ease of approval. The disadvantages include interest expense, additional paperwork, and lack of diversification of risk to other investors.

LO7 Criteria most lenders use in making the loan decision are the applicant's managerial ability, the proposal itself, and the applicant's background and creditworthiness.

DISCUSSION QUESTIONS

1. What is the cheapest source of funds? When all other sources turn down your request for funding, what source is most likely to say yes? Why is this the case?
2. What are the advantages and disadvantages of debt and equity financing?
3. What do you think are the advantages and disadvantages of angel investors?
4. Are investors on crowd-funding sites in need of some government protection, or do you agree that it is their money and they should be able to spend it as they see fit?
5. Should government provide loans for entrepreneurs starting new businesses? Should government guarantee loans for small businesses that are missing the necessary track record, assets, or other ingredients to obtain a commercial bank loan? What benefit do we, as a nation of taxpayers, receive from such loan guarantees?
6. An investor provides an entrepreneurial firm with the capital that it needs to grow. Over and above the capital, in what other ways can the investor add value to the firm? What are the possible downsides of having an angel or venture capitalist as an investor in the business?

APPLICATION QUESTIONS AND HANDS-ON ACTIVITIES

1. Indicate whether each of the following is a start-up cost (S), an ongoing operating cost (O), or both (B).
   a. $1000 for first month's rent
   b. $25,000 for store fixtures
   c. $1000 for third month's rent
   d. Weekly cleaning fee of $250
   e. Purchase of $50,000 of inventory
   f. Payroll expense
   g. $50,000 for TV advertising
2. Imagine you are preparing a business plan for a small manufacturing firm in your province or territory. Using Internet resources, determine what government programs are available for possible assistance. How could each program help your client's business?
3. Search the Internet for services that provide access to business angels or informal investors. How do these sites work? If you were an entrepreneur looking for funding, how much would it cost to use this service? How many business angels are registered on the typical database? How many entrepreneurs are registered on the typical database? How effective do you believe these services are? (Use data, where possible, to back up your answer.)
4. Interview an employee at one of the government agencies that offer equity or debt financing to small businesses. Determine the purpose, the merits, and the weaknesses of that program.
5. Interview a banker and someone at the Canadian Youth Business Foundation to determine what he or

she looks for in a loan application. Compare the differences.

6. Instructors can form groups in class into an equal number, label each group as either venture capitalist or entrepreneur. Inform each group that their job is to negotiate a deal with one another based on the following information—the entrepreneur has a company that has revenue of $2 million; expected annual growth is 25 percent a year for five years, and then 5 percent a year after that; looking for an investment of $5 million for 10 percent equity. Find out which VC firm and entrepreneur group negotiates the best deal.

7. Interview three small business owners about things they do (or have done) to bootstrap the financing of their business. How effective were these techniques? Be prepared to present this list to class and describe how the techniques work.

8. Go to a directory of venture capitalists and ascertain what percentage of funds for a typical venture-capital firm are invested in seed, start-up, expansion or development, and acquisitions or leveraged buyouts. What criteria do venture capitalists report using in their initial screening of business proposals?

Dan is quite proud of his business plan and realizes that he has learned a lot in preparing it. He also realizes, however, that for the business to get off the ground, he needs financing. Suzie will only let Dan use $20,000 of their savings for the venture, but Dan is of the opinion that this will at least help them get started. Once the business is up and running, additional funds will be generated through sales of the Ladder Rail.

Dan decides that he would rather establish the manufacturing facility from scratch than purchase the plant that is for sale. This way he can arrange the facility in a way that suits him, and he will not have to spend money to retrofit. In addition, Dan lives on an acreage and he already owns enough property on which to construct the building. He estimates that constructing a small building of 2000 square feet will cost about $100,000. Although he can use some of the metal-cutting and -bending equipment that he already has, another $30,000 is required to obtain the equipment required to move to commercial production of the Ladder Rail. Dan also thinks that he will need a truck to haul inventory to the plant and to deliver the finished product to purchasers. The estimated cost for a good used truck is $30,000. Initial inventory of aluminum is estimated at $10,000. The financing requirements total $170,000 (Figure 3-A).

Armed with his business plan and his estimate of start-up costs, Dan goes to his local bank to obtain the required financing. He is surprised that his banker is less than enthusiastic about his proposal. His banker's response is clear. "First, you need more equity than this before I could advance a loan to you. Second, you will need more detail on your costs. Third, I will need some indication that your business has the ability to make the loan payments." With his banker's words ringing in his ears, Dan is determined to show how this business could repay a loan. He goes home and starts to work up a proposed income statement, shown in Figure 3-B.

FIGURE 3-A	Ladder Rail Start-up Costs
Building	$100,000
Equipment	30,000
Truck	30,000
Inventory	10,000

FIGURE 3-B	Ladder Rail Income Statement
Revenue: 5000 units at $40	$200,000
Cost of goods sold: 5000 units at $10	50,000
Wages (Sid: $50,000; 2 workers at $30,000 each)	110,000
Utilities and phone	15,000
Net income	$ 15,000

When Dan takes this statement to the banker, he is still told that more work needs to be done. Dan goes home to Suzie feeling pretty discouraged and is not sure what to do next.

Suzie and Dan decide to spend some time researching other potential sources of money online. Both are surprised to learn about the number of angel investors and angel groups in their region. Suzie thinks pursuing angel support for their business would be ideal as the couple will not be burdened with interest costs, which are associated with traditional bank financing. Furthermore, if the business fails, they will likely lose less of their own money. Dan is not as excited about angel investors as Suzie is. He argues with her that he wants to be his own boss; business angels would want to influence his decisions, and starting the company is something they can do on their own. Dan also thinks that if he sells equity in his business, he could be giving up millions in long-term profits if the company succeeds nationally and then globally.

Questions

1. What items have been overlooked by Dan in both the start-up costs and the income statements for the Ladder Rail?

2. What additional statements would the banker likely require?

3. Do you think Dan should consider other forms of capital like equity? Why, or why not?

4. What advantages of angel financing is Dan missing out on in his assessment of this specific type of an investor? How might Suzie persuade him to change his mind?

5. Would crowd-funding be a good idea for Dan to pursue? What are some of the potential advantages and disadvantages of this strategy?

Clark's Sporting Goods   Kelly's Grill
Jensen Roofing   Second Cup
Conrad's Photographer's Supplies

Clark's Sporting Goods

D. Wesley Balderson, *University of Lethbridge*

Dave Clark plans to open a sporting goods store in London, Ontario, as soon as he graduates from university there in the spring. He did a market demand analysis for such a store for one of his course projects and is confident the opportunity exists.

Dave's major problem is determining the amount of funds he will require. His father, who is quite wealthy, will give him $30,000 as a graduation gift to invest. He has located a store that rents for $2,000 per month (in advance) and has made an itemized list of the start-up costs as follows:

Merchandise (4 months)	$100,000
Shelves, racks, displays	5,000
Remodelling	4,000
Cash register (used)	800
Check-out counter	500
Office supplies (4 months' supply)	200
Telephone: $50/month, $100 deposit, $25 installation fee	
Utilities: $200/month, $200 deposit	

Dave has made the following estimates:

- He can completely turn over his inventory every four months.
- In the first year, he plans a 60 percent markup on cost of merchandise.
- He can get by on a salary of $2000 per month.
- He plans to hire one full-time employee at $1500 per month and one at $1000.
- He plans to spend $2000 in opening promotion in the first month and $500 a month after the grand opening for advertising.
- He estimates that 50 percent of his sales will be on credit and will be paid in 30 days.
- The interest rate is 10 percent, payable every four months.
- The depreciation rate is 10 percent.

Questions

1. Estimate how much money Dave will need from outside sources to start his business.

2. Assuming Dave receives start-up financing from a bank, as calculated in question 1, will he require an operating line of credit during the first four months of operation? If so, how much?

3. Should Dave pursue debt or equity sources of funds to get started?

Jensen Roofing

D. Wesley Balderson, *University of Lethbridge*

Robert Jensen has just completed a short entrepreneurial course at a local college as preparation for establishing his own roofing business. One of the main things that he learned in the course was the necessity of preparing a business plan for the enterprise. As a result, Robert went to work and within a few days put together the following business plan for Jensen Roofing.

Background

I, Robert Jensen, will be the sole owner of this proprietorship, which will install and repair roofs in the Lethbridge, Alberta, market area. I have completed an entrepreneurial course at the Lethbridge Community College and have had several years experience in the roofing business working for Charles Hill Roofing, the largest roofer in the Lethbridge area.

I want to start my own business to be independent and to obtain a higher financial compensation than I am currently receiving. I want everyone in Lethbridge and surrounding areas to know my company and the quality work we do.

Market Approach

The target market will be every person who owns a house, apartment building, warehouse, condo, or office building. The services we provide will cater to all people who own buildings that need roof repair or construction. We will provide all types of roofing materials and services. Eaves-troughing will also be included in our business. Quality workmanship will be the building block of our business. We will ensure a one-year guarantee on all workmanship.

Because the service Jensen Roofing will provide is of high quality, I will charge a slightly higher price on our product. I will try to maintain a 20 percent markup over costs to keep our prices fair to every customer. Jensen Roofing will use several forms of promotion. Brochures and pamphlets will be prepared and sent through direct mail to every homeowner in Lethbridge. Newspaper ads and the Yellow Pages will also be used to promote the business.

Physical Facilities

The business will be located in my home at first. This will save a considerable amount of money until the business gets established. Equipment, supplies, and opening inventory will be purchased from local suppliers. The following schedule provides a listing of the equipment and supplies that will be needed to get started.

Physical Requirements

1 work truck (used half ton)	$ 5,000
3-tonne dump truck	5,000
1 hoist	500
4 ladders (25 foot)	1,500
Computer system	3,000
Office equipment and supplies	1,000
Total	$17,000

Financial

To estimate potential revenue for Jensen Roofing for new houses, I have multiplied the average roofing job for new houses ($8000) by the number of new houses constructed in Lethbridge (400) in 2004 for a total of $3,200,000. For repair jobs I have taken the average dollar expenditure per household for the Lethbridge area (Urban Family Expenditure Data) of $100 and multiplied it by the number of homes (26,000) for a total of $2,600,000. Of this total of $5,800,000, I estimate that Jensen Roofing will obtain a 10 percent market share for a total revenue of $580,000. There are currently eight other roofers in the city, but because of my quality workmanship, I hope to increase the market share of Jensen Roofing to 20 percent within five years.

Projected income based on these estimates are given below:

JENSEN ROOFING PROJECTED INCOME—YEAR 1

Sales	$580,000
Cost of goods sold (45%)	261,000
Wages	100,000
Depreciation	2,000
Advertising	2,600
Insurance	1,200
Repairs and maintenance	5,000
Licences and permits	200
Professional fees	800
Interest (8% on $15,000)	1,200
Total	374,000
Net Income	$206,000

Jensen Roofing will obtain a loan from a local bank to finance $15,000 of the start-up requirement. The remaining $2000 will be supplied by me, the owner. The financial records of the business will be prepared and maintained by an accountant.

Legal Requirements

The necessary business licences and permits will be obtained from the City of Lethbridge. Initially, the business will be operated as a proprietorship, and when the business becomes more established, I will consider forming a limited company.

Personnel

The personnel required to keep Jensen Roofing operating will vary from season to season. Due to the uncertainties of the weather, part-time employees will be used. Ads will be placed in the local newspaper to find workers for the business. I will also use the government employment agency of Canada Manpower. During the summer months, I may also look at hiring students. I estimate that on average I will have about five workers on the payroll. Training will take place on the job, which is appropriate for this type of work.

Question

1. Evaluate the Jensen Roofing business plan from an investor's and a lender's points of view.

Conrad's Photographer's Supplies

D. Wesley Balderson, *University of Lethbridge*

Richard and Karen Bingley are interested in going into a business related to their hobby—photography. For the last year, they have been good customers of Conrad's Photographer's Supplies, a sole proprietorship, owned by Shelley Conrad. Although the store is relatively new, they have become well-acquainted with Shelley, who is a well-known photographer in the community. Shelley told the Bingleys that the store was doing well considering she opened it just over year ago. More and more people have gotten involved in photography and with the introduction of digital cameras, the industry was in a growth position. An increasing number of people seem to prefer an outlet where they can get advice about taking pictures as opposed to buying only for low prices.

However, one day Shelley confides in Karen that although she enjoys operating the business, it was taking much more time to run than she expected, and she is considering selling the business to devote more time to her professional photography. Shelley thinks Richard and Karen might be interested in purchasing the business, since they are such good customers and know a lot about photography.

Richard and Karen are quite excited about the idea and meet with Shelley to go over the entire business. They are impressed with the operation as all the equipment and fixtures are new, and they are especially impressed with the extensive customer list. As they discuss the financial information (see below), Shelley indicates that she would sell the business for $80,000, slightly above the value of the assets of the company. Richard and Karen currently have $20,000 in equity and Shelley indicates that she is prepared to finance them over four years at 8 percent per annum, which is 2 percent less than Shelley is paying on her business debt. Because of her stature in the industry and her numerous connections in the community, Shelley has developed a good working relationship with her suppliers, which typically includes them granting 30-day credit on inventory. The store is located in a strip mall at the north end of the city of Winnipeg and has two years remaining on the three-year lease.

CONRAD'S PHOTOGRAPHER'S SUPPLIES
INCOME STATEMENT

Sales	252,000
Cost of Goods Sold	171,000
Gross Margin	81,000
Expenses	
Wages	38,000
Promotion	4,000
Rent	15,000
Utilities	6,000
Miscellaneous	2,000
Depreciation	5,000
Net profit	$11,000

CONRAD'S PHOTOGRAPHER'S SUPPLIES
BALANCE SHEET

Assets	
Cash	1,000
Accounts Receivable	8,000
Inventory	40,000
Fixtures	15,000
Goodwill	12,000
Total	76,000
Liabilities and Owner's Equity	
Accounts Payable	27,000
Debt	20,000
Equity	29,000
Total	$76,000

Questions

1. Suppose the Bingleys decided to start a photography store from scratch. Discuss how this decision would compare with the other two methods of getting into the business on (a) independence, (b) risk, and (c) information requirements.

2. In evaluating this business to purchase it, discuss concerns you would have about (a) the previous owner, (b) financial information, and (c) assets of the business.

3. Assuming the information in the financial statements is accurate, is Shelly Conrad's asking price a reasonable one? Use book value and capitalization of earnings methods to help you answer this question.

4. There is at least one adjustment to the balance sheet and two to the income statement that should be made to make these statements more accurate, which will affect the calculation of the price of the business. Make the adjustments and reevaluate the asking price based on your adjustments.

Kelly's Grill

D. Wesley Balderson, *University of Lethbridge*

Kelly Orr works as assistant department manager in the ladies' wear department of a large department store in Kingston, Ontario. She enjoys her work but sees that chances of further advancement in her $35,000-a-year job are limited. For the past few years, Kelly was thinking about starting her own business. As a teenager, she worked summers in a fast-food franchise and always wanted to own a restaurant. As she has two children, she resents having to work Thursday and Friday evenings and Saturdays, and thinks that by owning her own business she can more easily take time off to be with her family. Her husband, a schoolteacher, has supported her working in the past but is a bit hesitant about Kelly risking her savings of $20,000 to go out on her own. They agree, however, that Kelly should investigate a few possibilities and obtain as much information as she can about the restaurant industry in Kingston.

For the past six months, Kelly has visited with several of her friends, looked at some prospective businesses, and checked with public officials to find out what information was available. She has obtained the following information:

Population of Kingston	95,000
Per-family away-from-home food expenditures	$80/month
Number of families in Kingston	28,000
Number of restaurants in Kingston	110
Average square footage per outlet	1,500
Cost of goods sold as percentage of gross sales	50%
Bank's lending rate	10%

Operating expenses, excluding rent, interest, and franchise advertising royalties, are estimated to be 35 percent of gross sales.

From several restaurant possibilities, Kelly has narrowed the decision down to three: a site in a new shopping mall, a downtown restaurant that is for sale, and a fast-food franchise. All three involve a greater investment than Kelly was planning on. To get sufficient funds, the Orr's may have to remortgage their house.

Possibility A

The first potential site is a new shopping centre just nearing completion in a new and growing part of Kingston. The centre is anchored at each end by two national department stores. The space Kelly is considering is 3000 square feet and carries a rental of $10 per square foot, plus a royalty of 2 percent of gross sales. Although the rental costs would be high, Kelly is confident that the mall would generate considerable customer traffic, which would outweigh the rental costs. Also, the mall location is within a few minutes' drive from her home. However, the space is unfinished, and Kelly estimates she would need a minimum of $40,000 in equipment and $20,000 in leasehold improvements to get the restaurant started. Since not all the space was leased out, she was not able to find out how many other restaurants were planning to locate in the mall.

Possibility B

The second potential site is a 1500-square-foot, busy downtown lunchtime café that is for sale. The present owner is asking $50,000 for the restaurant and is willing to finance the sale at $25,000 down and $10,000 per year for three years. The space had been leased at $12,000 annually and is due to be renegotiated in three years. The location of this restaurant makes it attractive to lunchtime and late-afternoon customers. The restaurant has operated successfully for six years and is located close to several large office buildings.

Possibility C

The third possibility is to sign a franchise contract with a national fast-food franchise chain that wants to expand into Kingston. The typical outlet size is 2000 square feet. The initial franchise fee is $20,000, plus an additional $50,000 to be financed through Kelly's bank with the franchise guarantee, which would lower the interest rate by 2 percent. Kelly would also pay 6 percent of gross sales as a royalty. They would train Kelly in one of its company-owned outlets at no charge and help with the start-up of her own outlet. She would, of course, be constantly monitored by the franchise—a point that makes her a bit uneasy.

Kelly needs to make a decision soon. All three prospects might be lost if she waits too long.

Questions

1. How well has Kelly thought out and prepared for her decision to start her own restaurant?
2. Based on the information provided, which of the choices open to Kelly would you advise her to make?
3. What additional information should she obtain before making this decision?

Second Cup

D. Wesley Balderson, *University of Lethbridge*

Ken and Mary Hatch are in the process of making a major career change. Ken has been caretaker for a local high school in Markham, Ontario, for 20 years, rising to the position of supervisor. Mary has worked in a coffee shop for eight years since their children entered school. They are considering opening their own coffee shop and are interested in a Second Cup franchise.

Second Cup is a successful nationally known Canadian franchise that was established in 1975 in Toronto and has grown to more than 400 outlets across the country. Mary became aware from her employer that Second Cup was looking for franchisees in the Markham area and she has collected the following information from the company. The franchise fee is $20,000 and there is a promotional royalty of 9 percent of gross sales. Second Cup estimates that the total investment for an outlet is Markham to be an additional $200,000 for equipment and other start-up costs. This cost does not include the building, which Second Cup builds and then rents back to the franchiser.

Although the Hatches do not have $200,000, they have saved $20,000 and have been assured by Second Cup that the bank will finance the remainder at 5 percent by being signed up with the franchising company. One of the Hatches' concerns is that they have not managed a restaurant before, although Ken has supervised people in his caretaking job and Mary has worked in the coffee shop for eight years. The Hatches take some comfort in the fact that Second Cup offers a three-week course at their Coffee College to teach the fundamentals of the coffee and retail business.

They are both tired of taking orders from supervisors and see this opportunity as a way to be their own boss with minimal risk. There are currently five other Second Cup outlets in Markham and three Starbucks coffee houses, which are their major competitors. There are also many other independent coffee shops and other fast-food outlets that sell coffee. However, with the city and coffee sales growing, the Hatches are optimistic about their chances for success. They cite the fact that they will save considerably by purchasing all of their supplies from the parent company and the fact that the well-organized operating and monitoring system will ensure that they operate at peak efficiency as reasons for optimism.

Second Cup has supplied the following sample financial statement to help the Hatches in their planning:

Opening cash balance	$ 20,000
Sales	600,000
Cost of goods sold	320,000
Total	$300,000
Expenses	
Advertising royalty	$ 54,000
Other advertising	6,000
Rent ($30 at 1000)	30,000
Insurance	5,000
Repairs and maintenance	5,000
Telephone and utilities	15,000
Salaries	100,000
Miscellaneous	10,000
Total	$225,000
Net income	$ 75,000

The Hatches are most happy with the projections because the business would make $55,000. Ken estimates that half the salary total would be their own wage for working in the business. Ken and Mary note that combining these two would almost double what they are earning in their current jobs.

This couple is about to make the final decision to leave their employment and sign this franchise contract.

Questions

1. What further analysis should be done before making this decision?
2. What specific questions about the financial information as presented by Second Cup should be asked?

For more information on the resources available from McGraw-Hill Ryerson, go to www.mcgrawhill.ca/he/solutions.

PART III

MANAGING THE SMALL BUSINESS

Part 2 of this text dealt with issues relating to the organization and establishment of a small business. Once the business has been established, the owner-manager should follow several management fundamentals to ensure that the business stays viable and competitive. Part 3 discusses five of these management areas. Chapter 7 focuses on the marketing plan with a focus on industry and competitor analysis and market segmentation. Chapter 8 discusses the marketing mix with an emphasis on managing promotion in the digital age. Chapter 9 covers the recording and controlling of the financial aspects of the business. Both marketing and finance are areas in which many entrepreneurs lack training and competence. Chapter 10 discusses some fundamental components of the internal operations or production aspects of the business. Chapter 11 reviews the principles of personnel management applicable to the small organization. Chapter 12 outlines the most relevant tax considerations for the small business and extends some of the legal discussion from earlier in the text.

CHAPTER 7

MARKETING MANAGEMENT

LEARNING OBJECTIVES

By the end of this chapter, you should be able to:

LO1 Describe the role of marketing planning in a business enterprise.

LO2 List the major steps in a marketing plan.

LO3 Explain the need for an understanding of the external environment of the organization.

LO4 Discuss the importance of marketing research.

LO5 Describe the importance of and methods to employ effective customer relationship programs.

LO6 Discuss the importance of identifying goals and objectives.

LO7 Explain the importance of monitoring the marketing plan.

THE TALE OF PR AND SPIN MASTER LTD. *Destination Ceo*

The Canadian Press/Maclean's Photo/ Rick Chard

Ronnen Harary, Anton Rabie, and Ben Varadi, are living what for many would be a childhood dream. The trio and close friends are owners of their own toy company—Spin Master Toys. Harary and Rabie serve as co-CEOs, while Varadi is in charge of product development with the title of chief creative officer.

The 40-something Canadians have taken the toy world by storm over the last 15 years with such hot items as Bakugan Brawlers; Liv Dolls; Air Hogs, a plane that flies on air power; Bukuna Mighty Beanz collectibles; and Bella Dancerella, a home ballet studio and instructional kit. In addition, they have signed partnership agreements with some of the biggest companies in North America, including Disney and McDonald's, to develop such toys as the SpongeBob SquarePants–inspired Bounce Rounds (inflatable, portable play gyms) and a McDonald's McFlurry Maker.[1] The company has grown to reach almost $1 billion in sales in 2011 and is the third largest toy business in North America.[2]

One of the first and most common questions people ask after hearing the accomplishments of the three entrepreneurs is, "How did they break into a North American toy market that is characterized by large operators with equally large product development and marketing budgets?" A great deal of their success can be attributed to their initial marketing efforts and their focus on getting close to their customers so they understand their wants and needs. At the company's infancy stage it was clear the partners had a marketing plan they were following that focused on customer knowledge, relationship management, and low-cost strategies.

The company's first product was Earth Buddy, a replica of a small doll head constructed of pantyhose and filled with grass seed and sawdust. The Earth Buddy would sprout grass when watered and placed near light. With only $10,000 for marketing, the three developed a marketing plan that was heavy on non-traditional marketing and PR, selling the product and their story to anyone who would listen. Their marketing plan was based on getting to know retailers who would purchase their products and they created a positive relationship with Zellers, Canadian Tire, and eventually Walmart. The product was a huge success and they were on their way.

They followed the product with Devil Sticks, a game for children, and they managed to sell 250,000 units in six months without using any traditional promotional campaigns. Their marketing plan once again relied on non-traditional marketing whereas they hired college and university students to demonstrate the game at playgrounds, local events, and malls, which created a huge demand for the product.

With Devil Sticks becoming a commercial success, the company received its biggest break when it was approached by two inventors with the idea of an air-powered airplane. The concept was simple enough: Children pump the plane full of air and then launch it, watching it soar upwards of 15 metres. The result was a flying plane called Air Hogs. Rather than launch a massive retail and marketing campaign, Spin Master crafted a marketing plan where they focused on selling the product to specialty educational toy stores and through the Sears catalogue, using what they did well—PR and unconventional marketing methods. Knowing journalists, who in this case were their target market for PR would be looking for stories on non-conventional companies and products they built a suitcase to serve as a press kit and filled it with not only the plane but also a plastic airline cup, a bag of peanuts, and a barf bag, sending it out to numerous writers and editors. The campaign worked wonders as both *Time* and *Popular Science* magazines published stories on the airplane, with *Popular Science* calling it one of the best products of the year. Spin Master again hired students to travel from air show to air show demonstrating the product and creating a buzz among airplane enthusiasts. Sales were starting to boom. But the best was yet to come as the PR team at Spin Master managed to get the product on NBC's *Today* show and Rosie O'Donnell's talk show, creating major demand. The following year the company was ready to launch Air Hogs in traditional retailers and had a runaway hit on their hands.

A large part of Spin Master's success as mentioned above is an understanding of its customers and target markets. Iain Kennedy, the chief operating officer of Spin Master, says the firm is diligent in market research and compiles vast information on customers and their feedback. According to Kennedy, this understanding of customers has enabled them to develop some of the hottest toys in the industry. Kennedy also notes the firm tracks the success of its marketing strategist in their marketing plan and uses the information to determine a return on investment (ROI) for their initiatives.

The company, which pays close attention to trends in the toy industry, is in the process of re-positioning itself as a children's entertainment company. The result is due to changes in the business's environment where children are spending more time playing video games and mobile applications. As a result Spin Master has announced they will be releasing several new apps in 2013 all based on their most popular games. "The company is transforming itself and setting itself up for its next phase," said Anton Rabie, co-CEO and co-founder of the Toronto company. "We have been saying as a company for the last 10 years that we are not a toy company; we are a children's entertainment company focused on creating great content platforms for kids."[3]

THE ROLE OF MARKETING MANAGEMENT IN THE SMALL BUSINESS

Marketing activities are often overlooked by owner-managers after the business has been established. Some possible reasons for this are that (1) owner-managers do not fully understand what marketing is; (2) owner-managers may not think it is necessary—that is, they may believe that if they have a good enough product, it will sell itself; or (3) owner-managers tend to be so busy with the day-to-day activities and problems of the business that they do not take the time to assess the market and develop a marketing plan. For example, *Profit Magazine* columnist Lisa Shepherd recently stated that many businesses, in particular companies that focus on sales to other businesses, rarely have a good marketing plan and roughly 40 percent of firms have no plan at all.[4]

MANY BUSINESSES THAT SELL TO OTHER COMPANIES DO NOT HAVE MARKETING PLANS.
Alistair Berg/Getty Images

Regardless of the reasons for failing to apply marketing principles in the small business, it is critical that the owner-manager understand and apply those principles. The business will likely be unable to hire a marketing specialist. Therefore, the owner-manager will have to do a considerable amount of marketing, not only to potential customers but also to suppliers, employees, bankers, and perhaps even government agencies. The Small Business Profile of Spin Master Toys illustrates how important marketing was to the successful establishment of the company.

The major purpose of this chapter, then, is to introduce the fundamentals of marketing that can help sustain the growth of the business. Some of the principles also apply to establishing a business and were mentioned earlier in the text. Other marketing principles form an important part of a business plan and were discussed in Chapter 4.

An owner-manager may become involved in the following marketing activities:

- Writing and maintaining the marketing plan for the business
- Defining the target customer (market niche), target customer characteristics, and information concerning that customer's product or service wants and needs
- Understanding those influences outside the business that will affect its operations
- Developing the product or service
- Developing the channel(s) of distribution
- Setting price levels for the product or service
- Providing information or promoting the product or service to those who are influential in its purchase

This chapter will discuss the relevant aspects of marketing plans, market segmentation, target marketing, customer profiles, the impact of the external environment on the company, and relationship marketing. Chapter 8 will focus on the marketing mix, including a lengthy discussion on digital marketing and its impact on small and medium business. It is important to note, however, that these components need to be coordinated to prepare a marketing plan and managed together as a system to be most effective.

THE MARKETING PLAN   LO1

The marketing plan represents a significant element in the business plan for a new venture. It serves a number of important functions or purposes. Primarily the marketing plan establishes how the entrepreneur will effectively compete and operate in the marketplace and thus meet the business goals and objectives of the new venture. Once the strategies of how the business will operate have been established, the entrepreneur can assign costs to these strategies, which then serves the important purpose of establishing budgets and making financial projections. The marketing plan, like any other type of plan, may be compared with a road map used to guide a traveller. It is designed to provide answers to three basic questions:

1. Where have we been? When used as a stand-alone document (operational plan), this would imply some background on the company, its strengths and weaknesses, some background on the competition, and a discussion of the opportunities and threats in the marketplace. When the marketing plan is integrated as part of the business plan, this segment would focus on some history of the marketplace, marketing strengths and weaknesses of the firm, and market opportunities and threats.

2. Where do we want to go (in the short term)? This question primarily addresses the marketing objectives and goals of the new venture in the next 12 months. In the initial business plan, the objectives and goals often go beyond the first year because of the need to project profits and cash needs for the first three to five years.

3. How do we get there? This question discusses the specific marketing strategy that will be implemented, when it will occur, and who will be responsible for the monitoring of activities. For example, Winston Gust, owner of Crossdock Systems (http://crossdock-freight.com), a Mississauga-based transportation company and one of the fastest growing companies in Canada, uses social media, particularly LinkedIn, as a key component of its marketing strategy. "LinkedIn has become a very effective tool for us. Our theory now is: with all the social media at our fingertips, we should never have to make cold calls. There's always some way to connect with a person you want to talk to and get an

introduction, so when you make the call, it won't be cold."[5] The answers to these questions are generally determined from the marketing research carried out before the planning process is begun. Budgets will also be determined and used in the income and cash flow projections.

Management should understand that the marketing plan is a guide for implementing marketing decision making and not a generalized, superficial document. The mere organization of the thinking process involved in preparing a marketing plan can be helpful to the entrepreneur because to develop the plan, it is necessary to formally document and describe as many marketing details as possible that will be part of the decision process during the next year. This process will enable the entrepreneur not only to understand and recognize the critical issues but also to be prepared in the event that any change in the environment occurs.

Each year the entrepreneur should prepare an annual marketing plan before any decisions are made regarding production or manufacturing, personnel changes, or financial resources needed. This annual plan becomes the basis for planning other aspects of the business and for developing budgets for the year. Figures 7-1, 7-2, and 7-3 provide suggested outlines for

---

FIGURE 7-1   Marketing Plan for a Consumer Products Company

I.   ANALYZE AND DEFINE THE BUSINESS SITUATION—past, present, and future

An analysis of where we are, perhaps how we got there. Data and trend lines should go back three to five years.

Suggested items to cover:

A. The scope of the market (class of trade)

B. Sales history by products, by class of trade, by regions

C. Market potential, major trends anticipated

D. Distribution channels:

   1. Identification of principal channels (dealer or class of trade), sales history through each type

   2. Buying habits and attitudes of these channels

   3. Our selling policies and practices

E. The customer or end user:

   1. Identification of customers making the buying decision, classified by age, income level, occupation, geographic location, etc.

   2. Customer attitudes on product or services, quality, price, etc. Purchase or use habits that contribute to attitudes

   3. Advertising history: expenditures, media and copy strategy, measurements of effectiveness

   4. Publicity and other educational influences

F. The product or services:

   1. Story of the product line, quality development, delivery and service

   2. Comparison with other approaches to serve the customers' needs

   3. Product research; product improvements planned

II.   IDENTIFY PROBLEMS AND OPPORTUNITIES

A. In view of the facts cited in (I) above, what are the major problems that are restricting or impeding our growth?

B. What opportunities do we have for:

—Overcoming the above problems?

—Modifying or improving the product line or adding new products?

—Serving the needs of more customers in our market or developing new markets?

—Improving the efficiency of our operation?

III. DEFINE SPECIFIC AND REALISTIC BUSINESS OBJECTIVES

A. Assumptions regarding future conditions:

—Level of economic activity

—Level of industry activity

—Changes in customer needs

—Changes in distribution channels

—Changes beyond our control, increased costs, etc.

B. Primary marketing objectives (the establishment of aim points and goals). Consider where you are going and how you will get there. Objectives are the necessary base of any plan, since a plan must have precise direction.

C. Overall strategy for achievement of primary objectives. The division's overall strategy to accomplish its primary objective—sample: shifting of sales emphasis, products, or classes of trade; changes for improvement of sales coverage; etc.

D. Functional (departmental) objectives. In this section "explode" your primary objectives into sub objectives, or goals, for each department. Show the interrelation vertically, by marketing project. Show time schedule on objectives below:

1. Advertising and promotion objectives

2. Customer service objectives

3. Product modification objectives

4. New product objectives

5. Expense control objectives

6. Workforce objectives

7. Personnel training objectives

8. Market research objectives

IV. DEFINE MARKETING STRATEGY AND ACTION PROGRAMS—to accomplish the objectives

A. Here, *detail the action steps*, priorities, and schedules relating to each of the functional objectives above. If, for example, one of your estimates was "an increase in sales of product X from 10,000 to 20,000 units," now is the time to pinpoint specific customers. In order to explain who must do what, and when, you can show the interaction of the departments listed above (III-D) and how their objectives serve to meet this increased demand.

B. If one of your objectives was to introduce a new product by "x" date, now show the details and deadlines, production schedule, market introduction plans, advertising and merchandising support, sales and service training needed, etc. Define responsibility and dates for each step.

C. Alternatives—In the event of a delay in a project or program, what alternative plans are available?

V. CONTROL AND REVIEW PROCEDURES

How will the execution of the plan be monitored?

A. What kinds of "feedback" information will be needed?

B. When and how will reviews be scheduled (departments, regions, etc.)?

C. Date for full-scale review of progress vs. plan.

Source: David S. Hopkins, *The Marketing Plan*, The Conference Board, 1981. Reprinted with permission of The Conference Board.

FIGURE 7-2   Marketing Plan for a Business-to-Business Company

Marketing Plan Outline

For each major product/product category: Time Period—One, Three, and Five Plus Years

I.   MANAGEMENT SUMMARY

What is our marketing plan for this product in brief?

This is a one-page summary of the basic factors involving the marketing of the product in the plan period, along with the results expected from implementing the plan. It is intended as a brief guide for management.

II.   ECONOMIC OUTLOOK

What factors in the overall economy and industry will affect the marketing of the product in the plan period, and how?

This section will contain a summary of the specific economic and industry factors that will affect the marketing of this product during the plan period.

III.   THE MARKET—qualitative

Who or what kinds of market segments constitute the major prospects for this product?

This section will define the qualitative nature of our market segments. It will include definitive descriptions and profiles of major distributors, specifiers, users, and/or consumers of the product.

IV.   THE MARKET—quantitative

What is the potential market for this product?

This section will apply specific quantitative measures to this product. Here we want to include numbers of potential customers, dollar volume of business, our current share of the market—any specific measures that will outline our total target for the product and where we stand competitively now.

V.   TREND ANALYSIS

Based on the history of this product, where do we appear to be headed?

This section is a review of the past history of this product. Ideally, we should include annual figures for the last five years showing dollar volume, accounts opened, accounts closed, share of market, and all other applicable historical data.

VI.   COMPETITION

Who are our competitors for this product, and how do we stand competitively?

This section should define our current competition. It should be a thoughtful analysis outlining who our competitors are, how successful they are, and what actions they might be expected to take regarding this product during the coming year.

VII.   PROBLEMS AND OPPORTUNITIES

Internally and externally, are there problems inhibiting the marketing of this product, or are there opportunities we have not taken advantage of?

This section will include a frank commentary on both inhibiting problems and unrealized opportunities. It should include a discussion of the internal and external problems we can control, for example, by changes in policies or operational programs. It should also point to areas of opportunity regarding this product that we are not now exploring.

VIII.   OBJECTIVES AND GOALS

Where do we want to go with this product?

This section will outline the immediate short- and long-range objectives for this product. Short-range goals should be specific and will apply to next year. Intermediate to long-range goals will necessarily be less specific and should project for the next three to five years and beyond. Objectives should be stated in two forms.

(1) Qualitative—reasoning behind the offering of this product and what modification or other changes we expect to make.

(2) Quantitative—number of accounts, dollar volume, share of market, and profit goals.

IX. ACTION PROGRAMS

Given past history, the economy, the market, competition, etc., what must we do to reach the goals we have set for this product or service?

This section will be a description of the specific actions we plan to take during the coming plan period to ensure reaching the objectives we have set for the product in VIII. These would include the full range of factors comprising our marketing mix. The discussion should cover what is to be done, schedules for completion, methods of evaluation, and assignment of accountability for executing the program and measuring results.

Source: David S. Hopkins, *The Marketing Plan*, The Conference Board, 1981. Reprinted with permission of The Conference Board.

FIGURE 7-3   Marketing Plan for a Service Company

Marketing Plan Outline

For each major bank service:

I. MANAGEMENT SUMMARY

What is our marketing plan for this service in brief?

This is a one-page summary of the basic factors involving the marketing of the service next year along with the results expected from implementing the plan. It is intended as a brief guide for management.

II. ECONOMIC PROJECTIONS

What factors in the overall economy will affect the marketing of this service next year, and how?

This section will include a summary of the specific economic factors that will affect the marketing of this service during the coming year. These might include employment, personal income, business expectations, inflationary (or deflationary) pressures, etc.

III. THE MARKET—quantitative

IV. Who or what kinds of organization could conceivably be considered prospects for this service?

This section will define the qualitative nature of our market. It will include demographic information, industrial profiles, business profiles, and so on, for all people or organizations that could be customers for this service.

V. THE MARKET—quantitative

What is the potential market for this service?

This section will apply specific quantitative measures to this bank service. Here we want to include numbers of potential customers, dollar volume of business, our current share of the market—any specific measures that will outline our total target for the service and where we stand competitively now.

VI. TREND ANALYSIS

Based on the history of this service, where do we appear to be headed?

This section is a review of the past history of this service. Ideally, we should include quarterly figures for the last five years showing dollar volume, accounts opened, accounts closed, share of market, and all other applicable historical data.

VII. COMPETITION

Who are our competitors for this service, and how do we stand competitively?

This section should define our current competition, both bank and nonbank. It should be a thoughtful analysis outlining who our competitors are, how successful they are, why they have (or have not) been successful, and what actions they might be expected to take regarding this service during the coming year.

FIGURE 7-3   (continued)

VIII. PROBLEMS AND OPPORTUNITIES

Internally and externally, are there problems inhibiting the marketing of this service, or are there opportunities we have not taken advantage of?

This section will contain a frank commentary on both inhibiting problems and unrealized opportunities. It should include a discussion of the internal and external problems we can control, for example, changes in policies or operational procedures. It should also point to areas of opportunity regarding this service that we are not now exploiting.

IX. OBJECTIVES AND GOALS

Where do we want to go with this service?

This section will outline the immediate short- and long-range objectives for this service. Short-range goals should be specific and will apply to next year. Long-range goals will necessarily be less specific and should project for the next five years. Objectives should be stated in two forms:

(1) Qualitative—reasoning behind the offering of this service and what modifications or other changes we expect to make.

(2) Quantitative—number of accounts, dollar volume, share of market, profit goals.

X. ACTION PROGRAMS

Given past history, the economy, the market, competition, and so on, what must we do to reach the goals we have set for this service?

This section will be a description of the specific actions we plan to take during the coming year to ensure reaching the objectives we have set for the service in VIII. These would include advertising and promotion, direct mail, and brochure development. It would also include programs to be designed and implemented by line officers. The discussion should cover what is to be done, schedules for completion, methods of evaluation, and officers in charge of executing the program and measuring results.

Source: David S. Hopkins, *The Marketing Plan*, The Conference Board, 1981. Reprinted with permission of The Conference Board.

in-depth marketing plans. Variations of these outlines will depend on the market and nature of the product or service, as well as the general company mission. Lisa Shepherd, author of *Market Smart: How to Gain Customers and Increase Profits with B2B Marketing*, recently stated that an entrepreneur with no plan could start by taking four sheets of paper, conduct some research, and on each piece of paper answer four basic questions:[6]

1. Who is your target market?

2. What is your value proposition?

3. What is the message?

4. What tools will you use to connect to your target market?

While Shepherd obviously does not think this is an ideal marketing plan, given that many firms have no plan at all, this would be a good starting point.[7]

Entrepreneurs should recognize that the marketing plan is only as good as the information on which it is based. As such, most successful marketing plans are built on market research including secondary and primary data. A thorough discussion of market research can be found in Chapters 2 and 3 in the text. Business owners who want to create a successful marketing plan should normally engage in market research prior to drafting the plan and monitor customer feedback and amend the plan accordingly. As illustrated in the opening Small Business Profile, Spin Master Toys has invested time engaging in market research and evaluating their marketing efforts.

HOW TO FOCUS YOUR MARKETING PLAN

"Women in business often try to please everyone," says Barbara Densmore, a B.C.-based business consultant and coach, "But it takes a lot of energy to have a broad customer base and a broad product focus." Instead of casting your net wide, develop a focused marketing plan to give you the best return for your marketing dollars.

During a recent "training by telephone" workshop for the Women's Enterprise Society of B.C. (WESBC), Densmore offered five rules for creating a focused marketing plan:

Focus on the customer, not the product. Have you ever received a present you didn't like or need? Chances are, the giver thought you would appreciate it. The same situation often applies to potential customers presented with what a company offers, says Densmore. Not everyone likes receiving products or services the way businesses present them.

Instead of offering what you want to give, focus on providing what your best customers ask for. "Stop talking about yourself" and "listen, listen, listen," she says. "Get really curious about the needs of others and they'll tell you what they want. It allows you to give a gift that will be well-received."

Find the right customers. Most people believe that marketing success comes from having the right marketing message or marketing tools (such as ads or promotions), says Densmore. In fact, 60 percent of overall marketing success comes from finding the right customers. Spend more time discovering who your ideal client is, and you'll spend less time, energy and money on crafting the right message and tools.

Remember the 80–20 rule. If you remember the old adage that 80 percent of your business comes from 20 percent of your customers, it's easy to see that "you can waste a lot of energy marketing to a lot of people who aren't going to be your best customers," says Densmore. Once you find the right customers, focus your marketing energy on them and cut back on areas that offer little return on investment.

Remember "the rule of seven." On average, it takes up to seven exposures (such as ads, flyers, or even handshakes) for a customer to become familiar with you and up to another seven exposures for them to become comfortable enough to buy from you, says Densmore. "The thought of connecting with someone 49 times before you make a sale is tiring," but if you're not willing to repeat a marketing effort seven times "it's going to be a waste of time." If you don't have a large marketing budget, it's better to repeat a single effort directed at targeted customers than to try several approaches only once for a wider audience.

Spend your time wisely. Traditionally, we spend most of our time acting and very little time planning and researching that course of action, says Densmore. But according to *Seven Habits of Highly Successful People* author Stephen Covey, if you put more time and effort into "discovery" and planning, you'll be more productive and achieve your goals with a minimum of time, energy and stress. The Women's Enterprise Society of British Columbia (WESBC) is a non-profit organization committed to helping women entrepreneurs succeed in business. For more information about its resources, training opportunities, and free business counselling, visit www.wes.bc.ca.

Source: Reprinted with permission of Rogers Media, "How to Focus Your Marketing Plan," *Profit Magazine*, 2001, www.profitguide.com/magazine/article.jsp?content=538.

CHARACTERISTICS OF A MARKETING PLAN   LO2

The marketing plan should be designed to meet certain criteria. Some important characteristics that must be incorporated in an effective marketing plan are as follows:

- It should provide a strategy for accomplishing the company mission or goal.
- It should be based on facts and valid assumptions (Figure 7-4).
- An appropriate organization must be described to implement the marketing plan.
- It should provide for continuity so that each annual marketing plan can build on it, successfully meeting longer-term goals and objectives.
- It should be simple and short. A voluminous plan will be placed in a desk drawer and likely never used. However, the plan should not be so short that details on how to accomplish a goal are excluded.

FIGURE 7-4	Facts Needed for Market Planning

- Who are the users, where are they located, how much do they buy, from whom do they buy, and why?
- How have promotion and advertising been employed, and which approach has been most effective?
- What are the pricing changes in the market, who has initiated these changes, and why?
- What are the market's attitudes concerning competitive products?
- What channels of distribution supply consumers, and how do they function?
- Who are the competitors, where are they located, and what advantages/disadvantages do they have?
- What marketing techniques are used by the most successful competitors? By the least successful?
- What are the overall objectives of the company for the next year and five years hence?
- What are the company's strengths? Weaknesses?
- What are one's production capabilities by product?

- The success of the plan may depend on its flexibility. Changes, if necessary, should be incorporated by including "what if" scenarios and appropriate responding strategies.
- It should specify performance criteria that will be monitored and controlled. For example, the entrepreneur may establish an annual performance criterion of 10 percent of market share in a designated geographic area. To attain this goal, certain expectations should be made at given time periods (e.g., at the end of three months we should have a 5 percent share of market). If not attained, then new strategy or performance standards may be established.

It is clear from the preceding discussion that the market plan is not intended to be written and then put aside. It is intended to be a valuable document, referred to often, and a guideline for the entrepreneur during the next time period.

Since the term *marketing plan* denotes the significance of marketing, it is important to understand the marketing system. The marketing system identifies the major interacting components, both internal and external to the firm, which enable the firm to successfully provide products and/or services to the marketplace. In the marketing system, the external environment and the internal environment impact the entrepreneur or business owner, this, in turn, impacts marketing decisions and the development of marketing strategies through the marketing mix, which impact consumers. The customers, through their actions, provide feedback to the entrepreneur. The system can be seen in Figure 7-5.

As evident above, the environment (external and internal) plays a very important role in developing the market plan. These factors should be identified and discussed in the industry analysis section of the business plan. It should also be noted that while some of these factors are typically uncontrollable the owner-manager can do some things to effectively respond to some of these external influences:

- Identify which external conditions affect the business.
- Set up a system to continually monitor the relevant external influence(s). For the owner-manager, this might mean regularly obtaining reports, newsletters, and studies that contain up-to-date information on these conditions.

FIGURE 7-5   The Marketing System

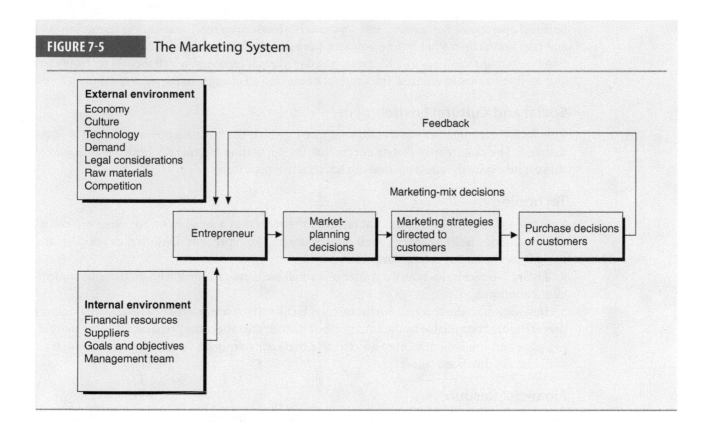

- Adjust internal operations to respond to changes in these external influences most effectively.
- Some of the most common external influences that can affect the small business and thus affect the information to be collected are the economy, the competition, legal restrictions, the social and cultural environment, and technology.

The Economy.   LO3

The state of the economy in the market area is a critical external condition. For many products and services, market demand is directly related to upturns and downturns in the economy. Small businesses often are able to react more quickly than large businesses to changes in the economy.

Competition.

As mentioned in Chapter 1, a small business usually finds itself competing against larger firms over which it has no control. New technology used by competitors is another factor in assessing competition, especially in many growth industries. In some cases, the small business may gain competitive advantages because of its size. By accurately identifying prospective competitors and their strengths as well as weaknesses, the entrepreneur can develop a more effective strategy. Attempts should be made to clearly identify the competitive advantage for the business. Many entrepreneurs have found that their competitors' websites are helpful resources when analyzing their strategy and future plans.

Legal Restrictions.

This potential influence includes the laws and regulations with which the business is required to comply. The owner-manager should keep up-to-date with any legislation that might affect business operations. Some entrepreneurs obviously have to pay more attention to changes in laws and regulations than other business owners. For example, firms such as Jeff Mann's Mann Mediation (www.mannmediate.ca), a Kingston-based mediation company, which focuses on family law and mediation, has to ensure it stays abreast of any and all changes in the legal system.[8]

Social and Cultural Environment.

This factor encompasses trends in the culture in which the business operates that may affect demand. The culture may dictate norms that the population is generally hesitant to violate or suggest new growth industries that can be attractive opportunities.

Technology.

New technology can be a significant factor in the success of a small business. Failure to recognize and adopt technology can spell disaster for the entrepreneur. Likewise, developing and using it can be an important competitive edge.

Figure 7-6 illustrates how the owner of a small business can work with all these uncontrollable conditions.

In addition to the external environmental factors, there are internal environmental factors that are more controllable by the entrepreneur but can also affect the preparation of the marketing plan and implementation of an effective marketing strategy. Some of the major internal variables are discussed below.

Financial Resources.

The financial plan, discussed in Chapter 4 and later in the text, should outline the financial needs for the new venture. Any marketing plan or strategy should consider the availability of financial resources as well as the amount of funds needed to meet the goals and objectives stated in the plan.

FIGURE 7-6   Management of the External Influences

EXTERNAL INFLUENCE	POSSIBLE CHARACTERISTIC	SYSTEM TO MONITOR	POSSIBLE INTERNAL ADJUSTMENT
Economy	Inflation rate Unemployment level	Relevant government and industry reports	Lower prices Increase advertising
Competition	Competitor strengths and weaknesses Competitor's use of new technology	Competitors' new products Competitors' reactions to your strategies	Alter product or service Select specific target market
Legal	Laws affecting your business	Legislative changes from government documents and industry reports	Alter product or service
	Pending changes in laws		Make promotional changes
Social and cultural	Lifestyle trends Demographic studies Purchase patterns	Industry and government reports recording social statistics and purchases	Provide new products or services Change distribution channel Change promotional themes and levels
Technology	Trends	New product reports Fast-growing company literature	Alter product

Employee Capabilities/Management Team.

It is extremely important in any organization to make appropriate assignments of responsibility for the implementation of the marketing plan. In some smaller organizations, the owner-manager may be solely responsible for implementing the marketing plan. Yet if she lacks the skills or capabilities the owner may want to make use of experts, enlist volunteers, or so forth. It does not make sense for a micro-enterprise to plan for an ambitious online marketing campaign to be implemented by the owner who lacks such skills. If the small business is larger the entrepreneur must be sure to build a management team who possess the skills to manage the marketing plan.

Suppliers.

The suppliers used are generally based on a number of factors such as price, delivery time, quality, and management assistance. In some cases, where raw materials are scarce or there are only a few suppliers of a particular raw material or part, the entrepreneur has little control over the decision. Since the price of supplies, delivery time, and so on, are likely to impact many marketing decisions, it is important to incorporate these factors into the marketing plan.

Company Mission.

As indicated in Chapter 4, every new venture should define the nature of its business. This statement that helps to define the company's mission basically describes the nature of the business and what the entrepreneur hopes to accomplish with that business. This mission statement or business definition will guide the firm through long-term decision making. For example, Dr. Julia Levy, executive chair and former CEO of the Canadian biopharmaceutical company QLT (www.qltinc. com), states, "Companies must define their collective values in a mission statement; the statement will define where the company goes in the next number of years and how it will get there."[9]

THE MARKETING MIX

The above environmental variables will provide important information in deciding what will be the most effective marketing strategy to be outlined in the marketing plan. The actual short-term marketing decisions in the marketing plan will consist of four important marketing variables: product or service, pricing, distribution or place, and promotion. These four factors are referred to as the *marketing mix*. Each variable will be described in detail in the strategy or action plan section of the marketing plan discussed in the next chapter. Although flexibility may be an important consideration, the entrepreneur needs a strong base to provide direction for the day-to-day marketing decisions. Some of the critical decisions in each area are described in Figure 7-7.

FIGURE 7-7	Critical Decisions for Marketing Mix

MARKETING MIX VARIABLE	CRITICAL DECISIONS
Product	Quality of components or materials, style, features, options, brand name, packaging, sizes, service availability, and warranties
Price	Quality image, list price, quantity, discounts, allowances for quick payment, credit terms, and payment period
Distribution/Place	Use of wholesalers and/or retailers, type of wholesalers or retailers, how many, length of channel, geographic coverage, inventory, and transportation
Promotion	Media alternatives, message, media budget, role of personal selling, sales promotion (displays, coupons, etc.), and media interest in publicity

STEPS IN PREPARING THE MARKETING PLAN

The major steps in preparing the marketing plan are as follows:

1. Examine the product/service and market situation.
2. Review company goals and restraints.
3. Set marketing objectives that are specific and measurable.
4. Determine the marketing strategies and prepare action programs.
5. Re-evaluate programs against objectives.
6. Draft marketing plan, with steps to monitor progress of programs.
7. Match feasibility of programs against resources.
8. Finalize the marketing plan,

Each of these steps, when followed, will complete the necessary information to formally prepare the marketing plan. The main steps are outlined and discussed using examples to assist the reader in fully understanding the necessary information and procedure for preparing the marketing plan. It is important for entrepreneurs to realize that the marketing plan must be updated frequently. Business owners must constantly ask themselves: Have my target customers changed? How has it changed? Do I need to reshape my marketing mix to reflect these changes? For example, Canadian retailer Harry Rosen (www.harryrosen.com) had to redesign its marketing mix when they realized that the average age of their customer had increased from 38 to 43. Additionally, Dennis Campbell of Atlantic Tours (www.atlantictours.com) had to change the long-term objectives of his tour company to increase usage by families. While the tour company is seeing the number of seniors who travel increase, the company has also realized that as people age they will eventually travel less. Thus the company must expand its reach into younger demographics if it wants to be successful.

DEFINING THE BUSINESS SITUATION

The *situation analysis* is a review of where we have been. It responds to the first of the three questions mentioned earlier in this chapter. It also considers many of the factors that were defined in both the environmental analysis section of the business plan (see Chapter 4) and the industry analysis discussed earlier in this chapter. Investors will also want to see your market potential and market share calculations for your business as well.

HARRY ROSEN HAD TO CHANGE SOME OF ITS PROMOTIONAL CAMPAIGNS DUE TO ITS AGING TARGET MARKET.
THE CANADIAN PRESS IMAGES/Jesse Johnston

To fully respond to this question, the entrepreneur should provide a review of past performance of the product and the company. If this is a new venture, the background will be more personal, describing how the product or service was developed and why it was developed (e.g., to satisfy consumer needs). If the plan is being written after the new venture has started up, it would contain information on present market conditions and performance of the company's goods and services. Any future opportunities or prospects should also be included in this section of the plan.

The industry and competitive environment have already been discussed in an earlier section of the business plan. Thus, at this point the entrepreneur should simply review some of the key elements of this section to help provide a context for the marketing segmentation and actions that will be stated in this section of the business plan.

MARKET SEGMENTATION AND TARGET MARKETING: BEYOND THE BASICS

Most entrepreneurs will have heard of the concept of target marketing and market segmentation prior to investigating their business idea. Market segmentation is simply defined as breaking a marketplace down into categories of buyers who share similar characteristics. Target marketing is the process of looking at what segment your company can most profitably serve and then modifying your product, price, placement, and promotion to deliver value versus your competition to your chosen targets. When textbooks describe the segmentation process, much attention is given to demographic information such as age or income and to geographic segmentation. Very little attention is paid to psychographic segmentation and the need to segment by buyer behaviour. As a result, these texts often contain examples such as "Jeannie's high-end clothing store is going to target middle-aged woman who have a university degree and earn an above average income." At first this might sound fine, but there are significant problems with that type of target, including the following:

- Not all women like to shop at the same location. Some may prefer a downtown district; others may prefer a shopping mall.

- Not all women are willing to pay the same amount for clothing regardless of income or education.

- Of the women who prefer extra advice and service with their clothing purchases, some are willing to pay a small premium for this, while others are willing to pay a large premium.

Now imagine that Jeannie's store is located in the downtown core, is relatively small (about 1000 square feet), offers modern business dress and a high level of service, and charges a moderate premium. Do you think the original segment of middle-aged, university-educated, above-average-income earners is a good target market? The obvious answer is no. Such a broad segment could have Jeannie wasting thousands of dollars promoting her products to people who are as likely to shop at a discount store such as Winners or Target as they are in her store.

What Jeannie has to do is take her market segmentation to the next level. This is sometimes referred to as *true target marketing* or *need based segmentation*. Lawrence Stevenson refers to this as "need segmentation" in his book, *Power Retail,* where he notes five characteristics that segmentation must have to be useful:

1. *Meaningful:* Segments must be different from one another to the point that two segments would be unlikely to be attracted to the same marketing strategy.

2. *Mutually exclusive*: Each segment must be mutually exclusive and collectively exclusive, meaning that each customer group only belongs to one segment.

3. *Measurable:* Each segment must be measurable in both market share and market potential to the business.

4. *Substantial:* Each segment must be large enough to represent a group of potential customers. If a large enough group of customers does not fit into the segment, then it may not be a segment at all.

5. *Actionable:* The entrepreneur should be able to promote his product offering to the segment. Look back at Jeannie's original target market, is it truly actionable?

MICHELLE STRUM, OWNER OF HALIFAX BACKPACKERS HOSTEL, HAS SAID THAT LISTENING TO FEEDBACK FROM HER CUSTOMERS HAS BEEN A KEY IN HER SUCCESS.
Photo courtesy of Michelle Strum, Halifax Backpackers Hostel

How does an entrepreneur develop segments that meet all the qualities discussed above? Through market research. Entrepreneurs must know the buying habits of their customers, their pre- and post-purchase behaviours, their motivation for buying, and so on. Simple demographic information is never enough. Barry Cohen and Michael Rybarski in their book, *Start-up Smarts: The Thinking Entrepreneur's Guide to Starting and Growing Your Business,* state that business owners should treat marketing as a science.[10] The pair recommends that entrepreneurs take the time and effort to fully understand their customers, what makes them buy certain products, and how they want to receive information. For example, Michelle Strum, owner of Halifax Backpackers Hostel (www.halifaxbackpackers.com), takes time to learn what her clients want and tailors her hostel to meet their needs. Her hostel has been open for over 10 years now, and she recently expanded it to include a coffee shop.[11]

Let us look at Jeannie's clothing store again. Jeannie should initially segment her market using demographic information, but then she should complete the segmentation process by conducting market research using observations, focus groups, and survey work. From this information, she would determine that four market segments meet the standards outlined by Stevenson above:

1. Price-conscious women who shop on the weekend in the suburbs

2. Bargain hunters

3. Price-insensitive women who seek advice and shop frequently

4. Price-insensitive women who seek advice and shop seasonally

By looking at the four categories, Jeannie can see that she cannot profitably appeal to the first group, as they likely have a family and will shop at malls and box stores. The second group will most likely frequent Winners, Walmart, and similar stores. But both the third and fourth groups are potentially profitable, large, mutually exclusive, measurable, and actionable. Jeannie can now fine-tune her marketing mix to appeal to these segments.

While this type of segmentation appears daunting to an entrepreneur, it is worth the time and investment. Proof can be found in the results of some of the largest companies in Canada.

Shoppers Drug Mart owes much of its success to the strategy of appealing to price-insensitive convenience shoppers and health-focused advice shoppers. The same is true for Canadian Tire, one of the few mass merchants that have thrived in the presence of Walmart and Costco. Canadian Tire reviewed their extensive database of credit-card holders to identify advice-seeking handymen and convenience shoppers as targets that they could profitably serve.

The key steps in moving your segmentation beyond the basics include the following:

1. Decide what general market or industry you wish to pursue.

2. Divide the market into smaller groups based on the characteristics of the customer and buying situation. These may include the following:

   • Demographic

   • Geographic

   • Psychographic (e.g., personality and lifestyle)

   • Motivation (e.g., rational, emotional)

   • Influencers (e.g., anyone else influencing decision, importance of opinion leaders)

   • Price sensitivity

   • Desired benefit (e.g., product features)

   • Usage (e.g., rate of use)

   • Buying conditions (e.g., frequency, time of year)

   • Awareness of buying intentions (e.g., familiarity of product and willingness to buy)

3. Make sure the segments are meaningful, mutually exclusive, measurable, substantial, and actionable.

4. Select a segment(s) to target.

5. Develop a marketing plan that integrates product, price, placement, and promotion.

A note of caution should be used in segmentation. Entrepreneurs often incorrectly assume the segment that produces the most revenue is the one that is the most profitable. This is incorrect and dangerous. Entrepreneurs must analyze the costs of each transaction, the time involved, the method of communication, and the cost of goods sold order to truly determine which segment offers the most profit potential. For example, John, an investment salesman, has determined that teachers in his area offer his business the most potential sales and thus the most potential profit. John, however, is ignoring that teachers take a great deal of time in deciding whether to purchase investments, and he will have to spend an average 12 to 15 hours per year acquiring each account and then another 10 to 15 hours per year speaking to each teacher about questions and concerns. Dentists, on the other hand, are fewer in number, and, while they offer less potential revenue, most dentists will only require an hour or two per year deciding whether or not to invest and then only two to three hours per year dealing with questions and concerns. Based on this information, dentists should be the target market as they offer the most profit potential.

Let us assume that an entrepreneur has developed a unique liquid cleaner that could clean a restaurant grill at operating temperatures; remove grease from household appliances; clean whitewall tires, bumpers, upholstery, and engines; and clean boats. At least four markets could be identified from its uses: restaurants, households, automobiles, and boats. Each of the markets is then segmented on the basis of the variables discussed above. The entrepreneur finds that in the restaurant market there is little competition, the product's advantages are most evident, and massive marketing resources are not necessary for entry. On this basis, the entrepreneur chooses the restaurant market. This market is then segmented by province, type of restaurant (e.g., fast-food, family), and whether the restaurant is part of a hospital, school, company, and so forth. Each of these segments is evaluated, and the entrepreneur chooses to initially target independent family restaurants in a specific region, such as within a single province.

This market offers the greatest opportunity because no other product exists that can perform grill cleaning at operating temperatures and without damage to the grill. The threats in this market include ease of entry and potential imitation by major competitors: in fact, a number of large firms such as Colgate-Palmolive and Procter & Gamble may be interested in the market. However, regardless of the threats, the greatest opportunity is presented in the restaurant grill-cleaning segment. This becomes the target market. Figure 7-8 gives a general example of purchase characteristics of various age groups.

CUSTOMER PROFILE

After selecting target markets, entrepreneurs should develop a comprehensive customer profile based on their needs and buying behaviour. The entrepreneur must be sure to include all the information from the segmentation process and expand on it to deal with such factors as the following:

- Demographic questions
- Customer attitudes on price and quality
- Where customer currently buys product
- Where customer wishes to buy product
- Influence of advertising
- Quantities and frequency of purchase
- Why customer buys product

FIGURE 7-8	Purchase Characteristics for Various Ages

In Their Teens

This group has an increasing amount of money to spend on clothing, cosmetics, and entertainment products. They also have a major influence with family purchases.

In Their 20s

This group is not yet financially secure. They demand instant gratification, lasting values, and tangible benefits. Purchase decisions are often based on subjective factors.

In Their 30s and 40s

These people have high incomes and high debt. They are individualistic, striving for self-fulfillment, and concerned about social and environmental issues. They look for information before buying.

In Their 40s and 50s

Prosperous and facing retirement, they purchase for sentimentality, brand loyalty, and convenience.

In Their 60s and 70s

They tend to have lots of leisure time. They seek financial security, quality, and value. They rely on knowledge and experience.

In Their 80s

This group spends heavily on health care, travel, and security products.

Based on this information, Jeannie's clothing store from the example earlier in this chapter would use a customer profile similar to the following:

- *Demographic information:* Women ages 40 to 55, income $75,000-plus, university degree, highly computer-literate
- *Frequency:* Shop frequently in the downtown core, often weekly or bi-weekly
- *Products:* Willing to pay a premium for quality products upwards of 20 percent compared with shopping district stores
- *Service:* Associate service with quality and are willing to pay a premium for upper-scale service
- *Motivation:* Can be motivated by both rational and emotional influences
- *Lifestyle/personality:* Read frequently, travels, share a desire to be perceived as fashionable and upper-class by society, want to be trendy and hip, influenced by friends and fashion magazines
- *Advertising:* Most susceptible to online and one-to-one marketing or one-to-small-group marketing
- *Buying decision:* This group will buy from me because I have connections in Paris that will allow me to bring the latest fashion trends to the region. In addition, I have built a database that will allow me to know each customer on a personal level and engage in one-to-one marketing, and I have hired experienced salespeople to provide meaningful advice.

INCIDENT 7-2

TARGET MARKET FOR A HYPOTHETICAL SMALL RESTAURANT

The following is a proposed target market for a high-end small restaurant.

Demographics
　Age: 30–49
　Income: higher than average ($40,000–$80,000)
　Occupation: professionals, managers
　Education: university graduates

Lifestyle (Psychographics)
　Activities: exercise and participation in sports, high social interaction; low TV usage and high reading; husband and wife both work, enjoy the outdoors, attend cultural events
　Interests: appearance, health, fashion
　Opinions: conservative economically, liberal on social issues
　Personality: achievement-oriented, outgoing, independent

Purchase Characteristics
　What: higher quality and higher priced menu items
　Where: higher class restaurant, international cuisine
　When: evenings and weekends
　How much: frequently eat away from home, 50 percent higher than national average

Purchase Motivations
　Benefits sought: superior quality of food, service, atmosphere, variety of the menu

Influencers
　Reference groups and social class the main influencers in choice of restaurant, through word of mouth

Discussion Questions

1. Review the target market, discuss areas where it is strong, and identify weaknesses.

2. What information could be added to enhance the target market?

3. Develop a target market and a customer profile for a well-known Canadian chain such as Lululemon or Sports Chek. Compare your customer profile with others in the class to identify areas for improvement.

4. Do you think small business should spend significant time and resources on creating customer profiles? Why, or why not?

CONSIDERING STRENGTHS AND WEAKNESSES

It is important for the entrepreneur to consider strengths and weaknesses in the target market. For example, referring to the liquid grill cleaner, the primary strength in its market is clearly its unique application: It can be used on a hot operating grill with no discernible odour. Other strengths might relate to the fact that the company has experience in the restaurant business and understands the customer.

Weaknesses could relate to the production capacity limited by space and equipment. In addition, the company lacks a strong distribution system for the product and would have to depend on manufacturers' representatives. Lack of cash to support a heavy promotional effort could also be identified as a weakness.

CUSTOMER RELATIONSHIP MARKETING   LO5

Investors often want to see some information in the marketing plan that focuses on how the company plans on building a relationship with its most profitable customers. Even if investors are not looking for this, most entrepreneurs should be trying to establish long-term relationships with customers. The key to proper relationship marketing is the realization that 70 to 80 percent of a business's profits can actually come from a very small percentage of customers. It is with these customers that the entrepreneur is going to want to build a relationship. Previously, much has been written about relationships with all customers—and in some businesses this is possible—but for many businesses it is not feasible and the entrepreneur can waste time and money trying to build relationships with people that do not offer much in return. For example, if a local car dealership tried to build a relationship with all its customers, it might end up allocating the same amount of marketing and research dollars to someone who buys a new car every two years and someone who buys a new car every 10 years. Entrepreneurs should focus on building relationships with their most profitable customers and customers that show the most potential to offer profits in the future. Therefore the car dealership should focus its energy on building a relationship with the person who buys a car every two years and attempt to convert the person who buys a car every 10 years into a more frequent purchaser.

One of the best tools in customer relationship marketing (CRM) is the use of a database to track customer buying habits, personal information, and anything else that is relevant. By analyzing this information, the entrepreneur can select with which customers he should build a relationship. Ken McLean, a financial planner with Investors Group, realizes the simple principle that he must build a relationship with his most profitable customers to be successful. Ken has identified that 70 percent of his profits come from only 20 percent of his clients, and so he spends extra time servicing the needs of this key group. Ken offers accounting services at tax time, takes clients golfing, and hosts annual Christmas and summer events. Furthermore, Ken has built an extensive database of these clients, learning birthdays, career aspirations, retirement goals, and anything else that may be relevant so that he can tailor his products to his target market. Harry Rosen, one of Canada's most successful retailers, has adopted the same principle as Ken and serves as a great example of how relationship marketing can work for larger businesses. The retailer makes use of an extensive customer database that goes beyond just recording basic demographic information. The database will typically include information on vacation destinations, size, time of year the person shops, personal relationships, and so forth. Rosen then builds its sales and marketing strategy around this information and two simple premises: 1. clients always come first; 2. keeping clients for life.

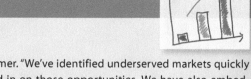

KNOW THY CUSTOMER

When founder Dennis Goll got West Wind Aviation (www.westwindaviation.ca) off the ground 25 years ago, it was a one-aircraft operation fuelled by high ambition. Today, the president and CEO has transformed this humble business into Western Canada's largest general aviation services company, employing more than 250 people. It has recently been recognized as one of Canada's 50 Best Managed Companies. Goll attributes success of the company primarily to understanding the consumer. "We've identified underserved markets quickly and honed in on those opportunities. We have also embedded customer service into our corporate culture. It's not just idle talk here. I've often told employees to not worry about numbers and think about customers' needs first." As a result the company is committed to customer service training for everybody in the company, from maintenance staff to accountants.[12]

The keys to establishing an effective relationship marketing program are the following:

- Start with proper segmentation and target marketing.
- Identify the most profitable customer groups.
- Identify groups that show potential of becoming more profitable.
- Solicit further information on customers.
- Develop products and services that are mutually beneficial.
- Allocate your marketing budget so that you spend the majority of money appealing to your most important customers.

THE DATABASE INFORMATION SYSTEM

A critical part of most effective CRM is the development of a database information system focused on the consumer. The emergence of database marketing is based on the premise that past behaviour is the best indicator of future purchase patterns. The increase in computer power and storage capabilities, coupled with decreasing costs, now enables organizations to deal directly with customers on an individual level.

DATABASE MARKETING FOR THE SMALL BUSINESS

A customer database is an organized collection of comprehensive data about individual customers or prospects, including geographic, demographic, psychographic, and behavioural data. The database can be used to locate good potential customers, tailor products and services to the special needs of targeted consumers, and maintain long-term customer relationships. Database marketing is the process of building, maintaining, and using customer databases and other databases (products, suppliers, resellers) to contact and transact with customers.

A small business can use databases for both business-to-business as well as business-to-consumer marketing. In business-to-business marketing, the salesperson's customer profile may contain such information as the products and services the customer has bought, past volumes and prices, key contacts, competitive suppliers, status of current contracts, estimated customer expenditures for the next few years, and assessments of competitive strengths and weaknesses in selling and serving the account. In consumer marketing, the customer database may contain a customer's demographics, buying behaviour, and other relevant information. Several simple

THE LOYALTY PUZZLE

Sunterra Markets (www.sunterramarket.com), an Alberta-based independent grocery operation, knows about customer relations. The company first introduced its loyalty program, Fresh Rewards, in 2000 and has seen steady growth, with five stores in Calgary and two in Edmonton.

What differentiates Sunterra's loyalty program with others is that it is not discount based—it is pure rewards. The program is simple and easy: The customer gets one point for every dollar

spent in any store; Sunterra pays them back at about three cents on the dollar. So, if you have 3330 points, you get a $100 gift certificate for Sunterra. There are two modes of redemption for Sunterra's reward program, high level and low level. High level is when you fill in a form and send it in or place your redemption online. Low level is done in the stores for items such as a $10 gift card or something even as small as a cookie.

Sunterra is expanding and always looking for more ways to connect with their customers. They have a birthday mail-out that allows any customer who signs up for the rewards program to receive a card in their birth month, along with a coupon for a free piece of cake or cup of coffee.[13]

WHILE SOME LARGER CANADIAN FIRMS ARE ABANDONING LOYALTY PROGRAMS, SUNTERRA MARKETS IS EXPANDING THEIRS TO BETTER CONNECT WITH CUSTOMERS.
© Daniel Koebe/Corbis

Discussion Questions

1. Do you think reward programs such as the one described above make a difference to the company's bottom line? Why, or why not?

2. In recent years, some larger Canadian companies such as Second Cup have abandoned their reward's program. What are some of the advantages and disadvantages of using rewards as a way to retain customers and generate sales?

3. If you were starting a small retail business, would you implement a rewards program? Why, or why not?

and inexpensive database software programs are now available to assist small businesses in being more responsive to their customers.

There are five steps in developing a database information system.

1. Begin with the customer information that the organization already has. Such information might include sales records, requests for information, credit files, and other customer data.

2. The next step is to obtain more information. This might be received through warranty cards, surveys, mail-in coupons, rebates, and contests. A relatively new method of obtaining information is to use the Internet. Not only can companies manually track some online activity but there are also a variety of companies and software applications that will enable a business to learn more about its customers by monitoring web habits. Care should be taken in obtaining information and permission should be sought for this information to be shared with other organizations.

3. Organizations may be able to supplement this data by accessing information available from a variety of public and private sources. Government and private market studies may profile different types of consumers and their purchase behaviours. Other databases might be obtained from credit card companies and banks.

INCIDENT 7-5

SOCIAL MEDIA MONITORING

Social media monitoring has become quite important for businesses. Not only do companies want to share information on social media sites about their products and services but they want to learn what you are saying about their organizations. Social media dashboards such as HootSuite are becoming increasingly common tools to monitor what people are saying about a company on the Internet. But other tools exist, for example Google Alerts notifies a business if their company's name comes up anywhere online. Businesses such as New Brunswick-based Radian6 identify trends in online communities and assist businesses in dealing with complaints. Other software tools such as KISSmetrics have been developed to help businesses identify the behaviour of web users. Users of KISSmetrics can not only identify who is visiting their site but their actions as well. This information can be used to tailor offerings and improve sales. Since the company's inception they have tracked the web use of 4.5 billion people and their 36 billion interactions.[14] Some companies have become even more creative when tracking its users and likely have breached privacy laws in Canada and the United States. Aaron's, a rent-to-own store, has recently gotten into hot water for installing software in laptops, which enabled the company to use the computer's web cam to see what its customers were doing. The software, called PC Rental Agent, has been the subject of a number of consumer complaints because of its use to capture pictures and video of people in very intimate moments. While Aaron's appears to have crossed the line with their software, the use of other tools such as Google Alerts, HootSuite, and KISSmetrics are considered to be perfectly legal and acceptable business practices.

Discussion Questions

1. Do you think organizations should be able to track who visits their websites and their online behaviour?

2. Do you think it is a worthwhile investment for businesses to monitor and respond to social media discussions about their companies? Why, or why not?

3. Did Aaron's cross the line with its monitoring tools?

4. If you started a business would you make use of social media tracking tools? Why, or why not?

---

4. The organization must then process the information. The acquisition of a database software system will be required. There are now a number of inexpensive systems available, or the business may need to have a customized model developed to suit its purposes. Such a system should allow the business to see the relationship between the data and the behaviour of the customer.

5. The last step in the development of a database system is to use the data to develop a highly specific profile of the company's customers.

CRM DATABASES AND RETENTION

As discussed above, one of the most critical keys to the success of the small business is retaining its customers. An increasing number of organizations are realizing that the cost is much higher to attract a new customer than to retain an existing one. As a result, expenditures for customer retention activities have now surpassed expenditures on customer attraction in North America.[15] By getting to know customers and creating a database, entrepreneurs are more likely to be able to target clients and offer products and services they are interested in. For example, Olivier Soapery (www.oliviersoaps.com) has created a unique family approach to business from the beginning. The New Brunswick-based company manufactures eco-skincare and their founder and president, Isabel Gagné, believes that the secret of a successful business lies in creating long-lasting relationships with customers. Her family approach to selling is what makes her business different than others. "Whenever you call, you get a real live person and never a machine. And that's fundamental to my company," Gagné says. The firm sells quality products through retail stores, a company website, a comprehensive distribution network, and through loyal clients. Olivier now markets 140 products and has started franchising the business.[16]

The small business should have a natural advantage over large businesses in the area of customer service and retention because of the ability to develop a more personal relationship with the customer. Many large businesses, in their attempts to increase volume of sales, simply cannot provide the level of service that a small business can. This is because service tends to be individualized and time-consuming to provide. The small business needs to remember that in most situations, the offering of excellent service is what will set it apart from large business and provide an important competitive advantage.

To provide effective customer service and retention, the small business should do the following:

- Identify the types of service to offer. These service activities, of course, should be tailored to the needs of the target market of the business. As discussed above the effective use of customer databases and customer profiles will assist the entrepreneur in achieving this goal.

- Budget adequate funds for this activity. Employee training, guarantees, and other service activities will require a financial investment.

- Handle customer concerns and complaints effectively. Research has shown that if a business handles a complaint quickly and satisfactorily, 70 to 95 percent of customers will continue to patronize the business.

- Do not disappoint the consumer. Although the business may need to advertise the service, many have found that the best policy is to provide better service than their customers expect. Christine Magee, founder of Sleep Country Canada, reflects this point of view. "When a customer comes in the door, we want to exceed their expectations."[17]

- The chances of retaining a customer primarily depend on the level of satisfaction received through the experience with the business. Specific activities that can be used to increase the chances of satisfaction are quality products and services, rebates and rewards, follow up contacts and thank-yous, requests for suggestions, and guarantees.

- Regularly evaluate customer service and retention programs to ensure their effectiveness and that they meet the needs of customers.

ESTABLISHING GOALS AND OBJECTIVES LO6

Before any marketing strategy decisions can be outlined, the entrepreneur must establish realistic and specific goals and objectives. These *marketing goals and objectives* respond to the question: "Where do we want to go?" and should specify such things as market share, profits, sales (by territory and region), market penetration, number of distributors, awareness level, new product launching, pricing policy, sales promotion, and advertising support.

For example, the entrepreneur of a new frozen diet product may determine the following objectives for the first year: 10 percent market penetration, 60 percent of market sampled, distribution in 75 percent of the market. All these goals must be considered reasonable and feasible given the business situation described earlier.

All the above goals were quantifiable and could be measured for control purposes. However, not all goals and objectives must be quantified. It is possible for a firm to establish some goals or objectives as: research customer attitudes toward a product, set up a sales training program, improve packaging, change name of product, or find new distributor. It is a good idea to limit the number of goals or objectives to between six and eight. Too many goals make control and monitoring difficult. Obviously, these goals should represent key areas to ensure marketing success.

DEFINING MARKETING STRATEGY AND ACTION PROGRAMS

Once the marketing goals and objectives are established, the entrepreneur can begin to develop the marketing strategy and action plan to achieve them. These strategy and action decisions respond to the question "How do we get there?" As indicated earlier, these decisions reflect on the marketing mix variables that will be discussed in-depth in the next chapter.

BUDGETING THE MARKETING STRATEGY

Effective planning decisions must also consider the costs involved in the implementation of these decisions. If the entrepreneur has followed the procedure of detailing the strategy and action programs to meet the desired goals and objectives, costs should be reasonably clear. If assumptions are necessary, they should be clearly stated so that anyone else who reviews the written marketing plan (e.g., a venture-capital firm) will understand these implications.

This budgeting of marketing action and strategy decisions will also be useful in preparing the financial plan. Details of how to develop a financial plan are discussed in Chapter 9, Financial Management.

MONITORING PROGRESS OF MARKETING ACTIONS   LO7

Generally, monitoring of the plan involves tracking specific results of the marketing effort. Sales data by product, territory, sales rep, and outlet are a few of the specific results that should be monitored. What is monitored is dependent on the specific goals and objectives outlined earlier in the marketing plan. Any "weak" signals from the monitoring process will provide the entrepreneur with the opportunity to redirect or modify the existing marketing effort to allow the firm to achieve its initial goals and objectives. Remember all marketing efforts need monitoring. Swiss Media Inc., the natural health producer and frequent user of guerrilla marketing (free samples), measures the impact of its sampling program by monitoring regional sales and its website traffic comparing the data before and after the completion of its sampling program. Other measures can be simpler. Brian Scudamore, owner of 1-800-Got-Junk?, a Canadian-based international junk-hauling franchise, established a customer relations program that focused on wowing customers starting with their call centre and the customer's first contact with the company. To measure this program, he employs a great deal of formal metrics, but he is also known to simply call his own call centre to see how workers are treating potential customers.

CONTINGENCY PLANNING

Generally, the entrepreneur does not have the time to consider many alternative plans of action should the initial plan fail. However, as stated earlier, it is important for the entrepreneur to be flexible and prepared to make adjustments where necessary. It is unlikely that any marketing plan will succeed exactly as expected.

WHY SOME PLANS FAIL

Marketing plans are ineffective or fail in meeting marketing goals for different reasons. In fact, failure may also be considered a matter of degree, since some goals may be met and others missed completely. The overall failure of the plan will be judged by management and may depend on the mere solvency of the organization. Some of the reasons for failure can be avoided if the entrepreneur is careful in preparing the marketing plan. Some of the more common reasons for failure that can be controlled are as follows:

- *Lack of a real plan*—The marketing plan is superficial and lacks detail and substance, especially regarding goals and objectives.
- *Lack of an adequate situation analysis*—It is invaluable to know where you are and where you have been, before deciding where you want to go. Careful analysis of the environment can result in reasonable goals and objectives.
- *Unrealistic goals*—This generally results because of a lack of understanding of the situation.
- *Unanticipated competitive moves, product deficiencies, and acts of God*—With a good situation analysis, as well as an effective monitoring process, competitive decisions can be assessed and predicted with some degree of accuracy. Deficiencies in the product often result from rushing the product to the market. For an act of God—such as an oil spill, flood, hurricane, or war—the entrepreneur has no control.

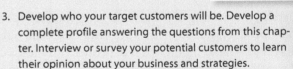

TIME TO TAKE ACTION

1. Conduct additional research on your industry, competitors, and customers. Start to build a profile of your main competitors, including such things as their target market(s) and their marketing mix. Expand this profile to identify your competitors' strengths and weaknesses.

2. Review the major factors in the external environment that can influence your business. Identify any potential changes in the environment that can impact you business.

3. Develop who your target customers will be. Develop a complete profile answering the questions from this chapter. Interview or survey your potential customers to learn their opinion about your business and strategies.

4. Use the Internet to review some of the common social media monitoring tools. Which ones would you consider using? Why? Create a table outlining the name, use, price, strengths, and weaknesses of each tool.

LEARNING OBJECTIVES SUMMARY

LO1 The marketing plan designates the response to three questions: Where have we been? Where are we going? How do we get there? Market planning is a key part of business planning, and much like a business plan, it must be monitored and updated frequently.

LO2 The marketing plan entails a number of major steps, including defining market segments, selecting target markets, and developing customer profiles.

LO3 Some of the most common external influences affecting the small business are the economy, the competition, legal restrictions, the social and cultural environment, and technology. In dealing with external influences, the owner-manager must identify which external conditions affect the business and then set up a system to monitor and effectively respond to changes in those influences.

LO4 To be able to respond effectively to these questions, it is generally necessary for the entrepreneur to conduct some marketing research. This research may involve secondary sources or a primary data collection process. Information from the research will be very important in determining the marketing mix factors or the marketing strategy to be implemented in the marketing plan.

LO5 Customer relationship management is important to the long-term success of business. One important tool in customer relations management is the use of databases.

LO6 Goals and objectives must be established. These goals and objectives must be realistic and detailed (quantified, if possible).

LO7 The marketing plan should be monitored to discern the success of the action programs. Any "weak" signals will provide the entrepreneur with the opportunity to modify the plan and/or develop a contingency plan. Even with careful scrutiny of the marketing plan, many plans will fail.

DISCUSSION QUESTIONS

1. What are the advantages of developing a very detailed marketing plan compared with a short plan that could be drafted on a few pages? Do you think it is valuable for businesses to invest a considerable amount of time developing a detailed marketing plan? Why, or why not?

2. As noted in the chapter many businesses do not have a marketing plan. How does this affect your opinion on the usefulness of the document?

3. One argument in favour of market segmentation and target marketing for small companies is they often lack the resources to market to large groups of people. Is this still true with the technology available today?

4. What is the difference between traditional target marketing and the more enhanced target marketing discussed in this chapter?

5. Is market segmentation just a nice way of using "stereotypes" to sell your products? Can people really be classified so easily into groups that share common needs, wants, and demands?

6. Segmentation is the process of breaking a population down into smaller groups. Is it possible for a small business to oversegment? How might that be detrimental to the success of the business?

7. Many businesses both large and small are using online tools, specifically social media, to track Internet use of customers and potential customers. Do you think this is ethical? Why, or why not?

8. Why is customer retention so important? What are some of the things businesses can do to improve retention?

9. What are some of the key steps in establishing successful goals for a business? Do you think goals have to be quantifiable? Why, or why not?

1. Define the target market(s) for your university or college. What are the target market demographics, lifestyle characteristics, purchase characteristics, and purchase motivations? Create a customer profile for one of the target markets.

2. Identify the major competitors for your local college or university. What are their strengths and weaknesses? Where do you see an opportunity in the market to create value and grow enrolments for your school?

3. Review the external environment for your university or college. What changes are you anticipating which could impact business? What can your school do to benefit from these changes?

4. Develop an idea for a new business that will operate in the local economy. Define the target market(s), create a customer profile, and examine in detail the factors in the external environment that will impact the business.

5. Develop a marketing mix (i.e., product, promotion, price, distribution) for a high-end restaurant that you would like to open.

6. Interview a local small business owner and find out what his or her marketing strategy is. Determine the promotional strategy. Are these strategies similar to those discussed in the chapter?

For more information on the resources available from McGraw-Hill Ryerson, go to www.mcgrawhill.ca/he/solutions.

CHAPTER 8

MANAGING THE MARKETING MIX

By the end of this chapter, you should be able to:

LO1 Recognize the importance of the marketing mix.

LO2 Explain how products are created.

LO3 Discuss the three methods of setting price.

LO4 Explain the different pricing strategies employed by small and medium businesses.

LO5 Identify the major elements in a promotional campaign.

LO6 Compare and contrast the different promotional tools.

LO7 Discuss the difference in marketing to consumers compared with marketing to businesses.

Shopify (www.shopify.ca) is one of Canada's fastest growing technology companies and one many consumers may have yet to hear about. While consumers may not know specifically about Shopify, many of them have no doubt visited one of Shopify's thousands of online stores and likely made a purchase. Shopify, a first-to-market Canadian success story, offers retailers an all-in-one platform where they can create and maintain an online presence all from one site. Shopify has managed to grow users at an exponential rate, and reports indicate that annual revenue is in the millions and growing by over 100 percent a year. Shopify's 65,000 users have annual online revenues of 1.5 billion, represent over 100 countries, and include such well-known businesses as Gatorade, General Electric, Pixar, and Penny Arcade. Businesses are attracted to Shopify's easy to use but feature rich template that enables micro to large businesses to sell products online. You may be wondering where did the company come from? Who owns the business? Well much like many successful ventures its founding and the entrepreneur behind the story are quite interesting.[1]

Shopify was founded in 2006 by a German immigrant, Tobias Lütke, who was actually selling snowboards out of a shop in his Ottawa garage, at the time using an online storefront produced by Yahoo! Lütke became frustrated with the lack of features available to small companies and businesses in general with Yahoo! stores and decided to create his own online shopping platform. Lütke, who had programming experience, wrote the code for Shopify's original template. Lütke says, "We did a lot of online retail using Yahoo! stores, but it wasn't very good." Lütke goes on to state, ". . . to make a long story short, after trying a series of existing online store software packages I got so disgusted with the quality of the whole lot, that I wanted to do something to spite them."[2]

Lütke's original product was a basic template for an online store where businesses could provide pictures and some description of their products. Lütke quickly saw the real opportunity was not in selling snowboards but in selling Shopify's templates, which were described as easy to use and feature rich.[3]

Lütke, much like any other entrepreneur, then had to create a marketing mix where consumers or in this case other businesses

Photo: Mark Hayes

could see and understand how his product offered superior value. The product component of the marketing mix was obvious, a user-friendly platform with various features that both big and very small businesses could use. Distribution would be online or direct to customers. Lütke still had two important questions left, how would he price his product and where would he promote his online template. Lütke opted to make a couple of decisions that were untraditional compared with other Internet start-ups. First, he almost immediately started charging for his service, something which was not common among start-ups at that time. Lütke says, "Most companies particularly start-ups, don't charge any money and just try to grab as much land as possible (market share)…I think it's wrong to offer a product for free…I like making a product people really like and charging money for it."[4]

Lütke also adopted a very non-conventional promotional strategy including blogs, word of mouth advertising, and his Build-A-Business competitions. The first Build-A-Business competition attracted a tremendous amount of attention and users to Shopify. Lütke offered a $100,000 prize to a start-up that had the highest six months' sales using his Shopify's online platform. The contest resulted in 1300 entries who sold $3.5 million of goods and services on their Shopify sites. Lütke followed the successful competition with Build-A-Business II in 2011 and Build-A-Business III in 2013.[5] Combined the competitions had 13,000 entrants, sales of $67 million and approximately $700,000 in prizes.[6]

Lütke is now focused on the mobile market and investing roughly 50 percent of his company's research and development into building a better mobile platform. Lütke points out the growth in mobile commerce is quite strong, and at the start of 2012 about 10 percent of the population made a purchases on mobile devices, this number climbed to 22 percent by August. Lütke expects the mobile market to grow quickly as smartphones and tablets become even more common.[7]

Lütke's long-term plans are to take the company public by 2016, to maintain his company's status as the preferred platform for retailers looking to create an online store, and to further develop the mobile side of his business.[8]

THE ROLE OF THE MARKETING MIX IN SMALL BUSINESS
LO1

As mentioned in the previous chapter marketing activities are sometimes overlooked by entrepreneurs. A key element in the marketing plan is establishing the correct marketing mix. A good marketing mix will create value and long-term relationships with target customers and distinguish a business from its competitors. For example, Shopify, which is discussed in the opening Small Business Profile, has created value for its target customers, businesses who want to sell products online, by creating an easy to use product, pricing it competitively by charging a royalty on a percentage of sales, and marketing the business using a number of non-traditional promotions that appeal to their target audience. The remainder of this chapter will discuss elements of the marketing mix and provide entrepreneurs with a variety of strategies to appeal to targeted customers.

DEVELOPING THE PRODUCT OR SERVICE
LO2

As mentioned in the previous chapter, the product or service to be offered should be designed to meet target market demand. To ensure responsiveness to consumer demand, the owner-manager should think of the product or service in terms of the ways and extent to which it satisfies consumer need. A prototype of the product should be prepared and tested with a representative sample of the market. This type of information should be collected before finalizing the production decision.

Some major decision areas about which the small business owner should be knowledgeable when developing a product strategy are discussed next.

Develop Product or Service Policies.

Product policies should cover such items as quality level, product or service depth and width, packaging, branding, level of service, and warranties.

Decide How the Product Will Be Manufactured.

For many small businesses, contracting with another firm to manufacture the product is advantageous. This may be an especially viable alternative during the early stages of a business, when the risk is usually higher. Once the product has achieved market acceptance and the volume of production has increased, it may be more cost effective to acquire the manufacturing capability.

Understand the Product Life Cycle.

All products and services have a life cycle, as Figure 8-1 shows. As the product moves from the introduction to the decline stage in its life cycle, the marketing strategy for the product and even for the business may also change. This means changes may be required in pricing, in distribution, in promotion, and even in the product or service. Knowing that the product or service has a life cycle helps the owner-manager plan for any necessary adjustments to the marketing strategy when the maturity stage is reached. Such modifications can help prolong the life cycle of the product or service. Strategies include the following:

- Appeal to a new target market.
- Adjust the product or service to meet changes in customer needs.
- Increase promotion to enhance frequency of purchases.
- Emphasize different uses or characteristics of the product or service.
- Offer a new product or service.

FIGURE 8-1 Product Life Cycle

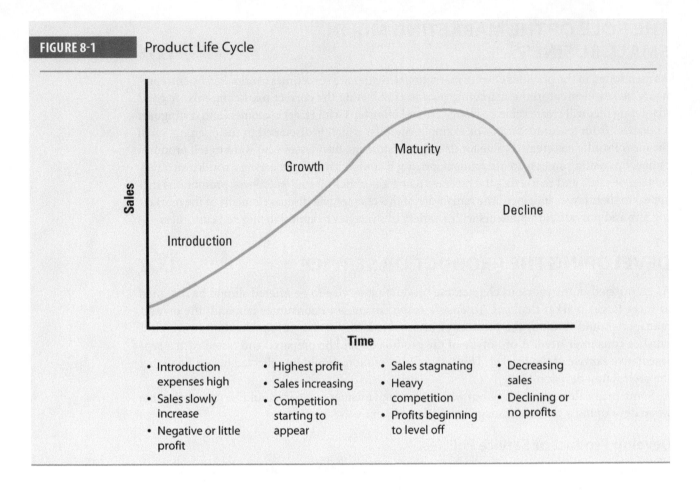

- Introduction expenses high
- Sales slowly increase
- Negative or little profit

- Highest profit
- Sales increasing
- Competition starting to appear

- Sales stagnating
- Heavy competition
- Profits beginning to level off

- Decreasing sales
- Declining or no profits

Product life cycles in many industries, notably the high-technology areas, are getting shorter. This has an impact on the long-term planning of the entrepreneur.

Determine Factors That May Accelerate Product or Service Adoption.

Research shows that consumers generally adopt new products or services at different rates. Those who purchase first are the innovators or early adopters. In Canada, there are an estimated 3.8 million early adopters who are often the opinion leaders in a social group. The innovators and early adopters typically make up about 15 percent of the market, but they have a far greater influence because the rest of the market usually looks to this group before purchasing.[9]

After the small business owner has identified the innovators and early adopters within the target market, every attempt should be made to test market the product or service to that group first. In Canada, early adopters are heavy Internet users and 23 percent more likely to use public transportation. If the early adopters accept the product or service, they may even do much of the initial promotion on social networking sites such as Facebook, Twitter, Pinterest, Instagram, Tumblr, and so forth. Early adopters also have higher income levels ($90,000 in Canada), are better educated, more socially active, and more willing to take risks and have greater exposure to printed media. Firms that are interested in appealing to these groups will often use social networking sites and print ads in subways and buses. For example, Snakes and Lattes (www.snakesandlattes.com), a Toronto-based board game and coffee shop that does not offer WiFi, uses social media to attract early adopters to its business. According to Snakes and Lattes owner, 27-year-old Ben Castanie, social media such as Facebook and Twitter have been essential in attracting clients to his business.[10]

In addition to understanding the characteristics of innovators and early adopters, the small business owner should be aware of the factors that can speed up product adoption and attempt to capitalize on them. Some of the more important factors are discussed below.

Relative Advantage.

If the product or service appears to have a significant advantage over existing ones, and if this advantage can be communicated effectively, it is more likely to have a faster adoption. This is the case in Shopify, which is featured in the opening profile. Not only was the company's online store building platform easy to use but it was also richer in features when compared with competitors.

TORONTO'S BOARD GAME AND COFFEE SHOP, SNAKES AND LATTES, HAS RELIED ON SOCIAL NETWORKING SITES TO ATTRACT EARLY ADOPTERS TO ITS BUSINESS.
THE CANADIAN PRESS/ Toronto Star—Steve Russell

Complexity.

If the product or service is difficult to understand, the adoption rate is typically longer. In such a case, promotion should have informational or educational content. For example, Halifax-based Lorax Systems Inc. (www.loraxsystems.com) has developed an oil and diesel filtration system that will eliminate fuel leaks and spills at residential and commercial properties. Given that the product is new, and the system somewhat complex, a great deal of Lorax's marketing initiatives include explaining how the product works.

Divisibility.

A product or service that can be purchased in small amounts with a minimum of social or financial risk usually has a quicker adoption rate. For example, the RimRoller (www.rimroller.com), a small tool that enables users to roll up the rim on Tim Hortons' cups amassed large sales after appearing on CBC's *Dragons' Den*. The product no doubt benefitted from not only the publicity but also its relative ease of use.[11]

Communicability of Results.

If the results of using the product or service are quickly evident and easily communicated to others, its adoption will be more rapid. For example, GoTire, is a mobile tire changing service which has spread rapidly across Canada. The business concept is simple, GoTire goes to people's homes to complete tire changes. This saves consumers the time and inconvenience associated with going to a service shop to have this done.[12]

In summary, the less risk associated with the purchase decision, the more rapid the adoption rate. The owner-manager therefore should do whatever is possible to reduce such risk when introducing a new product or service. Providing information and offering a guarantee or warranty as part of the purchase are commonly used methods for reducing risk.

Understand How the Consumer Classifies the Product or Service.

Marketers use a standard classification system in categorizing consumer products. This system can be valuable in developing the marketing strategy for the small business. The classifications are as follows:

- *Convenience products.* Convenience products are purchased with minimal effort. They may be necessities, unplanned purchases, or emergency goods.
- *Shopping products.* Shopping products are purchased only after comparison with similar products. Comparisons may be made on the basis of price if competing

FIGURE 8-2   Strategy Implications for Product Classifications

TYPE OF PRODUCT	PRICE	DISTRIBUTION	PROMOTION
Convenience	Although usually lower priced goods, the markups tend to be high. Within a certain range, price is not important to consumer.	Products should be located close to consumers, either in relation to where they live or within the store. Availability is important to the customer.	Promote availability. Use point-of-purchase displays for impulse goods.
Shopping	For similar products, the price must be competitive, as consumers are price sensitive. For dissimilar products that are still competitive, price is not as important to the consumer.	Products should be located close to competing products to aid comparison.	Promote price advantage for similar products or quality/style advantage for dissimilar products.
Specialty	Within a certain range, price is not important to the customer.	Location is not important to the customer.	Promote the outlet that carries the product or brand.

products are viewed as similar or in terms of quality or style if competing products differ.

- *Specialty products.* Consumers have substantial brand or product loyalty with specialty products or services. As a result, they are willing to spend considerable effort to locate and purchase the brands and products they desire.

Figure 8-2 illustrates strategy implications for each of these classifications. The focus of the marketing strategy is determined by how the target consumer classifies the product or service.

DEVELOPING THE DISTRIBUTION SYSTEM

Many entrepreneurs develop an excellent product but lack the knowledge about the best way to get it to the consumer. An effective distribution system should provide the product or service to the right consumer, at the right place, at the right time, and in the right quantity. For example, when Eryn Green and Tamar Wagman founded a frozen organic baby food company called Sweatpea, they struggled with getting their product into stores. At first, they started slowly selling their products at baby groups, yoga classes, trade shows, and using some small store demonstrations. However, they realized that to make this product a commercial success, they would have to obtain distribution in large retail stores. In Ontario, they sold directly to some of the supermarkets, but in Western Canada, they realized they would have to enlist the services of a distributor with a wide distribution network that could also represent their specialty product adequately to compete with other natural baby foods. They were successful in signing with SunOpta (www.sunopta.com), who achieved distribution in over 100 stores in the west.[13] This, coupled with their growing Ontario distribution, now means Sweetpea products are in over 350 stores nationwide.[14]

The distribution channel is the path the product or service follows from the producer to the consumer. It includes the different organizations or individuals who will assist in this movement toward consumption.

The small business owner needs to address three main distribution decision areas: the type of channel to use, the length of the channel, and the number of distributors authorized to sell the product.

CHANNEL OPTIONS

A small business can follow essentially two channel paths, although various combinations of these types of channels are possible.

Manufacturer to Consumer (Short-Direct Channel).

This type of channel involves distributing the product or service directly to the consumer. The transportation and selling functions are carried out by the owner-manager or the sales staff. While many small businesses often lack the financial capacity or expertise to hire and train their own salesforces, the Internet has enabled many small firms to pursue this strategy at low costs. For example, Halifax restaurant manufacturing company SureShot Dispensing sells some of its products direct to businesses using the Internet.

Manufacturer to Wholesaler/Retailer to Consumer (Long-Indirect Channel).

In this type of distribution channel, the wholesaler or retailer purchases the product and resells it to another channel member or to the consumer. The manufacturer assumes less risk with this method but generally has a lower profit margin and less control over the distribution. The small business may use this type of distribution channel by going to a retailer or wholesaler directly or visiting a tradeshow attended by these intermediaries. Many products receive their initial start from successful tradeshow experience.

CHANNEL LENGTH

The decision regarding channel length will depend on the concerns of the manufacturer mentioned above. It also involves examining the product and market characteristics listed in Figure 8-3.

CHANNEL INTENSITY

Another channel decision is how many distributors/dealers will be allowed to sell the product. Generally, products that require greater selling effort, seller knowledge, and sales expertise are best distributed through a more exclusive type of arrangement. For example, when Spin Master Toys (see opening profile in Chapter 7) started selling Air Hogs, an air powered toy plane, the company initially focused distribution efforts on hobby shops and specialty toy stores, where merchants would be more likely to take the time to explain the product. Standardized or convenience-type products usually call for a more intensive channel system. Because product availability is important in such a system, many dealers are allowed to carry the product.[15]

MULTI-LEVEL MARKETING

An increasingly popular form of distribution channel used by small and large organizations is the multi-level system. In a typical multi-level marketing or network marketing arrangement,

FIGURE 8-3   Deciding Channel Length

DIRECT-SHORT CHANNEL (MANUFACTURER TO CONSUMER)	INDIRECT-LONG CHANNEL (MANUFACTURER TO WHOLESALER/ RETAILER TO CONSUMER)
Implications for Manufacturer	
More expensive to set up	Cheaper to set up
Greater potential return	Least return
More risk	Less risk
More expertise needed	Less expertise needed
Product Characteristics	
Perishable	Standardized
Technical	Inexpensive
Large, bulky	Proven demand
Expensive	
Market Characteristics	
Geographically concentrated	Geographically dispersed
Low product awareness	High product awareness
Sales effort required	Less sales effort required

individuals associate with a parent company as an independent contractor or franchise and are compensated based on their sales of products or service, as well as sales achieved by the people they bring into the business. This type of selling is typically through personal contacts or at group social gatherings. Multi-level marketing organizations (MLMs) typically provide the entrepreneur with well-prepared training manuals and motivational meetings. The attractions of this type of marketing to the individual entrepreneur include flexibility, the ability to work from home, and the promise of high income. Careful evaluation of MLMs should be carried out, however, because with many of these organizations, the promised income is never realized, and some systems are illegal. More and more products and services have been added to multi-level marketing systems in recent years, and expansion to the Internet has vastly increased the market average for organizations and entrepreneurs. Despite the potential difficulties, multi-level marketing may be an excellent distribution method for the entrepreneur.

SETTING THE PRICE FOR THE GOOD OR SERVICE   LO3

Another marketing strategy variable within the control of the owner-manager is the setting of price for the product or service. Pricing is a critical part of the marketing strategy; the small business cannot afford to make a pricing mistake in a competitive industry. Unfortunately, many small business owners struggle with this element of the marketing mix and a common criticism is many small entrepreneurs are pricing their products too low. Additionally, small- and medium-sized businesses are facing competitors who are using a variety of pricing tools to gain a competitive advantage and consumers who have easy access to pricing information on the Internet. For example, Walmart and Target use psychological pricing strategies to help them maximize profits and online retailer Amazon uses "dynamic pricing," which uses algorithms to track past shopping habits and adjust the price of items based on the personal habits of individual shoppers.[16]

To approach price setting effectively, one must understand the factors that affect prices. These factors can be classified as either external or internal. External influences, as discussed in the previous chapter, include the state of the economy in the market area, the extent of competition, possible legal restrictions, cultural or societal attitudes toward certain price levels, and target market demand. Typical internal influences on pricing policy are internal costs, the firm's long-run objectives, and pricing policies as set by the owner-manager.

In setting price levels for the product or service, one may find that some of these factors are more influential than others. As a result, businesses use three general bases for price setting that take these influences into account: cost, demand, and competition.

COST-BASED PRICING

In cost-based pricing, the major influence is the cost of producing the product for the manufacturer, of purchasing and selling the product for the retailer, and of providing the service for the service firm (internal influence). Figure 8-4 illustrates the use of cost-based pricing in each of these types of business.

Once the costs have been determined, a percentage markup is added to reflect the profit objective of the firm. The owner-manager should realize, however, that the initial markup is

FIGURE 8-4	Cost-Based Pricing Methods

Manufacturing Firm	
Direct material cost per unit	$ 18.00
Direct labour cost per unit	21.00
Variable overhead (manufacturing)	10.00
Fixed overhead (factory)	30.00
Total manufacturing cost per unit	79.00
Selling cost per unit	3.00
General overhead (allocated per unit)	5.00
Total cost per unit	87.00
Desired profit	13.00
Selling price	$100.00
Retail Firm	
Cost of merchandise	$ 50.00
Selling and storage (estimated)	20.00
Estimated markdowns	5.00
Desired profit	25.00
Selling price	$100.00

In retailing, the difference between the price and the cost of inventory is known as *markup*. In this example, it is $50 and is usually expressed as a percentage in the following manner:

$$\text{Percentage} = \frac{100 - 50}{100} = 50\%$$

Service Firm	
Estimated cost of providing service per customer	$ 60.00
Estimated overhead costs per customer	20.00
Desired profit per customer	20.00
Selling price	$100.00

seldom achieved. Markdowns and inventory shrinkage should be estimated (see Figure 8-4) and built into the markup calculation.

DEMAND-BASED PRICING

Demand-based pricing uses consumer sensitivity to price as the major factor in arriving at the final price level (external influences). Usually primary research in the form of surveying will be required to assess acceptable prices for new products. Figure 8-5 illustrates the results of such a survey incorporated into a demand curve. Each point on the line shows the quantity demanded at the related price. For example, at a price of $30, demand would be 10 units; at $20, demand increases to 16 units. In this example, the total revenue at the $30 price is $300 (30 × 10), whereas at $20 the total revenue is $320 (20 × 16). This situation can be described as *price elastic*. In price-elastic situations, price increases result in a negative effect on demand. For some types of products (convenience and specialty) and some industries (those with little direct competition), price may be less important to the purchaser, and thus a change in price may not significantly affect demand. If this condition exists, it means the business has much more freedom and flexibility in setting prices than it would in a more competitive and price-sensitive situation. For example, Canada Goose has established that consumers are not very price sensitive when purchasing their branded products especially their winter jackets. As such, the company has established a policy where retailers are not allowed to discount their products.

For products and services already on the market, existing price levels and industry experts may provide valuable information to assist in setting demand-based prices.[17]

COMPETITION-BASED PRICING

Firms in a growing number of industries are using competitive pricing in which the major considerations in setting prices are the price levels and policies of competitors (external influences).

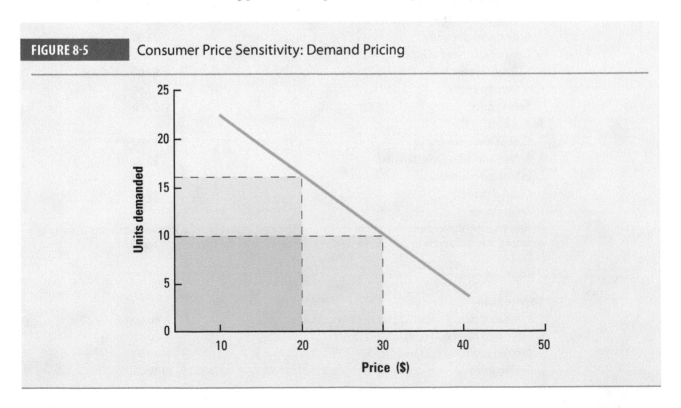

FIGURE 8-5   Consumer Price Sensitivity: Demand Pricing

Many firms conduct ongoing price checks on the competition to guide their own pricing. The small firm may want to set prices at a fixed percentage above, equal to, or below competitors' prices. Most markets today tend to be very price sensitive. As a result, entrepreneurs may have to resort to discounting prices to attract customer attention and patronage. However, in doing so, the entrepreneur should be aware of the final markups and be careful that discounting price does not conflict with the product or business image.

VALUE-BASED PRICING

Business experts are starting to argue that small business owners should not rely too heavily on only one of the above methods of pricing as they are problematic. Andreas Hinterhuber, an Austrian pricing consultant, says that most SMEs tend to set their prices based on their costs or what the competition charges. By slavishly matching rivals' prices, he says, "you completely abdicate pricing [control] and let someone else dictate your destiny." "In general," he continues, "pricing is undermanaged, in both small and large companies."[18] Hinterhuber is one of many who argue that small firms should embrace value-based pricing, which is becoming more popular with businesses. With value-based pricing, the entrepreneur makes sure that a clear association with the product or service and its benefits takes place. Such value components might be service, quality, or environmental factors. If this is done effectively, the seller has an easier time attracting and selling to target customers because they can more readily see the benefits. In addition, this strategy facilitates reaching customers who care more about value than cost alone.

PROMOTION   LO4

Gone are the days of the philosophy "Build a better mousetrap, and the world will beat a path to your door." Today, most businesses must actively provide information to the purchaser. For the entrepreneur, finding low-cost but effective ways to promote the business or product is a challenge. Knowledge of the options and the use of creativity can help stretch the promotional dollar. When drawing-up promotional plans, entrepreneurs may choose from a number of different media to convey their message, including TV, radio, newspapers, and magazines. While all offer some advantages and disadvantages, they share one common characteristic: They all cost money. Rather than spend a great deal of time discussing traditional promotional methods, which are sometimes not feasible for start-ups and/or small enterprises, we will briefly discuss them, then focus on tools that offer entrepreneurs significant potential at low costs. They include guerrilla marketing, public relations (PR), and the Internet.

STEPS IN A PROMOTIONAL CAMPAIGN   LO5

How does the owner-manager prepare the promotional program for the product, service, or business? The following steps are essential in carrying out a promotional program that can be used as a guide for the small business.

1. Set Promotional Objectives.
Specific objectives should be set before the promotion. Typical examples are the desired percentage increase in sales, the amount of traffic to be generated, and the percentage of awareness increase desired.

2. Determine the Target of the Promotion.

Although, in many cases, the target will be the ultimate consumer, often it will be an intermediary in the distribution channel or another group that has considerable influence over the purchase.

3. Understand the Target's Needs and Perceptions of the Product or Service.

Once the target of the promotion has been determined, it is essential that information be gathered about members of that group with regard to their needs, media habits, and perceptions of the product category or specific product or service.

4. Develop the Relevant Theme.

The next step is to develop a theme for the promotion that will reflect responsiveness to target needs and perceptions and help achieve the promotional objective. It is important that only one theme be used, since too many themes or too much information can confuse the consumer and lead to unsatisfactory results.

5. Determine the Method or Media to Use.

The decision about which promotional type to use often depends on the relative importance of creating awareness or closing the sale. Figure 8-6 lists the strengths of each previously mentioned type of promotion with respect to these purposes. As the figure illustrates, advertising, public relations, and some sales promotions tend to be more effective in creating awareness, whereas personal selling tends to work better for achieving or closing the sale.

6. Develop a Specific Promotional Message.

Once the theme and medium have been determined, it is possible to develop the specific type of message to be used. As Figure 8-6 points out, some types of information are not appropriate for certain types of media. Care should be taken to ensure that the benefits of the product are clearly communicated.

7. Set the Promotional Budget.

Once the method of promotion is determined, it is possible to estimate the cost of the promotion. Several methods are used to determine amounts to spend on promotion. The most common approach is the percent of sales method. Standard percentages for various businesses

FIGURE 8-6	Effectiveness of Promotion Types			
	PERSONAL SELLING	SALES PROMOTIONS	PUBLIC RELATIONS	ADVERTISING
Create awareness of product or business	Weak	Weak	Strong	Strong
Develop interest in product	Weak	Medium	Weak	Strong
Increase desire to purchase product	Medium	Medium	Weak	Medium
Achieve product purchase	Strong	Medium	Weak	Weak

can serve as a guide in using this method. The percent of sales method is theoretically weak but simple to apply, which explains its high rate of use by small businesses. A business owner should remain flexible in using these percentages, however, as market and product conditions may necessitate a deviation from the averages.

8. Implement the Promotional Program.

An essential feature of implementing the program is proper timing. Certain times of the year, the week, and even the day may be inappropriate for promoting the product or service to the target market.

9. Evaluate the Effectiveness of the Promotion.

The owner-manager should attempt to evaluate the promotional effectiveness to aid in future promotions. Evaluating effectiveness is much easier if specific objectives such as those mentioned earlier are set. Observations of results and surveys may be used in this evaluation. The mechanics of using primary research methods were discussed earlier in the text.

As this chapter illustrates, many aspects are involved in the marketing plan of a small business. The way all these aspects are integrated so that they compose a clear and coordinated strategy often spells the difference between a successful and an unsuccessful business.

TYPES OF PROMOTION   LO6

A small business can use a variety of methods to provide information about its product or service: advertising, sales promotions, personal selling, traditional promotions, non-traditional promotions (including guerrilla marketing and public relations), and Internet marketing.

Advertising.

Advertising is a non-personal form of promotion. It is directed at a mass audience through various forms of media such as television, radio, newspapers, magazines, billboards, the Internet, and direct mail. A small business owner should be aware of the strengths and weaknesses of each of these types of media and exactly when each is appropriate. This information is presented in Figure 8-7 and discussed in further detail below. One of the most rapidly growing vehicles for small business advertising is through the Internet. Recent research carried out by Statistics Canada revealed that Canadian online sales topped $122 billion in 2012, which is double what they were only five years ago. The Internet is not only an effective means of advertising but also an excellent tool for securing customer feedback. More will be discussed about small business and the Internet later in this chapter.

Because the small business typically does not have a lot of money to spend on advertising, it is important that the entrepreneur find effective ways to promote the business economically. Co-op and shared advertising are two ways of doing this.

With co-op advertising, the manufacturing company shares the cost of advertising with the small retailer, if the retailer features the manufacturer's products in those ads. Both the manufacturer and the retailer get more advertising per dollar by sharing expenses. Co-op advertising is used most frequently by small retailers, but unfortunately, many small retailers do not take advantage of this type of assistance.

In shared advertising, a group of similar businesses forms a syndicate to produce generic ads that allow the individual businesses to dub in local information. This technique is especially suitable for small businesses that sell relatively standardized products or services. The result of this form of advertising is higher quality ads and significantly lower production costs.

FIGURE 8-7 Advertising for Small Business

MEDIA TYPE	ADVANTAGES	DISADVANTAGES	PARTICULAR SUITABILITY	TYPICAL COSTS

Newspapers	Flexible
	Timely
	Local market
	Credible source
		May be expensive
		Short life
		Little "pass along"
		Non-selective
		  audience
			All local retailers
			  or for definable
			  market areas
			  similar to
			  circulation
				One-page ad: large
				  market
				  ($2,000–$4,000)
				  small market
				  ($500–$800)
				  (prices dependent on
				  length of contract)

Television	Sight, sound,
	  and motion
	Wide reach
		Cost
		Clutter
		Short exposure
		Less selective
			Definable market area
			  surrounding the
			  station's location
			  for certain products
				30 seconds of
				  prime time:
				large local market
				  ($750–$1000)
				small local market
				  ($200–$300)

Direct mail	Selected audience
	Personalization
	Flexible
		Relatively expensive
		  per contact
		High "throwout" rate
			New and expanding
			  businesses; those
			  using coupon
			  returns or catalogues
				Approximately $1
				  per contact

Radio	Wide reach
	Segmented audience
	Inexpensive
		Audio only
		Weak attention
		Short exposure
			Business catering to
			  identifiable groups:
			  teens, commuters,
			  housewives
				30 seconds of
				  prime time:
				large local market
				  ($175–$250)
				small local market
				  ($35–$60)

Magazines,
  including trade
  publications
  and catalogues
	Very segmented
	  audience
	Credible source
	Good reproduction
	Long life
	Good "pass along"
		Inflexible
		Long lead times
		Costly
			Restaurants
			Entertainment
			Identifiable target
			  markets
			Mail order
			Chains
				Approximately
				  $30,000 for
				  one-page, four-
				  colour ad in
				  Chatelaine (French
				  and English)

Outdoor	Flexible
	Repeat exposure
	Inexpensive
		Mass market
		Very short exposure
			Amusements
			Tourist businesses
			Brand name retailers
				One month of prime
				  location billboard,
				  large market
				  ($2,500–$3,000)

Telephone
  directories
	Users in market
	  for goods or
	  services
	Continuous ads
	Costs relatively low
		Limited to active
		  shoppers
		Limited visibility
		Not dynamic
			Services
			Retailers of brand
			  name items
			Highly specialized
			  retailers
				Inexpensive—
				  depends on size
				  of ad

Internet	Inexpensive
	Requires computer
	  hardware and
	  expertise
		Limited market
		  (but growing)
		Cannot see and try
		Lack of privacy
		Viruses
			Products that do
			  not require trial
			Information products
				"Sign on" fee
				  varies by type of ad

Tradeshows	Many buyers High exposure Time saving	Cost	Product sold in chain stores	Varies

Sales Promotions.

Sales promotions are also non-personal forms of promotion, but they are directed at a much more restricted audience than is advertising. Examples of sales promotions are point-of-purchase displays, coupons and discounts, tradeshows and exhibitions, and contests. Sean O'Reilly, owner of Barrie-based Shorex Roofing Corp. (www.shorex.ca), says that his firm has successfully used coupons from day one. When he first started his business, he had staff visit people door to door, and hand them brochure with a 25-percent off coupon. O'Reilly notes that customers who were thinking about hiring a roofing company had a choice, they could go to the phone book and start making calls or they could talk to the salesperson at the door who was handing them a paper worth 25 percent off the cost of a job.[19] Recently, online coupons, especially "deal of the day" coupons, have become an emerging trend in business as they offer consumers deep discounts and entrepreneurs a new method of promoting their product (see Incident 8-1 for additional information).

Tradeshows are also a cost-effective method of promotion for the small business. Research indicates that more than 80 percent of visitors at tradeshows are decision makers, and more than 60 percent plan to make a purchase. Cheryl Ng, president of FouFou Dog (www.foufoudog.com), a Richmond Hill-based distributor of designer doggy wear, notes that tradeshows are tailor made for the small business as the cost to participate is low and exposure is high. All these mechanisms are very effective forms of advertising for the small business, and some are relatively inexpensive.[20]

Personal Selling.   LO7

The conditions conducive to a short distribution channel or an emphasis on personal selling were discussed earlier in this chapter. Most businesses will require some personal selling as part of their marketing strategy and in some cases personal selling is essential to success. For example, Dwight Gerling, managing director of Toronto-based DG Global Inc. (www.dgglobal.ca), visits Japan and other Asian countries three to six times a year to build relationships with customers. Gerling says, "The Asian culture is all about relationships...they appreciate me coming over, as they see me more as a friend than just as a business partner."[21] Owner-managers will undoubtedly be required to promote themselves, their businesses, and their products to customers, bankers, suppliers, and government agencies through personal selling. If salespeople are employed, they will need to be trained, not only with respect to product or service knowledge but also in selling skills. Other aspects of training, supervision, and motivation of a salesforce are discussed in detail later in the text.

As discussed above, there are many methods for small- and medium-sized enterprises to promote their products. Generally, they can be classified into three broad categories: traditional promotional methods, untraditional promotional methods, and Internet marketing. The three categories will be discussed below, highlighting their uses along with some advantages and disadvantages.

Traditional Promotional Methods

Traditional promotional tools use a variety of media for the delivery of a company's message. As mentioned above, these tools include direct mail, newspapers, TV, radio, telephone directories and tradeshows. While these methods can be effective, they generally have higher costs than other forms of promotions, sometimes have limited exposure time, and are rarely interactive.

Direct Mail.

This is one of the most effective methods for SMEs to promote their business. Firms can tailor direct mail packages to certain segments of the population, and it is relatively easy to produce

GROUPON AND TEAM BUY—A DIFFERENT KIND OF COUPON

Traditionally, coupons offered customers a small savings off the price of a product. For example, you may receive 10–25 percent of your money back after purchasing laundry detergent at a grocery store or local restaurants may offer a two for one coupon in the daily newspaper. This all changed in 2008 when Groupon (www.groupon.com) was founded. The company, which can be described as an online social buying website, promotes "deal of the day" coupons that offer consumers deep discounts ranging from 50–90 percent off the cost of a purchase. Team Buy (www.teambuy.ca), which was founded in Toronto in 2009, was the first Canadian "deal of the day" site.[22]

Groupon, Team Buy, and a number of other "deal of the day" sites operate around the same basic concept, interested consumers agree to purchase a coupon but no sales occur until a minimum number of buyers are reached. Once a targeted number of buyers have been reached, the deal becomes unlocked, the consumer's credit card is charged, and they can print the coupon. Since consumers want the deal, they often share the details with their peers using social media sites such as Facebook and Twitter. Some sites, including Groupon and Team Buy, will actually pay consumers for providing referrals to deals if the person buys the coupon. The majority of "deal of the day" companies operate in most urban centres in North America.

When "deal of the day" sites first emerged, many companies liked the concept because they saw it as a low cost way to acquire consumers. Firms who used these online promotions paid no upfront money and had their name and logo emailed out to thousands, and in some larger urban centres, millions of people. But reviews from participating businesses have not all been favourable as many have citied the high cost of participating in the program as a deterrent. For example, at a minimum the coupons usually offer consumers a savings of 50 percent off the cost of a purchase. So, a participating restaurant would offer $100 worth of food for $50. This closely resembles traditional coupons discussed above where consumers could buy one meal and get another for free. But "deal of the day" sites need to make money as well, and they normally charge 50 percent of the sale price of the coupon, or in this example, $25. So a participating restaurant would be selling $100 worth of food for only $25. Given that most restaurants only net a small percentage of gross sales they would be incurring a substantial loss to participate in the program. Other complaints are that using these coupons creates a negative image about the business and "deal of the day" site operators such as Groupon and Team Buy are slow to pay the participating business their share of the money, resulting in businesses incurring hefty expenses to deliver the product or service without seeing the money come into their business for weeks if not months.[23]

Proponents of "deal of the day" sites argue that these coupons can work for some businesses. For example, some products and services have a high enough markup where businesses can afford to offer them at a deep discount. Furthermore, some companies, especially those in the service industry, are more prone to see repeat customers after a successful purchase. Coupon sites are also useful for businesses that are trying to generate sales during slow periods, get rid of unwanted inventory or for those with high fixed costs such as hotels, cruise ships, or even small tour operators. For example, Tennis Canada has used Groupon to sell tickets at some major events. Given that most of their costs are fixed, selling tickers at a deep discount is likely better than having the seats sit empty.

Discussion Questions

1. What are some of the potential advantages and disadvantages to firms who offer "deal of the day" coupons?

2. The case above cites some examples where "deal of the day" coupons may make sense. Develop some additional alternatives where participating in "deals of the day" programs would be beneficial to firms.

3. Do you think Tennis Canada is making a good business decision selling tickets at 50 percent off using Groupon? What are the benefits of this? What are the disadvantages?

4. If you ran a business would you offer consumers "deal of the day" coupons? Why, or why not?

5. Given the increasing competition among sites offering "deal of the day" coupons, is there a chance consumers will start to ignore their messages? Why, or why not?

materials that result in measurable results. In general, direct mail packages will include a letter that is written to grab a reader's attention and then a sales/promotional package. The general rule of thumb is a good direct mail campaign will produce two customers (responses) for each 100 sent, although there has been returns that have produced much higher results. So when costing your campaign, keep this 2 percent in mind—determine the costs of your package and the potential results based on a 2 percent response rate, and determine if it makes financial

TELEPHONE DIRECTORIES WERE USED FOR YEARS BY BUSINESSES THAT WANTED TO ENSURE LOCAL CUSTOMERS COULD FIND THEIR LOCATION AND CONTACT INFORMATION. TODAY DIRECTORIES ARE BEING REPLACED BY ONLINE LISTINGS AND WEBSITES THAT CAN PROVIDE MUCH MORE INTERACTIVE INFORMATION TO CONSUMERS.
©Brand X Pictures/PunchStock; Robynmac/Dreamstime.com

sense. Tom St. Louis, who specializes in SME marketing, advises companies to spend their marketing money on direct mail to current customers first. Then and only when there is money left over should SMEs spend money on lead generating marketing. Another advantage of direct mail is the ability to test different messages. SMEs can easily compare one direct mail package with another one to see if the response rate varies and then select the more effective package.[24]

Telephone Directories.

This is a common form of advertising for small businesses. Essentially, firms take out an advertisement or listing in the local directory. The ads are considered credible and have a longer shelf life compared with those in newspapers and magazines. They are, however, costly, and more and more consumers are shunning large, printed directories in favour of Internet solutions.

Newspapers/Magazines.

Entrepreneurs will generally advertise in newspapers/magazines using display ads or classifieds. The ads allow for some targeting of consumers can be run at different times of the year and are considered a credible source of information. The downside is the short life for many publications and the costs. Classified ads are usually less effective than display ads, but they cost substantially less. While some firms only use display ads, there has been some remarkable stories of businesses getting strong results by using classified advertising. A small Montreal retail spa business runs a weekly classified ad advertising a hot tub for sale. The ad reads like an individual is selling a new hot tub that is still the box—but in all actuality the business is selling the tub. The firm keeps running the ad because it has been highly effective. Much like many forms of traditional advertising newspaper and magazine advertising is being impacted by the Internet. As more people are relying on tablets and mobile devices to read newspapers and magazines, some businesses are questioning the value of print ads.

Radio.

Radio commercials are usually less costly than TV ads but they offer the ability to tailor a message to a specific audience. The disadvantages of radio advertising are the costs, audio only, and the short exposure.

Television.

SMEs usually advertise on TV by purchasing time to run commercials. Larger firms are now engaging in product placements but the costs associated with these are often beyond the scope of new entrepreneurs. The advantage of commercials is they include sight and sound and can be aimed at a specific audience. The biggest downside is the high costs and their short exposure. Former restaurant owner Jim MacAulay believes differently. MacAulay argues that too many small firms overestimate the cost of advertising on TV and underestimate the value. He notes that he spent less than $10,000 to advertise his restaurant, The True North Diner, throughout Atlantic Canada on TV and the results were a 30 percent increase in sales over the two-month period the ads ran. MacAulay says the ads also resulted in strong sales after they stopped running. For his business, TV was much more effective than other forms of media.

Non-traditional Promotional Methods

Non-traditional promotional methods can be defined as pursuing traditional business goals of sales and profits through non-conventional means. Non-traditional methods are usually low in cost, generate both exposure and sales, and may or may not be interactive with consumers. The two major types of non-traditional promotions are guerrilla marketing and public relations (PR).

Guerrilla Marketing.

Guerrilla marketing consists of entrepreneurs developing creative, catchy, and—most importantly—low-cost methods to attract attention to their business and to sell their products. For example, some companies have hired college students to stand in airports with signs sporting a company's web address to lure online visitors. Other companies stage contests, hire mascots, or arrange for special events, all of which draws attention to their business at very little cost. Shopify, which was featured in the opening profile, generates a great deal of business and buzz for itself by running Build-a-Business competitions. Calum McGuigan, 27-year-old owner of Fervent Events (www.ferventevents.com), a guerrilla marketing company based in Toronto, says, "Guerrilla marketing is about being innovative and creative."[25] His firm has staged flash mobs, fake public weddings, handed out free samples, created side walk art, used murals, and held parties to promote products and services. McGuigan says, guerrilla marketing shocks people out of their normal routine and leaves a lasting impression. ". . . one day you walk to work and you see something peculiar like a tug-of-war, a flash mob, chalk art, a free sample, a Guinness world record attempt etc…you take a second and then perhaps a third look. You're intrigued, and hopefully it's left a positive emotional experience with you. Guerrilla marketing reaches smaller more concentrated groups than traditional methods, but leaves more memorable impressions."[26]

Other examples of successful guerrilla marketing include, Montreal-based Lezza Distribution Inc., a high-end manufacturer of countertops and flooring surfaces, had nearly naked male models serving drinks to potential customers at a recent tradeshow. In addition, the company hosts an annual "Seven Sins" party, where barely clothed wait staff distribute drinks, highlighted by a game of strip poker. Company president Mark Hanna says, "Parties give us a chance to showcase our core values of passion, risk, and creativity, and they give us a cool factor that distinguishes us from our competitors."[27] Hanna spends upward of $90,000 per party, but he also sets sales goals to go along with his events and so far he has met or exceeded them all. Spindles, Stairs & Railings (www.greatstairs.com), a designer staircase company owned by Kevin Halliday of Calgary, Alberta, also embraces non-traditional marketing. Halliday visits unfinished homes and staples quotes, pictures of his work, and business cards to the staircases.[28]

One mistake entrepreneurs often make with guerrilla marketing is to wrongly associate it with smaller enterprises. This is simply not the case, as demonstrated by lululemon. To promote their high-end and high-cost yoga pants, the retailer has taken to giving free clothes to yoga instructors, offering discounts to customers who shop in the nude, and using inspirational

GUERRILLA MARKETING SUCH AS FLASH MOBS CAN SHOCK PEOPLE INTO TAKING A SECOND LOOK AND LEAVE A LASTING IMPRESSION.
Martingraf / Dreamstime.com

sayings on chalkboards to promote products.[29] Lululemon also relies heavily on the Internet and buzz from social media to promote its products.[30]

Other examples of guerrilla marketing efforts include the following:

- Contests or raffles
- Artists hanging pictures in doctors' offices
- Sticking Post-it notes where people can see them
- Offering free samples
- Public demonstrations
- Having people wear or use a company's product

It should be noted that guerrilla marketing is different than stealth marketing (see Incident 8-2 box). When companies engage in guerrilla marketing, consumers are generally aware of the company's intentions. Stealth marketing attempts to fool or mislead consumers into buying products. For example, in guerrilla marketing, a company may post something online or in a chat group and let users know the post came from a business or an individual representing a business. If the company was engaged in stealth marketing, it would post information online and pretend to be a regular consumer. The stealth marketer is hoping to mislead consumers into thinking a peer is recommending a product or service.

Public Relations (PR).

Public relations is defined as generating positive awareness of your company. PR is a highly effective form of promotion that has been effectively used by large and small firms. Spin Master Toys, the third largest North American toy company, shunned traditional advertising for years and instead concentrated on PR. PR offers the benefits of being free and is often viewed more

INCIDENT 8-2

STEALTH MARKETING VERSUS NON-TRADITIONAL MARKETING— CAN YOU TELL THE DIFFERENCE?

Stealth marketing are promotions undertaken by a company intending to be unbeknown to consumers. Stealth marketing often uses deception to convince consumers to buy products or to create awareness for a company. Stealth marketing often uses deception to convince consumers to buy products or to create awareness for a company and is different from unconventional marketing such as PR and guerrilla marketing, as the objectives of the company are often concealed from consumers. For example, CBC recently ran an expose on the use of stealth marketing in Canada and discovered a marketing firm that hired people to set up fake social networking accounts on such sites as Facebook. The people would befriend others and then make products and service recommendations on behalf of clients. Given that people, especially young people, put a higher value on peer recommendations, the business was successful in promoting products and events throughout the country. Another common form of stealth marketing is to post fake reviews on such sites as Yelp or TripAdvisor. Some business owners and/or managers will create false accounts, pose as customers, and draft favourable reviews about a product or service. Given that research has found that a slight increase in ratings can positively impact sales, the motives for entrepreneurs and managers are quite clear.[31]

Yet the lines between stealth marketing and untraditional marketing are becoming blurred. For example, the use of product placements and celebrity endorsements, while considered acceptable to some, is seen as unethical to others. People are often increasingly unsure whether to classify marketing activities as non-traditional or stealth in nature. For example, some alcohol companies have hired attractive or popular people to use their products in public; businesses have urged online friends to support their company or products in online contests; and some videos on YouTube, while appearing to be shot by amateurs, are actual professionally concealed product placements or endorsements.[32]

So far, the Canadian government has not adopted any laws to regulate or eliminate stealth marketing. While some consumer groups are advocating for rules to protect consumers, others are stating that the lines between stealth marketing and non-traditional marketing have become so close that rules or laws would not work.[33] Furthermore, companies that have engaged in stealth campaigns risk consumer backlash, which serves as its own deterrent.[34]

Discussion Questions

1. Do you think stealth marketing is ethical? Should it be illegal?

2. Should government create laws to protect consumers from fake or misleading recommendations on Facebook, Yelp, and TripAdvisor? Would it be possible to enforce such a law?

3. From the examples above, do you think alcohol companies that hire attractive or popular people to use their products are engaging in unethical behavior? Why, or why not?

4. Are companies such as Apple, which spend millions on product placements, engaging in stealth marketing? Do you think product placements are an acceptable form of advertising? Why, or why not?

5. Would you use stealth marketing to help you sell a product or service? Why, or why not?

6. How would you differentiate between stealth marketing and guerrilla marketing? Could you argue they are one and the same? Why, or why not?

SOME BUSINESSES HAVE HIRED PEOPLE TO ESTABLISH NUMEROUS SOCIAL NETWORKING ACCOUNTS UNDER FALSE NAMES TO PROMOTE PRODUCTS OR SERVICES. THIS IS REFERRED TO AS "STEALTH MARKETING" AND, WHILE NOT ILLEGAL, IS UNETHICAL.
Frui / Dreamstime.com

favourably by consumers. Business author Pamela Bartlett argues that PR should be incorporated into every business plan as it leads to an increase in credibility and sales. Bartlett says, "When a third party, such as the media, endorses a product or service, the company gains credibility. Consumers are much more likely to make a purchase based on third party endorsement than an advertisement."[35] Unfortunately, many new and smaller firms do not engage in PR as

INCIDENT 8-3

WRITING EFFECTIVE PRESS RELEASES

Effective press releases follow a formula, much like the one presented by Mia Wedgbury, president of High Roads Communications, a Toronto-based public relations agency, in a recent edition of the *Globe and Mail*. Wedgbury states that there are four sacred rules to writing press releases:

- Lead with your strength—What do you want the press to read first? Remember this is not a promotional piece but you are alerting the media about something that their readers will find interesting. Do not waste time with fluff; rather, get to the point, and sell the story.

- Answer the question, "So what?"—Demonstrate to the media why there is a demand for your company, product, or service, and why their readers will be interested.

- Let others do the talking—Offer expert opinion, testimonials from customers, and so forth. This adds credibility.

- Send it off with a pitch—Use email to send it to reporters. Ensure that the message entices them to read the message.

Source: www.theglobeandmail.com/report-on-business/what-are-they-saying-about-you/article1056425/?page=all.

they often believe it costs a lot of money or is nothing more than having a newspaper story written about their grand opening. PR consultant Susan MacDonald disagrees that PR is only for large firms noting that PR is actually a democratic process that rewards those who learn how the media works. She says firms that work hard and commit to the process can expect good results through PR.

Examples of good public relations include the following:

- Develop a press kit. Many entrepreneurs wonder how their competitor is always in the local paper and on TV. Chances are they have developed a press kit that consists of company information, pre-written stories, and pictures, which they have sent to reporters, editors, and so on.
- Write articles for a newspaper, newsletter, or community guide.
- Write letters to the editor.
- Participate in discussions either online or through traditional mediums.
- Host events.
- Offer services as a guest speaker.

Internet Marketing

The Internet offers small and new businesses a cost-efficient method of reaching customers anywhere in the world. Much has been made in the press about using the Internet as a central point of all marketing activities, as Internet marketing allows entrepreneurs to present consumers with a significant amount of information at lower cost than traditional methods. Additionally, and perhaps more importantly, Internet marketing, which is sometimes called "digital marketing," enables companies to reach out to consumers and engage in interactive conversations with them using a variety of tools including websites, social networks, and mobile applications.

Company Web Pages.

As previously noted, websites enable companies to post a great deal of information on the Internet for pennies, enable interactive communication between firms and consumers, allow for direct sales of products to customers, assist in procuring supplies, and so forth. Excellent

DRAGONS' DEN EFFECT

One of the best forms of PR is to get your product or service on TV. Whether it is the nightly news, serving as an expert on a televised panel, or just having your company in the background of a story, these can often cause sales and public awareness of your company to rise. In the U.S. the gold standard for companies was to get on the *Oprah Winfrey* show. Entrepreneurs knew having their business featured on *Oprah* would increase sales and customer awareness. Some entrepreneurs like Brian Scudamore, founder of 1-800-GotJunk? actually made appearing on *Oprah* a key goal for his company, a measure if he was successful, and something to springboard expansion plans around. Scudamore did eventually land a spot on *Oprah*, and shortly after the episode aired, the firm received 3000 calls from customers—up 300 percent from usual—and 500 franchise inquiries.[36]

In Canada, the equivalent of the Oprah show is CBC's hit series the *Dragons' Den*. As discussed in several chapters in this book, *Dragons' Den* has entrepreneurs pitch their business to a group of angel investors called "Dragons." Successful bidders can leave with an investment in their business, while unsuccessful entrepreneurs leave empty handed and occasionally have their business skills degraded by the investment panel. Occasionally, entrepreneurs are criticized so much that viewers may wonder why people would want to appear on the show, as it is not unusual for some Dragons to refer to entrepreneurs as crazy or insane.[37]

Yet the entrepreneurs who get on the show are far from crazy. While many pitchers are no doubt interested in the investment money from the Dragons, the PR benefits even from a rejected pitch can be significant. In fact, the positive boost in sales and awareness companies experience after being on the show has been given an official reference by CBC—"The *Dragons' Den* Effect." For example, Zane Caplansky appeared on the show looking to get money to franchise his food truck concept, Caplansky's Delicatessen (www.caplanskys.com), which featured what he claimed was the best smoked meat sandwiches in Toronto. While the Dragons enjoyed his product, they did not think his business was worth an investment, and one Dragon, Kevin O'Leary, started calling Caplansky, Insane Zane. The result of his rejection on air, a 50 percent rise in sales a month after the show aired. Other failed pitches report strong results as well, including the Stilt Guys (www.stiltguys.com),

performers . . . on stilts. While the company was unsuccessful in raising any money, the owners note that being on the show for less than a minute led to other PR opportunities that helped them expand the business. "Despite being on air for only a minute, we were able to make a big impression. Local media has loved talking to us and finding out what the experience was like. Considering most TV ads are only 30 seconds, having a full minute on one of Canada's most watched national TV shows is like winning a huge advertising grand prize!"[38] The most successful example of the "*Dragons' Den* Effect" goes to Holy Crap cereal. After appearing on the show company co-founder Brian Mullins was hoping to see annual sales increase to $600,000 a year. Instead sales skyrocketed to over $5 million.

What accounts for such strong results? The show is the number one in Canada and two in five Canadians watched an episode this past year. Faythe Pal, chair of the Canadian Institute of Marketing and CEO of Hands of Time, Inc. (www. handsoftimeinc.com), a Toronto management corporation, says it is a great coup to appear on the show. "All of that exposure, all of the commercial lead-ups, all of the promotional marketing. Even if you don't win, to get that full engagement where your products can then be sold on [the CBC] website, and your story can continue being told. It's amazing."[39]

Discussion Questions

1. What are the advantages and disadvantages of appearing on *Dragons' Den*?

2. Many entrepreneurs appear to be quite upset by some of the Dragons comments about their businesses and ideas. Do you think the potential of being called insane on national TV is worth the PR for a company?

3. If you had a business, would you try to get on *Dragons' Den*? Why, or why not?

4. Many of the so-called successful bidders do not end up receiving any financing support from the Dragons after the show has aired. Given this information, are you more or less likely to recommend the show to an aspiring entrepreneur? If the Dragons agree to invest in a concept on the air, should they not have to honour their investment? Why, or why not?[40]

websites are fast, facilitate communication with visitors, contain all essential information that customers are looking for, are easy to navigate, and have a domain name that is painless to remember. Unfortunately, having a website is not enough; for a website to assist your business, it has to get visitors—one way to do this is to register with search engines and build a search friendly site as is discussed below.

In developing a website, an entrepreneur needs to remember that a website is a communication vehicle and should address the following questions: Who is the audience? What are the objectives for the site? What do you want the consumers to do upon visiting the site? Is the website an integral part of the venture's total communication program? In addressing these questions, the entrepreneur needs to structure the website and organize the information to effectively engage the target market. This requires that the material be fresh, with new material added on a regular basis. The material should be interactive to engage the individual. And, of course, the website needs to be known and as visible as possible.

Search Engine Optimization (SEO).

When consumers use Google, Bing, or Yahoo! to search for a company, a product or service businesses want to ensure their firm not only comes up in the search results but is featured prominently on the list. Evidence indicates that firms who appear frequently and higher up search lists have more visitors to their web pages. SEO attempts to create websites that result in more frequent and higher ratings. While this is not an exact science, entrepreneurs will want to be sure to build a site that has clear title tags, have content pages that use words that relate to the purpose of the site, clearly link all documents, update the site frequently, and have lots of pages.

Additionally SEO experts recommend business owners who want to achieve better search results consider the following recommendations:

- Use words customers actually use to describe their service.
- Avoid changing a website's address, as Google search has a tendency to favour older sites.
- Increase the number of external links, as these strongly influence Google algorithms.

Embrace social networking by providing clear links to the business's social media sites. In general search engines favour websites that are shared, liked, or discussed more frequently.

Pay-Per-Click Advertising (PPC).

PPC advertising allows firms to bid on key words or phrases relevant to their target market. When a consumer enters in the phrase or word in the search engine, the company will appear under the results section, and their ads will appear on the side of the viewer's screen. Common PPC advertisers are Google AdWords, Yahoo! Search Marketing, and Microsoft adCenter. Prollenium Medical Technologies (www.prollenium.com), an Aurora, Ontario-based manufacturer of cosmetics, serves as a successful example of PPC advertising. The company purchased specific search terms using Google AdWorks and Yahoo! for $2000 per month, which have resulted in an increase from 1000 to 50,000 monthly visitors. The company now attributes 90 percent of company sales to PPC advertising. The other popular form of PPC advertising is when companies place ads on websites but only have to pay for them when their ad is clicked.[41]

Online Newsletter.

These can be created as standalone websites or be sent to customers via email. Since the newsletters are almost always permission based containing material your customers are interested in, they can build and strengthen relationships with customers and drive traffic to your website at a very low fee.

Direct Email to Customers.

Email marketing is just direct marketing to customers via the Internet. Since the Internet is used to communicate with customers, businesses can send a great deal more information compared with traditional direct mail at a substantially reduced cost. Email has almost unlimited number of uses and can be used to: welcome customers, encourage people to visit your website or make a purchase, provide additional information, and/or be used as a mechanism to send videos, blogs, newsletters, and podcasts. Emails can also be used to supplement other forms of marketing and research indicates that including email as part of a direct mail campaign increases response rates by 40 percent; when used in conjunction with telemarketing the response rate jumps by 76 percent. It should be noted that email marketing is not SPAM, a practice where companies send out emails to random lists of people; rather it is permission-based marketing.

Banner Advertisements.

Banner ads were one of the first forms of Internet marketing. Banner ads are placed on websites (for a fee) in an attempt to attract visitors to your website, purchase a product, and/or solicit further information. Banner ads can be advantageous as they allow entrepreneurs to target customers and may or may not be cost effective, depending on their placement. The key to using banner ads is to place them on sites that are appropriate to your target audience, have attractive ads that are visually appealing, and offer consumers some benefit by clicking on the advertisement.

Affiliate Programs.

These are online partnerships where one company posts links to your website if you do the same in turn. Affiliate programs are attractive to entrepreneurs because of their low cost and ability to target a specific audience.

Online Classified Advertising Sites.

Kijiji, BackPage, and Craigslist all allow users, including businesses, to post online classified ads. Kijiji, the most popular of the three in Canada, is the country's eighth most visited site. Unlike Craig's List and BackPage, Kijiji allows companies to post individual classified advertisements and banner ads that appear at the top of a user's computer screen. A variety of small and large businesses make use of Kijiji. For example, Chris Neville, who owns a landscaping and real estate business in Nova Scotia states, "Kijiji is actually my most effective form of advertising. I use Facebook and other forms of social media, but most calls for our services and/or apartments come from Kijiji."[42]

Online Auction Sites.

There are a number of online auction sites that allow businesses and consumers to sell items in an auction type format. Generally, individuals or companies post items for sale and take bids on their products or services. eBay is the best known of all these sites and one of the most commonly visited sites in the world. eBay allows users to sell items in online auctions or operate online eBay stores. Many small businesses are attracted to the site for its global reach, ease of use, and custom rich features. For example, Tina Kantana invested $500 in 2006 and started auctioning 10 pieces of designer clothes on eBay. Kantana was shocked how quickly her clothes sold and decided to pursue selling high-end fashion on the auction site. Today, she has her own eBay store, Fashion à la Carte (http://myworld.ebay.com/fashionalacarte_com), which has over 2000 items for sale, and she boasts that she has sold items in over 70 different countries. Every year eBay celebrates the achievements of successful Canadian entrepreneurs with eBay awards.[43] Last year's winner, Gatineau's Jean-Francois Lapointe, operates an online bicycle part store, Bhdbikestore, which has annual sales in excess of $1 million.[44]

Gamification.

Gamification is applying the concepts and application of game thinking to affect behaviour. Simple gamification concepts include having consumers collect points, badges, or other incentives. Common examples of gamification on websites and mobile applications include providing rewards for people or players who accomplish certain tasks, establishing levels of participation and enabling consumers to track their progress through various levels, providing virtual currency or coupons, adding elements of competition to a website, and so forth. For example, Cheryl Ng's company FouFou Dog, a Canadian retailer of high-end pet products, makes use of numerous gamification features on her website. FouFou Dog web visitors can play games on the site, including trying to move a dog through a maze and collect various rewards.[45] Other examples include consumer feedback sites that rank the users' level of participation; users are urged to provide additional feedback or participate more to unlock the next level. Sometimes, unlocking levels comes with awards, and in other cases, the achievement itself is the award.

Online Games.

In addition to adding gamification elements to websites and apps, many companies are delivering promotional messages during game play or sponsoring games as a way to communicate with consumers. These can take the form of virtual product placements, online scavenger hunts, and so forth.

Podcasts.

They are either audio and/or video clips that can be downloaded on a wireless device such as the Ipod, an MP3 player, or a BlackBerry. The keys to creating a good podcast include getting to your point quickly, creating something entertaining, and using conversational language. Podcasts are not just for reaching young consumers either; in fact, research indicates that podcasts influence B2B purchase decisions as well. As one buyer noted, "It's nice sometime just to listen to the information."

Webinars.

They have been described by entrepreneurs as the best sales tool to come along since the advent of the Internet. Webinars are web-based seminars where you can engage in a full sales pitch with a customer regardless of their location. One Nova Scotia entrepreneur stated that it is like a conference call on steroids. Sales staff can use the full interactivity of the web to sell clients on the wonders of their products but at a low cost.

Social Networking.

In addition to the Internet marketing methods mentioned above, more and more businesses are using social networking to promote their businesses with consumers. Social networking sites are online communities where people can meet new people, talk to current friends, and build their networks. Businesses are using social networking sites to talk to customers, create online communities, promote and sell products and services, and to learn more about consumers and competitors. Popular social networking sites include Facebook, LinkedIn, Twitter, Tumblr, Pinterest, Instagram, Flickr, Youtube, and Vine.

Facebook.

Facebook is the number two visited site in Canada and globally has over 835 million active viewers, of which more than 50 percent visit the site daily. Facebook allows companies to create profiles, distribute information such as product details or coupons, share pictures and videos, and encourage people to engage in online discussions. Most small businesses use Facebook to share information, pictures, and sales with consumers.[46]

LinkedIn.

LinkedIn has been described as Facebook for professionals. The social networking site currently has 120 million members, whose profiles appear online very much like a resumé. Members can network with one another, join specific groups, and communicate back and forth. Businesses have been using LinkedIn to recruit employees, to find out information about potential clients, and to strengthen relationships through communication.[47]

Foursquare.

This is a mobile-driven social networking site, where users check in at various locations or venues. Venues are identified using GPS enabled software in mobile devices and users can earn check-in awards or badges. The company had approximately 20 million users in 2012. Businesses have been using foursquare to encourage consumers to visit certain locations by offering discounts or coupons.[48]

Twitter/Tumblr/Online Blogs.

Blogs are websites where people can express their opinion on any issue that they see fit to post. Twitter and Tumblr are two of the most popular sites in Canada, but others exist as well. Twitter limits people to messages or tweets of 140 characters in length and is frequently in the top 10 monthly visited websites by Canadians. Tumblr, like Twitter, allows people to express opinions but does not limit what people can say. Many small businesses are using Twitter and Tumblr to post information about their business, to answer questions from consumers, and to attract people to their firm's websites.

Some businesses are also blogging, but doing so from their company webpage or using blogging software. These blogs have a tendency to be longer and offer more information than that on Twitter and Tumblr. Jim Estill, CEO of Symex Canada (www.sysmex.com) located in Ontario, says blogs allow him to stay in touch with key stakeholders.[49] Michael Jagger, president of Vancouver-based Provident Security and Event Management Corp. (www.providentsecurity.ca), dedicates a set number of hours a week to his blog and notes that it is part of the company's overall marketing strategy. Jagger thinks blogging leads to closer ties with current customers and generate new sales.[50] The advantages of blogging include low costs, ability to reach wide audiences, and to reach customers on a personal level.

Photo Sharing Sites (Pinterest, Instagram, and Flickr).

A number of photo sharing sites have emerged that allow users to post and share photos with their friends online. Companies have been using these sites to tell stories about their products, to build their brand, to interact with consumers, and to generate traffic back to their main sites. While the three most popular sites offer some similarities as discussed in Incident 8-5, they do have some functional differences and appeal to different audiences.

Video Sharing Sites (YouTube, Vine).

YouTube enables companies to share videos with millions of daily visitors. The site allows participants to load video clips onto their websites and display them for the public to see. The videos can act as mini-commercials for products or service, infomercials, attract prospective employees, or serve as a means to generate PR for a company. Entrepreneurs that want to use YouTube should ensure that their movies appeal to their target markets, are unique, run no longer than five minutes, and have a trailer with the video that provides a link to the company's website. For example, the worldwide Free Hugs campaign has relied on YouTube to promote its initiative throughout Canadian cities.

Vine is a new video sharing site that is focused on mobile devices. People use smartphones to shoot six second videos that they can share online using Twitter and Facebook. Given the time constraints of the video, businesses using Vine have to be quick and straight to the point. A big advantage of Vine is companies can create short videos to tell stories about their business or engage consumers in contests.

Other methods of using social networking for marketing include "deal of the day" coupon websites such as Team Buy and Groupon, which were discussed above, and the use of both online crowds and crowd-funding sites, which have been discussed at length in previous chapters. As previously discussed, crowd sites allow companies to seek consumer feedback from large numbers of online followers, and crowd-funding sites often allow companies to pre-sell products or services.

Mobile Marketing.

Mobile marketing is the use of mobile devices to communicate marketing messages. The most common mobile marketing methods are:

- *Apps or Application:* Companies are now creating applications, or, as they are better known, "apps," to be used on smartphones. For example, Tim Hortons has an app that allows users to find the nearest Tim Hortons location.

- *Text/SMS Messages:* Many companies use smartphones to send quick text messages to potential customers. For example, at the recent World Beach Volleyball Championship in Halifax, several sponsors used text messages to alert people about drink specials and opportunities to win prizes. As text messages are normally read within four minutes of receipt, customers are likely to receive them and respond.

- *QR Codes:* These are block bar codes that link print and other forms of media advertising to websites using a mobile device, which scans and reads the code. Some retail store owners have been posting QR codes near the entrance of their store to

PINTEREST VS. INSTAGRAM VERSUS FLICKR

Photo Sharing is quickly becoming one of the most popular forms of social media for small businesses. Entrepreneurs are now uploading pictures of their products, services, and customers to the three largest photo sharing sites on the Internet—Pinterest, Instagram, and Flickr. Given the time it takes to upload and maintain effective promotions, entrepreneurs may not have the time to successfully engage with audiences using all three platforms. So, many business owners are asking: If they can only pick one photo sharing site, which one should they use? While all three allow users to share photos, they have different uses and users.

Pinterest is the fastest growing and third largest social media website site in North America. Pinterest allows users to manage pictures and videos (named Pins) to an online bulletin board, known as a Pinboard. Themed Pinboards allow users to easily manage Pins, to share their content, and to search Pins posted by other users. Users can also Pin content they find on the Internet and easily upload it to their Pinboard. Pinboard users take great pride in creating attractive Pinboards to share. Pinterest's focus is on social networking. It refers to users as friends and lets you know when friends are logged into Twitter and Facebook. Additionally, the company allows you to follow others, comment on their Pinboard, and quickly load photos to their website. Businesses use Pinterest to tell stories about their firm, to engage in conversation with consumers, run contests, and promote their websites. Pinterest users are predominantly white, well-educated females who have higher household incomes compared with the other photo-sharing sites. Frequent Pinterest users have a tendency to spend more time on the site compared with Flickr and Instagram users. One criticism of Pinterest is in an increasing mobile world the site works best on traditional computer screens, although improvements have been made to its appearance on tablets.[54-57]

Flickr, the previous leader in online photo sharing, was traditionally aimed at professional photographers. The site enabled anyone to post up to 200 photos for free did not allow users to easily share pictures on other social media sites. Flickr had a separate account for people who wanted to post more than 200 photos a month called Flickr Pro. In May 2013, in response to losing market share, Flickr announced major changes to its website. Users can now store up to 600,000 photos for free, making Flickr Pro obsolete and resulting in the elimination of the service. Flickr is also embracing social media and allowing users to share pictures on Facebook, Twitter, and Pinterest. Businesses can use Flickr much like Pinterest, but the users, with number in the millions, are dwindling compared with Pinterest and Instagram. Furthermore, the recent changes to the site have upset long-time photographers, who do not like the changes to the site. Charlotte Henry, an online journalist says, Pinterest has clearly won the battle for online photo sharing when compared with Flickr, "In terms of advertising and building an online presence, the choice is simple. The ability to categorize images, the deep social interaction, not to mention the attractive interface, make Pinterest the clear winner. You can really build a brand image on Pinterest and display your products. Flickr remains important to photographers but has been overtaken by Pinterest by almost every other kind of user." Users of Flickr, much like Pinterest, are predominantly women between the ages of 18–39, with very few users under the age of 18.[58,59]

Instagram, which has 100 million monthly users, allows people to post photos onto their site using their smartphones as the primary camera and to share the photos using other social networking sites. Instagram, unlike Pinterest, is aimed at mobile devices, as users can quickly share, view, and upload pictures. Much like the other three sites, companies are using Instagram to host contests, tell stories about their brand, and to connect with consumers. Instagram is especially popular among people under the age of 24 and has very little users older than 35. Instagram users also tend to be more diverse, and have less education and income compared with Pinterest followers. Advocates of Instagram state that much of this has to do with the demographic profile; since Pinterest users have a tendency to be older than Instagram followers, it makes sense they are better educated and have higher income levels.[60]

Discussion Questions

1. What are the advantages and disadvantages of using photo sharing sites to promote your company?

2. Based on the following business descriptions, which photo sharing site would you choose, and why:

   a. Downtown nightclub that is trying to appeal to a broader audience between the ages of 25–35.

   b. A daycare hoping to increase its clientele.

   c. A large community event in the downtown core.

3. Flickr is attempting to re-invent itself as a social networking company. Given the changes they are making do you think they will be successful? Why, or why not?

attract people in by offering coupons, information on popular products, and pictures or videos.

- *Proximity/Location-Based Marketing:* Software can now allow companies to send out real-time advertising and communication to potential customers when they are in close proximity to a business. For example, a restaurant located on St. Catherine Street in Montreal can send out ads, menus, and/or coupons to potential customers walking in the area, via their mobile device. Twitter has recently announced that it will be able to support location-based advertisements or tweets.

LEARNING OBJECTIVES SUMMARY

LO1 The marketing strategy will differ for each type. The major decision areas in distribution include being aware of the channel options, deciding on the length of the channel, and determining the channel intensity.

LO2 Product development involves idea generation, product testing, and ultimately, if successful, commercialization.

LO3 The three methods of setting price are cost-based, demand-based, and competition-based pricing.

LO4 There are a variety of methods of providing information about a product or service: advertising, sales promotion, personal selling, public relations, Internet marketing, and so forth.

Businesses are becoming increasingly reliant on the Internet and social networking sites to promote their business.

LO5 Within a marketing plan, businesses usually have a promotional plan that includes goals, strategies, and controls. Today, businesses are using a mix of traditional media, public relations, and Internet marketing, including social networks, to sell their products or services.

LO6 The major points of difference among promotional tools are cost, impact, and level of consumer engagement.

LO7 Consumer marketing involves less detail and a shorter buying cycle compared with business marketing.

1. What elements make up the marketing mix? What is the purpose of the marketing mix in a marketing plan?
2. Where is Kellogg's Corn Flakes in the product life cycle? What has Kellogg done to prolong the life cycle of this product?
3. Why is appealing to early adopters important to a firm?
4. What methods of pricing do small firms normally use? What are some of the problems with pricing products using these methods?
5. Do you think there is a difference between guerrilla marketing and public relations? Why, or why not?
6. What are the advantages of using the Internet and social networking sites as a company's major form of advertising?

APPLICATION QUESTIONS AND HANDS-ON ACTIVITIES

1. Develop a marketing mix (i.e., product, promotion, price, distribution) for a bakery.
2. Form small groups and develop public relations and guerrilla marketing activities for your college or university. Select the best five ideas, and present them to the class.
3. Which pricing system would you use for the following products? Why?
   a. Campbell's soup
   b. Toronto Blue Jays season tickets
   c. Patio furniture
   d. Automobiles
4. If the cost of merchandise is $100 and it is sold for $150, what is the markup on cost? On selling price?
5. You have been approached to develop an advertising campaign for a new local discount golf franchise. The owners realize they need to develop awareness among consumers but have a very limited amount of funds available for advertising. Which media type would you use for the advertising campaign? Justify your decision to use or not use each media type.
6. Interview a local small business owner, and find out what his or her marketing strategy is. Determine the promotional strategy. Are these strategies similar to those discussed in the chapter?

For more information on the resources available from McGraw-Hill Ryerson, go to www.mcgrawhill.ca/he/solutions.

CHAPTER

9

FINANCIAL MANAGEMENT

LEARNING OBJECTIVES

By the end of this chapter, you should be able to:

LO1   Review the fundamentals of small business accounting.

LO2   Discuss the various types of accounting systems a small business can use.

LO3   Describe the considerations in purchasing a computer for the small business.

LO4   Illustrate how to evaluate the financial operations of the small business.

LO5   Explain the important aspects of credit management for the small business.

SMALL BUSINESS PROFILE

CHRIS NEVILLE *Entrepreneur Finds Accounting and Controlling Costs Are Keys to Success*

Photo courtesy of Chris Neville

Chris Neville of Sydney, Nova Scotia, was always interested in entrepreneurship and owning his own business as long as he could remember. Neville states his dream was to be an entrepreneur, to be able to set his own destiny, and to have unlimited earning potential as long as he could remember. So it was no surprise to his friends when Neville started his first business, a hockey identification camp for aspiring players when he was only 20 years old. The camp was highly successful, and Neville quickly jumped into another business manufacturing and selling calendars to university students. With two successful ventures under his belt, and still a university student at the University of New Brunswick, where he eventually earned his Masters of Business Administration degree, Neville began looking for larger ideas. He soon discovered online gaming and successfully started www.lifeofsports.com, an online gaming site specializing in poker tournaments aimed at University students, which he grew to over 100 employees in six different countries. Neville went on to sell the company to www.Gr88.com in 2010 when he felt the timing was optimal to maximize his value in the business.

Now with some time on his hands, Neville decided to venture into real estate and started KayJim Developments, a company he named after his parents in 2010. The company flourished, and he quickly acquired 139 units, mostly in his home town of Sydney, Nova Scotia. Neville states he was always fascinated with real estate and felt it was great way to grow his investment. One initial problem was he quickly grew his company but was not 110% prepared for the financial management involved with being a large landlord. Neville says, "We went from a few buildings to over 100 rather quickly, and managing rental units is different than other businesses in so many ways. For one, people want to pay using a variety of methods, and in some buildings we bought, rent was collected in cash, late collections were the norm, and the book keeping systems were often scribblers or loose paper." Undaunted, Neville very quickly developed formal rules for collecting rent, standardized the accounting systems from previous building owners, and started working with a professional accountant. Neville also notes that with so many rental units, controlling costs was vital to maximizing revenue. He states saving money on home heating oil, snow removal, and garbage collection are often overlooked by other growing property developers, and by spending time with his accountant and by negotiating hard with vendors, he managed to save thousands. Neville soon expanded into other businesses, including Vision Landscaping and Vision Snow Removal, and he recently purchased two Spas. Neville notes a big key to his long term success is his belief in strong financial management practices and working closely with his accountants to control costs. "As I expand into other areas, I always look to my costs and setting up strong financial management practices. By working with my accountants I can ensure systems are in place and my businesses all run well."

THE NEED FOR FINANCIAL RECORDS

Financial management skills are important for a small business. However, as Incident 9-1 shows, these skills are frequently lacking. One survey found that from 24 percent to 45 percent of Canadian small business owners did not understand basic financial measurement ratios used in evaluating their businesses.[1] Failure to understand and manage the financial aspects of a business can be disastrous for the small business owner. The need for competence in this area is continually growing as new technology and greater competition in many markets require closer monitoring of operations and quicker decision making. Keeping proper records can warn the owner-manager in advance of future financial difficulties and help plan the growth of the business.

Another reason for proper record keeping is to satisfy government requirements. Although most owner-managers do not revere the Canada Revenue Agency (CRA), the fact that this agency requires accurate record keeping to calculate a business's tax liability may actually benefit the small business.

Record keeping is also necessary if a business must borrow money. Lenders will require that proper record keeping be followed to ensure that debt obligations are met. The availability of accurate and current records of the operations of the business is also essential for the evaluation and control of business operations. Figure 9-1 illustrates the various uses of accounting information.

Small business owners may be tempted to neglect the financial aspects of the business in favour of the day-to-day operational aspects such as production, personnel management, and marketing. Often this is because they have an incomplete understanding of how to manage the record-keeping system effectively. Understanding the managerial aspects of record keeping requires reviewing some basic accounting fundamentals.

THE ACCOUNTING CYCLE   LO1

Figure 9-2 illustrates the basic process by which transactions of the business are translated into financial statements.

RECORDING TRANSACTIONS

Transactions are recorded chronologically (as they occur) in a record called a *journal*. Many types of journals are used. In a business in which few transactions occur, these entries may be

---

INCIDENT 9-1

MANAGING CASH FLOW

Pieter Spinder is president of Calgary-based Carmen Creek Gourmet Meats (www.carmencreek.com). This company processes bison meat throughout Canada and the United States. A large part of the success of the business (Carmen Creek was ranked the second-fastest growing company in Canada by *Profit Magazine* in 2009) is Pieter's thorough and detailed working with the financial numbers. He updates his Excel workbook several times a day and sends cash-flow updates to staff every two or three days. He also distributes weekly margin reports so that the firm can quickly trim spending if rising costs eat into margins. Being on top of the numbers provides Carmen Creek with the flexibility to make cost saving changes and move quickly to take advantage of new market opportunities. It has also improved relations with the company's banker. Because Spinder is such a meticulous bookkeeper, the bank was convinced to increase the company's line of credit to cover extra expenses that arise from time to time.

Source: Adapted from Annette Bourdeau, "Cash Flow," *Profit*, June 2009, p. 23.

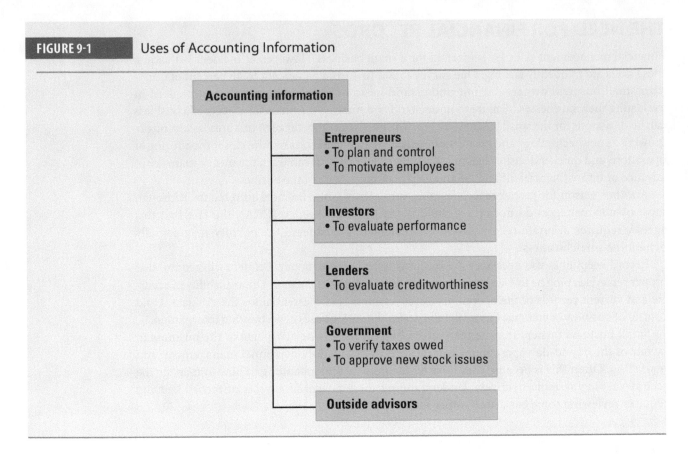

FIGURE 9-1   Uses of Accounting Information

Accounting information

Entrepreneurs
- To plan and control
- To motivate employees

Investors
- To evaluate performance

Lenders
- To evaluate creditworthiness

Government
- To verify taxes owed
- To approve new stock issues

Outside advisors

made manually. In many retail businesses, the daily cash register tape total may be used to record the revenue journal entries. The cheque register can be used to record payments or disbursements. In businesses with a large number of transactions, the journal may be kept mechanically by a bookkeeping machine or by a computer.

Accounting uses double-entry recording. This means the amounts of each transaction are recorded twice. This procedure accurately reflects the fact that each transaction affects two parts (accounts) of the business. Often a decrease in one means an increase in another. For example, if a desk costing $400 is purchased and paid for in cash, the amount of cash in the business decreases by $400 and the value of the office furniture in the business increases by $400. The use of double-entry accounting also allows for double-checking of the accuracy of the entries.

Figure 9-3 illustrates how some typical recording entries might appear in a small business journal. In each of these transactions, for every increase in one account, a corresponding decrease occurs in another account. At the end of the period, the totals of increases and decreases at the bottom of the page for a number of transactions should be equal.

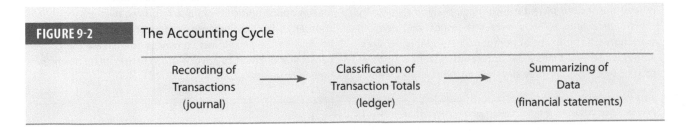

FIGURE 9-2   The Accounting Cycle

Recording of Transactions (journal) → Classification of Transaction Totals (ledger) → Summarizing of Data (financial statements)

FIGURE 9-3

Typical Journal Entries

		DR.	CR.
Jan. 1, 2014	Cash...	2,000	
	Accounts receivable		2,000
	Received from Bill Smith on account.		
Jan. 5, 2014	Equipment	4,500	
	Cash		4,500
	Purchased equipment for cash.		
Jan. 20, 2014	Inventory...	2,000	
	Accounts payable....................................		2,000
	Inventory is purchased on account.		
Jan. 31, 2014	Accounts payable..	500	
	Cash		500
	Liabilities of $500 are paid with cash.		
Jan. 31, 2014	Cash..	8,000	
	Sales revenue		8,000
	Sales of $8,000 are made during the month.		

CLASSIFYING TRANSACTION TOTALS

Once the transactions have been accurately and properly recorded, the next step is to group or classify similar transactions together. These groupings or classifications are called *accounts* and are entered into a book called a *ledger*. The ledger keeps a running balance of the dollar amounts in each account so that the net totals may be known at the end of each period. Like journal entries, a ledger may be kept manually or by computer. Figure 9-4 shows some accounts of a typical ledger for service, retail, and manufacturing firms. The recording and classifying steps of the accounting cycle are usually referred to as *bookkeeping*. Many small businesses have found it valuable to hire an accountant to set up the bookkeeping system most appropriate for their businesses.

SUMMARIZING DATA

The third step in the accounting cycle (which is usually carried out by an accountant) involves taking the account totals from the ledger and putting them together to form the financial statements. These statements indicate the past success and current position of the business. It is important that the small business owner understand what financial statements mean and how to use them.

Essentially three financial statements are important to the small business owner: the balance sheet, the income statement, and the cash flow statement.

Balance Sheet (Statement of Financial Position).

The balance sheet presents, in summary form, a snapshot of what the business owns and owes at any point in time. Those items the business owns

MANY SMALL BUSINESSES EMPLOY PROFESSIONAL ACCOUNTANTS TO PUT TOGETHER THEIR FINANCIAL STATEMENTS.
© Rob Daly / age fotostock

FIGURE 9-4 Typical Ledger Account Titles Used for Some Types of Businesses

SERVICE FIRM	FOR A RETAIL FIRM ADD THESE ACCOUNTS	FOR A MANUFACTURING FIRM ADD THESE ACCOUNTS
Sales	Sales returns and allowances	Machinery
Cash	Sales discounts	Accumulated depreciation: Machinery
Accounts receivable	Furniture and fixtures	
Accounts payable		
Land	Accumulated depreciation: Furniture and fixtures	Cost of goods sold: Raw materials Direct labour Factory overhead
Building		
Accumulated depreciation: Building	Merchandise inventory	
Office equipment		
Accumulated depreciation: Office equipment Office supplies inventory Retained earnings Salaries expense Telephone expense Advertising expense Office supplies expense	Cost of goods sold: Purchases Purchase returns Purchase discounts Transportation in	
Depreciation expense: Building		
Depreciation expense: Equipment		
Miscellaneous expense		
Salaries payable		
Utilities expense		
Licences and taxes expense		
Insurance expense		
Accounting and legal expense		

are termed assets, and those owed are either liabilities (owed to sources outside the business) or equity (owed to owners). Figure 9-5 illustrates a balance sheet for a hypothetical small business. Assets and liabilities are generally listed in order of liquidity, with the most liquid being first. Usually, assets and liabilities are divided into current (to be consumed in one year) and non-current (in more than one year).

Income Statement (Statement of Profit and Loss).

The income statement shows the results of the operations of the business for a given period. This statement, introduced in Chapter 3, is an integral part of the feasibility analysis and the business plan. The profit or income is determined by taking revenue from operations and

FIGURE 9-5   Balance Sheet

SMALL BUSINESS CORPORATION
BALANCE SHEET
AS OF DECEMBER 31, 2014

Assets

Current assets:

Cash	$ 3,449	
Accounts receivable	5,944	
Inventories	12,869	
Prepaid expenses	$ 389	
Total current assets		$22,651

Fixed assets:

Land, buildings, and equipment cost	26,926	
Less accumulated depreciation	$13,534	
Total fixed assets		$13,392

Other assets:

Investments	$ 1,000	
Total other assets		$ 1,000
Total assets		$37,043

Liabilities and Shareholders' Equity

Current liabilities:

Accounts payable	$ 6,602	
Other current liabilities	$ 825	
Total current liabilities		$ 7,427

Other liabilities:

Mortgage payable	3,000	
Total liabilities		10,427

Shareholders' equity:

Common stock	15,000	
Retained earnings	11,616	
Total shareholders' equity		26,616
Total liabilities and shareholders' equity		$37,043

subtracting expenses incurred in earning that revenue. Figure 9-6 illustrates an income statement for a hypothetical small business.

Cash Flow Statement or Statement of Changes in Financial Position.

The importance and format of the cash flow statement was discussed in Chapter 6. This statement is similar to the income statement except that only cash inflows and outflows are shown.

In recent years, it has been common to examine not only the cash flow position of a firm but also all the asset and liability accounts over time. This practice has led to the popularity of a statement called "the statement of changes in financial position." As the name implies, this

FIGURE 9-6 Income Statement

SMALL BUSINESS CORPORATION
INCOME STATEMENT
FOR THE YEAR ENDED DECEMBER 31, 2014

Net sales..	$197,000	
Cost of goods sold..................................	123,000	
Gross margin on sales..............................	74,000	
Operating expenses		
Selling expenses		
Advertising expense	1,200	
Sales salaries expense.........................	18,300	
Depreciation expense—store equipment.......	2,000	
Total selling expenses.......................	21,500	
General expenses		
Depreciation expense—building	3,000	
Insurance expense	675	
Miscellaneous general expenses..............	425	
General salaries expense	7,200	
Total general expenses......................	11,300	
Total operating expenses	32,800	
Net operating margin..............................	41,200	
Other expenses		
Interest expense..................................	2,750	
Net income before income taxes	38,450	
Income taxes	14,350	
Net income...	$ 24,100	

statement presents balance sheet account changes from one period to the next. It can help explain why a business has a positive net income but a decrease in cash for the same period of operation, a situation that mystifies some small business owners. The examination of the statement of changes in financial position can be complex. An example of a cash flow statement for a hypothetical small business appears in Figure 9-7.

ACCOUNTING SYSTEMS FOR THE SMALL BUSINESS   LO2

Small businesses use several types of accounting systems. Variations occur because of differences in company size, type of business (retail, service, manufacturing), industry, number of transactions, and expertise of the owner. The following is a brief description of some of the more common general systems used.

MANUAL SYSTEMS

Although few businesses use manual accounting systems today, some very small enterprises may find them useful, particularly at start-up. A recent survey found that nearly one million

FIGURE 9-7 Cash Flow Statement

SMALL BUSINESS CORPORATION
CASH FLOW FORECAST 2014

	JAN.	FEB.	MAR.	APR.	MAY	JUNE
Cash receipts:						
Sales in 2008.........................	—	$25,000	$ 7,500	$10,000	$10,000	$ 10,000
Accounts receivable for 2007	$19,000	13,000	6,000			
Other:						
Equity funding......................		10,000				
Total cash receipts.....................	$19,000	$28,000	$ 13,500	$10,000	$10,000	$ 10,000
Cash disbursements:						
Cost of sales						
Labour	$ 5,000	$ 5,000	$ 5,000	$ 7,000	$ 7,000	$ 7,000
Materials	400	800	800	1,000	1,100	1,100
Transport..........................	300	400	400	500	400	400
Accounts payable from 2007...........	12,000	10,000	10,000	6,000		
Selling expense	400	800	800	800	800	800
Administration	250	550	550	550	550	550
Fixed-asset investment						
Long-term repayment			2,500			2,500
Income tax installment			3,000			3,000
Interest on debt						
Long-term debt.....................			680			640
Bank loan (other cash source)........	$ 400	$ 350	$ 270	$ 370	$ 430	$ 440
Total cash disbursements	$18,750	$17,900	$ 24,000	$16,220	$10,280	$ 16,430
Monthly cash surplus (deficit)........	$ 250	$10,100	$–10,500	$–6,220	$ –280	$–6,430
Accumulated cash surplus						
(deficit) for 2008	250	10,350	−150	−6,370	−6,650	−13,080

Canadian small businesses still do their accounting manually.[2] Examples of such systems are the One Book, One Write, and Multi Journal systems. The basic accounting steps of journal and ledger entries are made in these systems. An example of a simple one-book system is shown in Figure 9-8.

OUTSOURCING FINANCIAL ACTIVITIES

A business can outsource financial activities such as cash receipts and disbursements, payroll, accounts payable, bank reconciliations, general ledger maintenance, budgeting, preparing interim financial statements, and information technology activities. Some small businesses have found that this option can be quicker, easier, and less costly and does not require financial expertise.

Another outsourcing option for many small businesses that cannot afford their own computerized accounting system is to use a computer service bureau. Most of these services are

FIGURE 9-8   Illustration of a One-Book Accounting System

1	2	3	4	5	6	7	8	9	10
			BANK		REVENUE		EXPENSES		
		CHEQUE			SALES/		WAGES/ADVERTISING/		
DATE	DESCRIPTION	NUMBER	IN	OUT	MISCELLANEOUS		OTHER		
Sept. 1/14	Wages paid for August	25		5,000			5,000		
Sept. 8/14	Sales for week 1		8,000		8,000				
Sept. 12/14	Paid utility bill	26		800					800
Sept. 15/14	Sales for week 2		6,500		6,500				
Sept. 19/14	Paid advertising bill	27		400				400	

offered by accounting firms. For a monthly fee, a small business can take its journal or ledger totals to this type of bureau and within a few days receive detailed financial statements for the period (usually monthly). Much of the bookkeeping will still need to be carried out by the business, but a good portion of steps 2 and 3 of the accounting cycle can be provided by the service bureau. The big advantage is that the details contained in the reports can be valuable in operating the business.

SMALL BUSINESS COMPUTER SYSTEMS   LO3

A valuable use of technology is in the management of the financial aspects of the business. Many software programs have been developed specifically for small businesses. This software may maintain bookkeeping and accounting of transactions, maintain a database of inventories, assist in making capital investments, and allow financial performance evaluation.

These applications allow for increased speed and accuracy of maintaining records, improved service to customers, improved and more timely information to managers, and reduced operating costs. Note that the selection of software is the most important aspect of the computer decision. Software that will carry out the operations the small business requires should be

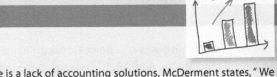

INCIDENT 9-2

FRESHBOOKS (WWW.FRESHBOOKS.COM)

FreshBooks is the Toronto-based world leader in cloud-based accounting systems. The company, which was founded by Mike McDerment in 2003, has transformed itself to offer accounting and billing solutions for small companies via the cloud. The "cloud" essentially means firms can access information from "any" and "every" where they want to. By being in the cloud, FreshBooks also had an easier time expanding globally, as they did not have to fight for shelf space or look for distributors.

While FreshBooks was originally aimed at small IT firms, it now specializes in service-based firms, where McDerment says

there is a lack of accounting solutions. McDerment states, " We are particularly focused on service-based businesses, where people—including butlers, bakers, and dog walkers—are paid for their time and expertise, and whose needs are not particularly well-met by generalized accounting software." FreshBooks allows for people to maintain easy and accurate billing records, accept various forms of payment, and create financial statements.

FreshBooks continues to grow, with five million users in 120 countries and $8 billion in annual invoices.

Source: Becky Reuber, "From His Parents' Basement, Entrepreneur Builds Accounting Powerhouse," www.theglobeandmail.com/report-on-business/small-business/sb-digital/biz-categories-technology/from-his-parents-basement-entrepreneur-builds-accounting-powerhouse/article6230133/, accessed July 15, 2013.

INBOX MARKETER'S SIX-MILLION-DOLLAR DISEASE

Randall Litchfield, co-founder of Toronto-based Inbox Marketer (www.inboxmarketer.com), says his growing firm was recently infected with a disease he calls $3 millionitis. No sooner did he think his firm was cured than $6 millionitis occurred. The cause of Inbox's disease was quickly growing sales to $3 million and then $6 million and his realization that his company's accounting and financial processes were not equipped to deal with sales of this size. Litchfield says while the sales numbers may differ from firm to firm and industry to industry, eventually all growing companies have to take control of their financial and accounting systems to ensure their growth is well managed. He says at his firm, the lack of systems and procedures negatively impacted administrative staffing, budgeting, and calculating of ratios, cash flow, and made his firm more vulnerable to fraud.

Rather than let his firm stay sick . . . from an accounting and financial perspective, Litchfield opted to deal with the problem. He had an accountant audit his financial systems and make recommendations. Now moving forward, Inbox Marketer has an accrual-based accounting system that will allow for quarterly comparisons. They are preparing budgets and forecasts and are striving to have a strategic plan, including financials for the next three to five years. Litchfield says the changes have left management with a much better sense of control of the company's finances and future.

Discussion Questions

1. Why is it important to have an accrual-based system?

2. Up to this point Litchfield was using a cash-based accounting system. What are some of the advantages and disadvantages of a cash-based system?

3. What are the advantages and disadvantages of more formal accounting systems?

4. Given that Litchfield has grown his business to $6 million in sales without spending much time on financial and accounting systems, do you think the company's corporate culture will easily adapt to more formal controls and planning? Why, or why not?

Source: Randall Litchfield, "Accounting That Kills," www.profitguide.com/manage-grow/financing/accounting-that-kills-30171?print, accessed July 1, 2013.

selected first, followed by the hardware on which the software will run. This ensures that the hardware is powerful enough to handle the demands the software places on the computer. Some of the more popular small business software accounting programs for small businesses are Quickbooks, Simply Accounting, Peachtree Systems, Sage Accounting, and Microsoft Office. A new trend in accounting systems is Internet-housed software solutions such as Canadian market leader FreshBooks. Businesses, especially service businesses find FreshBooks appealing as they can access key information regardless of where they are located.

MANAGEMENT OF FINANCIAL INFORMATION FOR PLANNING

The first part of this chapter dealt with the fundamental aspects of collecting and maintaining the financial information within the business. This information is of minimal value, however, unless it is used to monitor, evaluate, and control current operations, as well as plan for the future.

SHORT-TERM FINANCIAL PLANNING

Short-term financial planning consists of preparing an estimated future financial result of operations of the business. Such pro forma (projected) financial statements serve as a blueprint for planning operations. The projected income statement is generally referred to as a budget and was described in Chapter 3 in the preparation of the feasibility analysis. Although budgets can provide many benefits to an organization, relatively few small businesses prepare or work with budgets. A budget, however, can be a very valuable financial tool for the following reasons.

Clarification of Objectives.

A budget forces an organization to anticipate future operations and set goals and procedures to accomplish them.

Coordination.

The budgeting process draws employees and departments together and brings them into the planning process to input into the budget information relevant to their responsibilities.

Evaluation and Control.

A budget allows the owner-manager to quickly determine discrepancies that may require investigation. Such an investigation is often called *variance analysis*. It also allows comparison of planned (budgeted) amounts with actual results, which can improve effectiveness in the long term. Figure 9-9 shows how to establish and use a budget. After the comparison of budgeted (planned) and actual results, attempts can be made to explain the reasons for any differences. Consequently, changes might be made to correct the differences or refine the budgeting process.

LONG-TERM FINANCIAL PLANNING

Three types of long-term financial planning decisions could affect the small business—decisions regarding capital investment, capacity, and expansion.

INCIDENT 9-4

LEAN MANAGEMENT YIELDS SUCCESS

Anne Arcade, president and COO of Sequel Lifestyle Hotels and Resorts (www.sequelhotels.com), has found that running a lean company by paying attention to financial information has allowed the company to offer lower prices and be successful in a very competitive industry. One key aspect of this policy is to have no office space by having all managers and back-office staff work from home. That yields savings of close to $100,000 per year. It also increases employee creativity and productivity. Sequel has also embraced technology to run leaner. Understanding the financial aspects of business, Arcade has found, has been a key to profitable operations as well. Sequel teaches all 250 staff to read financial statements so they better grasp cost management. Call centres are not used, unlike competitors, and this also results in significant savings. Lean overheads allow Sequel to charge 30 percent lower property-management fees than its competitors. This advantage helps the firm increase revenues and profits each year, much higher than the industry average.

SEQUEL LIFESTYLE HOTELS AND RESORTS HAS MANAGED TO KEEP PRICES DOWN BY CONTROLLING COSTS.
Photo courtesy of Sequel Hotels and Resorts

Source: Adapted from Chris Atchison, "Running as Lean as a Greyhound," *Profit*, May 2009, p. 23.

FIGURE 9-9 Use of a Budget

SMALL BUSINESS CORPORATION
INCOME STATEMENT
FOR THE YEAR ENDED DECEMBER 31, 2014

	BUDGETED	ACTUAL	DIFFERENCE	EXPLANATION
Net sales	$197,000	$180,000	$17,000	Sales targets not reached
Cost of goods sold	123,000	120,000	3,000	Material costs increase
Gross margin on sales	74,000	60,000	14,000	
Operating expenses				
Selling expenses				
Advertising expense	1,200	1,200	0	
Sales salaries expense	18,300	18,300	0	
Total selling expense	19,500	19,500	0	
General expenses				
Depreciation expense—store equipment	2,000	4,000	2,000	Additional equipment purchased
Depreciation expense—building	3,000	3,000	0	
Insurance expense	675	1,200	525	Premium increase
General salaries expense	7,200	7,200	0	
Miscellaneous general expenses	425	600	175	
Total general expenses	13,300	16,000	2,700	
Total operating expenses	32,800	35,500	2,700	
Net operating margin	41,200	24,500	16,700	
Other expenses				
Interest expense	2,750	3,200	450	Rate increase
Net income before income taxes	38,450	21,300	17,150	
Income taxes	14,450	7,455	6,995	Marginal rate decrease
Net income	$ 24,000	$ 13,845	$10,155	

The Capital Investment Decision.

Most long-term planning includes the question of future capital purchases. This may involve the acquisition of land, buildings, equipment, or even another business. The small business owner needs to have a simple but accurate way to determine whether the decision will be financially sound. Some of the more commonly used methods of estimating future return for capital investments are discussed below.

Rate-of-Return Method.

This method estimates the annual rate of return of the new investment. After this value has been determined, it can be compared with alternative investments. Figure 9-10 shows how a rate of return for a capital asset is determined.

FIGURE 9-10

Rate-of-Return Method

STEPS	EXAMPLE
1. Calculate total cost of investment.	$50,000
2. Estimate depreciable life of investment.	5 years
3. Calculate average value of investment over life. Beginning value ($50,000) plus end value (0) divided by 2 equals average value.	$\dfrac{\$50,000}{2} = \$25,000$
4. Estimate average annual profit over depreciable life (net of depreciation).	$10,000
5. Average profit divided by average investment.	$\dfrac{\$10,000}{\$25,000} = 40\%$

A reasonable rate of return on a capital investment is between two and three times the prime rate of interest. Using this criterion, the 40 percent rate of return in this example represents an attractive investment.

Present Value Method.

This method employs the time value of money in looking at future cash inflows and outflows. Future inflows and outflows of cash are discounted because cash held today is worth more than cash received or paid in the future. Present value rates are collected from present value tables, which most accounting and finance texts provide. The rate required to equalize discounted outflows (for the purchase of the assets) and discounted inflows (income from the assets) represents the discounted rate of return of the asset.

Payback Method.

This method, which is similar to the rate-of-return method, estimates the number of years required for the capital investment to pay for itself. Figure 9-11 illustrates how the payback method is used.

FIGURE 9-11

Payback Method

STEPS	EXAMPLE
1. Calculate total cost of investment.	$50,000
2. Estimate depreciable life of investment.	5 years
3. Calculate annual depreciation charge.	$10,000
4. Estimate average annual profit over depreciable life.	$10,000
5. Cost of investment divided by cash inflow (profit + depreciation)	$\dfrac{\$50,000}{\$10,000 + \$10,000} = 2.5 \text{ years}$

The payback period for the capital investment would be 2.5 years. As this is considerably less than the depreciable life of the asset, it appears to be an attractive investment.

The Capacity Decision.

Another important financial planning decision for the small business, especially the small manufacturer, is the size and extent of operations. Financial management techniques related to capacity help answer such questions as how many units should be produced and how large the plant should be. A useful technique for answering these questions is break-even analysis.

The *break-even point* is the point at which the level of output (in units or dollars) is equal to fixed and variable costs. By applying break-even analysis, the small business owner can determine the minimum level of operations required to financially break even. The use of break-even analysis could form an important part of the feasibility analysis discussed in Chapter 3. The formula for break-even analysis is shown below:

$$\text{BEP} = \frac{\text{Fixed costs}}{\text{Profit per unit}} = \text{BEP in units}$$

or

$$\text{BEP} = \frac{\text{Fixed costs}}{\text{Profit as percent of sales}} = \text{BEP in dollars}$$

where

Fixed costs = Costs that will not vary as production increases (e.g., costs of plant, equipment, and some overhead expenses)

Profit per unit = Selling price − Variable costs

The resulting graph (Figure 9-12) illustrates at what price and output the break-even point occurs given fixed and variable costs.

The Expansion Decision.

Break-even analysis can also be used to help the owner-manager decide whether to expand the scope of operations. The same formulas can be used but only on an incremental basis, as follows.

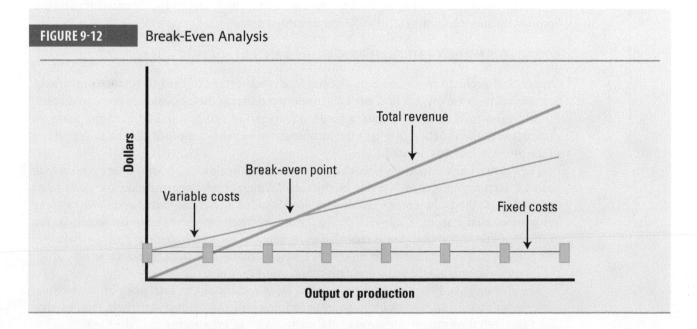

FIGURE 9-12 Break-Even Analysis

The Effect of Fixed-Cost Adjustments

$$BEP = \frac{\text{Additional fixed costs}}{\text{Profit per unit}} = \text{Additional unit volume needed to cover additional fixed costs}$$

$$BEP = \frac{\text{Additional fixed costs}}{\text{Profit as percent of sales}} = \text{Additional sales volume needed to cover additional fixed costs}$$

The Effect of Variable-Cost Adjustments

Another use of incremental break-even analysis is to measure the effects of changes in the components of the formula such as variable costs. The following example illustrates this calculation:

$$BEP = \frac{\text{Fixed costs}}{\text{New profit/unit}} - \frac{\text{Fixed costs}}{\text{Old profit/unit}}$$

= Additional unit volume needed to cover additional variable cost

$$BEP = \frac{\text{Fixed costs}}{\text{New profit as percent of sales}} - \frac{\text{Fixed costs}}{\text{Old profit as percent of sales}}$$

= Additional sales volume (in dollars) needed to cover additional variable costs

EVALUATION OF FINANCIAL PERFORMANCE LO4

Quantitative evaluation of the performance of the business is an essential management task. Because they lack a financial background, many small business owners rely on their accountants to look after the complete financial end of the business. An accountant may be essential for preparing year-end financial statements, but few small businesses can afford ongoing financial management advice from this source. The small business owner is well advised to acquire a basic working knowledge of some key financial evaluation components of the business. This can enable the owner to monitor and control operations throughout the year, not just at year-end.

Several measures also can be used to evaluate the results found in the financial statements. Some of the more common techniques are described next.

MANAGEMENT OF CURRENT FINANCIAL POSITION

One critical problem many small businesses face is a shortage of cash to finance operations. Some small business owners find it hard to understand that as their businesses become successful and grow, this tends to create a strain on operating funds. Equally hard for many to understand is the situation in which the income statement shows a profit but the cash position of the business has deteriorated.

The reason these situations occur is that most small businesses do not operate on a cash basis of accounting. (Some service businesses, farmers, and fishermen do use cash basis accounting methods, however.) The system used is called an *accrual-based accounting system*. With an accrual system, a transaction need not involve a cash transfer to be recorded. For example, a sale of merchandise is recorded as revenue for income statement purposes whether it is paid for in cash or purchased on credit. Likewise, many non-cash transactions may affect the income statement, whereas some cash transactions may not.

The above discussion illustrates the need to closely monitor the cash position of the business. As indicated, this is difficult to do by examining only the income statement. The balance sheet and cash flow statements are essential components of monitoring cash position.

LEGENDARY STORY—TED ROGERS, FOUNDER OF ROGERS COMMUNICATION AND CASH FLOW MANAGEMENT

The story goes something like this: "During Ted Rogers' early years of business, his company often lacked the cash to pay creditors. Rather than pick and choose who would be paid,

TED ROGERS, FOUNDER OF ROGERS COMMUNICATIONS, WOULD USE A VARIETY OF METHODS TO PAY HIS ACCOUNTS PAYABLE.
Toronto Star / GetStock.com

he would put all of their invoices into a hat and draw them out one at a time until the money was gone. The following week he would repeat the process. When one supplier heard about this selection method, he would call hollering and yelling, urging the company's owner to pay him and abandon the "invoice hat." Ted Rogers' reply was straight, to the point, and quieted down his angry creditor, "If you keep yelling at me, I won't put your company's invoices in the hat next week." While the story has been told time and time again, it does give you some insight into how even the most successful entrepreneurs had to stretch out accounts payable during the early and lean days of doing business. Of course, this was very early in Rogers' career, as he eventually would start Rogers Communications, one of Canada's most successful companies, a company he remained involved with until the time of his death in 2008.

Source: Created by author.

If the cash position of the business needs to be improved, an effective way to do so is to reduce the length of time from payment for inventory to receipt of payment for the inventory once it is sold. This cycle has three essential components:

1. Time taken to pay accounts payable
2. Time taken to sell inventory
3. Time taken to receive payment for inventory

Figure 9-13 illustrates how to use these components in reducing this cycle for a hypothetical business. Additional information about estimating cash requirements for an increase in sales is provided later in the text.

EVALUATION OF FINANCIAL STATEMENTS

Once the financial statements have been prepared, several relationships between various account totals can assist in evaluating the operations of the business. This evaluation of relationships is called *ratio analysis*. It can be used to compare the financial performance of the business with those of other similar businesses or with previous results for the same business.

Reports of financial ratios for other businesses are prepared by industry associations and Statistics Canada and can be found on the Statistics Canada, Strategis, and GDSourcing websites. These reports are collected from many businesses across the country; thus, when using them, it is important to use comparable businesses from the same industry.

Financial ratios can also help in isolating and analyzing weaknesses within the business. Four categories of ratios are commonly used in evaluating a small business. Each is discussed next with a general statement regarding whether the ratio is acceptable. The ratios of certain

FIGURE 9-13   Financial Management

SMALL BUSINESS CO. LTD.
BALANCE SHEET
AT DEC. 31, 20—

ASSETS		LIABILITIES	
Accounts receivable	$100,000	Accounts payable............................	$ 40,000
Inventory	50,000	Bank loans..................................	100,000
Fixed assets	$140,000	Shareholders' equity.........................	$150,000
		Total liabilities and shareholders'	
Total assets	$290,000	equity	$290,000

SMALL BUSINESS CO. LTD.
INCOME STATEMENT
FOR YEAR ENDED DEC. 31, 20—

Sales...	$750,000
Cost of goods sold...	500,000
Gross profit..	250,000
Expenses...	200,000
Net profit..	$ 50,000

1. Time taken to pay accounts

$$= \frac{\text{Accounts payable}}{\text{Cost of goods sold}} \times 365 \text{ days}$$

$$= \frac{\$40,000}{\$500,000} \times 365 \text{ days}$$

$$= 29.2 \text{ days}$$

This means that, on average, it takes 29.2 days to pay for inventory purchased.

2. Time to sell inventory

$$= \frac{\text{Inventory}}{\text{Cost of goods sold}} \times 365 \text{ days}$$

$$= \frac{\$50,000}{500,000} \times 365 \text{ days}$$

$$= 36.5 \text{ days}$$

This means that, on average, it takes 36.5 days to sell the inventory.

3. Time to receive payment

$$= \frac{\text{Accounts receivable}}{\text{Sales}} \times 365 \text{ days}$$

$$= \frac{\$100,000}{\$750,000} \times 365 \text{ days}$$

$$= 48.67 \text{ days}$$

This means that, on average, it takes 48.67 days to receive payment for inventory sold. The business cycle for this company is:

$$36.5 \text{ days} + 48.7 - 29.2 = 56 \text{ days}$$

To increase the cash position, suppose the business was able to increase the accounts payable and decrease the turnover and receivable day totals for each component by five days. The result of these actions is shown in the paragraphs below.

FIGURE 9-13   continued

1. *Time taken to pay accounts:* A five-day increase substituted in the formula would increase accounts payable from $40,000 to $46,849 with a resulting increase in cash of $6,849 (46,849 − 40,000) by using the above formula. This five-day increase might be accomplished by obtaining extensions from suppliers or simply not paying accounts payable until absolutely required.

2. *Time to sell inventory:* A five-day decrease substituted in the formula would decrease inventory from $50,000 to $43,150 with a resulting increase in cash of $6,850 (50,000 − 43,150). Such a decrease might be a result of increased advertising, more careful purchasing, or greater incentive to salespeople.

3. *Time taken to receive payment:* A five-day decrease substituted in the formula would decrease accounts receivable from $100,000 to $89,733 with a resulting increase in cash of $10,267 (100,000 − 89,733). Such a decrease might be accomplished by increasing the intensity of collection procedures or submitting charge card receipts more often.

The total effect of these measures on the cash position of the company would be $6,849 + $6,850 + $10,267 = $23,966 increase. The owner-manager, of course, would have to balance this increase in cash against the costs of accomplishing the five-day increases or decreases.

---

industries, however, may deviate from these averages. Illustrations of these ratios for a small business appear in Appendix 9A.

Liquidity Ratios.

Liquidity ratios assess the business's ability to meet financial obligations in the current period. Two liquidity ratios are commonly used: the current ratio and the acid test or quick ratio. The calculations for these ratios are as follows:

$$\text{Current ratio} = \text{Current assets} : \text{Current liabilities}$$

This figure, expressed as a ratio, should be higher than 1:1 and usually between 1:1 and 2:1.

$$\text{Acid test or quick ratio} = \text{Current assets} - \text{Inventories} : \text{Current liabilities}$$

The quick ratio is more suitable for businesses that have a high level of inventories. A ratio of 1:1 is considered healthy. If the liquidity ratios are lower than they should be, the business may have difficulty meeting obligations within the year and will have a hard time raising further debt capital. Actions that could improve the liquidity ratios are increasing current assets without a corresponding increase in current liabilities such as equity financing or increased long-term debt.

Productivity Ratios.

Productivity ratios measure the efficiency of internal management operations. They include the inventory turnover ratio and the collection period ratio.

The calculation of the inventory turnover ratio is as follows:

$$\text{Inventory turnover} = \frac{\text{Cost of goods sold}}{\text{Average inventory at cost}}$$

or

$$\text{Inventory turnover} = \frac{\text{Sales}}{\text{Average inventory at retail price}}$$

Inventory turnover reveals the number of times the inventory is turned over (sold) in a year. Average turnover rates vary considerably by industry but usually should not be lower than two to three times. An inventory turnover that is too low may reflect poor inventory buying in terms of either being overstocked or buying low-demand inventory.

The collection period is calculated as follows:

$$\text{Collection period} = \frac{\text{Accounts receivable}}{\text{Daily credit sales}}$$

This ratio reflects the average number of days taken for purchasers to pay their accounts to the business. Normal collection periods are in the 20-day to 40-day range. If the collection period is too long, it may mean the credit-granting policy is too loose, the administration of billing is too slow, or the collection of accounts is too lax. Solutions to poor productivity ratios include better buying and more emphasis on selling and collections.

Profitability Ratios.

Profitability ratios measure the effectiveness of operations in generating a profit. There are four ratios in this category.

The first ratio is gross margin:

$$\text{Gross margin} = \text{Sales} - \text{Cost of goods sold}$$

This figure, usually expressed as a percentage of gross sales, can be used for comparisons. Gross margin for an individual product is calculated by subtracting cost from selling price and is commonly called *markup*. Average gross margins usually range from 20 percent to 50 percent. If gross margins are lower than they should be, the cause may be poor buying, failure to emphasize high-margin items, theft or spoilage, or price levels that are not current.

The profit-on-sales ratio measures profit as a percentage of gross sales:

$$\text{Profit on sales} = \frac{\text{Net profit (before tax)}}{\text{Sales}}$$

Typically, the average percentages fall within 1 percent to 5 percent. A lower than average profit-to-sales percentage can reflect a problem with either pricing or expenses. Pretax profits are normally used, since the tax rates may vary by jurisdiction and industry. In addition, reporting agencies that publish industry standards may use pretax profits as a comparison.

The third profitability ratio is the expense ratio:

$$\text{Expense ratio} = \frac{\text{Expense item}}{\text{Sales}}$$

Many specific expenses on the income statement may be expressed as a percentage of gross sales. These figures can then be compared with those for similar businesses.

The return-on-investment ratio reflects the profitability of the owner's investment:

$$\text{Return on investment} = \frac{\text{Net profit (before tax)}}{\text{Owner's equity}}$$

This ratio may be compared not only with those for other similar businesses but also with alternative investments. If compared with the bank rate of interest, it is important to remember the risk associated with the business. Thus, the return on investment should be higher than the bank rate to compensate for this.

Debt Ratio.

The debt-to-equity ratio measures the solvency of the business, or the firm's ability to meet long-term debt payments:

$$\text{Total debt to equity} = \text{Total debt : Owner's equity}$$

Acceptable debt ratios vary, but generally, it should not be greater than 4 to 1. A lender normally will not provide further financing to a firm with a higher ratio. To improve the debt ratio, the small business may need to increase the equity investment or reduce debt through operations.

CREDIT AND THE SMALL BUSINESS   LO5

A major concern for many small businesses in their attempt to reduce the length of the business cycle is control of credit. The owner-manager should understand the fundamentals of credit granting and management to effectively control receivables. Before deciding to extend credit, the owner-manager should be aware of the costs and potential difficulties involved in granting credit, as well as the advantages of its use. The attractiveness of such a program is less today, since the majority of consumers can use bank credit or debit cards for their purchases. However, many small businesses have found success by offering gift cards and loyalty rewards programs as a form of credit.

ADVANTAGES OF CREDIT USE

The advantages of offering credit include the following:

- A credit program will undoubtedly result in increased sales and will probably be necessary to remain competitive.
- Credit customers are more likely to be loyal to the store or business.
- Credit customers tend to be more concerned than are cash customers with quality of service as opposed to price.
- The business can maintain information about and a record of credit customers and their purchases that can help in formulating future plans.

DISADVANTAGES OF CREDIT USE

A credit program can also create certain difficulties:

- There will generally be some bad debts when using a credit program. The number of bad debts depends largely on how strict the credit-granting policy is and how closely accounts are monitored.
- Slow payers cost the business in lost interest and capital that could be used for more productive investments. It is estimated that in many businesses, losses resulting from slow payers are greater than losses from bad debts.
- A credit program increases bookkeeping, mailing, and collection expenses. Purchase records need to be kept, statements mailed, and accounts monitored and collected. As a result, many small businesses decide against offering their own credit programs.

MANAGEMENT OF A CREDIT PROGRAM

If the small business owner decides to use a credit program, some essential steps should be followed to ensure maximum effectiveness.

Determine Administrative Policies.

This includes such items as application forms, credit limits for customers, procedures to follow on overdue accounts, determining which records to keep, and deciding when to send statements.

Set Criteria for Granting Credit.

A small business owner-manager may want to assess many of the same areas a lender would evaluate in considering a small business loan, although perhaps not in the same detail. Some essentials would be past credit history, other accounts held, monthly income, references, and bank used. A small business is well advised to use the services of a credit bureau located in most cities or a commercial agency such as Dun and Bradstreet to evaluate customers' creditworthiness.

Set up a System to Monitor Accounts.

Proper management of accounts receivable involves classifying accounts by the length of time they have been outstanding. This process is called *aging of accounts receivable*. Common categories used are under 30 days, 30 to 60 days, 60 to 90 days, and over 90 days. Experience shows that the longer an account is outstanding, the smaller is the chance of collecting it. Therefore, special attention should be paid to overdue accounts.

Establish a Procedure for Collection.

A uniform procedure should be set up regarding the use of overdue notices, phone calls, credit supervision, legal action, and a collection agency. Lax supervision of accounts has led to many small business failures, so this is an area of credit management that cannot be ignored. An example of such a collection policy appears in Figure 9-14.

One form of collection sometimes used by small businesses is a factoring company, which, as discussed in Chapter 6, can also be a source of small business financing. This type of company purchases accounts receivable for cash and attempts to collect them. In some cases, a factoring company handles the overall credit program for the business and even provides debt financing.

FIGURE 9-14	An Example of a Collection Policy				
	30 DAYS	**45 DAYS**	**60 DAYS**	**75 DAYS**	**90 DAYS**
Communication	Letter, telephone; copy of statement	Letter, telephone; copy of statement	Letter, telephone	Letter, telephone	Registered letter or lawyer's letter
Message	Overdue account, please remit	Pay in 15 days, or deliveries will be stopped	Deliveries stopped; pay immediately	Pay in 15 days, or account will be turned over for collection	Action is being taken
Action	None	None	Stop deliveries	None	Use collection agency or small claims court

Source: *Small Business Review*, pamphlet (Toronto: Thorne Riddell Chartered Accountants).

USE OF BANK DEBIT AND CREDIT CARDS

Because of the high costs and risks involved in operating their own credit programs, many small businesses find the most effective way to offer credit is to use bank debit and credit cards such as Visa and MasterCard. The use of credit cards and electronic banking by consumers has now surpassed that of cash and cheques in Canada. The credit card companies assume the risk of bad debts and cover much of the administration costs of bookkeeping and issuing of statements in return for a fee—usually from 1.5 percent to 6 percent of sales, depending on volume. Because of the high ownership of these cards by consumers, most retail and service firms find their use essential to enhancing sales. Recently in Canada, small business owners are becoming increasingly vocal about what they see are ever increasing transaction fees for some credit cards, notable reward or premium cards (see Incident 9-6). Visa Canada's recent, "So, you think you want to smallenfreuden?" marketing campaign urging consumers to charge everyday items such as milk and bread to their credit cards has been particularly bothersome to the Canadian Federation of Independent Businesses (CFIB). The CFIB are arguing that the campaign is increasing the costs of doing business for smaller firms, the ones that can least afford it and want Visa to end their marketing efforts.[3]

Most businesses allow the use of debit cards such as Interac. Much like the bank credit card, the debit card automatically transfers the sale amount from the customer's account at the bank to the business's account. The obvious advantages of debit cards are the quick repayment and reduction of accounts receivable. For a monthly fee, the business can be assured of on-the-spot transfers to its bank for a transaction. The costs of offering this service are approximately $50 per terminal per month and/or a percent of sales

INCIDENT 9-6

REWARDS CARDS—WE BENEFIT BUT WHO PAYS?

Aeroplan, TD Rewards, and RBC Travel Card are just some of the growing number of premium reward cards in Canada and the trend is growing. People love taking out their rewards card and charging anything from small convenience items to large purchases such as entertainment centres. After all, who does not love getting something for nothing? Provided you pay off the balance every month, you can enjoy rewards such as travel, gift cards, coupons, and so forth that do not cost you a dime.

Of course, someone has to pay for these free items, and who that someone is may surprise you. It is not Visa (www.visa.ca) or MasterCard (www.mastercard.ca) that issues the cards or the banks that supply them. Rather, it is the merchants who pay in the form of fees. Last year, merchants in Canada paid $5 billion in total credit card fees, and a growing percent of the fees are from premium or reward type cards. These premium cards come with higher transaction fees for the merchants, which can amount to 3 percent or more for every sale. Unlike regular credit cards, debit cards, or cash, where transaction and bank fees are relatively low, premium cards come with much higher fees, sometimes more than double of what a regular transaction fee would be. Many small business owners are

CONSUMERS IN CANADA LOVE EARNING REWARDS SUCH AS FREE TRAVEL WHEN THEY USE THEIR CREDIT CARD. UNBEKNOWNST TO MANY CANADIANS, THESE FREE TRIPS AND OTHER REWARDS ARE USUALLY PAID FOR BY MERCHANTS IN THE FORM OF HIGHER FEES.
Chris Ryan/Getty Images

saying the extra fees these premium cards are charging are hurting their business's bottom line.

Visa counters that the cost of accepting credit cards really amounts to the cost of doing business and merchants enjoy many benefits as a result. Visa says, "Retailers also receive many benefits, including guaranteed payment, faster checkout times, enhanced security and fraud protection, reduced cash handling costs, and access to hundreds of millions of cardholders from around the world." Furthermore, Visa points out that the average credit card transaction fee in Canada is 1.6 percent and the fee has been stable for 10 years now.

The Canadian Federation of Independent Businesses (CFIB) has brought the matter of higher transaction fees for premium cards to the Canadian Competitive Bureau where they are asking for changes to the transaction system. In their arguments, the CFIB is pointing out that average transaction fees are higher in Canada than in Australia, Denmark, the United Kingdom, and New Zealand and are asking that changes be made to the current system. The CFIB is asking that merchants be allowed the right to refuse to accept certain premium credit cards and have the ability to charge a surcharge to consumers who want to use them. Under the current system, Visa and Master Card can stipulate that a merchant must accept all their cards not just the ones they want to accept. Furthermore, merchants are not currently allowed to charge a surcharge to credit card purchases in Canada.

Discussion Questions

1. Do you think Visa and MasterCard are acting ethically in passing the cost of paying for consumer rewards cards to merchants in the form of higher fees? Why, or why not?

2. Do you think Visa is correct in that the transaction fees ranging from 1.5–3 percent are worth the advantages of being able to accept credit cards?

3. As a consumer, how would you feel if merchants could refuse to accept certain credit cards you use? Would you accept paying an extra fee for the right to use a rewards card? Why, or why not?

4. Do you support CFIB's position as outlined in the case above?

Sources: Tijana Martin, "Credit Card Issue," www.therecord.com/news-story/2629115-merchants-hit-hard-by-premium-credit-card-fees-round-table-participan/, accessed July 1, 2013; and Tracy Shelock, "Merchants Up in Arms Over Credit Card Fees," www.vancouversun.com/business/Merchants+arms+over+credit+card+fees/7597414/story.html, accessed June 15, 2013.

TIME TO TAKE ACTION

1. Create a personal financial snapshot for yourself. Where do you want to be financially in one, three, five, and 10 years?

2. If you are writing a business plan, prepare a financial snapshot for your business. Where do you want your company to be?

3. Create a list of start-up expenses. Wherever possible, verify these expenses with sources. Estimate only when you have to. Where do you think you could save money on start-up expenses? Bring your list to others who have started companies, and ask them if the list is complete and if it is possible to save money in certain areas.

4. Prepare cash flow and income statements. Bring these to other entrepreneurs and people in your network. Solicit their advice to determine if the numbers are realistic.

5. Prepare a balance sheet. Solicit advice from your network once again.

LEARNING OBJECTIVES SUMMARY

LO1 The three-step process of the accounting cycle includes (1) recording the transactions (journal), (2) classifying the transaction totals (ledger), and (3) summarizing the data (financial statements). The three financial statements important to the owner-manager of a small business are the balance sheet, the income statement, and the cash flow statement.

LO2 The common types of bookkeeping systems used by small businesses today are manual systems (the one-book system, the one-write system, the manual multi-journal system), out-sourcing certain functions, computer service bureaus, and small business computers.

LO3 Some of the more common operations computers can perform are word processing, general ledger, database files, payroll, financial planning, and capital investment decisions. Some potential disadvantages of computer ownership are cost, obsolescence, employee resistance, restricted capabilities, and set-up time.

LO4 Ratio analysis enables the small business owner to compare the financial performance of the company with that of other firms in the industry and with the company's own past performance. Common financial ratios include liquidity ratios, productivity ratios, profitability ratios, and debt ratios.

LO5 The advantages of offering credit are a likely increase in sales, increased store loyalty, and improved information about purchases. The disadvantages are bad debts, slow payers, and administration costs. Essential aspects of administering a credit program are defining administrative policies, establishing credit-granting criteria, setting up a system to monitor accounts, and establishing a procedure for collection.

DISCUSSION QUESTIONS

1. Is it more important for an entrepreneur to track cash or profits? Does it depend on the type of business and/or industry? What troubles will an entrepreneur face if he or she tracks only profits and ignores cash? What troubles will an entrepreneur face if he or she tracks only cash and ignores profits?

2. How useful is a financial plan when it is based on assumptions of the future and we are confident that these assumptions are not going to be 100 percent correct?

APPLICATION QUESTIONS AND HANDS-ON ACTIVITIES

1. Research the software packages available to help entrepreneurs with the financials for a business plan. Which do you believe is the best? Why?

2. Companies planning to make an initial public offering (IPO) must submit a financial plan as part of their prospectus. From the Internet, collect a prospectus from three different companies, and analyze their financial plan. What are the major assumptions made in constructing these financial plans? Compare and contrast these financial plans with what we would expect of a financial plan as part of a business plan.

3. Have students draw up pro forma statements for their venture ideas. (Note that the students must source these.) Then have the students break into small groups to review their expenses and try to find ways to generate savings. Ask the groups to try to reduce expenditures by at least 20 percent per business plan.

4. For the following transactions, indicate which accounts are changed and by how much:
   a. Feb. 14, 2014—Received $1,000 from Frank Johnson on account.
   b. Feb. 14, 2014—Purchased equipment for $1,500 (paid cash).
   c. Feb. 15, 2014—Paid owner Bill Cartwright $2,000 for January's salary.
   d. Feb. 18, 2014—Paid telephone bill of $90.87.
   e. Feb. 19, 2014—Bought ice cream on account, $395.00.

5. Calculate the rate of return for the following investment. The total cost of the investment is $250,000, the depreciable life of the investment is 10 years, and the annual profit (net of depreciation) is $30,000. What considerations other than financial ones exist?

6. Assume the annual depreciation charge for the investment in Problem 3 is $25,000. Determine the payback period of the investment.

7. Determine the break-even point, in dollars, for an investment with fixed costs of $100,000 and an estimated contribution of 60 percent. How much revenue would it need to produce before you would invest?

8. a. From the balance sheet and income statement of Sam's Paint and Drywall, determine the following ratios:

(1) Current
(2) Inventory turnover
(3) Profit to sales
(4) Return on investment
(5) Total debt to equity

b. From Dun and Bradstreet's *Key Business Ratios* on industry norms, evaluate each of the above ratios.

SAM'S PAINT AND DRYWALL
For Year Ended December 31, 2014
(in thousands of dollars)

ASSETS		LIABILITIES AND NET WORTH	
Cash	$ 12	Accounts payable........................	$ 15
Inventory	41	Notes payable—bank.....................	4
Accounts receivable	18	Other	20
Total current assets.................	71	Total current liabilities	39
Fixed assets:		Long-term liabilities	41
Vehicles.............................	10		
Equipment...........................	15		
Building	22		
Land.................................	23	Total net worth (owner's equity)..........	61
Total fixed assets...................	70		
Total assets.............................	$141	Total liabilities and net worth	$141

Income Statement
December 31, 2014
(in thousands of dollars)

Sales...	$280
Less: Cost of goods sold	186
Gross margin on sales	94
Less: Operating expenses...	81
Net profit	$ 13

9. Dick's Draperies has gross sales of $15,000 per month, half of which are on credit (paid within 30 days). Monthly expenses are as follows: wages, $3,000; utilities and rent, $2,000; advertising, $300; and miscellaneous, $500. Inventory is purchased every three months and totals $30,000 for each order.

Yearly expenses paid for in advance are insurance of $1,000 and a rent deposit of $700. Prepare a six-month cash flow statement for Dick's Draperies. What advice would you give this business based on the cash flow statement?

USE OF FINANCIAL RATIOS FOR A SMALL BUSINESS (AUTOMOTIVE DEALER)

RATIO	METHOD OF COMPUTATION	LAST YEAR	MOTOR VEHICLE DEALER		EXPLANATION
			PREVIOUS YEAR	INDUSTRY AVERAGE	
1. Liquidity a. Current	Current assets: Current ratio	1.09 times liabilities	1.05 times	1.1 times	Satisfactory: This dealer has the same ability as is common in this industry.
b. Quick ratio	Current assets — inventories : Current liabilities	0.33 times	0.45 times	Not available	
2. Productivity a. Inventory turnover	Cost of goods sold/Average inventory (at cost) or Sales/ Average inventory (at retail)	7.41 times	7.41 times	6.0 times	Good: This dealer has a higher turnover rate than the average dealer. This may indicate a higher sales level or lower inventory levels.
b. Collection	Average inventory at retail/Daily credit sales	13.56 days	16.01 days	12 days	Fair: The collection period is longer than average, which may indicate the need to tighten the credit policy; however, it seems that some action has already been taken.

RATIO	METHOD OF COMPUTATION	LAST YEAR	PREVIOUS YEAR	INDUSTRY AVERAGE	EXPLANATION
3. Profitability a. Gross margins	Gross sales − Cost of goods sold as a percent of sales	10.71%	12.28%	16.70%	Poor: The inventory may be obsolete, or company prices may be too low.
b. Profit on sales	Net profit (before tax)/Gross sales	0.85%	− (0.6%)	0.6%	Good: Expenses are being kept in line.
c. Expense ratio	Expense item/ Gross sales	11.69%	13.59%	Not available	Good: The company is making an effort to cut expenses.
d. Return on investment	Net profit (before tax)/ Owner's equity	10.49%	− 1.74%	9.0%	Good: This company is more profitable than most in the industry. It is clear that action is being taken to improve profitability of this firm.
4. Debt a. Total debt to equity	Total debt/ Owner's equity	325.89%	376.09%	398.20%	Good: This dealer depends less on debt financing than is common in this industry. An intentional move has been taken in this direction.

Note: The symbol / denotes division.

Despite the problems identified with marketing the Ladder Rail, Dan perseveres, and within a few months, he is able to secure enough orders to keep production steady. Dan is especially pleased to see that sales through the Internet and some local hardware chains are increasing and that there has been some repeat orders.

Although Dan underestimated many of his expenses and start-up costs, he provided much of the labour and expertise himself to defray part of this shortfall. As the year progresses, orders for the Ladder Rail continue to increase, and Dan begins to think that the business has turned the corner.

Suzie has kept track of the receipts and disbursements and at the end of the first year of operations takes all the financial information to their accountant. A couple of weeks later, the accountant calls them in. They are very disappointed in the results (see Figure 9-A). While reviewing the statements with their accountant, he provides some industry averages to help them in planning for the next year (see Figure 9-B). They are quite nervous about taking the statements to their investors, including their banker. Dan and Suzie are hopeful their investors will see that sales are increasing and will be satisfied with this.

FIGURE 9A

The Ladder Rail Income Statement: Year 1

Sales	4500 @ $30	$135,000	
	250 @ $40	10,000	$145,000
Cost of Goods Sold	4750 @ $12	57,000	
Wages		80,000	
Employee Benefits		6,000	
Utilities		17,000	
Repairs & Maintenance		4,500	
Insurance		1,000	
Amortization		17,000	
Interest and bank charges		10,400	$192,900
Net Income			($ 47,900)

The Ladder Rail Income Statement: End of Year 1

Assets	
Cash	$ 2,250
Accounts Receivable	3,800
Inventory	10,250
Building & Equipment	153,000
Land	50,000
Total Assets	$219,300
Liabilities & Owner's Equity	
Accounts Payable	$ 36,800
Bank Loan—Current Payable	23,400
Bank Loan—Long Term	117,000
Owner's Equity	42,100
Total Liabilities & Owner's Equity	$219,300

	Selected Ratios for Metal Fabricating Companies
Current Ratio	1.52 : 1
Gross Margin	23.2%
Profit on Sales	6.1%
Profit on Net Worth	21.13%
Collection Period	59 days
Inventory Turnover	4.2
Debt to Equity	1.1 : 1

Before Dan saw the statements, he had contemplated expanding his small factory by building an addition and adding some new equipment at a cost of $80,000 with a life of 10 years. He had estimated that this addition would bring in an additional income of $10,000 per year. With the first year's performance, however, Dan is not sure whether he should make this investment.

Questions

1. Evaluate Dan and Suzie's financial management practices.

2. Using the ratios provided by the accountant, evaluate Dan's business, and make suggestions for improvement.

3. Using the financial information provided, calculate a break-even point and rate of return for the new addition. What additional information would Dan need to do a payback analysis of the proposed expansion?

For more information on the resources available from McGraw-Hill Ryerson, go to www.mcgrawhill.ca/he/solutions.

CHAPTER 10

OPERATIONS MANAGEMENT

SMALL BUSINESS PROFILE

COSTA ELLES *Ela Greek Taverna*

Photography by Joseph Robichaud

Costa Elles came to Canada with his parents in the 1970s after fleeing Greece as a political refugee. Elles' father, who was a priest, stressed on two important things to being successful in life: education and work ethic. Elles recalls that he grew up playing and loving soccer. While his father was pleased to hear that he was working hard on the field, most of his father's focus was on school and education. With his love of soccer and a strong belief in education, Elles eventually moved to Halifax, where he attended St. Mary's University and was a student athlete. After graduating with a commerce degree, Elles ventured back to Greece, where he embarked on a professional soccer career for a short while before returning to Halifax. During Elles' early career, he coached soccer and worked as a sales representative for Moosehead Brewery. During this time as a sales rep, Elles noticed there were no authentic Greek restaurants in Halifax, and the idea of creating a great Greek restaurant became his passion. A short time later, Elles and his partner Chris Tzaneteas opened Opa in the Halifax downtown core. From the start, Elles

envisioned that Opa would provide guests with an authentic Greek experience, and the partners put in a number of controls and processes in place to ensure this would happen. Sourcing products was essential to the company, and they established the practice of only using the freshest and the highest-quality ingredients. In addition, controls were put in place to ensure the dishes were cooked and served properly and authentic high-quality food was consistently served. Elles states that they wanted Opa to be a top-notch Greek restaurant, and this could only occur with the finest products and attention to detail.

Opa soon became a hit in the Halifax community, and Elles and Tzaneteas expanded their company, Eat It Two Entertainment, to include various restaurants and bars, including Seven (a high-end restaurant), Argyle Bar and Grill, Mosaic, and eventually two other Opa locations. The pair attributed much of their success to attention to detail and a core belief of being committed to using the finest ingredients. It was during this time that Elles thought there could be a franchising opportunity for Opa and renamed the chain ela! Greek Taverna, which was a name they could trademark. Elles notes that a key to establishing a franchise is about finding the right people and putting in systems which they can follow in order to be successful. A franchisee has to be able to produce the same authentic meal, and rules and controls have to be in place to ensure consistency. Furthermore, as Elles states, controlling costs is very important in the restaurant business, and a franchisor wants to know that in addition to great food, they are buying into a great that includes cost and portion controls. After a number of years, which included an amicable split from his business partner, Elles thinks he has these systems in place to ensure a positive Greek experience and is looking to grow his restaurant chain using the franchise model.

ELA GREEK TAVERNA
www.elagreektaverna.com

Source: Interview by Peter Mombourquette, October 23, 2013.

MANAGEMENT OF INTERNAL OPERATIONS LO1

The management of internal operations is part of the physical facilities section of the business plan (see Chapter 4). Operations management is one area in which many small business owners have their greatest strength. They know how to produce a quality product or provide a quality service, and their primary interest often lies with this aspect of the business. Incident 10-1 illustrates the potential problems of inefficient management and production. Although they may have production expertise, many entrepreneurs lack the management skills of maintaining quality and control. Typical areas needing attention might be cash flow, production costs and product quality, inventory management, and physical facilities issues. As mentioned in earlier chapters, the entrepreneur is typically weaker in the areas of marketing and financial management than in managing the production process. As a result, many entrepreneurs find it advantageous to outsource some of these services. A recent study by PricewaterhouseCoopers found that 73 percent of Canadian businesses outsource one or more business processes.[1] Some of the typical services are financial management, human resource management, income tax preparation, marketing, call centre and customer care, and mail-room operations.

THE PRODUCTION PROCESS

The production process involves the conversion of inputs such as money, people, machines, and inventories into outputs—the products or services provided. Figure 10-1 illustrates this application for manufacturing, wholesaling, retailing, and service businesses. The owner-manager's task is to organize the production process of the business so that the outputs (products) can be produced efficiently.

The priority evaluation and review technique (PERT) and other flowchart systems have been developed to help organize the production process. A simple example of such a system is shown

---

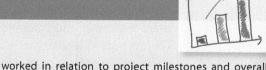

INCIDENT 10-1

MIND YOUR METRICS

Chris Bolivar, former president of Optamedia Inc., an Edmonton-based advertising agency that successfully merged with a rival marketing company McRobbie in 2009 to form McRobbie Optamedia (www.mcrobbieoptamedia.com), says during the first few months after establishing Optamedia, he noticed that although sales were good, the net income was off by as much as 10 percent. "I'd look at projects and wonder why they were taking so long," he says. He then realized that neither he nor his staff was keeping track of time spent on client work, which meant the firm was regularly underestimating how long it took to complete projects. Bolivar corrected the problem by introducing a time-accounting program that employees must fill out to get paid. Each month, he runs reports on accounts, tracking

hours worked in relation to project milestones and overall budget. As a result, net income has doubled, productivity is up, and estimating new jobs is more accurate. This and other improvements helped Optamedia to be named as one of Profit Magazine's Hot 50 start-up companies.

Discussion Questions

1. Given that Optamedia was a start-up when Bolivar instituted the operations procedures, do you think this made the implementation easier or more difficult?

2. Do you think employees would be responsive to this rigour in reporting work? Why, or why not?

Source: Adapted from Eleanor Beaton, "Launch and Learn," *Profit*, October 2008, pp. 45–47.

FIGURE 10-1   Examples of Production Systems

TYPE OF BUSINESS	INPUTS	PROCESS	OUTPUTS
Apparel manufacturer	Cloth, thread, buttons	Store—Cut—Sew—Press—Ship	Dresses
Wholesaler	Large volume per order of each product	Store—Sort—Package—Ship	Smaller volume of a product in each order
Retailer	A volume of each of many products to the ultimate customer	Store—Customer display—Package	Low volume of a few products to each customer
Laundry (service firm)	Dirty clothes	Sort—Wash—Press—Store	Clean clothes

Source: Adapted from Curtis E. Tate, Jr., Leon C. Megginson, Charles R. Scott, Jr., and Lyle R. Trueblood. *Successful Small Business Management*, 3rd ed. (Georgetown, Ont.: Irwin-Dorsey of Canada, 1982), p. 244.

in Figure 10-2 for a manufacturing firm. By visually plotting the tasks and required time, the owner-manager can minimize down time and ensure the most efficient production. Continual efforts should be made throughout the process to ensure quality control.

TOTAL QUALITY MANAGEMENT

Many small businesses have been able to develop a competitive advantage by ensuring superior quality in their products and services. This is referred to as *total quality management.* Total quality management (TQM) is a philosophy of management focusing on problem solving and control. An organization that focuses on TQM uses factors such as consumer-driven product quality, efficient distribution, quick response, continuous improvement, elimination of waste, and top management leadership and commitment as measurement tools. These systems are often developed in conjunction with other business and engineering disciplines using a cross-functional approach.

To achieve this type of standard, the business must meet several requirements:

- Realize that the business is going to exist in the long run, so it is more concerned with long-term performance than short-term profits.
- Involve employees in decision making so that they also see the need to ensure overall superior quality.
- Invest time and effort in training employees adequately.
- Develop standards by which quality performance can be measured.
- Continually measure internal performance through internal systems and externally by surveying customers and other key parties.

Some small businesses, particularly those interested in exporting their products, have found it advantageous to get their products quality certified through the International Standards Organization (ISO 9000). Although costly for the small business, certification can be an effective marketing tool. ISO 9000 is an international reference for quality requirements in

FIGURE 10-2   Priority Evaluation and Review Techniques (PERT)

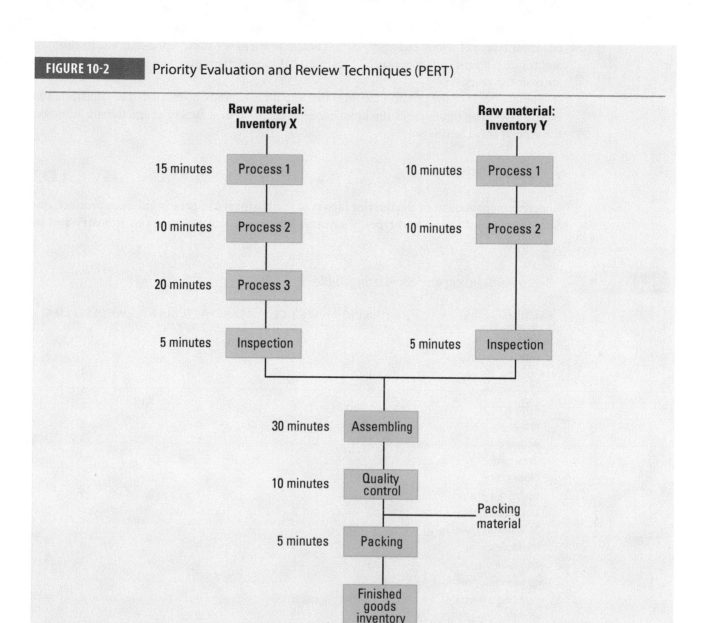

	Raw material: Inventory X		**Raw material: Inventory Y**	
15 minutes	Process 1	10 minutes	Process 1	
10 minutes	Process 2	10 minutes	Process 2	
20 minutes	Process 3			
5 minutes	Inspection	5 minutes	Inspection	

30 minutes — Assembling

10 minutes — Quality control

Packing material

5 minutes — Packing

Finished goods inventory

Total work time = 120 minutes   Critical path time = 95 minutes

business-to-business dealings. Quality Management Standards (QMS) are used by leading businesses worldwide to implement a management system that guarantees conformity and quality of their processes followed to output their products and services.[2]

PHYSICAL FACILITIES   LO2

Planning the physical facilities was discussed briefly in Chapter 3 as part of the preparation of the feasibility analysis. Selection of the location for the business was introduced in Chapter 4 as one of the steps in organizing a business.

Although it is not necessary to review that information again, it is critical for the owner-manager to recognize that the physical facilities must be closely monitored and maintained to ensure they are efficient and up-to-date. Locations are never static—populations, businesses, and traffic patterns shift continually. This trend has caused many excellent locations to deteriorate over the years.

Some aspects of the physical facilities that should constantly be evaluated are illustrated in Figure 10-3. The figure ranks the importance of each physical facility characteristic based on the type of small business.

LAYOUT LO3

Effective management of the interior layout of the business can greatly enhance productivity. Small businesses use several types of layouts. The layout selected varies by industry and by

FIGURE 10-3	Business Building and Site-Rating Table			
FACTORS	**RETAILING**	**SERVICE**	**MANUFACTURING**	**WHOLESALING**
Building feature:				
Age	1	4	3	4
Space	1	3	1	4
Configuration	1	4	4	3
Appearance	1	3	3	4
Frontage	1	4	4	4
Access	1	2	1	1
Interior use:				
Floor space	2	3	1	1
Room dimensions	1	3	1	4
Ceiling heights	2	2	2	4
Stairways, elevators	3	3	1	1
Window space	1	3	4	4
Utility services	3	1	1	3
Improvement potential:				
Building exterior	1	3	4	4
Building interior	1	3	2	2
Site	1	2	3	4
Surrounding	2	2	3	4
Streets and walks	2	3	3	3
Access	1	3	2	1
Expansion	2	1	1	1
Site and environment:				
Street and service areas	1	2	2	3
Setback and frontage	1	3	4	4
Parking	1	2	2	3
Surrounding businesses	2	3	4	4
Area environment	2	3	4	4

Key to ratings: 1 = critical; 2 = very important; 3 = not ordinarily important; 4 = minimum importance

Source: John B. Kline, Donald P. Stegall, and Lawrence L. Steinmetz. *Managing the Small Business* (Homewood, Ill.: Richard D. Irwin).

scope of operations. In determining layout, it is advisable to draw up a floor plan to better use available space.

LAYOUTS FOR MANUFACTURING FIRMS

Here are some key areas to consider in planning the interior of a manufacturing plant:

- Location of utility outlets for machines
- Location of receiving and shipping areas for raw materials and finished goods
- Safety aspects
- Adequate lighting capability throughout
- Provision for ease of maintenance and cleaning of the plant

Small manufacturing firms use essentially three types of layouts: product layout, process layout, and fixed-position layout.

Product Layout.

The product layout is suitable for the business that manufactures just one or only a few products. It closely resembles the production line of a large factory. Figure 10-4 illustrates the floor plan of a typical product layout. The product layout generally allows for economy in both cost of and time required for production, as each part of the manufacturing process is carried out in sequence.

Process Layout.

The process layout is designed for factories that manufacture many different or custom-made products. In this layout, similar processes are grouped together and the product moves back and

THE PRODUCT LAYOUT CLOSELY RESEMBLES ONE IN A PRODUCTION LINE.
John A. Rizzo/Getty Images

FIGURE 10-4 — Product Layout

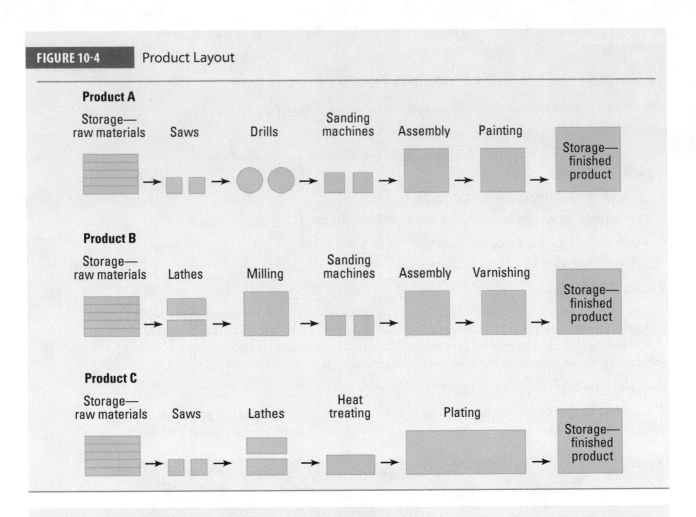

Product A

Storage—raw materials → Saws → Drills → Sanding machines → Assembly → Painting → Storage—finished product

Product B

Storage—raw materials → Lathes → Milling → Sanding machines → Assembly → Varnishing → Storage—finished product

Product C

Storage—raw materials → Saws → Lathes → Heat treating → Plating → Storage—finished product

FIGURE 10-5 — Process Layout

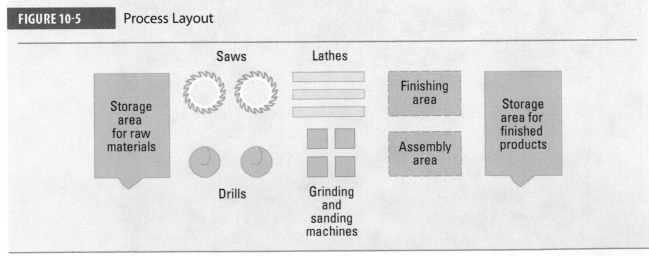

Storage area for raw materials

Saws

Lathes

Drills

Grinding and sanding machines

Finishing area

Assembly area

Storage area for finished products

forth among those areas until completed. The process layout is often more expensive and requires more management time to ensure efficiency. Figure 10-5 above illustrates a process layout for a small factory.

Fixed-Position Layout.

In the fixed-position layout, the product remains in a fixed position throughout its manufacture. The production processes move to the product. As one might expect, this type of layout is

FIGURE 10-6　Fixed-Position Layout

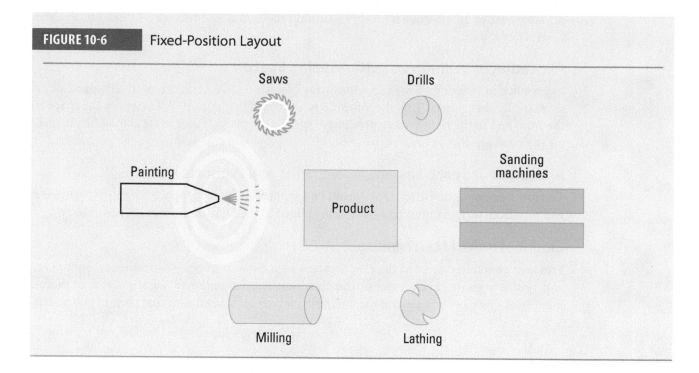

used for very large and cumbersome products and is used infrequently by small businesses. Figure 10-6 above illustrates the fixed-position layout.

LAYOUTS FOR RETAIL FIRMS   LO4

As noted in Figure 10-3, interior layout and creative display are important factors in the success of a retail store. Sensitivity to consumer needs and shopping patterns is critical to the

INCIDENT 10-2

PRODUCTION IMPROVEMENT

Chris Wood is president of Marwood Metal Fabrication Ltd. (www.marwoodmetal.com) located in Tillsonburg, Ontario. In 2008–2010, the auto industry was in crisis. As his business provided automobile parts to the major auto makers, he knew things were going to be difficult. So Wood turned to a lean management philosophy known as "Kaizen"—Japanese for continuous improvement—to help usher in a more efficient way to producing the components. This system allows groups of workers from throughout a company to brainstorm intensively about the way they do their work, to identify waste, and to cut out processes that add cost but not value. The production line began tightening up, and productivity increased. Wood says the changes in production methods brought in as a result of the exercise have saved the company millions of dollars and helped it survive the recession. His advice to small manufacturers is that you cannot afford to do things as you have always done them, especially when the economy and consumers are rapidly changing.

Discussion Questions

1. Do you think implementing changes, like the ones discussed above, is easier or more difficult in times of financial crisis?

2. Do you think there is a danger in the Kaizen system of making change for the sake of change? How can companies ensure this does not happen?

3. List additional benefits outside of the ones mentioned above for adopting a Kaizen system.

Source: Adapted from *Profits*, "Get The Edge," Business Development Bank of Canada, Fall 2009, pp. 7–9.

development of an effective layout. In planning the layout, the retailer will need to analyze several key areas.

Allocation of Selling versus Non-selling Space.

Experience in retailing shows that some areas of a retail store are more productive and draw more traffic than others. This phenomenon is illustrated in Figure 10-7. Generally, the space at the front and to the right is more productive space. Obviously, selling space should be planned for the most productive areas of the store.

Allocation of Space among Departments and Products.

The same principle discussed above should be applied in allocating space among departments and products, with the most profitable being placed in the high-traffic areas, if possible.

Classification of Merchandise.

Previous chapters discussed the classification of consumer goods—convenience, shopping, and specialty goods. Each merchandise classification may require a slightly different placement in the retail store based on the purchase motives associated with that class of goods. For

---

FIGURE 10-7 Rankings of Space Importance in a Typical Retail Store

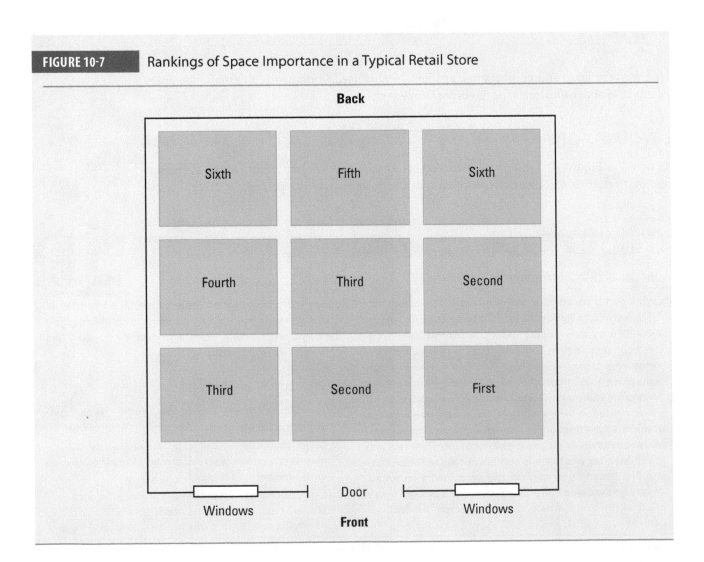

example, convenience items are often found close to heavier customer traffic flow. Shopping goods might be placed by competing brands and specialty or demand items at more inaccessible parts of the store.

Location of Displays and Products on the Shelf.

The small retailer should acquire expertise in a number of display techniques. Placement of merchandise on a shelf or counter can lead to increased sales, as certain areas are more productive than others. Merchandise placed at eye level and at the ends of aisles generally sells better. Two types of layouts are used by retail stores: the grid layout and the free-flow layout.

Grid Layout.

The grid layout is organized with customer convenience and retailer efficiency in mind. Grid layouts have traditionally been used in stores such as supermarkets and hardware stores. Figure 10-8 illustrates a grid layout.

Free-Flow Layout.

Some types of merchandise are purchased in a more relaxed atmosphere that allows customers more time to browse. For such merchandise, it is common to use the free-flow layout illustrated in Figure 10-9. This type of layout is suitable for clothing and many specialty types of merchandise.

Many larger retail stores use combinations of the grid and free-flow layouts. Most small retailers, however, generally use one or the other type. Incident 10-3 describes the innovative layout of a well-known retailer.

FIGURE 10-8 Grid Layout

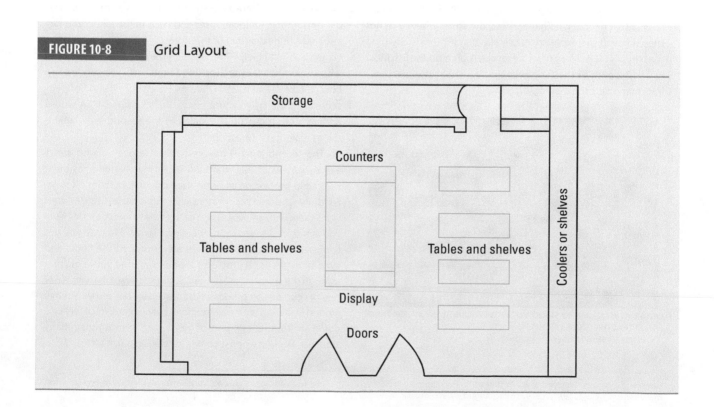

FIGURE 10-9   Free-Flow Layout

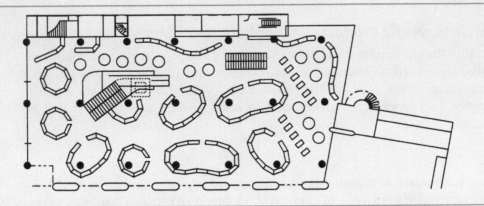

LAYOUTS FOR SERVICE FIRMS

Because the operations of service firms are so diverse, it is difficult to provide standard information on layouts. Some service firms such as restaurants more closely approximate the layouts of retail stores. Many of the principles discussed earlier for retailing apply here. For those service

INCIDENT 10-3

NAVIGATING IKEA

Although it may seem odd to talk about a store solely in terms of its layout, if anyone deserves the honour, it's IKEA (www.ikea.com). Most people who have visited the store, whether or not they enjoyed the experience, can say that if there is anything that makes IKEA different, store layout is high on the list. Most will admit even further, however, that IKEA has some awesome information architecture going on.

IKEA HAS MANAGED TO STAND OUT IN THE INDUSTRY BY MAINTAINING AN ATTRACTIVE STORE LAYOUT.
Jackbluee / Dreamstime.com

In the main lobby, you'll find an array of sensible and well-marked services. There are restrooms and payphones, and even phone numbers for local buses and taxis. In the lobby, you can also find a huge diagram of the store.

On the first level, IKEA has everything laid out for people who know what they are looking for. As well, you can browse bins of "take-me-home-now" items. Here you will also find self-serve furniture aisles and a bistro. But of course, IKEA would prefer you to move up the stairs, to the second level, where things really get interesting.

The second level is devoted to those people who aren't exactly sure what they want. All IKEA's merchandise has been laid out in context or, as some have called it, in room displays. For those who aren't decorator savvy, this is perfect, as IKEA provides them with an IKEA vision of "real life." As well, on this level you are guided to move in one direction. And in case you get confused, just look down! There are arrows on the floors and even signs at critical junctures that explain that you're moving through the store in the planned, straightforward manner. All of this, of course, is on purpose. And while you can certainly move around in IKEA in your own manner, chances are you'll feel odd doing so. But that's all part of IKEA's plan, proving that, if any store has an edge when it comes to retail layout, it's IKEA.

Source: S.L. Wykes, "Navigating IKEA: Tour of Emeryville Store Provides Tips for Future P.A. Shoppers," *The Mercury News*, www.mercurynews.com/mld/mercurynews/news/local/6606519.htm?1c, August 24, 2003; and IKEA website, 2013.

firms that are more similar to manufacturing firms such as repair shops, the principles of manufacturing layouts may be more appropriate.

PURCHASING AND CONTROLLING INVENTORIES   LO5

The cost of purchasing and holding inventories can be substantial. Because a small business generally has limited economic resources, it is critical that it give inventory management a high priority. The following sections discuss areas about which the small business owner should be knowledgeable in purchasing and controlling inventories.

SOURCES OF SUPPLY

The chapters on marketing and business planning discussed various aspects of the distribution channel from the seller's point of view. The same principles apply in this section, but from the buyer's position. The owner-manager should know which suppliers are available. Purchases can usually be made directly from the manufacturer, from an agent of the manufacturer, from a wholesaler, or from a retailer. Although sources vary considerably among industries, most small businesses purchase their inventories from wholesalers.

One question most small businesses face is whether to purchase from one supplier or many. In purchasing from only one supplier, the buyer is assured of consistent quality and will probably receive favourable treatment such as discounts and guaranteed supply in case of shortages, although orders may be too small to divide. Conversely, other suppliers may periodically offer lower prices. The business may also spread risk by purchasing from many suppliers. The small business owner must weigh these pros and cons in making this decision.

Many small business owners find it advantageous and cost effective to pool purchases with other companies. This may be done on an informal basis but usually involves the business joining a purchasing group or franchise system. This type of arrangement may also be used to purchase group insurance and benefit plans for employees.

Other methods of achieving potential savings on purchasing include buying in large quantities, seasonal buying, consignment buying, and receiving price discounts for paying in cash.

EVALUATING SUPPLIERS

Small business owners generally use certain criteria to evaluate suppliers. The following are some of the more common criteria.

Dependability.

The owner-manager should evaluate how dependable the prospective supplier will likely be. Dependability will undoubtedly be more important for some companies and even for some types of products than for others.

Cost.

Obviously the cost of inventories will play a major role in supplier selection for the small firm.

Services Offered.

Typical services offered by suppliers are delivery, discounts, credit, promotion, promotional support materials, return policies, guarantees, and technical assistance. Willingness and ability to provide these services at all hours may be an important factor in the selection of a supplier.

DETERMINING ORDER QUANTITIES

Estimating the quantities of inventories to order requires several essential items of information.

Order Lead Time.

Estimate the time taken to process the order at both shipping and destination points as well as to transport the item(s). This is called *order lead time* and is illustrated by the distance between points B and C in Figure 10-10. An increasing number of businesses have instituted a just-in-time (JIT) inventory policy. In this approach, the order is placed so that the inventory arrives "just in time" to be used in the production process. This system is appropriate for manufacturers that have computer capabilities, are confident of the dependability of suppliers, and require large amounts of inventory.

The basic idea of JIT is to reduce order sizes and time orders so that goods arrive as close to the time they are needed as possible. The intent is to minimize a business's dependence on inventory and cut the costs of moving and storing goods. JIT is used more by producers than by retailers. There are notable differences between a JIT approach and a more traditional approach. Figure 10-11 illustrates these differences.

Sales or Production Estimate.

The owner-manager will need to make a realistic projection of inventories to be sold or consumed in the manufacture of the finished product for the period. Methods of obtaining this type of information were discussed in Chapter 3. This rate of sale throughout the period is shown by the diagonal line A–C in Figure 10-10.

Minimum Inventory Levels Required.

No business wants to run out of inventory, especially if the inventory consists of important items. It is therefore common to carry a minimum basic inventory for many items. This inventory is often called *safety stock* and is shown as the distance between D and E in Figure 10-10.

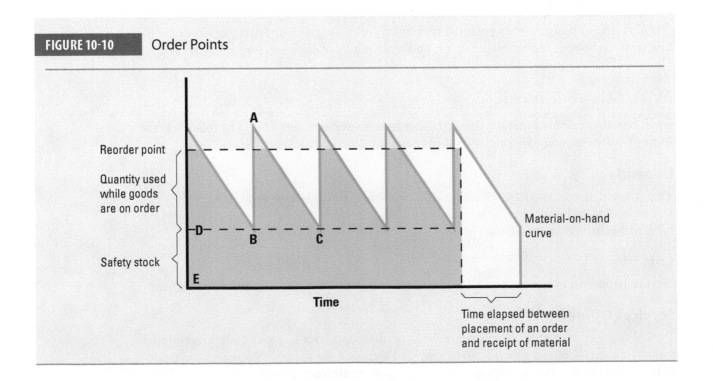

FIGURE 10-10   Order Points

FIGURE 10-11 | JIT and Traditional Inventory Comparison

JIT INVENTORY	TRADITIONAL INVENTORY
Small orders and frequent deliveries	Large orders and infrequent deliveries
Single-source supplier for a given part with long-term contract	Multiple sources of suppliers for same part with partial or short-term contracts
Suppliers expected to deliver product quality, delivery performance, and price; no rejects acceptable	Suppliers expected to deliver acceptable level of product quality, delivery performance, and price
Less emphasis on paperwork	Requires more time and formal paperwork
Delivery time and quantity can be changed with direct communication	Changes in delivery time and quantity require new purchase orders

Source: Sang Lee and Marc Schniederjams, *Operations Management* (Houghton Mifflin, Boston, 1994), p. 256.

The size of safety stock usually depends on such factors as the importance of the inventory, volatility of demand, and dependability of sources of supply.

Inventory Currently on Hand.

The owner-manager should have an accurate estimate of inventories on hand. To monitor current inventory levels on a continual basis, a perpetual inventory system can be used. Details of this type of system will be discussed later in this chapter. For many businesses, a perpetual system requires a computerized inventory system, which an increasing number of small businesses can now afford such systems. Once current inventory levels have been determined, the owner-manager can incorporate those amounts into various methods to determine order quantities.

Methods for Determining Order Quantities.

Some of the more common methods used to determine order quantities follow.

Minimum-Turnover Method.

This method uses the inventory turnover formula for the business in determining amounts of inventory required. For example, if inventory turnover for the business is 4 (four times per year) and projected sales for the period are $200,000, the required inventory is calculated as follows:

$$\frac{\text{Sales}}{\text{Inventory}} = \text{Inventory turnover}$$

$$\frac{\$200,000}{\text{Inventory}} = 4$$

$$\text{Inventory} = \frac{\$200,000}{4} = \$50,000$$

Hence, the minimum required inventory at retail value for the period is $50,000.

Maximum-and-Minimum Method.

Some small businesses set acceptable maximum and minimum limits on inventory levels. Whether inventory is measured in dollar amounts or number of units, reaching these limits indicates when it is time to order and specifies the amount to order. This method is frequently used by small businesses for merchandise of lower unit values.

Open-to-Buy Method.

This method of calculating order quantities, used extensively in retailing, uses the following formula (the components were discussed earlier):

Open to buy = Maximum inventory − Merchandise on order − Merchandise on hand

where

Open to buy = Inventories that can be purchased

Maximum inventory = Expected sales + Safety stock required

A-B-C Analysis.

This method of inventory management recognizes that some items of merchandise are more important to the business than others. The level of importance is influenced by such factors as higher sales, high unit value levels, higher profitability, or importance in the manufacture of the finished product.

With A-B-C analysis, the most important inventory (A items) is watched more closely to ensure it is managed efficiently. The B and C items, being less important, may require less detailed monitoring and control. Figure 10-12 gives an example of A-B-C analysis.

Administration of the Buying Process.

The owner-manager should be familiar with the mechanics of purchasing. Knowledge of the different kinds of discounts and purchase terms and conditions is essential, as are efficient receiving, checking, and marking of merchandise to minimize inventory costs and reduce shrinkage.

INVENTORY CONTROL

As discussed earlier, efficient purchasing requires proper monitoring and control practices. Three essential aspects of inventory control are determining the unit of control, the method of valuing inventories, and the method of monitoring inventory levels.

Unit of Control.

Most firms keep track of their inventories by dollar amounts. This approach is called *dollar inventory control*. Dollar inventory control is suitable for firms with large amounts of inventory at a relatively low per-unit value.

FIGURE 10-12 A-B-C Analysis

	A ITEMS	B ITEMS	C ITEMS
Percent of total inventory value	65%	25%	10%
Percent of total list of different stock items	20%	20%	60%
Inventory method used	Minimum turnover EOQ Maximum turnover	Minimum turnover	Eyeballing
Time allocation	Time-consuming and precision needed	Less time-consuming estimates	Rough estimates only

Some businesses that have relatively small amounts of inventory keep track of inventories in numbers of units. This method is called *unit control*.

Valuation.

Generally accepted accounting principles allow inventories to be valued at the lower of cost or market value. It is very important that an accurate valuation of inventory levels be calculated, because, as Figure 10-13 shows, inventory levels directly affect the net income of the business at the end of the period.

Monitoring.

There are essentially two methods of monitoring inventories. The first, periodic inventory, involves physically counting and recording the merchandise to determine inventory levels. Periodic inventory calculation is required at least once each year for income tax purposes. It is costly and time-consuming to carry out, however, so most businesses use this method no more frequently than required.

The second type of inventory monitoring, perpetual inventory, involves continuous recording of inventory increases and decreases as transactions occur. Historically, this system was feasible only for a small business with low levels of high-unit-value inventory. Recently, however, microcomputer database management programs have made the perpetual inventory system a reality for many small businesses. These systems use the bar codes that identify inventory purchases and sales. By using this system, sales can be tracked, inventory levels can be monitored, and orders can be made. Inventory software programs that small businesses can use are Peachtree Complete Accounting and QuickBooks Pro. These programs are relatively inexpensive and are regularly updated. Some small businesses find that developing a customized program, even though more costly, better suits their needs to manage inventory effectively. Inventory control is also enhanced by performing various evaluation analyses such as calculating turnover, comparing budgeted amounts with actual inventories, and analyzing inventory disappearance (shrinkage).

Security of Inventory.

Preventing loss of inventory (shrinkage) is a major challenge for most small businesses. The business should develop a detailed procedure for ordering, receiving, marking, handling, and monitoring all inventories. The system selected will vary, depending on the type of business. Additionally, some small businesses are investing greater attention and money to better security of inventory throughout the supply chain. Such devices as radio frequency identification (RFID) are being used on an increasing basis to track inventory as it moves through the distribution channel.

FIGURE 10-13   Valuation of Inventories

Sales − Cost of goods sold − Other expenses = Net income

where

Cost of goods sold = Beginning inventory + Purchases − Ending inventory

Using the relationships in these formulas, one can see that if ending inventory is overstated, cost of goods sold will be understated by the same amount and net income overstated by that same amount. Therefore, a valuation error of $100 will translate into either an overstatement or an understatement of net income by $100.

THE SMALL BUSINESS-SUPPLIER RELATIONSHIP

One critical key to the success of operations management is the relationship that the business maintains with its suppliers. Because of the size of the business and relatively small volumes of purchases, the small business tends to be at a disadvantage compared with large businesses in receiving favourable treatment from suppliers. It is therefore important that the owner-manager implement policies and procedures that can ensure a successful relationship with the supplier. Examples of such policies and procedures are as follows:[3]

1. Define clear, identifiable, and measurable objectives for your supplier management strategy.

2. Be prepared to work with the supplier to identify and define the roles that each will perform. Consider your relationship a partnership to achieve the goals stated in number one above.

3. Attempt to employ technology to share data relating to forecasting, product movement, and financial evaluation.

4. Evaluate suppliers regularly with an objective standardized framework that is both quantitative and qualitative.

SUPPLY CHAIN MANAGEMENT

Many successful small businesses recognize the value in developing a network of interconnected businesses to provide products and services to the end customer. Supply chain management includes the movement and storage of raw material, work-in-process inventory, and finished goods from point of origin to point of consumption. This means that the small business places high priority with the coordination and collaboration with channel partners such as suppliers, intermediaries, third party service providers, and customers.

TIME TO TAKE ACTION

1. Depending on your business or business plan, start to create standard operating procedures. Be sure to address such questions as how will you maintain quality control, standards, and so forth. You may find it helpful to contact entrepreneurs or managers with similar companies and ask for their advice.

2. If your business is a retail location, then start to visit other retailers. Take pictures and notes about their store layout. Create a document, using your computer, on how your store will be laid out. Ask experienced entrepreneurs to comment on the layout of your store.

LEARNING OBJECTIVES SUMMARY

LO1 The production process involves the conversion of inputs such as money, people, machines, and inventories into outputs—the products or services provided.

LO2 The physical facilities must be continually monitored, as the conditions that contribute to their effectiveness will not remain static.

LO3 The three types of layouts used by small manufacturing firms are the product layout, process layout, and fixed-position layout. The product layout is used when the business manufactures large numbers of just one product or a few products. The process layout is designed for factories that manufacture smaller numbers of many different or custom-made products. The fixed-position layout is used for very large or cumbersome products.

LO4 In planning the interior layout of a retail store, the retailer needs to analyze the allocation of selling versus non-selling space, the allocation of space among departments and/or products, classification of the merchandise, and the location of displays and products on the shelf. The two types of layouts used by a retail store are the grid layout and the free-flow layout. The grid layout, typically used in a supermarket, is organized with customer convenience and retail efficiency in mind. The free-flow layout has a more relaxed atmosphere that is conducive to browsing. This type of layout is suitable for clothing and many specialty types of merchandise.

LO5 In estimating the quantities to order, the essential items of information required are the order lead time, the sales or production estimate, minimum inventory levels required, and the inventory currently on hand. Some methods used to determine order quantities include the minimum-turnover method, which uses inventory turnover calculations; the maximum-and-minimum method, which indicates the time and amounts to order; the open-to-buy method, used in retailing; the economic order quantity, which calculates the minimization of the ordering and storage costs of inventory; and A-B-C analysis, which prioritizes types of inventory.

DISCUSSION QUESTIONS

1. What kind of layout should be used for the following manufacturing firms?
   a. Golf club manufacturer
   b. Independent bottler
   c. Bob's Machine Shop
2. What kind of layout should be used for the following retail firms?
   a. Clothing store
   b. Motorcycle shop
   c. Small grocery store
3. Answer the following questions regarding the location of food items in a grocery store:
   a. Where are bread and milk located? Why?
   b. Where are chocolate bars and other candies located? Why?
   c. Where on the shelf are the top name-brand items located? Why?
   d. Where are the high-margin items positioned in the store and on the shelves? Why?

APPLICATION QUESTIONS AND HANDS-ON ACTIVITIES

1. Visit a small retail store or manufacturing plant, and evaluate the layout.
2. Frank Newhart is opening a new DVD electronics store but has not determined which DVD supplier to use. Frank has narrowed the choice to two sources. Supplier 1 is newly established and sells the units for $60 apiece. Supplier 2 is a well-established firm and sells the units for $75 each, with a 7 percent discount on orders over 50 units. Evaluate each supplier from the information given. With this information, develop different scenarios in which Frank would choose supplier 1 or supplier 2.
3. Interview three business owners to determine which inventory ordering system they use and why.
4. Interview a small business owner to learn why he or she selected a particular supplier. Find out what criteria were important to the owner in making the choice.
5. How could a small business improve the quality of a product or service that it offered? Discuss the information provided in this chapter.

Dan worked long and hard to improve the financial condition of the business as a result of the statements received at the end of the first year of operations. He was able to make some adjustments in operations, move some short-term debt to long term, and obtain additional equity that allowed the business to receive adequate financing for the second year. His banker was also influenced positively by the upward sales trends for the Ladder Rail. In addition to allowing the existing operation to receive stable financing, the bank also agreed to finance the addition to the building that Dan had been contemplating. It was felt that this building was needed to meet the growing demand for the product.

With the new addition, Dan is now considering revising the interior space of the plant. Until now, he has employed an assembly-line type of production process, as he makes only one product. However, Dan is starting to get orders for different-sized ladders (which require a variation in the size and type of Ladder Rail), as well as for other accessories, such as safety braces to prevent ladders from moving sideways when placed against a building or roof. Given the possibilities for increasing his line of products in the future, Dan wonders whether his current manufacturing layout is still effective.

Another concern Dan is dealing with is inventory levels. Dan started out using the industry average for manufacturing plants to order initial inventory, but he soon realized that the industry average did not apply to a small plant like his. He then tried to order high volumes of inventory to get a better price, but he found that if the metal was sitting too long in inventory, it was costing him in interest expenses. Conversely, Dan does not want to run out of metal and cause a stoppage in the production process.

Dan is currently purchasing the metal used in fabricating the Ladder Rail from a local plant in Hamilton. He is, however, continually receiving calls from salespeople from outside the area offering better prices. This is also a concern for Dan. All these dilemmas are weighing heavily on Dan and are taking him away from making the Ladder Rail units. He often thinks how nice it would be to just be involved in the manufacturing part and not have to worry about such things as buying metal and selling Ladder Rails.

Questions

1. Discuss the layout options for Dan's company, considering the increased space and changes in product line.

2. What advice could you give Dan regarding his inventory ordering and management practices?

3. Discuss the criteria that Dan could use to evaluate suppliers for metal.

For more information on the resources available from McGraw-Hill Ryerson, go to www.mcgrawhill.ca/he/solutions.

CHAPTER
11

HUMAN RESOURCES MANAGEMENT

By the end of this chapter, you should be able to:

LO1 Explain the importance of human resources management to the small business.

LO2 Illustrate the methods of planning for hiring and training employees.

LO3 Identify the principles of effective human resources management for the small business.

LO4 Discuss skill areas the owner-manager can strengthen to improve personal leadership and people skills within the organization.

LO5 Identify the legal requirements relating to personnel of the small business.

LO6 Review the procedures of administering a small business payroll.

CHARLIE SPIRING *Wellington West Capital Inc.*

Wellington West was founded in 1993 by one of Canada's top investment advisers, Charles Spiring. Charlie walked away from a successful career at a major financial institution to create a top-quality, local investment boutique. In 1996, he added financial planning capability to complement the full-service brokerage. Charlie's vision was to create a brokerage owned by brokers. He was committed to selecting only the best and brightest talent in the industry—people who lead and inspire their communities.

Photo courtesy of Charlie Spiring

Wellington West had become one of the largest and fastest growing independent full-service investment firms in Canada. This is particularly significant because the major banks in Canada control 70 percent of the brokerage business. Wellington had more than 40 offices, 585 employees, and nearly $9 billion in client assets under administration. This led to several #1 placings in the Canadian Investment Executive Brokerage industry over the past decade.

The secret to Wellington's success, according to Spiring, included several personnel practices that are unique to the industry. First, brokers are offered an ownership share of the company. This allowed Wellington to attract many well-respected analysts to the firm. These brokers, although successful with their previous company, had not "experienced ownership, entrepreneurialism, culture, independence and autonomy," according to Spiring. Even though this practice of employee ownership had led to Spiring's ownership equity dropping to less than 20 percent, he was not worried. He realized that the company's success was completely dependent on employees' individual skills, personalities, and attitudes.

Other unique personnel practices were that the company disclosed sales numbers daily, conducted complete accounting quarterly, and publicly released an annual report, even though the company was private. Wellington also held regular town hall meetings with its employees, ensuring open communication. Flexibility was also a feature of the employee work environment. World and Canadian curling champion Jennifer Jones was an in-house corporate lawyer for Wellington and was allowed to take the necessary time off work to participate in competitions.

The results of Wellington's personnel practices had garnered it many awards. Some of them included Canada's second best workplace in the 2008 Hewitt Associates survey of Canadian companies (#1 in 2007), #33 in *Profit Magazine's* top 100 fastest growing companies in 2008, and six consecutive years ranking among the Canadian 50 Best Employers survey. Charlie Spiring has personally been awarded the "top 40 under 40" business award, and he won the 2009 Entrepreneur of the Year Award in Finance at the Ernst and Young Awards Dinner.

Wellington's personnel practices led to financial success as well. Wellington had shown revenue growth of 585 percent from 2003–2008, with offices and employees across Canada. Although still a small company by industry standards, Wellington had shown that success and growth are possible by using creative personnel management practices and showing employees that they are valued.

In 2011, Wellington West was sold to National Bank, and in 2012, Wellington West Financial Services (a division of Wellington West Holdings) was subsequently sold to Manulife. One of the biggest assets in the sale to National Bank was Wellington's employees, whose motivation and performance made them attractive to large organizations. Both National Bank and Manulife stated they wanted to maintain the positive management practices of Wellington West in their respective business practices.

WELLINGTON WEST CAPITAL INC.
www.wellingtonwestcapital.com

Source: Used with the permission of Charlie Spiring.

HUMAN RESOURCES MANAGEMENT AND THE SMALL BUSINESS

LO1

Management in an organization has often been defined as getting things done through other people. Small business owners are personnel managers, even if their main strength or interest lies in the production, financial, or marketing aspects of the business.

Often small business owners are reluctant to learn human resources management (HR) fundamentals because they believe these principles apply only to larger organizations. The result is often HR problems such as frequent turnover of staff, lack of motivation and initiative, lack of harmony among employees, high absenteeism, frequent grievances, and high overall employee costs. The incidence of these problems appears to be high in small business. A recent study by Industry Canada found that successful entrepreneurs believe that owner-managers' number one challenge and most time-consuming activity is personnel.[1] Another study pointed out that the demands of running the business usually prevented owner-managers from paying as much attention to their employees as they should.[2] A third study, conducted by the Canadian Federation of Independent Business, found that more than half of small businesses had difficulty finding qualified labour at a reasonable wage.[3] Another study conducted by American Express in co-operation with *Profit Magazine* found that 74 percent of Canadian firms said it was hard to find employees, especially managers and tradespeople.[4] Moreover, the Conference Board of Canada predicts that business will experience employee shortages of 1 million by the year 2020 due to the retirements of baby-boomers.[5] Despite these predictions and trends, CFIB has also found that employees in small companies are significantly more likely to rate their workplace as "good" than those in large firms, as shown in Figure 11-1. The reasons for this apparent high level of satisfaction are increased flexibility in the workplace and a closer relationship with the owner.[6] Small businesses have a natural advantage over large businesses in these areas. It is critical that the entrepreneur use the techniques described in this chapter to maintain that advantage.

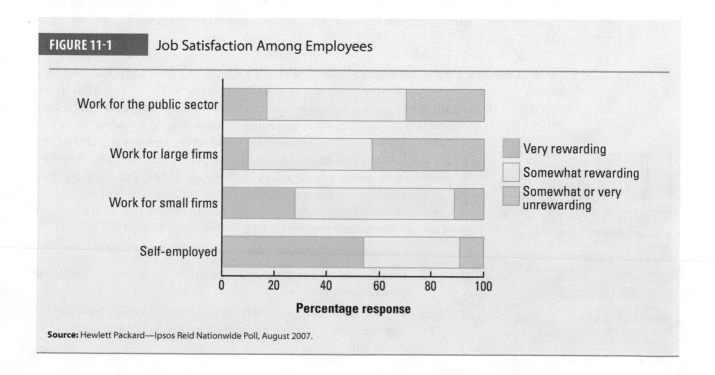

FIGURE 11-1 Job Satisfaction Among Employees

Source: Hewlett Packard—Ipsos Reid Nationwide Poll, August 2007.

As the business grows, the owner-manager's workload generally expands. Because there is a limit to what one person can do, the business may suffer if the owner fails to hire new employees and delegate responsibilities to them. In most cases, when this occurs, the entrepreneur will have difficulty making the transition from a start-up to a growing, well-managed business that maintains its success over a long period of time. If a company is successful eventually an entrepreneur will have to share the management of the firm or create what is known as a *management team*.

The reputation of a business in the community can be affected by employees' satisfaction with their jobs. The level of employee satisfaction can be enhanced or lowered by the owner-manager's use of personnel management principles. This is especially true in the retail and service industries. Motivated and competent personnel are one characteristic of a business that the competition may find difficult to duplicate.

A recent survey found that 56 percent of small business owners increased the time and money invested in employee training, with only 2 percent indicating a decrease.[7] The majority report that the responsibility for training employees lies mainly with the owner.

Given all these factors, it is essential that the owner-manager have some knowledge of personnel administration principles to sustain the success of the business. This chapter covers planning for personnel, hiring, and ongoing personnel management in the small business.

PLANNING FOR HUMAN RESOURCES   LO2

There is an old saying in business, "If I hire someone and they fail to perform, then I have made a mistake." What this essentially means is that a person is responsible for the people they hire; if they fail to live up to expectations or—worse—steal, lie, or harm the company's reputation, then the person who hired them is ultimately responsible. If the saying does not convince you of the need for a detailed human resources plan, then simple math might. The cost of a poor hiring decision to a company's bottom line is a net loss of two to four times that person's annual salary. This calculation includes the costs associated with the original staffing process, training the person, the realization that they are ineffective, removing them from the organization, and then hiring a replacement, all of this would cost a company thousands of dollars.

To avoid poor hiring decisions and to ensure productive and engaged people are working for a small business, a human resources plan should be developed. Questions to consider in a human resources plan include how many employees the company will have and need in the next one to three years, when employees will be needed, what training programs will be provided, where candidates will come from, what job requirements will need to be met, how and what employees will be compensated, and what employee policies will be in place. While this sounds like a substantial amount of work, investors will want to know your answers to these questions. Furthermore, this information will assist you when it comes time to hire and administer people in your organization. The best way to ensure that all these questions are addressed is by completing the following tasks:

1. Determine the requirements.

2. Establish an organizational structure (for every planned hire, draw a new chart).

3. Prepare job descriptions including job titles, qualifications, duties, reporting lines, compensation, training necessary, and potential career paths.

THERE IS A SAYING IN BUSINESS, THE PERSON WHO MAKES THE HIRING DECISION IS RESPONSIBLE FOR WHO THEY HIRE.
© Blend Images/Alamy

4. Develop a hiring plan.

5. Develop human resources policies such as sick leave, bereavement leave, tardiness policy, and so on.

Determine Personnel Requirements.

The first step in planning for personnel is to determine the number of jobs or tasks to be done, shift schedules if applicable, and determine the level of expertise required and the number of people needed to perform those tasks. This process may already have been carried out as part of the feasibility analysis discussed in Chapter 3 or in business planning in Chapter 4.

Set Organizational Structure.

The second step in personnel planning is to integrate tasks and employees so that the owner can visualize how the different parts of the plan will work together. This formalized plan is commonly called an *organizational chart.* In the very small (two- or three-person) business, the organizational chart may simply be a division of responsibilities, as in Figure 11-2. In a larger business, the organizational chart shows the lines of responsibility for each member of the organization. An organizational chart for a small retail store appears in Figure 11-3. Each business possesses unique characteristics that dictate how to set up the organizational chart. Some of the more common approaches are to organize by (1) function performed such as sales, purchasing, or promotion; (2) type of merchandise or department, as in Figure 11-3; or (3) geographic territory.

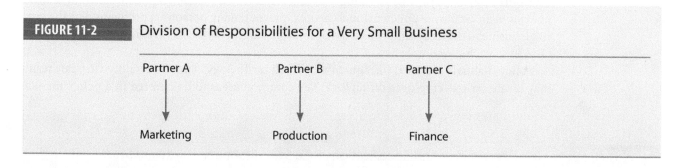

FIGURE 11-2   Division of Responsibilities for a Very Small Business

Partner A	Partner B	Partner C
↓	↓	↓
Marketing	Production	Finance

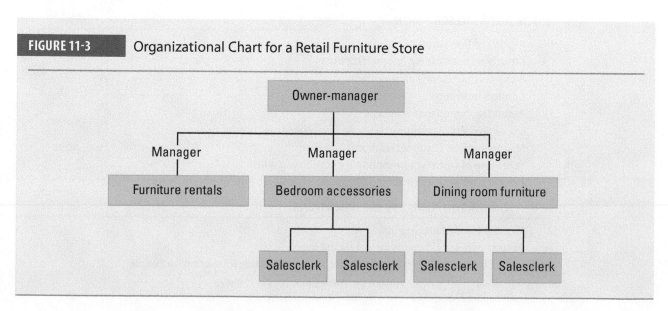

FIGURE 11-3   Organizational Chart for a Retail Furniture Store

In setting up the organizational structure, some rules of thumb have been found to contribute to a successful operation:

- Each employee should report to only one supervisor. This arrangement is called *unity of control or command.*
- Similar functions should be grouped together, if possible.
- There is a limit to an individual's span of control. Span of control is the number of people who can be directly supervised by one person. The proper span of control varies according to the combined characteristics of the manager, the subordinates, and the job.

Prepare Job Descriptions.

The third step in personnel planning is to prepare job descriptions and specifications. Before hiring employees, a detailed listing of the job or task duties (job descriptions) must be made. The job description briefly explains what is to be done, how it is to be done, and why it is done. This information goes into the job specification—a statement of the skills, abilities, physical characteristics, and education required to perform the job. As mentioned earlier, part of the job description may be included in the policy manual. Figure 11-4 illustrates a job description and specifications for an employee of a small business.

Develop Personnel Policies.

The fourth step in personnel planning is to formally develop personnel policies. Including these policies in an employee policy manual can help prevent many personnel problems. For the very small business, this may simply be a list of some do's and don'ts; a larger business may provide a booklet to each new employee.

Policy manuals are used infrequently in small businesses. The uncertainty that can result may create serious employee difficulties. The common areas to be covered in a policy manual

| FIGURE 11-4 | Job Descriptions and Specifications for a Sales Manager, Hardware Store |

JOB DUTIES DESCRIPTION

Reports to the general manager
Directly responsible for floor salespeople
Suggests markdowns on slow items
Controls inventory
Authorizes merchandise returns
Occasionally meets with suppliers to learn about new products
Maintains good customer relations at all times
Takes care of written correspondence concerning sales
Does any other task relevant to the job as requested by the general manager

PERSONAL REQUIREMENTS SPECIFICATIONS

High school diploma or equivalent
At least two years' experience in a similar job
Initiative; "instinct" for sales; convincing manner; aptitude for managing people
Self-disciplined; good appearance; willing to work overtime

are described below. Minimum standards for many of these areas are set by government labour departments in each province and territory.

- Job descriptions clearly outline the duties, responsibilities, and reporting lines for employees, as mentioned previously.

- Working conditions include such things as hours of work, coffee breaks, and other expectations of management.

- Holidays and leaves outline statutory holidays, paid vacations, and procedures for taking a leave of absence.

- Remuneration and pay consist of a listing of details of the payroll such as date of payment, time periods included, and reviews of pay levels.

- Employee benefits provided by the firm such as bonuses, profit sharing, medical-dental insurance plans, and employee discounts should be clearly stated.

- The grievance procedure consists of a description of the procedure employees are to follow if they have a concern or grievance within the organization.

THE HIRING PROCESS

Once the personnel plan has been developed, the next step is to review various sources for potential employees and make the selection.

SOURCES OF EMPLOYEES

A study by the Canadian Federation of Independent Business indicated that the most common methods of recruitment for small businesses were referrals from friends and employees (used by 69 percent of companies), media ads (used by 41 percent), unsolicited applications (used by 37 percent), and government agencies (used by 17 percent).[8] The following are some other potential sources of employees for small businesses.

Recruitment from Within.

For most organizations, recruiting from within the firm is the most common course if current employees have the qualifications. Hiring an outsider to perform a supervisory job instead of someone within the organization usually has a negative and disruptive effect on the business.

Other Businesses.

To reduce training costs, employees from competing firms or similar industries can be hired. Such employees generally will have some background in the industry or business that can be easily transferred. The recruiter, however, will have to use this approach carefully to avoid a negative reaction from the competition, particularly in smaller markets.

Employee Referrals.

Current employees may be asked to recommend acquaintances to fill available jobs. This method has the advantage of some prior knowledge of the individual's background. Some firms such as Toronto-based Achievers provide employees with incentives for make successful referrals. A downside of this method is it may have a negative effect, however, if the new employee proves unsatisfactory.[9]

Advertising and Using Social Media.

MANY COMPANIES ARE POSTING JOBS AND SEARCHING FOR LEADS ON LINKEDIN, FACEBOOK, TWITTER, YOUTUBE, AND SO FORTH.
Cifotart/Dreamstime.com

Small businesses frequently advertise for employees in local newspapers or using online ads on national sites such as such as Workopolis (www.workopolis.com) or Monster (www.monster.ca), or they use region-specific sites such as Career Beacon (www.careerbeacon.ca). Since the cost of newspaper advertising is rising, more and more firms are finding online advertising optimal, as they can often post more details about the job online for less money. In addition the Internet has replaced newspapers as the traditional source of information for job hunters.

Small and large companies alike are also using social media to post jobs and to find qualified leads. Many companies are posting jobs and searching for leads on LinkedIn, Facebook, Twitter, YouTube, and so forth. Business author Shannon Bowen-Smed says social media allows firms to go beyond traditional job posting and should be a key component of recruitment strategies. Bowen-Smed says social media can be used to reach passive job searchers by creating conversations on social networking sites such as LinkedIn and firms can highlight their positive corporate culture on Twitter and Facebook making their company more appealing to job seekers.[10] For example, Toronto-based Razor Suleman recently distributed job postings for 17 positions to his employees, who then placed them on their Facebook status updates, tweeted them to friends who re-tweeted them, and shared them through LinkedIn networks. Mr. Suleman explains that the average cost of a newspaper ad is $5000, while an online job board costs $700. Another comparison would be with recruitment firms that charge a percentage of a new hire's salary; the price tag of using one to fill these 17 positions would be $260,000. Instead, he is paying a total of $1800 for wine and

---

INCIDENT 11-1

LINKEDIN'S IMPACT ON EMPLOYEE RECRUITMENT

While LinkedIn was originally founded as a social networking site for professionals, it has transformed itself into a site where people expand their networks, look for work, or are found by potential employers who often browse the site for qualified leads. In addition to job postings, LinkedIn now offers companies the following tools to assist them in recruiting candidates:

1. LinkedIn Recruiter allows companies to browse the profile of all LinkedIn users so they can contact people who may be interested in working for their firm.

2. LinkedIn Employment Branding services allow companies to build a career website on LinkedIn to network and attract employees.

3. LinkedIn Talent allows firms to manage incoming applications and manage recruitment marketing.[11]

Spark Internet Marketing Corp. (www.sparkinternetmarketing.com), a Toronto-based firm, recently used LinkedIn to fill a position with a unique technical skill set—SEO management. Rather than advertise the job, Spark's executives posted information about the job in some of LinkedIn's groups and quickly filled the position.[12]

The major advantage of using social media recruitment is the low cost, as sites such as LinkedIn and Facebook do not charge. Additionally firms can access passive job seekers—people who would consider applying for a job they see but are not actively looking for work. The other major advantage is reach; not only will postings easily reach all the followers, people are inclined to share information they see on social media that they think others will be interested in.

Discussion Questions

1. What do you think are the advantages and disadvantages of using social media sites to recruit for employees?

2. What types of companies do you think are best suited to use LinkedIn and other social media sites for recruitment? Which types of companies do you think are poorly suited to use LinkedIn? Why?

---

cheese at the open house that applicants are invited to. Companies such as Future Shop, Best Body Bootcamp, and many others are using similar means to find new employees. Experts say that for reach, speed, and recruitment branding, social media are here to stay.[13]

Employment Agencies.

Employment agencies sponsored by provincial governments are one source. Human Resources Development Canada (www.hrdc-drhc.gc.ca) offices also have lists of employees looking for work. This can be a potentially valuable source of employees, particularly for positions that do not require highly technical expertise. Private employment agencies typically are not used by small businesses to recruit employees, but they may be helpful in recruiting highly skilled employees.

Educational Institutions.

Some small businesses that require employees with technical expertise use universities or colleges as sources. These sources can be helpful in manufacturing, some service businesses, and retailing.

THE SCREENING PROCESS   LO3

Once potential employees have been identified from one or more of the above sources, the owner-manager faces the task of selection. Several screening devices can be used to help select employees.

Application Form or Resumé.

Many small businesses will have a potential applicant submit a resumé or an application form. These documents can be a valuable screening tool and a time saver for the owner as they provide the candidate's education, work experience, and skills. Applicants who do not have the required background or skills do not have to be interviewed or hired. An application form need not be lengthy to be useful, as Figure 11-5 illustrates.

The Employment Interview.

Although the application form or the submission of a resumé may screen out several potential employees, an interview is normally required to make the final decision. The employment interview is particularly important for jobs requiring interpersonal contact, as it allows the interviewer to judge appearance, poise, and communication ability. A helpful tool in interviewing is an interview guide, which focuses the discussion and provides a constant base of information with which to compare applicants. Interviews normally start with an introduction, questions are asked about the resumé, open-ended question may be asked followed by PAR (problem–action–result) questions (see below). At the end of the interview it is common for the potential employee to make additional comments and/or ask questions. Jerry Fitch, president of Toronto-based Marberg Staffing (www.marberg.com), says preparation is the key to a successful interview. Fitch advises employers to start by formulating a job description and basing the questions on the corresponding skills. Research on interviews indicates that while PAR questions are very common, there are no magic questions that will help employers find the best person.[14] For example, Rowan O'Grady, president of Hays Recruitment Canada says he likes going through a candidate's job history one position at a time and find out what they enjoyed about the company and what they found frustrating. O'Grady says it helps him pick out inconsistencies.[15]

FIGURE 11-5

Application for Employment for a Small Business

Name _____   First Name _____

Address (Home) _____   Tel. _____

Address (Work) _____   Tel. _____

Social Insurance No. _____

Languages: Spoken _____   Written _____

Secondary Education

_____

Years   School   City   Diploma

Post-Secondary Education

_____

Years   School   City   Degree

Work Experience
(begin with most recent)

From _____ To _____   Employer _____

Title _____   Nature of Duties _____

Salary _____

Reason for Leaving _____

_____

_____

Work Experience

From _____ To _____   Employer _____

Title _____   Nature of Duties _____

Salary _____

Reason for Leaving _____

_____

Other Information

References   Name   Address   Title

1.

2.

3.

Signature   Date

Checking References.

The third screening device is the checking of references. Most application forms require the applicant to list both personal and business references. As might be expected, business references are more valuable because they provide information regarding the individual's past work record.

Checks made by telephone or in person with business references are preferred to written responses. The writer of a letter of reference may have little or no idea of the requirements of the job. Also, past employers are sometimes reluctant to write uncomplimentary letters of reference. Specific questions should be asked about the candidate's performance as well as about whether employers would consider rehiring the person. Recently, more and more companies are using social media sites to screen out candidates or to learn more about applicants. The issue is discussed in more detail below.

Tests.

Many large businesses use various types of intellectual, ethical, and physical tests as part of the screening process. Some specific tests being used increasingly in small businesses are proficiency and skill tests (to perform a particular trade, craft, or skill), vocational interest tests (to assess long-term interest in the job or company), aptitude tests (to determine how a person might perform on a given job), and polygraph tests (to measure level of honesty). Because some of these tests are technical, the owner-manager should seek professional assistance in administering them.

INCIDENT 11-2

USING SOCIAL MEDIA TO REFERENCE CHECK

More and more business owners and human resources professionals are now screening applications by visiting an applicant's social media sites. *Forbes* magazine recently reported 37 percent of employers use social networks to screen potential job candidates. These companies are scanning social media sites to see if a person presents a professional image, if the person will fit into the company's corporate culture, and to learn more about a person's credentials and experiences. Not only are companies attempting to learn more about potential employees by scanning social media sites but roughly 33 percent of businesses that engage in the practice have opted not to hire someone based on what they have discovered on social media.[16]

Some social media users, particularly younger users, may find this use of social media reference checking disconcerting, as they think social media sites are private and employers should recognize this when screening applicants. Many business owners and human resources professionals counter with the fact that the information is publicly available and should be considered. A recent study by Dr. Amy Thurlow, a professor at Halifax-based Mount Saint Vincent University, on the acceptable use of online information may shed some light on the opposing viewpoints. Dr. Thurlow discovered that older people thought all information in the public domain, including information on social media sites, was public content and it was fair to use such information in any way that they saw fit. Others, in particular younger people, indicated that it was not the poster's responsibility to control what they put on their social media site; rather, the visitor of the site should be expected to know what is private and what is intended for public viewing.[17]

Discussion Questions

1. Do you think potential employers should look at people's social media pages as part of the hiring process? Is this practice ethical or unethical? Why?

2. Once employees are hired, do you think employers should monitor their social media usage? Why, or why not?

3. Who is responsible for privacy on social media sites—the person who posts the information or the person who visits the site?

4. If you managed or owned a business, would you visit a candidate's social media sites as part of the hiring process? Why, or why not?

NOTIFICATION OF THE HIRING DECISION

Once the hiring decision has been made, an offer of employment should be made to the successful applicant. This notification should be in writing, with a clear indication of the terms and conditions associated with the job. Most businesses require written confirmation of acceptance of the offer by the applicant.

All unsuccessful applicants should also be notified. Failure to provide this courtesy can have a detrimental effect on the reputation of the business.

INCIDENT 11-3

DO'S AND DON'TS OF HIRING

Poor hiring can be as much of a problem as not controlling cash flow. Entrepreneurs should always start with a job description and then develop a plan to staff each position. The following is a list of do's and don'ts that will assist in the process:

Do:

1. Write a detailed job description. You will be lost without one.
2. Prepare interview questions in advance, and ask everyone the same questions. You could be subject to a human rights complaint if you do not follow this procedure.
3. When interviewing, screen the resumé to verify that the facts are true. Then move on to PAR-type questions.
4. Provide candidates with a reasonable description of the job and a timeline of the hiring process.
5. Take notes throughout the interviewing process. It is impossible to remember everything.
6. Try to limit the number of candidates that you interview.
7. Make sure that you check references thoroughly. Prepare questions in advance, and make sure that the reference can provide an accurate assessment of the candidate's work record.
8. Test the candidates. For example, if you want them to speak in public, design a simulation where they have to speak to a room; if they need to speak another language, give them a language test.
9. Make use of any external testing tools such as ethics, honesty, or aptitude tests. Even small companies can make use of online testing tools that range in price from as little as $10–$250. Thomas Savundra uses psychometric tests to ensure that new employees share his web hosting company's values.

Don't:

1. Rely only on the interview process as a selection method. The interview has proven to be a poor tool in selecting candidates.
2. Become stuck on one key qualification. If you originally wanted an MBA and someone applied for the position without one but has 10 years of job experience, do not dismiss them from the process.
3. Rely on non-work-related references. Many resumés are filled with references from volunteer commitments, politicians, or religious leaders, and they will rarely speak poorly about people who volunteer their time or vote for them.
4. Ever assume the candidate is telling the truth. In fact, one prominent HR group notes that 25 percent of job applications contain a major falsehood.

When interviewing candidates for the job it is best to rely on the PAR method of questioning to be sure that you have a true idea about the candidate's skills in certain areas. The PAR method is based on a simple premise that the best predictor of future behaviour is past behaviour. The PAR process is as follows:

*   **P:** Present the candidate with a problem that he or she would have had to overcome in the past job that is related to the position for which you are hiring. If you are hiring for a sales position, ask questions such as, "Can you give me a time when you had to close a particularly tough sales call?" or "Can you tell me about a time that you had a problem dealing with angry customers?"
*   **A:** Ask the candidate what action he or she took to resolve the problem.
*   **R:** Ask if the result was positive or negative. Note that the entrepreneur should pay close attention to the result segment of the answer. Some candidates may come up with innovative solutions to problems, but if the results are not positive, this is a strong indicator that they probably did not take the right course of action.[18]

PERSONNEL MANAGEMENT LO4

Once employees have been hired, the owner-manager's responsibility is to see that they are properly trained, satisfied enough with the working conditions to continue working there, and—probably most important—motivated to work hard and show initiative. Most small businesses are not in a position to hire a professional personnel manager to ensure that these desirable conditions exist. However, the owner-manager can foster these conditions by using the concepts of personnel management discussed in this section.

THE INTRODUCTION PERIOD

The first few months on the job are crucial to the employee's overall satisfaction and length of stay with the business.

The First Week.

One of the most frequently mentioned characteristics of good working conditions is the way the owner-manager makes the employees feel like part of the organization.[19] Much can be done in the first week to communicate to employees that they are a valued member of the business. New employees should be introduced to co-workers, shown the locations of employee facilities, informed of any company regulations, and encouraged to ask for additional information needed. Employees should be talked to frequently during the introductory period, not simply left alone to read the company policy manual as larger companies sometimes do.

Many employers find it helpful to set some short-term goals toward which the new employees can work within the first week or two. These goals can be discussed at the conclusion of the agreed-on time. This communicates not only that the employer is interested in the employee but also that the business is results- and goal-oriented.

THE PROBATIONARY PERIOD

Most employers find it advantageous to use a probationary period of three to six months for new employees. The probationary period allows the employer to further assess the new employee's suitability for the job. At the conclusion of a satisfactory probation period, the employee becomes permanent and may be entitled to a pay increase and other benefits of a permanent employee.

TRAINING

The purpose of the training program is to increase productivity. In addition, successful training programs can reduce employee turnover, allow for less supervision, and increase employee morale. Properly trained employees acquire a sense of worth, dignity, and well-being, as well as increased skill levels. Businesses use many forms of employee training. Two of the more common are discussed next.

On-the-Job Training.

This is the least structured and most frequently used method by small businesses. It is perhaps the best method of training for routine and repetitive types of work. The business may assign another worker to work closely with the new employee in a buddy system or apprenticeship. Formal apprenticeship programs are offered by many educational institutions and are growing rapidly, with approximately 300,000 apprentices currently registered in Canada.[20]

Just-in-Time (JIT) Training.

One of the more common types of employee training that is becoming particularly suitable for small business is short term or project training. Because of rapid advances in technology, many jobs are changed or displaced every three to five years.[21] It is predicted that in the future, an organization's core workforce will need to be continually training as new skills are required. This just-in-time (JIT) training may be provided by professional training agencies or simply downloaded onto employee computers.

Formal Classroom Training.

Businesses use many varieties of formal classroom training, but only a few have been used by small businesses. One such system is a co-operative type of program with an educational institution. This allows the employee to attend classroom instruction and training on a part-time basis. In Canada, the government provides financial assistance for employee training programs. These programs are discussed later in this chapter. Some businesses hold periodic seminars in which they bring experts from various fields to the business. Recent research indicates that 43 percent of small businesses in Canada use a combination of the above methods, while 43 percent use only informal on-the-job training.[22]

THE OWNER-MANAGER AS LEADER AND PERSONNEL MANAGER

Leadership Style.

Entrepreneurs are often the primary managers in their business, and their ability to lead and their leadership style is quite important to the success of the firm. While some people are natural leaders, it is a skill which can be developed and taught. Successful business author and researcher Jim Collins notes that successful leaders put the company first, surround themselves with highly qualified people, and then provide them with the decision making tools and resources to do their job.[23] Leadership experts Jim Kouzes and Barry Posner, co-authors of *The Leadership Challenge,* state that leadership can be learned and that great leaders follow several basic principles that they refer to as the Practices of Exemplary Leadership.[24] They have found that such strategies work with large and small companies alike. The practices are as follows:

- *Find your personal voice by clarifying your personal values:* Essentially successful leaders establish expectations for themselves and then must reinforce these values daily in their actions.
- *Model the way:* Great leaders act as exemplary role models to employees.
- *Inspire a shared vision:* Create a vision of where you want your company to be. Then enlist others that share the same dream.
- *Challenge the process:* Do not accept any process or problem as unchangeable. Leaders should continuously search for new opportunities to grow their company.
- *Enable others to act:* Collaborate as it improves performance, create a climate of trust, and strengthen others by providing confidence and fostering accountability.
- *Encourage the heart:* Recognize contributions, pay attention to what is occurring, expect the best, and recognize those who perform well, celebrate victories, create a spirit of community.[25]

Often another step in this process is a self-evaluation to obtain an understanding of one's own leadership or management style. Sometimes, owners are so preoccupied with running the technical or market side of the business that they give little thought to the kind of leadership example they set for employees.

For entrepreneurs, several styles appear to be successful. A recent study of Canadian entrepreneurs found five different types of leadership. Figure 11-6 describes each type.[26]

The effectiveness of the owner-manager's leadership style may vary, depending on the characteristics of the business and its employees. However, certain styles generally are more successful in the long run. Whatever the owner-manager's style, concern for both the people within the organization and the production process is important.

Time Management.

A second critical aspect of successful people management is efficiently managing one's own time. Time management is often difficult to apply in small businesses. So many operating crises and interruptions take place in the normal course of a day that the owner-manager may feel that much of the advice in time management literature is impossible to employ. However, some basic time management concepts can be used successfully in a small business. Some of the more important concepts are discussed next.

Recognize the Importance of Time.

Much time wasting results from a failure to recognize the importance of one's time. The first step in improved time management, therefore, is to have a sincere desire to use time more efficiently.

Re-examine and Clarify Priorities.

Priority planning may be long or short term. Long-term planning involves setting objectives that the owner and business are projected to meet over a period of months or years. Long-term objectives, which are a part of the business plan, as discussed in Chapter 4 as part of the establishment plan of the business, provide direction for the firm. This strategic plan serves as the guideline for all operations of the business. Short-term priority planning deals with the use of time on a daily or weekly basis. It involves prioritizing tasks and working on those that are most important.

Analyze Present Time-Consuming Activities.

This step requires keeping a diary of the daily activities of the owner-manager. Most people find the results of this step surprising. Often they find they spend time on less important items at the

---

FIGURE 11-6	Leadership Styles in Canadian Small Business

SOLO	OSMOSIS	MANAGERIAL	SYSTEMS	FIGUREHEAD
Does everything	High level of control over business but does spend time developing managers	Sets objectives and lines of authority	Develops systems and direction	Owns business but has little to do with it
Little delegation		Controls results but delegates more on procedures	Allows employees to set some objectives and determine how they are met	Complete delegation
Very small firms	High level of contact with employees	Less employee contact		

expense of more important ones. One small business owner spent several hours arguing over a $25 increase in building rental instead of using that time to evaluate the suitability of the overall location.

Implement Time Management Principles.

The owner-manager may be able to eliminate common time-wasting traps and use time more efficiently by implementing the following practices:

- Avoid procrastinating on difficult but important decisions in favour of easier but less important ones.
- Use the most productive time of the day for the more important decisions or analyses. For some people, this may be early in the day, and for others it may be later. Many have found it beneficial to schedule routine or enjoyable tasks during their least productive time.
- Read only relevant information. Stop reading, and start searching. Use travel, waiting, or otherwise unproductive times for reading.
- Use letters less and the telephone more. If possible, handle letters only once in a given period of time.
- Operate with a minimum of meetings. Make sure meetings are results oriented and have definite starting and ending times.
- Delegate as much work as possible, recognizing that the owner manager is still ultimately responsible for the decision or action. A more detailed discussion of delegation in small businesses appears in Chapter 13.

ORGANIZATION CULTURE

In addition to managing employees and setting the vision for the company, the actions of the founding entrepreneur will also define the organization culture. Organizational culture is the blend of attitudes, behaviours, dress, and communication styles that make one business different from another. Business owners should recognize that their decisions will impact the way their employees interact with one another and with customers. For example, Costa Elles, owner of Ela (www.elagreektaverna.com), a Halifax-based Greek restaurant, is in the process of creating a customer first culture. He recently had a staff meeting where he wrote the word "yes" on a board. He then gave a speech in which the central theme was "just say yes" to what customers want. If customers want to substitute food—say yes; if customers want to order off the lunch menu at dinner—say yes; and so forth. Later in the week, Elles observed an exchange in which a chef was questioning a server's order as she allowed for uncommon substitutions in the three-course meal. Elles said the server listened to the chef saying that the substitution would be difficult and then reminded him that their motto was, "say yes." The chef then agreed with the server and made the food. The end result, according to Elles, is a happy customer, and happy customers come back. Elles is in the process of buying pins and other signs for the employees displaying the word "yes" to get the message across.[27]

When creating a corporate culture, the owner must ensure it is aligned with the strategy in the business plan. For example, Fran Bigelow, founder of Fran's Chocolates (www.franschocolates.com) in Seattle, has been able to get her employees, including her management team, to consider themselves artisans, focus on detail, and strive for perfection. Fran feels that this strategy is effective for her venture because of her premium product line but might result in disaster for someone marketing a high-volume, low-cost manufactured product. Owners must then ensure

INCIDENT 11-4

BUILDING A GREAT COMPANY

Jim Collins, book, *Good to Great*, is widely considered one of the best management books ever written, with over two million copies sold. Inside the book are tips and lessons on how to lead and build a great company. Entrepreneurs will want to pay close attention to Collins's thoughts on leadership, management, and culture:

Great companies have great leaders. Great leaders put the company first, are less about ego and more about results, give credit to employees, and are tireless workers.

Great companies have great employees. Leaders must recognize what characteristics are needed in their management team at different stages in their company's growth and make the appropriate hires and/or changes. The right employees are a company's best assets.

If you hire the right people, they will already be motivated. Focus on hiring right, and don't waste time on motivation. Great leaders spend little time on motivation.

A great culture is one of both freedom and accountability. A leader must allow his managers the freedom to make decisions but they must be held accountable.[28]

---

their actions confirm the chosen culture. For example, Elles has taken to waiting tables in his restaurants and always goes above and beyond to ensure customer satisfaction. Other employees see this and follow his lead. After establishing the culture, the entrepreneur must ensure he hires people who have the personality to fit within the culture. For example, if the business owner wants people with a positive attitude, then he should create a hiring process that weeds out people who are pessimistic. Sophie Bond, publisher of the *Upper Canadian Antiques Showcase* (www.theuppercanadian.com), a Grimsby-based magazine, wants a positive corporate culture and places an emphasis on personality when hiring. Bond recently posted a job with the following: "Complainers need not apply." Finally the reward system must encourage people to act in a way that reinforces the corporate culture. For example, if a firm wants people to be innovative, even those who try innovations and fail must be rewarded.[29]

MOTIVATION, ENGAGEMENT, AND LOYALTY

Successful managers are able to generate employee engagement and strong loyalty from their employees. Engaged employees are motivated employees working toward company goals. Engaged employees work hard and are creative and productive. Entrepreneurs and managers in engaged workplaces have open communication lines and creative benefits that provide a comfortable work environment. Employee engagement expert Mark Royal of Hay Group says the key to an engaged workforce is having leadership that lays out a clear plan for the company so people know they are working in a winning organization. The second aspect is one of reciprocity where people want to know when they perform they will get something in return. Roy states, "Employees have to know that when they do go above and beyond, they'll be noticed and recognized for it."[30]

It is no accident, however, that these conditions exist in some companies and not in others. In a recent Angus Reid survey, reasons for employees' dislike of their jobs were examined. The results are shown in Figure 11-7. Some owner-managers understand and are able to apply these critical principles in human relations management. Two important principles concern working conditions and employee needs.

Working Conditions.

Employee satisfaction with general working conditions has been shown to reduce employee turnover. Although these factors may have minimal motivational impact, they are important in

FIGURE 11-7 Reasons Employees Dislike Their Jobs

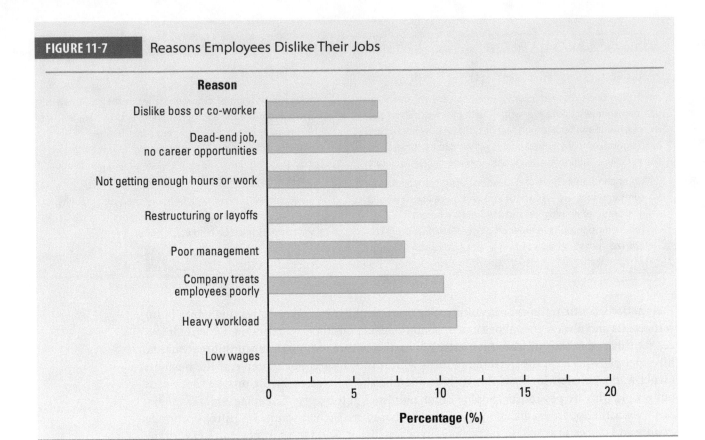

developing loyalty to the organization.[31] Some working conditions that may have this effect are the physical characteristics of the workplace, the level of supervision, relationships with co-workers, and company policies.

Employee Needs.

Understanding employee needs and providing the means whereby employees can fulfill unmet needs can be a powerful motivational tool for the owner-manager.[32] Employees' needs include adequate pay, feedback from management, feeling they are a valued part of the organization, the

---

INCIDENT 11-5

PAY FOR PROFIT

Trevor Wasney, owner of Arctic Spas (www.arcticspas.ca) Oakville Group Inc., has seen the benefit of switching to profit-based compensation, which pays sellers for generating margin rather than revenue. Prior to the switch, Wasney paid his employees on a revenue-based commission tied to listed product prices and began running into trouble when poor performing salespeople began slashing prices and throwing in free merchandise just to secure a sale. On the advice of a fellow hot tub retailer, Wasney decided to make the switch, and almost immediately his sales reps cut down on both price-chopping and free product throw-ins. Since implementing the system, Arctic Spas has held its profit margins during slow years and increased them during good ones. Wasney has also seen how the system has helped motivate and retain his best employees.

Source: Adapted from Eleanor Beaton, "Pay for Profit," *Profit*, May 2008, pp. 39–41.

INCIDENT 11-6

IS FIDO THE KEY TO EMPLOYEE HAPPINESS?

A growing trend in business is the practice of employees bringing pets, especially dogs, to the workforce. In fact, June 21 is International Take Your Dog to Work Day, and some companies such as HootSuite.com are allowing employees to bring their pet to work on a daily basis. HootSuite's CEO Ryan Holmes brings his own dog into work daily and says allowing pets in the office is an inexpensive way to improve employee's physical and mental health. His comments are echoed by Liz Palika, author of the book, *Dogs at Work*, who states, "Employees are generally happier with a dog in the workplace."[33]

Not everyone agrees that dogs in the workplace is acceptable, and some opponents raise issues of productivity, safety, and potential allergic reactions. In a small survey conducted by *Profit Magazine,* it was found that the key to successfully integrating dogs into the workplace was to create dog-free zones and policies around appropriate care and handling of the animals.[34]

Discussion Questions

1. What do you think are some of the advantages and disadvantages of allowing pets, specifically dogs, in a workplace?

2. Given the research on the impact of animals in the workplace is rather limited, would you allow employees to bring pets to work if you were in charge? Why, or why not?

3. Conduct some research on the Internet about pets in the workforce. What is the current position of the literature on employee morale and productivity?

MANY FIRMS ARE STARTING TO ALLOW PETS, ESPECIALLY DOGS, TO COME TO WORK WITH EMPLOYEES. MANAGERS THINK THIS PRACTICE CREATES MORE ENGAGED AND LOYAL EMPLOYEES.
Monkeybusinessimages/Dreamstime.com

possibility for advancement, extra responsibility or authority, recognition and praise by management, esteem of peers, a sense of achievement, and the challenge of the job.

One real challenge to the owner-manager is to encourage employees to have the same interest and enthusiasm for the business that he or she has. A recent Angus Reid survey found that 46 percent of Canadian workers are encouraged and expected to think of new and innovative ways of doing things.[35]

PAYING EMPLOYEES

Small business owners face stiff competition from large companies and even government in paying their employees. In 2009, people in companies with fewer than 100 employees earned an average of $723 a week, compared with those in companies with upward of 500 workers who earned an average of $874.[36] In addition, a recent CFIB study found that the federal government is the fastest growing sector among all industries, with a 23 percent wage and benefits advantage over its private sector counterparts.[37] Many think they cannot afford to meet this competition. However, the value of a key employee cannot be overstated for many small businesses. As a result, many owner-managers have recognized that they must be competitive in paying key employees.

Employees are concerned about both absolute and relative wage levels. This means employees are usually aware of and concerned about their level of pay relative to those of their co-workers.

Employee pay levels are very difficult to keep confidential in a small business. Often a wage increase for one employee will be seen by other employees not as a reward for that employee but as a decrease in pay for themselves. This, of course, can cause unrest within the organization.

Wage levels are generally set using external and internal factors as a guide. Externally, the owner-manager may want to assess wage levels in similar or competing industries. Many provincial governments publish wage survey data that can assist in this regard. Most owner-managers can find out what the wage levels are in their communities through an informal survey. Other external considerations in arriving at wage levels might be cost-of-living increases, the demand/supply situation for employees, and government regulations. Internally, considerations employers use in setting salary levels are ability to pay, employee performance levels and requirements, and, as just mentioned, relative pay relationships.

Remuneration for employees can offer employees security and also have a motivational effect. There are many methods of paying employees, each with advantages and disadvantages. The owner-manager needs to tailor the pay plan to meet the needs of employees and the goals of the organization. Figure 11-8 lists some of the more common methods of paying employees in small businesses and describes their advantages and limitations. Many organizations use combinations of these plans. A recent survey of top employees who left large organizations to work for smaller companies revealed that the main reason was the possibility of owning equity in the firm.[38]

FRINGE BENEFITS

Although one survey found that fewer than half of Canadian small businesses offer incentive plans,[39] increasingly small businesses need to provide fringe benefits to attract and retain

| FIGURE 11-8 | Salary Plans for a Small Business |

TYPE OF PLAN	HOW CALCULATED	ADVANTAGE	LIMITATION	BUSINESSES USING THE PLAN
Salary	Per hour or per month	Security Simplicity	Lack of incentive	Many businesses—routine tasks
Commission	Percentage of sales	Incentive	Lack of control Lack of security Lack of simplicity	Automobile sales Housing industry Some retail products requiring extra selling effort
Cash bonus on individual performance	Bonus on reaching objectives or quota	Security Incentive	Can be complicated	Retailing Manufacturing
Profit sharing on company performance	Percentage of profits distributed	Incentive Cooperation in organization	Can be complicated Amounts too small to motivate	Manufacturing Retailing Knowledge based/service
Stock bonus	Predetermined percentage to employees based on objectives	Long-term interest in organization Incentive	Some employees want only cash	Manufacturing Knowledge based/service

employees. A recent survey of the 100 fastest-growing small businesses in Canada indicated that only 65 to 75 percent of employee compensation should be salary. The rest can be made up of bonus, profit sharing, stock options, and commissions.[40] Profit sharing has become increasingly common as entrepreneurs have found that linking employee compensation to the success of their business helps motivate employees. For example, QuickContractors.com's (www.Quick-Contractors.com) president Trevour Bouchard says profit sharing helps keep employees focused and more concerned about keeping expenses low to maximize profits as a result.[41, 42] Other common benefits include bonuses, employee discounts, pension plans, disability and life insurance, and dental insurance.

If the small business has enough employees, it may be able to qualify for group insurance plans that reduce the cost of providing this benefit. Frequently, these plans are available through industry associations. Total costs of providing employee benefits are rising, and the owner-manager should monitor such costs closely. The Employee Benefit News Canada Organization reports that employee benefit programs typically cost from 2.5 to 9.1 percent of total payroll, depending on which benefits are offered.[43] The business may benefit by comparing costs and services of several benefit providers to ensure which is the most cost effective.

Other work-related fringe benefits the business might offer to increase employee satisfaction and motivation are discussed next.

Job Rotation.

With job rotation, employees are periodically allowed to exchange jobs with other employees. Used in factory situations, this program can not only increase employee interest and motivation but also assist in training workers.

Job Sharing.

Some firms have found success in allowing employees to share their jobs. The possibility of two part-time workers may satisfy the job requirements and increase the satisfaction of those who may not want to work full time. It is estimated that over 170,000 Canadians job-share, according to Statistics Canada.[44]

Working from Home.

An increasing number of businesses are allowing employees to complete some or all of their work at home. This may not be appropriate for all types of small business but may be viewed as a valuable benefit to some employees. Statistics Canada has found that close to 10 percent of working Canadians do at least part of their jobs from home.[45]

Flexible Hours.

Some firms have experienced increases in productivity by allowing employees a work schedule other than the nine-to-five schedule common in many industries. A recent survey found that 60 percent of Canadian employers offered flexible work schedules.[46] The 2012 Small Business Monitor Survey found that 72 percent of employees rated flexible hours as an effective retention tool on par with bigger paycheques. *Profit Magazine's* 2013 survey found similar results with 84 percent of employees citing it as an important consideration in retention.

Employee Suggestion Systems.

Many companies have some form of employee suggestion system. Recently, some companies have taken this idea a step further by offering employees money and/or time to implement their suggestions. For example, Arrow Group (www.arrowgroup.ca), one of the fastest growing

FIGURE 11-9 Five Hottest Employee Benefits

1. Spending Accounts	Many firms that cannot afford flexible-benefit plans are turning to spending accounts, funded by company or employee contributions. They can be used to cover a range of health or dental expenses. When employees contribute a portion of their salaries (say 2 percent) to these funds, that income is not taxed.
2. Health Promotion	More employers offer non-medical benefits aimed at "wellness." Staff is allowed certain sums for such items as gym memberships, health-risk assessments, psychological counselling, and personal training.
3. Increased Choice	There is more choice in structuring benefit plans. Staff choices depend on how much they wish to spend, or on other variables such as their state of health or access to other benefits.
4. Flexible Work Hours	To help families juggle increasingly complex schedules, more firms let workers set their own hours. It could be 9 to 5, 7:30 to 3:30, or four 10-hour days.
5. Employee Input	More employees are being asked for their input on operational matters, but at a cost. Staff who suggest benefits changes, for instance, are held responsible for the program's success. If costs exceed plan, they must make up the balance.

Source: "Employee Benefits—What's Hot and Not in Workplace Perks," *Canada News Wire Service*, September 5, 2008.

companies in 2013 according to *Profit Magazine*, provides employees with Arrow time. This is time to work on individual projects from home or the office. Arrow's president Sam Ibrahim says, "Some of our best innovations have come from people thinking on their independent time." The National Association of Suggestion Systems (www.benefits.org) reports that some 3000 formal suggestion systems operate in the United States, generating more than 300,000 ideas and saving companies more than $800 million annually.[47]

Figure 11-9 above provides a description of five fast-growing employee benefit programs. Additional assistance benefit programs may be available through a number of private companies that specialize in this area, such as Benefits Interface Inc.

CONTROLLING AND EVALUATING EMPLOYEE PERFORMANCE

Many of the practices previously mentioned may contribute to a more motivated and loyal workforce. It is essential, however, that this motivation be directed toward achieving the firm's objectives. In this regard, the owner-manager needs to effectively evaluate progress toward goals and objectives and inform employees of their progress. This can be done through a regular performance appraisal.

Another method for accomplishing this is the management by objectives approach (MBO), which is used in many organizations. A simplified version of MBO that is suitable for the small business is described in *Putting the One Minute Manager to Work*.[48] The five steps in this method (called the *PRICE system*) are as follows:

- *Pinpoint:* Define the performance area to be evaluated (e.g., sales for a retail clerk).
- *Record:* Set up a system to monitor, and record performance in that area (e.g., the cash register tape).
- *Involve:* Manager and employee jointly set goals and a strategy for reaching those goals in that performance area (e.g., dollar sales per month).

- *Coach:* The manager observes performance periodically, perhaps making suggestions but allowing the employee considerable freedom to work toward the agreed-on goals.

- *Evaluate:* At the end of the agreed-on period, assess performance; reward positive results, and set future goals.

The value of the PRICE system is the clear line of communication between employer and employee in directing the employee toward goals and evaluating the employee's progress.

HANDLING GRIEVANCES

Employee grievances, or concerns, arise in most organizations. They can have a negative effect on the morale of the organization, but they can also be positive and helpful if handled properly. The following are some principles for effective grievance management:

1. Implement a precise method whereby employees can express grievances. It is important that the organizational lines of authority be followed in this case. If at all possible, the grievance should be expressed to the immediate supervisor. This procedure should be laid out in the policy manual.

2. Employees need assurance that expressing their concerns will not jeopardize or prejudice their relationship with the employer. A wise employer will recognize that many grievances are legitimate and, if acted on, can help the organization.

3. There should be minimal red tape in processing complaints. Employees need to feel that someone is really listening to their concerns.

4. Owner-managers need to understand that some employees may be hesitant to raise a concern directly. In these situations, the suggestion box is effective.

TERMINATING THE EMPLOYEE

If the owner-manager makes a decision to terminate an employee, it is important to follow due care to legislation and regulations concerning this matter. While legislation varies by province, the following should be adhered to: justifiable reasons for the termination provided, adequate notice provided, appropriate severance and vacation pay provided (if applicable), necessary documentation completed (such as the Record of Employment), and if warranted, letters of explanation or reference for the employee provided.

UNIONIZATION AND THE SMALL BUSINESS

Most small businesses do not have unions operating within the organization. As the firm grows, however, and as employees become farther removed from the owner, the possibility of union-related activity increases. The owner-manager should recognize that unions are formed when a majority of employees believe that a union would better serve their employment needs than the existing system. For example, Just Us Coffee (www.justuscoffee.com), a Nova Scotia-based coffee roaster, had one of its retail locations unionize in 2013, as workers at the Halifax store expressed concern about working hours and distribution of tips. The owners of the firm, a co-operative, expressed surprise at the union movement and dismissed the union's organizers. After the dismissed employees filed complaints with the labour board, they were hired back, and Just Us accepted a union in the Halifax location. Union organizer Shay Enxuga says, "One of the biggest reasons we wanted the union was to put a system in place to negotiate things within our collective agreement. We don't want to just count on the benevolence of our bosses. But also because unless we have a union, there's a power dynamic going on between us and our bosses where we're not protected. One of the reasons we want to have a union is to have a grievance process, where we could be legally protected in case of mistreatment, like being dismissed."[50]

Effective human relations policies can go a long way toward discouraging union establishment in the firm. Some small businesses in certain industries may be required to hire unionized employees.

In both these situations, there are certain requirements for both the employer and the union as set out in the Labour Relations Act in each province and territory. Some of the more common aspects of collective bargaining that may affect the small business owner are the following:

- The contents of an agreement must deal with wages, benefits, and working conditions.
- Both parties must meet and bargain in good faith. However, an employer need not reveal company data that he or she prefers to keep confidential.
- The owner cannot discriminate against an employee for union involvement.
- Both employers and unions are bound by the terms and conditions of the collective agreement.
- Disputes concerning interpretation of the agreement must be resolved by an arbitrator.

GOVERNMENT REQUIREMENTS AND ASSISTANCE LO5

The owner-manager should be aware of relevant government labour laws and programs that affect the management of personnel. A brief discussion of such laws and programs for all levels of government follows.

FEDERAL GOVERNMENT

The federal government provides training and employment programs to 400,000 Canadians each year. Through the Canadian Jobs Strategy program, approximately $1.7 billion is spent to increase training and expand opportunities.[51] Some specific programs of Jobs Strategy include the following:

- *The job entry program* provides training for unemployed or undertrained people for up to one year.
- *Skill shortage and skill investment programs* provide financial assistance and training for up to three years for skill upgrading as a result of technological change within the company.
- *The job development program* provides training and financial assistance for the unemployed, disadvantaged persons, women, persons with disabilities, older workers, and visible minorities.
- *Innovation programs* provide funds to test new solutions to labour-market-related problems.
- *The Community Futures Program* helps finance local committees for development training and employment initiatives in areas experiencing economic hardship.

For more information on each of the above programs, contact the local Canada Employment Centres.

The federal government also has some legislation in the areas of employment standards, employment and pay equity, and hiring practices. Because of some overlaps in jurisdiction with the provinces and territories, details are discussed in the next section.

PROVINCIAL AND TERRITORIAL GOVERNMENTS

Each province and territory in Canada, through its human resources or labour department, has set labour standards with which every owner-manager should be familiar.

Job Discrimination.

Each provincial and territorial government has passed legislation concerning human rights in the workplace. Entitled *Bills or Codes of Human Rights,* they are administered by provincial and territorial human rights commissions; this legislation has jurisdiction over businesses not federally owned or regulated. Like their federal counterparts, these regulations are designed to prevent discrimination in the workplace.

Pay and Employment Equity.

Recently, some provinces and territories have enacted legislation to ensure equality of pay and employment opportunity regardless of gender, race, religious affiliation, or ethnic origin.

Working Conditions and Compensation.

Numerous legal requirements govern the conditions under which retail employees work. Of importance to the small business owner are wage and hour requirements, restrictions on the use of child labour, provisions regarding equal pay, workers' compensation, unemployment benefits, and the Canada Pension Plan.

Employment Standards.

Both the federal and provincial or territorial governments administer a considerable amount of legislation related to employment standards and labour relations. At both levels of government, ministries of labour have primary responsibility in this field of regulation. In addition, both levels have legislation that allows for the establishment of unions and collective bargaining agents in the form of provincial or territorial labour relations acts and the federal Canada Labour Code (http://laws.justice.gc.ca/en/L-2/index.html). The Canada Labour Code also deals with many aspects of fair labour standards, labour relations, dismissal procedures, severance allowances, and working conditions. Similarly, each province and territory enforces statutes covering minimum wage rates, hours of work, overtime, holidays and leaves, termination notices, employment of young people, and information requirements on the statement of earnings and deductions.

Employment Safety and Health.

Employment safety and health programs are designed to reduce absenteeism and labour turnover. Most provinces and territories have passed industrial safety acts to protect the health and safety of workers. These laws govern such areas as sanitation, ventilation, and dangerous machinery. In addition to legislation, provincial and territorial governments, as well as employers, provide programs and training designed to accomplish similar purposes.

Workers' Compensation.

Workers' compensation is an employee accident and disability insurance program required under provincial and territorial law. It covers employees who are accidentally injured while working or who are unable to work as a result of a disease associated with a particular occupation. Although these programs vary, they generally provide for medical expenses and basic subsistence during the period of disability. Employers help pay for the program through assessments from the Workers' Compensation Board or Workplace Safety and Insurance Board. The assessment rates represent a substantial operating expense; thus, they must be planned for and managed with considerable care.

Wage Subsidy Programs.

These programs provide financial assistance for up to six months for small businesses that hire unemployed persons.

Provincial and Territorial Training Programs.

These programs provide job training and skill development incentives to upgrade the labour force. Often such programs include a wage subsidy to small businesses that hire new employees. Contact a local labour department for details of these programs.

MUNICIPAL GOVERNMENTS

Local or municipal government regulations related to industry generally are confined to such areas as licensing, zoning, hours of operation, property taxes, and building codes. For example, one issue of current debate in some areas relates to Sunday openings of retail stores. Generally, authority has been left to the municipal government. This issue has significant implications in terms of operating costs and competitiveness.

Municipal authorities also exercise an especially strong influence over food establishments. For instance, a municipal licensing system for restaurants and other food services establishments may be in effect. Health inspectors may make periodic and sometimes unannounced inspections. (Any store that sells wine, beer, or liquor may require a licence from provincial or territorial liquor-licensing authorities.)

RECORD KEEPING FOR EMPLOYERS   LO6

Every employer should maintain an employee file that includes such information as the employee's original application form, work record, salary level, evaluation reports, and any other pertinent information. One of the most important employee record-keeping tasks for the owner-manager is completing the payroll. There are several essential steps in managing a payroll system for employees.

Employee Remittance Number.

As an employer, the owner-manager collects employee income tax on behalf of the government as a deduction from the employee's wage. Before remitting this amount to the Receiver General, the employer must obtain a remittance number, available by contacting the nearest office of the Canada Revenue Agency.

Payroll Book.

The employer should obtain a payroll book or record that contains space for recording time worked as well as all the required deductions. These books can be obtained from most business supply or stationery stores.

Monthly Remittance.

As mentioned above, each payday the employer is required to make the appropriate deductions and remit them, as well as the employer's share of Canada Pension Plan (CPP) and Employment Insurance (EI), to the Canada Revenue Agency. This remittance is made on a prescribed form similar to that in Figure 11-10. This form contains the remittance number, the current payment amount, and a cumulative record of payments to date.

FIGURE 11-10   Remittance Form

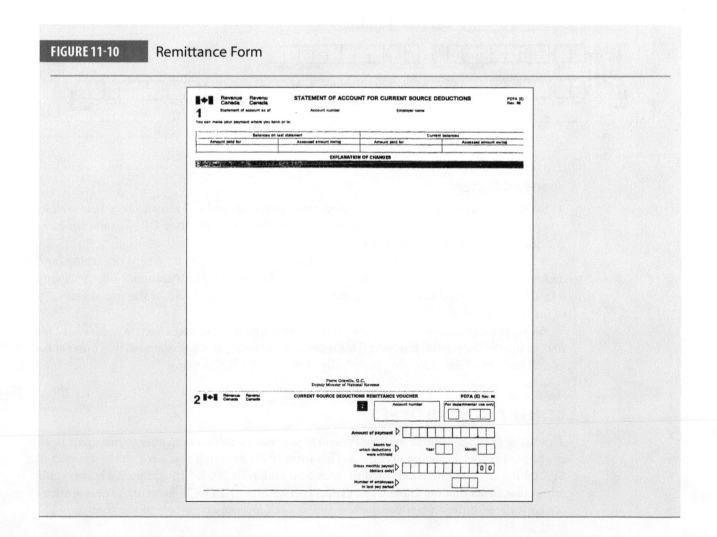

FIGURE 11-11 T4 Slip

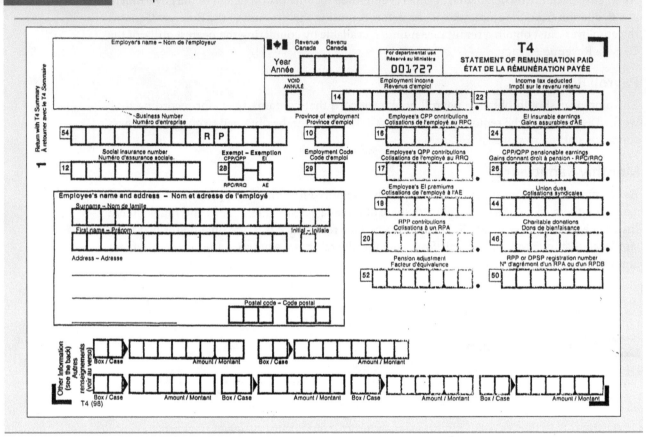

Year-End Statements.

At the end of the calendar year, the employer is required to total and reconcile the year's remittances with the Canada Revenue Agency's totals. This is done on a T4-A summary form provided by the Canada Revenue Agency.

It is also the employer's responsibility to fill out for each employee a record of earnings and deductions for the year on the T4 slip. The T4 slip (Figure 11-11) is completed by reviewing totals from the payroll book and is required to be sent to the employee by the end of February of the following year.

An increasing number of small businesses have found it to be cost effective to hire another firm to handle the payroll function. This is called *outsourcing* and has extended into other areas as well because of the increasing complexity of some of these functions.

CONTRACT EMPLOYEES

A growing number of small businesses owners may use a contract employee to meet part or all of the business's labour requirements. This form of outsourcing was used in the amount of $1.7 billion in 2003 and is expected to reach $2.8 billion by 2008.[52] In addition, a recent study found that firms that outsourced can expect cost savings of 20 to 25 percent.[53] These workers are considered independent contractors and as such are not employees of the company. The

By this stage in the entrepreneurial process readers should be working on their business plan or even perhaps running their business. Entrepreneurs should consider the following action steps:

1. Complete a personal SWOT analysis. In what areas of management will you need help?

2. Complete an organizational chart and staffing plan for your business.

contractor or the contracting company simply invoices the small business for services rendered. Contract employees may be hired for a particular project and could be long term. They could also be hired for temporary purposes and paid a fee to provide a short term service. Although the owner-manager still manages these people, the calculation of CPP, EI, or other benefits are not required. This typically results in a reduction in costs to the small business of about 10 to 15 percent. However, some companies have experienced increased costs. It must also be remembered that some positions and tasks may not be suitable for the contract employee, and issues of motivation and loyalty may be a problem for contract workers. Therefore, a contract employee may be more appropriate for temporary or project-type jobs. Other difficult issues relating to contract employees involve new privacy legislation, labour standards, performance appraisal, and terminations. The owner-manager should be aware of the legal differences in managing contract and traditional employees.

LEARNING OBJECTIVES SUMMARY

LO1 Sound personnel management is a key to the success of a small business because motivated and competent personnel is one aspect of a business that may be unique and difficult to duplicate.

LO2 The organizational chart integrates tasks and employees so that the owner can visualize how the different aspects of the plan will work together. An effective way to prevent many personnel problems is to have a policy manual covering such areas as job description, working conditions, holidays and leaves, remuneration, and employee benefits.

LO3 The screening devices used in hiring employees include an application form or resumé, the employment interview, references, and various kinds of tests. An interview guide helps focus the interview and provides a constant base of information with which to compare applicants.

LO4 The owner-manager should apply the following concepts of personnel management: assess his or her leadership style, work on time management by avoiding procrastination on important decisions or tasks, assess priorities, and use the most productive time of the day for the more important decisions.

LO5 Legal requirements for the personnel aspects of small business are applicable from federal, provincial or territorial, and municipal governments.

LO6 The steps in administering a payroll system are: obtain an employee remittance number, obtain a payroll book, make the appropriate deductions and remit them with the employer's share to the Canada Revenue Agency, total and reconcile the year's remittance at the end of every calendar year, and send out T4s.

DISCUSSION QUESTIONS

1. Discuss the relative advantages and disadvantages of the various compensation plans used in small businesses.
2. What industries can you think of in which profit sharing would be less successful? Why?
3. Discuss the relative advantages and disadvantages of the different types of fringe benefits for a small manufacturing company. If possible, interview employees of such a business to find out which of these benefits are the most attractive.
4. Recently, a small business increased the wages of its employees, but its productivity is still inadequate. What could be some possible reasons for this low level of productivity?
5. After reading this chapter, what do you believe will be the most critical small business personnel problem in the future?

APPLICATION QUESTIONS AND HANDS-ON ACTVITIES

1. Interview two small business owners to find out their personnel policies and how they communicate those policies to their employees.
2. Ask three employees of small businesses what they like and dislike about their jobs. What personnel policies could be used to remedy the dislikes?
3. Determine how three employees of various small businesses were recruited for their present positions. What seems to be the most popular source from which to recruit employees for small businesses? Why?
4. Study the local newspaper, and choose three examples of good job advertisements and three examples of poor job advertisements. Be prepared to explain your choices.

Dan resolved the inventory and layout concerns with the help of a consultant whom his banker had suggested. With the expansion of the plant, Dan was able to meet demand for orders of the Ladder Rail and some additional products. Sales were increasing, and the problems with finances and marketing that had caused concern earlier seemed to be less troublesome.

However, partway through year two an additional problem began to surface. It involved his personnel. With increased demand and plant expansion, Dan had hired four additional employees. Three were put to work in the metal fabricating part of the business, and the other was hired to work full time with marketing and distribution. The two employees who had started with Dan had both left for higher paying jobs, so Dan had hired a total of six new employees in a short time. The first couple of hires were found through ads in the local newspaper, but lately Dan had simply gone down to the local Canada Manpower office and found the required workers.

Dan is becoming increasingly discouraged with the time and hassle involved in managing employees. On many occasions, he would have liked to have fired an employee, but the hiring and training processes seem to take so long that Dan feels that he cannot afford a slowdown of the production process with demand being what it is. He realizes that the type of employee he is hiring possesses little education, but as a small business owner, he simply cannot afford—nor does the job require—better trained employees. He currently pays employees $1 above minimum wage, which is well below union rates, but he increases the wage as the employee finishes the on-the-job training. He also intends to give all employees a raise each year based on seniority. Because the business is losing money, however, Dan does not feel that he can afford raises to employee wages at this time.

Some of the employee problems that particularly bother him are employees wanting more money and better benefits; workers threatening to leave for higher union steelworker wages if he does not increase their wages; work slowdowns when he is not physically present at the plant; poor quality work and too much wasted metal as a result of fabricating errors; and the appearance and conduct of some of the younger workers. This last problem especially annoys Suzie, who is frequently in the plant working on the finances.

In addition, on some occasions, Suzie has been in the plant and has given some direction to the workers when Dan is away. The employees simply ignore her because she is not the boss.

Questions

1. Evaluate Dan's personnel procedures.
2. How could Dan motivate his employees?
3. What should be done differently for the marketing person? Why?
4. What outside assistance might be available to help Dan with his personnel problems?

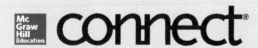

For more information on the resources available from McGraw-Hill Ryerson, go to www.mcgrawhill.ca/he/solutions.

CHAPTER 12

MANAGING TAXES AND GETTING MANAGEMENT ASSISTANCE

LEARNING OBJECTIVES

By the end of this chapter, you should be able to:

LO1 Illustrate how advisers, boards of directors, or boards of advisers can be used.

LO2 Explain the importance of understanding the nature of the Canadian tax system.

LO3 Discuss key tax management principles the owner-manager can follow.

LO4 Describe specific tax-related programs that apply to small business.

SMALL BUSINESS PROFILE

DEVON BROOKS *Blo Blow Dry Bar*

Devon Brooks may be young, but her talent, ability to triumph through great challenges, and her clarity on value-based leadership have already earned her extraordinary recognition.

In 2012, *PROFIT Magazine* acknowledged Devon aptly when they named her "1 of the 30 most fabulous entrepreneurs in Canada," alongside heavy hitters such as Joe "Fresh" Mimran, Guy Laliberte, and Steve Nash.

Thus far, her entrepreneurial journey or "adventure," as she has put it, "resembles a path and no path at all"—and, for the wisdom it has allowed her, she would not have it any other way. Devon had sailed around the world by 16. At 21, she actualized her second-year school project, at the London College of Fashion, founding a category-defining franchise, Blo Blow Dry Bar, along with her co-founders, and loved ones, Judy Brooks and Val Litwin.

"The Blo concept is a simple one," explains Brooks, "choose off a 'hair menu' and get your hair washed and styled in a short period of time for less than then you would pay in a salon format. It is what my founders and I called 'fast, affordable, catwalk quality hair,'" she says. Brooks and her mother and co-founder, Judy Brooks came up with the idea when reminiscing about how frazzled attendees looked at a previous "top 100 women in business" event . "It was a gender equality issue as far as we were concerned. The time and cost of services at that point were forcing women to sacrifice self-care in their very busy schedules . . . It's difficult to factor in the time for aesthetics you'd like, the modern woman has much to do."[1] The Blo concept made that luxury affordable and fast. Six months after Devon submitted the business plan as a school project, the founding team of three launched their first location.[2] They innovated strong franchise systems and were quickly recognized for their edgy brand, with taglines such as "cause you can't blo yourself" and "you're not cheating on your hairdresser." "Hair cadets" (the "Blocabulary" name for its clients) were rolling in and so were franchise requests. They were onto something big, and it was not just the hair.

Photo: www.AlexJowett.com

The Canadian-born business has been credited for igniting what has become a global market category. Today, the business is managed by the Toronto-based operating team the founders merged with in 2010. Blo has 32 locations around the world and continues to grow.

Working with that volume ignited something for Devon and completely altered her lens on leadership. She notes, "It can't just be effective, it has to be meaningful and connected to the roots of the lives of it's people." "If you don't know what people are dealing with, you can't know what they need," she explains. The lack of authenticity in the sharing of business stories compelled her. "We all have a perception issue, when we look at what we think is the success of others. Almost nothing is what it seems." She began speaking publicly about the abuse and violence she had endured at 18, when she was raped, and again at 21, just after launching Blo, when an assailant forced his way into her home, attacked her, and held her against her will until she was able to free herself. She never looked back. Devon activates personal evolution, from mental wellness to sex and relationship, with raw conversation: Speaking to thousands, on many stages, including TEDX and Pecha Kucha; Joining the board of directors, and spearheading the marketing committee, of a feminist anti-violence organization (www.wavaw.ca) to make her hometown, Vancouver, a safer place for women; and supporting, mentoring, and advising businesses and aspiring entrepreneurs who want to make a cause-based impact in their communities. At 24, she became the youngest-ever mentor of the Canadian Youth Business Foundation (CYBF) and went onto represent Canada at two G20 Young Entrepreneur Summits. Devon has a hunger for greatness and is skilled in awakening greatness in others. Her CYBF mentees noted, ". . . . as our business grows, our mentoring grows as well. Each session is more helpful than the last. We are extremely grateful for what Devon has brought to us, and we hope to continue to grow with her."[3, 4]

For bookings, press, or a whole lot of inspiration, find Devon, and her team, at www.devsdevelopment.com.

BLO BLOW DRY BAR
www.devsdevelopment.com

ADVISERS AND SMALL BUSINESS

As entrepreneurs are engaged in planning and starting their business, they will often seek out assistance from more experienced entrepreneurs or mentors. Many successful entrepreneurs such as Brian Scudamore, founder of 1-800-Got-Junk? state that seeking the advice of experienced leaders helped them grow their company. In addition to mentors, many entrepreneurs will form actual boards of advisers or directors to assist them in growing their company. Entrepreneurs should also be willing to engage in discussions with lawyers, accountants, and business counsellors as they move their business from just an idea, to start-up to a growing enterprise. The chapter will first introduce the concept of mentoring and advisers and then proceed to discuss tax management, a very important topic in small business.

USE OF ADVISERS

Entrepreneur will usually use outside advisers such as accountants, bankers, lawyers, advertising agencies, and market researchers on an as-needed basis. These advisers, who are separate from the more formal board of adviser s discussed below, can also become an important part of the organization and thus will need to be managed just like any other permanent part of the new venture.

The relationship of the entrepreneur and outside advisers can be enhanced by seeking out the best advisers and involving them thoroughly and at an early stage. Advisers should be assessed or interviewed just as if they were being hired for a permanent position. References should be checked and questions asked to ascertain the quality of service as well as compatibility with the entrepreneur and/or the management team.

Hiring and managing outside experts can be effectively accomplished by considering these advisers as advice suppliers. Just as no manager would buy raw materials or supplies without

BUSINESSES OFTEN RELY ON OUTSIDE ADVISERS SUCH AS CPAS AND LAWYERS TO ENSURE THEY ARE MAKING APPROPRIATE DECISIONS.
© Rob Daly/age fotostock

knowledge of their cost and quality, the same approval can apply for advisers. Entrepreneurs should ask these advisers about fees, credentials, references, and so on, before hiring them.

Even after the advisers have been hired, the entrepreneur should question their advice. Why is the advice being given? Make sure you understand the decision and its potential implications. There are many good sources of advisers such as other small business owners, chambers of commerce, universities, friends, and relatives.

Mentors

Often the first stage in formal advice is the use of a mentor. Mentors can be used on an ad hoc basis or formally assist the entrepreneur in running the company on an ongoing basis. Mentoring often takes the form of a new business owner forming a relationship with an experienced mentor. The experienced entrepreneur offers advice and guidance to an entrepreneur who is in the early stages of running their business. For example, the founders of Canadian toy giant, Spin Master Toys, relied on several business mentors in the toy industry as they were building their company. Brian Scudamore of the above mentioned 1-800-Got-Junk? still uses mentors even as his company has surpassed $100 million in sales.[5] The major benefit of mentoring is it allows for one-on-one communication and will enhance your skill set. The Canadian Youth Business Foundation (CYBF) believes so strongly in the mentoring process that they insist all loan applicants who receive funding from the organization establish a formal mentor relationship. Devon Brooks, who is discussed in the opening profile, is one of CYBF's current mentors.

Todd O'Keefe's story is typical of many CYBF successes; while Todd O'Keefe was enrolled in his PR degree course, he was soon sure about two things: One, he enjoyed PR and marketing, and, two, he wanted to run his own consulting firm rather than work for someone else. Todd states, "Running my own company is a dream and I had to make it happen." Rather than wait till he graduated, Todd started writing his business plan and soliciting clients in his fourth and final year of his degree. Todd decided to focus on small and micro-sized businesses as a way to build his portfolio and work with clients that normally would not be able to afford the services of larger firms. O'Keefe says, "Small firms need PR work, too; they may not need it all the time, but no one is trying to specifically serve this market, as most firms would rather deal with larger clients who have bigger budgets." Todd quickly found a couple of clients and successfully earned a CYBF loan that comes with a mandatory mentorship program to further finance his enterprise. Todd notes, "Getting the financing was wonderful, but equally valuable was their insistence that I work with a mentor. My mentor has assisted me every step of the way in starting my firm, and I will continue to rely on them in the future."[6] Todd's advice to other PR and marketing grads who dream of working for themselves is to find mentors that can assist you and go for it as being your own boss can be just like a dream that comes true.

GREIG CLARK, FOUNDER OF COLLEGE PRO PAINTERS, SAYS USING A BOARD OF ADVISERS ASSISTED HIM IN GROWING HIS BUSINESS.
Hannamariah/Dreamstime.com

Board of Advisers

Some entrepreneurs will form a board of board of advisers occasionally referred to as a *board of directors*. Brian Scudamore notes that having a board for 1-800-Got-Junk? has greatly assisted him in running his business. Scudamore notes, "If you (entrepreneurs) don't have a mentor board of advisers, get one soon—it offers the best education money can't buy." Greig Clark, founder of College Pro Painters, says that forming a formal advisory board of seasoned business leaders greatly assisted him in running his company. Clark then proceeds to point out that 28 percent of private firms among the fastest growing firms in Canada use

THE ABCS OF BOARDS[7]

Many entrepreneurs cringe when they think of forming a board of directors or advisers. They are concerned with giving up control of the company or losing their ability to make quick decisions. What is important to remember is that any company that is going public will require a board. An effective board, whether it is a board of directors or advisers, is often cited as the main reason that businesses have thrived rather than just survived. A strong board should provide entrepreneurs with the following:

- *Access:* A board will link entrepreneurs to people and capital that they may not have normally met on their own.
- *Credibility:* Board members are usually experienced entrepreneurs. Investors will be more willing to invest knowing that entrepreneurs can draw on the advice of knowledgeable advisers.
- *Strategic thinking*: Board members will be able to draw on their experience and provide advice to entrepreneurs.
- *Education:* Entrepreneurs should think of board members as a mentoring club. Most board members are usually willing to mentor individuals as well as companies.

Planning

1. Start with an assessment of the strengths and weaknesses of the company's owner or management team. You should try to find board members that fill gaps.
2. Determine how many board members you want in advance. The optimal number for a small- to medium-sized company is five to seven members, although new and smaller companies can use fewer.
3. Establish a list of firm objectives for the board. The board should focus more on strategy and not on daily administrative tasks.
4. Determine how you will compensate board members. If you expect to have them meet and conduct real work, you should expect to compensate them with either money or a small amount of equity.

Recruiting

1. Avoid family and friends. They have no objectivity.
2. Start with your own network of accountants, lawyers, and other business associates and build referrals.

3. Try to recruit people with experience that have managed similar companies in the past or at least worked in the industry. As baby boomers start to retire, the number of potential board members increases substantially.
4. Do not over-recruit. Sometime entrepreneurs ask anyone and everyone to be on their board—remember that you are trying to address gaps in the management team and make the company more attractive to investors.
5. Do not use the first three people who agree. Rather, take your time, and find the right people.

Managing the Board

1. Growing companies should schedule monthly meetings. At the very minimum, an effective board should meet bi-monthly. Remember that technology today allows for members to be in different locations for meetings.
2. At board meetings, entrepreneurs should consider themselves to be a team leader or as a leader among equals. Entrepreneurs must be willing to give up some control if the board is to be effective.
3. Ensure that every meeting has an agenda that allocates the majority of meeting time on strategic issues. Reviewing reports and daily administrative matters should be kept to a minimum.
4. Do not be afraid to assign homework. If board members are willing, and they will be if they are getting paid, assign some work for them to do outside of the actual meeting.
5. As your company evolves, so should the board of directors. New board members should be added and other members replaced as the company grows.

Discussion Questions

1. What do you see as some of the advantages and disadvantages to using an advisory board?
2. Do you think brand new companies should spend money and pay members of an advisory board? Why, or why not?
3. Would smaller businesses be better off using mentors and paid outside advisers or should all firms form an advisory board? Why?

Source: Adapted from Eleanor Beaton, "Pay for Profit," *Profit*, May 2008, pp. 39–41.

a board of advisers. Rob Bracey, president of a Toronto-based IT firm started a board of advisers after attending a Microsoft partners' conference.[8] He says the speakers pointed out that those firms with a board are on average much more profitable than those without one.

The board of advisers may serve a number of functions:

- Reviewing operating and capital budgets providing accountability and discipline
- Developing longer-term strategic plans for growth and expansion
- Supporting day-to-day activities
- Resolving conflicts among owners, partners, or shareholders
- Ensuring the proper use of assets
- Developing a network of information sources for the entrepreneurs

Boards can provide an important reality check for the entrepreneur or owner of any non-corporate type of business. Robin Chase, the founder of Zipcar, a self-service car rental business, regularly calls on a group of advisers to help her hash out ideas, provide recommendations for advancing her company, or just get a sanity check. Chase finds that the flexibility of a board of advisers in size, background requirements, number of meetings, and compensation makes these boards a very desirable alternative to the more formal boards of directors.[9]

The purpose of the board of advisers is they provide important leadership and direction for the new venture and participants should be carefully chosen. Entrepreneurs should do the following when selecting board members:

- Select individuals who can work with a diverse group and will commit to the venture's mission.
- Select candidates who understand the market environment or can contribute important skills to the new venture's achievement of planning goals.
- Select candidates who will show good judgment in business decision making.
- Candidates should be identified using referrals of business associates or from any of the external advisers such as banks, investors, lawyers, accountants, or consultants.

TAXATION AND SMALL BUSINESS   LO2

Chapter 4 presented a brief outline of small business tax requirements. It was noted that various types of business and property taxes are levied by federal, provincial, and municipal governments. The calculation of and liability for most of those taxes are relatively straightforward and are not discussed again in this chapter. Income taxes, however, can be more complicated, be more subject to interpretation, and have a greater impact on the planning and cash flow of the business. This chapter therefore focuses primarily on this area.

The Canadian Federation of Independent Business (CFIB) reports that the total tax burden is the top concern of small and medium size enterprises (SME), as shown in Figure 12-1. Individuals who reside and corporations that operate in Canada are liable for federal and provincial income taxes. These taxes are applied on income that is received or receivable during the taxation year from all sources minus less certain deductions. Federal and provincial or territorial tax agreements govern the procedures by which the federal government is empowered to collect taxes and remit portions to the provinces and territories. Some provinces and territories, including Quebec and Alberta, now collect their own corporate income taxes.

FIGURE 12-1 Total Tax Burden Remains Top SME Concern

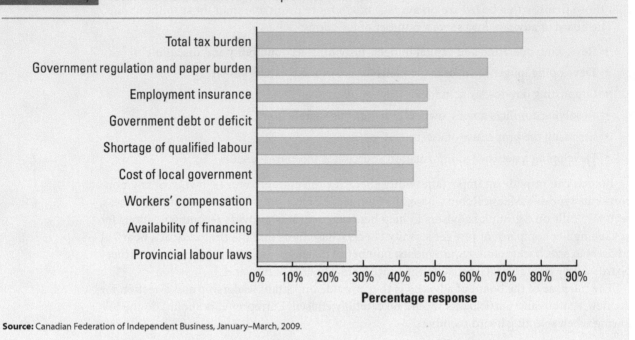

Total tax burden
Government regulation and paper burden
Employment insurance
Government debt or deficit
Shortage of qualified labour
Cost of local government
Workers' compensation
Availability of financing
Provincial labour laws

0% 10% 20% 30% 40% 50% 60% 70% 80% 90%

Percentage response

Source: Canadian Federation of Independent Business, January–March, 2009.

Because of the complexity of tax principles, the frequency of legislative changes concerning taxes, and the provincial differences in application, a detailed treatment of tax management for small business is beyond the scope of this book. This chapter briefly discusses some general tax management principles and programs. Although it is essential for owner-managers to have some knowledge of these principles in managing and planning their businesses, they are

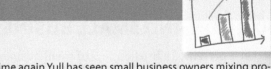

INCIDENT 12-2

THE LITTLE SHOEBOX OF HORRORS

Karen Yull, a tax specialist at Grant Thornton LLP and author of *Smart Tax Tips*, describes as the "little shoebox of horrors" the experience where a client arrives with a box or bag full of receipts. It is then the accountant's job to make sense of the business expenses while keeping the tax payable and the accountant's fees to a minimum. Yull knows the frustration that can accompany this task and suggests that a small organization can go a long way in managing personal and business expenses for tax purposes. Small business owners are usually the ones who pay for things with cash and often have all their personal and business expenses coming out of the same account. A lot of time and money can be saved by simply keeping business affairs separate from personal banking and by keeping track of all expenses. Although it may sound like a simple solution, time

and time again Yull has seen small business owners mixing professional and personal expenses, leaving the difficult task of sorting expenses to the accountant.

Yull offers a few suggestions to business owners to help at tax time. Because small business owners do not usually have their own pension plans, it is important to plan for retirement. If members of your family are working in your business, consider paying them a salary, which will help the tax situation. By using small business credit cards solely for business purposes, you can separate personal and business expenses. Also, maintaining your own ledger will make the accountant's job easier and will save money in accounting fees. The last piece of advice is perhaps the most important; if you are unsure about what you are doing, seek help from a professional.

Source: Adapted from Sasha Nagy, "The Little Shoebox of Horrors," *Globe and Mail Update*, March 21, 2006; www.theglobeandmail.com; Ronald L. Johnson C.A., 2010.

FIGURE 12-2   Impact of Tax Rate on a Business

Taxable income	$50,000
Increase in tax rate from 20% to 30%	20% of 50,000 = $10,000
	30% of 50,000 = $15,000
Increased tax liability	15,000 − 10,000 = $5,000
Profit as a percentage of sales	5%
Sales required to offset tax	5,000/5% = $100,000

Note: The extra $100,000 in sales would also incur an additional $1,500 tax liability.

strongly advised to seek professional advice in preparing tax returns and investigating methods of minimizing tax liability. An accountant or bookkeeper who is up-to-date with tax changes and is experienced in working with small businesses can help the entrepreneur avoid many difficulties. This person may also assist with personal income taxes for the entrepreneur, as often business and personal tax considerations are closely interrelated.

The organization's income that the government requires the small business owner to report refers to the profits the business makes (for tax purposes). This should not be confused with the income the owner makes from the business, which may or may not be taxable, depending on the legal form of the organization. This chapter deals primarily with the income tax considerations of the organization.

Some owner-managers may not be overly concerned with income taxes and thus may do little tax planning. This lack of concern may be due to one of two factors. First, the business may currently have no tax liability; in other words, it is losing money. This situation, of course, will be only temporary because the business will eventually become profitable or cease to exist. Second, the owner-manager may not understand the impact of taxes on the cash flow of the business. As Figure 12-2 above illustrates, an increase in the tax rate of only 10 percent translates into a tax liability that would require an additional $100,000 in sales to offset. When owner-managers understand the full effects of a lower or higher tax liability, they will want a working knowledge of tax principles and programs.

GENERAL TAX MANAGEMENT PRINCIPLES   LO3

Small business owner-managers should be aware of 10 fundamental areas of tax management.

CONTINUAL TAX PLANNING

One of the most disturbing aspects of tax statement preparation for owner-managers is learning that they have incurred an unnecessary tax liability. This situation usually arises because the accountant received and prepared the return too late to take advantage of favourable programs and deductions.

It is critical, therefore, that owner-managers be aware of the tax consequences of business operations throughout the year, not just at or after the year-end. Up-to-date income statements can assist in forecasting income trends, allowing some advance tax planning. Many simple software programs are now available that can help entrepreneurs in the information and tax management function.

The Canada Revenue Agency (CRA), formerly Revenue Canada, requires that income tax be paid in installments throughout the year. Individuals operating proprietorships and partnerships are required to remit quarterly installments for the amount of taxes they incur. Corporations must submit monthly installments based on their prior year's tax liability. Again, prior planning will be required to allow compliance with this regulation.

TAX DEFERRAL

One unwritten rule of tax management concerns tax deferral. This means that owner-managers should attempt to put off paying taxes as long as legally possible. There are at least two good reasons to defer taxes. First, they have the use of the tax money for the period of the deferral. This money can be put to productive use in the business or other investments. Second, tax laws may change, resulting in a decreased liability in the future.

Several specific programs facilitate deferral of tax liability. Some of these programs are discussed later.

INCOME SPLITTING

The tax system for individuals in Canada is a progressive system whereby a higher taxable income results in a higher percentage tax liability (see Appendix 12A [on Connect] for current tax rates for individuals in Canada and Appendix 12B [on Connect] for tax rates for corporations). Because of the progressive nature of taxes, splitting incomes between spouses and other family members or among partners will result in a reduced overall tax liability, as Figure 12-3 shows. If done within a family, the spouse and children will likely be taxed at lower rates, which would further reduce this tax liability.

MARGINAL TAX RATES

The marginal tax rate is the tax rate applied by the Canada Revenue Agency to the next dollar of income earned. Knowledge of an individual's marginal rate can be helpful in planning income and expenses. For example, if an owner-manager has a marginal tax rate of 30 percent, each dollar of income earned will incur a tax liability of 30 cents, whereas each dollar of expense incurred will save 30 cents in tax liability. Thus, awareness of the current marginal rate allows the owner-manager to calculate the after-tax effects of extra income and expenses.

FIGURE 12-3   Impact of Tax Rate on a Business

Business income = $60,000

A. If one person declared the income:

Income = $60,000

Tax rate = $6,108.90 + 22% of $19,274

Tax liability = $10,349.18

B. If two people split the income:

Income = $60,000

Partner A = $30,000

Partner B = $30,000

Tax rate for each = 15% of $30,000

Tax liability A = $4,500

Tax liability B = $4,500

Tax liability for A & B = $9,000

Tax savings by splitting income = $10,349.18 − $9,000 = $1,349.18

VICTORIA SOPIK AND JENNIFER NASHMI: KIDS AND COMPANY

Victoria Sopik was running non-profit daycare centres in Toronto in 2001 when she recognized a need in the childcare market that was not being met by existing services. "I also realized that the non-profit service I was running was limited because it was in schools, the space was limited, and it catered to children age two and older," said Sopik, herself a mother of eight.

As a result, she set up Kids and Company with Jennifer Nashmi, a chartered accountant who had worked with Victoria in her previous business. Together they targeted the lucrative corporate market. They spent a year preparing a business plan and doing market research by interviewing potential corporate clients. They discovered that there was a significant need for childcare for company employees but these companies did not want to provide it themselves. They set up centres in downtown locations close to company offices and outfitted them with webcams so parents could view their children occasionally from work. Sopik and Nashmi also offered emergency backup services that parents could use when they had no access to regular childcare.

Although they felt that they had a winning concept, the start-up was not without its difficulties. Obtaining the necessary funding when each centre took almost $500,000 to open up was a problem. Although banks were interested in using their service, they would not lend Sopik and Nashmi the money to get started. Finally, the two entrepreneurs were successful in obtaining start-up financing from an angel investor friend. Once adequate financing was in place, signing up clients happened quickly.

Sopik and Nashmi's success has been due to more than identifying a niche in the market. Their background and experience has also been a major factor. Victoria had a long and distinguished career in the childcare industry. She also has a business degree from the University of Western Ontario, which has been helpful in the management aspects of the business. Jennifer Nashmi's accounting and financial experience covered over 10 years with various high tech and service organizations. Her expertise in the financial aspects of the business has allowed Kids and Company to successfully manage and minimize the tax consequences of the company's growth and success. Nashmi indicates that a rapidly growing company in a difficult economy and continually changing tax environment needs considerable expertise to navigate through such volatile times.

The results of Sopik and Nashmi's efforts have been outstanding. Although their goal to become a $50 million business has been slower to reach than they desired, Kids and Company's growth has still been phenomenal. It was recognized as the #1 growth company in Canada by *Profit Magazine* in 2008 and #38 in 2009, with revenues of over $16 million. The number of employees has risen from 12 in 2003 to 370 in 2008, and it has over 23 centres across Canada. Key client companies include Royal Bank, CIBC, Rogers, Coca Cola, Procter and Gamble, Deloitte, and Manulife Financial.

Discussion Questions

1. What are some of the factors that enabled the company to be successful?

2. Do you think their company will be able to reach its lofty growth targets? Why, or why not?

3. Given that anyone can start this type of business, are you surprised more competition has yet to emerge? Why?

4. What type of advisers should someone look for if they wanted to start a firm similar to the one above?

Sources: Adapted from Stephanie Whittaker, "Childcare For Career Set," Canwest News Service, June 2008; Rick Spence, "New Twist On An Old Business," *Profit*, June 2008, pp. 57–58; Kids and Company website, 2010.

Another benefit of knowing the marginal rate is the possibility of moving that rate to a lower bracket by incurring some additional expenses before year-end—provided, of course, that the expenses are necessary. Like income splitting, this principle has the most value for the proprietorship and partnership.

DEDUCTIBLES

The small business owner should be familiar with those expenses that are deductible in the calculation of taxable income. The onus is on the taxpayer to keep proper records, since the burden of proof for these expenses lies with him or her. This means the owner-manager must keep receipts of business expenses. An often neglected aspect of this practice is the failure to obtain or keep receipts of expenses for which the owner-manager paid personally on behalf of the business. These expenses may seem too small to justify keeping track of them. However, if the tax rate is 25 percent, a mere $4 of unrecorded expense can result in an increased tax liability of $1. According to Generally Accepted Accounting Principles, an expense is defined as a payment or a liability created to earn income. To determine whether certain expenses are deductible, the owner-manager should consult an accountant, CRA, or such publications as the *Master Tax Guide* published by Commerce Clearing House. Some of the more common small business expenses that may require explanation follow.

Accounting and Legal Expenses.

Only those expenses incurred to earn income are deductible. Expenses incurred to incorporate the business or prepare a personal tax return are not deductible.

Advertising.

Advertising expenses are deductible only if used in Canadian media and targeted to Canadian consumers.

Business Entertaining.

Business entertaining expenses incurred in one's home are not deductible. Neither is the purchase of club memberships or yachts. Other types of legitimate business entertaining, however, are deductible.

Automobile Expenses.

For a personal auto, the portion of expenses used for business purposes is deductible, but records must be kept to verify those amounts. Usually, the business portion is the number of kilometres expended on business travel prorated to the total kilometres travelled. In addition, automobile lease costs and interest costs on vehicle loans are also deductible business expenses.

Interest Expense.

Interest expense is deductible for business loans but not for personal loans. Some experts counsel that to maximize this deductible, personal savings should be used to finance personal expenses, if possible, rather than business expenses.

For a corporation, another interest-related matter is a loan to the business by a shareholder. This is a fairly common form of financing a business because it offers some significant advantages. The interest is a deductible expense to the business, but the repayment terms may remain flexible, depending on the ability of the business to pay and the wishes of the owner-lender. In a sense, the shareholder's loan combines the advantages of both debt and equity financing. Note that interest paid to shareholders must be included in their income.

Repairs and Improvements.

Repairs are deductible expenses, but improvements should be depreciated at the specified CCA (capital cost allowance) rates. CCA rates are percentages that can be subtracted from a capital asset cost and allocated as a business expense. It is often unclear what portion of the expenditure is a repair and what portion is an improvement. An accountant should be consulted in making this allocation.

Office Expenses.

Office expenses are deductible and can be an important area for the owner-manager whose office is in the home. In such a case, a portion of household expenses such as utilities, mortgage interest, insurance, repairs, and taxes can be listed as business expenses. The portion to deduct depends on the size of the office relative to the size of the house. Care should be taken in including depreciation as an office expense, since it could be deemed to be recaptured and added to taxable income and result in the loss of the principal residence capital gains exemption. Small business owners should consult with an accountant to verify the level of home expenses that qualify as a deduction.

An increasingly popular way of taking advantage of these expenses is contracting out. Many employees have left employment with an organization and have contracted out their services to that company. Although this may allow them to take advantage of some of the above deductions, care must be taken to be sure that it is not an employment arrangement. Discussion with a tax accountant should be held if such a plan is being contemplated. Also, consult the CRA guide for the distinction between an employee and subcontractor.

GOVERNMENT TAX-RELATED PROGRAMS   LO4

Numerous government programs and policies in Canada affect the tax management practices for the small business. It is important that the entrepreneur be aware of these programs to take advantage of their benefits, as Incident 12-4 advises. The following is a summary of some of the more important items for the owner-manager.

Special Tax Rate Deductions

Small Business Deduction (SBD).

The small business deduction is 17 percent (from 28 percent to 11 percent) of active business income for an incorporated, Canadian-controlled, private business. This special rate applies to the first $400,000 of income. For income above this limit, the federal tax rate is 19.5 percent (28 percent minus 8.5 percent). Figure 12-4 illustrates the significance of this program for a small business. In addition provincial tax rates for small businesses range from 3 percent (Alberta) to 8 percent (Quebec). These lower rates allow small businesses to retain more of their earnings in the business for reinvestment.

Investment Tax Credits.

Some provinces allow residents to be eligible for investment tax credits on purchases of qualified property. All taxpayers are eligible for tax credits on qualified scientific research

---

INCIDENT 12-4

CAN A COMPUTER SOLVE TAX PROBLEMS?

The answer is no. Software cannot do your thinking for you, although it can keep accurate records and work more efficiently. At CFIB, horror stories are shared about how business owners did not understand the tax rules or their software and ended up in all sorts of trouble. This can be avoided by hiring a bookkeeper to handle day-to-day affairs or by hiring an accountant to set up your system and answer questions. An accountant is completely liable to give you accurate advice, so you will be insured against any loss.

If you do make a mistake, all is not lost. Simply contact your accountant, and follow his or her instructions. It is also a good idea to get expert advice before contacting the Canada Revenue Agency so that you can describe the situation accurately.

Source: Adapted from Catherine Swift, "Ask Catherine," *Report on Small Business*, Summer 2006, p. 41.

FIGURE 12-4

Effect of the Small Business Deduction

	Business income = $50,000
No small business deduction:	Small business deduction:
Tax rate = 28%	SBD = 28% − 17% = 11%
Tax liability = $12,500	Tax liability = $550
	Difference in tax liability = $6,950

expenditures (SRTCs). Canadian-controlled private corporations may apply for a 35 percent SRTC, while all other taxpayers may apply for a 20 percent SRTC. Other tax credit programs that may be of interest to small businesses are the Apprenticeship Job Creation and Investment Credits for creating childcare spaces.

Deferral Programs.

Some programs that allow tax deferrals are very popular with owner-managers of small businesses:

1. *Deferred profit sharing.* DPS allows for a deferral of part of the business profits that have been registered for payment in the future to employees. The payment amount is taxable to employees only when received but is a deductible expense in the year in which it is set aside or registered. The entrepreneur should see an accountant regarding this deferral program.

2. *Registered retirement savings plan.* RRSPs allow the owner-manager to put money into a registered plan that will be taxed only when received at a future date, presumably when the taxpayer is in a lower tax bracket. Budget changes have increased the contribution limits of RRSPs.

3. *Bonus deferral.* This program permits the business to deduct an accrued bonus or wage as an expense, but allows a certain time period (180 days) to pay the amount. This amount is not taxable until received. The bonus deferral thus may effectively allow the business an expense in one year but defer tax liability in the hands of the recipient to the following year.

4. *Tax Free Savings Account.* Similar to the RRSP, this relatively new program allows the small business owner to shelter $5000 in savings from tax each year (without a specific level of earned income as required with RRSP contributions).

Accelerated Capital Cost Allowance.

This program allows an increased depreciation rate (capital cost allowance) to be applied as non-cash expenses to certain classes of assets in calculating taxable income. Capital cost allowance rates can be obtained from an accountant or the tax department or by consulting the *Master Tax Guide.*

Small Business Financing Programs.

For the incorporated business, these programs allow the business to borrow money from a chartered bank at a reduced interest rate. This is made possible because of special tax treatment these banks receive from the CRA. Only businesses unable to obtain ordinary debt financing are eligible for this program.

THE INCORPORATION QUESTION

One decision regarding the establishment or growth of the business that owner-managers face is incorporation. Chapter 4 discussed the relative merits and weaknesses of the proprietorship, the partnership, and the incorporated company. Some significant differences in tax treatment also exist among these different forms of business.

As mentioned above, with the small business deduction the federal tax rate for an incorporated business is about 11 percent. If the business is a partnership or a proprietorship, the business income is brought into the owner-manager's personal tax return. This return includes various other personal deductions and exemptions. The individual's personal rate (see Appendix 12A on Connect) may be higher or lower than the rate for an incorporated business (see Appendix 12B on Connect). If the minimization of tax liability were the major concern, the owner-manager would pursue incorporating when the tax rate for the business was lower than the personal rate. The incorporation question is influenced by more than just the tax liability for the different legal forms of business; many government programs are available only to incorporated businesses. Examples of the tax consequences of the different legal forms of business are shown in Figure 12-5.

THE REMUNERATION QUESTION

Another difficult decision owner-managers must make is how to be paid by the business. In the proprietorship and the partnership, payment to the owner is treated as a drawing from the business and is not a deductible expense (or taxable income). In the corporation, an owner can be paid with a salary or with dividends. These methods of payment receive significantly different tax treatment and vary by province. The owner-manager should consult with an accountant before making a decision in this area, as federal budgets have changed the difference in tax treatment of salary and dividends. Currently, surtaxes imposed by the federal and some provincial governments result in a slightly higher income tax paid when remuneration is taken in dividends if the owner's taxable income exceeds $55,000. Since 2000, dividends paid to children under the age of 18 became taxable to the parent, although a family trust can still be used. This change reduces the effectiveness of income splitting with family in an incorporated business.

FIGURE 12-5	Income Tax for Different Legal Forms of a Business		
	BOB JOHNSON LTD. CORPORATION	**BOB JOHNSON PROPRIETORSHIP**	**BOB AND SUE JOHNSON PARTNERSHIP**
Revenue	100,000	100,000	100,000
Expenses	80,000	80,000	80,000
Net Income	20,000	20,000	20,000
Tax Consequences	Taxed at the corporate rate. (Bob's salary is a business expense.)	Income brought into and taxed at personal rate. (Bob's salary not a business expense.)	One-half of income partner's income and rates. (Salary to Bob and Sue not business expenses.)

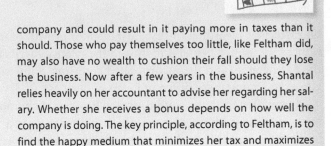

INCIDENT 12-5

ENTREPRENEUR COMPENSATION

Shantal Feltham started Stiris Research Inc., a clinical research business, in London, Ontario, with just enough cash to operate for a few months. She was seriously underfunded during the start-up, during which she took no salary for herself. This situation allowed the company to survive, but it created considerable stress on Feltham. Like Shantal, many entrepreneurs pay themselves too little and are not sure how much and which combination of salary, bonuses, and perks to pay themselves. This can lead to an artificial positive performance for the company and could result in it paying more in taxes than it should. Those who pay themselves too little, like Feltham did, may also have no wealth to cushion their fall should they lose the business. Now after a few years in the business, Shantal relies heavily on her accountant to advise her regarding her salary. Whether she receives a bonus depends on how well the company is doing. The key principle, according to Feltham, is to find the happy medium that minimizes her tax and maximizes the value of the company.

Source: Adapted from Sandra Martin, "Do You Earn What You Should?" *Profit*, November 2009, pp. 93–94.

TRANSFERRING THE BUSINESS: CAPITAL GAINS

Many small business owners wanting to transfer their businesses to others have encountered considerable difficulty. Some tax considerations significantly affect how the business is transferred. Tax changes involving capital gains exemptions have made it much easier to transfer the business to family members or others. Currently, CRA allows a $750,000 lifetime capital gains exemption on the shares of a small business corporation.

GOODS AND SERVICES TAX (GST) AND PROVINCIAL SALES TAXES (PST)

Although the GST and PST are value-added taxes that are not levied on the income or profits of the small business, they are taxes on sales revenues achieved by the small business and require a significant amount of effort on the part of the small business. The federal GST is currently set at 5 percent of the sale price, whereas the PST rates vary by province or territory. The amount of both taxes (Harmonized Sales Tax [HST]) is added to the retail price of the product. Accurate record keeping is required to collect, record, and remit GST amounts to the government. Figure 12-6 illustrates the type of information required for submission to the

TIME TO TAKE ACTION

By this stage in the entrepreneurial process, readers should be working on their business plan or even perhaps running their business. Entrepreneurs should consider the following action steps:

1. Complete a personal SWOT analysis. What areas of management will you need help? Consider finding some formal mentors who can offer you advice.

2. Form a board of advisers to assist you in starting and running your business. The board can be as few as three people. Ensure that they can add depth and breadth to your company.

FIGURE 12-6   Goods and Services Tax Return

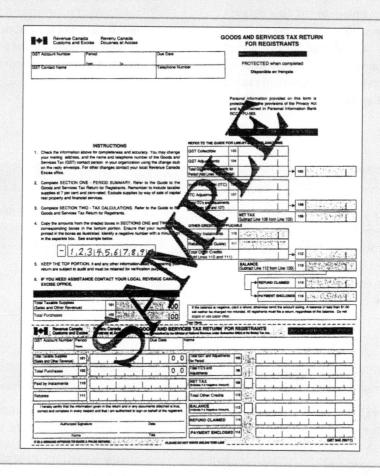

Canada Revenue Agency by the small business. If the small business has sales of less than $30,000 per annum, no GST collection and remittance is required. The small business owner should consult the CRA or the provincial or territorial revenue department for information about how the GST and PST applies to his or her business.

LEARNING OBJECTIVES SUMMARY

LO1 Advisers will often be necessary in the new venture. Outside advisers should be evaluated as if they were being hired as permanent members of the organization. Information on their fees and referrals can help determine the best choices. A board of directors or board of advisers can provide important management support for the entrepreneurs in starting and managing the new venture. The board of advisers is a good alternative to a board of directors when the stock is held privately or in a family business.

LO2 Basic tax knowledge allows the small business owner to save money that would otherwise be paid in taxes. Continual tax planning ensures that the owner-manager is aware of the tax consequences of business decisions throughout the year rather than just at year-end.

The 10 fundamental areas of tax management of which the owner-manager should be aware are (a) continual tax planning, (b) tax deferral, (c) income splitting, (d) marginal tax rates, (e) deductibles, (f) knowledge of government tax-related programs, (g) the incorporation question, (h) the remuneration question, (i) capital gains, and (j) GST and PST.

LO4 Some of the more important government tax-related programs are the small business deduction, manufacturing and processing deductions, investment tax credits, deferral programs, accelerated capital cost allowances, and small business financing programs.

DISCUSSION QUESTIONS

1. What are the advantages of using a mentor compared to a board of advisers?
2. Does the old saying "You get what you pay for" apply to a board of directors or a board of advisers?
3. Explain why the year-end date is significant in tax planning.
4. Which variables affect the decision to incorporate?
5. Discuss with an accountant the advantages and disadvantages of the different owner compensation methods in a corporation.

APPLICATION QUESTIONS AND HANDS-ON ACTIVITIES

1. The year-end for Wave Waterbeds is soon approaching. The proprietor, Tom Newcombe, estimates that the company currently has taxable income of $5500. He would like to purchase a new cash register worth $2000. Determine the tax liability if Newcombe purchases the cash register before or after year-end (use Appendix 12A on Connect); cash registers are depreciated at 20 percent. When would you advise Newcombe to purchase the cash register? Why?
2. The owner-manager of L.A. Construction has just incurred the following expenses. Which expenses are tax deductible?
   a. Incorporation expenses
   b. Advertising expense in the United States and in Canada
   c. Truck repairs of $2000
   d. Costs of maintaining a residential phone used for business purposes
3. What is the tax liability for the following proprietorship's taxable incomes?
   a. $5496
   b. $10,942
   c. $34,999
   d. $63,000
4. Determine the federal tax liability for the following companies using Appendix 12A (on Connect):
   a. A Canadian-controlled incorporated company with $25,000 taxable income
   b. A Canadian-controlled incorporated company with $25,000 taxable income that qualifies for a small business deduction
   c. Same as part b, but the business qualifies for the 5 percent manufacturing credit
   d. A proprietorship with taxable income of $25,000
5. Ask a consultant or an accountant when a business should incorporate. What are the important considerations?
6. Assemble a board of advisers/directors for your venture idea. Make sure you can justify each person's placement on the board, and state the attributes that they are bringing to the venture. If you are not seriously pursuing a business venture, you could complete an assessment of a peer's company and board.
7. Interview five entrepreneurs about their use of a board of advisers. Ask who is on the board, how the members were selected, how they were encouraged to join the board, how useful the board has been, and so on.

Derocher's Market
Home Mart
Hardware Store
Martha's Designs
Sadie's Country
n'Western Store
Dale's Sport Pursuit

Susie's Fashions

Taylor Construction Company
The Barrel Bracket

Threadz
Garner Men's Wear
Boomerang Bouncers Entertainment

Derocher's Market

D. Wesley Balderson, *University of Lethbridge*

Derocher's Market opened a new store in Quebec City in January 2009. Although the firm has been in business for three generations, the neighbourhood in which the original store stood had become shabby, and many of its loyal clientele had moved to the suburbs. The present owner, Claude Derocher, decided to follow the population move. The new store is located in a small shopping centre adjacent or close to more than 70 four-storey apartment buildings that housed more than 400 families. Many more apartment buildings are under construction, as well as three- and four-bedroom, single-family homes in several nearby housing developments. The nearest competition is located approximately 3 km northeast of the present shopping centre.

In preparation for the grand opening, Claude Derocher purchased many varieties of canned juices, fruits, and vegetables. In addition, he carries a number of varieties and lines of cheeses, frozen foods, other dairy products, fruits, vegetables, and meats. To display and sell all the stock, it is necessary to use valuable aisle space as islands for various bulk cheeses, canned fruits, and dry groceries such as potato chips, pretzels, and the like. The store size is 17 by 27 metres. The store layout, shown in Figure 1, is as follows:

- A: display area for crackers, breads, and cookies
- B: refrigerated area for frozen foods, frozen desserts, and packaged cheeses
- C: display area for olives, pickles, other condiments, canned fruit, and fruit juices
- D: display area for canned vegetables, canned fish, breakfast cereals, and dried fruits.

FIGURE 1 | Present Store Layout—Derocher's Market

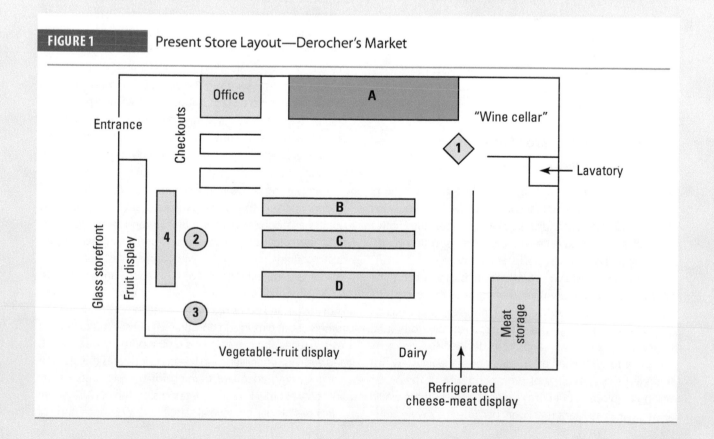

- 1: island display for bulk cheeses
- 2, 3: island display for soft drinks
- 4: area for shopping carts

The store employs eight full-time people. These consist of six clerks and two assistant managers—one manager for meat and dairy and the other for grocery, produce, and frozen foods.

During the first four weeks of operation, it was determined that:

1. There are far too many employees for the type of work needed.
2. There is far too much congestion of shoppers at certain in-store locations.
3. There is a build-up of customers at the check-out stations.
4. Many customers have inquired as to where to find various food items.
5. Several of Derocher's employees have indicated that some changes need to be made to the interior layout of the store.

After receiving this input, Derocher is not sure what to do. The present layout seems unsatisfactory, but he does not want to spend a lot of money making changes.

Questions

1. Based on Figure 1 and the observations of the first four weeks, what are the weaknesses of the present store layout?
2. Develop a layout that might solve these problems.

Home Mart Hardware Store

D. Wesley Balderson, *University of Lethbridge*

Home Mart is a small hardware store located in Weyburn, Saskatchewan, an agricultural community with a population of about 9000. Merchandise stocked includes automotive and farm supplies, furniture and appliances, sporting goods, plumbing and electrical supplies, and giftware.

The owner is David West, a prominent businessman in the community who also owns another business that occupies a large portion of his time. Because of this, West has delegated considerable authority to the manager of the store, John Burns. In July 2013, West and Burns decided to hire a new employee to be trained as an assistant manager. They first discussed the possibility of promoting one of the store's existing employees, but Burns thought none of them would be suitable as assistant managers because they were either too old or did not want the extra responsibility. Doug Burns, John's uncle, was already 63 years old and, though working full-time, had indicated he wanted to work fewer hours and begin to ease into retirement. Sue Mikita, 52, had been with the company for 12 years but had concentrated on the gift-ware side of the department. Burns did not think she had an adequate knowledge of the farm supply side of the business, which produced the most revenue in the store. Ruth Huddy, 61, had worked for the company for only six years, mostly part time, and although she was very competent and knowledgeable, Burns felt she was also too old to fill the position. The only other employees were part-time students who worked Saturdays and summers.

West and Burns decided to advertise for an assistant manager in the local paper. This resulted in a few enquiries, but no applicants who met the two criteria Burns and West considered most important: familiarity with the people in the community and knowledge of agriculture. West and Burns met again in August to discuss the lack of prospects. West suggested that he might contact Noel Branlen, an acquaintance who lived in Weyburn, about coming to work for the company. Branlen currently worked in a town some 40 km away, and perhaps he could be attracted back to his home town. Branlen was young—only 25—and knew the people in the community. West approached him and found out he was interested in working for him but required a salary higher than West and Burns had planned for this position. If they agreed to pay the salary he requested, Branlen would be paid a higher wage than the other hardware department employees except Burns himself. Although West and Burns were worried about this, they decided to hire Branlen and requested that his salary be kept confidential. Branlen would be in a training position for approximately six months and would then assume the position of assistant manager of the store.

Things went smoothly at first, but after a few months, it is evident to West that some problems are surfacing. West notices antagonism between Branlen and the other three regular employees, and so do the store's customers. In discussing Branlen's progress with Burns, West learns that Branlen is frequently late for work, his appearance is unsatisfactory, he is very slow in gaining essential product knowledge, and Burns has had several complaints from customers about him. In addition, Branlen himself has contacted West directly and expressed his disillusionment with the job and with his supervisor, John Burns. He indicates that Burns is not providing adequate training for the products or the authority to order inventory, set prices, and so on. Also, when Burns has his day off, several sales are lost because none of the employees knows the information customers required. Branlen also mentions that as assistant manager he should not have to sweep the floors as he has been required to do on several occasions. He further requests that he be granted time off two afternoons a week to take a management course at a local college to help him prepare for the managerial aspects of his job.

West discusses the problem again with Burns, who says that as soon as Branlen proves himself, he will be given the requested authority—and he is very opposed to letting Branlen take time off for a management course, so this request is turned down.

Toward the end of November, Branlen contacts West to see if he can take some of his vacation just before Christmas. When West mentions this request to John Burns, Burns is very opposed to it because this is the busiest time of the year for the store; furthermore, in the past employees had worked for a year before they took their holidays. However, West allows Branlen to take the vacation.

The store gets through the Christmas rush and inventory taking without serious incident, but things get progressively worse thereafter. Nine months after his hiring, Branlen hands in his resignation, saying he is going back to university. West is relieved that this problem employee is leaving and hopes that the same problems will not recur next time.

Questions

1. Comment on the possible reasons why Noel Branlen's employment did not turn out successfully.
2. How could Home Mart successfully compete against the threat of competition from Walmart or Home Depot?

Martha's Designs

D. Wesley Balderson, *University of Lethbridge*

Martha Millwork needs to make some important decisions regarding her clothing manufacturing business. Started as a hobby in the 1990s, the business has grown to the point where she has opportunities to expand the scale of operations so that it can become a full-time commercial enterprise. She is unsure of which markets to pursue, which marketing channels to use, and the extent of product line that would be the most effective.

Martha lives in Grenfel, Saskatchewan, and she had started sewing clothing for herself and her children in the 1990s. Her skill and talents were first shown publicly during the summer Agribition celebration in Regina in 2002, at a fashion show she organized. As a result of this initial show, she received orders from interested buyers, and the hobby soon became a part-time business that she operated out of her home in Grenfel. Company sales have grown steadily since that time and reached close to $30,000 in the latest fiscal year. Although this only brought a profit of $5000, Martha has fine-tuned the business so that an increase in sales also means a larger profit percentage.

Martha's Designs specializes in high-quality, fashionable women's and men's coats made from canvas, denim, and Hudson's Bay and Pendleton wool blankets. The coats are designed to be comfortable, sophisticated, and original. They also feature fur and leather trims. Several coat designs are available and Martha modifies existing designs and creates new ones on an ongoing basis. The coats are well-made, with high-quality materials, and are priced from $300 to $600. The clothes are fashionable and modern. This blend of fashion, function, and tradition make a unique finished product that she has successfully sold to buyers from across North America and Europe.

As the owner-manager, Martha designs the coats and cut the fabric. She usually orders materials only after receiving an order for a particular coat. The cut pieces, trim, and notions are sent to one of two part-time local seamstresses who do the sewing in their own homes. Martha carefully inspects each garment upon completion. The purchasing of materials is an important aspect of the production process, since the cost of materials is such a large part of the cost of goods. Fabric is purchased at the lowest possible price, but Martha is aware that better prices are available as she increases the size of her orders. The unique trims used on the coats are purchased primarily from local suppliers.

Recently, Martha was approached by the town of Wolseley (estimated population 1000), which is about 15 km from Grenfel, to be a part of a sewing plant that the village is planning to establish. The village intends to purchase sewing machines and other equipment and contract out the sewing services of the workers to interested firms such as Martha's Designs. Martha realizes that to make such a change in operations worthwhile, Martha's Designs will have to increase its production volume dramatically. This proposal is attractive because of its low financial risk, the opportunity for increased production efficiencies, and the flexibility to produce a greater volume of coats.

Martha's marketing efforts to date consist primarily of fashion shows, displays at events, some newspaper advertising, and a brochure. Each year she organizes several fashion shows in Alberta, Montana, North Dakota, and Saskatchewan. In the past, some of these were in conjunction with other events such as the agricultural exhibitions, rodeos, and athletic events. Each show is the result of coordinating the individual efforts of models, commentators, hairdressers, make-up artists, sound specialists, musicians, and publicity staff. Displays are set up at various trade shows and even at such events as the Calgary Winter Olympics. A small amount of advertising has been done in newspapers such as the *Regina Leader Post* and other local papers. Martha uses advertising to promote general awareness and to promote good community relations.

With a potential increase in production capacity, Martha has to plan the company's future marketing strategy. She is confident that demand for her company's unique clothing exists and that volume could be increased enough to result in significant material purchase savings, which would lower production costs. A major decision is which marketing channel to use. Until now, sales have been made directly to purchasers of the clothing. Martha thinks she might achieve an increase in volume by selling through retail stores or clothing wholesalers, but she is unsure which type of retail store would most effectively reach her target customer. An alternative is to continue selling directly to customers and expand on these efforts by distributing a mail-order catalogue.

Another important decision is where to focus the firm's marketing efforts. Her sales, to date, have been mainly through buyers from Alberta, Saskatchewan, and North Dakota, but there is also the possibility of increasing sales to other parts of Canada, the United States, and Europe. Martha is also thinking about increasing the sales of men's and children's coats. Although this strategy would add to her product line and create additional design work, it could also make the line more marketable by broadening its appeal.

A final decision to be made is how to support the sales efforts. Should she use more advertising, or should she concentrate on setting up sales booths at trade shows? There are many trade shows, and deciding which to attend would be difficult.

As Martha considers the alternatives available to her, she is beginning to realize that her company is at an important crossroads—to continue its growth, it would have to enter new markets and expand production capacity. Martha's Designs is a cottage industry on the verge of becoming a small manufacturer.

Questions

1. Discuss the implications of Martha Millwork's potential expansion.
2. Evaluate the distribution channel options and promotional implications associated with them if Martha's business expanded.

Sadie's Country n' Western Store

D. Wesley Balderson, *University of Lethbridge*

Sadie Rogers is the owner of a western-wear clothing and gift store located in Champion, Alberta. Champion is a small town of 500 located about 150 km south of Calgary and 100 km north of Lethbridge Alberta. There are several other smaller communities within a 100 km radius of Champion, as well as numerous rural farmers. Champion is located on one of two major highways from Lethbridge (and the United States) to Calgary. Other amenities located in the small town include a school, bank, post office, restaurant, hotel, grocery store, hardware store, farm machinery dealership, and services such as insurance, beauty salon, and a small library.

Sadie established her store two years ago after a successful five-year experience owning the town's grocery store. With this first venture, she was pleasantly surprised that such a small community could support a grocery store, and she was especially pleased that she was able to draw residents from some of the other communities to her store. The margins in the grocery industry were not very high, however, and she contemplated using her experience, expertise, and knowledge of the community with a clothing and gift store. She reasoned that if she could have the same success in drawing customers with higher margin merchandise, the business could really be profitable. She therefore sold the grocery store and started her current business. She named it Sadie's Country n' Western Store.

Sadie's Country n' Western is located on the main street and is part of a mini-mall with a beauty salon, grocery store, and bank. Sadie's features a huge selection of clothing for men, women, and children (including jeans, shirts, jackets, footwear, hats, and accessories), gifts, collectibles, toys, furniture, jewellery, cards, and gift wrap. She has maintained a close working relationship with Wrangler, which has become her most profitable brand. The store also carries a line of rancher supplies such as saddles, bridles, and other cowboy accessories. She imports many of these products from the United States, which allows her to carry products that are exclusive to Southern Alberta.

Sadie defines her target market as customers within a 90-minute drive of her store. Interestingly, the majority of her market comes from outside the town of Champion. There are few direct competitors to her store in many of the towns within a 100 km radius. However, Sadie feels that the main reason she is able to draw customers from outside her community is because of her marketing efforts and low prices.

Because of her low overhead, Sadie makes sure that her prices are lower than her competitors'. She regularly visits these stores in other communities and does price checks. Sadie's promotion includes direct mail flyers distributed throughout southern Alberta, highlighting low prices on standard products and some of her unique products. Sadie's also offers discounts to 4H and rodeo club members, guest appearances by well-known rodeo professionals, and various contests and giveaways.

Sadie has been very pleased with sales as she nears the end of her second year of operations. Results have been remarkable considering the small size of the community in which she is located. Although sales have exceeded expectations, she has some concerns about the profitability of the business and is anxiously awaiting the year-end results.

Questions

1. How do you account for the ability of Sadie's Country n'Western Store to attract customers from outside of the local community?

2. Evaluate Sadie's marketing strategy. What additional things might be done to enhance sales?

3. Evaluate Sadie's pricing strategy. Relate your evaluation to the classification of consumer goods.

Dale's Sport Pursuit

D. Wesley Balderson, *University of Lethbridge*

Dale Jorgensen has developed a new board game for sports enthusiasts similar to Trivial Pursuit except that the questions are about sports. The game involves asking questions about various players, teams, statistics, and records in all of the major North American professional and amateur sports. As the participants answer the questions correctly, they move around the board, which is patterned after a racetrack. The first participant to cross the finish line is the winner.

Dale has made a few prototypes of the game in his home and is now in the process of developing the marketing plan. Dale currently works for a national sporting goods chain in Toronto as a retail sales associate. Dale is now 38, and he would like to turn this idea into the type of business that would allow him to leave retailing and be his own boss. Dale has an extensive background in athletics, having played major junior hockey for three seasons and participated in amateur baseball until he was 16. He enjoys attending professional sporting events, and most of his good friends meet often to discuss various sports. He has tested the prototype of his game with these friends and they have indicated to him that he has the makings of a million-dollar product if he can market it effectively.

Assume that Dale has come to you for guidance in developing the marketing plan for his product. As Dale has little experience in marketing or managing a business, he wants you to help him develop a marketing strategy for Sport Pursuit.

Questions

1. Discuss how the concept of product classification would provide Dale direction regarding price, distribution, and promotion strategy.

2. What considerations would help Dale determine whether personal selling on the Internet or selling to a national chain such as Toys-R-Us would be the most effective distribution method?

3. What factors could help determine whether to emphasize personal selling or advertising as the major promotional method?

4. Give an example of how public relations could work with this product. Mention an advantage and a disadvantage of using this promotion.

5. If Dale wanted to export the product, briefly discuss some things that he should know about each country he planned to market to.

Susie's Fashions

D. Wesley Balderson, *University of Lethbridge*

As part of his MBA course requirements at Simon Fraser University in British Columbia, Darren Richards has received a student consulting assignment with a small clothing manufacturer in Vancouver. The firm has been in operation a little over a year and has received funding from the government agency funding small businesses. However, it is experiencing cash flow problems. There is a concern that the business, Susie's Fashions, will have to either close or obtain additional funds. Richards spends considerable time wading through the financial data and finally comes up with the approximate statements shown in Figure 1.

Susie Mikado had emigrated to Canada from Hong Kong about five years earlier. Being a hard worker and having worked in a clothing factory in Hong Kong, she got a job immediately at a dress-manufacturing factory. After three-and-a-half years, she accumulated some funds and decided to start her own small business making selected clothing primarily for the large Asian population in the Vancouver area. Susie has an obvious talent for selecting fabrics and designing garments and, through her family and friends, has developed a reputation as a skilled seamstress.

FIGURE 1 Income Tax for Different Legal Forms of a Business

SUSIE'S FASHIONS BALANCE SHEET
AS AT JANUARY 31, 2013

ASSETS			LIABILITIES AND OWNER'S EQUITY	
Current assets:			Current liabilities:	
Cash	$ 95		Accounts payable	$ 8,450
Accounts receivable	3,815		Current portion of debt	1,000
Inventory	4,765		Total current liabilities	9,450
Prepaid expenses	275		Long-term liabilities	
Total current assets	8,950		Debt	4,000
Fixed assets:			Total liabilities	13,450
Equipment	3,500		Owner's equity	(1,000)
Total assets	$12,450		Total liabilities and owner's equity	$12,450

INCOME STATEMENT
FOR YEAR ENDED JANUARY 31, 2013

Sales:		
352 dresses	$17,600	
298 robes	11,920	
Other miscellaneous	5,200	
Total sales		$ 34,720
Cost of goods sold:		
Dresses	6,336	
Robes	7,152	
Other miscellaneous	2,500	
Total cost of goods sold		15,988
Expenses:		
Wages (including Susie's)	20,400	
Rent	4,800	
Utilities and phone	3,200	
Interest	1,000	
Repairs and maintenance	3,000	
Total expenses		32,400
Total cost of goods sold and expenses		48,388
Net profit (loss)		**$(13,668)**

Susie located her business in the Chinatown district of Vancouver in a leased space of about 1800 square feet. To make renovations, buy equipment, and pay other initial expenses, she borrowed $5000 and put $2000 of her own funds into the venture. She hired two full-time employees, paying them $6 per hour to assist in sewing the clothing items. The production process is simple: Each employee and Susie make a garment from beginning to end.

Darren Richards visits Susie's Fashions to assess the situation and determine what can be done to solve the cash flow problem. He is impressed with the product line, which exhibits quality craftsmanship. Susie's produces primarily two garments. The first is a Chinese-style dress retailing at $55, and the second is a kimono-like robe retailing at $45. Sales are based almost entirely on word-of-mouth, as Mikado spends no money advertising. In examining the production process, Darren notices numerous interruptions occur as family and friends of the workers frequently come by to visit. He estimates, however, that on average the dresses take four hours to make and the robes take three hours. The average dress takes about three yards of material, and the robes average four yards. The fabric for both items cost Susie about $6 per yard.

Richards is concerned about the management of the firm. Although Susie hired two full-time employees, she often hires family or friends to help for a few days at a time when they, as she put it, "need some money." He is most concerned, however, with the financial procedures Susie is following. Because there is no record-keeping system, he has difficulty determining paid and unpaid bills from the assortment of receipts, scraps of paper, invoices, and notes Susie keeps. Deposits and withdrawals from the bank account have been made but not recorded. Susie salary is not recorded, but Richards learns that she withdraws $200 per week. Credit sales are frequent and informal, with Susie allowing customers to take garments without leaving a down payment.

Questions

1. Briefly evaluate Susie Mikado's approach to starting her own business.

2. Examine the pricing system for Susie clothes.

3. Assuming miscellaneous clothing and robe sales stay the same, how many dresses would Susie's have to sell to break even?

4. Evaluate the financial statements prepared by Darren Richards in both form and content.

5. What kind of financial recordkeeping system would you advise for Susie's Fashions?

Taylor Construction Company

D. Wesley Balderson, *University of Lethbridge*

In September 2013, George Taylor realized a lifelong dream by starting his own construction company. He had worked for several construction firms in the province of Quebec over the years, and prior to the time he started his own firm, he had been a foreman on several large projects. He is a hard worker and has developed a reputation as a capable and sought-after foreman by many companies. Since starting Taylor Construction Company, George has succeeded in obtaining several profitable contracts, which keep him very busy.

One day he was visiting with a friend, Rob Dumont, over lunch. The following conversation reveals that things are not so great at Taylor Construction.

Rob: How is your business doing, George? You've sure been busy lately.

George: Yes, we've got lots of work, but you can't imagine the problems I've had with employees. I never dreamt it would be such a hassle.

Rob: What kinds of problems are you talking about?

George: Take your pick! When we started up and got our first contract, I needed six labourers, so I ran an ad in the paper. I got 19 applicants, and I was surprised that most hadn't finished high school. Even the ones I hired were lazy and undependable. I spent half my time replacing those who quit or whom I fired. Since then things haven't really improved much.

Rob: Maybe you should spend more time training them.

George: More time? As it stands now, I have to be with them almost constantly on a job and tell them what to do every step of the way. If I leave one of them in charge when I have to be away, the others resent it. It seems like they're always bickering with each other.

Rob: I wonder if you should train a foreman to supervise the workers.

George: I tried that. The work that he supervised was poorly done, and on top of that he padded his hours. I even noticed a few tools missing. When I confronted him with it, he up and quit.

Rob: Can't you spend a little more money and find some better-qualified and motivated employees?

George: My labour costs are too high already! Even though I don't hire union workers, I have to pay pretty close to those rates, and they are high. Once in a while a hard worker comes along, but before long peer pressure from the others seems to drag him down to their level.

Rob: It sounds pretty hopeless.

George: The worst part is that just last month I gave all my employees a bonus. I distributed it based on how long they had worked for me and thought I had explained it to them. However, after I gave it out, several of them were upset, and I even had two quit on the spot. Can you believe that? I'm seriously considering shutting down the business and going back to working for my old firm.

Questions

1. Why do you think George has gotten into this situation?

2. What recommendations would you make to George?

The Barrel Bracket

D. Wesley Balderson, *University of Lethbridge*

Gary Anderson operates an accounting firm in Fredericton, New Brunswick. Although his accounting business is successful and he enjoys it, Gary has always wanted to invent a product and take it to market. In his spare time, Gary recently developed a metal bracket that, when attached to a wall, allows you to hang a wheelbarrow on the wall of a garage or shed. Gary feels that this simple metal product could provide wheelbarrow owners with a major saving of space. Named the "Barrel Bracket," the product has received positive comments from several friends and some retail hardware store owners. Gary has obtained a patent on the product and has made a number of them in his garage. He believes that the Barrel Bracket would be an ideal product for most homeowners who own wheelbarrows, and it may even be of interest to some businesses and retail stores.

With his steel press located in his garage, Gary can make 100 Barrel Brackets per day with the material costing him $5. He is hoping that he can sell the product for $10 and that eventually sales will increase to the point that he can build his own manufacturing facility and retire from his accounting practice.

The major decision facing Gary at this time is to determine the most effective way to market the Barrel Bracket. He has identified three distribution channel options, which all seem viable. The first is to sell to a national retail hardware chain such as Canadian Tire or Home Depot. This method would guarantee substantial sales, but Gary is unsure of the profit margin he could make on each bracket. The second option is to hire manufacturer representatives to sell the Barrel Bracket. Manufacturer representatives are independent salespeople who sell to retail stores and receive a commission on these sales. These salespeople typically represent several manufacturers as they travel around to various retail stores. The third option is to hire some salespeople himself and sell the product door to door.

Since Gary does not have a lot of expertise in marketing, the decision of the appropriate marketing channel is especially troublesome to him. In addition, Gary does not want to spend a lot more money on the venture because he has already invested most of his spare cash to develop the product and obtain the patent.

Questions

1. Evaluate the three distribution options for Gary using the information provided in the textbook regarding long and short channels.
2. Discuss the implications for setting the price of the Barrel Bracket for each of the three distribution options mentioned.
3. What other marketing costs may Gary have overlooked?

Threadz

D. Wesley Balderson, *University of Lethbridge*

Threadz is a small independent retail women's clothing store located in London, Ontario. London is a city of 336,000 in southwest Ontario and has a large young adult population due to the university and colleges located in the area. The owner-manager of the store is Jennifer Byers. Byers established Threadz eight years ago after graduating from university with a bachelor's degree in business management. During her high school and college days, she worked in various retail clothing stores and gained valuable experience for this kind of business. Her father, a successful entrepreneur, provided start-up capital and other assistance for the venture.

Although sales have increased steadily each year, Jennifer has been concerned recently that this success is starting to fade and will be short lived unless something is done soon. Last year, sales were virtually the same as the previous year, and the rate of growth in sales has declined in each of the last three years. Because Threadz is an independent retailer, Jennifer is concerned that stiff competition from the well-known chains is luring away her customers due to lower prices, greater choice, and large advertising budgets.

The Threadz outlet contains 500 square metres of selling space and targets the 20–35-year-old aspiring professional woman. Jennifer's competition comes from such stores as Benetton, Mexx, Esprit, Banana Republic, Club Monaco, Savannah, and Suzy Shier. In addition, there are many other clothing retailers that are somewhat competitive, but Jennifer is of the opinion that they are not focused on the exactly the same customer that Threadz targets. Byers describes her target market as the upper-middle-class woman who is "on the go" and requires clothes that are easy to "mix and match" and are "for any occasion." Threadz's target market comprises a decreasing circle of women who enjoy the shopping experience. Because of career obligations, women in this market tend to shop during lunch breaks, in the evenings, and on weekends. Threadz is located in a large mall in downtown London and is accessible to a large work population as well as the residential market. The downtown has many eating places and night clubs, which also contribute to mall patronage at midday and in the evenings.

Jennifer has operated the store in the past with herself as manager, an assistant manager, and two sales clerks. Recently, she hired a new assistant manager, Sarah Hetherington, who has graduated from a retail management diploma course at a local college. As she is discussing Threadz's current sales dilemma with Jennifer, Sarah asks her if she has thought of establishing a database program in an attempt to retain the customers she suspects she is losing. Sarah indicates that such a system would help in better customer relationship management (CRM), something that successful retailers are recently giving much more attention to. Although she is aware of CRM, Jennifer thinks that such systems are far too expensive for a small, independent retailer like Threadz. She is not sure that she can afford another marketing cost as she is already spending 4 percent of sales on promotion, above the industry average.

Threadz's promotion budget comprises special events, newspaper advertising, and participation in various mall promotions. In the past, Jennifer had also considered developing a website to further advertise the business but felt the costs did not outweigh the expected benefits. However, Sarah explains that technology costs have come down and that a website and a database system might help Threadz to provide better service to its existing customers. Such a system could profile these customers and monitor their purchasing behaviour to tailor special offers to them. As the system is developed further, Sarah explains that it could also be used to target new customers.

Another use would be to exchange this information with other organizations such as restaurants, jewellery stores, and shoe stores that have the same target market as Threadz. A main benefit, according to Sarah, would be that this system could provide in-store sales personnel with immediate information about its customers so that the store could provide more personal treatment to them. Jennifer sees some of the advantages of the system that Sarah is suggesting but is unsure whether it is worth the financial investment.

Questions

1. Evaluate the advantages of the system that Sarah Heatherington is suggesting.
2. What concerns should be explored with this system?
3. What steps should be followed in setting up a CRM system for Threadz?
4. What other promotional suggestions might improve Threadz's performance?

Garner Men's Wear

D. Wesley Balderson, *University of Lethbridge*

Garner Men's Wear is a relatively small independent men's wear retailer located in Oshawa, Ontario, that has been operating for more than 20 years. The owner, Adam Garner,

previously worked for 10 years at Tip Top Tailors, a national chain of men's formal clothing, before starting his own store. Although the first few years were difficult as the business was getting established, Adam was eventually able to develop the business and provide superior service while offering high-quality men's clothing at competitive prices. His target market is made up of middle-aged executives and professionals, most of whom he knows on a first-name basis. Adam has always felt that if he takes care of his best customers, the financial part of the business will take care of itself. He is comfortable with this philosophy because he really does not enjoy all the bookwork that is part of running a business.

Recently, however, he is becoming concerned about the performance of the business. One of his concerns includes the financial aspects of the business. He seems to always have lots of customers, but when he gets his financial statements from his accountant about two months after the year-end, he is surprised and disappointed to find that the net income of the business has dropped to $10,000 and there is no cash in the business bank account. Assume that you have been called in to evaluate Adam's business. He provides you with the following financial statements for the last two years:

Garner Men's Wear Ltd. Balance Sheet

ASSETS	2012	2013
Cash	$ 10,000	$ 0
Accounts Receivable	90,000	120,000
Inventory	50,000	80,000
Fixed Assets	140,000	130,000
TOTAL	$290,000	$330,000
LIABILITIES		
Accounts Payable	40,000	50,000
Long-Term Debt	100,000	120,000
Owner's Equity	150,000	160,000
TOTAL	$290,000	$330,000

Garner Men's Wear Ltd. Income Statement

Sales	$750,000	$720,000
Cost of Goods Sold	500,000	490,000
Gross Profit	250,000	230,000
Expenses	200,000	220,000
Net Profit	$ 50,000	$ 10,000

Questions

1. Comment on the financial management practices of Adam Garner in managing Garner Men's Wear.

2. Calculate and discuss the significance of each of the following for Garner Men's Wear:
   a. Current ratio
   b. Inventory turnover
   c. Debt ratio
   d. Return on investment
   e. Return on sales

3. How many days are there in this company's business cycle? (That is, how long is it taking to convert cash spent back to cash available?)

4. Where did the $10,000 cash from the 2012 statement go in 2013, even though the business made $10,000 income during 2013?

Boomerang Bouncers Entertainment

Jim Clark, *University of Lethbridge*

As Cam Bean sits at his desk on March 1, 2013, he feels he needs to make some decisions about his strategy for using e-commerce tools to take his business to the next level. Cam has decided that April 1, 2013, would be his last day as a tax trust lawyer for a firm that employs 175 other lawyers just like him. He is not enjoying this profession, but it pays the bills. After three years of running a small part-time business, Cam and his wife/business partner feel the time is right to take the business on full-time and devote all his energies into making his business a full-time endeavour.

Cam Bean is 32 years old. His wife, Janet, is also his business partner. They have four young children. Cam has a joint law/MBA degree, and Janet has an education degree. Cam grew up in a family with a small-business and entrepreneur background. Janet's parents worked for very large aerospace firms. Three years ago, Cam decided to make some extra income on weekends by renting out air bouncers to people for recreational activities. Bouncers are large inflatable tent-like structures. They are sometimes known as moonwalks, spacewalks, jumps, inflatables, among several other names. They come shaped in themes such as Barney, Spiderman, Cinderella, and so on. Cam got the idea for the air bouncers from a college friend who had a thriving business in bouncers in Kansas City, Kansas. Cam lives in Calgary and thought this might be a nice way to bring in extra income on the weekends.

Cam and Janet called their small part-time venture Boomerang Bouncers Entertainment. The bouncers are usually rented for five hours at a time at a cost of $225. Boomerang Bouncers Entertainment delivers and sets up the jumps. They make sure everything is safe, clean, and dependable. At the end of the rental time, Boomerang then picks up the jump and takes it back to inventory to be rented out again. The market for these jumps includes daycares, schools, family parties, church and club socials, and corporate parties. Weekends are usually the busiest time. The business is seasonal and things slow down from November to February each year.

In their first year, Cam and Janet invested in two bouncers at a cost of $4500 each. With these two bouncers, they generated sales of $32,400 on 72 unit bookings. The next year, Cam thought they would expand this business with two more bouncers and another $9000 investment. In year two, they generated sales of $72,000 on 320 bookings. In year three, they went to a total of six bouncers and sales went to $108,000 on 480 bookings. They almost always have multiple requests for bouncer rentals on weekends that they cannot fulfill because all the bouncers are already booked out. Cam has found that he really enjoys the business and can hardly wait for his work day as a tax lawyer to end so he can take time for Boomerang Bouncers Entertainment. He decides to quit his tax job and operate Boomerang Bouncers full-time, with a total of 20 bouncers.

This decision to go full-time with 20 bouncers means Cam has to make a number of other decisions. He has to hire more drivers for delivery and increase his marketing efforts to keep all the bouncers rented as much as possible.

Cam advertises in local community papers read by moms of school-aged kids, uses word-of-mouth, and also makes some person-to-person sales. Most orders are received over the phone by Janet. She makes sure the particular jump the customer wants is available. As these jumps are visually stunning, it is hard to describe them adequately over the phone. Cam knows that keeping these jumps rented out as much possible is the key to expansion. He feels he needs a Web strategy of some sort to increase his marketing and sales efforts to keep his jumps booked at a high capacity. Cam and Janet feel the Web would graphically show the potential customer the variety of products that they have in inventory.

Cam is a fairly sophisticated computer user, skilled with PCs and networking. He feels that with his business growing, he can use the Web for marketing and sales. He also wants to use a database to keep track of sales and human resources needs.

Cam knows he has to make a number of decisions regarding his use of e-commerce tools and that he needs to make them very soon. In 30 days, his whole livelihood depends on making Boomerang a success.

Questions

As a consultant to Cam, answer the following questions:

1. What are the advantages of a Web presence for Boomerang Bouncers?

2. Identify what Boomerang Bouncer's website objectives should include.

3. Cam will need to host his website once it is developed. What would you recommend he should do about choosing a web-hosting strategy? Why?

4. What are the five top ways that Boomerang Bouncers could attract customers to their website? Why did you choose them?

For more information on the resources available from McGraw-Hill Ryerson, go to www.mcgrawhill.ca/he/solutions.

PART IV

LOOKING TO THE FUTURE

Part 4 focuses on management of the small business for the long term. If a business is being managed effectively and increasing sales and profitability have resulted, the owner-manager will face the question of expansion. If growth of the business is desired, some changes will be required within the organization. Chapter 13 discusses the preparations needed in such a situation.

Chapter 14 discusses the methods of transferring ownership of the business to someone else. Many key considerations in this regard have legal and tax implications with far-reaching consequences for the owner-manager. An option other than transferring ownership to another person is involving family members in the business. The majority of small businesses are, in fact, family-owned and family-operated. Chapter 14 also examines the special characteristics of such businesses.

CHAPTER 13

MANAGING GROWTH

LEARNING OBJECTIVES

By the end of this chapter, you will be able to:

LO1 Describe the potential problems that success and growth can bring to the small business.

LO2 Review the characteristics of the stages in the business life cycle.

LO3 Discuss how to sustain the business despite the difficulties created by growth.

LO4 Illustrate the importance of planning for growth.

SMALL BUSINESS PROFILE
MABEL'S LABELS

Photo courtesy of Mabel's Labels

Mabel's Labels (www.mabelslabels.com) does not sound like a high growth company. But you may not want to tell that to the four company founders, Julie Cole, Cynthia Esp, Julie Ellis, and Tricia Mumby, who reside in southern Ontario. The company does exactly what the name suggests—they make labels for children's clothes or, as the company slogan states, "Labels for stuff kids lose." "The idea of labels just came to us," Cole says. "After seeing countless masking tape labels on toddlers' Sippy cups, we said, 'We can do better than that'."[1] While Mabel's Labels started out of a basement, it now employs 40 people out of a 14,000 sq. foot facility in Hamilton, and they have just announced a major deal with Walmart Canada to sell their labels in their stores.

The partners who wanted to grow their firm beyond local moms have successfully used social media and online sales to sell over 50 million labels in 97 countries. Their initial social media objectives were to first get visibility for their firm and then engage followers. The company initially targeted highly influential mommy bloggers who are always looking for new content. The partners sent free labels to bloggers and held contests with them in order to gain visibility. Mabel's Labels also created volunteer Buzzmamas, women who would post positive news about the company on their social media pages. After using bloggers and Buzzmamas to gain visibility, the company used their own social media pages and website to develop a community of followers. "Moms talk about products they love and hate like it's their job," says Cole. In order to keep their community engaged they hold online events and discussions about things mothers are interested in.[2] For example, the company recently hosted an online discussion about whether parents should send their children to camp. The discussion had a camp counsellor as a guest, and he answered questions from many of the followers. Cole says their online business, which has become a true community of followers and supporters, was recently recognized by Inc.com as one of the top 20 Awesome Facebook Fan Pages and Hubspot's The 15 Best Facebook Pages You've Ever Seen.

As Mabel's Labels grew, the founders also made several business decisions aimed at supporting growth. The partners realized they had to let go of minor aspects of the company to focus on the big picture. They brought in consultants to assist with their human resource development and to fill the gaps in other areas, they hired a PR firm to grow sales in the U.S., and perhaps most importantly, they hired a retail consultant, Gerald Harris to help them pitch to Walmart. Harris along with the partners visited Walmart armed with a new product—blank non-custom labels that can survive both the dishwasher and washing machine—along with market research supporting the concept. The meeting was a success, and the company landed a contract with Walmart Canada. Mabel's Labels shows no signs of slowing down, and with a growing online and retail business, the four partners think the sky is the limit for their company.

MABEL'S LABELS
www.mabelslabels.com

SMALL BUSINESS AND GROWTH LO1

As illustrated below, short-term success and subsequent growth do not always lead to a trouble-free business operation. Often success and growth may compound the complexities and difficulties of managing the business.

But even with the challenges discussed in the chapter, there are many advantages to growing a business. Many entrepreneurs work the same amount of hours regardless if the business is pursuing a growth strategy or simply providing an income for its founder. One of the difference between a business pursuing a growth strategy and a business opting to stay small is the earning potential of the growth business is much more significant. Former CEO of Lakeport Brewing Income Fund, Teressa Casciola says, "One of the only differences between a small and large business is the size and volume of transaction. But the higher volume and larger transaction enables larger businesses to pay their owner much more money which translates into nicer homes, cars and vacations."[3] Rebecca MacDonald, CEO and founder of Toronto-based Just Energy (http://justenergygroup.com) states that larger companies are also better prepared to handle downturns in the economy, saying, "Unless your business is growing, it's stagnating. Keeping the business small, you don't have a diversification portfolio, so you are counting on all the eggs in one basket. You cannot sustain the bad times as much as big business can. You can get in trouble way quicker."[4] Victoria Sopik, president and CEO of Thornhill, Ontario-based Kids and Company (www.kidsandcompany.ca), a childcare that specializes in 24-hour care catering to corporate clients and emergency care says she has been growing her business as quickly as possible to gain market share and put the company in a position to fend off any potential competition. Other advantages of larger growing business include they have an easier time raising capital, can usually attract and retain employees compared with small stagnant companies, and can often be sold for more money than small firms with low growth stories.

To avoid the pitfalls of growth and changes in the market, owner-managers should try to ensure long-term viability early in the life of the business. First, owner-managers need to understand the life cycle of the business to effectively plan for the future. Second, they should be aware of some of the more common growth problems a business is likely to face. Finally, owner-managers should take specific steps in planning for growth of the business.

THE BUSINESS CYCLE LO2

The business cycle of the small enterprise is similar to the product life cycle discussed earlier in the text. For many small businesses that have only one or two products, the business cycle and the product life cycle may be the same.

Figure 13-1 illustrates the changes required by a small business as it moves through its life cycle. The vertical axis represents the growth index, usually measured by gross sales, market share, or profitability. The horizontal axis measures the time taken to pass through the stages of the cycle. The length of time a business stays in one stage depends on several variables. Many small businesses take several years to move through the life cycle, while others pass through all four stages within a couple of years. This shorter life cycle is common in high-technology industries. The characteristics of the stages of the business cycle are discussed next.

Introduction.

Stage 1 is the start-up stage of the small business. It is characterized by expenditures made for both product development and introductory promotion and by low profits, particularly at the beginning. Stage 1 also usually includes a narrow market, a very limited product line, and

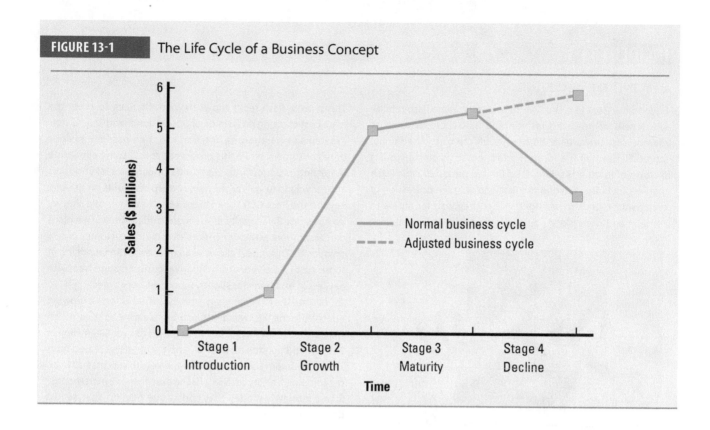

FIGURE 13-1 The Life Cycle of a Business Concept

Y-axis: Sales ($ millions)
X-axis: Time

— Normal business cycle
--- Adjusted business cycle

Stage 1 Introduction
Stage 2 Growth
Stage 3 Maturity
Stage 4 Decline

involvement in most aspects of the business by the owner-manager. The owner's role tends to be more technical and entrepreneurial in this stage. As discussed in the Opening Profile of this chapter, the founders of Mabel's Labels invested a significant amount of time in just gaining visibility for the company, and during the early stages of their business, they were involved in all aspects of running the company.

Growth.

Stage 2 of the business cycle, growth, is usually characterized by the establishment of a market share, or acceptance, and expansion of the product line or markets. It may also take the form of internal or external expansion such as a merger or franchising. During this period, sales grow at an increasing rate. At the end of the growth stage, however, competitive pressures begin to take their toll, necessitating changes in business strategy. Promoting the business to customers, investors, and employees is important at this stage of the business life cycle. Most small businesses find that this stage requires increased capital to finance the expansion. The business may have orders to purchase but only receives payment when the product or service is delivered. Therefore, financing to cover inventories, equipment, and employees is required before sales occur. Most high-growth firms indicate that this is the stage at which the most severe cash flow problems occur in the life of the business. As Incident 13-1 illustrates, even when Montreal e-retailer Beyond the Rack Inc. (www.beyondtherack.com), grew their sales from $4 million to $80 million, they continued to need outside capital to cover the costs of growth.

Maturity.

Stage 3 is characterized by a levelling of sales due to increased competition or a decrease in demand. During this stage, the owner-manager must make some important strategic decisions

INCIDENT 13-1

BEYOND THE RACK INC.

Beyond the Rack Inc., is a Montreal-based online flash retailer which sells name-brand fashion and household items to its members for upwards of 80 percent off the cost in traditional stores. Flash retail is a form of retail, where a company posts pictures of items it is selling for a limited period of time. Flash retailers, including Beyond the Rack, do not take possession of merchandise prior to selling it; rather they wait for orders to come in and then place demand orders with their suppliers.

MONTREAL-BASED BEYOND THE RACK IS THE LARGEST FLASH RETAILER IN CANADA WITH SALES IN EXCESS OF $80 MILLION. FLASH RETAIL ALLOWS THE COMPANY TO SELL ITEMS BEFORE INCURRING THE COST OF TAKING POSSESSION OF THEM. THIS ENABLES WWW.BEYONDTHERACK. COM TO SELL NAME-BRAND FASHION AT 80 PERCENT OF RETAIL PRICES.
Michele Constantini/PhotoAlto/Corbis

This type of flash retail allows Beyond the Rack to avoid the extra cost of taking possession of unsold merchandise and storing items in warehouses. The firm can then pass the savings onto consumers. While this process does add some extra time in getting products into the hands of consumers, shoppers appear willing to wait as they enjoy deep discounts on the site. Beyond the Rack CEO Yona Shtern says, "As a flash sale site, we do not stock the majority of the merchandise we sell; we place demand orders with our vendors after taking customer orders on our site. This model allows us to offer exceptional pricing at some cost to delivery time. Our loyal customers are happy to pay less in exchange for slightly longer delivery times."[5]

Beyond the Rack has been recently named as fastest growing e-retailer in the U.S. by *Internet Retailer* magazine as sales, which were under $4 million in 2009 have grown to over $80 million in 2011. In addition the number of employees has increased from 75 to 333. Shtern states that one of the keys to success has been the company's ability to raise what he describes as "smart money." Smart money is money that adds value beyond that of just dollars. The investors bring in connections or knowledge that can help grow the business.[6] Shtern says the process of raising capital is not easy and in order to raise funds entrepreneurs need to be committed to the process every day. Shtern states you need a good business plan and resilience to be successful. Shtern appears to be following his own advice, as he recently announced Beyond the Rack has raised an additional $36 million in order to fund continued growth.

to avoid moving into stage 4, decline. Out of necessity the strategy of the business will become more competitive. Such a strategy may involve adding new products, expanding to new markets, or adjusting or improving existing products in some way. The goal of such actions is to lengthen the life cycle, as illustrated by the increase in sales during the decline stage of the adjusted life cycle in Figure 13-1. The owner's responsibility becomes much more managerial during this stage. For example, Richard Abbas, founder and president of Deep Down Cleaning (www.deepdowncleaning.ca), a commercial cleaning business based in Halifax, says that growth during the early stage of his company was rapid. But eventually it started to slow.[7] To maintain growth and diversify income, Abbas started to rent out high-end cleaning equipment and expanded into industrial clean-ups.

Decline.

As Figure 13-1 shows, stage 4 involves a decrease in both sales and profits. Unless action is taken to reverse this trend, the business will fail.

Figure 13-2 shows an example of the growth of a business and subsequent operational and strategy changes that should take place. The actual dollar level of sales relating to the stages of

FIGURE 13-2   Stages of Growth

APPROXIMATE SALES LEVEL	MARKET	PRODUCT	OWNER-MANAGER
$0–$1,500,000	One market	One or limited line	Involved in day-to-day aspects of the business such as buying, selling, and financial management
$1,500,000–$4,000,000	Expanding into new markets	Adding new products in same category	Some organizational change allowing supervisor to oversee greater part of day-to-day operations
			Greater need for financial evaluation
			Greater need to obtain capital to finance growth
			Some delegation required
			Development of managers
$4,000,000+	Established markets: continued expansion to new markets	Adding new products in different categories	Managers run day-to-day operations and report to owner
			Communication and information important
			Training for management development
			Establishment of proper controls

Source: Ronald W. Torrence. *In the Owner's Chair: Proven Techniques for Taking Your Business from Zero to $10 Million,* © 1986, p. 259. Reprinted by permission of Prentice Hall, Inc., Englewood Cliffs, New Jersey. Updated 2005.

the life cycle will vary depending on the growth of the market, the type of industry, and the owner's objectives. However, Figure 13-2 points out the need to deal quickly with the changes that growth in sales can create.

PROBLEMS CREATED BY GROWTH   LO3

To be able to anticipate growth difficulties and make plans to minimize them, the owner-manager should be aware of some of the problems that can be expected to accompany growth.

Owner-Manager Fatigue and Stress.

Stress levels rise when the scope of the business and the magnitude of its problems increase. For example, John DeHart and Ken Sim, co-founders of Nurse Next Door Home Healthcare Services Inc., had successfully grown to 1000 employees and $20 million in revenue in four short years. Yet, one day at work, the pair realized that they no longer liked their business, nor did many of their managers actually like them. The founders of Nurse Next Door were so focused

was negatively impacting the work environment.[8] Rather than sell their firm, which they discussed, the pair opted to create a new vision, remove employees who they identified as problematic, and revamped some of their human resources practices, including their hiring process. In order to ensure an engaged workplace, the co-founders then invested more money in training managers. The result is an increase in growth and a happier work environment for the entrepreneurs and the employees.

Lack of Communication.

As the scope of operations grows, the former closeness between owner and business dissipates. Many owner-managers resent this loss of closeness and even curb their growth objectives as a result. As a firm grows, owners often have to let go of managing every part of their company, and this can be something that they struggle with. For example, Rebecca MacDonald says that when she first started the business, she was involved in every detail of managing the firm. But as the business grew, she had to let her managers do their jobs, which was something she struggled with. "At one point I was involved in everything, from sales to marketing to gas procurement," notes MacDonald. "It was almost like letting a child leave home. It was hard for me. But I wanted to allow my talented people to do what they were hired to do."

Human Resources Problems.

One of the biggest challenges facing growth companies is human resources related. Many companies are facing staffing challenges as they cannot find enough skilled workers, while other companies are adding employees so quickly that they failed to develop enough formal structures to manage their employees, often leading to low morale and high turnover. Both a lack of qualified staff and formal human resources practices can negatively impact growth. For example, Halifax-based make your own wine company, Noble Grape (noblegrape.ca) grew from one store to eight in Halifax over a short period of time. As the company grew, co-founders Stephen and Mark Haynes focused on sales and not creating any formal human resources structures.[9] Eventually employees started to complain that there was no consistency in how the firm was being managed. This eventually led Stephen to develop a formal human resources guide, including rules on sick leave, vacation days, and so on to ensure formal practices were used in all locations. Employees were happy with the consistency and that many of their benefits were now in writing.

Lack of Coordination.

Various aspects of the business may become specialized and less integrated with the overall operation as a business grows. This often results in increased conflicts among departments and individuals within the organization. Employees who in the early stages of the company life cycle performed many duties are often reluctant to give up some of those responsibilities to specialists. Such resentment often leads to conflicts within the organization.

Shortage of Cash.

Growth and expansion often require financing that the business has not yet generated. Merchandise may have been sold or services rendered but cash not yet received, even though cash is still needed to acquire new inventories or to fuel growth. *Profit Magazine* produces a list of the fastest growing companies in Canada and many of them, including 40 percent of the top 15, have yet to make any money. As noted above, Beyond the Rack has achieved sales in excess of $80 million but still needed to raise $36 million in capital to fuel growth.[10] Another example of firms that had to overcome a shortage of cash includes Aecometric Corp. (www.aecometric.com).

Its president Jill Anderson discovered the importance of managing cash-flow during the recession. Her firm, which makes custom burners and other heavy industrial equipment, narrowly missed going out of business because of the economic slump. Large-scale construction projects were brought to a halt and clients started taking longer to pay, which caused the firm to miss payroll three consecutive times. To keep the firm afloat, Anderson cut her workforce from 22 to six and re-mortgaged the family farm. Although sales are up, Anderson has become a very careful manager of cash flow. It is important that the owner-manager estimate the cash requirements of an increase in sales.[11] See Figure 13-3 for an illustration of how to do this.

Low Profitability.

Low profitability is common in rapidly growing businesses. As discussed above, approximately 40 percent of the 15 fastest growing companies in Canada according to *Profit Magazine* are not making any money. Considerable expenses are incurred in research and development of markets during the growth period.[12]

Breakdowns in Production Efficiency.

Declining production efficiency, as evidenced by unmet schedules, increases in quality assurance problems, and consumer complaints, are common in rapidly growing companies.

Lack of Information.

Lack of information with which to evaluate the business's performance often accompanies rapid growth. As the owner-manager becomes increasingly removed from day-to-day operations and the scope of the business outgrows manual information retrieval, a more automated system is often required to generate the required data.

FIGURE 13-3   How to Estimate the Cash Requirements for an Increase in Sales

To make the calculation, a business needs the following information:

- The increase in sales planned ($)
- The timeframe for adding new sales (days)
- The company's gross profit margin, gross profit ÷ net sales (percent)
- The estimated additional expenses required to generate additional sales ($) (extra overhead)
- The company's average collection period (days)

To calculate the amount of additional cash needed, use the following formula:

Extra cash required = [(New sales − Gross profit + extra overhead) × (Average collection period × 1.20*)] ÷ (Time frame in days for adding new sales)

*The extra 20 percent is added as a cushion.

Consider the following example:

The owner of Ardent Company wants to increase sales by $75,000 over the next year. The company's gross profit margin is 30 percent of sales (so its gross profit on these additional sales would be $75,000 × 30 percent = $22,500), its average collection period is 47 days, and managers estimate that generating the additional sales will require an increase in expenses of $21,300. The additional cash that Ardent will need to support this higher level of sales is:

Extra cash required = [($75,000 − $22,500 + 21,300) × (47 × 1.2)] ÷ 365 = $11,404

Ardent will need $11,404 in extra cash to support the additional sales of $75,000 it plans to bring in over the next year.

Source: Adapted from Norm Brodsky, *Paying for Growth: How Much Cash You Need to Carry New Sales*, Inc. Online Tools & Apps: Worksheet, October 2008.

INCIDENT 13-2

ISSUES WITH GROWTH

Jacqueline Shan had received a Ph.D. in pharmacology from her native China and a Ph.D. in physiology from the University of Alberta when she formed CV Technologies Inc. in Edmonton with her colleague, Dr. Peter Pang, in 1992. With $20 million in government grants and private investor money, their research led to the development of the cold and flu remedy COLD-FX (www.cold-fx.ca).

Using a combination of Asian natural preventive techniques and a proprietary extract of North American ginseng, Shan and Pang along with several other research scientists developed a product and system that became a commercial success. "I believed we had the best product in the world for the prevention and treatments of colds and flu," observed Shan.

Marketing the product, however, proved to be a challenge at first. It was not until Jacqueline was able to tap into public relations with well-known celebrities such as Don Cherry and the release of trial results showing COLD-FX's effectiveness that sales increased substantially.

Within a short time, COLD-FX became the #1 selling cold and flu remedy in Canada, with sales increasing from $1.5 million in 2003 to $41.3 in 2006. The company was one of the top growth firms in Canada, and it received the Marketer of the Year award in 2006 from *Marketing* magazine. Dr. Shan was selected as the Chinese Canadian Entrepreneur of the Year and was inducted into the Canadian Healthcare Marketing Hall of Fame.

The year 2007, however, was a difficult one for the company. Although growth in sales continued, CV Technologies lost $9.8 million. With its growth, the company had failed to control costs, had made a disastrous attempt to enter the U.S. market, and was experiencing management turmoil. Jacqueline quickly realized that changes were needed to move the company back to profitability.

In 2008, she stepped down as CEO, returned to the research area, and hired a professional manager to run the company. Many changes were made and the results were immediate. Sales rose to $49.4 million in 2008, with profits of $4.6 million. In 2009, the name of the company was changed to Afexa Life

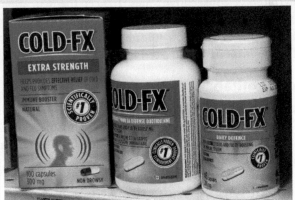

DR. JACQUELINE SHAN WHO DEVELOPED COLD-FX EVENTUALLY HAD TO STEP DOWN AS CEO OF THE FIRM SHE FOUNDED FOR MORE PROFESSIONAL MANAGEMENT.
Mike Cassese/Reuters /Landov

Sciences Inc. New products were added. Marketing efforts were rewarded, and the endorsements of Canadian doctors and athletes continued to provide positive media attention. COLD-FX was selected as the official cold remedy for the 2010 Olympics in Vancouver.

With sales of over $50 million in 2009, Afexa had climbed back into the top 50 fastest growing companies in Canada as selected by *Profit Magazine*. This growth was not lost on Valeant Pharmaceutical International Inc. (www.valeant.com) that purchased the company in 2011 and took it private.

Discussion Questions

1. Why do you think the founder of a business may hesitate to step down as CEO?

2. If the founder steps down as CEO, do you think it is possible for him or her to work in a lesser role in the business? Why, or why not?

3. Using Internet resources, find out the current state of the company today. Report back to the class what you found.

Source: Used with the permission of Dr. Jacqueline Shan and Afexa Life Sciences Inc.

Owner Lifestyle.

An often overlooked contributor to business failure due to growth relates to personal lifestyle decisions of the owner as the business begins to be successful. A larger house, bigger car, or exotic vacations based on the expectation of continued growth often leave the owner unable to meet personal obligations.

EVALUATING THE GROWTH QUESTION

Owner-managers should answer four important questions before proceeding to expand the business.

Is the Business One That Can Grow?

A preliminary step in dealing with the question of growth is to evaluate whether the product or business is one that can grow. Restricted markets or products that have volume production restrictions are difficult to expand. Many service businesses that rely on the special expertise of their owners also fit into this category. Rapidly changing industries such as those found in high technology suggest concerns of rapid obsolescence. This is particularly critical if the capital investment of growth is large.

Is the Business Owner Prepared to Make the Effort?

Expanding a business will require additional time and effort on the part of owner-managers. The decision owner-managers must make is whether they are ready to increase effort and prepare for the stress or be content with a smaller but less demanding business. Many successful small businesses have chosen not to grow for precisely this reason. This decision not to grow is one which has been applauded by U.S. business consultant Ed Hess. Hess states that some firms with owners who are not prepared to change and are run by people who do not want to grow are better off staying small.

Does the Owner-Manager Have the Capabilities to Grow?

The owner-manager should assess whether the needed capital, labour, and expertise can be obtained to deal effectively with growth. Some of these specific areas will be discussed in the following section.

How Should the Owner-Manager Pursue Growth?

If growth is desired, several approaches may be taken in pursuing it. The most common strategies (some of which were already mentioned) are as follows:

- Pursue new markets for the product or service. This may involve different geographic (domestic or foreign) or demographic markets. For example, Nat Bosa of Bosa Development Corp (www.bosadev.com), a successful Canadian condominium developer, has expanded his company to the United States. Bosa, on a trip to San Diego, was shocked by the lack of development in the downtown area and immediately started buying several blocks of prime, underdeveloped real estate. Bosa then proceeded to construct a wall of high-rise condominiums that reshaped the community so much that a local magazine recently ran the headline, "Welcome to Bosa Town."[13] Since Canada is relatively small on a global scale, many companies such as Bosa's are pursuing exporting or international expansion as their main strategy. Of the fastest growing companies in Canada identified by *Profit Magazine,* 58 percent of them are pursuing International expansion. For example, Toronto-based Varicent Software Inc. (www.varicent.com), an IT company that has developed compensation software to help firms manage their payroll, states that Canada only accounts for 6 percent of its sales and the firm was built to service the U.S. market.[14]

- Increase sales of existing products or services by increasing the frequency of use. This can be done through increased promotion.

- Add new products or services or modify existing ones to increase sales.

- Find new uses for the product or service and promote these uses to the market.

- Acquire other small companies or merge with another organization.

INCIDENT 13-3

SECURE KEY TECHNOLOGIES INC.

Have you ever ordered something online? Most people have. The process has become very simple. Consumers point and click on an item, enter a credit-card number, and wait for their package to arrive. If the item can be downloaded, consumers can access their order using a computer or mobile device in seconds.

As online sales have grown, so has online theft and fraud. In the transaction described above, all that is needed is a computer, tablet, or online device to place the order and credit-card numbers. The actual credit card is not required. Thieves, who can use a variety of tricks to get your credit-card number, including skimmers and mobile cameras, can then spend thousands of dollars online without ever stealing your card. Greg Wolfond, founder and CEO of Secure Technologies Inc. (http://securekey.com), wants to change this. His Toronto-based company is working with Intel to allow computers and mobile devices to recognize credit and bank cards. Online transactions would be more secure as people would have to have the physical card to make a purchase. Consumers would tap their cards against their computers or online device when making a purchase increasing the security of the system.

In addition to online credit-card recognition, Secure Key Technologies Inc. is working on a strategy to allow one set of online credentials to deal with multiple online sites or access points—the product is Secure Key Concierge. Customers using Secure Key Concierge would no longer have to memorize various usernames and passwords but would be able to securely access multiple sites using one secure sign-in system. Consumers would benefit from being able to access sites, some of which they may not frequently visit, relatively easily, while businesses would be able to ensure clients and employees are who they say they are. Secure Key has recently announced a pilot project where people will be able to access personal information from Revenue Canada using their online banking sites. Thus consumers can benefit from the security of their online banking system to access government documents and information.[15]

Discussion Questions

1. What are some of the advantages and disadvantages of Secure Key's systems described above?

2. Would you be more comfortable tapping your credit card against your iPhone or iPad compared with typing in your credit-card information? Why, or why not?

3. Do you think people would be comfortable accessing all of the websites they visit using one sign-in system? Why, or why not?

PLANNING FOR GROWTH   LO4

Once the decision to expand has been made and the method of expansion has been determined, a plan for growth should be developed. A growth or strategic plan is a blueprint of future actions. Planning is an essential but often overlooked part of management. One survey found that only 5 percent of all companies do formal short-term and long-term planning, and almost 50 percent do little or no formal planning.[16] Dan Shimmerman, president and CEO of Varicent Software Inc., which was discussed above, notes that planning is essential in expanding his company. Shimmerman who plans on reaching $100 million in sales over three years states that global expansion and a firm plan are central to managing his business.[17] Shimmerman's comments are echoed by Kevin Higgins, owner of Fusion Learning (www.fusionlearninginc.com), a salesforce training company with $5 million in sales. Higgins has developed a formal plan titled "Better, Stronger and Fitter" to help him manage and grow his firm.[18]

Some small business owners fail to plan for the future because they do not understand what a plan is. A plan is more than short-term sales forecasts and budgets. It includes setting long-term objectives and outlining procedures for reaching those objectives.

In addition, most small business owners feel snowed under by the daily operations and often think planning is a nuisance. However, small business owner-managers who are able to periodically step back from the organization and objectively assess its overall direction are generally better able to cope with the environmental changes that will affect the business. It may be advisable for owner-managers to employ professional management in the business if the management problems of rapid growth are due to their own limited capabilities. Many entrepreneurs have found that following this course of action has allowed them to focus on the areas that they have greater expertise and interest in.

Finally, conditions change so rapidly in many industries that plans have to be altered frequently. The need for constant adjustment discourages many small business owners.

THE EXPANSION PLAN

Chapter 4 discussed the essential elements of the start-up business plan. Many similarities exist between the start-up plan and the expansion plan. The business plan as introduced in Chapter 4 includes projecting for growth and expansion as well. The steps in the expansion plan are discussed below.

Set Objectives.

The first step in the planning process is to set the objectives the business is to accomplish. As mentioned previously, it is important to set objectives specifically so that the outcomes can be measured. Objectives may include dollar sales, market share percentage, or dollar profits.

Determine Alternatives.

The second step includes identifying possible strategies to achieve the set objectives. It also involves forecasting the possible outcomes of different alternatives.

Select the Best Alternatives.

Alternatives should be selected with a view toward long-term success. The components of this success are the company's capability and the potential growth of the area.[19] As mentioned previously, growth could occur geographically, by reaching new markets, or by adding new products.

UNDERSTANDING THE REQUIREMENTS OF GROWTH

Rapid growth will necessitate some fundamental changes within the organization. Some of the requirements of growth are discussed next.

Greater Management Depth.

Owner-managers must realize that an expansion of management depth must accompany the expansion of the business. This will require more skills or harder work on behalf of owner-managers. Because they may already be stretched to the limit, such expansion usually consists of training subordinates to handle some of the managerial responsibilities. This involves training and delegation, two personnel practices owner-managers are often hesitant to incorporate into their management styles. As the business grows, owners must spend more time thinking and less time doing. This also means they must move from task delegation to functional delegation, allowing key people to manage various functional areas of the business. Greater management depth can also be achieved through the use of functional specialists outside the company such as accountants, lawyers, directors, or mentors.

Staffing.

As firms grow, they will also require additional staff and or managers. Given the aging workplace in Canada many firms struggle to hire skilled employees. Any expansion plan should contain human resources recruitment strategies. Some firms such as Winnipeg-based Broad-view Networks Inc., has adopted programs to enhance the skills of its employees so they can meet the everchanging needs of the firm. According to Broadview's president Michael Orloff, the company has adopted a training program for every one of the firm's employees to grow the skills of the company.[20]

Intelligent Expansion.

A common problem among small business owners is that in their effort to succeed, they start too many diverse projects. They often do so without evaluating whether they have the productive or marketing expertise and resources to accomplish the expansion. They may also ignore the potential effects of unplanned expansion on their existing products. The decision to expand should incorporate continuity, experience, and intelligence.

Additional Capital.

Any expansion in the business will require additional money to finance added productive capacity, inventory, or personnel. Unless the business has a solid debt-equity ratio and a steady cash flow, it may have difficulty obtaining this needed financing.

One way to achieve high growth even with limited capital may be to franchise the business or the idea. Although becoming a franchisor requires a certain amount of capital, franchising may allow a firm to expand rapidly without needing large amounts of funds. Michael Gerber, author of the bestselling entrepreneurship book, *The E-Myth Revisited: Why Most Small Businesses Don't Work and What to Do About It*, has studied a number of the world's best brands and concluded that franchising their system is what enabled them to grow quickly but at a controlled pace.[21] Brian Scudamore, CEO of 1-800-Got-Junk?, a Canadian franchisor of junk removal businesses, notes that franchising has enabled him to grow

INCIDENT 13-4

ENVIRO PAVING CORP.

Enviro Paving Corp. (www.enviropaving.com) is using the franchise model to successfully grow its business throughout North America. The company, which uses recycled tires to pave driveways, is enjoying significant growth as people are looking for more environmentally friendly ways to do business. Unlike traditional asphalt driveways, Enviro-recycled driveways do not leak toxins into the ground and come with a five-year guarantee. Current franchise owner Ron Bristow tried the product at his home in Innisfail, Alberta, and liked the product so much he bought the franchise rights for two territories, including Central Alberta. Bristol says, "We can put it over asphalt, concrete, paving stone, sidewalk blocks," adding that there's a recycled plastic product that can be used to create the necessary base for the rubber coat elsewhere—such as on bare ground. "It'll support over 100,000 pounds per square foot."

ENVIRO PAVING CORP., A COMPANY THAT PAVES DRIVEWAYS WITH RECYCLED TIRES, IS USING THE FRANCHISE MODEL TO GROW ITS BUSINESS IN CANADA.
Marekusz/Dreamstime.com

Source: www.albertalocalnews.com/business/Driveway_leads_to_business_venture_103099979.html?mobile=true.

his company with partners (franchisees) into one of the most successful junk removal businesses in North America.

Financial Information.

Often, increased sales obscure the fact that the profitability of the business is declining or even negative. As the business grows, it is increasingly difficult—but more important—for owner-managers to obtain accurate information about the profitability and productivity of the business. The use of computers by many small businesses has greatly helped in this area. As the business grows, there is a greater need to use information technology. Owner-managers should regularly project future financial requirements so that cash shortages do not occur.

Organizational Change.

As owner-managers realize they can no longer be involved in every aspect of the business, the organizational structure will require alteration. This is necessary to establish a clear understanding of reporting and responsibility centres in the business. The aim is to reduce the owner's span of control, allow managers the space to make decisions and let owners focus on planning and long-term strategy development of the business. It can also allow the owner more time to foster coordination within the firm. Incident 13-5 illustrates how one entrepreneur found that organizational change was required for the firm to grow. As the firm grows, the owner can also make greater use of advisory boards and professionals.[22] At the same time, owner-managers must resist the temptation to "overdo" the bureaucracy of the organization. An entrepreneurial culture (which likely contributed to the business's success in the first place) must be retained if growth is to continue.

Implementing Managerial Controls.

As a business grows, it becomes more difficult to control. Through the use of informational and organizational methods, a system of goals, performance levels, and evaluations must be put into place. As discussed earlier in the text, the integration of new software into the small business's operations has greatly enhanced owner-managers' ability to control all aspects of the business. Such measures as ratio analysis, bench marking, inventory turnover, margins, and cost controls are examples.

INCIDENT 13-5

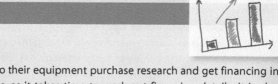

STRUCTURING YOUR GROWTH

Planning for growth is a sound business strategy that Phoenix Building Components (www.phoenixbuilding.ca) has fully exploited. The company, a rapidly growing manufacturer and wholesale distributor of engineered wood building products, has carefully staged its growth and has also made a point of investing in the future. Jeff Allan, vice-president, sales and marketing, says that continuing to invest in equipment is essential for a company with a lot of growth potential, such as this. He advises entrepreneurs to make sure they allow necessary time to do their equipment purchase research and get financing in place, as it takes time to work out financing details. It is also important to work with a clear and documented business plan. Phoenix Building Components had a very detailed plan that showed exactly where revenue would be generated, such as with equipment purchases. Allan believes that having a plan is very helpful when looking for the right lenders, as it adds credibility and lets lenders see exactly how the purchase will help the company grow.

Source: Adapted from, "Success Story: Structuring Your Growth," *Business Development Bank of Canada*, November 6, 2008, p. 1.

Monitoring the External Environment.

The final growth requirement is that owner-managers should focus greater attention on the external environment of the business. These external forces serve as a guide to the long-term strategic planning in which owner-managers now must engage. Important external forces are technological change, competition, consumer demand, social and cultural norms, legislation, and the state of the economy.

To keep their companies strong and encourage growth, managers need to:

- Invent new applications for products and services
- Find new sales and distribution channels
- Rethink internal processes
- Enhance technological content
- Provide employees with upgradeable, saleable skill sets
- Disseminate internal information effectively[23]

INCIDENT 13-6

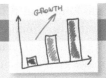

BNOTIONS.COM

Technology can change in a heartbeat, just ask Alkarim Nasser, founder of Toronto-based Bnotions.com, who started the company with a focus on Flash technology in 2008. Nasser, who at the time was only 26, quickly recognized the rise of mobile and social media would be the drivers of IT growth and decided to switch his firm's focus to developing mobile and social apps.[24]

Nasser's decision to focus on apps and games is paying off, as the company has grown from revenue of roughly $200,000 in 2009 to over $2 million in 2011. Much of the growth can be attributed to Bnotions ability to combine elements of social media such as community interactions to apps and games. Nasser notes that just because he and his employees loved online games did not make them experts. Rather they spent countless hours researching successful online games and apps and developed basic rules to social gaming success. He states that games and apps must be simple, fun, interactive, involve low stress, and users must have a desire to share gameplay and information. Bnotions' games and app strategy has led it to form relationships with numerous clients such as Johnson & Johnson, the SCORE, and Indigo, and the company has recently been recognized as one of the preferred app developers in Canada by Facebook.[25, 26]

Bnotions, like most technology companies, is having trouble getting enough skilled employees and Nasser has taken an innovative approach to solving this dilemma. The company creates and hosts educational events that allow them to meet prospective recruits. Nasser started by offering free nine-week training classes in digital media and has grown to hosting conferences in Toronto. He states that roughly 20 percent of his growing company's employees come from such events. Nasser also creates an open and collaborative environment allowing his staff freedom in accomplishing their goals. Nasser states, ". . . (we) trust our teams to collaborate and deliver. We believe that every team is only as strong as each individual it is comprised of. Surrounding ourselves with passionate and talented folks on the day-to-day give that extra burst of energy and that push for us to take things one step further."[27] Nasser also states that he relies on his employees to make sure Bnotions stays current in the everchanging technology field. Nasser says, "We hire folks that aren't satisfied with the way we use the internet today and the tools that are out there. There is this intrinsic curiosity that leads us to perpetually explore."[28]

Discussion Questions

1. What are some of the pros and cons of Bnotions unconventional hiring strategy?

2. Bnotions has created a very open and flexible environment for employees. What are some of the advantages and disadvantages of this type of work environment in a dead-line driven industry?

3. Bnotions maintains a very active social media presence. Visit their websites, and use the information to identify some of the emerging trends in online business. State what they are and what businesses you could start to profit from these trends.

TIME TO TAKE ACTION

If you are following the steps in this book, you are well on your way to your entrepreneurial dreams or hopefully at the very least a great grade in your course(s). The focus of this chapter is on growth strategies and dealing with the implications of growth. Whether you are running a growing business or hope to be, it is never too early to plan for growth. After this chapter, you should complete some or all of the following activities:

1. Determine what your business goals are. Look at your business idea or operating business. Is the business large enough to meet your goals? Generate some ideas that would grow your business. If necessary, review Chapter 2's discussion on creativity.

2. Check out the Internet or your local book store, and read material on people who have grown a small business into a large one. Try to determine what strategies they used. Comment on any changes in the management structure of the company. If possible, interview some entrepreneurs who have grown their business. Identify their strategies, and discuss with them what, if any, changes occurred in how they manage their company.

3. If you have not already done so, complete a list writing down your personal strengths and weaknesses. Now review where you want your company to grow to in the next three, five, and 10 years. Then note areas where you have to develop if you want to maintain your position as owner-manager.

LEARNING OBJECTIVES SUMMARY

LO1 Problems to anticipate as a result of growth are the owner-manager's increased fatigue and stress, lack of communication, human resources problems, lack of coordination, shortage of cash, low profitability, breakdown in production efficiency, lack of information, and possible decreases in employee morale.

LO2 The four stages of the business cycle are the introduction, growth, maturity, and decline stages.

LO3 To acquire the knowledge to deal with growth problems, the owner-manager should address three areas. First, review the business life cycle. Second, be aware of the common growth problems that arise. Third, know the steps to take to plan effectively for growth.

LO4 Growth planning is often overlooked because of the failure to understand the planning process, lack of time, and the constant changes occurring in the industry. The three steps in developing an expansion plan for a small business are (1) setting objectives, (2) identifying all the possible strategies or alternatives for achieving the objectives, and (3) choosing the best and most viable alternative.

DISCUSSION QUESTIONS

1. What are some of the advantages of growing a business?

2. What problems should the owners be aware of when expanding? How might these problems be dealt with?

3. What are the requirements for growth?

1. The owner-managers of a small, successful hair-cutting company want to expand their business. Their growth objective is to have 35 percent of the local hair-cutting market in two years' time.
   a. What steps could they take to determine the feasibility of their expansion?
   b. Outline a brief expansion plan.

2. Interview the owner-manager of a successful small business, and evaluate the potential for further growth. Would you recommend expansion for this firm? Why, or why not?

3. Visit three small businesses that you suspect have varying sales levels. Determine the market, product, and degree of owner-manager involvement in each business. Are your results significantly similar to those in Figure 13-2? Explain.

4. Identify three of the fastest-growing companies in the region. What opportunities have they pursued to achieve this level of growth? What growth mechanism have they used (internal, joint venture, acquisitions, franchising, etc.)?

5. Use research to come up with three examples of founding entrepreneurs that stepped aside once the firm had grown to a certain size and brought in a "professional manager." What relationship did the entrepreneur continue to have with the firm after the transition? Provide an example of a founding entrepreneur being forced out of the position of CEO to be replaced by a professional manager.

6. Form groups, and assume the roles of top management at your university or college. Develop expansion strategies and objectives to grow the business. Present your findings.

Despite the personnel problems, Dan is able to persevere and keep the plant running. Toward the end of the second year of operations, Dan's business seems to be really taking off. Sales have reached $700,000 by October, mainly because of distribution of the Ladder Rail and accessories across Canada, as well as a growing number of sales from the United States. He has added some accessory products and their sales are also contributing to the positive company performance. This expansion necessitated renting additional manufacturing space nearby and doubling production. Dan secured patent protection for the Ladder Rail and its accessories and now has several ideas for new but related products.

However, the major concern that Dan has is that the business has grown to the point that he is putting in 18-hour days. It seems that every day new crises arise and he is the only one who has either the expertise or the interest to deal with these problems.

Despite the sales success, the business continually experiences cash flow problems. Dan has to pay for the metal C.O.D., but the retail hardware chain that has exclusive rights for his products only pays him once per month. This results in a continual operating deficit until this payment is received.

The plant personnel problems continue to cause a lot of stress and with the additional plant, this is compounded. Dan finds that he is going from one plant to the other to try to ensure quality production. Times when he has been on the road, the quality has slipped and a number of customer complaints have been received. Although his marketing person is a hard worker and capable, Dan has to oversee marketing as well as review the financial condition of the business. Finally, he has to ensure that the loan payments to the bank are made.

His family life has essentially disappeared. The dream of owning his own business and having the freedom to do what he wants is turning into a nightmare. All the problems of trying to run the business were compounded when Suzie announced that something had to be done or they were through. Dan realized that he does not want to lose Suzie. He is contemplating selling the business or altering the organization somewhat to allow for more time for his family.

Question

1. Identify the problems that growth has caused with Dan's business and discuss possible solutions.

For more information on the resources available from McGraw-Hill Ryerson, go to www.mcgrawhill.ca/he/solutions.

CHAPTER 14

MANAGING THE TRANSFER OF THE BUSINESS

MOIRA AND LINDSAY G. MERRITHEW *Merrithew Health & Fitness™*

In 25 years, husband-and-wife entrepreneurial team Lindsay G. Merrithew and Moira Merrithew, co-founders of Merrithew Health & Fitness™ (www.merrithew.com), have parlayed their passions for fitness and business into an exercise empire. Blending his business savvy with her fitness expertise, they established Merrithew Health & Fitness as the world's only fully integrated company of its kind specializing in mindful movement education, equipment manufacturing, and video production. Their acclaimed, premier brand, STOTT PILATES®, is recognized as one of the world's most respected mind-body fitness brands.

Photography © Merrithew Corporation. Used with permission.

Forced to end her dance career because of a foot injury, Moira applied for and received a grant from Toronto's Dancers in Transition Centre to retrain as a Pilates instructor at Joseph Pilates' original studio in New York City. Lindsay, meanwhile, spent time in New York completing a second degree at the Juilliard Theater School before launching a successful acting career. When the two returned to Toronto in 1987, they began their entrepreneurial venture in Pilates with the philosophy that effective and responsible exercise is the foundation to a better lifestyle. Moira began offering private sessions in their Toronto apartment, attracting such celebrity clients as prima ballerina Karen Kain. Lindsay focused on the business side of their small but high-potential business while also working in film and television. The proceeds of his acting work were used to help finance the fledgling company's growth. Early positive media exposure, a demand for mind-body exercise among dancers, athletes, and the active baby boomer population, plus an incredible sense of ambition inspired the couple to think big.

Today, in addition to STOTT PILATES, Merrithew Health & Fitness has developed three other fitness programs: Total Barre™, CORE™ Athletic Conditioning and Performance Training™ and ZEN·GA™. The company produces its own line of DVDs and crafts high-caliber professional and consumer exercise equipment that is manufactured at their Toronto facility. The company has three Corporate Training Centers located in Toronto, New York and Denver as well as over 50 Licensed Training Centers that offer instructor training across the globe.

Merrithew Health & Fitness was ranked as one of the fastest-growing companies in Canada five years in a row by *Profit* Magazine. Merrithew's revenues grew 742 percent between 1998 and 2003, while the number of staff grew almost four-fold during the same period. Today, company performance is solid with more than100 full-time staff as well as over 38,000 instructors trained in more than 100 countries.

One challenge of making this business successful has been the working relationship with a spouse. The Merrithews have had to learn how to divide management duties and responsibilities to make a good partnership. As President and CEO, Lindsay is the driving force behind growing the fully integrated business from a visionary and strategic point of view. Moira, the company's Executive Director, Education, oversees the creation of the curricula and education materials and is often the lead instructor in their extensive library of DVDs. The current delineation of roles didn't come without significant growing pains. In hindsight, says Lindsay, they were blissfully ignorant about the challenges of building a business together. "We didn't know any better at the time."

They soon realized a clear growth plan was necessary. Having a clear game plan, understanding their markets, their customer needs and their product development strategy goes before anything else.

Lindsay and Moira agree. "We've got these growth pillars in place and are now focused on furthering our global reach to ensure strong, continued growth," says Lindsay. "With the launch of our new branded programs and our expanding line of exercise equipment for both the professional and consumer markets, we're able to cater to a global, diverse audience of fitness professionals and enthusiasts." Building on this strong foundation, the Merrithews look forward to tackling the challenges and seizing the opportunities that will undoubtedly come their way with the growing demand for health and wellness products and services.

MERRITHEW HEALTH & FITNESS™
www.merrithew.com

LONG-RANGE PLANNING

As mentioned in Chapter 13, relatively few owner-managers engage in formal long-range planning. One reason is the unpredictability of the future due to changes in the economy, technology, consumer demand, and legislation. However, one outcome that is predictable for small business is the fact that the owner-manager will not be able to manage the business forever. Someday the business will be transferred to others or be closed down. Because of the time, effort, money, and commitment owner-managers have put into their ventures, they generally want the business to continue to grow and prosper and hope to realize a financial gain for their efforts in starting and building the organization.

To ensure this continuity for the business, owner-managers need to plan early for the time when they will no longer be in charge. Many small business owners are uncomfortable about this prospect. As a result they often procrastinate, avoiding the issue until shortly before the transfer of ownership is a necessity. Most succession experts advise that planning should be done five to 10 years in advance.[1] Given today's legislation and tax laws, such a lack of planning can be extremely costly and damaging to both the owner-manager and the new owners of the business.

In addition, succession problems are predicted to be at a high level in the near future as many business owners who have an average age of 53 who started their businesses in the 1960s, 1970s, and into the 1980s are planning on retiring. According to the National Entrepreneurship survey conducted by *Profit Magazine,* roughly 50 percent of small and medium enterprise (SMEs) owners plan on selling their business within five to 10 years, with 16 percent looking to sell in fewer than five years. If business owners stick to their timelines discussed in the survey roughly 60 percent of Canadian SMEs will change hands in the coming decade. Research conducted by the Canadian Federation of Independent Business (CFIB) supports the findings with 71 percent of entrepreneurs reporting that they plan on selling their business within 10 years.[2] Benjamin Tal, deputy chief economist with CIBC world market, says that 310,000 Canadian SME owners plan to transfer control of their business in the next five years.[3] Some experts involved in the buying and selling of businesses, such as Brent Boyd, think the number of firms hitting the marketplace at the same time could be devastating to entrepreneurs looking to cash in on the sale of their firm. Boyd is forecasting that upwards of 80–90 percent of firms will not actually find a buyer.[4]

SOME EXPERTS ARE PREDICTING THAT THERE WILL BE SO MANY BUSINESSES FOR SALE IN THE COMING DECADE THAT 80–90 PERCENT OF THEM WILL NOT FIND A BUYER.
Photawa / Dreamstime.com

Jordan Gould, a Toronto-based specialist in succession planning, echoes Boyd's comments saying that many firms, especially those with less than $8 million a year in annual revenue may have no one to sell to.[5]

The key to successfully transferring ownership of a business is planning for succession in advance. Yet the majority of entrepreneurs do not appear to have any formal plans. In the above mentioned National Entrepreneurship survey, only 18 percent of respondents indicated they had a formal written plan, and 44 percent admitted to no plan at all. According to small business expert Mark Groulx it can take upwards of two years to just prepare for the sale of a business.[6] Succession expert Gould suggests that many small business owners have their heads in the sand when it comes to proper succession planning. Gould notes that succession planning is minimum a five to 10 year process and entrepreneurs who do not like planning for the long term lack the capacity to think about this.[7]

Given the number of businesses that could be sold in the coming decade, entrepreneurs should be familiar with the possible outcomes for the business, the relative merits of those outcomes, and some key implications of each.

ALTERNATIVE OUTCOMES FOR THE BUSINESS

The owner-manager can anticipate four possible outcomes for the business: transferring ownership to family members, selling the business to an employee, selling the business to outsiders, and closing down the business or declaring bankruptcy. Prior to transferring ownership of his business the entrepreneur should do everything possible to get the business in a condition to maximize the value of the firm. This maximization of the value of the firm is sometimes referred to as *harvesting*.

SUCCESSION PLANNING

Succession planning, much like traditional business and expansion planning, involves the entrepreneur first developing alternatives and then selecting the best strategy for his or her firm. In the case of succession planning, most entrepreneurs want to remove themselves from their business and maximize profits as a result. In some cases, especially in family businesses, entrepreneurs are motivated to leave control of their firm to certain individuals and may except less money to do so. They key steps in a strong succession plan are discussed below.

1. Plan Early.

Most experts agree the sooner an entrepreneur starts to plan for their exit, the better. For example, Ron Foxcroft, founder of Fox International Inc., recognized at age 55 that he needed a plan to eventually exit his business. Part of the plan should include the method or choice of exiting the business. Foxcroft, after learning neither of his sons wanted to manage the company, developed a plan where the chief operating officer would eventually take over the management of the firm.[8] The other aspect of the plan should include tax planning. In Canada, the owner and those who own shares in the firm in his family could be eligible for capital gains tax exemptions in the amount of $750,000. Doug Robbins, founder and president of Robbinex Inc., a brokerage specializing in selling businesses, says that most firms are saleable, but some need time to get their financial and management practices in condition where they are attractive to buyers. Robbins further adds that if you are in a hurry to sell your business it might be for a lot less than it could be worth.[9]

2. Start to Gradually Remove Yourself from the Business.

Many entrepreneurs, especially those in smaller businesses are so hands on that the company could not run without them. If an entrepreneur wants to sell their firm, then they have to start to build a management team or train employees to make decisions without them. The owner wants to ensure the business can be efficiently and effectively when they are gone. For example, Tom Duffey owns and operates Tom Duffey Hockey Schools (www.tomduffeyhockey.com) throughout Atlantic Canada, the name alone and the fact that he manages all on-ice sessions will make it difficult for him to sell his firm. As one business consultant said, what value does Tom Duffey Hockey Schools have without Tom Duffey? Entrepreneurs should also start to create a business plan or operations guide outlining how they manage their firm. This can be included in any sales package. Buyers will want to know about key suppliers, employees, customers, and internal plans and practices.

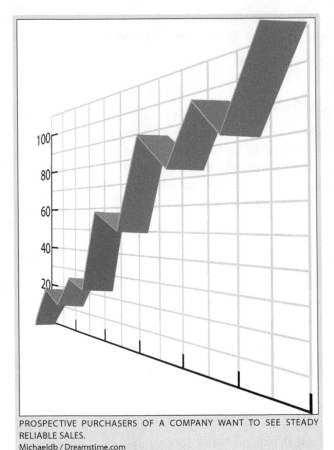

PROSPECTIVE PURCHASERS OF A COMPANY WANT TO SEE STEADY RELIABLE SALES.
Michaeldb / Dreamstime.com

3. Start to Prepare Financial Statements.

Potential purchasers of a business are normally interested in the cash flow a company can provide them with. Thus purchasers pay particular attention to EBITDA, or earnings before interest, taxes, depreciation, and amortization. As discussed in Chapter 5 on buying a business, purchasers will often look at net income or EBITA and multiple the amount by a number ranging from two to 10 times to determine a rough value of the firm. Often when entrepreneurs are preparing financial statements, especially income tax returns, they overstate expenses by running personal items through the company, engaging in travel to conferences or professional development events, or by employing family members who do not play an active role in the firm. Entrepreneurs who are looking to maximize the value of their firm should try to increase their EBITDA as much as possible by growing sales and eliminating non-essential expenses.

4. Grow Stable Revenue.

As stated briefly above, part of any succession plan should include maximizing incoming revenue. Of particular importance is regular revenue or income that occurs time after time. Prospective buyers like to know there is consistent revenue.

5. Get an Evaluation of the Firm.

One of the biggest shocks to entrepreneurs is what their business is actually worth. Some entrepreneurs describe getting the first offer as a "slap in the face moment" and as a result some business owners decide to not proceed with even investigating the sale of their company. Business consultant Mark Groulx says for many entrepreneurs the value of their firm puts their pride on the line. "It's the ultimate measure of what you (entrepreneurs) did with your

CONSULTANT MICHAEL LAMM SAYS WHEN SOME ENTREPRENEURS HEAR WHAT THEIR BUSINESS IS WORTH, THEY ARE SO UPSET THEY COMPARE IT TO A SLAP IN THE FACE.
© esolla/iStockPhoto

company." Michael Lamm, a merger and acquisition consultant states, "They (entrepreneurs) think their company is terrific, has all these bells and whistles, and is worth an enormous amount of money. When we tell them, 'Here's the reality,' some owners are able to accept that. But others say, 'I'm not going to sell my company, ever!' They'll take it to the grave."[10] By getting an evaluation done in advance, entrepreneurs can get a true sense of what their firm is worth and, in some cases, the time to recover from the shock of the valuation.

6. Consider Hiring Professionals.

Often buyers, especially larger companies, will have lawyers and accountants evaluating a potential purchase decision. Entrepreneurs may want to bring in consultants to assist them in not only getting their firm in a position to be sold but people to help negotiate the process. Business brokers, lawyers, and many accountants actually specialize in this area of expertise.

TRANSFERRING OWNERSHIP TO FAMILY MEMBERS   LO2

Keeping the business in the family is a common method of transferring the business. Many Canadian family businesses have been successful, and many small business owners wish to pass the business they have inherited or built up to their children. In a 2012 Pricewaterhouse-Coopers (www.pwc.com) survey, 51 percent of family businesses planned on passing the ownership of the company to family members.[11] Yet few owners of family businesses appear to be preparing for succession. In a recent survey by The Canadian Association of Family Enterprise (CAFE), 80 percent of family businesses had no formal succession plans. In some cases, this transfer occurs with considerable tension[12] (see Incident 14-1). Because a family-owned business has many unique characteristics, it is important to review the problems and potential solutions in managing this type of organization.

Estimates of the extent of ownership within a single family indicate that approximately 90 percent of all businesses in Canada are family-owned and family-operated[13] and employ close to 60 percent of the Canadian workforce. Although a majority of these firms are small businesses, a significant number of family-owned large companies exist. Almost 35 percent of the Fortune 500 companies are owned or controlled by a single family.[14] In Canada, family involvement in business is also significant as approximately 40 percent of the largest 100 companies on the Toronto Stock Exchange (TSX) have handed down control to a second or even later generation.[15] One survey of the 500 fastest-growing private corporations in America undertaken by *Inc.* and *USA Today* found that 33 percent of spouses and 28 percent of children are involved in family business operations.[16] Some facts on Canadian family business include the following:

- Account for 80 to 90 percent of firms
- Generate more than 50 percent of GDP
- Employ, directly and indirectly, around 6 million people
- Create 50 percent of all new jobs
- Represent roughly 40 percent of the largest 100 public companies started as family businesses (many still are)
- Outperform non-family businesses
- Stay in existence longer than non-family firms
- Generate approximately $1.3 trillion in revenue

Despite the predominance of family businesses in Canadian society, relatively few survive into the second and third generations. It is estimated that only 30 percent continue into the second generation and 10 percent into the third.[17] This succession problem also appears to be occurring more frequently today as many entrepreneurs who launched in an economic boom 30 years ago are now nearing retirement.[18] What are the reasons for this apparent lack of continuity? One of the major problems occurs in family business when the firm reaches the second and third generations and shares of the firm continue to be diluted among family members. For example, the Irving Group of New Brunswick, which was founded by legendary business icon KC Irving, originally had a simple succession plan. KC noted that his three sons would equally split the shares in the firm, and the oldest would be in charge.[19] While this plan initially worked, as his children's children had families, shares in the firm become more and more divided. Recent news stories have discussed internal succession struggles as

INCIDENT 14-1

McCAINS DISPUTE

Harrison and Wallace McCain, former owners of McCains (www.mccains.com), a billion-dollar frozen-food empire, provide an example of how difficult succession planning can be. For years, McCains' two founding brothers, Harrison and Wallace McCain, co-managed the company. The brothers often appeared to be a perfect management match, with Harrison the extrovert assuming the role of spokesman for the company, focusing attention on sales, expansion, and managing the overseas operation, while Wallace, three years Harrison's junior and an introvert, spent his time running the North American operations and looking after the smaller details of company business. The two brothers were co-CEOs, with each possessing a veto over final decisions; between them they controlled 66 percent of the company's shares, with the remaining 33 percent divided up among their two late brothers' children.[20]

The company successfully ran this way for over 30 years, reaching sales of approximately $3.5 billion in 1993 with operations in 11 different countries. Together the brothers were a perfect management match and best friends. Unfortunately, this would all unravel when the touchy subject of succession came to the forefront. Both men had sons who worked within the company at one time or another, but only Wallace's son, Michael, had managed to climb the corporate ladder and gain enough experience to take over as CEO. Wallace was becoming adamant behind closed doors that if the pair was to name a successor, Michael should receive the job. Harrison disagreed; he thought Michael was still too inexperienced and lacked people skills. He felt that their late brother's son, Allison, would be a better choice but admitted Allison needed more experience before he would be ready to lead the company. As an alternative, Harrison pushed to bring in an outsider (not a family member) to take over the reins of the company until Michael matured or Allison was ready to assume the leadership role.

The situation came to a head when Wallace flew to the company's head office in the United States to appoint Michael as CEO of McCain's U.S. operations. To outsiders, the move made sense as Michael had held a number of high-level management positions within the company and was currently serving as president of McCain's U.S. frozen juice company where he engineered a turnaround, reversing years of losses and turning the company into a money maker. But what few people knew is that Harrison was dead set against the promotion and asked Wallace not to proceed with the announcement. "I never claimed Michael was stupid or that he was lazy. I just felt that he wasn't ready and that his appointment made us look bad to the professional managers we employed around the world. I told Wallace his son's promotion wasn't justified

and was far too nepotistic." Wallace proceeded with the announcement and, for the first time, ignored the long-time mutual veto that either brother could use at his discretion.[21]

After this, it was only a matter of time before significant changes were made to the company's management team. The board of directors had the power to terminate one of the brothers, and Harrison gathered support from the other family members to successfully oust Wallace from his position as co-CEO. Wallace countered with a lawsuit, and the two brothers agreed to have Judge Ronald Stevenson adjudicate the matter with the binding authority of a court but behind closed doors. After hearing the case, the judge ruled that the board did have the legal right to oust Wallace but offered some recommendations with his ruling that might be seen as an acceptable compromise to both sides. He suggested that both brothers resign as co-CEOs as soon as an outsider could be found to fill the role, the brothers should stay on as consultants, family members with ambition should be patient, outside directors should be brought in to sit on the board, and the family should consider going public. Harrison refused the compromise that Wallace was now willing to accept and fired his brother.[22]

Rather than stay in New Brunswick, Wallace moved to Toronto and tried to find an alternative exit from the family business. He tried to sell his shares but could not find any takers outside the family who were willing to become a minority shareholder in a family enterprise. He considered selling his shares to Harrison, but they could never agree on a price. Finally, he used the leverage of his shares and his strong business connections to acquire the financing to purchase Maple Leaf Foods, a competitor of McCain's. His son Michael soon joined him under the Maple Leaf banner, taking over the role of president and CEO. Harrison and Wallace continued their feud almost up to the time of Harrison's death. Wallace died a short time later. Michael McCain is still the CEO of Maple Leaf; and Allison McCain, Harrison's choice of successor, has taken over as chairman of McCain's board of directors, although the day-to-day operations are managed by an outside CEO.[23]

Discussion Questions

1. Are you surprised by any elements in the case above? Which elements did you find surprising, and why?

2. What type of compromise would have been possible to avoid such a lengthy dispute?

3. Do you really think non-family members working in the company would have been surprised or objected to Michael McCain assuming the role of CEO? Why, or why not?

4. Were you surprised to learn that the brothers continued their feud almost up to the time of Harrison's death?

INCIDENT 14-2

SUCCESSFUL FAMILY BUSINESS

Before George Thomson, founder of Paradise Island Foods (www.paradise-foods.com), passed the family business on to his two sons Len and Kevin, he insisted that they first prove they were assets to the business. Len, now president of the Nanaimo, B.C.-based company, says that his father wanted them to first gain hands-on experience in the food industry, as well as learn to work for other people. The Thomson sons first learned the ropes in grocery retailing in other companies, and then moved up the ladder at Paradise Island Foods before finally taking over their father's enterprise in 2003.

The company worked closely with a chartered accountant and lawyer to structure a succession plan to help them through the business ownership transition. The transition was made over a three-year period so that the sons could reach their comfort level and make adjustments. They had experts work on tax planning, one of the more complex matters in the business. Businesses can benefit from a third-party point of view, and BDC Consulting offers entrepreneurs expertise regarding transition planning.

Communicating effectively to customers, suppliers, and employees in advance is a key factor in the success of the owner-ship transition. Thomson went to the senior management team six months in advance so that there would be no surprises and everybody would be prepared. Communicating to customers and suppliers was crucial in the process because of the strong rapport Thomson had built with them.

Today the Thomsons have proven themselves to be capable owners by bringing different strengths to the business. Kevin, vice-president, operations, is a natural for sales development, while Len is more focused on the production side of business. The business is achieving steady growth, and the Thomsons have seen highly positive results since taking over.

Discussion Questions

1. What are some of the benefits to planning for succession as outlined in the case above?

2. Did the family miss any steps in their planning process? If so, what steps were missed?

3. If you worked in a management capacity in the family business, knowing their intent to leave the company in the hands of family members, would you continue working for the firm? Why, or why not?

Source: Adapted from "Success Story: Family Succession Know-how," *Business Development Bank of Canada Newsletter*, November 2008, p. 2.

---

the growing family struggles to craft a clear succession strategy. Observation also shows that if some unique considerations in operating the family business are not recognized and planned for, they can cause considerable difficulties for the enterprise. Family involvement in a business may have a detrimental effect not only on the business but also on family relationships. Additionally, unique challenges result when spouses own and operate a business together. Statistics Canada estimates that 30.7 percent of all self-employed persons have their spouses as a partner.[24] The profile at the beginning of this chapter illustrates some of these considerations.

Planning for Succession in the Family.

The owner-manager has both a difficult task and an excellent opportunity in preparing children to become involved in the business. Some difficulties include providing proper training, adequate motivation, and a supportive atmosphere so that the child is able and willing to come into the business. Research shows that fewer than 50 percent of children who worked in family businesses expect to return after receiving their college or university education, and only 20 percent plan to return to the business within five years of their graduation.[25] For example, Dani Reiss, the current CEO of Canada Goose Jackets and son of the previous CEO David, noted that he had no intentions to work for the family business once he graduated from university. Dani only started to work there as a summer job, but once he became involved with the firm, he fell in love with the stories associated with the jackets. Much of the company's current success can be attributed to Dani's promotional efforts and his decision to continue to manufacture the jackets in Canada.[26] Other studies indicate that 70 percent of family businesses are either liquidated or sold after the founder retires.[27] It is apparently difficult for the parent to instill in the child the personal interest in the business the parent has. One school of thought is that parents may take too passive a role in attempting to interest their children in the business. They assume the children will find a profession more interesting and rewarding for them.[28] A common scenario is that of the parent-owner who is unwilling to give up control or allow the child a say in the business. For example, Shannon Bowen-Smed had to threaten her mother with her resignation from the family company if she continued to dismiss her input in the business. Bowen-Smed had joined Calgary-based Bowen Workforce Solutions Inc. (www.bowenworks.ca) in the early 1980s and had worked in more progressive jobs but she wanted to expand and diversify the company. She eventually took control of operations and has grown annual sales from $1 million to $33 million. Conversely, it is also common for the inexperienced child to want to make changes the parent believes will be detrimental to the business.

Running a family business also offers a great opportunity to provide on-the-job training and background for the child that is not otherwise possible. The parent-owner can also assess the child's progress and level of preparation over a longer period than would be possible if hiring an outsider to manage the business. In addition, the owner-manager's business philosophy and style may be taught to the child who is apprenticing for management and ownership of the business.[29]

Figure 14-1 provides questions that should be asked before transferring the business to an heir.

Tax and Legal Implications of Transferring the Business to Family Members.

An increasingly complex consideration in transferring a business to heirs is the legal and tax implications. One specific tax consequence of transfers of business ownership within a family concerns capital gains. In Canada, one-half of the capital gain (defined as the increase in value of the asset since acquisition of the business or since 1972, whichever is shorter) on the sale is added to the income of the person disposing of the asset (business). This rule applies a "deemed

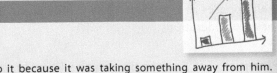

INCIDENT 14-3

CHARLES NORTHSTRUP

Life in a family business has its ups and downs, but Brett Northstrup knew more about the downs. He had worked for his parents in the family furniture store all his life. "I grew up with the idea that I was going to work in the business; my parents told me the business was for me," said Brett. So there was never any leeway or choice as to what he was going to do as an adult. He was going to work there, so he did. But when it came time for his dad, Charles Northstrup, to retire, he would not. He wanted Brett to take over the business, yet he did not want him to do it because it was taking something away from him. Charles Northstrup now said, "I don't know if I ever will want to retire. I'd just take it a little easier someday because I know I'd miss all the friends I've made, all the customers—they're just like friends. Besides, I'm not sure Brett can handle the business yet; he just doesn't run the business my way."

After 15 years with the business, Brett had finally had enough. He left and started over, leaving his parents to run the business their way.

Source: Rick Heyland, University of Lethbridge.

Consider this a final exam that your family business should take before it advances from one generation to the next. Developed by Scott E. Freidman, an attorney, author, and consultant specializing in family-business issues, the Family Business Scorecard is a comprehensive, 100-question survey designed to identify problem areas, especially those that can directly impact a planned succession. "Three types of people should take this quiz," Friedman explains. "Adult family members who work in the business, adult family members who don't work in the business but are stakeholders, and key non-family employees and advisers, such as the firm's lawyer, accountant, and financial planner. How much of a consensus there is among the participants can be as revealing as the answers themselves."

We have adapted 10 "yes" or "no" questions from the quiz to help give readers a quick take on how they are doing.

1. Our family has customized its decision-making process to require various levels of consent (by different family members or outside advisers) for issues of varying significance.
2. Our key non-family employees are satisfied with the manner in which family members are brought into and employed by our business.
3. All family members, regardless of sex or birth order, will be considered as possible successors for the business.
4. Our succession criteria include formal education, job experience outside our business, and job experience inside our business with increasing responsibility.
5. A written agreement establishes rules for buying, selling, and transferring ownership interest in our business.
6. If our business leader suffered a catastrophe, our family would be prepared to react.
7. Spouses of family members have a meaningful forum in which to air their views on subjects affecting the business.
8. Adult family members have begun working on their estate plan.
9. Senior family members approaching retirement age look forward to pursuing interests outside our business.
10. Our family has considered the merits of adopting an alternative dispute-resolution mechanism in the event of family conflict.

If you answered "no" to five or more of these questions, or if the people in your company who took the test gave different answers to the same questions more than four times, your business would benefit from a more complete analysis by an adviser. Freidman's law firm, Buffalo-based Lippes, Mathias, Wexier, and Friedman LLP (716-853-5100; sfriedman@lippes.com), charges for a complete survey and follow-up analysis.

Source: "Mom and Pop Quiz: How Succession-Ready is Your Company?" *Success*, December 1998, p. 80.

disposition" rule (to family) in that the business is "deemed" to have been sold at market price whether or not the market price was actually paid.

In the past, the federal government allowed a tax-free rollover or capital gains deferral to a spouse and children up to a maximum capital gain of $200,000. This applied to Canadian-controlled private corporations. If the heir sold the shares (or business) to someone outside the family, the capital gain would be realized and a resulting tax liability incurred. Canadian tax law also allows for a $750,000 lifetime capital gains exemption. This provision allows for the transfer of ownership of the business with little capital gains consequence, whether or not the business is an incorporated company.

Obviously, these changes have affected the tax consequences of transferring the business to heirs. Although most of these changes have been positive from the point of view of the small business, they are complex and may differ by province and territory. Therefore, counsel should be sought from a legal or tax expert before making a decision in this area.

Another important task when considering transferring or selling the business is determining its value. Assistance should be sought from an accountant or member of the Canadian Institute of Chartered Business Valuators in this regard.

Methods of Transferring the Business to Family Members.

In deciding which method to use in transferring all or part of the business to the heirs, owner-managers first need to clarify their own objectives in making the transfer. Some common transfer-related objectives are the following:

- Owner-managers want to keep a reasonable amount of control over the business until the heirs are of an age and competence level to assume their responsibilities.
- Although owner-managers want to maintain control of the business, they also want the heir(s) to maintain their interest in and commitment to the business.
- Owner-managers desire to distribute the business assets (ownership) so that the heirs (if more than one) will recognize this distribution as fair.
- Owner-managers want sufficient access to income or assets from the transfer of the business to maintain an adequate standard of living.
- Owner-managers want to achieve an orderly transfer of the business to minimize the tax consequences for both parties.

Some of the most common methods of transferring ownership to the heir(s) are discussed next.

Through a Will.

When the transfer is made through a will, ownership of the business does not pass to the heir until the owner dies. This method may satisfy the owner's objective of maintaining control of the business, but it fails to address any of the other objectives mentioned. For example, serious tax consequences may arise if the business is unincorporated. In such a situation, the previous owner's income is calculated at the date of death. If the business has an irregular business cycle and a death occurs at the wrong time of the year, a large income (and higher tax liability) may result. The heirs would then have to deal with this tax liability.

Purchase and Sale of the Business.

This method may not satisfy the owner's objectives unless it takes place gradually over a number of years. Such an agreement can remain flexible within the family to accomplish the objectives of both the owner and the heirs. A "deemed disposition" is viewed to have taken place at market value whether or not that amount was actually paid. Purchasing the business gradually may provide an incentive for the heir and also allow the parent to maintain the desired control for the required period of time.

Gifting Program.

In the absence of gift taxes, part or all of the business may be gifted to the heir(s). The most common method of doing this is gradually, over several years. This option is likely feasible only if the owner is not dependent on proceeds of the sale for his or her income.

INCIDENT 14-4

HAVE A SUCCESSION PLAN

The Storwick family is a good example of why having a succession plan and ensuring that the plan is understood and followed benefits the company as well as family members. The Storwicks own GreatWest Kenworth Ltd., the Calgary-based heavy duty truck dealership that has passed to the third generation from its founder. "At some point, my father and grandfather decided to start to transfer, not necessarily share, the responsibility for the growth of the business and the authority of the business," explains Jeff Storwick, Kenworth's current president. Storwick and his brother actively entered the business in the early 1980s and after working for over 10 years, their father gradually transitioned more control and authority to his sons. "It's been pretty gradual but pretty smooth because all parties understood the plan and were motivated to follow it." Although they have control of the day-to-day operations of the company, their father is still a presence, as he is chairman of the board.

Source: Adapted from Marzema Czarnecka, "Start Planning Today," *Alberta Venture*, September 2007, p. 157.

Life Estate.

A life estate is used primarily when the significant assets are real property. This method transfers the ownership or title of land or buildings to the heir, with the condition that the previous owner has a position of control until he or she dies. The extent of control can diminish as the heir becomes more involved in the business. Immediately on the parent's death, the title automatically passes to the heir. This method accomplishes many of the aforementioned objectives.

Joint Ownership of the Business.

In this method of succession, the parent can transfer shares of the business to the child (if the business is incorporated) or transfer an ownership interest to the child in the form of a partnership (if it is not incorporated). In both situations, the parent can retain control over the business by providing the child with a different form of ownership such as a different class of share (corporation) and a limited partnership interest (not incorporated).

In a corporation, this type of arrangement may also provide the beneficial tax advantage of freezing the value of the shares. In both methods, the voting or controlling interest may be transferred gradually as the interests, abilities, and conditions warrant.

Potential Problems in a Family Business.

Several problems may surface in the family-owned business. Recognition of these potential difficulties is essential for the owner-manager and even for the other family members so that they can take steps to prevent problems.

Overreliance on the Founder.

Most family businesses remain highly dependent for their success on their leader, who is typically the founder of the business. Most have no contingency plan covering the disability or death of this person.

Higher Emotional Level.

Because of existing family relationships, some of the business decisions and evaluations may be more emotionally charged than they would be in a non-family setting. For example, the evaluation of performance or supervision affecting a family member employee may be biased positively or negatively because of the relationship. Family members often bring their personal feelings and stress to the business, which often precludes them from making objective decisions.

Blurring of Roles.

In many family-owned businesses, the personal and business roles of individual family members may become blurred. For example, the chief executive officer of the business may in practice not really be in control because of his or her subordinate role in the family. This often occurs when children have "taken over" the business but their parents still exert informal control over both the children and the business.

Incompetence.

The problem of incompetence may arise in the family business in two areas. The first situation involves the relative who assumes the position of chief executive simply because of birthright. The experience, education, intelligence, and work ethic required to manage the business successfully may be lacking. The second situation involves hiring incompetent family members. Helping out an incompetent family member may not only lead to disappointment and damage to the business but can also have a disruptive effect on the non-family employees.

Non-family Employee Attitudes.

One common characteristic of family-owned businesses is high turnover of non-family employees. Many young employees see no chance for promotion to management in the company because they are not part of the family. As a result, they may gain experience in the business and then leave for other organizations that offer the opportunity for promotion.

Objectives of Family Owners.

In most family businesses, more than one member of the family owns shares or has an ownership interest in the business. Because these owners may be from different generations, have different levels of involvement in the business, and have various backgrounds and needs, differences of opinion regarding the operations of the business are common.

For example, owners who are actively involved in building up the business often want to reinvest more of the earnings in the business. The non-active owners or shareholders, however, may want their share of the profits to be distributed as dividends or payments to themselves.

Objectives regarding the growth of the business may also differ. Sometimes younger members of the family want to expand the business or make capital expenditures that older family owners are more conservative or cautious about making. Both situations can lead to conflicts that have a detrimental effect on the long-term progress of the business.

Principles of Success for Family Businesses.

The preceding section has demonstrated the many difficulties that can arise in a family business. As illustrated, these difficulties can be detrimental to the success of the business and damaging to family relationships. If the owner-manager is concerned about succession, planning for it should commence immediately rather than waiting until health or other circumstances force or prevent action. If you are involved in a family business or are contemplating bringing family members into the business, the practices discussed below may help prevent some of the aforementioned difficulties from arising.

Recognize the Importance of Objectivity.

Evaluations and supervision involving family members should be done on an objective basis. Even if tempted to do otherwise, the owner-manager must attempt to separate family discussions and emotions from business activities. Care should be taken to ensure that consistent policies are followed for both family and non-family employees. Many owner-managers have found it essential to separate their children physically and functionally from themselves and one another to prevent such difficulties from arising.

Create Clear Role Structures.

The solution to the problem of the blurring of roles may be difficult to implement, as much of the control may be exerted informally. A clear definition of the roles, objectives, and responsibilities of all associated family members may help solve the difficulty. Separation of business and family goals and systems has also been recommended to alleviate this problem.[30]

Ensure Competence.

Because an incompetent owner-manager can spell disaster for the business, providing the heir with technical and practical training, along with increasing decision-making authority, is vital. This may involve encouraging the family member to acquire some necessary skills outside the business at a college, a university, or another business before returning to become fully involved. Many potential inheritors of businesses appear to follow this route to the ownership of the family business.[31] If a competent family member is not available, the remaining family owners may be able to persuade the owner-manager to let a more capable individual run the day-to-day affairs of the company.

If training does not improve the performance of incompetent relatives, but for family reasons it is not possible to let the employee go, some owner-managers place such an employee in a position in which he or she can do the least harm to the company.

Provide Incentives for Non-family Employees.

To maintain the loyalty of non-family employees and ensure that they stay with the company, the owner-manager will need to devise various rewards and incentives. These incentives can be financial or may involve including employees in decision-making and educational programs. It may still be impossible to retain an energetic young employee who desires to eventually rise to the top of the organization unless the owner-manager is prepared to give up some of the ownership or authority of the business.

Clarify Objectives of Family Owners.

To prevent disharmony resulting from differing objectives of family members, it is important to formally clarify the long- and short-term objectives of the company. These might include objectives for such areas as expansion and distribution of profits. Some firms distribute a set percentage of profits in dividends or reinvest a specified amount back into the business annually.

Keep Communication Lines Open.

Perhaps the most effective aspect of operating a family business successfully is open communication. Given many potential areas of conflict, differences of opinion must be communicated to the relevant parties before they develop into a serious problem. Formalized objectives, plans, roles, and procedures can accomplish this.

SELLING THE BUSINESS TO AN EMPLOYEE

Another option for transferring the ownership of a firm is to sell the business to employees. Advance planning is still crucial for this type of succession. This type of transition is known as ESOP, or Employee Share Ownership Plan. Tomivino's a Halifax pizzeria recently went through a successful employee purchase where a couple working for the company bought the firm from its founder. The following steps should be a part of such a succession plan for an employee:

- Identify the timeframe and exit strategy.
- Develop a plan to maximize the value of the business and minimize the tax effects before the transfer date.
- Choose the successor.
- Make yourself replaceable. Install the procedures that will allow the company to grow without you.
- Find a way to fund the transition, such as debt financing or subordinate financing.
- Introduce the successor to clients, suppliers, and other contacts.
- Make sure that the new owner's vision ensures the continuity of the business.
- Manage the possible financial, fiscal, legal, and other impacts of the transition process, drawing on the support of professionals.

SELLING THE BUSINESS TO OUTSIDERS

If owner-managers are not able or do not want to keep the business in the family, they may decide to sell all or part of the business to someone outside the family. This action, of course, could be taken at any time, not just when the owner-manager is ready to retire. Often owners

DEAN HARTMAN, FOUNDER OF NUBODY'S FITNESS CENTRES INC., ATLANTIC CANADA'S LARGEST FITNESS CLUB, SOLD HIS BUSINESS TO GOODLIFE FITNESS, A NATIONAL CHAIN WHO WANTED TO EXPAND IN THE REGION.
The Canadian Press Images/Christian Lapid

sell the business as a way to maximize their return on their investment of time and capital. For example, Jonathan Latsky has sold two companies including the recent sale of Student Awards Inc. (www.studentawards.com), a Toronto-based scholarship-search website he co-owned. Latsky says selling a business is a way to exchange ownership or equity for money. "I'm always open to a discussion if I feel there's a good ROI for my investment, that might sound crass, but that's what it is."[32]

One possible outcome of selling the business may apply to a partner or other owner. As mentioned in Chapter 4, a buy/sell clause should be a part of the partnership agreement. This clause should be carefully worded to account for future differences in the value of the firm.

Sometimes small businesses are purchased by larger companies. The acquiring company is usually looking to expand or capitalize on some unique advantage or capability the small business has. For example, purchasing a small business may allow a company to capitalize on such strengths as a unique product, market access, or expertise it could not otherwise obtain. For example, Dean Hartman, founder and president of Nubody's Fitness Centres Inc., recently sold his growing business to GoodLife Fitness Clubs (www.goodlifefitness.com). Hartman who built Nubody's Fitness into the recognized Atlantic Canadian leader in exercise clubs with 26 clubs, 750 employees, and 50,000 active members sold to a national firm that was looking to grow. Through the purchase of Nubody's, Goodlife gets established exercise clubs and revenue from 50,000 members.[33] In a similar situation, Lori Van Opstal, owner of Cambridge-based Your Advantage Staffing Consultants Inc., an employment agency for truck drivers, became aware that a larger rival—Protrans Personnel of Mississauga wanted to expand. Opstal contacted Protrans and negotiated a deal in less than one day to sell her firm.[34] In some situations, the owner-manager of the smaller business is retained in the organization. Sometimes this works well as the owner-manager can help the buyer run the firm, but in some cases, it does not work, as the entrepreneur has difficulty transitioning to an employee. For example, surfboard designer Corran Addison was successfully running his Montreal-based firm Imagine Surf, but he lacked the capital to fuel growth. When he was approached by Manhattan Beach, a California-based company with a $2 million offer to buy the brand, invest in the company, and retain him as an employee, he jumped at the chance. He sold his controlling share in the business and moved to California where he assumed the role of an employee. Within a year, he started having some difficulties with the Manhattan Beach's management, the relationship worsened, and Manhattan Beach eventually sold the company for slightly more than they paid for it.[35]

Sometimes the owner-manager may want to sell only a part of the business. This is accomplished much more easily if the business is incorporated to allow a share transfer to take place. In such a case, the owner-manager may be able to retain control over the business while obtaining capital needed as payment for the shares.

Going Public.

Sometimes a small business that has been successful but has a need or desire for a significant amount of capital and is not planning to exit the business, sells shares to the public. This is called an *initial public offering (IPO)* and the corporate status changes from a private to a public company. Sometimes owners regret the move to go public rather than selling shares privately. Figure 14-2 illustrates a comparison of public versus private placement. Going public may also allow control of the business to remain with the owner-manager if more than 50 percent of the shares are not sold. The business should address the following issues if it is planning an IPO:[36]

- Improve the company's overall capital structure and financial performance.
- Review staff needs, including the need for a strong management team.
- Strengthen the organization through purchase or sale of particular business units.

FIGURE 14-2 — Implications of Selling Shares

	GOING PUBLIC	PRIVATE PLACEMENT
Shareholders	Many new shareholders	Few investors
Importance of earnings	High	Low
Importance of stock performance	Short term	Long term
Investor communication required	Extensive	Limited
Board of directors	Independent members	Strategic members

Source: *The Globe and Mail,* June 12, 1996, p. B7.

- Structure the board to include strong outside directors.
- Plan for effective distribution of earnings.

One or more of the following characteristics may indicate that the small business is in a favourable position to go public:[37]

- The company is in a popular specialized market.
- The company is in an above-average growth position.
- The business has a strong market niche and proven sales appeal in an emerging rather than a mature industry.
- The business can and does generate a return on equity of at least 20 percent to 25 percent.
- The company has at least $10 million in annual revenues.
- The company has strong management.
- The company has reached the point at which it needs a substantial amount of capital for growth and expansion.

If the owner-manager finds it necessary or desires that the firm's shares be offered to the public, the services of an investment dealer may be helpful. An investment dealer (or underwriter) will assist the owner by acting as the marketer for the stock. The investment dealer can use an over-the-counter market, one that includes securities that are not sold on the stock exchange. If this method is followed, a reputable investment dealer with substantial connections throughout the investment community should be selected.

CLOSING DOWN OR GOING BANKRUPT   LO4

The third possible outcome for the business—generally a result of unsatisfactory performance—involves closing down, being placed into receivership, or going bankrupt. These are, of course, the least desirable outcomes for the small business. As discussed in Chapter 2, however, each year many small businesses end up in this situation because of lack of profitability. Closing down is much easier for an unincorporated business than for a limited company. In theory, the incorporated company is required to file dissolution forms and notify government agencies. Although this is the case if the company does not have a large debt load, the incorporated company has more protection in a debt situation because of its limited liability.

TIME TO TAKE ACTION

Although you may be only at the start-up stage of your company or business plan, it is a good idea to include a harvesting strategy or at least be aware of the options. As such you may want to consider the following:

Interview some entrepreneurs who have sold their business. Ask them about the pros and cons of the sale process and what motivated them to sell.

LEARNING OBJECTIVES SUMMARY

LO1 Planning for the eventual transfer of the business is an important component of small business management. Some of the more common methods of transferring ownership of a business to family members are through a will, a sale of the business to the heirs, a gifting program, a life estate, and joint ownership.

LO2 The unique problems of a family business are higher emotional levels, blurring of roles, incompetence, non-family employee turnover, differing objectives among family owners, and planning for succession.

LO3 Sometimes a small business that has been successful but needs a significant amount of capital may sell shares to the public to meet financial needs while retaining control of the company.

LO4 A business that cannot be transferred can be closed down, be placed in receivership, or file for bankruptcy.

DISCUSSION QUESTIONS

1. Assume you owned a company that you wanted to keep in the family. One of your three children has been working in the business and is interested in taking over. However, the other two feel that they are entitled to their one-third share of the value of the business. What would you do?

2. Jim Duncan is the owner-manager of a local restaurant chain. In its earlier years, the three local family restaurants were very successful. Then a recession came, and the businesses did not do as well. Jim is 60 years old and is thinking about retirement or semi-retirement. He has a son who has managed one of the restaurants, but he is not sure Jim Jr. is ready for the problems of the whole operation. If you were Jim Sr., how would you transfer ownership? Explain your decision.

3. Your father has just made you president of the family sand and gravel company. You want to computerize the payroll and the accounts payable and receivable, but your father does not see the need for the extra expense when expenses are already too high. What two problems exist here? How would you resolve this conflict as the newly appointed president?

4. Your parents have just made you the manager of your family's grocery store. Since the transition, problems have seldom been brought to your attention, and you have received little feedback on your instructions. What problems might be evident? How would you solve these problems?

5. Hamilton Rogers is the owner-manager of a successful machine shop. In the last year, he has promoted his sons to floor managers. Recently, several employees have also left the company. What factors could be responsible for the employees leaving their jobs? How could Hamilton have prevented this problem?

6. Assume you owned a company that you wanted to keep in the family. One of your three children has been working in the business and is interested in taking over. However, the other two feel that they are entitled to their one-third share of the value of the business. What would you do?

1. Interview the manager of a family-owned and -operated business. What unique problems are evident?

2. Interview someone who is a future heir of a family business and is now going to school or gaining business experience. What problems are evident from his or her perspective? Does this person want to go back to the business? Why, or why not?

3. Pomaona Fastener Company has suffered several years of operating losses. Because of the unfavourable outlook for the firm, it filed for bankruptcy and was dissolved. On liquidation, $570,000 was received, to be split among the following creditors:

Accounts payable	$100,000
Secured loans from bank	400,000
Accrued wages	10,000
Rent due on building	20,000
Government loan	300,000
Trustee's fee	10,000

What would be the priority of payment, and how much would each class of creditor receive?

4. Interview the owner-manager of a small business that recently went public, and find out what he or she learned through the experience.

Bailey's Office Supply
Baker Hardware Ltd.
Brian Luborsky—Premier
   Salons International Inc.
ITI Educational Corporation
Company's Coming Cookbooks

BAILEY'S OFFICE SUPPLY

D. Wesley Balderson, *University of Lethbridge*

In 1976, John Bailey left a major department store chain where he worked as the hardware department manager to open his own office supply store. John worked for the chain for more than 15 years and was very knowledgeable about the business. He felt, however, that he could develop a successful business by offering more personalized customer service than the larger stores could. By 1986, the firm, Bailey's Office Supply, had become a large and well-known establishment in Toronto with three outlets. The firm had no particular specialties but did carry a very extensive line of all basic office supplies, typewriters, and adding machines, and a limited line of office furniture. Its strength was, as John Bailey had intended, its superior customer service. John was careful to properly train his employees to know not only their products but also their customers' needs.

In 1996, John Bailey's son Marty was finishing college in business administration and decided to join his father in the business. Marty had worked from time to time for his father and thought that he might enjoy the business. John had told Marty, however, to get an education first. If he decided to work at Bailey's, he would have a job. Although John made this offer to Marty, he was concerned because he had a younger son and an older daughter and wondered how they would react to Marty being brought into the company.

Marty joined Bailey's as assistant sales manager with the understanding that he would be given the job of sales manager on the retirement of Kenneth Harker, due to take place in another three years. At the same time Marty's brother and sister, along with Marty, were placed on the board of directors for Bailey's. Although the board met only sporadically, it did have the authority to ratify major management decisions.

During the late 1980s, both Baileys observed the phenomenal growth and development of the high-technology firms that occupied the Golden Triangle area in and around Toronto, Ottawa, and Montreal. This boom not only spawned the creation of many successful firms, but it also signalled the introduction of many strong competitors for Bailey's. Some of these were warehouse stores, which offered a large assortment of office merchandise at very low prices. John Bailey still maintained that if Bailey's continued to offer its personal "down home" service this new competition would not seriously affect Bailey's.

It was tempting for the Baileys to invest in newly created firms, knowing that the investments of several of their friends had been very successful. John Bailey, however, was fairly conservative and, having built the business to a success, was now looking forward to enjoying the fruits of his hard work by playing more golf and travelling with his wife for a month or two every year. He still retained controlling interest in the business and was opposed to making any outside investments. Marty, on the other hand, was anxious to take advantage of some of these opportunities and felt strongly that by adding lines of computer hardware and software to their merchandise line, Bailey's could increase sales. He felt, in fact, that Bailey's would have a difficult time competing with the office supply warehouses if they did not move into this area. As this would require a rather major reinvestment of earnings back into the firm, John and his other son and daughter were reluctant to move in this direction. These disagreements were a source of frustration for Marty and he contemplated leaving the family business and starting his own high-tech office supply store.

By 2008, the effects of the competition and a cutback in building construction had reduced the total income of business and the profit of Bailey's by some 20 percent. It was a sobering turn of events for a firm that had experienced a long, steady expansion. In thinking about this, John Bailey feels that it might be wise to turn the management of the business over to Marty, along with some of his ownership interest. Under John's proposal he would retain majority ownership of the company and still come in to work part-time, but Marty will be responsible for the day-to-day operations. When John approaches Marty with the proposal, he is shocked to hear that Marty has decided to leave the firm. John feels that he has given Marty a tremendous opportunity to learn about and then take over the business that he has built into a success. He cannot understand why Marty is turning down such an offer.

Questions

1. Why would Marty want to leave the firm instead of accepting his father's offer?

2. What could be done now to salvage the situation and keep Marty with the company?

3. Assuming that Marty remained with the firm, what suggestions could be made to turn the business around?

BAKER HARDWARE LTD.

D. Wesley Balderson, *University of Lethbridge*

Baker Hardware Ltd. is a hardware store in the town of Souris, located in an agricultural area of southern Manitoba. Souris is 48 km south of Brandon (population 55,000), which is the major trading centre for many smaller towns within a 100-km radius.

Mr. Baker, the owner of Baker Hardware, is contemplating expanding his merchandise offering to include lumber and building supplies. Currently Baker's, in addition to a standard selection of hardware merchandise, carries paint and building tools; therefore, Mr. Baker thinks this new line would be fairly compatible.

Baker Hardware is a part of the Home Hardware network of dealers, a nationwide group of hardware stores and home centres located primarily in smaller towns and cities. For the past few years, Home Hardware has been encouraging its dealers to expand into building supplies. Concerned that there is another lumber yard in Souris (which happened to be next door to Baker Hardware), Mr. Baker has shown little interest in such a move in the past.

Recently, however, he became aware that this lumberyard, Banner Building Supplies, is for sale or will be closed down. Mr. Baker gathers information from both the owners of Banner as well as from Home Hardware and is in the process of making a decision. As Mr. Baker sees it, he has three choices: (1) purchase Banner Building Supplies, (2) expand into building supplies through Home Hardware on his own premises, or (3) maintain current operations (not expanding into building materials).

The Market

As previously mentioned, Souris is a small town of about 2000 located 48 km from Brandon. The estimated population of surrounding area farms is 500. Over the years, the retail communities in most of the small towns close to Brandon have deteriorated because of the strong competition of retailers there and the increased mobility of consumers. The building supply industry is no exception. Such chains as Canadian Tire and Beaver Lumber, which have outlets in Brandon, have attracted numerous customers from these rural communities.

The population of Souris consists mainly of farmers, commuters who work in Brandon, and professionals such as teachers who work in the town. The town has experienced some growth in recent years because of its relaxed atmosphere and excellent recreational facilities. Projections indicate the population could reach 2500 by the year 2011.

Baker Hardware

Baker Hardware has operated successfully in Souris for many years. Mr. Baker purchased the store from his father and, with

changes and modernizations, increased sales from $450,000 in 1990 to $800,000 in 2011. Although sales show a significant increase, profits do not. The strong competition from hardware chains in Brandon in recent years has eroded Mr. Baker's profit margin. Baker Hardware's competitive strength has always been that it catered to the agricultural community. Unfortunately, farm incomes have experienced considerable volatility in recent years, and this trend directly affects Baker Hardware's profit performance.

Baker Hardware currently has 4000 square metres of selling space and a large (2700-square-metre) warehouse. Mr. Baker believes that if he goes into building supplies he could, with some renovations, free up about half of the warehouse space to house the new merchandise.

Baker Hardware's current financial situation, while not serious, is such that if a capital investment were made, Mr. Baker would have to borrow to finance it. At the current interest rate of 8 percent, this is a concern for Mr. Baker.

Home Hardware

Home Hardware Ltd. is a well-established franchise system of dealer-owners located across Canada. Originating in southern Ontario, it has expanded to become a dominant small-town retailer of hardware merchandise. Recently, Home Hardware moved into the building supply industry in an attempt to capitalize on the growth of the home centre concept. Home Hardware has been encouraging its dealers to branch into this area, and many have done so.

Mr. Baker obtains from Home Hardware a list of the recommended product assortment for a home building supply dealer. A summary of this list, along with space requirements and markups, appears in Figure 1. Home Hardware also suggests that Mr. Baker needs a forklift (estimated cost $15,000, used), a delivery truck (estimated cost $10,000, used), and a shed of at least 5000 square feet (estimated cost $5000).

Banner Building Supplies

Banner Building Supplies is a family-owned business that has operated in Souris for more than 40 years. It is owned by two brothers, both close to retirement age, who also owns a window and door manufacturing plant. As the manufacturing plant is much larger in size and scope of operations, the Banners have devoted most of their time and energy to this business. The retail building supplies outlet has, over the years, taken second priority in their business interests, although it provides a stable and needed outlet for the town.

Interest in selling the retail outlet results from two major factors. First, both brothers want to cut back on their work

FIGURE 1

Recommended Home Building Supply Full Product Assortment

PRODUCT	COST	SUGGESTED MARKUP ON COST	ESTIMATED TURNOVER	SPACE REQUIREMENT
Insulation	$ 4,000	25%	4.0	600
Doors and mouldings (complete assortment)	6,000	30	2.5	900
Plywood (complete assortment, 2 pallets each)	20,000	15	5.5	2,100
Drywall (complete assortment, 2 pallets each)	10,000	15	4.5	600
Cement	2,000	30	5.0	180
Roofing materials	5,000	25	3.5	600
Nails	1,000	30	5.0	120
Siding, soffit, facia	6,000	30	2.0	900
Dimensional lumber, 2 by 4, 2 by 6, etc. (complete assortment, 2 pallets each)	36,000	15	6.0	3,000
	$90,000			9,000

responsibilities, as both are approaching retirement age and have no family members interested in taking over the business. However, one brother has a son-in-law who is interested in the manufacturing part of the business. Second, the profitability of the retail outlet has suffered in recent years due to strong competition from larger hardware chains and home centres in Brandon. Some of these competitors can sell certain types of lumber and other supplies at lower prices than Banner's costs. The estimated profit and loss statement Mr. Baker obtained from Banners for 2008 is shown in Figure 2. Currently Banner Building Supplies has approximately $97,000 in inventory

FIGURE 2

BANNER BUILDING SUPPLIES
ESTIMATED INCOME STATEMENT FOR 2008

Sales	$230,000	
Cost of goods sold (85%)	195,500	
Gross profit		$34,500
Expenses:		
Wages	22,500	
Taxes and licences	2,000	
Insurance	1,000	
Professional fees and admin.	500	
Utilities	2,000	
Fuel (trucks, etc.)	1,200	
Bad debts	1,000	
Depreciation	1,800	
Repairs and maintenance	1,000	
Misc. supplies	$ 500	$33,500
Net income before taxes		$ 1,000

FIGURE 3

BANNER BUILDING SUPPLIES
INVENTORY ESTIMATE

Insulation	$ 6,000
Doors and mouldings	24,000
Plywood	12,000
Drywall	7,000
Cement	1,000
Roofing materials	2,000
Nails, etc.	1,200
Siding	2,000
Dimensional lumber	35,000
Paints	2,500
Tools and hardware	2,500
Carpet and linoleum	$ 1,800
	$97,000

(see Figure 3) and owns a large lot containing some sheds and a showroom next door to Baker Hardware. The estimated value of real estate and buildings is approximately $25,000. The company has no debt.

In looking at the merchandise requirements recommended by Home Hardware, Mr. Baker notes that Banner's inventory levels are different. Mr. Baker discusses this with the previous manager of Banner's and learns that some building supplies do not sell well in Souris. He informs Mr. Baker that the standard types of lumber (plywoods, 2 by 4s, etc.) are the steady sellers, although warpage causes considerable waste in dimensional lumber. He also mentions that it is very difficult to compete with the city building centres for the large contractors' business. The major market for Banner's has been the small contractor (renovators) and the do-it-yourself customer.

Armed with this information, Mr. Baker is determined to make a decision.

Questions

1. What other information should Mr. Baker obtain before he makes this decision?

2. Using the information provided, evaluate the alternatives Mr. Baker has identified. Be sure to evaluate the attractiveness of the proposed merchandise lines.

3. What other alternatives has Mr. Baker not explored?

BRIAN LUBORSKY—PREMIER SALONS INTERNATIONAL INC.

D. Wesley Balderson, *University of Lethbridge*

Brian Luborsky started out his business career as a chartered accountant with Coopers and Lybrand. It did not take long for him to realize, however, that he wanted to be part of something that was more growth-oriented and that allowed him to be more entrepreneurial. He still remembers the day he decided to quit. His boss wanted him to write a memo, but Luborsky, who was building and buying houses on the side, was working to save $50,000 on a property to buy. "The deal was worth more than my annual salary," he laughs, "I wasn't doing myself any favours, and I wasn't being fair to the company, so I resigned."

Meanwhile he became interested in a new hair salon franchise called Magicuts. Magicuts was established in 1981 as a discount haircut chain that attempted to bring the McDonald's efficiency principles to hair salons. Luborsky joined Magicuts as a franchisee, purchasing four franchises in 1984. What lured him was the math. "There is such a high ratio of sales to assets in haircutting it was hard to go wrong," he says. "Say, it costs $50,000 to set up shop. I can do $250,000 in sales in a year out of that store. Now, say, I make 10 percent on that: I'm getting a 50 percent return on investment, and that's hard to beat."

In 1993, Luborsky considered expansion to the United States. He felt that his company was in a position to grow and he became aware of a chain of hair salons that he felt could fit in with the system that he had developed for Magicuts. After difficult negotiations for financing, he was successful in acquiring a large financially troubled Minneapolis-based chain of hair salons—MEI Salons. MEI had 1600 outlets, three times as many as Magicuts, but was in need of financial and management stability, which Luborsky could provide.

Luborsky's goal for growth is now centred on three areas. First, he wants to continue to emphasize superior service to compete with the independent mom-and-pop salons that dominate the industry. Because of the size of the company, it can take advantage of economies of scale, and this allows investment in employees. As a result, Premier (as the salons were renamed) has invested heavily in extensive employee training. Premier's 76 trainers teach the latest styles and trends, as well as soft skills such as dealing with clients. Luborsky's second push involves "partnerships" with well-known retailers, most of which are department stores. Luborsky's third growth strategy is to seek out compatible chains and purchase them, similar to what occurred with MEI. Recently, Premier purchased 22 Boscov's salons in Pennsylvania.

Questions

1. What are some of the problems that Brian Luborsky will likely face with the expansion to the United States? What solutions can be suggested?

2. What questions should he have evaluated prior to the U.S. expansion?

ITI EDUCATIONAL CORPORATION

D. Wesley Balderson, *University of Lethbridge*

The idea for ITI began in 1984, when Gary Blandford, an MBA dropout, was studying computers at a failing private college in Halifax, Nova Scotia. When Gary learned that the college was in financial difficulty and was up for sale, he wondered if he could make it successful. Because computer training was a growing market and rather than lose a chance to graduate, the 28-year-old scraped together $60,000 to buy the school. Gary worked hard at improving the school and by 1995, the renamed Information Technology Institute boasted annual sales of more than $2 million.

Exploding demand for information technology workers told Blandford that it was time to expand to meet this growing demand. ITI went public in 1995, raising $3 million over the next two years to fund school openings in Moncton, Ottawa, and Toronto. The company also switched from a strictly technical program to a mixed curriculum aimed at

arts grads. Gary was able to partner with large organizations so that tuition for the course was often paid by many of these firms as they were interested in upgrading the skills of their employees. This type of arrangement ensured that ITI's classrooms were full. By the end of 1997, ITI was producing 1500 grads a year.

ITI continued its rapid expansion and by mid-2000, students in seven Canadian and three U.S. cities were each paying ITI $25,000 for its crash course in technology. Due to market growth, the ITI short course seemed to have unlimited potential. However, ITI's rapid expansion eventually stirred up rivals such as DeVry Canada, which was much larger and offered a more complete and longstanding training program. Aggressive competition from DeVry and others began taking sales from ITI, which devastated the bottom line.

In 1999, ITI lost $11.6 million on sales of $35.4 million. To revive the company, Blandford developed an $8 million marketing campaign to fight back, but his rivals were spending four times as much and ITI's message did not get effective exposure.

After the dot-com bubble burst, new enrolments plummeted. Suddenly, ITI was big and bloated. Blandford disbanded ITI's expansion team and slashed marketing, accounting, and curriculum spending by the millions, but ITI still lost $12 million in 2000 on sales of $50 million. By August, 2001, Blandford was forced to close down the business.

Questions

1. Identify the problems that led to ITI's demise.

2. What could Gary Blandford have done to prevent the failure of ITI?

COMPANY'S COMING COOKBOOKS

D. Wesley Balderson, *University of Lethbridge*

Cooking has always been an important part of Jean Paré's life. In 1963, when her four children had all reached school age, Jean volunteered to cater the 50th anniversary of the Vermillion School of Agriculture, now Lakeland College. Working from her home, Jean prepared a dinner for more than 1000 people. The dinner was so successful that Jean decided to start a catering business. This business developed into a flourishing catering operation that has continued for more than 18 years.

At first Jean single-handedly ran the business with part-time assistance from family members. It gave her an opportunity to try new recipes, and she soon wrote a cookbook that included some of her best ones. Jean also travelled across Alberta opening retail accounts to handle the book. As the business grew, Jean teamed up with her son Grant Lovig to form Company's Coming Publishing Limited. Between sales trips and publishing her second cookbook, she managed shipping and receiving, invoicing, and accounts receivable collections for her growing publishing venture.

Jean's first cookbook, entitled *150 Delicious Squares*, was very successful, and soon the company was publishing several cookbooks each year. By 2003, the company had published more than 60 titles and sold more than 20 million cookbooks worldwide with sales of more than $10 million annually. The head office is now a specially constructed building in Edmonton, where Grant oversees business operations in his role as president.

Printed in both English and French, Company's Coming cookbooks are available in more than 6000 retail stores across Canada. The cookbooks are also distributed in the United States and various overseas markets. A Spanish-language edition of Jean Paré's familiar and trusted recipes can even be found in Mexico.

Jean credits much of the company's success to the sales savvy of her son Grant, who was fresh from marketing school when he developed the retail plan for the cookbooks. Grant feels the family connection is one of their great strengths. Although Jean is the primary creative force behind Company's Coming, she confides that some of her best material comes from yet another son, Brian, who lives in Kelowna, B.C. Her daughter Gail Lovig has also been a part of the company since its inception. Gail currently oversees all marketing and distribution efforts, leading a team that includes marketing personnel located in major cities across Canada.

Questions

1. Which success principles for operating a family business discussed in the text does Company's Coming appear to be following?

2. As Jean Paré looks to the future, what concerns might she have about family members being involved in the business? How could she address these concerns?

For more information on the resources available from McGraw-Hill Ryerson, go to www.mcgrawhill.ca/he/solutions.

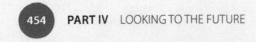

DIRECTORY OF SUPPLEMENTARY CASES

CASE TITLE	APPROPRIATE PART
CLOVIS JEWELLERS	**PART 3** Managing the Small Business
THOMSON GREENHOUSE	**PART 4** Looking to the Future
ROBINSON TEST PREP CO.	**PART 1** The Decision to Start a Business **AND** **PART 2** Preparing for Small Business Ownership
BLAKE LOCK AND SECURITY SYSTEMS	**PART 1** Managing the Small Business **AND** **PART 2** Preparing for Small Business Ownership
THE BEACH CARRIER	**PART 1** The Decision to Start a Business **AND** **PART 2** Preparing for Small Business Ownership
GOURMET EXPRESS	**PART 2** Preparing for Small Business Ownership **AND** **PART 3** Managing the Small Business
THE WINSLOW CLOCK COMPANY	**PART 2** Preparing for Small Business Ownership **AND** **PART 3** Managing the Small Business
WINDOW TECH INC.	**PART 3** Managing the Small Business **AND** **PART 4** Looking to the Future

CLOVIS JEWELLERS

D. Wesley Balderson, *University of Lethbridge*

Clovis Jewellers is a small jewellery store located in Brandon, Manitoba.* You have been called on by the owner to prepare an analysis of the business. The owners have supplied you with a detailed description of their operation and strategy. Critically evaluate each area described in the case.

Structure

Legal Structure.

Clovis Jewellers is an incorporated company under the name of Clovis Jewellers (1988) Limited. It is a privately held corporation. The only shareholders are Mr. and Mrs. Neudorf, each of whom owns 50 percent of the outstanding shares. As a corporation, Clovis Jewellers is authorized to issue an unlimited number of Class A, B, and C common shares. The only outstanding shares are 100 Class A shares. In the case of Clovis Jewellers, the shareholders are the owners, directors, and managers.

Financial Structure.

The capital structure of Clovis Jewellers is financed by a combination of debt and shareholder's equity. The debt constitutes roughly 75 percent of the capital and the shareholder's equity the other 25 percent. The shareholder's equity is made up of both class A share capital and retained earnings, of which the latter is, by far, the larger.

The debt financing is held with the Bank of Montreal and is in the form of a long-term loan. This loan is approximately $190,000. The first $150,000 is guaranteed through a provincial government small business assistance plan and carries an interest rate of 9 percent; the remaining $40,000 carries a rate of prime plus 1 percent. This long-term debt is covered by personal guarantees of Fred Meyer, a business associate of Mr. Neudorf, and by a mortgage on the Neudorfs' house.

The Bank of Montreal has also authorized an operating line of credit to Clovis Jewellers with a ceiling of $20,000. This line of credit is used to assist Mr. Neudorf in managing the cash flow in the slower summer months.

Organizational Structure.

There are four levels of employees in Clovis Jewellers' organizational structure (see Figure 1). The first level is the manager

*Although this case describes an actual business, the names of the business and owners, as well as the location, have been changed.

and is filled by Mr. Neudorf. The duties of this position include accounting and financial management, management of day-to-day store operations, and gemologist/diamond expert. Mr. Neudorf works together with both the assistant manager and the sales staff.

The second level in the organization is the assistant manager and is filled by Mrs. Neudorf. She works as the assistant manager approximately 50 percent of the time and as a salesperson the remaining 50 percent. The duties of the assistant manager include purchasing merchandise and controlling inventory. The inventory control function is done on a very informal basis, usually by a simple visual check.

The third level in the organization includes the sales staff and the repair service administrator. The job of overseeing the repair service is held by one of the full-time salespersons and requires approximately 20 percent of her time. The number of salespersons varies with the time of year, ranging from six to seven at Christmastime to two or three during the summer months.

The fourth level in the organization is the goldsmith and repairperson. This position is filled by Mr. Neudorf and requires a great deal of his time. Mr. Neudorf works together with the repair service administrator when acting as goldsmith.

There are two positions outside of the four-level organization. One is an accountant, and the other is a lawyer. Mr. Neudorf hires these two professionals on a part-time basis as demand calls for them. Both the accountant and the lawyer interact only with Mr. Neudorf.

Personnel

Clovis Jewellers experiences very little employee turnover (one staff member every two or three years) and therefore does not engage in recruiting procedures on a regular basis. When a new staff member is needed, a small advertisement is placed in the classified section of Brandon's daily newspaper. Although an advertisement is always placed, most hiring results through word of mouth and other contacts with neighbouring businesspeople.

When selecting a new employee, Mr. and Mrs. Neudorf look for individuals with an outgoing, friendly personality. Usually the person is middle-aged and has sales experience. Application forms are screened based on these qualifications, and the applicant who best meets the qualifications is asked to come in for a personal interview. Unless there is more than one "ideal" applicant, the new employee is hired after only one interview.

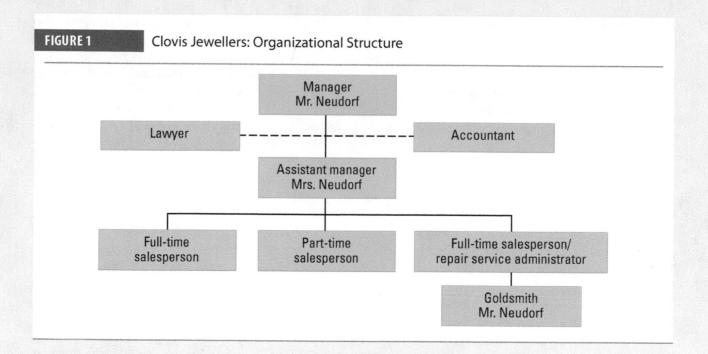

FIGURE 1 Clovis Jewellers: Organizational Structure

The training supplied to new employees comes in two forms: product training and operations training. The product training requires the employee to learn a great deal about jewellery—a very complex area. The individual must gain knowledge about watches, diamonds, gemstones, and qualities of gold. This product training occurs as the person works in the showroom selling jewellery and takes approximately one month.

The operations training is less involved than the product training and is completed in the first week or two of employment. This training involves learning the daily routine carried out at Clovis Jewellers, as well as cash register and receipt-writing operations.

The method of employee remuneration is a straight hourly wage; no commissions are paid. Employees' hours are recorded in a payroll register, and employees are paid every two weeks based on the number of hours worked. Mr. Neudorf tried to introduce a commission pay plan in the past, but employee resistance forced him to shelve the plan.

Employee morale appears relatively high compared with other retail stores. Mr. Neudorf believes this is because he and his wife treat the sales staff with respect and as friends. The employees know the importance of selling to the company's well-being, and Mr. Neudorf continually reinforces this by verbally acknowledging an individual for his or her sales efforts. A further indication of high morale is the fact that Clovis

Jewellers experiences an extremely low rate of absenteeism and lateness.

Marketing
Product.

A majority of Clovis Jewellers' yearly sales consists of ring and precious stone jewellery; for this reason, its product mix heavily favours these two items. Ring sales are responsible for the single highest sales total; therefore, great emphasis is placed on the ring inventory when the product mix is evaluated. Clovis Jewellers is known for carrying good-quality merchandise; this is reflected in the purchasing habits and quality control employed at Clovis. However, Clovis has shifted to a lower-quality selection of rings and jewellery to compete with the competition. This shift appears to be temporary, as the better-quality lines remain.

Mr. Neudorf believes seasonal fluctuations in sales do not seriously affect the product mix. Relative sales of most items remain constant throughout the year.

Distribution.

Clovis Jewellers is in the middle of a transition from using a traditional manufacturer-retailer distribution channel to a more direct channel. Jewellery and ring manufacturers are actually intermediaries in the supply of diamonds and precious gems (the manufacturers buy the gemstones from large diamond and gemstone suppliers). This method of purchasing was more convenient for Mr. Neudorf but inevitably meant higher-priced merchandise. Mr. Neudorf has now made arrangements to buy diamonds directly from the source of supply and therefore has greatly reduced merchandise costs. This shift also gives Mr. Neudorf much greater control over diamond and gemstone quality.

Pricing.

Mr. Neudorf uses several different methods in calculating the retail prices of the merchandise. Brand-name items such as watches are priced according to the manufacturer's suggested retail price, because Mr. Neudorf thinks customers will base their purchase decisions solely on price when shopping for brand names.

Merchandise whose quality the customer cannot differentiate easily, such as gold chains, are priced very competitively. Comparisons are often made with other jewellery stores to ensure that these items are priced competitively. Jewellery items such as earrings and pendants are priced according to a standard markup of keystone (50 percent), plus an additional 10 percent to make up for markdowns, which are often needed to sell the jewellery.

Mr. Neudorf finds rings the hardest items to price, as they carry no brand names or identifying trademarks. Each ring is priced individually, based on special features (or lack of them). A general markup formula is still used, but individual factors dictate the final selling price of the ring. For example, everyday solitaire engagement rings are priced below the standard markup, whereas individual modern engagement rings are priced above that markup.

Promotion.

Clovis Jewellers uses a wide range of media in its advertising program, including a daily newspaper, a local television station, AM and FM radio stations, and flyers. Advertising is used to convey both a specific promotional method and corporate image advertising. Mr. Neudorf prepares much of his own advertising, especially radio and newspaper ads. He also gives the ads a personal touch by recording many of the radio ads himself and including his picture in several newspaper advertisements. Mr. Neudorf claims that Clovis Jewellers targets its selling toward middle-aged women, but this target is not evident in the advertising; rather, the advertising appears to be general, with no real objectives or target market in mind. The advertising budget is prepared by taking a percentage of projected sales. This target percentage is between 4 percent and 5 percent.

Mr. Neudorf uses many different forms of sales promotion throughout the year. These include diamond remount plans, jewellery repair sales, graduation promotions, Mother's Day promotions, and other general markdown sales. The number of sales promotions has increased over the past few years due to an increase in competition. The trend in promotions has switched from using them to enhance slow selling periods toward bettering higher selling periods. That is, they are now timed in conjunction with a month of already higher-than-average sales.

Personal selling is heavily used at Clovis Jewellers. Mr. Neudorf believes jewellery requires a substantial selling push and therefore uses in-store personal selling as a major marketing tool. Emphasis is on making every sale count, large or small. Monthly sales totals are updated every day and then compared with the projected sales for the month. This information is then passed on to the salespeople to keep them aware of the importance of selling.

Public relations can also be an effective marketing tool, especially in a close-knit community such as Brandon. Mr. Neudorf is involved with many community clubs and events, which give him a fair amount of low-cost public relations. Clovis Jewellers sponsors sporting events for persons with disabilities and is a member of both the Rotary Club of Brandon and the Brandon Chamber of Commerce (of which Mr. Neudorf has been president and is currently a director). Mr. Neudorf gives talks to local women's groups and at high school career days. He has also had much interaction with the Brandon City Council and has served on committees such as the Brandon Parking Commission.

Location and Layout

Location.

Clovis Jewellers' trading area consists of the city of Brandon, surrounding towns and farmlands, and small communities that extend to the Ontario and Saskatchewan borders. The population of the area is slightly greater than 200,000, of which 55,000 live in the city of Brandon. The primary trading area (approximately 70 percent of the business) includes the entire city of Brandon and the surrounding towns of Virden, Souris, Minnedosa, and Neepawa.

The economy of Clovis Jewellers' trading area relies heavily on its two industries, farming and oil. Clovis Jewellers' sales experience large fluctuations due to the characteristics of each of these industries. The downturn in the oil industry has had a significant impact on the firm's profitability; sales have dropped significantly in the past three years.

Clovis Jewellers leases its site from a management firm located in Winnipeg. The basic rent is approximately $2400 per month. On top of this expense, Clovis pays a yearly management, property tax, and insurance fee for the building. The building is a single-storey structure located on Brandon's main downtown artery. The physical characteristics of the site follow the image Clovis is trying to portray; the storefront is pleasant and modern looking.

The buildings surrounding Clovis Jewellers host mostly banks and other independent retail stores. Several retail stores on the same city block appeal to Clovis's target market, including the Roset by Reid jewellery store located across the street. There is one vacant space on the street, located right next to Clovis Jewellers. The vacancy was caused by a fire over a year ago, and the building remains boarded up.

Clovis Jewellers is located on Ross Street, which is the centre downtown street. Ross Street has angle parking on both sides and is busy every weekday from 9:00 a.m. until around 6:00 p.m. This heavy vehicle traffic is due to the large number of banks in the area that deal with a high volume of customers every day. Ross Street also experiences a high volume of pedestrian traffic during the day, as it is situated in the heart of Brandon's retail and office sector.

Layout.

Clovis Jewellers' present location is 1000 square feet. Eight hundred square feet are used as selling space and the remaining 200 for office and storage space. The showroom is divided among rings, gold chains, watches, gift items, diamond jewellery, and regular jewellery. Although space is allocated to each section according to proportion of total sales, the allocation is based on rough estimates of both percentage of sales and space used.

The layout of the store is designed to make efficient use of high-traffic areas. The engagement rings, which are classified as specialty goods, are located at the back of the store, a spot that would normally see low-traffic volume. The shopping goods such as watches and gold chains are located in high-traffic areas around the cash register and front entrance.

Merchandise is displayed in either a locked showcase or behind a showcase out of the customer's reach. This method of displaying is necessary due to the high value and small size of individual pieces of merchandise. Each display case is lighted by two spotlights dropped from the ceiling. Florescent lights illuminate the general-purpose areas of the store; other lamps are suspended from the ceiling as part of the decor. The lighting appears adequate, as the store gives a "bright" first impression.

Purchasing and Inventory Control

Purchasing.

Mrs. Neudorf is responsible for purchasing the majority of the required merchandise. The salespeople often assist her, especially when the purchasing is done in Clovis Jewellers' showroom. Purchasing is done through a combination of jewellery and gift show attendance and meetings with individual supplier representatives.

The tradeshows Mr. and Mrs. Neudorf attend are held throughout Canada and the United States and include cities such as Hawaii, Vancouver, Brandon, Calgary, Winnipeg, and Toronto. Roughly 20 percent of total purchases are made at these tradeshows. Mr. and Mrs. Neudorf attend them to obtain new products and ideas as well as to make actual purchases.

Eighty percent of purchasing is done in-store and with the help of the salespeople. Mrs. Neudorf prefers in-store purchasing because it gives her the undivided attention of the company representative and allows her to compare items with Clovis's existing merchandise. Each company representative visits Clovis Jewellers two or three times a year, usually in the spring and early fall.

Mr. Neudorf has arranged special payment terms with approximately 75 percent of his suppliers. The credit terms are usually 30/60 days, 30/60/90 days, 30/60/90/120 days, or even up to six months; most companies will give these terms free of any interest charges. Mr. Neudorf finds these terms necessary for cash flow management, as the majority of purchases are made during slow sales periods.

Mr. Neudorf maintains a tight level of quality control, inspecting each piece of jewellery before it is put on sale. Each item is checked for diamond or gemstone quality, quality of stone settings, and adequate stamping of gold quality. Items that do not meet the strict quality standards are returned to the supplier for exchange.

A purchasing budget is prepared by multiplying the target gross margin percentage by the budgeted sales figure. This total purchase figure is then spread out throughout the year according to monthly sales, with the majority of purchases made in the pre-Christmas season.

Inventory Control.

No formal inventory control method is used at Clovis Jewellers. Mr. and Mrs. Neudorf rely on experience when it comes to controlling inventory levels. Visual inspections determine whether inventory levels are sufficient or need replenishing. No automatic reorder procedure is used; Mr. and Mrs. Neudorf believe automatic reordering would hurt rather than enhance sales because customers expect to find unique pieces of jewellery at Clovis.

Mr. Neudorf has insurance to cover fire, loss of merchandise stored in the safe, loss of customer goods stored in the safe, and business interruption (up to six months). Insurance to protect against theft of merchandise not stored in the safe is either not available or too expensive. All of the rings and diamond jewellery are placed in the safe after business hours; therefore, most of Clovis's inventory is insured in the event of a break-in. The business interruption insurance is related to inventory; a major loss or damage of inventory would not force Clovis Jewellers out of business, as the firm would continue to have a daily cash flow.

Accounting and Financial
Recording and Classifying.

The daily and weekly recording and classifying done by the staff at Clovis Jewellers basically follows a one-write system, with the addition of certain journals and a daily cash summary. The one-write system, kept by Mr. Neudorf, is used to maintain all of the sundry (non-merchandise) accounts, as well as the company payroll. The non-merchandise accounts are paid as they arise and therefore require almost daily attention; the payroll is calculated every two weeks.

Mr. Neudorf prepares a daily cash summary every weekday morning (Friday's and Saturday's are prepared on Monday). This cash summary includes a summary of the day's sales, both cash sales and charge sales; a summary of how the cash flow is distributed, including cash expenses and bank deposits; and a record of returned merchandise and cheques. The main purpose of this cash summary is to ensure that the cash transactions balance on a day-to-day basis.

Mr. Neudorf also keeps an accounts payable ledger, which he updates weekly. Proper managing of the accounts payable is important to Clovis Jewellers because it relies on trade credit to purchase all of its inventories. A journal of monthly purchases is kept to maintain control over the inventory and the merchandise purchases. Mrs. Neudorf is responsible for keeping this journal up to date; usually she adds all of the invoices to the journal at the end of the month, when a total can be calculated.

One final area in which recording is done on a day-to-day basis is the jewellery repair journal and record of ring sales. Clovis Jewellers has an extensive jewellery and watch repair department. The repair department is run by the sales staff and involves entering every repair job into a journal for easy reference. Because of the quick turnover of repair jobs (usually one to two days), they must be entered into the journal the same day they are received to prevent any bottlenecks in the system. Individual ring sales are also recorded in a book for quick reference, as needed.

Budgeting.

Five years ago, the budgeting process was almost non-existent at Clovis Jewellers. Except for some very rough, off-the-top-of-the-head figures, no budgets were prepared. This has changed in the last few years, and although the budgetary process still needs improvement, it has taken a definite shape and form.

The process starts with a sales budget. This budget is prepared by looking at last year's sales and then updating them based on any special considerations for the upcoming year. The budget is prepared monthly and used to make regular comparisons with actual sales figures.

Once the sales budget is complete, a merchandise purchases budget is prepared based on the specific level of monthly sales. The purchases budget includes all shares of merchandise purchases, including the cost of repairs.

Mr. Neudorf prepares an expense budget using previous years' expense totals. These expense totals are evaluated as being too high, too low, or correct over the past year and are then changed accordingly for the upcoming budgeted year. The budgeting of all the expense totals is very important, as it allows for better control of these expenses as they are incurred.

The final budget prepared is the cash flow project budget. This is done by combining the projected sales, merchandise payments, and expense budgets. This cash flow projection is very important for Clovis Jewellers, because the seasonal cash inflows it experiences often creates cash shortages; the cash flow analysis allows Mr. Neudorf to plan for these shortages.

Financial Statements.

Clovis Jewellers has a complete set of financial statements prepared once a year by a certified general accounting firm (see Figure 2). The statements are prepared after January 31 of each year, which Mr. Neudorf has chosen as the year-end date due to the low volume of business and low inventory count that occur at this time. All financial statements are prepared showing the previous year's figures for purposes of easy comparison.

The balance sheet is prepared in the traditional format, with assets on the left side of the statement and liabilities

FIGURE 2 Clovis Jewellers: Financial Statements

CLOVIS JEWELLERS (1988) LTD.
BALANCE SHEET (UNAUDITED)
JANUARY 31, 2010

	2010	2009
Assets		
Current		
Cash	$ 24,886.15	$ 32,834.17
Accounts receivable (trade)	4,885.34	5,725.74
(shareholders)	18,186.40	18,462.84
Inventory	190,612.90	197,318.70
Prepaid expense	8,437.01	9,150.01
	247,007.80	263,491.46
Assets		
Investments	1,045.00	—
Fixed	10,853.69	13,566.69
Other		
Goodwill less amortization	56,672.20	59,228.20
Incorporation costs	—	373.54
Due from Neudorf holdings	15,448.95	15,448.95
	$331,027.64	$352,108.84
Liabilities		
Current:		
Accounts payable and accruals	$ 70,987.17	$ 92,214.96
Employee remittance payable	1,447.75	1,539.07
Corporation taxes payable	925.40	834.85
Current portion of long-term	11,316.00	8,000.00
	84,676.32	102,588.88
Long-Term	199,961.77	214,156.14
	284,638.09	316,745.02
Shareholders' Equity		
Share Capital	$ 100.00	$ 100.00
Retained Earnings	46,289.55	35,263.82
	46,389.55	35,363.82
	$331,027.64	$352,108.84

CLOVIS JEWELLERS (1988) LTD.
BALANCE SHEET (UNAUDITED)
JANUARY 31, 2010

	2010	2009
Sales	$420,559.99	$472,035.50
Cost of Sales	218,332.01	261,016.36
Gross Margin	202,227.98	211,019.14
Selling Expenses	192,626.33	210,073.57
Operating Income	9,601.65	945.57

(continued)

Other Income:		
Interest earned	350.48	213.63
Gain from sale of assets	—	1,133.00
Income before Taxes	9,952.13	2,292.20
Income taxes	925.40	834.85
Net Income	$ 9,026.73	$ 1,457.35

CLOVIS JEWELLERS (1988) LTD.
BALANCE SHEET (UNAUDITED)
JANUARY 31, 2010

	2010	2009
Operating Expense:		
Accounting	$ 761.20	$ 1,039.30
Advertising	11,024.93	33,250.03
Amortization	4,556.00	4,556.00
Auto expenses	1,794.77	3,146.33
Bank charges and interest	4,318.90	4,549.10
Canada Pension Plan	1,201.94	1,296.32
Donations	350.00	350.00
Depreciation	2,713.00	3,391.00
Employment Insurance	2,492.46	2,539.19
Equipment rental	4,200.00	2,700.00
Interest	28,016.38	30,747.77
Insurance	3,047.00	3,079.41
Legal expenses	448.54	80.09
Memberships and dues	510.00	587.74
Postage and stationery	1,382.82	2,388.12
Rent	28,965.29	28,175.00

CLOVIS JEWELLERS (1988) LTD.
STATEMENT OF OPERATING EXPENSES *(CONTINUED)*
(UNAUDITED)
YEAR ENDED JANUARY 31, 2010

Repairs and maintenance	432.41	464.59
Salaries	82,180.91	74,505.54
Security	711.39	681.25
Supplies	2,224.87	2,308.94
Taxes	2,603.75	3,144.88
Telephone	983.67	1,104.04
Travel and promotion	3,764.89	1,621.14
Utilities	3,818.71	4,092.59
Workers' compensation	122.50	245.00
Total expenses	$192,626.33	$210,073.57

and equity on the right. Current assets constitute roughly 75 percent of the total assets; inventory is the largest and most important part of the current assets. Clovis Jewellers has a long-term loan payable, which makes up the largest part of the total liabilities. This loan contract is held with the Bank of Montreal and carries personal guarantees from both Mr. Neudorf and his business associate, Fred Meyer.

An income statement is prepared based on sales and expense figures supplied by Mr. Neudorf. This statement does not include a detailed list of the operating expenses. For this purpose, a detailed statement of operating expenses is prepared. This statement lists each expense totalled for the year and in alphabetical order.

A statement of changes in financial position is also prepared at year-end. This statement explains how funds were generated and used throughout the year. The purpose of this statement is to indicate any changes in the working capital of the business and explain how those changes occurred.

Planning

Long-Term Planning.

Management at Clovis Jewellers appears to be typical of most small businesses in that a serious lack of any long-term planning exists. The only long-term planning that has occurred is the signing of a five-year lease. Although this means of planning is extremely informal by even a liberal definition, it indicates that some consideration has been given to the long-range plans of Clovis Jewellers.

Short-Term Planning.

Mr. Neudorf engages in a number of forms of short-term planning, including budgeting for the upcoming year, planning promotions, and planning cash flow. Budgets are prepared early in the fiscal year and extend to the end of the year. The budgets include a sales budget, a purchases budget, and an expense budget. The budgetary process is still in the early stages of development, but an increased awareness on the part of Mr. Neudorf ensures that it will be an effective form of short-term planning in the future.

Promotions are planned on an informal basis; no concrete goals or objectives are stated. Most of the promotions are planned based on the success of the previous year's promotions. If a promotion proved successful one year, it is automatically considered for the next year. This method produces mixed results, as some promotions are successful one year and quite unsuccessful the next.

One area of short-range planning that requires attention is the planning of future cash flows. Mr. Neudorf prepares a complete cash flow analysis for the upcoming year based on projected sales, merchandise purchases, and expenses. This cash flow analysis does not always prove accurate due to extraordinary items that arise in the course of the year, but at least it gives Mr. Neudorf a plan for goals for which to aim.

THOMSON GREENHOUSE

D. Wesley Balderson, *University of Lethbridge*

Background

Thomson Greenhouse is located just outside Sudbury, Ontario, and is owned by Earl and Lisa Thomson. It is a seasonal operation, offering many different types of bedding plants, vegetables, annuals, perennials, and specialty plants and arrangements. The business also has a two-acre tree nursery and garden offering a wide range of trees from pines to fruit trees.

Earl and Lisa Thomson have been operating the business for 17 years after taking over the business from Lisa's parents. The original business was located on land on the outskirts of Sudbury that was annexed by the city. At that time, Earl and Lisa decided to move from the city to a small acreage so that they could continue the business and set up a new location. The structures were taken down and reassembled on the new acreage just northeast of Sudbury.

Much of the knowledge of the greenhouse business has been passed down from Lisa's parents, and as Earl and Lisa have three sons working in the business, it continues to be a solely family-run operation. Many of the aspects of the business have remained the same since it was established. Thomson Greenhouse has been serving the city of Sudbury and surrounding area for many years and has been fairly successful in establishing a name for quality products and good customer service.

Thomson Greenhouse is a form of second income to the Thomsons due to its seasonal nature and because Earl is the chief accountant for a local manufacturing company. It also has allowed the Thomsons' three sons to work in the business to help finance their schooling. The oldest son, Derek, is currently about to graduate with a bachelor's degree in business from the local university, while the other brothers Ryan and Russell are in Grades 10 and 12, respectively. Lisa's parents, Morris and Anna Slemko, also work in the business during the busy times.

Due to the success of the business and because their sons are getting to the age where they are about to leave home, the Thomsons are faced with some long-term decisions about the business.

Organization

Thomson Greenhouse is a general partnership with the two partners being Earl and Lisa Thomson. Earl feels that although they have unlimited liability under this arrangement, the tax and flexibility advantages of a partnership outweigh this risk. Both partners own an equal share of the business, although Lisa spends more time working in the business because Earl has a full-time job in Sudbury.

Earl and Lisa have equal authority with regard to the employees. Both are knowledgeable regarding horticulture and care for trees and plants. Earl is more responsible for the accounting, advertising, deliveries, and seeding. Lisa handles orders, daily operations in the greenhouse, transplanting, sales, and customer service. Both Earl and Lisa know their strengths and weaknesses and tend to do the things they each do well. Some overlapping occurs, but this is advantageous in some ways because some operations are too big to handle by themselves.

Over the years there have been few conflicts in the management of the operation or with employees, as it has all been within the family. All three of the Thomson sons have worked in the business throughout the summer as well as evenings and weekends for a number of years. During the busy season Lisa's parents, from whom Earl and Lisa purchased the business, help out. Because the business is family owned and operated, no formal personnel policies or training programs have been developed. Management of the company has been carried out on an informal basis. The employees are paid on a straight salary basis with considerable flexibility available for the sons as things come up that they need to do.

One of the major concerns that Earl and Lisa have is the future of the business when the children finish their high school and university studies. The business is not currently large enough to be a full-time occupation unless a considerable capital investment is made to expand the operation. Another difficulty is that the second-oldest son Ryan has expressed interest in becoming involved in the business, but the Thomsons are concerned about how to make this transition should it take place. They are wondering what effects such a move would have on their other two sons.

Location and Physical Facilities

Thomson Greenhouse is located just northeast of the city limits of Sudbury. The market area not only includes the city of Sudbury (population 90,000) but also many of the small communities around the city, which is estimated to have another 60,000 people. This location serves Thomson well because of its proximity to the city; as well, its rural location allows for plenty of space for production and expansion, if required. Distribution is carried out primarily by truck, and the highways and roads in the area are very well maintained.

Thomson Greenhouse is located on 20 acres, of which five are used for the greenhouse and the Thomsons' residence and the other 15 are rented out to a local farmer. The greenhouse building covers approximately 800 square metres. Although most of the area is taken up with plants and could be referred to as selling space, a small area at the front is devoted to customer service and a cash counter. A small greenhouse at the back is used for personal items and the holding of special orders. The building's age is a concern, as it has begun deteriorating. The frame is made of wood and the aging process has damaged many of the wooden glass frames. Much of the material for this greenhouse came from the original greenhouse that was moved from the previous site.

Recently Thomson Greenhouse purchased a new computer system. The Thomsons are in the process of converting their manual record keeping and inventory control over to the computer. Other equipment owned by the business are a small front-end loader/garden tractor, a truck used to deliver plants to commercial customers, a roto tiller, a dirt mixer, and a dirt purifier, and other miscellaneous garden tools and greenhouses devices.

Purchasing for Thomson Greenhouse is carried out by both Earl and Lisa. They purchase their supply of inventory from various seed processors located primarily in Southern Ontario and the United States. Quality, dependability, and price are all used to evaluate suppliers. Lead times for ordering are about 30 days for most items. No formal inventory-ordering method is used as the business is small enough that Earl and Lisa are able to adjust their inventory levels from visual inspection and from previous experience.

Marketing

The target market for Thomson Greenhouse consists of consumers who come to the greenhouse, as well as some large retail accounts to supermarkets such as Superstore and A&P. The consumer market tends to be older, those who have the resources and time to spend on their yards and gardens. The supermarket or commercial accounts purchase vegetables and some flowers, while those customers who come out to Thomson Greenhouse make greater purchases of bedding plants and trees. In terms of quality and price, the commercial accounts tend to be interested in low price. As a result, the margins that Thomson achieves with the commercial accounts are much lower than with the customer accounts. Those who come out to the greenhouse desire high quality and customer service, even if it means paying a slightly higher price. Earl Thomson realizes this and sets prices to meet these preferences and also to ensure that the business is able to achieve a profit. The profit margin has to be high enough to include the discounts that inevitably occur at the end of the season due to the perishability of the product.

The busy time of year for bedding plants is during May and June as most people are preparing their yards and gardens. During the summer and fall, produce sales increase, and during the winter months very little business is done.

There are several other greenhouses in the Sudbury area, and many customers do price comparisons. Thomson Greenhouse has always prided itself on superior customer service and, despite the competitive nature of the industry, seems to retain a fairly loyal following. The commercial contracts also add to the stability of operations for Thomson. Earl has an informal idea of Thomson Greenhouse market share through the monitoring of sales of their various products.

One of the trends the Thomsons have noticed is the increasing market share that has been obtained in the gardening-nursery product category by department stores such as Walmart and Canadian Tire. Thomson Greenhouse currently has contracts with only two supermarkets, and although these have provided steady volumes, purchases from these sources have not grown over the past few years. The Thomsons are considering attempting to obtain contracts with some of these department stores as a means of increasing sales. They realize that margins would be thin, however, and that price would be a major purchasing factor for the consumer. Many of the other greenhouses in the area are actively competing for the business of these stores. The Thomsons realize that they would have to be very competitive to be successful in obtaining a contract. If they were able to secure new purchasers, expansion of their current operation would seem to be necessary.

Thomson Greenhouse uses several forms of promotion. It places some ads in the local newspaper and uses the Yellow Pages. It also purchases a booth at the Home and Garden Tradeshow, which is held in Sudbury each spring. Occasionally, direct mail promotion is used to highlight special sales or end-of-season discounts. Thomson uses business cards and has been actively involved in sponsoring minor hockey teams and karate schools as part of its public relations promotion. Earl and Lisa realize, however, that word of mouth is their most effective form of promotion, so they ensure that they and their sales staff are knowledgeable about the product and courteous to the customer.

Financial Situation

Thomson Greenhouse has been profitable since its establishment, earning about $10,000 per year on about $40,000 in sales. (See Figure 1 for the latest income statement.) Although sales haven't increased over the past five years, Earl and Lisa have not been concerned about this because there has been an increase in competition and they are currently operating at capacity with their present facilities. They have been using a one-book system for accounting but are currently switching over to an accounting software program in conjunction with their computer purchase.

One of the concerns that Earl and Lisa have is the state of their current greenhouse, which is getting old. They are considering constructing a new one in addition to the current greenhouse. This would increase the capacity of the business and would allow for increased sales but would also increase the workload for the Thomsons, something that they are not sure they want. Alternatively, they could replace the existing greenhouse and maintain current operations, but at a more efficient level.

A new greenhouse of a similar size to the current one would cost approximately $12,000 and would last about 10 years. If the Thomsons decided to go ahead with this, they would finance $8000 at the local bank at 8 percent interest. They estimate that the annual sales for a greenhouse of this size would be $30,000.

Questions

1. Discuss the implications of the Thomsons' attempt to obtain additional commercial contracts (the department stores) for their products.

2. Evaluate the decision to construct another greenhouse from a financial as well as organizational point of view. (Use rate of return, payback, and break-even analysis in your evaluation.)

3. Comment on the financial health of the Thomson Greenhouse through a review of the financial statements.

4. Discuss the implications for succession of the business if the decision were to:

   a. Pass the business to one of the sons

   b. Sell the business to someone outside the family

FIGURE 1   Clovis Jewellers: Financial Statements

THOMSON GREENHOUSE INCOME STATEMENT
FOR THE YEAR ENDED DECEMBER 31, 2009

Revenue		$37,000
Expenses		
Cost of Goods Sold		
Seed and materials	$ 3,560	
Containers	3,150	
Fertilizer	290	
Water	305	
Soil	90	
Direct labour	3,000	$10,395
Contribution Margin		26,605
Occupancy and Selling Costs		
Building repairs	130	
Truck costs	2,300	
Office expenses	1,015	
Property taxes	1,560	
Heat and power	3,450	
Advertising	2,150	
Selling labour	3,150	
Depreciation	$ 3,800	$17,555
Profit before Income Taxes		$ 9,050

THOMSOM GREENHOUSE BALANCE SHEET
AS AT DECEMBER 31, 2009

Current Assets		
Cash	$ 1,000	
Accounts receivable	1,500	
Inventory	3,000	
Fixed Assets		
Land	26,000	
Buildings	58,000	
Equipment	$ 21,000	
Total Assets		$110,500
Liabilities and Owner's Equity		
Liabilities		
Accounts Payable	1,500	
Owner's Equity	$109,000	
Total Liabilities and Owner's Equity		$110,500

ROBINSON TEST PREP CO.

In the spring of 2004, Olivia Robinson felt that she had come to a crossroads with her business. As the founder and CEO of Robinson Test Prep, an Ontario company specializing in preparing people for the Chartered Accountant (CA) exam, the Uniform Evaluation (UFE), she felt that she was not achieving market share and growing in the right direction. After three years of providing prep classes to both students and professionals, Robinson had about 10 percent of the market and was facing fierce competition from her primary rival, Canadian Assessment Centres. Uncertain with which growth direction to take, Olivia contemplated several options.

Background

Olivia Robinson started Robinson Test Prep in the summer of 1998 after graduating with a master's degree in accounting. She began applying to accounting firms such as Ernst & Young, KPMG, Grant Thornton, and Pricewaterhouse-Coopers. Frustrated after receiving several rejections, Olivia began to consider other employment options. Her undergraduate degree was in business, and after graduation, Olivia worked for several years in the business office of a small test prep company based in San Francisco. The company prepared students who wanted to take primarily the SAT, GRE, GMAT, MCAT, and LSAT. Although her job was to manage the company's business affairs, she also began teaching math to students several nights a week. Olivia received training from the company in teaching basic testing skills, and she applied those skills toward teaching the math portion of the exams. She received positive feedback from her students as a conscientious and innovative teacher. Olivia eventually was hired by KPMG and returned to Canada.

Olivia felt that her experience as a teacher for the test prep company helped her when she began studying for the CA exam. She knew how to study efficiently, how to organize her notes, and how to practise for the various sections. Olivia was one of the 25 percent of students who passed all sections of the CA exam on the first try.

When contemplating what to do next, Olivia was struck by the fact that so many of her colleagues were unable to pass the exam. Convinced that she was not only skilled in the accounting and finance principles but also in knowing how to study effectively, she decided to start her own test prep business teaching specifically to the CA exam. She was confident that students and professionals wishing to become CAs would benefit from a full-service program that gave students full classes and individualized attention so that they could pass the exam.

Olivia put together a business plan and secured financing from a local venture capital firm specializing in small start-ups. She decided to focus her business and marketing efforts in the Toronto area. Based on her research and the area's concentration of different types of businesses, Olivia estimated that there was a market of about 1000 students a year.

Canadian Assessment Centres

Canadian Assessment Centres is Robinson's primary competition. CAC is a national test preparation company that has been in existence since 1962. The company focuses on virtually every standardized test that is offered and has programs for high school students, undergraduate students, and graduate students taking certification tests like the bar and CA exams. In addition, the company has a program designed for international students taking the Test of English as a Foreign Language (TOEFL) exam.

CAC is a full-service program that offers a variety of options for students taking any of these exams. Most courses offer the opportunity to have classroom lectures, home-study videotapes, books, software, online tests, or a combination of any of these options.

The CA course does not offer live classroom sessions but gives students the option of books, software, and online testing for one or all of the areas covered on the exam. Students also have a toll-free number that they can call if they have questions as well as online chats with CAC instructors to answer questions. CAC offers students a free repeat course if they do not pass the CA exam and boasted a 75 percent pass rate. The course is priced from $1000 to $1500, depending on which of the services the student chooses. Many of CAC's students are repeaters who initially chose to study on their own and use a book or software package. Such students are dedicated to passing the second time they take the exam and want the structure that the courses provide. CAC provides a study schedule, study techniques, and information about how to take the exam, which, it boasted, cannot be found in any other course on the market.

Many of CAC's students have also taken a CAC course for a previous entrance exam. CAC boasts a higher overall pass rate for all its courses than any other test prep centre in the country. People who had taken a course for another test and had passed, for example, felt confident that they would be equally prepared for passing the CA exam. In a survey of undergraduate students who had taken CAC, 85 percent said they would take another CAC course to prepare them for a graduate school entrance exam.

The Robinson Testing Advantage

Despite CAC's success, Olivia knew that with a pass rate of only 25 percent for first-time takers, there was a need to provide a comprehensive program to students so that they could pass on their first try. She devised a full-service program that lasted for six weeks and was three to six hours per day. She worked with accounting, finance, and law professors to design a curriculum to give students a comprehensive approach to studying for the exam. She hired the professors to give three live, one-hour lectures per day, and she taught the test-taking techniques and organizing skills necessary to easily assimilate the mountains of information that students needed to know. Olivia also provided audiotapes for students so that they could review the lectures at home and suggested that they listen to them in their cars to maximize the use of their time. The course also included several timed mini-tests for each topic and four practice essay questions, which Olivia and her professors graded. The responses to essays included many comments and much feedback to give students guidance on areas to improve.

Olivia also made herself completely available to her students. She felt that one-on-one attention was critical to their success, and she held bi-weekly meetings with each student to gauge progress and answer questions. In addition to the meetings, students could call Olivia or email her with questions, and she promised to get back to them within 24 hours.

Olivia held two sessions a year in March and September, allowing students to continue to study on their own before the exams. She also made herself available to students after the course to answer their questions and help them in any way she could. Pricing her course at $1100 per student, she felt that she was providing her students with more of an advantage and better preparation than any of the CAC options. She also offered a guarantee, allowing students to repeat the course if they did not pass the exam.

Olivia had taken a year to develop the materials and create a marketing plan for her company. She decided to place ads in Toronto area business schools to attract students contemplating taking the exam after graduation. She also created flyers to be placed in the schools and asked the school administrations if she could place them in students' mailboxes. She introduced herself to local businesses and tried to alert them to her program so that up-and-coming accountants would be encouraged to take her class if they wanted to take the CA exam.

The first year that she ran the program she had 10 students. Despite the small class size, students felt that they had been well prepared for the exam and appreciated the individual attention they received. All students passed the exam. The second course had 45 students, 70 percent of whom passed. The last session that she held had 105 students and 80 percent of those students passed. Olivia did not feel comfortable advertising her pass rate, however, because many of her students had taken the CA exam one or two times before and failed. She was not sure whether they passed after taking her course because of the quality of the program or because they were bound to pass it at some point.

Spring 2005

By the spring of 2005, Olivia had finished teaching the March course and was looking forward to the September class. Although she was pleased that the number of students in each session was rising, she felt concerned that she was not making enough of an impact in the market. With only 10 percent of the market tapped, Olivia wanted to know how to improve her marketing and gain market share. She also wondered if she needed to format the course differently to attract students who did not want to attend live lectures. She had initially believed that students would benefit from a structured program that kept them on track, but now she was not so sure. Many times students did not come to class but opted to listen to the tapes at home. Finally, Olivia realized that in her zeal to get her business up and running she had neglected to calculate her break-even point. How many students did Olivia need to break even, and at what point could she recognize a profit? She realized that these were all critical questions that needed answers to ensure the future success of her business.

BLAKE LOCK AND SECURITY SYSTEMS

Paul Blake was sitting back in his chair in his home office trying to understand why the new venture had not made him the rich man he thought he would be. Blake Lock and Security Systems (BLSS) had been established about two years ago and offered locksmithing services to residential and commercial customers as well as automobile owners in the greater Halifax area. These services included lock rekeying, lock and deadbolt installation and repair, master key systems, emergency residential lockouts, foreign and domestic automobile lockouts, and window security locks. In addition, BLSS was certified by the province to perform alarm installation and offered a full range of alarm products.

Financial results have been relatively poor, with losses of $6500 in the first year and a profit of only about $3500 in year 2. Currently, BLSS's target market is three local communities in the Halifax area with similar demographics (see Figure 1).

FIGURE 1 — Demographic Profile of Present Market

DEMOGRAPHICS	DARTMOUTH	BEDFORD	SACKVILLE
Total population	65,741	16,102	55,765
Total number of households	28,060	6,035	18,745
Total number of families	18,860	4,625	16,655
Number of married-couple families	12,195	3,685	12,965
Number of female householder families	3,760	495	1,815
Average household income	$41,107	$73,804	$60,365
Education			
Percent high school educated	87.0	90.5	87.3%
Percent college or higher educated	38.0	42.3	39.9%
Labour force			
Percent total population employed	59.9	65.9	68.3%
Percent female population employed	54.7	59.8	63.2%
Total number of housing units	28,060	6,035	18,745
Median number of rooms	5.9	7.9	6.4
Total number of owner-occupied housing units	14,790	4,390	16,180
Total number of renter-occupied housing units	13,275	1,645	2,565

Background

Paul Blake is the only child of parents who were both successful entrepreneurs. His parents are now deceased, and Blake received a substantial inheritance that would satisfy any of his financial needs for the rest of his life. He was not a great student but always seemed to get by. His summers were usually spent at the college, taking summer courses.

Upon graduation, his father had helped him get a job with a friend who owned a security and alarm manufacturing business in the western part of the province. Paul worked in various areas of the business learning a great deal about alarms and locks. After two years there, Paul decided that he would prefer to be his own boss and, using some of his inheritance, entered a special program to learn more about the locksmith business. His intent upon completion of the program was to start his own lock and security business. He felt from his experience and education that this market offered tremendous opportunities. Increased crime and residential house sales that often required new locks offered many opportunities to succeed in this business.

Paul did not want to offer alarm installations as part of his new venture, since he felt that they were bothersome to install. He also knew that there were many large competitors already in the alarm market that would be able to offer products and service at much lower prices.

Industry Structure/Competition

The locksmith industry was dominated by small operators, 60 percent of which consisted of an owner and one employee. Only about 20 percent of these firms had five or more employees.

Because of the low entry barriers, the number of small operators had grown dramatically in the past few years. These businesses were often operated out of the home with no storefront and concentrated mainly on the residential market. There were also a large number of family-owned businesses that usually had a retail store serving their communities for several generations of family members. The larger operators were the most sophisticated in terms of service and products and relied primarily on commercial accounts.

The Halifax area had 80 locksmiths all advertising in the area Yellow Pages. In the three communities on which BLSS concentrated, there were 18 other locksmiths.

Present Strategy

Excluding alarms, Paul offered just about every locksmith service. His company van was used to store these products and any necessary tools for servicing his clients. This company van was 10 years old with a few minor dents, but it ran quite well.

Paul had a beeper system and a cellular phone in order to respond to customer requests. After 5 p.m., however, Paul turned off the system and refused to take calls. During his operating hours he was able to respond to all requests fairly quickly even if he was not in the office, primarily because of the beeper and cellular phone. He had tried using an answering machine, but it did not allow him to respond to a customer fast enough, especially if he was at a job that kept him out of the office for a number of hours. He also knew that many job requests were emergencies and required a quick response.

During the past year, Paul had decided to advertise in the Yellow Pages. He felt that with all the locksmiths listed in the Yellow Pages he needed to be near the top of the list, so he decided to use his last name in his company name to form Blake Lock and Security Systems. The Yellow Pages ad seemed to help business and contributed to the $4000 profit (see Figures 2 and 3 for billing and expenses).

Paul spent a lot of his time in the office thinking of ways to increase his business, yet to this point nothing had been very successful. His understanding was that many of his competitors had found that the Yellow Pages were the most likely place for customers to find a locksmith. His ad identified the three communities, the services he offered, and a telephone number. In addition, he included that he was bonded and insured and a member of the Canadian Association of Professional Locksmiths. Competitors typically stressed products and services, 24-hour emergency service, follow-up guarantee service, being bonded and insured, and membership in the locksmith association.

FIGURE 2	BLSS Monthly Billings for Year Two
January	$ 1,200.01
February	2,260.85
March	2,777.26
April	1,748.62
May	922.20
June	1,414.12
July	1,595.18
August	1,652.37
September	2,264.64
October	2,602.19
November	4,087.37
December	1,905.80
Total	$24,430.61

FIGURE 3	Year Two Expenses
Business expenses	
Selling expenses	$ 9,454
Memberships (chambers of commerce and Canadian Association of Professional Locksmiths)	2,490
Telephone (includes beeper and cellular)	1,920
Office expenses (materials/supplies)	1,775
Yellow pages	4,200
Other promotional expenses	600
Total expenses	$20,439

Time was running out for Paul, and he was trying to think of other businesses that he could start up. He would often question his decision to enter the locksmith business, but then he would quickly decide that since he did not really need the money, it was no big deal. However, at some point he felt he should try to establish himself so he could settle down to a more routine life.

THE BEACH CARRIER*

Mary Ricci has a new product concept, The Beach Carrier, which she is ready to bring to market. Ricci is creative, optimistic, enthusiastic, flexible, and motivated. She is willing to put substantial time into developing and bringing The Beach Carrier to market. Although she lacks capital, Ricci is unwilling to license or sell the pattern to a manufacturer; she is determined to maintain control and ownership of the product throughout the introduction and market penetration phases. Ricci believes there is a significant amount of money to be made and refuses to sell her product concept for a flat fee.

The Product

The Beach Carrier is a bag large enough to carry everything needed for a day at the beach, including a chair. When empty, the bag can be folded down to a 30 cm by 30 cm square for easy storage. The bag's 91 cm by 91 cm size, adjustable padded shoulder strap, and various-sized pockets make it ideal for use in carrying chairs and other items to the beach or other outdoor activities such as concerts, picnics, and barbecues. The bag can also be used to transport items such as ski boots that are difficult to carry. Manufactured in a lightweight, tear-resistant, fade-proof fabric that dries quickly, the bag will be available in a variety of fluorescent as well as conservative colours.

Competition

Currently there are two competitive products sold online that Ricci felt would compete with the Beach Carrier. The first one, found at www.shadeusa.com, is the Caddy Sack and is advertised as a backpack-type product that can hold a beach chair, an umbrella, a boogie board, and even a small collapsing table. There is also an outside pocket for a towel, a snorkel, or fins. It is available in three colours and is priced at $16.95. Ricci purchased one of these and felt that it would not hold all the items advertised at one time. The chair had to be very small and room for extra beach accessories was very limited. This item was ideal for someone biking or walking to the beach with gear for only himself or herself.

The second item is called the Wonder Wheeler and can be found at www.4thebeach.com. It looks similar to a two-wheel shopping cart that might be used to carry purchased groceries while walking home from the store. This product is advertised as having oversized wheels; it weighs less than 10 pounds (5 kg) and folds up easily. It can hold a significant amount of beach gear such as multiple chairs, an umbrella, a cooler, beach towels, and toys. It has a list price of $59.99, and Ricci felt that even with the advertised oversized wheels it would be cumbersome to manoeuvre on the sand. Its high price was also felt to be a negative for many consumers.

Marketing Research

Ricci commissioned a consulting company to perform a feasibility study for the product, which included a demographic profile, cost estimates, packaging recommendations, and a patent search. The patent search revealed the above-mentioned products and a chair that could be folded and carried as a small tote bag that could also hold a few small beach items. None of these were felt to be a threat to Ricci's product, and she was optimistic that a patent could be obtained.

A focus group was used to determine potential consumer response. Results of the focus group indicated that several features of the product should be modified. For example, the material was perceived as durable; however, the fluorescent colour was see-through and considered "trendy," lessening the perceived quality of the bag. The size also represented an issue, as the bag was perceived as much larger than necessary.

Market Potential

People who use suntan and sunscreen products have been identified as the primary target market for The Beach Carrier. Research indicates that 48 percent of adult Canadians, or over 12 million, use sunscreen and sunscreening products. In the U.S., 43.9 percent or over 77 million people, use sunscreen and associated products. Beach bags are replaced every three years. The primary market for suntan and sunscreen products is described in Figure 1. The marketing share objectives for the first year of The Beach Carrier's sales have been determined based on the following assumptions:

- People who use suntan and sunscreen products represent the market for The Beach Carrier.
- Most men do not buy beach bags; consider women only (57.8 percent of population).
- Women buy new beach bags every three years on average; that is, one-third will buy a new bag this year.

Based on these assumptions, the unit sales needed to achieve market share objectives of 1 percent, 2 percent, and 5 percent of the total market during the first year of The Beach Carrier's sales are shown in Figure 2. Ricci is targeting 1 percent of this potential market.

Strategy

Ricci investigated several methods of marketing The Beach Carrier, including selling it in upscale (i.e., The Bay) or discount (i.e., Zellers) stores, licensing the product concept to a manufacturer,

FIGURE 1	The Beach carrier

SEGMENT	PERCENTAGE OF TOTAL USERS OF SUNTAN/SUNSCREEN PRODUCTS
Ages 18–44	66.9
High school graduate	40.2
Employed full time	60.5
No child in household	54.5
Household income of $30,000+	55.3

FIGURE 2

	POPULATION	SUNSCREEN USERS	REPLACE BAG THIS YEAR
Total adults	203,150,133	90,285,814	29,294,319
Females	117,420,776	60,219,277	19,872,361
		MARKET SHARE	
	1%	2%	5%
Total adults	297,943	595,886	1,489,716
Females	198,734	397,447	993,618

selling the idea for a flat fee, selling the bag to corporations for use as a promotional item, selling it on the Internet, and setting up a mail-order operation. Ricci believes that the mail-order option, while requiring the most effort, will provide higher margins, lower risk, and the overall best fit with Ricci's strengths and weaknesses, her market penetration objectives, and her limited financial resources. The Internet could also create opportunities but Ricci was unsure of this option.

The mail-order sales strategy will be implemented nationally using a regional roll-out and following a seasonal demand pattern. With three-month intervals between rollout phases, national market exposure will be achieved within 12 months. Ricci is also exploring how to set up a website with a local university team of student consultants.

Promotion

The product initially will be promoted in novelty and general interest mail-order catalogues and special interest magazines that appeal to beachgoers and boat owners.

Pricing

The costs of manufacturing have been estimated at $6.50 per unit for material, zippers, Velcro, and so on. The costs for assembly and packaging have been estimated at $3.50 per unit, bringing the total manufacturing cost to $10.00. After analyzing competitive products and focus-group results, a mail-order price in the $12.99 to $14.99 range has been established.

Distribution

The product will be manufactured at a local factory, drop-shipped to a storage facility, and shipped via UPS or Canada Post to the consumer. Initially, inventory can be carried at no cost in Ricci's house or garage. This same process could also be used if the website is developed.

Financing

A $30,000 small business loan is the minimum amount Ricci needs to fund her fixed costs for the first phase of the rollout for the mail-order program. Marketing the product through traditional retail channels would require approximately $250,000 for advertising and other selling costs associated with a new product introduction.

Break-Even Analysis

Break-even analysis was performed at three mail-order prices, as seen in Figure 3. Based on this analysis, Ricci must meet only one-fourth of her target sales goal, or one-quarter of 1 percent of the total market, in order to break even in the first year.

GOURMET EXPRESS

Today many households have two incomes. At the end of the day the questions arise: "Who will cook?" or "What do I cook?" Time is limited. After a long day at work, few people want to face the lines at the grocery store. Often the choice is to eat out. But the expense of dining out or the boredom of fast food soon becomes unappealing. Pizza or fast-food delivery solves the problem of going out but does not always satisfy the need for nutritious, high-quality meals. Some people prefer a home-cooked meal, especially without the hassle of grocery shopping, menu planning, and time-consuming preparation.

Jan Jones is one of those people. She is a hard-working professional who would like to come home to a home-cooked meal. She would not mind fixing it herself but, once at home, making an extra trip to the store is a major hassle. Jones thought it would be great to have the meal planned and all the ingredients at her fingertips. She thought of other people in her situation and realized there might be a market need for this kind of service. After thinking about the types of

FIGURE 3

	UNIT VARIABLE	COST PER UNIT	PRICE CONTRIBUTION
Materials	$ 6.50	$12.99	$2.99
Assembly	3.00	$13.99	$3.99
Packaging	0.50	$14.99	$4.99
Total unit VC	$10.00		

FIXED COSTS

	TOTAL
Advertising	$100,000
Warehousing	1,199
General S&A	10,000
Total fixed costs	$111,199

BREAK-EVEN UNITS

$12.99	37,190
Percent of total market	0.25
$13.99	27,869
Percent of total market	0.19
$14.99	22,284
Percent of total market	0.15

meals that could be marketed, Jones discussed the plan with her colleagues at work. The enthusiastic response led her to believe she had a good idea. After months of marketing research, menu planning, and financial projections, Jones was ready to launch her new business. The following is the business plan for Gourmet Express.

Executive Summary

Gourmet Express is a new concept in grocery marketing. The product is a combination of menu planning and grocery delivery; a complete package of groceries and recipes for a week's meals is delivered to a customer's door. The target market consists of young urban professionals living in two-income households in which individuals have limited leisure time, high disposable income, and a willingness to pay for services.

The objective is to develop a customer base of 400 households by the end of the third year after start-up. This level of operation will produce a new income of about $120,000 per year and provide a solid base for market penetration in the future.

The objective will be achieved by creating an awareness of the product through an intense promotional campaign at start-up and by providing customers with first-class service and premium-quality goods.

The capital required to achieve objectives is $258,000. Jones will invest $183,000 and will manage and own the business. The remainder of the capital will be financed through bank loans.

Product

The product consists of meal-planning and grocery-shopping services. It offers a limited selection of preplanned five-dinner packages delivered directly to the customer.

The criteria for the meal packages will be balanced nutrition, easy preparation, and premium quality. To ensure the nutritional requirements, Gourmet Express will hire a nutritionist as a consultant. Nutritional information will be included with each order. The most efficient method for preparing the overall meal will be presented. Meals will be limited to recipes requiring no more than 20 minutes to prepare. Premium-quality ingredients will be a selling feature. The customer should feel that he or she is getting better-quality ingredients than could be obtained from the grocery store.

Manufacturing and Packaging

Since the customer will not be shopping on the premises, Gourmet Express will require only a warehouse-type space for the groceries. The store location or decor will be unimportant in attracting business. There will be fewer inventory expenses, since the customer will not be choosing among various brands. Only premium brands will be offered.

It will be important to establish a reliable connection with a distributor for high-quality produce and to maintain freshness for delivery to the customer.

As orders are processed, the dinners will be assembled. Meats will be wrapped and ready for the home freezer. All ingredients will be labelled according to the dinner to which they belong. The groceries will be sorted and bagged according to storage requirements: freezer, refrigerator, and shelf. Everything possible will be done to minimize the customer's task. Included in the packaging will be the nutritional information and preparation instructions.

Customers will be given the option of selecting their own meals from the monthly menu list or opting for a weekly selection from the company.

Future Growth

Various options will be explored in order to expand the business. Some customers may prefer a three- or four-meal plan if they eat out more often or travel frequently. Another possibility might be the "last-minute gourmet"; that is, they can call any evening for one meal only.

Increasing the customer base will increase future sales. Expansion of Gourmet Express can include branches in other locations or even future franchising in other cities. With expansion and success, Gourmet Express might be a prime target for a larger food company to buy out.

Industry

The Gourmet Express's concept is a new idea with its own market niche. The closest competitors would be grocery stores and restaurants with delivery services.

Of the approximately 400 grocery stores in the Oshawa, Ontario, region, only two offer delivery service. They are higher-priced stores and will deliver for $4, regardless of order size. However, they offer no assistance in meal planning.

A number of pizza chains will deliver pizza as well as fried chicken. There is also a new service that will pick up and deliver orders from various restaurants. However, Gourmet Express would not be in direct competition with these services because the meals available from them are either of a fast-food type or far more expensive than a Gourmet Express meal.

Sales Prediction

The market segment will be households with an income of at least $65,000 per year. In the Oshawa Region, this will cover an area including over 18,000 households that meet the target requirements of income with an age range of 24 to 50 years. By the end of the third year, a customer base of 400 households will be developed (2.3 percent of the target market). At a growth rate of 2.73 percent a year, the target market of households should increase over three years to 19,000.

Financial

Various financial statements are included in Figures 1 through 8.

FIGURES 1	Start-Up Expenses	
Ad campaign		
Ad agency*	$3,000	
Brochures†	7,000	
Radio spots‡	8,000	
Newspaper ads§	7,000	
Total		$25,000
Pre-start-up salaries**		16,000
Nutritionist consulting		6,000
Miscellaneous consulting (legal etc.)		1,500
Pre-start-up rent and deposits		4,000
Pre-start-up utilities and miscellaneous supplies		2,000
		$54,500

*40 hrs. at $75/hr

†20,000 brochures; printing, development, etc. at $0.35/ea

‡4 weeks intense campaign: 20 spots/week (30 seconds); $100/spot

§50 ads at an average of $100/ad

**Jan Jones at 3 months; clerks, two at 2 weeks

FIGURE 2	Capital Equipment List		

Computers:			
Apple, MacIntosh Office System			
3 Mac systems		$3,000	
Laser printer HP2300 series		1,000	
Networking		2,000	
Software		3,000	
Total			$ 9,000
Delivery vans, Chevrolet Astro			66,000
Food lockers and freezers			15,000
Phone system (AT&T)			1,500
Furniture and fixtures			3,500
			$95,000

Marketing

Distribution.

The product will be delivered directly to the customer.

Sales Strategy.

Advertising will include newspaper ads, radio spots, an Internet web page, and direct-mail brochures. All four will be used during normal operations, but an intense campaign will precede start-up. A series of "teaser" newspaper ads will be run prior to start-up, announcing a revolution in grocery shopping. At start-up, the newspaper ads will have evolved into actually introducing the product, and radio spots will begin as well. A heavy advertising schedule will be used during the first four weeks of business. After start-up, a direct mailing will detail the description of the service and a menu plan.

Newspaper ads aimed at the target markets will be placed in entertainment and business sections. Radio spots will be geared to stations most appealing to the target market. Since the product is new, it may be possible to do interviews with newspapers and obtain free publicity.

Sales promotions will offer large discounts to first-time customers. These promotions will continue for the first six months of operations.

The service will be priced at $10 per week for delivery and planning, with the groceries priced at full retail level. According to the phone survey, most people who were interested in the service would be willing to pay the weekly service charge.

Management

The management will consist of the owner/manager. Other employees will be delivery clerks and order clerks. It is anticipated that after the business grows, an operations manager might be added to supervise the employees.

FIGURE 3 — Pro Forma Income Statement

YEAR 1

	MO. 1	MO. 2	MO. 3	MO. 4	MO. 5	MO. 6	MO. 7	MO. 8	MO. 9	MO. 10	MO. 11	MO. 12
Sales[1]	2,600	3,900	6,500	13,000	19,500	23,400	26,000	28,600	31,200	33,800	36,400	39,000
Less: Cost of goods sold[2]	1,700	2,550	4,250	8,500	12,750	15,300	17,000	18,700	20,400	22,100	23,800	25,500
Gross profit	900	1,350	2,250	4,500	6,750	8,100	9,000	9,900	10,800	11,700	12,600	13,500
Less: Operating expenses												
Salaries and wages[3]	7,400	7,400	7,400	7,400	7,400	7,400	9,800	9,800	9,800	9,800	9,800	9,800
Operating supplies	300	300	300	300	300	300	300	300	300	300	300	300
Repairs and maintenance	250	250	250	250	250	250	250	250	250	250	250	250
Advertising and promotion[4]	130	195	325	650	975	1,170	1,300	1,430	1,560	1,690	1,820	1,950
Bad debts	100	100	100	100	100	100	100	100	100	100	100	100
Rent[5]	1,667	1,667	1,667	1,667	1,667	1,667	1,667	1,667	1,667	1,667	1,667	1,667
Utilities	1,000	1,000	1,000	1,000	1,000	1,000	1,000	1,000	1,000	1,000	1,000	1,000
Insurance	600	600	600	600	600	600	600	600	600	600	600	600
General office	150	150	150	150	150	150	150	150	150	150	150	150
Licences	200	0	0	0	0	0	0	0	0	0	0	0
Interest[6]	310	310	310	310	310	310	530	530	530	530	530	530
Depreciation[7]	1,271	1,271	1,271	1,271	1,271	1,271	1,271	1,271	1,271	1,271	1,271	1,271
Total operating expenses	13,378	13,243	13,373	13,698	14,023	14,218	16,968	17,098	17,228	17,358	17,488	17,618
Profit (loss) before taxes	(12,478)	(11,893)	(11,123)	(9,198)	(7,273)	(6,118)	(7,968)	(7,198)	(6,428)	(5,658)	(4,888)	(4,118)
Less: Taxes	0	0	0	0	0	0	0	0	0	0	0	0
Net profit (loss)	(12,478)	(11,893)	(11,123)	(9,198)	(7,273)	(6,118)	(7,968)	(7,198)	(6,428)	(5,658)	(4,888)	(4,118)

[1]Sales—per Action Plan; see Exhibit 8 for details.

[2]Cost of goods sold—80% of retail grocery price, or $40.00 per household per week ($170.00/month household). (80% an average margin on groceries)

[3]Salaries and wages—Ms. Jones's salary will be $5000/month. Order clerks will be paid $1300/month, and delivery clerks will be paid $1100/month. One additional order clerk and delivery clerk each will be added once sales reach 100 households, and again at 200 households. Salaries will escalate at 6%/year.

[4]Advertising and promotion—The grocery industry standard is 1% of sales. However, Gourmet Express being a new business will require more than that level; 5% of sales is used in this plan. (Special prestart-up advertising is covered with other start-up expenses.)

[5]Rent—2000/ft.^{2} @ $10.00/ft.^{2}; $1667/month; escalate at 6%/year.

[6]Interest—Loans on computer ($9,000) and delivery vehicles ($22,000 ea.) at 12.0%/year. (Delivery vehicles will be added with delivery clerks.) (Debt service— based on three-year amortization of loans with payments of $1/3$ at the end of each of three years.)

[7]Depreciation—All equipment will be depreciated per ACRS schedules: vehicles and computers—3 years; furniture and fixtures—10 years.

| FIGURE 4 | Pro Forma Income Statement |

	YEAR 2				YEAR 3			
	Q1	**Q2**	**Q3**	**Q4**	**Q1**	**Q2**	**Q3**	**Q4**
Sales[1]	136,500	156,000	194,698	234,000	253,500	273,000	292,500	312,000
Less: Cost of goods sold[2]	89,250	102,000	127,302	153,000	165,750	178,500	191,250	204,000
Gross profit	47,250	54,000	67,395	81,000	87,750	94,500	101,250	108,000
Less: Operating expenses								
Salaries and wages[3]	31,164	38,796	38,796	38,796	41,124	41,124	41,124	41,124
Operating supplies	900	900	900	900	900	900	900	900
Repairs and maintenance	750	750	750	750	750	750	750	750
Advertising and promotion[4]	6,825	7,800	9,735	11,700	12,675	13,650	14,625	15,600
Bad debts	300	300	300	300	300	300	300	300
Rent[5]	5,301	5,301	5,301	5,301	5,619	5,619	5,619	5,619
Utilities	3,000	3,000	3,000	3,000	3,000	3,000	3,000	3,000
Insurance	1,800	1,800	1,800	1,800	1,800	1,800	1,800	1,800
General office	450	450	450	450	450	450	450	450
Interest[6]	1,280	1,940	1,720	1,720	1,410	1,190	970	970
Depreciation[7]	6,910	6,910	6,910	6,910	7,493	7,493	7,493	7,493
Total operating expenses	58,680	67,947	69,662	71,627	75,520	76,275	77,030	78,005
Profit (loss) before taxes	(11,430)	(13,947)	(2,267)	9,373	12,230	18,225	24,220	29,995
Less: Taxes	0							
Net profit (loss)	(11,430)	(13,947)	(2,267)	9,373	12,230	18,225	24,220	29,995

[1]Sales—per Action Plan: see Exhibit 8 for detail. Average unit sale is $40.00 for groceries plus $10.00 per week for delivery (Exhibit 1), making the monthly unit sales per household (2 people) $215.00.

[2]Cost of goods sold—80% of retail grocery price, or $32.00 per household per week ($138.00/month household). (80% an average margin on groceries—Progressive Grocer; April 1984; p. 94.)

[3]Salaries and wages—Ms. Jones's salary will be $4500/month. Order clerks will be paid $1000/month, and delivery clerks will be paid $900/month. One additional order clerk and delivery clerk each will be added once sales reach 100 households, and again at 200 households. Salaries will escalate at 6%/year.

[4]Advertising and promotion—The grocery industry standard is 1% of sales. However, Gourmet Express being a new business will require more than that level; 5% of sales is used in this plan. (Special prestart-up advertising is covered with other start-up expenses.)

[5]Rent—2000/ft.^{2} @ $8.00/ft.^{2}; 1333 $1/month; escalate at 6%/year.

[6]Interest—Loans on computer ($10,000) and delivery vehicles ($12,000 ea.) at 12.5% year. (Delivery vehicles will be added with delivery clerks.) (Debt service-based on three-year amortization of loans with payments of $1/3$ at the end of each of three years.)

[7]Depreciation—All equipment will be depreciated per ACRS schedules: vehicles and computers—3 years; furniture and fixtures—10 years.

FIGURE 5 Pro Forma Cash Flow Statement

YEAR 1

	MO. 1	MO. 2	MO. 3	MO. 4	MO. 5	MO. 6	MO. 7	MO. 8	MO. 9	MO. 10	MO. 11	MO. 12	TOTAL
Cash receipts													
Sales	2,600	3,900	6,500	13,000	19,500	23,400	26,000	28,600	31,200	33,800	36,400	39,000	263,900
Other													
Total cash receipts	2,600	3,900	6,500	13,000	19,500	23,400	26,000	28,600	31,200	33,800	36,400	39,000	263,900
Cash disbursements													
Cost of goods sold	1,700	2,550	4,250	8,500	12,750	15,300	17,000	18,700	20,400	22,100	23,800	25,500	172,550
Salaries and wages	7,400	7,400	7,400	7,400	7,400	7,400	9,800	9,800	9,800	9,800	9,800	9,800	103,200
Operating supplies	300	300	300	300	300	300	300	300	300	300	300	300	3,600
Repairs and maintenance	250	250	250	250	250	250	250	250	250	250	250	250	3,000
Advertising and promotion	130	195	325	650	975	1,170	1,300	1,430	1,560	1,690	1,820	1,950	13,195
Bad debts	100	100	100	100	100	100	100	100	100	100	100	100	1,200
Rent	1,667	1,667	1,667	1,667	1,667	1,667	1,667	1,667	1,667	1,667	1,667	1,667	20,004
Utilities	1,000	1,000	1,000	1,000	1,000	1,000	1,000	1,000	1,000	1,000	1,000	1,000	12,000
Insurance	600	600	600	600	600	600	600	600	600	600	600	600	7,200
General office	150	150	150	150	150	150	150	150	150	150	150	150	1,800
Licences	200	0	0	0	0	0	0	0	0	0	0	0	200
Interest	310	310	310	310	310	310	530	530	530	530	530	530	5,040
Debt service (principal)												10,333	10,333
Total cash disbursements	13,807	14,522	16,352	20,927	25,502	28,247	32,697	34,527	36,357	38,187	40,017	52,180	353,322
Net cash flow	(11,207)	(10,622)	(9,852)	(7,927)	(6,002)	(4,847)	(6,697)	(5,927)	(5,157)	(4,387)	(3,617)	(13,180)	(89,422)

FIGURE 6
Pro Forma Cash Flow Statement

	YEAR 2				YEAR 3			
	Q1	Q2	Q3	Q4	Q1	Q2	Q3	Q4
Cash receipts								
Sales	136,500	156,000	194,698	234,000	253,500	273,000	292,500	312,000
Other								
Total cash receipts	136,500	156,000	194,698	234,000	253,500	273,000	292,500	312,000
Cash disbursements								
Cost of goods sold	89,250	102,000	127,302	153,000	165,750	178,500	191,250	204,000
Salaries and wages	31,164	38,796	38,796	38,796	41,124	41,124	41,124	41,124
Operating supplies	900	900	900	900	900	900	900	900
Repairs and maintenance	750	750	750	750	750	750	750	750
Advertising and promotion	6,825	7,800	9,735	11,700	12,675	13,650	14,625	15,600
Bad debts	300	300	300	300	300	300	300	300
Rent	5,301	5,301	5,301	5,301	5,619	5,619	5,619	5,619
Utilities	3,000	3,000	3,000	3,000	3,000	3,000	3,000	3,000
Insurance	1,800	1,800	1,800	1,800	1,800	1,800	1,800	1,800
General office	450	450	450	450	450	450	450	450
Licences	0	0	0	0	0	0	0	0
Interest	1,280	1,940	1,720	1,720	1,410	1,190	970	970
Debt service (principal)		7,333		10,333	7,333	7,333		10,333
Total cash disbursements	141,020	170,370	190,054	228,050	241,111	254,616	260,788	284,846
Net cash flow	(4,520)	(14,370)	4,643	5,950	12,389	18,384	31,712	27,154

FIGURE 7
Pro Forma Balance Sheets

END OF:	YEAR 1	YEAR 2	YEAR 3		YEAR 1	YEAR 2	YEAR 3
Assets				**Liabilities**			
Current assets				Accounts payable	12,750	21,217	31,875
Cash	3,000	5,000	7,000	Notes payable	0	0	0
Accounts receivable	19,500	32,450	48,750	Total current liabilities	12,750	21,217	31,875
Inventory	12,750	21,217	31,875	Long-term liabilities			
Supplies	300	300	300	Bank loans payable	42,667	47,000	22,000
Prepaid expenses	1,667	1,767	1,873	Personal loans payable	0	0	0
Total current assets	37,217	60,734	89,798	Total long-term liabilities	42,667	47,000	22,000
Fixed assets				Total liabilities	55,417	68,217	53,875
Furniture and fixtures	18,000	16,000	14,000	Owner's equity			
Vehicles	33,000	32,780	8,140	Paid-in capital	133,889	62,897	28,068
Equipment	6,750	3,330	0	Retained earnings	(94,339)	(18,271)	29,995
Total fixed assets	57,750	52,110	22,140	Total owner's equity	39,550	44,627	58,063
Total assets	94,967	112,844	111,938	Total liabilities and equity	94,967	112,844	111,938

FIGURE 8 — Sources and Uses of Funds

Sources of Funds

Jan Jones (personal funds)	$182,913
Bank loans for computer and vehicles*	75,000
Total sources	$257,913

Uses of Funds

Computer, peripherals, and software	$9,000
Food lockers and freezers	15,000
Delivery vehicles	66,000
Phone system	1,500
Miscellaneous furniture and fixtures	3,500
Start-up expenses†	54,600
Working capital‡	108,313
Total uses	$257,913

* Total for initial 3-year period. Computer and one delivery van will be acquired prior to start-up, one delivery van will be added 6 months after start-up, and another will be added 15 months after start-up. Financing will be handled simultaneously with procurement.

†To cover negative cash flow over first $1\frac{1}{2}$ years of operation. (See pro forma cash flow statements.)

‡See detail, following.

THE WINSLOW CLOCK COMPANY

For the third time, Dr. Winslow sat up in bed, flipped on the light, and reached for The Winslow Clock Company business plan. Maybe reading through it again would calm his growing fears. As he flipped through the pages, he recalled again all the years of thinking, tinkering, and discovery that had gone into the development of his alarm clock. How could something he spent so much time and energy on be wrong? It was such a good idea, this "throwable" alarm clock: Millions of Canadians would want to get this kind of revenge on their daily call to the rat race. And, in its final design, it contained all kinds of computer-age technology. Surely, the investors tomorrow will love it!

What had happened to his confidence? He had been sure enough to invest all his savings in the clock's development. What a time to get second thoughts! Didn't he use the best technical help available to design the clock and plan the production and marketing? Maybe that was his problem—too much dependence on "experts." Being a practicing psychiatrist, he considered himself a good judge of character and motivation, but maybe his obsession with his clock had clouded his perception. Should he take more time to personally study the different production and marketing scenarios? He did not have any more time, if he wanted to get production started in time to hit the Christmas season. Should he wait another year, or risk going to market at a slow time of year, or…?

The more he thought, the more the doubts and worries grew. He had to put a stop to this pointless mental exercise. The business plan he held in his hands was what he had to sell tomorrow at the meeting, so he had better have confidence in it. If things went badly, then he could think about changes. For now, he would read over the business plan for The Winslow Clock Company (which follows) just once more, concentrating on the favourable arguments his business "experts" had made.

Summary

The attached five-year business plan for The Winslow Clock Company is based primarily on the estimated potential of the company's first product, an alarm clock designed and patented by Dr. Michael Winslow, a psychiatrist by profession. He expected the sales and profits generated by this product to reach $8.5 million and $1.5 million, respectively, within three years, which would provide sufficient resources to enable the company to expand its line into related products now under consideration.

History of the Product.

Under development for 10 years, the concept for the clock stems from Dr. Winslow's thought that it would be fun to have the liberty to "get back at" the alarm that so readily awakens everyone each morning. The "fun" part—and what makes the alarm unique—is that you throw it to turn it off.

Development of the microchip and related technology in recent years has made the design of such a clock possible at a reasonable cost. The technical assistance on the clock was provided by students at Queen's University. The business and marketing planning for the clock was done with the help of Queen's Small Business Consulting (QSBC) under the direction of its faculty associate.

In addition, Dr. Winslow has contracted with a number of professional consultants in the areas of product design, product engineering, marketing and advertising, production, legal matters, and accounting.

Market Acceptance.

Early reaction from such major retailers as Sears Canada has been very positive, thus supporting the belief that the targeted levels of sales are achievable.

Thus, in what might otherwise be considered a mature market, new design and technology are eagerly sought by retailers and customers anxious to provide or find a refreshing selection of alternatives. The company's projected level of sales in its first year represents less than 1 percent of this growing segment of the Canadian clock market.

Competition.

Although several major manufacturers account for most clock sales (with Japanese manufacturers dominating the sale of quartz movements), there is, nevertheless, a significant annual volume attributable to smaller specialty designers, most of whom purchase the clock movements on an OEM (original equipment manufacturer) basis from the larger producers and concentrate on unique housing designs.

Seiko, the company supplying the movement for Dr. Winslow's clock, has made impressive strides in Canada in the last four years by increasing its annual OEM business from 400,000 to 2 million units. Besides selling its own Seiko and Picco brands, it is developing a reputable supplier business. This strategy allows Seiko to enjoy some of the profit opportunity created by an expanded market without all the marketing costs and risks.

In addition, a number of large retailers contract with the major manufacturers for private-label production. This somewhat fragmented structure has created profitable opportunities for products designed for niches within the large clock market.

The question is: If the product is attractive enough to create a niche in the market, how soon will it have competition? The concept of a "throwable" alarm and several components designed specifically for the product are patented. In addition, it would require some time and expense for potential competitors to develop the impact switch and the microchip used in Dr. Winslow's clock.

Financial Projections: Opportunities and Risks.

Financial projections for the first five years of the company are summarized below. (Sales are based on only the first product, to be introduced in 2006.)

Since components and subassemblies would be purchased, rather than manufactured by the company, and then assembled and shipped by an outside contractor, the capital investment required is minimal, estimated at less than $50,000, the majority of which would be for tooling. Another $50,000 for start-up expenses, prototypes, and preproduction operating expenses would also be required in the first two months of 2006.

By March, however, the commitment increases. Because of the company's lack of credit history, all indications suggest that suppliers will require letters of credit to accompany the $814,000 in parts orders placed between March and

September of 2006, when shipments are expected to begin. In addition, operating expenses between March and October are forecasted at $176,000.

Given the projected level of sales in the first two years, the company is seeking equity capital of $600,000 as early as possible in 2006. An additional term loan of approximately $650,000 would be needed by June to carry financing and operating costs through year's end.

It should be emphasized that although this combined cash injection of $1.2 million is at apparent risk for at least the six to eight months prior to the beginning of shipments (and, of course, beyond), two factors diminish this risk. First, the initial selling effort in the spring of 2006 to secure orders for the Christmas season should provide a clear indication of market acceptance by the end of April. The long lead time required to order components then becomes a positive factor. Orders for 40,000 of the first season's production of 50,000 units could be cancelled without penalty a month in advance on standard items such as the clock movement. This alone would save almost $730,000. In addition, many operating expenses could be curtailed accordingly and alternative marketing plans put into place. (Direct mail-order marketing, for example, is an approach that will be explored from the beginning anyway and, in a downside case, certainly would be a viable alternative.)

The second factor that diminishes the risk is that low fixed costs allow the break-even point to be projected at 16,000 units, which should be achieved in October, the second month of actual shipments.

According to its projected cash flow, the company should be able to repay its term loan in full within 18 months. From that point on, it can fund its continuing operations from the generated working capital.

The returns on investment are calculated at 19, 33, and 37 percent in the first three years, respectively, with returns on net worth at 34, 46, and 45 percent. Net present value for the original investors would be $1.7 million, based on five years of net cash flow and not including the salable value of the firm or its continuing earning power after that time. Payback is expected in one year, based on the forecast of sales and profits. Specific financial details are found in Figures 1 through 7.

Industry Information

The clock market in Canada has been growing at a rate of between 8 and 10 percent per year, with significantly higher growth (three times the industry average) recorded in the segments where innovative design or a technological change has been offered. The recent introduction of

FIGURE 1

THE WINSLOW CLOCK COMPANY
PRO FORMA INCOME STATEMENTS
FIVE-YEAR PROJECTION

	YEAR 1	YEAR 2	YEAR 3	YEAR 4	YEAR 5
Unit sales	50,000	150,000	200,000	150,000	125,000
Price	$42.50	$42.50	$42.50	$40.00	$40.00
Net sales (000s)	$2,125	$6,375	$8,500	$6,000	$5,000
Bad debt allowance (2%)	43	128	170	120	100
Adjusted net sales	2,082	6,247	8,330	5,880	4,900
Cost of goods sold	1,093	3,253	4,630	3,655	3,267
Gross margin	989	2,994	3,700	2,225	1,633
Operating costs	323	552	695	663	642
E.B.I.T.	666	2,442	3,005	1,562	991
Taxes (50%)	333	1,221	1,502	781	495
Net income	$ 333	$1,221	$1,503	$ 781	$ 496

FIGURE 2

THE WINSLOW CLOCK COMPANY
PRO FORMA BALANCE SHEET
AS OF DECEMBER 31 ($000S)

	YEAR 1	YEAR 2	YEAR 3	YEAR 4	YEAR 5	YEAR 6
Assets						
Cash	5	203	256	1,019	2,722	3,539
Accounts receivable	—	1,345	2,044	2,726	1,924	1,283
Inventory						
Finished goods	—	73	44	48	53	58
Work-in-process	—	106	—	78	—	—
Raw materials	55	—	141	155	171	188
Net fixed assets	40	36	32	29	26	24
Total assets	100	1,763	2,517	4,055	4,896	5,092
Liabilities						
Accounts payable	40	50	141	155	171	181
Accrued liabilities	—	—	560	581	626	309
Est'd tax liability	—	70	—	—	—	—
Short-term debt	—	650	—	—	—	—
Long-term debt	—	—	—	—	—	—
Common stock	—	600	600	600	600	600
Paid-in capital						
(M. Winslow)	60	60	60	60	60	60
Retained earnings	—	333	1,156	2,659	3,439	3,935
Total liabilities	100	1,763	2,517	4,055	4,896	5,092

FIGURE 3

THE WINSLOW CLOCK COMPANY
STATEMENT OF SOURCES AND USES OF FUNDS*
YEAR ENDED DECEMBER 31 ($000S)

	YEAR 1	YEAR 2	YEAR 3	YEAR 4	YEAR 5
Sources					
Funds provided by operations					
Net income after taxes	333	823	1,503	780	496
Plus depreciation	4	4	3	3	2
Inc.—accounts payable	10	91	14	16	17
Inc.—accrued liabilities	—	560	21	45	—
Inc.—taxes payable	70	—	—	—	—
Inc.—common stock	600	—	—	—	—
Inc.—short-term debt	650				
Dec.—accounts receivable	—	—	—	802	641
Dec.—inventories	—	—	—	57	—
Total sources	1,667	1,478	1,541	1,703	1,156
Uses					
Inc.—cash	198	53	763	1,703	817
Inc.—accounts receivable	1,345	699	682	—	—
Inc.—inventories	124	6	96	—	22
Dec.—accrued liabilities	—	—	—	—	317
Dec.—taxes payable	—	70	—	—	—
Dec.—short-term debt	—	640	—	—	—
Total uses	1,667	1,478	1,541	1,703	1,156

*Based on pro forma balance sheets and income statements.

battery-operated quartz mechanisms combined with sleek styling to create lightweight, portable, wireless clocks has led to at least a 25 percent annual growth rate for decorative or kitchen wall clocks and to almost a 29 percent increase for alarm clocks.

Clocks are in most households and constitute an enduring and important retail gift category. As with many items that are so inherently useful that they might be considered a household necessity, the greater the opportunity to differentiate the product, the greater is the ability to segment the market by appealing to consumers through unique designs that are fashioned to suit a wide variety of tastes and income levels.

A handful of major competitors serve as the dominant force in the industry and often not only sell their own brands but also make private-label brands for large retailers as well. (Seiko, for example, produces the private-label quartz alarm

---

FIGURE 4 Break-Even Quantity Calculation

1. Contribution margin per unit is estimated to be $20.81 in 2006 and 2007. (See unit sales, cost, margin analysis.)
2. Fixed costs for unit sales in the first year of 50,000 units are estimated to be $332,910, including $10,200 paid for prototype development in 2003. Break-even quantity would be $332,910/20.81 = 16,000 units.
3. Based on the expected seasonality of sales in the first year of selling, the break-even point should be reached in mid-October 2006, in the second full month of product shipments.

FIGURE 5 — Financial Data Backup

Unit sales, cost, margin analysis	
Retail suggested list	$85.00
Dealer margin	42.50
Mfr. selling price (dealer cost)	42.50
Cost of goods sold*	14.60
Gross margin	$27.90
Other variable costs*	
Warranty	.05
Quality control allowance	.29
Shipping & handling contribution	.20
Co-op advertising allowance	2.13
Selling commissions	4.25
Designer/developer fee	.17
Subtotal variable costs	7.09
Net margin	$20.81
Note: Total cost of goods	$21.69

*Backup detail provided.

FIGURE 6 — Financial Data Backup

Cost of goods sold analysis		
Item		
Movement*	$2.77	$ 3.87
(and circuit board)	$1.10	
Chip (production model)		$.79
Capacitors (3)		.30
Impact switch		1.03
Battery holder		.20
Photo transistor		.30
Ball		.87
Moulded sphere		.20
Velcro®		.07
Molded cube (housing)		2.00
Batteries		.95
Face, crystal, hands, etc.		.60
Board		.40
Board assembly		1.00
Feet		.05
Speaker, lamp, socket		1.08
Assembly		.50
Product subtotal		$14.21
Package (inc. inside corrugated)		.24
Printed inserts		.05
Portion (1/6) master carton		.10
Package subtotal		$14.60

*Add $0.30 premium per unit for air shipments.

Note: Tooling not amortized in these calculations because first production run estimated to be 10K units; all other costs listed here based on runs of 100K. Tooling at this point treated as a capital expenditure and listed under fixed costs.

clocks for Walmart and Sears.) As a result, clock movements are inexpensive and -readily available, which in turn spawns a significant opportunity for a number of smaller companies to specialize in unique designs that range from the very inexpensive to one-of-a-kind collector's items.

Clocks are sold through a variety of retail outlets that include mass merchandisers, department and specialty stores, furniture and interior design stores, jewellery stores, shops that deal exclusively in clocks, and museum gift stores.

Catalogue sales are also an important means of reaching the clock consumer. Furthermore, within a department store, clocks can be found in various departments that include gifts, luggage, electronics, fine collectibles, furniture, jewellery, and occasionally even in their own clock department.

This diversity of product as well as placement makes the clock market a natural arena in which independent sales representatives may operate. This fact simplifies, to some extent, the problems that the smaller producers face in trying to get their product to the national marketplace without incurring a disproportionate expense for the hiring, training, and support of a sales force.

It is apparent, then, that the market for clocks has ample room for product differentiation. Dr. Winslow's clock, we believe, presents an exciting opportunity to capitalize on a segment of this significant market.

The Product: Present and Future

The product will first be described and then discussed in terms of its future potential.

Product Description.

The battery-operated quartz alarm clock consists of two basic parts, the first of which is a lightweight black foam ball, approximately 4 inches in diameter, that contains the "brains" of the clock—a microchip, circuit board, impact switch, small batteries, and the audio device for the alarm. These are held inside a plastic capsule that is secured by a Velcro enclosure within the larger foam ball. The second part of the clock is the quartz movement that is housed in a handsomely styled cube of moulded plastic.

Listed below are those areas of particular concern and importance to the management.

1. *Timing* will play a critical role in the success of this venture. The key variables are:
   - Product readiness
   - Financing
   - Approach to the marketplace
   - Production, from delivery of components to assembly, inventory, and shipping procedures

2. *Projections* used are "best" estimates, and all financial needs and operating costs have been based on what is considered to be the most likely volume of sales achievable. Because selling activities will begin early in 2006, reaction from the marketplace should be clear by late spring. Decisions can still be made to cut back—or to gear up—for the 2006 season.

   The first commitment to Seiko for 10,000 units (cost of $4.17 each) will have been made by mid-March, and estimates for the entire year will be in their production plan by then. While cutbacks can be made as late as a month in advance, increased production might be a problem since it would bump into Seiko's heaviest production season.

3. *Financing* would be another major consideration if sales were much in excess of expectations, particularly because we must assume that early orders are going to require an accompanying letter of credit. For this and other reasons, the marketing plan is meant to guard against some of these problems and is specifically geared to reach upscale stores and catalogues that will commit early to carry the "limited production" of the first year.

4. *Ironing out production* and assembly problems will be of major importance in June and July. Although the process is not complex, it will be totally new, and the production rate is currently scheduled at 5,000 units in July and 10,000 in August in order to meet anticipated shipping requirements in September and to build minimal inventory requirements. For these reasons, selection of an experienced production manager will be critical.

What makes the clock functionally unique is that throwing the ball turns off the alarm. Great care was taken to use materials that have virtually no chance of damaging the wall or any other object. The specifically designed impact switch is sensitive enough that even a light impact will stop the alarm. On the other hand, a throw of considerable force will not disturb the contents of the inner capsule. Two insurance companies specializing in product liability testing have been consulted. They both feel that the product is safe and free enough from liability risk that they have quoted. The Winslow Clock Company the minimum premium for liability insurance.

Several achievements have made the clock technologically possible. There is no need for an electrical connection between the clock base and the ball because an ultrasound device signals the alarm to go off. A receiver in the inner capsule "reads" the signal and triggers the humorous crescendo of the alarm; upon "advice" from the impact switch, a satisfying tone of demise is produced when the alarm hits the wall. In addition, a timing device has been built into the circuitry that automatically shuts off the alarm after one minute if the ball is not thrown.

The overall design and finish of the clock are clean and sophisticated in order to eliminate any sense of gimmickry that might lessen the perceived value of the clock. This elegant styling and the sophisticated electronics, combined with both the psychological satisfaction and the sense of fun and playfulness inherent in being able to throw one's alarm clock, should appeal to a significant cross section of consumers, from executives to athletes. The product has a strong appeal to retailers as well, who look for "something refreshing and new to pull people into the stores."

Technical specifications of the product are as follows:

Dimension: Base—4½" × 4½" × 4½" Ball—4½" diameter

Colour: Model A—white clock housing with black face, charcoal ball, white, yellow, and red hands

Model B—black housing with other colours in Model A

Accuracy of movement: +/− 20 seconds per month

Hands: Luminescent minute and hour hands

Foam ball: 35 ppi Crest Foam

Future Potential.

The new technologic innovations that have emerged during the development of this first product have significance for the future of the company as well. First, extensions of the basic concept are possible in a variety of clocks with other features. Obvious examples are clock radios and snooze alarms. In addition, as production quantities increase, specialty designs for the premium market become possible at reasonable cost.

A family of related products such as posters, a wall-mountable target, and other clocks—all dealing with the frustration people feel with time, alarm clocks, and schedules—are natural offshoots of the throwable alarm, and their development is currently being explored.

Marketing Plan and Strategy

Given the clock's unique function, design, and appeal, the first year's marketing plan will focus on placing the clock in upscale department stores, clock specialty stores, and catalogues that reach upper-middle-income and upper-income executives and families. The early strategy is to keep the clock out of the mass market and discounters' trade, instead making it readily available to consumers more interested in its characteristics and uniqueness than its suggested list price of $85. The sales, cost, and margin analysis is based on the assumption that the suggested list price of $85 and dealer price of $42.50 will be held constant for three years. The goal is to introduce the product with a large enough margin for the dealer in the higher-end retail and catalogue business to make an adequate return and to allow the company to recapture its fixed costs as quickly as possible.

While the suggested list and dealer prices at this time are expected to remain the same in the second and third years, part of the strategy will be to refine the production and assembly costs, negotiate volume discounts with suppliers, and devise other cost-saving measures in order to offer more marketing support to the expanded dealer base without sacrificing profitability. If necessary, cost-saving measures will be adopted that will make it possible to lower the price dramatically as a means of defence against competitors in years 3 and 4 of the product's life.

Sales Tactics.

The principals of the firm will contact potential buyers directly at first, beginning in early 2006 when there are still budgets available for merchandise for the 2006 Christmas season. Sales in 2006 are planned at 50,000 units, on a first-come, first-served basis, unless a retailer will commit for a guaranteed order prior to June 1. A sales rep organization will also be retained to continue these early sales efforts and to expand distribution after the first season. A commission averaging 10 percent of the dealer price per unit has been incorporated into the cost of sales to cover the activities of these sales reps.

In addition, an experienced, full-time, in-house sales manager will coordinate the selling and promotional activities of the independent rep organization. Other responsibilities of the sales manager will include (1) making direct contact with buyers, (2) making direct contact with sales reps and evaluating their performance, (3) coordinating the marketing support and promotional activities of the sales rep force, and (4) developing other possible avenues for marketing the company's products. The direct marketing approach referred to earlier is an obvious example of this.

Advertising and Publicity

A publicity campaign aimed at generating interest in the clock's development, its state-of-the-art technology, and its founder's concept of "functional fun" will be launched in early fall 2006. This publicity and accompanying new product announcements will target the "executive toy" purchaser.

In addition, a print ad campaign slated for the 2006 Christmas retail market and a cooperative advertising plan to help participating dealers are expected to aid sell-through in the clock's first major season on the market.

Expanded advertising marketing support for the second season will include the following: attendance at trade shows (notably the EPTECH electronic trade show and at least one of the major gift shows); an in-store promotion plan highlighted by a 90-second video spot; continuation of the co-op advertising plan; and an overall advertising budget slated at 5 percent of anticipated sales for the year.

Operations Management

Since all assembly and subassembly operations will be handled by independent contractors, with final shipment emanating from the final point of assembly, the need for an office, a production staff, and overhead would be kept to a minimum.

Although Dr. Winslow will oversee all operations, his regular staff will supervise the critical functions of marketing and business development, administration (including office management, billing, accounts receivable and payable), and production management (the control of all facets of outside assembly and vendor supplies and relations).

Marketing and business development (including sales in the initial stages) would be managed by Ms. Kristen Jones, who has 15 years of experience in marketing and finance in both domestic and international operations for Fuji Photo Film Canada. She has an MBA from University of Toronto and a BA from Brock University.

The production management area (including product engineering) is currently handled in an advisory capacity by several consultants, including Mr. Steve Canon (see enclosed profile). As the company approaches actual production (now slated for June–July 2006 start-up), a full-time production manager will be hired. Several candidates are presently being considered for this position.

Strong relationships with highly responsible subcontractors have already been established. These include Seiko, for the precision quartz movement and related technology; Finproject N.A. Inc., Quebec, QC, for the ball; Cocor Aero Products Inc., Markham, ON, for the switch; and Bramcan Plastics Ltd., Brampton, ON, for the plastic moulding.

An outside contractor in the Toronto area will handle the assembly operation, which includes packaging and shipment to fulfill sales orders. Several companies are being considered and will be submitting quotes on the specifications early in 2006. A decision is expected to be made by the beginning of February. The possibility of an assembly operation outside Canada will be investigated as a cost-saving measure once production is being handled efficiently here.

The administrative position will have the responsibility of handling all office functions, including billing, receivables, credit, and payables. Two candidates are now being considered. It will be important to fill this function as soon as possible, even if it is on a part-time basis for the first few months. The candidates are available for such a schedule, if necessary.

Other critical areas that are now, and will continue to be, handled by consultants are advertising (including sales promotion and publicity)—Bill Barlow—and product design—John Edwards.

Management

Dr. Michael Winslow is the inventor of the clock and founder and president of the company. His profession is psychiatric medicine, and he is currently practising at the Kingston Regional Psychiatric Centre and is also a lecturer in the Department of Psychiatry at Queen's University. He also maintains his own private practice. Dr. Winslow earned his undergraduate B.Sc. degree at Dalhousie University and his medical degree at the University of Western Ontario.

It was while he was a resident in psychiatry that he conceived of the idea for the clock. He first pursued the concept as a hobby, trying to find a way to throw the clock without damaging either it or the surface it hit. Within the last two years, as it became apparent that it would be possible to create and produce such a clock at a reasonable cost, further development of the idea became another full-time occupation for Dr. Winslow.

Dr. Winslow is a man of great energy, but part of his success in bringing the product from the initial concept to the prototype stage lies in his effectiveness in finding and utilizing the outside resources he has needed. He has also had enough confidence in, and received enough encouragement about, the ultimate marketability of the product that he has invested his own savings in development costs, a sum of approximately $60,000 to date.

Because his profession is very important to him, Dr. Winslow intends to continue his private medical practice. But he will also serve as president of The Winslow Clock Company, hiring professional managers to run the day-to-day operations for him and using consultants in those aspects of the business where a particular expertise is needed.

Kristen Jones joined Fuji Photo Film Canada, where her experience and responsibilities grew over a broad range of marketing and finance assignments.

During the years in which Fuji dramatically increased its market share, Jones was responsible for sales planning and forecasting for all its amateur photographic products. Later, as a financial analyst, her job was to assess the company's distributor markets around the world for potential as profitable wholly owned subsidiaries, as well as to carry out new product profitability analyses.

She then joined the domestic marketing division, where her assignments ranged from sales administration to marketing manager in charge of a test program to assess the potential of selling the company's Frontier System on a direct basis. In her last position as national merchandising manager, she created and managed the merchandising programs to support the national sales efforts for all consumer products.

In February 2000, she took advantage of the company's voluntary severance program to complete work on her master's degree in business administration at the University of Toronto. Ms. Jones earned her BA degree at Brock University in Ontario.

Steve Canon is a consultant, teacher, and businessman whose broad range of experience covers many aspects of new product design, development, and marketing. He presently has over 35 products of his own on the market and also teaches marketing and business law at the University of Western Ontario. In addition, he published a book in the spring of 1996 that deals with invention, product development, and marketing.

Among his numerous accomplishments, he has taught product design at Dalhousie, Laval, University of Toronto, and Western. He has won awards for his contributions to the field, including two from Ford Motor Company for innovative product development. Canon has appeared on television talk shows, as both guest and host, discussing product marketing.

Although his primary contributions to The Winslow Clock Company are in the fields of product development and manufacturing/production, his knowledge of new product introductions has been very helpful in a number of other areas as well.

Bill Barlow has been president and creative director of Bill Barlow Advertising since 1998. Prior to establishing his own company, Barlow was director of advertising for Bose Canada, a national sales promotion manager and creative director at Polaroid Corporation, and a creative supervisor for Bell Canada.

In his five years as an entrepreneur, Barlow has built an impressive list of clients and has won numerous awards and honours for excellence in advertising. His current list of clients includes Polaroid Corporation and Hewlett-Packard.

He will be responsible for advertising, promotional support materials, and publicity for The Winslow Clock Company.

John Edwards is the founder of Edwards Design Associates, Inc., a firm that specializes in industrial design, product development, and graphic design. For the past seven years, this company has provided an integrated approach to the design of both products and the packaging and collateral materials to support the products.

Among his clients, primarily in the fields of consumer products and finance, are Polaroid, Revlon, Chaps, and Hallmark.

Edwards has a B.Sc. degree in mechanical engineering from École Polytechnique and an M.Sc. degree in industrial design from the University of Ottawa.

In addition to designing Dr. Winslow's product, Edwards has also provided invaluable help in finding sources for the manufacture of several components, for injection moulding and for packaging.

WINDOW TECH INC.

Ahmed Raj had been in the housing restoration business for 15 years when, in 2001, he designed a machine that could remove old windows from their frames without destroying the wooden panes known as muntins and mullions that surround the glass (see Figure 1). One of the big advantages of the tool is that it was built around a routing drill piece that moved on a three-dimensional plane. This allowed Raj to replace windows that up until then could not be serviced. Once the small panes were removed, they would be replaced by one large pane of double glass. The muntins and mullions would be inserted over the window to give it the same look as before.

Raj applied for a patent as soon as he realized his machine was unique, and the patent was granted in August 2002. He has been operating the business since that time under the name of Window Tech Inc. He and his wife, Saira, are the sole owners and employees of the company. She oversees the advertising and promotional aspects, and Ahmed does the actual installing. They both engage in the selling process, particularly in the colder months when the actual installation business is slower. Their current geographic market is the Edmonton area, although they have done business outside it. They generally have concentrated on the residential market, but have periodically completed commercial jobs.

The restoration market is affected by several factors that include the state of the overall economy, local employment levels, and the amount of a consumer's disposable income. Since the company began operations, the economy has been favourable. The GNP has been increasing, real disposable income has risen moderately, and there has been a decrease in unemployment in the Edmonton area. The restoration of windows is a relatively large expense, costing between $3000 and $7000, depending on the number of windows installed in a house. Home owners are more likely to invest in this type of restoration when their level of net disposable income is greater and when the economy is good. Today, there is a trend toward less saving on the part of many Canadians, and consumers are tending to borrow for expenditures such as home renovations. Therefore, the level of interest rates affects Window Tech's business. Fortunately, interest rates have been low recently, so consumers have been able to afford such renovations.

Another factor that affects the renovation market is the cost of energy. In the late 1970s, the energy crisis forced many people to see energy as a limited resource. Since that time, people have generally tried to conserve energy. Consumers are faced with finding alternative sources of energy to heat and cool their homes and offices. This concern with conservation gives Window Tech an advantage in that it is replacing single-pane non-insulated windows with energy-efficient dual-pane insulated windows.

Due to the favourable economy and Window Tech's unique method of installing double-pane glass, the Rajs have had more business than they can handle. They have advertised in the Yellow Pages and have sent direct mail to the subscribers of a regional home improvement magazine. Their customers have referred their friends to the Rajs, so business has expanded considerably. Ahmed has two ideas on how to handle his growing business. He could hire and train a staff of salespeople and installers, or he could franchise his business. He enjoyed the selling and the actual installing of the windows, but neither he nor his wife was interested in managing a staff of workers. Therefore, franchising was more appealing to him. He felt that one of Window Tech's big advantages was

FIGURE 1

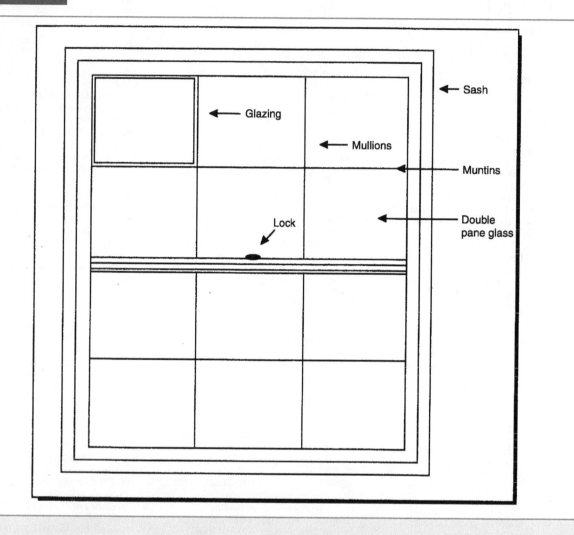

the patented cutting tool, and he could bring the name Window Tech to more customers if he franchised the business. Several contractors he contacted had expressed an interest in the Window Tech machine and wondered if he was interested in franchising.

Ahmed decided that his goal was to franchise the business. There were three groups of people he could contact regarding franchising. First, he could sell the rights of the product to contractors who were in the business of restoring residential homes or commercial offices. He felt that their reach with consumers could help to broaden the exposure of the Window Tech name. He also thought that glass companies in the Edmonton area might be interested in a Window Tech franchise. Since his tool could cut odd-shaped glass, it

had an advantage over existing methods, which glass companies would benefit from. Saira mentioned that individuals who wanted to get into the restoration business might also be potential targets for franchising.

Ahmed needed to know how to go about franchising the business. What kind of legalities were involved? He knew that he had patent protection on the machine, but what kind of procedures should he follow in terms of setting up guidelines for owning a Window Tech franchise? Which group should he target for franchising? How much should the franchise cost? He wanted to sell his franchise to the group or groups that would give the Window Tech name the most exposure and continue to emphasize the quality of the work. How should he proceed?

ENDNOTES

CHAPTER 1

1. Josh O'Kane, "Canada Goose CEO's 'Aha' Moment: I Realized the Brand was Real," April 11 2013, www.theglobeandmail.com/report-on-business/small-business/sb-growth/day-to-day/canada-goose-ceos-aha-moment-i-realized-the-brand-was-real/article10982951/.
2. John Lorinc, "The Golden Goose," October 17, 2012, www.profitguide.com/manage-grow/strategy-operations/the-golden-goose-42172/2.
3. Hollie Shaw, "Canada Goose's Made-in-Canada Marketing Strategy Translates into Success," May 18, 2012, http://business.financialpost.com/2012/05/18/canada-gooses-made-in-canada-marketing-strategy-translates-into-success/.
4. Josh O'Kane, "Canada Goose CEO's 'Aha' Moment: I Realized the Brand was Real," April 11 2013, www.theglobeandmail.com/report-on-business/small-business/sb-growth/day-to-day/canada-goose-ceos-aha-moment-i-realized-the-brand-was-real/article10982951/.
5. Hollie Shaw, "Canada Goose's Made-in-Canada Marketing Strategy Translates into Success," May 18, 2012, http://business.financialpost.com/2012/05/18/canada-gooses-made-in-canada-marketing-strategy-translates-into-success/; and John Lorinc, "The Golden Goose," October 17, 2012, www.profitguide.com/manage-grow/strategy-operations/the-golden-goose-42172/2.
6. John Naisbitt, *Global Paradox* (New York: William Morrow and Company, 1994).
7. As reported in *Success*, February 1999, p. 12.
8. *Growing Small Business* (Ottawa: Industry Canada/Statistics Canada, February 1994).
9. Global Entrepreneurship Monitor 2012 Global Report, www.gemconsortium.org/docs/download/2645.
10. G.E.M. Report, as reported in *Business Research Newsletter*, June 18, 2007.
11. *Small Business Quarterly*, Industry Canada, May 2009, p. 8.
12. *Small Business Quarterly*, Industry Canada, August 2006, p. 1.
13. As reported in GDSourcing.com, CIBC, October 2003.
14. Genius Factor Games, www.geniusfactorgames.com/about; and Matthew Braga, "Was This a $4.8-Million Fraud?" August 2, 2012, www.theglobeandmail.com/report-on-business/small-business/sb-tools/small-business-briefing/was-this-a-48-million-fraud/article4457675.
15. Canadian Economic Observer, November 1997, CAICS 11-010-XPB, January–December, V-10, Statistics Canada.
16. Jim Reid, presenter, Business and Tourism Conference 2009 and 2011, Mount Saint Vincent University, Halifax, Nova Scotia.
17. Skoll Foundation, www.skollfoundation.org.
18. Joe Castaldo, "Kick-start a Radical New Funding Model," March 21, 2013, www.canadianbusiness.com/technology-news/kick-start-a-radical-new-funding-model/; and Opportunity 2013: Social Financing, www.profitguide.com/opportunity/opportunity-2013-social-financing-45887.
19. Wallace Immen, "Venture Capital Rejection Leads to Funding Record," April 18, 2012, www.theglobeandmail.com/report-on-business/small-business/sb-money/business-funding/venture-capital-rejection-leads-to-funding-record/article4170756/#dashboard/follows/.
20. Joe Castaldo, "Kick-start a Radical New Funding Model," March 21, 2013, www.canadianbusiness.com/technology-news/kick-start-a-radical-new-funding-model/; Wallace Immen, "Venture Capital Rejection Leads to Funding Record," April 18, 2012, www.theglobeandmail.com/report-on-business/small-business/sb-money/business-funding/venture-capital-rejection-leads-to-funding-record/article4170756/#dashboard/follows/; and "Pebble: The First Great Smartwatch," April 21, 2013, http://datkin.net/blog/2013/04/21/pebble-the-first-great-smartwatch.
21. "The Entrepreneurial Numbers Game," *Inc.*, May 1986, pp. 31–36.
22. "Small Businesses Fuel Growth," *Success*, July/August 2000, p.16.
23. *Small Business Quarterly*, Industry Canada, August 2009, p. 2.
24. *Key Small Business Statistics*, Statistics Canada, July 2009.
25. *Key Small Business Statistics*, Statistics Canada, July 2009; *Key Small Business Statistics*, Statistics Canada, July 2012, www.ic.gc.ca/eic/site/061.nsf/vwapj/KSBS-PSRPE_July-Juillet2012_eng.pdf/$FILE/KSBS-PSRPE_July-Juillet2012_eng.pdf; and www.ic.gc.ca/eic/site/061.nsf/eng/02719.html.
26. CIBC Study as reported in *Business Research Newsletter*, February 27, 2006.
27. *Small Business Quarterly*, Industry Canada, November 2009, p. 4.
28. *Key Small Business Statistics*, Statistics Canada, July 2009.
29. *Key Small Business Statistics*, Statistics Canada, July 2009; *Key Small Business Statistics*, Statistics Canada, July 2012, www.ic.gc.ca/eic/site/061.nsf/vwapj/KSBS-PSRPE_July-Juillet2012_eng.pdf/$FILE/KSBS-PSRPE_July-Juillet2012_eng.pdf; and www.ic.gc.ca/eic/site/061.nsf/eng/02719.html.
30. *Key Small Business Statistics*, Statistics Canada, July 2012, www.ic.gc.ca/eic/site/061.nsf/vwapj/KSBS-PSRPE_July-Juillet2012_eng.pdf/$FILE/KSBS-PSRPE_July-Juillet2012_eng.pdf.
31. David Smith, *Why Small Business Is So Important* (Budget Brochure, Ministry of State for Small Business and Tourism, Government of Canada, 1984).
32. *Small Business Quarterly*, Industry Canada, May 2009, p. 8.
33. "Entrepreneurship Education," *Technological Entrepreneurship and Engineering in Canada, Canadian Academy of Engineering Report*, Chapter 9, Ottawa, 1997, pp. 149–160.
34. Thomas Peters and Robert H. Waterman, Jr., *In Search of Excellence* (New York: Harper and Row, 1982).
35. Ibid.
36. Stephanie Melita, "Small Talk," *Wall Street Journal*, May 21, 1998, pp. 28–29.
37. Canada: About Us, Canadian Federation of Independent Business (CFIB), www.cfib-fcei.ca/english/about-us/canada/178-about-us.html.
38. *The Globe and Mail*, June 12, 1995, p. B7.
39. "How the Dragons' Den Effect Works," http://money.ca.msn.com/small-business/insight/how-the-dragons%E2%80%99-den-effect-works?page=0.
40. *Small Business Statistics*, Statistics Canada, July 2008.
41. R. Peterson, *Small Business—Building a Balanced Economy* (Erin, Ontario: Press Porcepic Ltd., 1977), p. 64.
42. *Key Small Business Statistics*, Statistics Canada, July 2012, www.ic.gc.ca/eic/site/061.nsf/vwapj/KSBS-PSRPE_July-Juillet2012_eng.pdf/$FILE/KSBS-PSRPE_July-Juillet2012_eng.pdf.
43. Ibid.
44. Ibid.
45. Ibid.
46. Ibid.
47. Ibid.
48. Ibid.
49. Ibid.
50. Frank Condron, "Profit Magazine Reveals Canada's Top Young

Entrepreneurs, 2012," November 13, 2012, www.profitguide.com/topic/fuel-awards.

51. Ibid.

52. "The Young and the Restless," *Profit*, June 1993, p. 48.

53. As reported in *Costco Connection*, March–April 2005, p. 16.

54. Tracey Hanes, "Whats New: The Secret to a Lasting Business: Create Something You Want for Yourself," May 1, 2012, http://holycrap.ca/whats-new/the-secret-to-a-lasting-business-create-something-you-want-for-yourself; and "The World's Most Amazing Breakfast Cereals," http://holycrap.ca/about-corin-mullins-and-brian-mullins-co-founders-holy-crap-cereal/.

55. *Small Business Statistics*, Statistics Canada, July 2009.

56. Ibid.

57. *Women in Management 9*, no. 2 (University of Western Ontario, December–January 1999), p. 2.

58. *Small Business Quarterly*, Industry Canada, February 2009, p. 1.

59. *Small Business Quarterly*, Industry Canada, August 2009, p. 2.

60. Jim McElgunn, "Canada's Top Female Entrepreneurs, 2012: Overview, October 1, 2012, www.profitguide.com/manage-grow/success-stories/canada%E2%80%99s-top-female-entrepreneurs-2012-overview-41318.

61. CIBC World Markets, *Small Business in Canada, Trends & Prospects*, September 2006.

62. "Canadian Small Business—A Growing Force," *CIBC World Markets*, September 2006, p. 2.

63. *Key Small Business Statistics*, Statistics Canada, July 2012, www.ic.gc.ca/eic/site/061.nsf/eng/02720.html.

64. Zoltan J. Acs and David B. Audretsch, "Innovation in Large and Small Firms," *The American Economic Review* © 1988, www.jstor.org/action/showPublisher?publisherCode=aea%, p. 678; and "Small Business Resource," www.2-small-business.com.

65. Small Business Innovations Institute, *Intuit* (Palo Alto: California, 2009).

66. *CFIB Small Business Profile*, December 2009, p. 2.

67. HootSuite, http://hootsuite.com/leadership; Trevor Melanson, "Is HootSuite Canada's Next Billion-Dollar Tech Titan?" January 9, 2013, www.canadianbusiness.com/technology-news/is-hootsuite-|canadas-next-tech-titan; "11 Questions for Ryan Holmes," March 5, 2013, www.huffingtonpost.ca/2013/03/05/11-questions-for-ryan-holmes-hootsuite_n_2793294.html.

68. Peters and Waterman, *In Search of Excellence*.

69. Ibid.

70. Shannon Skinner, "Extraordinary Women: TV," www.extraordinarywomentv.com/category/.../entrepreneurs/.

71. *Statistics on Foreign Ownership, Small versus Large* (Ottawa: Statistics Canada, Inter-Corporate Ownership, 1984), p. 252.

72. "Would You Want Your Son to Marry a Marketing Lady?" *Journal of Marketing*, January 1977, pp. 15–18.

73. Ivan I. Stefanovic, "Sidestepping Socialism in Yugoslavia," *Venture*, September 1984, p. 60.

74. *Global Entrepreneurship Monitor*, London Business School, Summer 2000.

75. Frank Condron, "Philanthropy: Small Business, Big Difference," October 10, 2012, www.profitguide.com/news/philanthropy-small-business-big-difference-41921.

76. Ten Tree Apparel, www.tentree.org/about; and www.tentree.org/dragons-den.

77. Randall Litchfield, "Turn Change into Advantage," *Small Business*, June 1989, p. 19.

78. Robert D. Hisrich, Michael P. Peters, Dean A. Shepherd, and Peter Mombourquette, Entrepreneurship, 2nd Canadian edition (Toronto: McGraw-Hill Ryerson Ltd., 2009), p. 75.

79. "Canadian Small Business—A Growing Force," *CIBC World Markets*, September 2003, p. 2.

80. "Opportunity 2013: Gen Y Enters Its Family Years," December 14, 2012, www.profitguide.com/opportunity/opportunity-2013-the-gen-y-family-45593.

81. *North America Free Trade Agreement*, Chapter 10.

82. *North America Free Trade Agreement*, Chapter 3.

83. *North America Free Trade Agreement*, Articles 1202 and 1204.

84. Joe Dangor, "Thriving on Change," *Small Business Magazine*, June 1989, " p. 32.

85. Alain Hailley, *A Study of Outsourcing of Canadian Business*, Montreal, 2000.

86. Angus Reid Studies, June 2009.

87. GEM Report in Business Research Newsletter, February 28, 2005, p. 2.

88. World Bank, "Doing Business" as reported in *Small Business Quarterly*, November 2008, p. 8.

89. *Growing Small Business*, p. 1.

90. John Bulloch, "Policy Guidelines to Help Make Your Venture Work," *The Financial Post Special Report*, November 24, 1984, p. 53.

91. CFIB, "Prosperity Restricted by Red Tape," January 2010.

92. *Growing Small Business*.

93. "Canada's Red Tape Report with U.S. Comparisons," www.cfib-fcei.ca/english/article/4791-canada-s-red-tape-report-with-u-s-comparisons.html.

94. *Profits*, Business Development Bank of Canada, Winter 1999, p. 2.

95. "Canadian Small Business—A Growing Force," *CIBC World Markets*, September 2003, p. 2.

CHAPTER 2

1. Frank Condron, "Canada's Young Entrepreneur of the Year, 2012," December 5, 2012, www.profitguide.com/manage-grow/innovation/canadas-young-entrepreneur-of-the-year-2012-44540; and Frank Condron, "Q&A: The Game Changer—Chris Ye," November 26, 2012, www.profitguide.com/startup/best-practices/fuel-award-winners-startup-lessons-chris-ye-44098.

2. Mathew Ingram, "Uken Games Lets You Take Your Game with You," October 15, 2010, http://gigaom.com/2010/10/15/uken-games-lets-you-take-your-game-with-you/; and Frank Condron, "Q&A: The Game Changer—Chris Ye," November 26, 2012, www.profitguide.com/startup/best-practices/fuel-award-winners-startup-lessons-chris-ye-44098.

3. Frank Condron, "Canada's Young Entrepreneur of the Year, 2012," December 5, 2012, www.profitguide.com/manage-grow/innovation/canadas-young-entrepreneur-of-the-year-2012-44540.

4. Frank Condron, "Canada's Young Entrepreneur of the Year, 2012," December 5, 2012, www.profitguide.com/manage-grow/innovation/canadas-young-entrepreneur-of-the-year-2012-44540; Mathew Ingram, "Uken Games Lets You Take Your Game with You," October 15, 2010, http://gigaom.com/2010/10/15/uken-games-lets-you-take-your-game-with-you/; and Herbert Lui, "How to Stay Hyper-Competitive: Secrets from Uken Games," August 8, 2012, www.techvibes.com/blog/how-to-stay-hyper-competitive-secrets-from-uken-games-2012-08-08.

5. Herbert Lui, "How to Stay Hyper-Competitive: Secrets from Uken Games," August 8, 2012, www.techvibes.com/blog/how-to-stay-hyper-competitive-secrets-from-uken-games-2012-08-08; and Frank Condron, "Q&A: The Game Changer—Chris Ye," November 26, 2012, www.profitguide.com/startup/best-practices/fuel-award-winners-startup-lessons-chris-ye-44098.

6. "*Inc. and U.S.A. Today* Survey of 500 Fastest Growing Private Companies," *Inc.*, June 1986, p. 48.

7. Kenzie MacDonald, in-class presentation, "Small Business Management," Mount Saint Vincent University, May 2010, Halifax, Nova Scotia.

8. Frank Condron, "Bill Hennessey, 2012 Fuel Award Winner," December 12, 2012,

www.profitguide.com/startup/success-stories/qa-bill-hennessey-2012-fuel-award-winner-45073.

9. CIBC World Markets, January 2005, p. 4.
10. Pat Thompson, "Characteristics of the Small Business Entrepreneur in Canada," *Journal of Small Business and Entrepreneurship,* vol. 4, no. 3 (Winter 1986–87), p. 5.
11. Frank Condron, "Ronald Richardson, 2012 Fuel Award Winner," December 12, 2012, www.profitguide.com/startup/success-stories/qa-ronald-richardson-2012-fuel-award-winner-45078.
12. "Small Business Starting Out: Accidental Entrepreneurs Find Purpose and Success," http://m.theglobeandmail.com/report-on-business/small-business/starting-out/accidental-entrepreneurs-find-purpose-and-success/article7509740/?service=mobile.
13. *The Globe and Mail,* April 17, 1995, p. B4.
14. Karl Vesper, "Freedom and Power: What Every Entrepreneur Craves," *Success,* May 1988, p. 48.
15. Frank Condron, "Reid Campbell, 2012 Fuel Award Winner," December 12, 2012, www.profitguide.com/startup/success-stories/qa-reid-campbell-2012-fuel-award-winner-44933.
16. As reported in *Costco Connection,* September/October, 2003.
17. Linsey Knerl, "5 Successful Mompreneurs," January 11, 2011, www.nbcnews.com/id/40969268/ns/business-small_business/t/successful-mompreneurs/.
18. The Mompreneur website, www.themompreneur.com.
19. Linsey Knerl, "5 Successful Mompreneurs," January 11, 2011, www.nbcnews.com/id/40969268/ns/business-small_business/t/successful-mompreneurs/.
20. GEM Report as reported in *Business Research Newsletter,* February 2005, p. 6.
21. David P. Boyd and David E. Gumpert, "Coping with Entrepreneurial Stress," *Harvard Business Review,* March–April 1983, pp. 44–64.
22. "Small Business Starting Out: Accidental Entrepreneurs Find Purpose and Success," http://m.theglobeandmail.com/report-on-business/small-business/starting-out/accidental-entrepreneurs-find-purpose-and-success/article7509740/?service=mobile.
23. Public lecture, Mount Saint Vincent University, October 22, 2011.
24. "*Inc.* and *U.S.A. Today* Survey of 500 Fastest Growing Private Companies."
25. RBC Study, as reported in *Business Research Newsletter,* February 2005, p. 5.
26. *Statistics Canada Survey of Employment,* July 2008, p. 10.
27. *Small Business Quarterly,* vol. 5, no. 3, November 2003, p. 6.

28. *Small Business Statistics,* Statistics Canada, July 2008.
29. *Key Small Business Statistics,* Statistics Canada, July 2012, www.ic.gc.ca/eic/site/061.nsf/eng/02726.html.
30. *Small Business Quarterly,* Statistics Canada, August 2010.
31. "State of the Entrepreneur Nation," www.profitguide.com/news/state-of-the-entrepreneur-nation-41932.
32. *Small Business Quarterly,* vol. 5, no. 3, November 2008, p. 6.
33. *Profit,* June 1993, p. 49.
34. Ali Asaria, www.aliasaria.ca/.
35. Ali Asaria, www.aliasaria.ca/; and Virginia Galt, "A Case Study on Luring Investment Angels," September 20, 2010, /www.theglobeandmail.com/report-on-business/small-business/sb-money/business-funding/a-case-study-on-luring-investment-angels/article555794/.
36. Virginia Galt, "A Case Study on Luring Investment Angels," September 20, 2010, /www.theglobeandmail.com/report-on-business/small-business/sb-money/business-funding/a-case-study-on-luring-investment-angels/article555794/.
37. *The Globe and Mail,* June 17, 1995, p. B5.
38. *Self-Employment in Canada—Trends and Prospects,* CIBC Economic Analysis, December 2000, p. 16.
39. *Small Business Quarterly,* Industry Canada, August 2008, p. 5.
40. *Small Business Quarterly,* Industry Canada, November 2009, p. 2.
41. Ibid; and Canadian Entrepreneurship Status, 2010, www.bdc.ca/Resources%20Manager/misc/CES_2010_EN%20Final.pdf.
42. Kathleen Martin, "Reinventing Yourself," www.progressmedia.ca/article/2011/12/reinventing-yourself.
43. T. Corcoran, "Entrepreneurial Drive, and Innovation," *National Post,* December 1, 2009, p. 1.
44. Brett Wilson, "Calgary Business Experts Encourage Risk Taking," April 26, 2012, www.itbusiness.ca/news/calgary-business-experts-encourage-risk-taking/17353.
45. "Ontario Entrepreneur of the Year: Risk Taker Has Midas Touch?" October 23, 2012, http://business.financialpost.com/2012/10/23/ontario-entrepreneur-of-the-year-risk-taker-has-midas-touch/?__lsa=a1a9-eaec.
46. Amex, December 2005, as reported in GDSourcing.com, January 2006.
47. Charles A. Garfield, *Peak Performers* (New York: William Morrow, 1985).
48. "Networking and the Art of the Pitch," March 25, 2013, www.cybf.ca/cybf_press_media/networking-and-the-art-of-the-pitch/.
49. Thompson, "Characteristics of the Small Business Entrepreneur in Canada."
50. Frank Condron, "Derrick Fung, 2012 Fuel Award Winner," December 12, 2012,

www.profitguide.com/news/profile-derrick-fung-2012-fuel-award-winner-45297.
51. "A Nation of Entrepreneurs," *Report on Business Magazine,* October 1988.
52. *Self-Employment in Canada—Trends and Prospects,* CIBC Economic Analysis, December 2000, p. 16.
53. *Canadian Economic Observer,* November 1997, Statistics Canada, Catalogue #11-010-XPB, p. 19.
54. "Networking and the Art of the Pitch," March 25, 2013, www.cybf.ca/cybf_press_media/networking-and-the-art-of-the-pitch/.
55. Janet MacMillan, class presentation October 2012.
56. Carter Henderson, *Winners: The Successful Strategies Entrepreneurs Use to Build New Businesses* (New York: Holt, Rinehart and Winston, 1985), p. 178.
57. John Lorinc, "Rethink Your Business Like It's Brand New," October 22, 2012, www.profitguide.com/manage-grow/innovation/rethink-your-business-like-its-brand-new-42218.
58. Ibid.
59. Schleese Saddlery Services, www.profitguide.com/microsite/profitw100/2011/94-Schleese-Saddlery-Service.
60. Rob Lewis, "Canadian Entrepreneur on Raising Venture Capital at Age 17," January 16, 2013, www.techvibes.com/blog/canadian-entrepreneur-on-raising-venture-capital-at-age-17-2013-01-16.
61. Sarah Perez, "AppHero Raises $1.8 Million for App Recommendation Service Which Learns Your Interests from Facebook," July 5, 2012, http://techcrunch.com/2012/07/05/apphero-raises-1-8-million-for-app-recommendation-service-which-learns-your-interests-from-facebook/; and Rob Lewis, "Canadian Entrepreneur on Raising Venture Capital at Age 17," January 16, 2013, www.techvibes.com/blog/canadian-entrepreneur-on-raising-venture-capital-at-age-17-2013-01-16.
62. Jeffrey A. Timmons, Leonard E. Smollen, and Alexander L. M. Dingee, *New Venture Creation: A Guide to Entrepreneurship* (Homewood, Illinois: Richard D. Irwin, 1985), p. 28.
63. Jeffry Tannenbaum, "On Their Own," *Wall Street Journal,* May 21, 1998, p. R20.
64. Joel Corman and Robert Lussier, *Entrepreneurial New Ventures* (Cincinnati, Ohio: Thomson Learning, 2001), pp. 1–18.

CHAPTER 3

1. Entrepreneur of the Year, 2012, www.ey.com/CA/en/About-us/Entrepreneurship/Entrepreneur-Of-The-Year/2012-EOY-National-Winners.

2. Deborah Aarts, "Advice You Should Ignore," April 1, 2013, www.profitguide.com/industry-focus/retail/advice-you-should-ignore-49929.

3. Life Choices Foods, www.lifechoicesfoods.com.

4. Terry Lee, "New Electronic Parking Pay Stations in Appleton Bring in More Than Twice the Haul," March 14, 2013, wydrthedrive.com/news/articles/2013/mar/14/new-electronic-parking-pay-stations-in-appleton-bring-in-more-than-twice-the-haul/; and Digital Payment Technologies, www.digitalpaytech.com/aboutus.

5. "Who We Are: The Fox 40 Story," www.fox40world.com/index.cfm?pagepath=ABOUT_US/Who_We_Are__The_Fox_40_Story&id=4099.

6. Frank Condron, "Michael Kaye, 2012 Fuel Award Winner," December 12, 2012, www.profitguide.com/news/profile-michael-kaye-2012-fuel-award-winner-44620.

7. "Gord Dickie: Sometimes You Don't Have to Talk," www.bluteaudevenney.com/business-insights/gord-dickie-sometimes-you-dont-have-to-talk.html.

8. "Blade Runner on Ice," www.progressmedia.ca/article/2011/11/small-business-blade-runner-ice.

9. *Micro-Enterprises Survey 2000, A Progress Report.* Industry Canada, June 7, 2001, p. 10.

10. *Small Business Quarterly,* Industry Canada, August 2008, p. 2.

11. *The Financial Post,* October 29, 1994, p. S24.

12. Ryan Charkow, "5 Young Canadian Entrepreneurs Reveal Secrets to Success," October 6, 2011, www.cbc.ca/news/business/smallbusiness/story/2011/09/28/f-smallbiz-young-entrepreneurs.html; and Sassy Cassy's, Boots, www.sassycassys.com/business-fraser-valley-article/.

13. *Market Research Handbook,* 2009, Statistics Canada; Metro Toronto Information, 2009; and *Average Household Expenditures, 2009,* Statistics Canada.

14. Frank Condron, "Growing Great Ideas," June 28, 2012, www.profitguide.com/manage-grow/innovation/growing-great-ideas-36633.

15. Canadian Franchise Association website, 2010.

16. Innovate Calgary, www.innovatecalgary.com/Learn-About-Us.

17. Canadian Association of Business Incubation, www.cabi.ca/business-incubation.php.

18. National Business Incubation Association website, January 2010.

19. "Incubator Update," *Inc.,* January 1993, p. 49.

20. Canadian Association of Business Incubation, website, 2010.

21. Ibid.

22. Kim Hart McNeill, "A New Way to Kickstart a Business," September 5, 2012, www.profitguide.com/startup/best-practices/mass-appeals-40210; "Awkward, Clunky and Just Plain Ugly: The Cane Gets a Much Needed Makeover," May 6, 2013, www.theglobeandmail.com/report-on-business/small-business/starting-out/awkward-clunky-and-just-plain-ugly-the-cane-gets-a-much-needed-makeover/article11730586/.

23. Brenda Bouw, "Here's a Twist: Developers Ask Residents What Stores They Want," April 15, 2013, www.theglobeandmail.com/report-on-business/small-business/starting-out/heres-a-twist-developers-ask-residents-what-stores-they-want/article11165548/.

24. Jeff Quipp, "Adapt or Die: The Revolution in Marketing," February 26, 2013, www.profitguide.com/manage-grow/sales-marketing/market-research-through-social-networking-has-limits-30340.

25. Lyndsie Bourgon, "The No-Money Startup Miracle," January 3, 2013, www.profitguide.com/startup/best-practices/the-no-money-startup-miracle-45604; and Jeff Quipp, "Adapt or Die: The Revolution in Marketing," February 26, 2013, www.profitguide.com/manage-grow/sales-marketing/market-research-through-social-networking-has-limits-30340.

CHAPTER 4

1. *Business Research Newsletter,* GDSourcing.com, vol. 3, no. 12, November, 2000, p. 9.

2. 1-800-Got-Junk?, www.entrepreneur.com/franchises/1800gotjunk/293278-0.html#.

3. Joe Mancuso, president of the Centre for Entrepreneurial Management.

4. "Secrets of Successful Business Planning," *Profit,* March 2007, p. 35.

5. Donald Rumball, *The Entrepreneurial Edge* (Toronto: Key Porter Books, 1989), pp. 225–33.

6. Adapted from "Success Story: Strategic Planning Sharpens Jonoke Software's Competitive Edge," *Business Development Bank of Canada newsletter,* March 2009, p. 1.

7. Will Moniz, "Young Entrepreneur Profile: Notable TV's Julian Brass," August 5, 2009, http://talentegg.ca/incubator/2009/08/05/young-entrepreneur-profile-notabletvs-julian-brass/.

8. Mount Saint Vincent University Business and Tourism, March 8, 2013, www.youtube.com/watch?v=rZAKSPogwYE.

9. Classroom presentation, Mount Saint Vincent University, October 2012.

10. "Secrets of Successful Business Planning," *Profit,* March 2007, p. 35.

11. Will Moniz, "Young Entrepreneur Profile: Notable TV's Julian Brass," August 5, 2009, http://talentegg.ca/incubator/2009/08/05/young-entrepreneur-profile-notabletvs-julian-brass/.

12. C. Bart, "Words to Grow By," *Profit,* March 2006, p. 66.

13. Shockbox, *Dragon's Den,* November 25, 2012, www.cbc.ca/dragonsden/2012/11/shockbox.html.

14. Russ Bitely, "Making Sensor Out of Concussions," February 29, 2012, www.examiner.com/article/making-sensor-out-of-concussions.

15. Shockbox, *Dragon's Den,* November 25, 2012, www.cbc.ca/dragonsden/2012/11/shockbox.html.

16. Jerry White, "Canada's Free Trade Winners," *Small Business Magazine,* July–August 1990, p. 38.

17. Robert Morent, "Seven Principles of Admirable Business Ethics," About.com website, 2010.

18. Edmee Metivier, "Against the Grain," Business Development Bank of Canada website, 2010.

19. *Ipsos-Reid SOHO Syndicated Study,* 2001.

20. *Small Business Statistics,* Statistics Canada, July 2008.

21. *Profit,* December–January 1998, p. 46.

22. *The Globe and Mail,* April 10, 1995, p. B6.

23. PublicServicePrep, About Us, www.publicserviceprep.com/Public/about.aspx; and Kim Shiffman, "5 Smart Strategies of Super Startups," June 11, 2007, www.profitguide.com/startup/best-practices/5-smart-strategies-of-super-startups-29182.

24. *Small Business Quarterly,* Industry Canada, February 2009, p. 9.

25. *The Globe and Mail,* June 19, 1995, p. B7.

26. Just Us! Coffee Roasters Co-op, About Us, www.justuscoffee.com/our-co-op/beginnings.

27. "Secrets of Successful Business Planning," *Profit,* March 2007, p. 35.

CHAPTER 5

1. Harvey Schachter, "Don't Grow It . . . Buy It," *Profit,* June 1998, p. 161.

2. Joanna Pachner, "Breakthrough: Dealmaker Slays His Competition with One Perfect Purchase," February 21, 2013, www.profitguide.com/manage-grow/success-stories/big-moments-in-entrepreneurial-lives-48565.

3. Adapted from Cheryl Devoe Kim, "Takeover Helps Company Meet Its Target," *The Globe and Mail,* March 24, 2009, pp. 1–3.

4. Chris Atchison, "Acquisitions: Buying a Business," December 8, 2011, www.

profitguide.com/manage-grow/strategy-operations/acquisitions-buying-a-business-30314.

5. Used with the permission of Karina Birch and Cameron Baty and the Rocky Mountain Soap Company website, 2010.
6. Chris Atchison, "How to Acquire Your Worst Enemy," April 5, 2013, www.profitguide.com/manage-grow/strategy-operations/how-to-acquire-your-worst-enemy-49866.
7. Ibid.
8. Chris Atchison, "Acquisitions: Buying a Business," December 8, 2011, www.profitguide.com/manage-grow/strategy-operations/acquisitions-buying-a-business-30314.
9. Ibid.
10. Ibid.
11. Ibid.
12. Grant Thornton LLP Study as reported on *About Small Business,* February, 2007.
13. Joanne Pachner, "Want to Buy a Business?" *Report on Business,* November 19, 2009, p. 2.
14. Peter Thomas, "Negotiate to Win," *Profit,* October 1991, p. 34.
15. Ian Portsmouth, "Ask the Legends: Mac Voisin," February 16, 2011, www.profitguide.com/manage-grow/leadership/ask-the-legends-mac-voisin-30092.
16. James Foster, "Franchises Lead to Business Careers," *New Brunswick Business Journal,* January 17, 2009, pp. 1–2.
17. Noemi LoPinto, "The Joy of Giving," *Alberta Venture,* July 2007, pp. 11–12; and Basket Boutique website, 2010.
18. *The Globe and Mail,* October 1995, p. B7.
19. Franchise Law e-Communique, April 4, 2013, www.casselsbrock.com/CBNewsletter/Franchise_Law_e_COMMUNIQUE___April_2013.
20. Frank Zaid, "Mediation and Arbitration of Franchise Disputes—The Path of the Future," February 2012, www.oba.org/en/pdf/sec_news_adr_feb12_Franchise_Art.pdf.
21. Faye Rice, "How to Succeed at Cloning a Small Business," *Fortune,* October 28, 1985, p. 60.
22. *Franchising in the Canadian Economy 1990–92,* Canadian Franchise Association and Price Waterhouse, 1992.
23. *Canadian Capabilities: Key Facts about Canadian Franchise Expertise,* Industry Canada, March 4, 1998, p. 1.
24. Franchising in Canada website, October 2006.
25. Canadian Franchise Association website, 2010.
26. Gordon Brockhouse, "The Franchise Advantage," *Small Business Magazine,* July–August 1990, p. 48.
27. *Franchising in the Canadian Economy 1990–1992* (Toronto: Canadian Franchise Association and Price Waterhouse), p. 3.
28. Tom Hortons, FAQs, www.timhortons.com/ca/en/join/franchise-ca-faq.html.

29. Eve Lazarus, "Building the Perfect Franchise," February 9, 2006, www.profitguide.com/manage-grow/strategy-operations/building-the-perfect-franchise-28811.
30. Ibid.
31. Joanna Pachner, "Secrets of the Sunshine Girl," February 18, 2010, www.profitguide.com/manage-grow/success-stories/secrets-of-the-sunshine-girl-29689.
32. Tony Martin, "Love Thy Franchisees," April 30, 2008, www.profitguide.com/manage-grow/strategy-operations/love-thy-franchisees-29388.
33. Ibid.
34. Rice, "How to Succeed at Cloning a Small Business."
35. Adapted from "Smoothie Chain Booster Juice Finds Expanding Globally Is Not Always Smooth," *Canadian Business,* January 30–February 12; Mark Sutcliffe, "Booster Juice Founder," *Ottawa Citizen,* September 12, 2007; and the Booster Juice website, 2010.
36. Elizabeth Sile, "Edible Arrangements in Legal Hot Water," July 22, 2011, www.inc.com/news/articles/201107/edible-arrangements-lawsuit.html.
37. Eve Lazarus, "Building the Perfect Franchise," February 9, 2006, www.profitguide.com/manage-grow/strategy-operations/building-the-perfect-franchise-28811.
38. David Joseph, "Why I Sold My Kumon Franchise," April 26, 2010, www.franchisepublicity.com/kumon-"why-i-sold-my-kumon-franchise.
39. "Reading the Fine Print," *CBC Venture,* February 2000.
40. U.S. Department of Commerce, *Franchising in the Economy, 1977–79* (Washington, D.C.: U.S. Government Printing Office, 1981), Table 3, p. 34.
41. Andraya Frith, Jennifer Dolman, Gillian S.G. Scott, Evan Thomas, and Frank Zaid, "Franchising in the Courts," www.osler.com/NewsResources/Default.aspx?id=3136.
42. Ibid.
43. *Machias v. Mr. Submarine Ltd.,* April 2, 2002, www.intelligentfranchising.com/case22.html.
44. "A&W CEO Kevin Bazner Responds to Unhappyfranchisee.com," August 15, 2012, www.unhappyfranchisee.com/category/franchisor/aw-restaurants-franchise/.
45. Rice, "How to Succeed at Cloning a Small Business."
46. Kenneth Barnes and Everett Banning, *Money Makers: The Secrets of Canada's Most Successful Entrepreneurs* (Toronto: McClelland and Stewart, 1985), p. 84.
47. Adapted from Derek Sankey, "Life's a Beach for High-Tech Spa Franchisee," *Financial Post,* February 23, 2009, pp. 1–2.
48. Kenneth Barnes and Everett Banning, *Money Makers: The Secrets of Canada's*

Most Successful Entrepreneurs (Toronto: McClelland and Stewart, 1985), p. 72.
49. Ibid., p. 144.
50. Eve Lazarus, "Building the Perfect Franchise," February 9, 2006, www.profitguide.com/manage-grow/strategy-operations/building-the-perfect-franchise-28811.
51. Ibid.
52. Joanna Pachner, "Secrets of the Sunshine Girl," February 18, 2010, www.profitguide.com/manage-grow/success-stories/secrets-of-the-sunshine-girl-29689.

CHAPTER 6

1. Kim Girard, "Razor Suleman, CEO of I Love Rewards, on Engaging Employees," March 4, 2011, http://digitalpuck.ca/the-digital-puck/razor-suleman-ceo-of-i-love-rewards-on-engaging-employees/; and "I Love Rewards Is Now Achievers," September 18, 2011, www.achievers.com/about-us/press-release/i-love-rewards-now-achievers.
2. Kim Girard, "Razor Suleman, CEO of I Love Rewards, on Engaging Employees," March 4, 2011, http://digitalpuck.ca/the-digital-puck/razor-suleman-ceo-of-i-love-rewards-on-engaging-employees/.
3. *The Canadian Business Failure Record, 1999* (Toronto: Dun and Bradstreet Business Education Division, 1998).
4. "Small and Medium Sized Enterprise Financing in Canada," www.sme-fdi.gc.ca/eic/site/sme_fdi-prf_pme.nsf/eng/01052.html; and "Access to Finance for the Small and Medium Sized Enterprise Sector, Evidence and Conclusions," October 2009, www.cga-canada.org/en-CA/ResearchReports/ca_rep_2009-10_sme_joint.pdf.
5. "Small and Medium Sized Enterprise Financing in Canada," Government of Canada Publication, 2003, p. 58.
6. "The Success Secrets of Gerry Schwartz," May 16, 2011, www.profitguide.com/manage-grow/success-stories/the-success-secrets-of-gerry-schwartz-29394.
7. Rebecca Gardner, "PROFIT 100 Fundraising Secrets," May 10, 2005, www.profitguide.com/manage-grow/financing/profit-100-fundraising-secrets-28646.
8. "CIBC and Advancing Canadian Entrepreneurship Name Amanda Harburn Student Entrepreneur of the Year," May 12, 2004, www.prestigedance.com/downloads/PrestigedanceMedia_CIBC_StudentoftheYear.pdf.
9. "Opportunity 2013: Gen Y Enters Its Family Years," December 14, 2012, www.profitguide.com/opportunity/opportunity-2013-the-gen-y-family-45593; and R. Spence, "Stuck in the Middle," *Profit,* October 2007, p. 17.

10. Armina Ligaya, "The Dark Side of Crowdfunding: Startups Face Unique Hurdles When Turning to the Public for Money," March 13, 2006, http://business.financialpost.com/2013/05/06/crowdfunding-comes-with-its-own-set-of-entrepreneurial-hurdles/.
11. Ibid.
12. Kara Aaserud, "Private Investing: After the Handshake," April 30, 2008, www.profitguide.com/manage-grow/financing/private-investing-after-the-handshake-29390.
13. Ibid.
14. Jim McElgunn, "Financing Strategies for Your Startup," February 6, 2012, www.profitguide.com/startup/best-practices/financing-strategies-for-your-startup-30353.
15. Ibid.
16. Karen Geier, "Your Start-Up Business: How to Find an Angel Investor," January 10, 2013, www.huffingtonpost.ca/karen-geier/angel-investor_b_2210768.html.
17. Eleanor Beaton, "What Investors Want," August 29, 2011, www.profitguide.com/manage-grow/financing/what-investors-want-2-30220.
18. Kim Hart Macneill, "Pitching to an Angel," July 25, 2012, www.profitguide.com/manage-grow/financing/pitching-to-an-angel-38604.
19. Deborah Aarts, "Financing Foreign Sales," December 7, 2011, www.profitguide.com/manage-grow/financing/financing-foreign-sales-30309.
20. Jim McElgunn, "Financing Strategies for Your Startup," February 6, 2012, www.profitguide.com/startup/best-practices/financing-strategies-for-your-startup-30353.
21. "Where's the Money? Angel Investment in Canada," October 19, 2012, www.writeahead.ca/2012/10/19/angel-investment-in-canada/; and "Investment Activity by Canadian Angel Groups," 2011 Report, https://nacocanada.com/wp-content/uploads/2012/12/NACO-2011-Report-Investment-Activity-By-Canadian-Angel-Groups.pdf.
22. Kim Hart Macneill, "Pitching to an Angel," July 25, 2012, www.profitguide.com/manage-grow/financing/pitching-to-an-angel-38604.
23. "Venture Capital: More Money, Still Choosy," *The Magazine That's All about Small Business,* May 1984, p. 49; Canadian Venture Capital Association website, October 2006.
24. "Canada's Venture Capital Market in 2012: VC Investments at $1.5 Billion, Fund Raising Highest Since 2002," February 19, 2013, www.newswire.ca/en/story/1116517/canada-s-venture-capital-market-in-2012-vc-investments-at-1-5-billion-fund-raising-highest-since-2002.

25. Financial Report, September 30, 2012, www.bdc.ca/EN/Documents/doc_corpo/FR_2013_Q2_En.pdf.
26. "Recyc PHP: Of Vision and Volume," April 2008, www.butler-consultants.ca/news_profit.html.
27. *Canadian Year Book 2008,* Statistics Canada, p. 443.
28. Ibid.
29. "Statistics Canada Survey on Financing," as reported in *The Globe and Mail,* March 24, 2006.
30. *Small Business Quarterly,* Industry Canada, May 2009, p. 1.
31. "Venture Survey—Financing," *Venture,* October 1986, p. 24.
32. "Small and Medium Sized Enterprises: Lending and More," October 11, 2012, www.cba.ca/en/media-room/50-backgrounders-on-banking-issues/124-small-and-medium-sized-enterprises.
33. *CFIB Banking Study,* October 7, 2003.
34. Business Development Bank Annual Report 2009.
35. Doug Bruce and Queenie Wong, "Battle of the Banks: How Small Businesses Rate Their Banks," May 2013, www.cfib-fcei.ca/english/article/5171-battle-of-the-banks-how-small-businesses-rate-their-banks.html.
36. "Small and Medium Sized Enterprises: Lending and More," October 11, 2012, www.cba.ca/en/media-room/50-backgrounders-on-banking-issues/124-small-and-medium-sized-enterprises.
37. Doug Bruce and Queenie Wong, "Battle of the Banks: How Small Businesses Rate Their Banks," May 2013, www.cfib-fcei.ca/english/article/5171-battle-of-the-banks-how-small-businesses-rate-their-banks.html.
38. Ibid.
39. "Cozy Corner Saunas: The Relaxation Business That Almost Wasn't," http://s3images.coroflot.com/user_files/individual_files/337558_Dg7vsl2wkdC8BX7xODR6nhDJl.pdf.
40. Canadian Youth Business Foundation, www.cybf.ca/about/.
41. *Business Research Newsletter,* GDSourcing.com, vol. 4, no. 1, June 2001, p. 8.
42. "Canadian Banker's Association Survey, October 2009," CBA website.

CHAPTER 7

1. Spin Master—Company Overview, www.spinmaster.com/company-overview.php.
2. Hollie Shaw, "Spin Master Joins Digital Gaming Ranks," December 21, 2012, http://business.financialpost.com/2012/12/21/spin-master-joins-digital-gaming-ranks/; and Kate

Rockwood, "How Spin Master Mixes Tech and Toys—and Keeps Mattel Looking over Its Shoulder," April 1, 2010, www.fastcompany.com/1579439/how-spin-master-mixes-tech-and-toys%E2%80%94and-keeps-mattel-looking-over-its-shoulder.
3. Hollie Shaw, "Spin Master Joins Digital Gaming Ranks," December 21, 2012, http://business.financialpost.com/2012/12/21/spin-master-joins-digital-gaming-ranks/.
4. Lisa Shepherd, "Why Your B2B Company Needs a Marketing Plan," November 2, 2010, www.profitguide.com/manage-grow/strategy-operations/why-your-b2b-company-needs-a-marketing-plan-30399.
5. "7 Sales Strategies of High-Growth Companies," June 3, 2013, www.profitguide.com/manage-grow/sales-marketing/the-7-best-sales-tactics-of-high-growth-companies-53035.
6. Lisa Shepherd, "Why Your B2B Company Needs a Marketing Plan," November 2, 2010, www.profitguide.com/manage-grow/strategy-operations/why-your-b2b-company-needs-a-marketing-plan-30399.
7. Ibid.
8. Jim Barber, "Profile of a Kingston Entrepreneur: Mann Mediation," March 18, 2013, http://kingstonentrepreneurs.ca/success-stories/profile-of-a-kingston-entrepreneur-mann-mediation/.
9. P. Crescoe, *The Mavericks* (Toronto: McGraw-Hill Ryerson Ltd., 1999), pp. 311–312.
10. "Great Ideas: Smart Marketing for Startups," October 17, 2010, www.profitguide.com/startup/best-practices/great-ideas-smart-marketing-for-startups-29376.
11. Class presentation and interview, 2012.
12. Adapted from *Profit Magazine,* "Entrepreneur's Diversification Strategy Takes Off," Business Development Bank of Canada, Fall 2009, pp. 12–13.
13. Adapted from Rhona Macinnes, "The Loyalty Puzzle," *Grocer Today,* January–February 2008, pp. 10–12.
14. "Neil Patel (entrepreneur)," http://en.wikipedia.org/wiki/Neil_Patel_%28entrepreneur%29.
15. *Marketing,* Fourth Canadian Edition (Toronto: McGraw-Hill Ryerson, 1997).
16. "All in the Family," *BDC Success Stories,* p. 3, and the Olivier Soapery website, 2010.
17. Lawrence N. Stevenson, Joseph C. Shlesinger, and Michael R. Pierce, *Power Retail: Winning Strategies from Chapters and Other Leading Retailers in Canada* (Toronto: McGraw-Hill Ryerson, 1999), p. 67.

CHAPTER 8

1. Shopify—Company Overview, www.crunchbase.com/company/shopify.
2. Mark Anderson, "Canada's Smartest Company: Shopify," November 28, 2012, www.profitguide.com/industry-focus/technology/canadas-smartest-company-44283.
3. Duryee, Tricia, "Shopify Picks Up $15 Million As It Faces New Competition from eBay," October 17, 2011, http://allthingsd.com/20111017/shopifys-picks-up-15-million-as-it-faces-new-competition-from-ebay/.
4. Mark Anderson, "Canada's Smartest Company: Shopify," November 28, 2012, www.profitguide.com/industry-focus/technology/canadas-smartest-company-44283.
5. "Shopify—Build a Business," www.shopify.ca/build-a-business.
6. Samantha Burns, "Announcing Shopify's 3rd Build-a-Business Competition Winners," April 24, 2013, www.shopify.ca/blog/7751369-announcing-shopifys-3rd-build-a-business-competition-winners#axzz2hKAnFFsk.
7. Mark Anderson, "Canada's Smartest Company: Shopify," November 28, 2012, www.profitguide.com/industry-focus/technology/canadas-smartest-company-44283.
8. Duryee, Tricia, "Shopify Picks Up $15 Million As It Faces New Competition from eBay," October 17, 2011, http://allthingsd.com/20111017/shopifys-picks-up-15-million-as-it-faces-new-competition-from-ebay/.
9. Everet M. Rogers with F. Floyd Shoemaker, *Communication of Innovation* (New York: Free Press, 1971), p. 270.
10. David Kates, "Unique Idea Strategy Fuel Game Cafe's Success," April 17, 2012, http://o.canada.com/life/unique-idea-strategy-fuel-game-cafes-success/.
11. Rimroller—Company website, http://www.rimroller.com/.
12. GoTire—Company website, http://gotire.com/.
13. A. Holloway, "Try It! You'll Like It," *Profit,* November 2006, p. 65.
14. "Profit 100 Growth Strategies," *Profit,* November 2007, p. 17.
15. Rachel Beck, "Spin Master Toys Soars to Success with Air Hogs," *Los Angeles Times,* March 24, 1999, http://articles.latimes.com/1999/mar/24/business/fi-20523.
16. "Dynamic Pricing Helps Keep Pack with Savvy Consumers," May 17, 2013, www.emarketer.com/Article/Dynamic-Pricing-Helps-Keep-Pace-with-Savvy-Consumers/1009897.
17. Noel Hulsman, "Why Canada Goose Will Never Go on Sale," January 16, 2013, http://ca.finance.yahoo.com/blogs/insight/why-canada-goose-never-sale-171840302.html.
18. John Lorinc, "Case Study: Sweet Tooth," February 11, 2013, http://www.profitguide.com/?p= 47908&preview=true.
19. Laura Pratt, "Profit Hot 50: Safer Passage," August 31, 2009, www.profitguide.com/manage-grow/success-stories/profit-hot-50-safer-passage-29600.
20. Eleanor Beaton, "Sell More, Spend Less on Marketing," March 1, 2009, www.profitguide.com/manage-grow/sales-marketing/marketing-painless-promotion-29890.
21. Kim Shiffman, "3 Deadly Pricing Sins," May 27, 2013, www.profitguide.com/manage-grow/sales-marketing/3-deadly-pricing-sins-52300.
22. Ibid.
23. Rick Spence, "The 5 Winning Strategies of High-Growth Companies," June 1, 2011, www.profitguide.com/opportunity/the-5-winning-strategies-of-high-growth-companies-30184.
24. Susanne Baillie, "How to Measure Your Marketing Effectiveness," Februrary 2, 2004, www.profitguide.com/manage-grow/sales-marketing/how-to-measure-your-marketing-effectiveness-28401.
25. Ryan Lum, "Agency News: Interview with Calum McGuigan, Founder of Fervent Events," June 28, 2011, www.creativeguerrillamarketing.com/guerrilla-marketing-agency-news/agency-news-interview-calum-mcguigan-founder-fervent-events/.
26. Ibid.
27. Eleanor Beaton, "How to Sell More, More, More," May 27, 2010, www.profitguide.com/manage-grow/sales-marketing/sales-marketing-how-to-sell-more-more-more-29740.
28. Elaine Davidson, "Two Steps at a Time," January 3, 2004, http://albertaventure.com/2004/01/two-steps-at-a-time/.
29. Kathryn Lamb, "Lululemon and FITiST Team Up to Give Free Yoga Classes in January" (Video), January 5, 2013, www.examiner.com/article/lululemon-and-fitist-team-up-to-give-free-yoga-classes-january.
30. Emily Wexler, "Brands of the Year: Lululemon Takes Local to the Next Level," September 28, 2012, http://strategyonline.ca/2012/09/28/brands-of-the-year-lululemon-takes-local-to-the-next-level/.
31. CBC News, "Stealth Marketing," May 16, 2011, www.cbc.ca/player/News/Technology+and+Science/Audio/ID/1928239861/?page= 11&sort=MostPopular.
32. "Stealth Marketing – the 21st Century Con," June 7, 2011, http://ethicstechnologyandsociety.wordpress.com/2011/06/07/stealth-marketing-the-21st-century-con/.
33. CBC News, "Stealth Marketing," May 16, 2011, www.cbc.ca/player/News/Technology+and+Science/Audio/ID/1928239861/?page= 11&sort=MostPopular.
34. "Stealth Marketing – the 21st Century Con," June 7, 2011, http://ethicstechnologyandsociety.wordpress.com/2011/06/07/stealth-marketing-the-21st-century-con/.
35. Pamela Bartlett, "How Public Relations Can Help Your Small Business Grow," 2013, www.prnewswire.com/knowledge-center/small-business-pr/How-Public-Relations-Can-Help-Your-Small-Business-Grow.html.
36. Brett Nelson, "Bang for Your Marketing Buck," June 9, 2005, www.forbes.com/2005/09/06/marketing-advertising-entrepreneurs-cx_bn_0906marketing.html.
37. Ibid.
38. Stilt Guys website, "Dragons' Den Effect," October 27, 2012, http://stiltguys.com/2012/10/27/dragons-den-effect/.
39. Jason Buckland, "How the Dragons' Den Effect Works," April 19, 2012, http://money.ca.msn.com/small-business/insight/how-the-dragons%e2%80%99-den-effect-works.
40. Ibid.
41. Eleanor Beaton, "How to Sell More, More, More," May 27, 2010, www.profitguide.com/manage-grow/sales-marketing/sales-marketing-how-to-sell-more-more-more-29740.
42. Interview with Chris Neville, Halifax, Nova Scotia, June 20, 2013.
43. Notable.ca, "Tina Kastana: Today's Notable Young Entrepreneurs," June 5, 2013, http://notable.ca/nationwide/entrepreneurs/Tina-Kastana-Todays-Notable-Young-Entrepreneur/.
44. CNW.ca, "eBay Recognizes Canadian Excellence in eCommerce," October 1, 2012, www.newswire.ca/en/story/1044659/ebay-recognizes-canadian-excellence-in-ecommerce.
45. Fou Fou Dog—company website, www.foufoudog.com.
46. Alexa—Top Sites by Country, www.alexa.com/topsites/countries/CA.
47. Laura Hazard Owen, "LinkedIn Earnings Up As Membership Hits 120 Million and Mobile Usage Soars," August 5, 2011, http://paidcontent.org/2011/08/05/419-linkedin-earnings-up-as-membership-rises-16-to-115-8-million-users/.
48. Sarah Kessler, "Foursquare Tops 20 Million Users," April 16, 2012, http://mashable.com/2012/04/16/foursquare-20-million/.
49. Jim Estill, "Super Strategies for Small Guys," November 30, 2008, www.profitguide.com/manage-grow/strategy-operations/super-strategies-for-small-guys-29503.

50. Kara Aaserud, "Bonded by Blogging" *Profit*, October 1, 2006, http://www.providentsecurity.ca/press/31.

51. Trevor Melanson, "Is HootSuite Canada's Next Billion-Dollar Tech Titan?" January 9, 2013, www.canadianbusiness.com/technology-news/is-hootsuite-canadas-next-tech-titan/.

52. Ingrid Lunden, "HootSuite Gets Creative, Now Integrates Vimeo for Video, WordPress for Blogs, and Pinterest Tracking," December 6, 2012, http://techcrunch.com/2012/12/06/hootsuite-gets-creative-now-integrates-vimeo-for-video-wordpress-for-blogs-and-pinterest-tracking/.

53. Trevor Melanson, "Is HootSuite Canada's Next Billion-Dollar Tech Titan?" January 9, 2013, www.canadianbusiness.com/technology-news/is-hootsuite-canadas-next-tech-titan/.

54. Caroline Beavon, "Flickr, Instagram and Pinterest," December 22, 2012, http://carolinebeavon.com/2012/12/22/flickr-instagram-and-pinterest/.

55. Michael Stelzner, "Pinterest Success: Creative Ways to Use Pinterest for Your Business," June 14, 2013, www.socialmediaexaminer.com/pinterest-success-creative-ways-to-use-pinterest-for-your-business/.

56. FindTheBest.com, "What Type of Site Is Flickr Social Networking Site?", http://social-networking.findthebest.com/q/83/355/What-type-of-site-is-Flickr-social-networking-site.

57. Flickr—Company Weblog, "A Better, Brighter Flickr," May 20, 2013, http://blog.flickr.net/en/2013/05/20/a-better-brighter-flickr/.

58. Charlotte Henry, "Pinterest vs. Flickr – The Battle for Photo Dominance," March 6, 2013, http://wallblog.co.uk/2013/03/06/pinterest-vs-flickr-the-battle-for-photo-dominance/.

59. Flickr—Company Weblog, "A Better, Brighter Flickr," May 20, 2013, http://blog.flickr.net/en/2013/05/20/a-better-brighter-flickr/.

60. Sarah Perez, "Flickr Grows Post-Relaunch, Tumblr Now 7.2% of Site's Referral Traffic," August 29, 2013, http://techcrunch.com/tag/flickr/.

CHAPTER 9

1. "Small Business Magazine's First Annual Survey of Canada's Entrepreneurs," *Small Business,* June 1987, pp. 49–53.

2. "Intuit Canada," as reported in GDSourcing.com, February 27, 2006.

3. "Small Business Fights Visa's 'Smallenfreuden' Campaign," www.thestar.com/business/2013/06/11/small_business_fights_visas_smallenfreuden_campaign.html, accessed July 1, 2013.

CHAPTER 10

1. *Profit,* December/January, 1999, p. 48.

2. ISO website, www.iso.org/iso/home.html.

3. Naomi Levinson, "7 Steps to a Successful Relationship," *Canadian Retailer,* May/June 2000, p. 15.

CHAPTER 11

1. "Grant Thornton, L.L.P., October 2001," as reported in GDSourcing.com, April 2003.

2. *Small Business in Canada, 1990* (Ottawa: Industry, Science and Technology Canada), p. 19.

3. Canadian Federation of Independent Business, News Release, April 6, 2006.

4. David Pimentel, "To Find and to Keep: How to Recruit and Retain Good Employees," December 8, 2011, www.profitguide.com/manage-grow/human-resources/entrepreneurs-and-the-hunt-for-good-staff-30316.

5. *Profit Guide,* April 6, 2006, p. 4.

6. "Linda Duxbury and Christopher Higgins," as reported in *The Globe and Mail,* September 21, 1999, p. B1.

7. Canadian Federation of Independent Business, News Release, November 18, 2003.

8. Ibid.

9. Catief, "Achievers Publishes Guidelines for Successful Employee Referral Programs," June 24, 2013, www.achievers.com/about-us/press-release/achievers-publishes-guideline-successful-employee-referral-programs.

10. Shannon Bowen-Smed, "3 Ways to Win the Best Employees," February 8, 20913, www.profitguide.com/manage-grow/human-resources/how-to-win-the-talent-game-47950.

11. Tavia Grant, "Employers Sidestep Recruiters to Tap Social Media," August 23, 2012, http://m.theglobeandmail.com/report-on-business/employers-sidestep-recruiters-to-tap-social-media/article1359961/?service= mobile.

12. Susan Heathfield, "Use LinkedIn for Recruiting Employees," 2013, http://humanresources.about.com/od/recruiting/a/recruit_linked.htm.

13. Deborah Aarts, "Social Media Recruiting," December 6, 2010, www.profitguide.com/manage-grow/human-resources/its-a-gr8-way-2-hire-30018.

14. Kim Hart MacNeill, "The Perfect Interview Formula," May 17, 2013, http://www.profitguide.com/manage-grow/human-resources/interview-hiring-tips-52306.

15. Ibid.

16. Jacquelyn Smith, "How Social Media Can Help (or Hurt) You in Your Job Search," April 16, 2013, http://www.forbes.com/sites/jacquelynsmith/2013/04/16/how-social-media-can-help-or-hurt-your-job-search/.

17. Interview with Dr. Amy Thurlow, Mount Saint Vincent University, Halifax, Nova Scotia, June 5, 2013.

18. Robert D. Hisrich, Michael P. Peters, Dean A. Shepherd, and Peter Mombourquette, *Entrepreneurship,* 2nd Canadian Edition (Toronto: McGraw-Hill Ryerson Ltd., 2009).

19. Robert Levering, Milton Moscowitz, and Michael Katz, *The 100 Best Companies to Work for in America, 1984* (Scarborough, New York: New American Library, 1985).

20. Canadian Apprenticeship Forum, *Costco Connection,* July/August 2008, p. 11.

21. Cyberspace Industries 2000 Inc. website, 2007.

22. Canadian Federation of Independent Business, News Release, November 18, 2003.

23. Jim Collins, *Good to Great* (New York: HarperCollins Publishers Inc., 2001).

24. Jim Kouzes and Barry Posner, *The Leadership Challenge,* (San Francisco, Wiley, 2012).

25. Ibid.

26. For a complete discussion, see Donald Rumball, *The Entrepreneurial Edge* (Toronto: Key Porter Books, 1989), pp. 159–179.

27. Interview with Costa Elles, Halifax, Nova Scotia, July 5, 2013.

28. David Pimentel, "To Find and to Keep: How to Recruit and Retain Good Employees," December 8, 2011, www.profitguide.com/manage-grow/human-resources/entrepreneurs-and-the-hunt-for-good-staff-30316.

29. Jim Collins, *Good to Great* (New York: HarperCollins Publishers Inc., 2001).

30. Deborah Aarts, "The Real Reasons Your Staff Is Disengaged," June 26, 2013, www.profitguide.com/manage-grow/human-resources/the-real-reasons-your-staff-is-disengaged-54015.

31. Frederick Herzberg, *Motivation to Work* (New York: John Wiley and Sons, 1959).

32. Abraham H. Maslow, *Motivation and Personality* (New York: Harper and Row, 1970).

33. Liz Palika and Jennifer Fearing, *Dogs at Work: A Practical Guide to Creating Dog-Friendly Workplaces* (New York: Humane Society Press, 2008).

34. Lisa Evans, "Your Best New (Furry) Employee," June 21, 2013, http://www.profitguide.com/manage-grow/human-resources/your-best-new-furry-employee-53877.

35. "Angus Reid Group Survey for Royal Bank, September 1997," as reported in *Profit,* October 1998, p. 16.

36. *Small Business Statistics,* Industry Canada, July 2010.

37. CFIB Mandate Newsletter, December 2003, p. 4.

38. *The Globe and Mail*, February 20, 1995, p. B6.

39. "Small Business Magazine's First Annual Survey of Canada's Entrepreneurs," *Small Business*, June 1987, pp. 49–53.

40. "Work Arrangements in the 1990s," Statistics Canada, May 1998, as reported in *Profit*, October 1998, p. 14.

41. Deborah Aarts, "The Business-Boosting Alternative to Snitch Lines," July 24, 2013, www.profitguide.com/manage-grow/human-resources/the-business-boosting-alternative-to-snitch-lines-55354.

42. "6 Innovative HR Tactics," June 3, 2013, www.profitguide.com/manage-grow/human-resources/6-innovative-hr-practices-52983.

43. "Work Arrangements in the 1990s," Statistics Canada, May 1998, as reported in *Profit*, October 1998, p. 14.

44. Ibid.

45. "Mercer Human Resources Consulting," as reported in *Alberta Venture Magazine*, November 2003, p. 12.

46. Kenneth Blanchard and Robert Lorber, *Putting the One Minute Manager to Work* (New York: Berkley Books, 1984).

47. "7 Sales Strategies of High-Growth Companies," June 3, 2013. www.profitguide.com/manage-grow/sales-marketing/the-7-best-sales-tactics-of-high-growth-companies-53035.

48. Susanne Ruder, "The Best Advice I Ever Got: Karen Flavelle," October 25, 2005, www.profitguide.com/manage-grow/strategy-operations/the-best-advice-i-ever-got-karen-flavelle-28741.

49. *Small Business in Canada*, 1990, p. 61.

50. Hillary Bain Lindsay, "Just Us and Them?," April 2, 2013, http://halifax.mediacoop.ca/story/just-us-and-them/16963.

51. *Outsourcing Institute Study*, 2005, Jericho, New York.

52. "Colleen Gordon, Deloitte Touche," as reported in *Profit*, May 2009, p. 44.

53. *Profit*, December 2003, Advertising Supplement.

CHAPTER 12

1. "Fab 30: Devon Brooks, Co-Founder, Blo Blow Dry Bar," July 18, 2012, www.profitguide.com/industry-focus/retail/fab-30-devon-brooks-co-founder-blo-blow-dry-bar-38164.

2. Frances Bula, "Blow-Dry Bar Concept Heats Up," December 8, 2011, http://www.theglobeandmail.com/report-on-business/small-business/sb-growth/success-stories/blow-dry-bar-concept-heats-up/article4180474/.

3. Ibid.

4. Anthony Reinhart, "Branding Blow-by-Blow: Q&A with Devon Brooks," May 25, 2012, www.cdmn.ca/branding-blow-by-blow-qa-with-devon-brooks/.

5. Brian Scudamore, "World's Greatest MBA," June 1, 2006, www.profitguide.com/manage-grow/human-resources/worlds-greatest-mba-28887.

6. Interview with Todd O'Keefe, Halifax, Nova Scotia, June 1, 2013.

7. Ian Portsmouth, "Podcast 9 - Advisory Board: Why You Need One," October 10, 2008, www.profitguide.com/business-coach-podcast/podcast-9-advisory-board-why-you-need-one-31670.

8. Rahim Kanani, "Robin Chase, Founder & Former CEO of ZipCar, On Leadership and Innovation," March 19, 2012, http://www.forbes.com/sites/rahimkanani/2012/03/19/robin-chase-founder-former-ceo-of-zipcar-on-leadership-and-innovation/.

9. Robert D. Hisrich, Michael P. Peters, Dean A. Shepherd, and Peter Mombourquette, *Entrepreneurship*, 2nd Canadian Edition (Toronto: McGraw-Hill Ryerson Ltd., 2009).

CHAPTER 13

1. Becky Reuber, "Mabel's Label's Social Media Strategy Sticks," August 24, 2012, http://m.theglobeandmail.com/report-on-business/small-business/sb-marketing/mabels-labels-social-media-strategy-sticks/article600065/?service=mobile.

2. Francine Kopun, "Mabel's Labels at Walmart Canada," June 25, 2012, www.thestar.com/business/2012/06/25/mabels_labels_at_walmart_canada.html.

3. Kim Shiffman, "Profit W100 Overview: Big Is Beautiful," July 11, 2007, www.profitguide.com/manage-grow/success-stories/profit-w100-overview-big-is-beautiful-29188.

4. Ibid.

5. Jerry Langton, "Did You Know This Shopping Website is Canadian?" November 7, 2012, www.theglobeandmail.com/report-on-business/economy/canada-competes/did-you-know-this-shopping-website-is-canadian/article5061065/.

6. Louis Rheaume, "Beyond the Rack's Yona Shtern Shares Advice for Entrepreneurs at Accelerate MTL 2012," May 25, 2012, www.techvibes.com/blog/beyond-the-racks-yona-shtern-shares-advice-for-entrepreneurs-at-accelerate-mtl-2012-2012-05-25.

7. Interview with Richard Abbas, Halifax, Nova Scotia, July 7, 2013.

8. Chris Atchison, "Middle Managers' Engagement Key to Company Success," February 8, 2012, http://www.profitguide.com/manage-grow/human-resources/middle-managers-engagement-key-to-company-success-30341.

9. Stephen Haynes, in-class presentation, "Small Business Management," Mount Saint Vincent University, May 2013, Halifax, NS.

10. Jerry Langton, "Did You Know This Shopping Website Is Canadian?" November 7, 2012, www.theglobeandmail.com/report-on-business/economy/canada-competes-did-you-know-this-shopping-website-is-canadian/article5061065/.

11. Tony Martin, "Financing Solutions: Crossing the Cash Chasm," May 31, 2008, www.profitguide.com/manage-grow/financing/financing-solutions-crossing-the-cash-chasm-29407.

12. Ian Portsmouth, "Canada's Fastest-Growing Companies," Profit 500, June 3, 2013, www.profitguide.com/news/profit-500-overview-canadas-fastest-growing-companies-52841.

13. J.K. Dineen, "Nat Bosa Puts His Money Where He Thinks People Will Buy," October 28, 2011, http://www.bizjournals.com/sanfrancisco/print-edition/2011/10/28/nat-bosa-puts-his-money-where-he.html?page=all.

14. Rick Spence, "The 5 Winning Strategies of High-Growth Companies," June 1, 2011, www.profitguide.com/opportunity/the-5-winning-strategies-of-high-growth-companies-30184.

15. Grant Buckler, "Tiny Tech Firm Scores One for Universal Passwords," November 26, 2012, http://www.theglobeandmail.com/report-on-business/small-business/sb-digital/biz-categories-technology/tiny-tech-firm-scores-one-for-universal-passwords/article5610227/; Secure Technologies Inc - About Us Company Website, www.securetechnologies.ca/?page=about.

16. Donald L. Sexton and Philip M. Van Auken, "Prevalence of Strategic Planning in Small Business," *Journal of Small Business Management*, July 1982, p. 20.

17. Rick Spence, "The 5 Winning Strategies of High-Growth Companies," June 1, 2011, www.profitguide.com/opportunity/the-5-winning-strategies-of-high-growth-companies-30184.

18. Ibid.

19. Richard M. Hodgetts, *Effective Small Business Management*. Reproduced by permission of Academic Press Inc., 1982, p. 197.

20. Rick Spence, "The 5 Winning Strategies of High-Growth Companies," June 1, 2011, www.profitguide.com/opportunity/the-5-winning-strategies-of-high-growth-companies-30184.

21. Michael Gerber, *The E-Myth Revisited: Why Most Small Businesses Don't Work and What to Do About It* (New York: HarperCollins Publishers, 1995); 1-800-GOT-JUNK— company website, About Brian Scudamore, www.

1800gotjunk.com/ca_en/about/brian_scudamore.aspx.

22. *The Globe and Mail,* October 12, 2005, B13.

23. *Profits* (Business Development Bank of Canada, Winter 1999), p. 4.

24. Facebook post about BNotions, posted on May 23, 2013, https://www.facebook.com/BNOTIONS/posts/529098543812901.

25. Eleanor Beaton, "Recruiting By Stealth," August 29, 2012, http://www.profitguide.com/industry-focus/technology/profit-hot-50-11-recruiting-by-stealth-39769.

26. "Q&A with President and Founder of BNotions, Alkarim Nasser," DEM Society website, blog post, January 2012.

27. Trina Boos, "Inside the Industry with Alkarim Nasser, Founder/Partner, Product Investments at BNotions," August 21, 2012, http://www.boostagents.com/interviews/inside-the-industry-with-alkarim-nasser-founderpartner-product-investments-at-bnotions/.

28. Ibid.

CHAPTER 14

1. Myles Marchison, "Successful Succession Planning," *Profit,* September 2005, p. 75.

2. Rick Spence, "Tsunami Warning," September 17, www.profitguide.com/prosper/tsunami-warning-40276.

3. Jim McElgunn, "Why It's a Lousy Time to Sell Your Business," July 31, 2013, profitguide.com/manage-grow/financing/why-its-a-lousy-time-to-sell-your-business-55684.

4. Rick Spence, "Tsunami Warning," September 17, www.profitguide.com/prosper/tsunami-warning-40276.

5. Ibid.

6. Mark Groulx, "Selling Your Business 101," August 16, 2011, www.profitguide.com/prosper/selling-your-business-101-30193.

7. Rick Spence, "Tsunami Warning," September 17, www.profitguide.com/prosper/tsunami-warning-40276.

8. Susanne Baillie, "Eight Steps to a Profitable Exit," September 30, 2004, http://www.profitguide.com/manage-grow/strategy-operations/eight-steps-to-a-profitable-exit-28530.\

9. Rick Spence, "Tsunami Warning," September 17, www.profitguide.com/prosper/tsunami-warning-40276.

10. Jim McElgunn, "Selling Your Baby," January 31, 2009, http://www.profit-guide.com/prosper/selling-your-baby-29522.

11. PwC website, Family Business Survey 2012, www.pwc.com/gx/en/pwc-family-business-survey/index.jhtml.

12. P. C. Rosenblatt, L. deMik, R. M. Anderson, and P. A. Johnson, *The Family in Business* (San Francisco: Jossey-Bass, 1985), p. 5.

13. "Succession Planning for Small Businesses," Grant Thornton, October 2006, p. 1.

14. S. I. Lansberg, "Managing Human Resources in Family Firms: The Problem of Institutional Overlap," *Organizational Dynamics,* Summer 1983, pp. 39–46.

15. *Canadian Business,* May–June, 2005, p. 55.

16. Curtis Hartman, "Main Street Inc.," *Inc.,* June 1986, pp. 49–54.

17. "Succession Planning for Small Businesses," Grant Thornton, October 2006, p. 1.

18. *The Globe and Mail,* October 9, 1995, p. B7.

19. Ralph Douglas and Costello How, *K.C.: The Biography of K.C. Irving* (Toronto: Key Porter Books, 1993).

20. Statistics Canada, *Small Business Quarterly,* January 2001.

21. S. Birley, "Succession in the Family Firm: The Inheritor's View," *Journal of Small Business Management,* vol. 24, no. 3 (July 1986), p. 36.

22. John Lorinc, "The Golden Goose," October 17, 2012, www.profitguide.com/manage-grow/strategy-operations/the-golden-goose-42172/2.

23. Jennifer Low, "Dad, When Are You Going to Let Go?" *Profit,* October 1991, p. 28.

24. Marshall Paisner, "Myths about Succession," *Inc.,* October 1986, p. 146.

25. Joanna Pachner, "When Kids Run The Family Business," April 11, 2010, www.profitguide.com/manage-grow/strategy-operations/when-kids-run-the-family-business-2-29711.

26. "McCain Business Empire Has Deep Roots," March 19, 2004, www.cbc.ca/news/business/mccain-business-empire-has-deep-roots-1.518215; Clyde Farnsworth, "Canadian Family's Feud," October 30, 1994, www.nytimes.com/1994/10/30/business/canadian-family-s-feud.html.

27. Robert D. Hisrich, Michael P. Peters, Dean A. Shepherd, and Peter Mombourquette, *Entrepreneurship,* 2nd Canadian Edition (Toronto: McGraw-Hill Ryerson Ltd., 2009).

28. Clyde Farnsworth, "Canadian Family's Feud," October 30, 1994, www.nytimes.com/1994/10/30/business/canadian-family-s-feud.html.

29. Gordon Pitts, "McCain Brothers Unlikely to End Feud," December 24, 2001, http://www.theglobeandmail.com/report-on-business/mccain-brothers-unlikely-to-end-feud/article1035633/?page=all.

30. Rosenblatt, deMik, Anderson, and Johnson, *The Family in Business,* p. 274.

31. Birley, "Succession in the Family Firm."

32. Jim McElgunn, "Selling Your Baby," January 31, 2009, http://www.profitguide.com/prosper/selling-your-baby-29522.

33. "Nubody's Founder to Step Down – GoodLife to Acquire Chain," August 13, 2009, http://www.progressmedia.ca/article/2009/08/nubodys-founder-step-down-goodlife-acquire-chain.

34. Kim Shiffman, "Business Exit Strategy: Company Sold in One Day," February 8, 2012, http://www.profitguide.com/manage-grow/strategy-operations/business-exit-strategy-company-sold-in-one-day-30334.

35. Tenille Bonoguore, "Surfboard Designer Finds Buyout a Rough Ride," May 28, 2012, http://www.theglobeandmail.com/report-on-business/small-business/sb-money/valuation/surfboard-designer-finds-buyout-a-rough-ride/article4216665/.

36. "Your Going Public Checklist," *Profit,* November 1998, p. 47.

37. Mark Stevens, "When to Take Your Company Public," *Entrepreneurial Manager's Newsletter,* vol. 7, no. 4 (1986), p. 4.

INDEX

3twenty Solutions, 15–16

A

A-B-C analysis, 346
absenteeism, 353, 376
accelerated capital cost allowance, 394
accessibility of site, 102
accountants, 384
accounting cycle, 303–308, 304*f*
accounting expenses, 392
accounting information uses, 304*f*
accounting software, 310–311
accounting systems, 106, 308–311
accounts receivable, 160
achievement orientation, 40
Achievers, 197
action programs, 267
Adams, Doug, 59
advantages
    of a corporation, 112*f*
    of debt financing, 224
    of equity financing, 206
    of franchising, 170–173
    of organizing a small business from
        scratch, 90–91
    of a partnership, 108*f*
    of purchase of business, 152–153
    of small business ownership, 33–36
    of a sole proprietorship, 108*f*
advertisement
    for employee recruitment, 358–359
    expenses, 392
    as promotion, 283–284*f*
    and social media, 358–359
advisers
    board of advisers, 385–387
    mentors, 385
    and small business, 384
    use of, 384–387
affiliate programs, 294
age, and self-employment, 17*f*
alertness to change, 44–45
Allan, Jeff, 425
Amack, John, 172
analytical method, 163–164
angel investors, 205
    characteristics of, 214*f*
    defined, 212–213
    finding and soliciting, 213, 215–218
    information on Canadian angel groups, 220*f*
    organizations, 218–219
applicant, for loan, 229, 231
application form, 359, 360*f*
Apprenticeship Job Creation, 394
apps (application), 297
Arcade, Anne, 312
Arctic Spas, 368
artisan entrepreneur, 48
Asaria, Ali, 11, 37
assets, 159–160
asset value, 161–162

Association of Canadian Venture Capital
    Companies, 220
automobile expenses, 392
autonomy, 23

B

baby-boomers, 26
Bailey's Office Supply (case), 449
Baker Hardware Ltd. (case), 450–452
balance sheet, 305–306, 307*f*, 318*f*–319*f*
Balderson, D. Wesley, 83, 84, 236–237,
        237–238, 238–239, 239–240, 399,
        400, 401, 402, 403, 405, 406, 407,
        449, 450, 452, 453
bankruptcy, 446
banner advertisements, 294
The Barrel Bracket (case), 405–406
Baty, Cameron, 155
BC Angel Forum, 219*f*
Belvedere Place Development, 23
Beyond the Rack Inc., 416
bias for action, 22, 40
Big D's Painting Company (case), 84–85
Birch, Karina, 155
BlackBerry, 11
Blanchard, Kenneth, 372
Blanshay, Jonathan, 89
Blo Blow Dry Bar, 383
blogs, 69, 296
blurring of roles, 442
Bnotions.com, 426
board of advisers, 385–387
board of directors, 385–387
Bolivar, Chris, 333
bonus deferral, 394
bookkeeping systems, 106
book value, 161–162
Boomerang Bouncers Entertainment (case),
    408–409
Booster Juice, 172
bootstrap financing, 222–223
brainstorming, 58
Brass, Julian, 95
break-even analysis, 315*f*
    feasibility analysis, 78
breaking into the market, 60–61
Brian Luborsky-Premier Salons International
    Inc. (case), 452–453
Bristow, Ron, 424
Brock, Derek, 110
Brooks, Devon, 383
Brouwer, Zora, 167
budget
    financial planning, 313*f*
    marketing management, 267
building, as asset, 160
burnout, 47
business angels. *See* angel investors
business building and site-rating table, 336*f*
business counsellors, 384

business cycle, 414–417
Business Development Bank of Canada
    (BDC), 13, 14, 16–17, 221–222
business entertaining expenses, 392
business opportunities
    assessment of, 58–60
    breaking into the market, 60–61
    collecting information, 64–70
    opportunity assessment, 59–60
    qualitative assessment, 58–59
    quantitative assessment, 70–78
    self-assessment for, 78*f*
    strategic competitive advantage, 61–63
business plan
    background statement, 97
    business objectives, 97–98
    checklist, 121–123
    components of, 94–96
    described, 90
    executive summary, 97
    financing plan, 106
    importance of, 92–93
    legal requirements. *See* legal
        requirements
    management team, 97
    marketing approach, 98–100
    marketing program, 100
    measuring plan progress, 117–118
    online templates, 96
    organizing a small business from scratch,
        90–92
    personnel plan, 107
    physical facilities, 104
    samples, 124–139, 139–149
    selection of location, 101–104
    small business plan, 92–93
    table of contents, 96
    updating, 118–119
    writing the plan, 93–94
business start-ups, 8–10, 90–92
business-to-business company
    database marketing, 263–265
    marketing plan for a, 248*f*–249*f*
business-to-consumer, and database
    marketing, 263–265
buying patterns, 26
buy-or-lease location, 102–103

C

CAFE (Canadian Association of Family
    Enterprise), 435
Campbell, Anne, 151, 159
Canada Customs and Revenue Agency. *See*
    Canada Revenue Agency (CRA)
Canada Goose, 3
Canada Pension Plan (CPP), 377
Canada Revenue Agency (CRA), 11, 14, 377,
    378, 390
Canadian Association of Family Enterprise
    (CAFE), 435

Canadian Bankers' Association, 14, 226
Canadian Business Week, 13
Canadian Competitive Bureau, 324
Canadian Federation of Independent
    Business (CFIB), 12, 323, 324, 353,
    357, 387
Canadian Franchise Association, 167
*The Canadian Franchise Dealership
    Guide*, 177
Canadian Opportunities Investment Network
    (COIN), 156
Canadian ownership, 23
Canadian Small Business Finance Program
    (CSBF), 225, 226–227
Canadian Social Enterprise Foundation, 8
Canadian Youth Business Foundation
    (CYBF), 17, 225, 227
capabilities, 58–60
capacity decision, 315
capital gains, 396
capital investment decision, 313–314
capitalization of earnings formula, 163f
capitalization of earnings value, 164f
capital requirements, 106, 424–425
Career Beacon, 358
career path, preferences, 5f
Carmen Creek Gourmet Meats, 303
cases
    See also comprehensive cases
    Bailey's Office Supply, 449
    Baker Hardware Ltd., 450–452
    The Barrel Bracket, 405–406
    Big D's Painting Company, 84–85
    Boomerang Bouncers Entertainment,
        408–409
    Brian Luborsky–Premier Salons
        International Inc., 452–453
    Clark's Sporting Goods, 236
    Company's Coming Cookbooks, 453–454
    Conrad's Photographer's Supplies,
        237–238
    Dale's Sport Pursuit, 403
    Derocher's Market, 399–400
    Garner Men's Wear, 407–408
    Home Mart Hardware Store, 400–401
    ITI Educational Corporation, 453
    Jensen Roofing, 236–237
    Katie's Custom Engraving Logos, 85–86
    Kelly's Grill, 238–239
    Martha's Designs, 401–402
    Petite Shop (A), 83
    Petite Shop (B), 83–84
    Sadie's Country n' Western Store, 402–403
    Second Cup, 239–240
    Susie's Fashions, 403–405
    Taylor Construction Company, 405
    Threadz, 406–407
cash flow
    feasibility analysis, 75, 78
    managing, 303
    shortage in growth companies, 418–419
cash flow statement, 202f, 203f, 307–308, 309f
cash requirements for increased sales, 419f
challenge, 34–35
change
    alertness to change, 44–45
    and the future of small business, 25
    organizational change, 425

channel intensity, 277
channel length, 277
channel options, 277
chartered banks, 225, 226
Chaworth-Musters, Bob, 216
Chilton, David, 71
Clark, James D., 85
Clark, Jim, 408
Clark, Scott, 99
Clark's Sporting Goods (case), 236
closing down, 446
Cohen, Barry, 258
COIN (Canadian Opportunities Investment
    Network), 156
COLD-FX, 420
Cole, Julie, 413
collateral, 230–231
collection policy, 322f
Collins, Jim, 364, 367
combination methods for pricing a business,
    163–165, 165f
Commerce Clearing House (CCH), 392
Committee for Economic Development
    (U.S.), 14
communicability of results, 275
communication, lack of, 418
communication skills, 42, 443
company mission, 255
Company's Coming Cookbooks (case),
    453–454
company websites, 291–293
competition
    extent of, 100
    and marketing plan, 253
    in the trading area, 101
competition-based pricing, 280–281
competitive advantage, 61–63
competitive aspects of markets, 26–27
complexity of product or service, 275
comprehensive cases
    See also cases
    Dan Kim, part 1, 81–82
    Dan Kim, part 2, 189
    Dan Kim, part 3, 235
    Dan Kim, part 4, 329–330
    Dan Kim, part 5, 350
    Dan Kim, part 6, 381
    Dan Kim, part 7, 429
Comprehensive Economic and Trade
    Agreement (CETA), 27
Conference Board of Canada, 353
Conrad's Photographer's Supplies (case),
    237–238
consumer price sensitivity, 280f
consumer products company, marketing plan
    for, 246f–247f
consumers
    baby-boomers, 26
    buying patterns of, 26
    demographics of, 26
    manufacturer to consumer channel, 277
    manufacturer to wholesaler/retailer to
        consumer channel, 277
    millennial generation, 26
    staying close to, 45
content of work, 58
contingency planning, 268
continual tax planning, 389–390

contract, franchise, 180
contract employees, 378–379
contributions of small businesses, 21–24
controls, and marketing management, 267
convenience products, 275
Cooper, Adam, 44, 108
cooperative, 113–115
coordination, lack of, 418
corporate investors, 219–220, 221f
corporate lenders, 224–225
corporations, 111–112, 114f
cost-based pricing, 279–280
costs
    of franchise, 174
    of land and buildings, 101
    of lease, 103
    merchandise costs, 175
    ongoing operating costs, 201
    site costs, 102
    start-up costs, 199–201, 205f
Counselling Assistance for Small
    Businesses, 14
coupons, 286
courses, small business, 11
CPP (Canada Pension Plan), 377
CRA. *See* Canada Revenue Agency (CRA)
Crazy Plates, 71
credit, 321–323
credit cards, 323
credit program, 321–322
credit unions, 225
creditworthiness, 231
crowd-funding, 9, 45
    equity financing, 211–212
crowd-sourcing, 9, 69
cultural environment, and the marketing
    plan, 254
Cunningham, Jason, 110
customer database marketing, 263–265
customer-focused interview (CFI), 68
customer profile, and the marketing plan,
    260–261, 263
customer relationship marketing (CRM)
    and customer retention, 265–266
    database information system, 263
    described, 262–263
customer retention, 265–266
customers
    database marketing, 263–265
    direct email to, 293–294
    external relationships, 161
    loyalty programs, 264
    staying close to, 22

D

Dale's Sport Pursuit (case), 403
Dan Kim (case), 81–82, 189, 235, 329–330,
    350, 381, 429
data
    primary data, 66–68
    secondary data, 64–66
    summarizing, 305–308
database information system, 263
database marketing, 263–265
deal of the day websites, 286
debit cards, 323

debt financing, 202
    advantages of, 224
    corporate lenders, 224–225
    disadvantages of, 224
    government lenders, 225–228
    private lenders, 224
    private lending institutions, 225
    sources of, 224–228
    use of, 223
debt-to-equity ratio, 321
decline stage, 416–417
deductible expenses, 391–392
deferral programs, 394
deferred profit sharing, 394
demand-based pricing, 280
Densmore, Barbara, 251
Derocher's Market (case), 399–400
Dickie, Gord, 63
Dickinson, Arlene, 19
Dinn, Michael, 230
direct mail, 285–287
disadvantages
    of a corporation, 112*f*
    of debt financing, 224
    of equity financing, 206
    of franchising, 173–177
    of organizing a small business from
        scratch, 92
    of a partnership, 108*f*
    of purchase of business, 153–156
    of small business ownership, 36–39
    of a sole proprietorship, 108*f*
distribution system development
    channel intensity, 277
    channel length, 277, 278*f*
    channel options, 277
    described, 276–277
    multi-level marketing, 277–278
divisibility of product or service, 275
division of responsibilities, 355
Dogs at Work (Palika), 369
dogs at work, and employee happiness, 369
dollar inventory control, 346
Dragons' Den (TV show), 13, 17, 19, 24, 97,
    109, 212, 215, 218, 292
Dun and Bradstreet, 13

E

earnings value, 162–163
echo generation, 26
economic base, 101
economy
    contributions by small businesses, 12*f*,
        16*f*, 24
    and marketing plan, 253
    recession, slow growth after, 27–28
    small business in gross domestic
        product, 15*f*
    state of the economy, 100
educational institutions, 359
EI (Employment Insurance), 377
Elles, Costa, 332, 366
Ellis, Julie, 413
email marketing, 293–294
emotional level, 441–442
employee remittance number, 377

employees
    See also personnel management
    attract and retain, 45
    benefits, 372*f*
    capabilities, and marketing plan, 255
    contract employees, 378–379
    engagement, 367–369
    evaluation of, 372–373
    fringe benefits, 370–372
    grievances, 373–374
    hiring process, 357–362
    job dissatisfaction reasons, 368*f*
    job satisfaction, 353*f*
    lean staff, 23
    loyalty, 367–369
    motivation, 367–369
    needs, 368–369
    number of, and government funding, 14
    number of, in businesses, 10
    productivity through, 23
    recruitment, 107
    referrals, 357
    remuneration, 369–370
    revenue-based commission, 368
    sale of business to, 444
    sources of employees, 357–359
    termination, 373–374
    training, 107, 363–364
    turnover, 353, 363, 367
    weekly hours worked, 38*f*
    working conditions, 367–368
Employee Share Ownership Plan (ESOP), 444
employee suggestion systems, 371–372
employment agencies, 359
employment equity, 375
Employment Insurance (EI), 377
employment interview, 359
employment reference checks, 361
employment safety and health, 376
employment screening tests, 361
employment standards, 375–376
Emsley, Derrick, 24
Emsley, Kalen, 24
*The E-Myth Revisited: Why Most Small
    Businesses Don't Work and What To
    Do About It* (Gerber), 424
Enactus, 16
enjoyment, 35
entrepreneurial process
    ideas, 55
    sources of new ideas, 55–58
Entrepreneurial Research Consortium, 35, 38
entrepreneurial skills, 48
entrepreneurs
    artisan entrepreneur, 48
    characteristics of, 39–44, 39*f*
    compensation, 396
    education levels, 39
    and equity financing, 209
    founders of business, 48
    as franchisor, 183–186
    immigrant entrepreneurs, 19–20
    male entrepreneurs, 18–19
    mompreneurs, 35
    and parents of entrepreneurs, 41
    personality characteristics of, 39–44
    promoter, 48
    senior entrepreneurs, 17

    sources of stress, 36*f*
    suitability checklists, 52
    traditional managers, compared to, 50*f*
    women. *See* women entrepreneurs
    young entrepreneurs, 15–17, 46
entrepreneurship
    and autonomy, 23
    courses at post-secondary schools, 11
    described, 4
    development of, 4–8
    image of, 12–13
    by industry, 20*f*
    and intrapreneurship, 11
    motivators for, 5–8
    nature of, 4–8
    by region, 20–21*f*
    small business management, *vs.*, 48–49
    small business ownership, *vs.*, 4
    students studying, 4
Entrepreneurship and Small Business
        Office, 11
environment, and marketing plan,
        252–253, 254*f*
Enviro Paving Corp., 424
equipment, as asset, 160
equity financing, 202
    advantages of, 206
    angel investors. *See* angel investors
    corporate investors, 219–220, 221*f*
    crowd-funding, 211–212
    disadvantages of, 206
    and entrepreneurs, 209
    family and friends, 209–211
    government programs, 220–222
    informal risk-capital market, 205,
        212–213
    personal funds and retained earnings,
        207–209
    small, slow growth businesses, 207*f*
    sources of, 205
    venture-capital companies, 219–220, 221*f*
e-retailer, 416
ESOP (Employee Share Ownership Plan), 444
Esp, Cynthia, 413
European Union (EU), 27
evaluation of business for sale
    See also purchase of business
    asset conditions, 159–160
    customers, 160–161
    financial condition of the business,
        158–159
    industry analysis, 157
    previous owner, 157–158
    quality of personnel, 160
    records, condition of, 161
    suppliers, 160–161
evaluation of franchise opportunity
    contract length, renewal and
        termination, 180
    current owners' feedback, 180
    financial stability of franchise, 179
    potential market, 179
    profit potential for new franchise, 179
    territorial protection, 180
    training and operations assistance, 180
    unproven *vs.* proven franchise, 178–179
exaggeration of financial success, 176–177
excise taxes, 115–116

expansion decision, 315–316
expansion plan, 423
experience, 60
external environment, 426
external shocks, 47

F

Facebook, 69, 295, 358
failures
common failure factors, 47f
small businesses, 46–47
family, as source of capital, 209–211
family business
blurring of roles, 442
clear role structures in, 443
communication, 443
competence, 443
emotional level, 441–442
facts and statistics, 435
and incompetence, 442
legal implications of transfer, 438–440
non-family employee attitudes, 442
non-family employees, incentives for, 443
objectives of family owners, 442
objectivity, importance of, 443
overreliance on the founder, 441
owners' objectives, 443
potential problems in a, 441
principles of success for, 442–443
successful, 437
succession planning, 435, 437–438
tax implications of transfer, 438–440
transfer methods, 440–441
Family Business Scorecard, 439f
fatigue, 417–418
feasibility analysis
example, 76f–78f
market potential, 71–72
market share for manufacturing firm, 73–74
market share for retail firm, 73
market share for service firm, 74–75
preparation of, 70–71
federal government
See also government
human resources requirements and
assistance, 374–375
licences and taxes, 115
Federation of Independent Business, 28
female entrepreneurs. *See* women
entrepreneurs
finance companies, 225
financial information, 425
financial management
accounting cycle, 303–308, 304f
accounting information uses, 304f
accounting systems, 106, 308–311
balance sheet example, 318f–319f
credit, 321–323
evaluation of financial performance,
316–321
financial planning, 311–316
financial records, need for, 303
outsourcing financial activities, 309–310
financial performance measurement
of business, 158–159
current financial position, 316–317

financial ratios, 317, 319–321, 327–328
financial statements, evaluation of,
317–321
financial planning
capacity decision, 315
capital investment decision, 313–314
expansion decision, 315–316
long-term financial planning, 312–316
short-term financial planning, 311–312
financial ratios, 317, 319–321, 327–328
financial records, 303
financial resources for marketing plan, 254
financial rewards, 34, 37–38
financial statements
evaluation of, 317–321
income statement, 306–307, 308f
succession planning, 434
validity of, 158
financing
accounting systems, 106
amount of funds needed, 199–202
bookkeeping systems, 106
bootstrap financing, 222–223
and business stages, 202–205
capital requirements, 106
collateral, 230–231
debt financing, 202, 223–228
determining amount of funds needed,
199–202
equity financing. *See* equity financing
evaluation measures, 106
feasibility projections, 106
government lenders, 225–228
importance of, 198–199
lender relations, 231
lending programs, 13–14
matching to assets, 228f
net worth, personal, 204f
net worth of owner, 201
ongoing operating costs, 201
private lenders, 224
proposal to obtain financing,
229–231
small business, 198
sources of funding, 106
stages of business development
funding, 208f
start-up costs, 199–201
start-up costs schedule, 200f
start-up firms, 205f
term of financing, 228–229
types of, used to maintain activities, 206f
types of financial instruments, 207f
First Angel Network, 219f
fixed-cost adjustments, 316
fixed-position layout, 338–339
flash mobs, 289
Flavelle, Karen, 373
flexibility of small businesses, 23
flexible work hours, 45, 371
Flickr, 296, 298
focus groups, 57, 68
formal classroom training, 364
founders of business, 48
Foursquare, 296
Franchise Annual Directory,
The, 177
franchisee, 185–186, 192–195

franchises
risk assessment, 181f
selling, 184
top 10 new franchises, 178f, 183f
franchising
See also evaluation of franchise
opportunity
advantages of, 170–173
background of, 166–169
checklist for potential franchisee, 192–195
defined, 169–170
disadvantages of, 173–177
exaggeration of financial success,
176–177
finding a franchise, 177–178
franchise sales in Canada, 168f
future of, 186
history of, 166–169
by industry, 168f
legal requirements, 184–185
trends in, 177f
types of businesses, 183–184
types of franchises, 170f
franchising company, 170
franchisor
becoming a, 183–186
establishing a prototype, 184
establishing a support system, 185
finding franchisees, 185–186
legal requirements, 184–185
obtaining financing, 185
preparing necessary information, 184
services provided by, 171–173
standardized program of operations, 185
Freedman, David, 28
free-flow layout, 341–342f
Freidman, Scott E., 439f
FreshBooks, 25, 310
friends, as source of capital, 209–211
fringe benefits, 370–372
funds
crowd-funding, 9
obtaining capital, 45
future of small businesses, 24–29

G

gamification, 294–295
Garfield, Charles A., 39
Garner Men's Wear (case), 407–408
Generally Accepted Accounting
Principles, 392
general partnership, 110–111
Gerber, Michael, 424
Global Economic Entrepreneurship, 18
Global Entrepreneurship Monitor, 5, 28
global markets, 26–27
Global Paradox (Naisbitt), 4
The Globe and Mail, 13
Goalline, 63
goals, 58
going public, 445–446
Golden Horseshoe Venture Group, 219f
goods and services tax (GST), 115–116,
396–397
Good to Great (Collins), 367
goodwill, 160

government
    See also municipal governments;
        provincial and territorial governments
    criteria for small businesses, 14
    equity financing programs, 220–222
    human resources requirements and
        assistance, 374–376
    laws, rules, and regulations, 45
    lenders, 225–228
    licences, 115–116
    outsourcing, 27
    programs for small businesses,
        10–11, 13
    as source of businesses for sale, 156
    support for social entrepreneurship, 8
    taxes, 115–116
government tax-related programs,
    393–395
graduates, starting a business, 18
Grass Frames, 8
GreatWest Kenworth Ltd., 441
grid layout, 341
grievances, 373–374
Groupon, 286
growth
    business cycle, 414–417
    capital requirements, 424–425
    evaluation of growth question, 421
    expansion plan, 423
    external environment, monitoring, 426
    financial information, 425
    intelligent expansion, 424
    management depth, 423
    managerial controls, 425
    organizational change, 425
    planning for growth, 422–426
    problems created by growth, 417–421
    requirements of growth, 423–426
    and small business, 414
    staffing, 423–424
    stages of growth, 417f
growth stage, 415
GST (goods and services tax), 115–116,
    396–397
guerrilla marketing, 288–289

H

hands-on-value driven, 23
HapiFoods Group Inc., 17
Harary, Ronnen, 243–244
harmonized sales taxe (HST), 396
harvesting, 433
Herjavec, Robert, 19, 212
High Roads Communications, 291
Hipp, Linda, 54
hiring process
    do's and don'ts of hiring, 362
    notification of the hiring decision, 362
    screening process, 359–361
    sources of employees, 357–359
historical method, 165
Holmes, Ryan, 22, 297, 369
home-based business, 103–104
Home Mart Hardware Store (case), 400–401
HootSuite, 22, 297, 369
Human Resources Development Canada, 359

human resources management (HR)
    contract employees, 378–379
    government requirements and assistance,
        374–376
    grievances, 373–374
    growth companies, 418
    hiring process, 357–362
    job descriptions, 356
    job satisfaction among employees, 353f
    personnel management, 363–373
    planning for, 354–357
    record keeping, 376–379
    and small business, 353–354

I

ideas
    defined, 55
    sources of new ideas, 55–58
IKEA, 342
immigrant entrepreneurs, 19–20
Impakt Protective, 99
Inbox Marketer, 311
income splitting, 390
income statement, 306–307, 308f
income taxes, 115–116, 395f
incompetence, 442
incorporation, 113, 395
independence, 33–34, 40–41
independence, lack of, 174
independence vs. risk, 90f
industry, entrepreneurship by, 20f
industry analysis, 157
Industry Canada, 11, 14, 111, 353
informal risk-capital market, 205, 212–213
information, lack of, 419
information collection
    assessing market feasibility using
        secondary data, 65f
    customer-focused interview (CFI), 68
    importance of, 64
    observation, 66–67
    primary data, 66–70
    secondary data, 64–66
    sources of, 64
    surveys, 67–68
    test marketing, 68–70
initial public offering (IPO), 445
innovations, 21–22
innovativeness, 41–42
In Search of Excellence (Peters and
    Waterman), 11
Instagram, 296, 298
insurance, 103, 104–106
intellectual property, 116
intelligent expansion, 424
interest expenses, 392
International Standards Organization
    (ISO 9000), 334
International Take Your Dog to
    Work Day, 369
Internet
    advertisement for employee recruitment,
        358–359
    and the future of small business,
        25–26
    and information collection, 69

marketing, 291–297
    as source of businesses for sale, 156
    surveys, 68
Internet marketing, 291–297
    See also promotion
    affiliate programs, 294
    banner advertisements, 294
    blogs, 296
    company websites, 291–293
    direct email to customers, 293–294
    Facebook, 295
    Foursquare, 296
    gamification, 294–295
    LinkedIn, 296
    mobile marketing, 297, 299
    online auction sites, 294
    online classified advertising sites, 294
    online games, 295
    online newsletter, 293
    pay-per-click advertising (PPC), 293
    photo sharing sites, 296
    podcasts, 295
    search engine optimization
        (SEO), 293
    social networking, 295
    Tumblr, 296
    Twitter, 296
    video sharing sites, 296–297
    webinars, 295
intrapreneurship, 11, 27, 49–50f
Intrapreneur's Ten Commandments of
    Success, 49
introduction period, 363
inventions, 21–22
inventory
    A-B-C analysis, 346
    control, 346–347
    dollar inventory control, 346
    evaluation of, 160
    on hand, 345
    just-in-time (JIT), 344
    just-in-time (JIT) vs. traditional, 345f
    maximum-and-minimum method, 345
    minimum levels required,
        344–345
    minimum-turnover method, 345
    monitoring, 347
    open-to-buy method, 346
    order lead time, 344
    order points, 344f
    order quantities, 344–346
    periodic inventory, 347
    perpetual inventory, 347
    purchasing, 343–347
    sales or production estimates, 344
    security of, 347
    shrinkage, 347
    software programs, 347
    sources of supply, 343
    suppliers, evaluation of, 343
    unit control, 346–347
    valuation, 347
inventory turnover formula, 345
Investment Credits, 394
investment tax credits, 393–394
IPO (initial public offering), 445
ITI Educational Corporation
    (case), 453

J

Jensen Roofing (case), 236–237
Jessop, Deland, 44, 108
job descriptions, 356
job discrimination, 375
job dissatisfaction reasons, 368*f*
job rotation, 371
job satisfaction, 353*f*
job sharing, 371
joint ventures, 115
journal entries, 303–305*f*
Jugo Juice, 110
Jumpstart Our Business Start-ups (JOBS) Act (U.S.), 211
just-in-time (JIT) inventory, 344, 345*f*
just-in-time (JIT) training, 364

K

Kaizen, 339
Katie's Custom Engraving Logos (case), 85–86
Kelly's Grill (case), 238–239
Kickstarter, 9
Kids and Company, 391
Kouzes, Jim, 364

L

labour intensity, 21
Labour Relations Act, 374
Lamoureux, Patrick, 167
Lampert, Mark, 32
large businesses
    intrapreneurship in, 11, 27, 49–50*f*
    outsourcing, 27
    productivity and profitability, 22–23
    response of, 27
    small businesses, *vs.,* 13–14, 21, 27
lawyers, 384
layouts
    described, 336
    fixed-position layout, 338–339
    free-flow layout, 341–342*f*
    grid layout, 341
    manufacturing firms, 337–339
    process layout, 337–338, 338*f*
    product layout, 337, 338*f*
    rankings of space importance in retail store, 340*f*
    retail firms, 339–342*f*
    service firms, 342–343
The Leadership Challenge (Kouzes and Posner), 364
leadership styles, 364–365, 365*f*
lease, 103
leasehold improvements, 103
ledger account titles, 306*f*
legal expenses, 392
legal requirements
    franchising company, 184–185
    intellectual property protection, 116
    legal structure, 107–116
    licences, 115–116
    taxes, 115–116
legal restrictions, and the marketing plan, 253–254

legal structure
    cooperative, 113–115
    corporations, 111–112, 114*f*
    income tax, 395*f*
    incorporation, 113
    joint ventures, 115
    partnership, 108–111, 114*f*
    sole proprietorship, 107–108, 108*f*, 114*f*
legislation, 99
lender relations, 231
lending programs, 13–14
licences, 115–116
life cycle of a business concept, 415*f*
lifestyle, 58, 420
Lija Style Inc., 54
limited financial rewards, 37–38
limited partnership, 109–110
LinkedIn, 296, 358
liquid assets, 159
liquidity ratios, 319
Litchfield, Randall, 311
loan proposal, 229–231, 229*f*
location, 101–104, 152, 171
long-indirect channel, 277
long-range planning, 432–433
low profitability, 419
loyalty programs, 264
Luba, David, 24
Lütke, Tobias, 272

M

Mabel's Labels, 413
MacDonald, Amanda, 18
mail surveys, 68
male entrepreneurs, 18–19
management
    ability, 229
    entrepreneurship, *vs.,* 48–49
    lean management, 312, 339
    managerial skills, 48–49
    problems, 47
management by objectives (MBO), 372
management by walking around (MBWA), 23, 45
management-ownership structure, 14
management team, 97, 354
    marketing plan, 255
managerial skills, 48–49
manual accounting systems, 308–309
manufacturer-directed franchise, 169
manufacturer to consumer (short-direct channel), 277
manufacturer to wholesaler/retailer to consumer (long-indirect channel), 277
manufacturing firm
    feasibility analysis, 73–74
    layouts, 337–339
    ledger account titles, 306*f*
Maple Leaf Angels, 219*f*
market feasibility, 65*f*
marketing
    approach, 98–100
    Internet, 291–297
    mobile marketing, 297, 299
    multi-level marketing, 277–278
Marketing magazine, 420

marketing management
    action programs, 267
    budgeting, 267
    contingency planning, 268
    controls, 267
    customer relationship marketing (CRM), 262–263
    database marketing, 263–265
    goals and objectives, 266–267
    marketing mix, 255
    marketing plan. *See* marketing plan
    marketing strategy, 267
    monitoring progress of actions, 267–268
    role of, in small business, 244–245
    and social media, 265
    target marketing, 257–260
marketing mix
    critical decisions for, 255*f*
    distribution system development, 276–278
    pricing for the good or service, 278–281
    product or service development, 273–276
    promotion. *See* promotion
    role of, in small business, 273
marketing of the product or service, 98–100
marketing plan
    for a business-to-business company, 248*f*–249*f*
    characteristics of, 251–255
    company mission, 255
    and competition, 253
    for consumer products company, 246*f*–247*f*
    cultural environment, 254
    customer profile, 260–261, 263
    defining the business situation, 256–257
    described, 245–246, 250
    and the economy, 253
    employee capabilities, 255
    environment, external and internal, 252–253
    external influences, 254*f*
    facts needed for, 252*f*
    failure of, 268
    financial resources, 254
    focused marketing plan, 251
    legal restrictions, 253–254
    management team, 255
    marketing system, 253*f*
    market segmentation, 257–260
    for a service company, 249*f*–250*f*
    social environment, 254
    steps in preparation, 256–268
    strengths and weaknesses, 262
    suppliers, 255
    target marketing, 257–260
    technology, 254
marketing program, 100
marketing strategy, 267
marketing system, 253*f*
Marketplace (TV show), 13
markets
    breaking into the market, 60–61
    competitive aspects of, 26–27
    cultural norms, 100
    global markets, 26–27
market saturation, 174–175
market segmentation, 257–260

market value, 161
Martha's Designs (case), 401–402
Marwood Metal Fabrication Ltd., 339
Master Tax Guide (CCH), 392
maturity stage, 415–416
maximum-and-minimum method, 345
McCain, Harrison, 436
McCain, Wallace, 436
McCains, 436
McCrea, Bryan, 15
McDerment, Mike, 25, 310
McRobbie Optamedia, 333
media, and entrepreneurship, 12–13
mentors, 385
merchandise costs, 175
Merrithew, Lindsay G., 431
Merrithew, Moira, 431
Merrithew Health & Fitness, 431
microbusinesses, 14
Migicovsky, Eric, 5–6, 9, 45, 211, 212
millennial generation, 26
Mindfirst Angels, 219f
minimum-turnover method, 345
Ministry of State for Small Business, 14
mobile marketing, 297, 299
mobile technology, 25–26
MOMpreneur Magazine, 35
mompreneurs, 35
Mompreneur Showcase Group Inc., 35
Monster, 358
monthly remittance, 377
Mullins, Brian, 17
Mullins, Corin, 17
multi-level marketing, 277–278
Mumby, Tricia, 413
municipal governments
    human resources requirements and
        assistance, 376
    licences, 116
    taxes, 116

N

Naisbitt, John, 4
Nashmi, Jennifer, 391
Nasser, Alkarim, 426
National Angel Capital Organization
        (NACO), 218, 219f
National Association of Suggestion
        Systems, 372
National Post, 13
need segmentation, 257
negotiating the deal, 166
neighbouring businesses, influence of, 102f
net income, and feasibility analysis, 75, 78
net worth of owner, 201, 204f
Neuralitic, 222
Neville, Chris, 302
newspapers/magazines, 287
New Venture Strategies (Vesper), 40
Noble, Heidi, 230
non-family employees, 442, 443
North American Free Trade Agreement
        (NAFTA), 26
Northstrup, Brett, 438
Northstrup, Charles, 438
Notable.ca, 95

NovaScotian Crystal, 151, 159
numerical skills, 42

O

objectives of family owners, 442
objectivity, importance of, 443
observation, 66–67
office expenses, 392–393
Okanagan Angel Network, 217
O'Leary, Kevin, 97, 212, 216, 292
O'Leary and Lang Exchange (TV show), 13
one-book accounting system, 310f
online auction sites, 294
online classified advertising sites, 294
online games, 295
online newsletter, 293
on-the-job training, 363
open-to-buy method, 346
operating capital, 45
operating costs, 201
operating details, 45
operations assistance, 180
operations management
    business-supplier relationship, 348
    described, 333
    inventory control, 346–347
    layouts, 336–343
    physical facilities, 335–336
    production process, 333–334
    purchasing inventory, 343–346
    supply chain management, 348
    total quality management (TQM),
        334–335
opportunity assessment, 59–60
Opray Winfrey (TV show), 292
order lead time, 344
order points, 344f
organizational change, 425
organizational chart, 355
organizational culture, 366–367
organizational evaluation, 44–47
organizational structure, 355–356
Original Basket Boutique, 167
outsiders, selling business to, 444–446
outsourcing
    business process, 333
    financial activities, 309–310, 378
    large business and government, 27
Overholt, Greg, 8
overreliance on the founder, 441
owner lifestyle, 420
owner-manager as personnel manager,
        364–366
ownership. *See* small business ownership

P

Palika, Liz, 369
Pang, Peter, 420
Paradise Island Foods, 437
partnership, 108–111, 114f
Patent Gazette, 48
payback method, 314
pay equity, 375
pay-per-click advertising (PPC), 293
payroll book, 377

Peak Performers (Garfield), 39
Pebble Watch, 6, 9, 212
peer-to-peer lending, 211
people conflicts, 38
periodic inventory, 347
perpetual inventory, 347
perseverance, 42–44
personal contact with people, 34
personal funds, as source of capital, 207–209
personal interviews, 68
personality characteristics, 39–44, 43f
personal net worth, 204f
personal selling, 285
personnel, quality of, 160
personnel management
    See also employees
    control of employee performance,
        372–373
    employee motivation, engagement, and
        loyalty, 367–369
    employee needs, 368–369
    employee remuneration, 369–370
    evaluation of employee performance,
        372–373
    first week, 363
    fringe benefits, 370–372
    grievances, 373–374
    introduction period, 363
    leadership styles, 364–365, 365f
    organizational culture, 366–367
    owner-manager as personnel manager,
        364–366
    probationary period, 363
    record keeping, 376–379
    revenue-based commission, 368
    salary plans, 370f
    termination, 373–374
    time management, 365–366
    training, 363–364
    unionization, 374
    working conditions, 367–368
personnel policies, 107, 356
personnel requirements, 355
Peters, Thomas, 11
Petite Shop (A) (case), 83
Petite Shop (B) (case), 83–84
philanthropy, 24
Phoenix Building Components, 425
photo sharing websites, 296, 298
physical characteristics of site, 102
physical facilities, 104, 335–336
Pinchot, Gifford, 49
Pinterest, 296, 298
planning, and capital, 198–199
podcasts, 295
Podleski, Greta, 71
Podleski, Janet, 71
Police Prep, 44, 108
political climate, 27–28
political power of small businesses, 12
Po Po's Ponchos, 104
Posner, Barry, 364
potential financial rewards, 34
Power Retail (Stevenson), 257
Practices of Exemplary Leadership, 364
present value method, 314
press releases, 291
previous owner, 157–158

PRICE system, 372
PricewaterhouseCoopers, 333, 435
pricing
    a business. *See* valuation of business
    for good or service, 278–281
primary data
    observation, 66–67
    surveys, 67–68
priority evaluation and review technique
        (PERT), 333, 335*f*
priority planning, 365
private lenders, 224
private lending institutions, 225
probationary period, 363
problem-solving abilities, 42
processes, as asset, 160
process layout, 337–338
product development
    See also service development
    adoption, 274–275
    consumer classification of product,
        275–276
    manufacturing of product, 273
    policies, 273
    product classification, 276*f*
    product life cycle, 273–274, 274*f*
production efficiency breakdowns, 419
production estimates, 344
production process, 333–334
production systems, 334*f*
productivity, 22–23
productivity ratios, 319–320
product layout, 337, 338*f*
product life cycle, 273–274, 274*f*
product pricing
    See also service pricing
    competition-based pricing, 280–281
    consumer price sensitivity, 280*f*
    cost-based pricing, 279–280
    demand-based pricing, 280
    setting, 278–279
    value-based pricing, 281
products
    adoption, 274–275
    classification, 276*f*
    consumer classification, 275–276
    convenience products, 275
    distribution system development,
        276–278
    manufacturing of, 273
    product development, 273–276
    proven market for, 170–171
    setting price for the, 278–281
    shopping products, 275–276
    specialty products, 276
professionals, as source of businesses for
        sale, 156
profitability, 22–23
profitability ratios, 320
Profit Magazine, 13, 23, 24, 38, 62, 244, 303,
        353, 369, 372, 421, 432
profits, 14
profit trends of industry, 157
promoter, 48
promotion
    See also Internet marketing
    advertising, 283–284*f*
    campaign, 281–283

described, 281
direct mail, 285–287
effectiveness of, 175–176, 282*f*
guerrilla marketing, 288–289
newspapers/magazines, 287
non-traditional promotional methods,
        288–291
personal selling, 285
press releases, 291
public relations (PR), 289–291
radio, 287
sales promotions, 285
stealth marketing, 290
telephone directories, 287
television, 287–288
traditional promotional methods,
        285–288
promotional campaign, 281–283
property taxes, 116
proposal to obtain financing, 229–231
prospectus, 211
provincial and territorial governments
    financial assistance programs, 227–228
    human resources requirements and
        assistance, 375–376
    licences and taxes, 115–116
provincial sales taxes (PST), 396–397
proximity/location-based marketing, 299
public-equity market, 205
public relations (PR) as promotional tool,
        289–291
purchase characteristics for various ages, 260*f*
purchase of business
    See also evaluation of business for sale
    advantages of, 152–153
    checklist of considerations, 190–191
    combination methods for pricing a
        business, 165*f*
    disadvantages of, 153–156
    evaluation of a business for sale, 157–161
    negotiation of deal, 166
    price or value, determination of, 161–165
    purchase transaction, 165–166
    sources of businesses for sale, 156–157
    steps in acquisition, 166
purchase transaction, 165–166
purchasing inventories, 343–346
Purdy's Chocolates, 373
Putting the One Minute Manager to Work
        (Blanchard), 372
Pyrotek Special Effects Inc., 59

Q

QR codes, 297, 299
qualitative assessment, 58–59
quantitative assessment, 70–78
Quicksnap, 109

R

Rabie, Anton, 243–244
radio, 287
radio frequency identification (RFID), 347
Ramsden, Kelsey, 23
rankings of space importance in retail
        store, 340*f*

rate-of-return method, 313–314*f*
Rathod, Kalpesh, 108
real estate, as asset, 160
real estate brokers, as source of businesses for
        sale, 156
reference checks, 361
region, entrepreneurship by, 20–21*f*
registered retirement savings plan, 394
Reiss, Dani, 3
relative advantage, 275
remittance form, 377*f*
remuneration question, 395–396
repair and improvement expenses, 392
repairs, 103
replacement value, 162
representative survey sample, 67*f*
research. *See* information collection
research and development, 22
restrictions of site, 102, 103
restrictions of the contract, 174
résumé, 359
retail firms
    feasibility analysis, 73
    layouts, 339–342*f*
    ledger account titles, 306*f*
revenue-based commission, 368
Revenue Canada. *See* Canada
        Revenue Agency
Revision Military, 89
reward cards, 323–324
reward programs, 264
Reynolds, David, 109
risk assessment, 116–117, 181*f*
risk-capital markets, 205
risk management, 104*f*
risk of failure, 36
risk taking, 40
risk *vs.* independence, 90*f*
Roback, Al, 8
Rocky Mountain Soap Company Inc., 155
Rogers, Ted, 317
Rogers Communication, 317
Rybarski, Michael, 258

S

Sadie's Country n' Western Store (case),
        402–403
safety stock, 344–345
salary plans, 370*f*
sales estimates, 344
sales promotions, 285
sales taxes, 116
sales trends of industry, 157
Satok, Jordan, 46
Sciemetric, 41
scientific research expenditures (SRTCs),
        393–394
screening process, 359–361
screening tests, 361
search engine optimization (SEO), 293
*Second Annual Global Entrepreneurship
        Monitor*, 24
secondary data, 64–66
Second Cup (case), 239–240
Secure Key Technologies Inc., 422
security, lack of, 175

security of inventory, 347
self-assessment for a small business
        opportunity, 78f
self-assurance, 40–41
self-confidence, 40–41
self-employment/self-employed
    education levels, 39
    growth and extent by age, 17f
    main reasons for, 33f
    as percentage of labour force, 6f
    by region, 20–21f
    by sector, 20f
    weekly hours worked, 38f
selling shares, 446f
selling skills, 42
senior entrepreneurs, 17
Sequel Lifestyle Hotels and Resorts, 312
service development
    See also product development
    adoption, 274–275
    consumer classification of service,
        275–276
    policies, 273
service firms
    feasibility analysis, 74–75
    layouts, 342–343
    ledger account titles, 306f
    marketing plan for a, 249f–250f
service pricing
    See also product pricing
    competition-based pricing, 280–281
    consumer price sensitivity, 280f
    cost-based pricing, 279–280
    demand-based pricing, 280
    setting, 278–279
    value-based pricing, 281
services
    franchisor services, 171–173
    proven market for, 170–171
Shan, Jacqueline, 420
Shark Tank (TV show), 97, 212
Shopify, 272
shopping products, 275–276
short-direct channel, 277
short-term financial planning, 311–312
shotgun clause, 111
shrinkage, 347
Shtern, Yona, 416
SigPod, 41
site, the, 101–102
site costs, 102
site history, 102
site proximity to other businesses, 102
situation analysis, 256–257
skills, 34, 37, 42
Skoll, Jeff, 7
Skoll Foundation, 7
small and medium-sized enterprises (SMEs)
    contribution to Canadian economy, 16f
    female entrepreneurs, 17–18, 19f
    number of employees, 14
    research and development, 22
    and taxes, 387–389
    types of financing used by, 207f
small business
    See also large businesses
    accounting systems, 106, 308–311
    advertising, 283–284f

and advisers, 384
alternative outcomes, 433
business-supplier relationship, 348
and consumer demographics, 26
contributions of, 21–24
courses at post-secondary schools, 11
and credit, 321–323
criteria for lending programs, 14
current state of, 14–21
database marketing, 263–265
defined, 13–14
division of responsibilities, 355
economic contributions by, 12f, 15, 16f, 24
economic recovery, 27–28
employee numbers, 10, 14
evaluation of, 13
failures, 46–47
financing. See financing
financing programs, 394–395
financing small, slow growth
        businesses, 207f
firm size, 10f
flexibility of, 23
future of, 24–29
government programs, 10–11, 13
and growth, 414
growth in, 8–13
human resources management (HR),
        353–354
image of, 12–13
innovation enablers, 21–22
large businesses, vs., 13–14, 21, 27
lending programs for, 13–14
management vs. entrepreneurship, 48–49
marketing mix, role of, 273
number of, 8–10, 21f
organizational evaluation, 44–47
ownership. See small business
        ownership
performance comparison, 13
political climate, 27–28
political power of, 12
by province, 20–21f
representative survey sample, 67f
salary plans, 370f
self-assessment for an opportunity, 78f
social climate, 28–29
successes, 44–46
tax breaks for, 11
tax deduction, 394f
and taxes, 387–389
tax management, 389–397
tax rate, 389f, 390f
unionization, 374
Small Business Administration (U.S.), 14
small business decision
    advantages of small business ownership,
        33–36
    demographic characteristics of
        entrepreneurs, 39
    disadvantages of small business
        ownership, 36–39
    entrepreneurship and small business
        management, 48–49
    organizational evaluation, 44–47
    personal evaluation, 33–39
    personality characteristics of
        entrepreneurs, 39–44

small business failures, 46–47
small business successes, 44–46
Small Business Deduction (SBD), 393
small business ownership
    advantages of, 33–35
    described, 4
    disadvantages of, 36–39
    entrepreneurship, vs., 4
    number of, 8–10
    personal evaluation, 33
Smart Tax Tips (Yull), 388
social climate, 28–29
social contributions, 24
Social Enterprise Council of Canada, 8
social entrepreneurship
    government support, 8
    as motivator, 6–7
    young social entrepreneurs, 8
social environment, and the marketing
        plan, 254
social media
    deal of the day websites, 286
    employee recruitment, 358–359
    innovation in small business, 22
    Notable.ca, 95
    and photo sharing websites, 296, 298
    reference checks, 361
    and stealth marketing, 290
social networks
    Facebook, 69, 295, 358
    Foursquare, 296
    and information collecting, 69
    LinkedIn, 296, 358
    and marketing, 265
    and promotion, 295
    Twitter, 69, 296, 358
    Yelp, 69
sole proprietorship, 107–108, 108f, 114f
Sopik, Victoria, 391
sources of new ideas
    brainstorming, 58
    deliberate searches, 57–58
    drawing from experience, 56
    existing products and services, 56–57
    focus groups, 57
    hobbies, 55–56
    observations, 56
    occupations, 55
Spark Internet Marketing Corp., 358
specialty products, 276
Spinder, Pieter, 303
Spin Master Ltd., 243–244
Spiring, Charlie, 352
staffing, 423–424
stages of business development funding, 208f
stages of growth, 417f
Start, Karen, 104
start-up costs
    financing, 199–201, 205f
    schedule, 200f
Start-up Smarts: The Thinking Entrepreneur's
        Guide to Starting and Growing Your
        Business (Cohen and Rybarski), 258
start-up stage, 414–415
statement of changes in financial position,
        307–308
Statement of Financial Position, 305–306
Statement of Profit and Loss, 306–307

Statistics Canada, 10, 13, 14, 17, 19, 37, 39, 42, 47, 111
stealth marketing, 290
Stevenson, Lawrence, 257
Storwick, Jeff, 441
STOTT PILATES®, 431
strategic competitive advantage, 61–63
strategic planning, 42
stress, 36–37, 417–418
Students Offering Support (SOS), 8
succession planning
    evaluation of the firm, 434
    failure, 438
    family business, 435, 437–438, 441
    Family Business Scorecard, 439f
    financial statements, preparation, 434
    hire professionals, 434–435
    plan early, 433
    remove yourself from the business, 433
    stable revenue, 434
Suleman, Razor, 197, 209
Sunterra Markets, 264
suppliers
    evaluation of, 343
    and evaluation of business for sale, 160–161
    marketing plan, 255
supply chain management, 348
supply sources, 343
support system for franchisee, 185
SurveyMonkey, 69
surveys, 67–68, 67f
Susie's Fashions (case), 403–405
systems, as asset, 160

T

T4 slip, 378f
target market
    clear concept of, 98
    for a hypothetical small restaurant, 261
    needs, wants, and purchasing habits, 98
target marketing
    marketing plan, 257–260
    strengths and weaknesses, 262
Taverna, 332, 366
tax computer software, 393
tax deferral, 390
taxes, 115–116
    as burden to small and medium-sized businesses (SMEs), 388f
    and small business, 387–389
tax free savings account, 394
tax management
    accelerated capital cost allowance, 394
    capital gains, 396
    continual tax planning, 389–390
    deductible expenses, 391–392
    deferral programs, 394
    goods and services tax (GST), 396–397
    government tax-related programs, 393–395
    harmonized sales tax (HST), 396
    income splitting, 390
    income tax for different legal forms of business, 395f
    incorporation, 395

investment tax credits, 393–394
    marginal tax rates, 390–391
    provincial sales tax (PST), 396–397
    remuneration, 395–396
    Small Business Deduction (SBD), 393
    small business financing programs, 394–395
    special tax rate deductions, 393–394
    tax deferral, 390
tax rate, 389f, 390f
Taylor Construction Company (case), 405
Team Buy, 286
technology
    and the future of small business, 25
    marketing plan, 254
    mobile technology, 25–26
    monitoring new technology, 100
telephone directories, 287
telephone surveys, 68
television networks, 13
television promotion, 287–288
Ten Commandments for Intrapreneur Success, 49
Ten Tree Apparel, 24
territorial protection, 180
test marketing, 68–70
text/SMS messages, 297
Thomson, George, 437
Threadz (case), 406–407
Thurlow, Amy, 361
time-accounting program, 333
time demands, 38–39
time management, 365–366
times earnings method, 163
Tim Hortons, 176
total quality management (TQM), 334–335
total revenue, 14
trade journals, as source of businesses for sale, 156
trading area, 101
training, 107, 180, 363–364, 376
transactions, recording, 303–304
transaction totals, 305
transfer of business
    alternative outcomes, 433
    to employee, 444
    Employee Share Ownership Plan (ESOP), 444
    to family. See family business
    going public, 445–446
    implications of selling shares, 446f
    long-range planning, 432–433
    sale to outsiders, 444–446
Treliving, Jim, 215
trust companies, 225
Tumblr, 296
turnover, 353, 363, 367
Twitter, 69, 296, 358
Tzaneteas, Chris, 332

U

Uken Games, 32
unfulfilled promises, 174
UnhappyFranchisee.com, 182
unionization, 374

unit of control, 346–347
unity of control or command, 356

V

valuation of business
    asset value, 161–162
    combination methods, 163–165, 165f
    earnings value, 162–163
    market value, 161
valuation of inventory, 347
value-based pricing, 281
Vancouver Angel Forum, 216
Varadi, Ben, 243–244
variable-cost adjustments, 316
Venture (TV show), 13
venture-capital companies, 219–220, 221f, 222
venture-capital market, 205
verbal skills, 42
Vesper, Karl, 40
video sharing sites, 296–297
video sharing websites, 296–297
Vine, 296–297

W

wage subsidy programs, 376
Warren Industries Ltd., 28
Wasney, Trevor, 368
Waterman, Robert, 11
webinars, 295
websites, company, 291–293
Wedgbury, Mia, 291
weighted-average earnings, 162f
Well.ca, 37
Wellington West Capital Inc., 352
wholesaler-retailer-directed franchise, 169
Willoughby, Evan, 16
Wishewan, Dale, 172
Wolfond, Greg, 422
women entrepreneurs
    facts about, 19f
    increase of, 17–19
    men entrepreneurs, vs., 18–19
Women Entrepreneurs of Canada (WEC), 18
Women Presidents Organization (WPO), 18
Women's Enterprise Society of B.C. (WESBC), 251
Wood, Chris, 339
word of mouth, as source of businesses for sale, 157
workers' compensation, 376
working conditions, 367–368
working from home, 371
Workopolis, 358

Y

Ye, Chris, 32
year-end statements, 378
Yelp, 69
young entrepreneurs, 15–17, 46
YouTube, 296–297, 358
Yull, Karen, 388